VIEWS ON CAPITALISM

SECOND EDITION

RICHARD ROMANO

Associate Professor and Chairman
Department of Economics
Broome Community College,
State University of New York

MELVIN LEIMAN

Associate Professor
Department of Economics
State University of New York
at Binghamton

GLENCOE PRESS
A division of Benziger Bruce & Glencoe, Inc.
Beverly Hills

Printed in the United States of America

GLENCOE PRESS
A division of Benziger Bruce & Glencoe, Inc.
8701 Wilshire Boulevard
Beverly Hills, California 90211

Collier-Macmillan Canada, Ltd.

Library of Congress Catalog Card Number: 74-6628

First printing, 1975

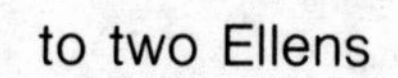
to two Ellens

CONTENTS

PREFACE vii

THE CONSERVATIVE VIEW 1

ADAM SMITH 6

from: AN INQUIRY INTO THE NATURE AND CAUSES OF THE WEALTH OF NATIONS 8

HENRY C. SIMONS

A POSITIVE PROGRAM FOR LAISSEZ-FAIRE 22

MILTON FRIEDMAN 35

from: CAPITALISM AND FREEDOM 38

MONEY AND ECONOMIC ACTIVITY 55

EDWARD C. BANFIELD 61

from: THE UNHEAVENLY CITY 63

NIXON, THE GREAT SOCIETY, AND THE FUTURE OF SOCIAL POLICY 68

MURRAY ROTHBARD 74

THE GREAT SOCIETY: A LIBERTARIAN CRITIQUE 75

AYN RAND 81

A COMMENT BY MELVIN LEIMAN 81

BIBLIOGRAPHY 89

THE LIBERAL VIEW 91

JOHN STUART MILL 95

from: PRINCIPLES OF POLITICAL ECONOMY 96

JOHN MAYNARD KEYNES 104

THE END OF LAISSEZ-FAIRE 106

ECONOMIC POSSIBILITIES FOR OUR GRANDCHILDREN 111

JOSEPH A. SCHUMPETER 117

from: CAPITALISM, SOCIALISM, AND DEMOCRACY 119

PAUL A. SAMUELSON 132

PERSONAL FREEDOMS AND ECONOMIC FREEDOMS IN THE MIXED ECONOMY 133

MICHAEL D. REAGAN 142
from: THE MANAGED ECONOMY 143

JOHN KENNETH GALBRAITH 151
from: THE NEW INDUSTRIAL STATE 154
MANDATORY AND PERMANENT WAGE-PRICE CONTROLS 184

DANIEL P. MOYNIHAN 187
THE PROFESSIONALIZATION OF REFORM 188

WALT W. ROSTOW 198
THE STAGES OF ECONOMIC GROWTH 201

ROBERT L. HEILBRONER 212
THE FUTURE OF CAPITALISM 213

BIBLIOGRAPHY 233

THE RADICAL VIEW 235

KARL MARX AND FRIEDRICH ENGELS 239
from: A CONTRIBUTION TO THE CRITIQUE OF POLITICAL ECONOMY 242
from: SOCIALISM: SCIENTIFIC AND UTOPIAN 243
from: THE COMMUNIST MANIFESTO 255
from: THE CAPITAL 269

THORSTEIN VEBLEN 273
from: THE THEORY OF BUSINESS ENTERPRISE 276

PAUL BARAN AND PAUL SWEEZY 303
from: MONOPOLY CAPITAL 305

HERBERT MARCUSE 340
from: AN ESSAY ON LIBERATION 341

DANIEL R. FUSFELD 350
THE RISE OF THE CORPORATE STATE IN AMERICA 352

HERBERT GINTIS 367
ALIENATION IN CAPITALIST SOCIETY 369

BIBLIOGRAPHY 380

PREFACE

Over the past ten years, the market has been flooded with political economy readers which cover every conceivable contemporary economic topic from urban affairs to international money problems. This book differs from most in that its selective coverage examines some of the more fundamental, although sometimes less visible, problems which our society faces. Confronted here are the questions of the connection between economic and political freedom, the proper role of the government, and the forces and directions of change within the system. The focus is on the changing institutional structure of capitalism and on the variety of reactions to that changing structure.

As in the first edition, we have tried to present excerpts of sufficient length to allow the student to get the proper perspective on each author's particular view of the world. We do not believe that this feeling can be captured by reading excerpts of a page or two in length. The readings are divided into three broad categories of opinion—Conservative, Liberal, and Radical. Admittedly these terms have suffered from overuse and have undergone significant semantic change during the time span over which these selections were written. We do believe, however, that the categories, properly defined, can be a useful device for sorting out and understanding the competing ideological positions presented here. The general introduction to each of the three parts outlines the basic approach that the readings in that section follow. The introductions preceding the individual selections provide additional background material on the authors and a certain amount of editorial analysis. Since this criticism reflects the editors' own biases, let us state at the outset what those biases are. Professor Romano's views are influenced primarily by the mainstream of reform liberalism, while Professor Leiman's are in the radical tradition. Although the introductions represent the combined efforts of both editors, chief responsibility for each piece is indicated by the initials that follow it.

These essays have been used as a supplement in the principles of economics and political economy courses at Broome Community College and in the introductory social science course at the State University of New York at Binghamton. We are gratified that the first edition found acceptance outside these areas and in revising the volume we have attempted to take account of the suggestions sent to us by its users.

January 1974
Binghamton, New York

RICHARD ROMANO
MELVIN LEIMAN

THE CONSERVATIVE VIEW

An economic conservative places the primary responsibility for the organization and distribution of production on the market system. He views government intervention as undesirable and generally defines the government's role as one of protecting individual property rights, promoting competition, maintaining law and order, and defending the country against foreign military aggression. Although conservatives differ over the specific functions which they believe government should perform within the economy, it is fair to say that they all feel its role should be a limited one.

Freedom of choice, economic efficiency, and a rising standard of living are the benefits the conservative feels will accrue to a society that allows the market to allocate resources without governmental controls. The case for economic efficiency and growth is based firmly on orthodox neoclassical economic theory. The market is efficient because flexible prices and profits divert resources away from areas where society wants them least and into areas where they are wanted the most. Although fluctuations in economic activity cannot be completely eliminated, the free interaction of individuals and a sound monetary policy will propel the society in an upward direction. Perhaps the most interesting issue raised by the conservatives, however, is the connection between the economic system they admire and man's pursuit of freedom. They agree with those in the radical group that essential human freedoms are linked to the institutional framework under which production is carried out. The conservative feels that freedom, which he defines as the absence of coercion, is maximized under a system of competitive capitalism, while the radical feels that capitalism stifles freedom. Both have a great deal of faith in individual human potential, but they disagree sharply on its affinity for the capitalist system.

To better understand the conservative model of the operation of the market economy, one needs to know its underlying premises. These include the assumptions that:

- each individual understands perfectly the alternative actions open to him in any situation and the consequences of those actions;
- each individual has the mobility that gives him the option of alternative courses of action;
- each individual acts rationally and consistently to serve his own self-interest;
- each individual can act to maximize his own self-interest better than other individuals or groups (i.e., governments) could serve him;
- each individual who acts to serve his own self-interest maximizes the welfare of society.

Essential to the conservative position is the view that the market generates a high degree of economic freedom because it permits voluntary interactions among individuals which benefit all parties involved. Government intervention into this system reduces its efficiency, makes it less responsive to change, and contracts individual economic freedoms. In addition, the conservative views the growing power of government as leading to authoritarianism. Thus the powerful state poses a serious threat to human rights and political freedom. Following this philosophy, the economic conservative (believer in laissez-faire) might also argue against government action in other areas. If, for instance, the solution of a noneconomic problem, say civil rights, threatens to infringe on the right of private property, then the conservative is likely to revert to the philosophy that "that government governs best which governs least." Modern liberals, on the other hand, tend to stress the positive role that government can play in expanding and guaranteeing individual freedoms.

The selections in this section reflect the laissez-faire philosophy and share a concern about the future of capitalism. As these authors look at the system, they are obviously disturbed by what they see. For Adam Smith, this concern emerges in a condemnation of the mercantalist system, which artificially diverted capital toward the trade sector and stimulated the growth of government-protected monopolies. For Simons, Friedman, Banfield, and Rothbard, this concern focuses on the increasing size and power of the federal government and the movement toward the welfare state. Each presents his own case against the growing power of the state, but all feel that the future of capitalism lies in a reversal of the direction in which it seems to be going; all warn of the dangers inherent in a system that deviates from the laissez-faire philosophy.

An excerpt from Adam Smith's *Wealth of Nations,* published in 1776, is included here because it is the classic statement on the virtues of competitive capitalism. This book is still widely read by students, and its influence on contemporary thinking is reflected in the numerous references to it by the other authors in this volume. At the time the *Wealth of Nations* appeared, Britain was in the early stages of the Industrial Revolution. The philosophy of Smith and his followers, the Classical economists, provided the theoretical underpinnings for the rising industrial sector that moved Britain close to a laissez-faire economy by the middle of the nineteenth century. These Classical economists were not considered conservatives. Indeed, in the Lockean tradition they were liberals who fought the existing power structure in an effort to establish free trade, a competitive market, and Parliamentary reform. Thus Smith is a liberal in the nineteenth-century tradition, but a conservative when viewed against a modern background. Simons, Friedman, Banfield, and Rothbard can also be considered either nineteenth-century liberals or modern conservatives. The approach here is to view them as the latter.

The selections by Henry C. Simons and Milton Friedman are modern expressions of the laissez-faire philosophy espoused by Adam Smith. "A Positive Program for Laissez-Faire" has become a classic and provides an interesting contrast to other laissez-faire proposals in its heavy reliance on positive governmental action. Reacting against the economic regulation of the New Deal era, but almost as if he had accepted the increased role of the government in the economy as inevitable, Simons shows how the power of the federal government can be used to move the economy toward laissez-faire rather than away from it. His program would result in a radical restructuring of the economy as we know it today. He argues for more flexible wages and prices, an elimination of tariff barriers, tax reforms to redistribute income, a responsible monetary policy to promote economic stability, the restriction of wasteful advertising, and the breakup or governmental takeover of large corporations. While Simons' essay is policy oriented, that of his student, Milton Friedman, is more philosophical. Friedman is modern America's best-known conservative economist. His views have been linked with the political campaigns of Barry Goldwater and Richard Nixon. In his book *Capitalism and Freedom* he shows his distaste for the liberal approach, which he sees as moving the country toward the welfare state. Like Simons, Friedman links this movement to increased limitations on individual freedom. The main part of the selection reprinted here examines the connection between economic and political freedom. The last part is a criticism of the current use of macroeconomic planning. Building on the earlier analysis of Simons, Friedman argues that monetary policy has a more important influence on economic activity than does fiscal policy and that its use to offset business cycles is most often disruptive. As a substitute for the discretionary policy of the Keynesians, Friedman proposes a neutral monetary policy geared toward long-term economic growth. His idea of increasing the money supply at a steady, rather than widely fluctuating, rate has a good deal of support among academic economists.

The selection by Edward C. Banfield is taken in part from his popular book *The Unheavenly City,* which applied the conservative framework to modern urban problems. His contention is that these problems are not as severe as we might think and that if the federal government would reduce its attempts to "solve" them they would eventually "dwindle into unimportance."

The Murray Rothbard piece is a historical note on the growth of private and public power. Rothbard argues for a return to laissez-faire, but his analysis is similar to that of the New Left. He is perhaps most accurately described as an extreme libertarian (one who places individual liberty above all) and would argue that even the limited governmental intervention proposed by Friedman and other conservatives is too much of a threat to individual freedom. Another representative of this extreme right-wing position is Ayn Rand. Breaking slightly from the format of the volume, Professor Leiman has written a critical analysis of her position from his own radical perspective.

R R

ADAM SMITH

(1723–1790)

Adam Smith did not set out to predict the future of capitalism. As this selection indicates, however, he was concerned that those forces which would ensure a bright future be allowed to operate. Writing in a period of commercial capitalism, he preached the partially heretical notion that abandonment of comprehensive mercantile regulations and adoption of laissez-faire rules of the game would unleash a country's vast economic potential. The "invisible hand" (the competitive market system) would efficiently allocate society's human and material resources among the various sectors so as to foster economic development and class harmony.

Reacting against the mercantilist tendency to concentrate its capital in the tariff-protected foreign trade sector, Smith advocated a gradual, balanced growth pattern in which investment in agriculture received top priority at an early stage followed in due time by manufacturing and trade. Facilitating this growth would be, according to Smith, the increased employment of productive labor (those engaged in turning out tangible products) and the utilization of the division-of-labor principle (illustrated by his famous "pin factory"). A component of the latter factor is represented in modern times as technological change, and Smith placed great emphasis on its role within the laissez-faire system. He undoubtedly felt that the two were consistent with one another, a view which may be contrasted with those of Schumpeter and Galbraith. Growth, then, was Smith's chief concern, and the crucial initiator of this economic activity was the savings of the propertied class. These savings set in motion a dynamic growth process in which the "wages fund" (money available for wage payments) advanced by the capitalists in the current period, out of earnings in the previous period, was replenished by the productive workers in an amount greater than the advance. This in turn aided economic growth in the following period. The possibilities of uninvested savings or inadequate effective demand (which would cause unemployment) were not explored by Smith. His perspective was the grand theme of economic development within the framework of a competitive capitalist order, rather than short-run cyclical phenomena. Operating under a competitive system, with the profit motive as the main incentive for production, the concentration of economic power would be limited, and an efficient allocation of resources as well as a growing economy would result. Smith mentions the possibility of a stationary state at some advanced stage of capitalism, but this possibility is not fully explored until the middle of the nineteenth century by John Stuart Mill.

An adequate appraisal of Smith's economic thinking requires historical perspective. Smith represents a fusion of the economic theorist and the political statesman. His *Wealth of Nations* is both an economic treatise and a practical political program. It represents the thinking of an intellectual keenly aware of the mainstreams of theoretical political economy, and a cautious reformer attempting to influence public policy. The England of Smith's day was one where the mercantile restrictions and subsidies were becoming more and more arbitrary and oppressive, and where commercial and military rivalries imposed a drain on the economy. With England, the world's leading commercial center, on the threshold of the Industrial Revolution, it was not unreasonable for Smith to believe that the free market was a more effective instrument for furthering the wealth of nations and maintaining political freedom than the "planned economy" administered by the mercantilist statesmen.

Monopoly privileges, public corruption, and economic inefficiency were all too obvious, and invasion of personal political rights was becoming more and more so. In championing free trade and a decentralized economy, which separated the business sector from governmental control, Smith was providing a rationale for a widely prevalent practice—mass evasion of the burdensome mercantile regulations by a growing entrepreneurial class actively and skillfully pursuing its self-interest. It was the pursuit of this self-interest which Smith characterized as economic man's basic psychological drive. Because of his belief in the existence of a natural order in the universe, Smith felt that this drive would automatically work for the betterment of society as a whole. To ensure that this natural order would be preserved, a noninterventionist government was necessary. The role of the government, according to Smith, ought to be restricted to military protection, administration of laws, and erection of a limited number of public works which the private sector had insufficient economic incentive to engage in. Smith's arguments and those of his followers, combined with the success of the system which seemingly operated under their principles, became so dominant that they helped to foster the idea of a relationship between economic and political freedom and competitive capitalism. This feeling has carried down to the present time and is expressed here, with various personal twists and modern connotations, by Simons, Friedman, and Rothbard.

Even though Smith underestimated the thrust that the mercantilist system had imparted to early capitalist economic development, he did recognize that the interests of society could not be best served by operating under that institutional arrangement. Despite the ready adaptability of his doctrines to the propertied interests, Smith's sympathies were with the laboring class and the actual tiller of the soil. Although Smith is sometimes regarded by businessmen and modern conservatives as being favorable to big business, a close examination of the selection presented here will show this view to be a false one. He believed, and probably with validity under the existing institutional arrangements, that impersonal competitive markets could more effectively restrain the ability of the capitalists to exploit the public than a government he regarded as an "engine of oppression." The irresponsibility of the business class and the State toward the condition of the masses in the period of industrial mobilization does not destroy the historical validity of Smith's theory. It was not unreasonable for him to assume that capital accumulation would necessarily raise the standard of living of the working class, since it was not yet typical for capital accumulation to take the form of fixed capital (such as machinery and factories) which could result in economic growth without an accompanying rise in economic welfare.

Two of Adam Smith's notions deserve attention because they are of concern to many of today's undeveloped countries. They are the alleged benefits of stressing agriculture at an early stage of development as opposed to industry or commerce, and the idea that free trade is beneficial from the standpoint of growth and welfare. There are serious shortcomings to both of these positions. A strong case can be made for the view that free trade, based on the principle of comparative advantage, could freeze a country's productive pattern and prevent the diversified development of industry. The all-too-frequent result is a reinforcement of the circle of poverty and a widening gap between the advanced and backward countries. The stress on agriculture also has certain weaknesses except in cases, like early America, where the land:labor ratio is exceptionally favorable. Agriculture is likely to be carried on in an unproductive manner in a society with a weak industrial sector. Although agricultural development may, under certain favorable circumstances, ease the transition to an industrial society, in a world characterized by rapidly rising expectations the peoples of undeveloped countries will almost certainly view the price of gradual balanced growth as too severe.

Smith's *Wealth of Nations*, nevertheless, remains one of the great classics of economic thought. It gave a precision and rigor to economic analysis that was indispensable for the development of the discipline. But more than that, it presented a model of an economic system that is rigorously defended by a number of modern theorists, some of whom have expanded its implications far beyond the scope of economic theory. The mystique of Smith's market system remains the ideal to which American capitalism often pays lip service but which it refuses to practice.

M L

From

AN INQUIRY INTO THE NATURE AND CAUSES OF THE WEALTH OF NATIONS

(1776)

ECONOMIC GROWTH AND THE DIVISION OF LABOR

The annual labor of every nation is the fund which originally supplies it with all the necessaries and conveniences of life which it annually consumes, and which consist always either in the immediate produce of that labor or in what is purchased with that produce from other nations.

According, therefore, as this produce, or what is purchased with it, bears a greater or smaller proportion to the number of those who are to consume it, the nation will be better or worse supplied with all the necessaries and conveniences for which it has occasion.

But this proportion must in every nation be regulated by two different circumstances: first, by the skill, dexterity, and judgment with which its labor is generally applied; and, secondly, by the proportion between the number of those who are employed in useful labor and that of those who are not so employed. . . .

The abundance or scantiness of this supply too seems to depend more upon the former of those two circumstances than upon the latter. . . .

The greatest improvement in the productive powers of labor and the greater part of the skill, dexterity, and judgment with which it is anywhere directed, or applied, seem to have been the effects of the division of labor. . . .

To take an example . . . from a very trifling manufacture, but one in which the division of labor has been very often taken notice of, the trade of the pinmaker; a workman not educated to this business (which the division of labor has rendered a distinct trade), nor acquainted with the use of the machinery employed in it (to the invention of which the same division of labor has probably given occasion), could scarce, perhaps, with his utmost industry, make one pin in a day, and certainly could not make twenty. But in the way in which this business is now carried on, not only the whole work is a peculiar trade, but it is divided into a number of branches, of which the greater part are likewise peculiar trades. One man draws out the wire, another straightens it, a third cuts it, a fourth points it, a fifth grinds it at the top for receiving the head; to make the head requires two or three distinct operations; to put it on is a peculiar business, to whiten the pins is another; it is even a trade by itself to put them into the paper; and the important business of making a pin is, in this manner, divided into about eighteen distinct operations, which, in some manufactories, are all performed by distinct hands, though in others the same man will sometimes perform two or three of them. I have seen a small manufactory of this kind where ten men only were employed, and where some of them consequently performed two or three distinct operations. But though they were very poor, and therefore but indifferently accommodated with the necessary machinery, they could, when they exerted themselves, make among them about twelve pounds of pins in a day. There are in a pound upward of four thousand pins of a middling size. Those ten persons, therefore, could make among them upward of forty-eight thousand pins in a day. Each person, therefore, making a tenth part of forty-eight thousand pins, might be considered as making four thousand eight hundred pins in a day. But if they had all wrought separately and independently, and without any of them having been educated to this peculiar business, they certainly could not each of them have made twenty, perhaps not one pin in a day; that is, certainly, not the two hundred and fortieth, perhaps not the four thousand eight hundredth part of what they are at present capable of performing in consequence of a proper division and combination of their different operations.

In every other art and manufacture the effects of the division of labor are similar to what they are in this very trifling one; though, in many of them, the labor can neither be so much subdivided nor reduced to so great a simplicity of operation. The division of labor, however, so far as it can be introduced, occasions, in every art, a proportionable increase of the productive powers of labor. The separation of different trades and employments from one another seems to have taken place in consequence of this advantage. This separation too is generally carried furthest in those countries which enjoy the highest degree of industry and improvement, what is the work of one man in a rude state of society being generally that of several in an improved one. . . .

This great increase of the quantity of work which, in consequence of the division of labor, the same number of people are capable of performing is owing to three different circumstances; first, to the increase of dexterity in every particular workman; secondly, to the saving of the time which is commonly lost in passing from one species of work to another; and, lastly, to the invention of a great number of machines which facilitate and abridge labor and enable one man to do the work of many. . . .

It is the great multiplication of the productions of all the different arts, in consequence of the division of labor, which occasions, in a well-governed society, that universal opulence which extends itself to the lowest ranks of the people. Every workman has a great quantity of his own work to dispose of beyond what he himself has occasion for; and every other workman being exactly in the same situation, he is enabled to exchange a great quantity of his own goods for a great quantity or, what comes to the same thing, for the price of a great quantity of theirs. He supplies them abundantly with what they have occasion for, and they accommodate him as amply with what he has occasion for, and a general plenty diffuses itself through all the different ranks of the society. . . .

This division of labor, from which so many advantages are derived, is not originally the effect of any human wisdom, which foresees and intends that general opulence to which it gives occasion. It is the necessary, though very slow and gradual, consequence of a certain propensity in human nature which has in view no such extensive utility; the propensity to truck, barter, and exchange one thing for another. . . .

Among men, . . . the most dissimilar geniuses are of use to one another; the different produces of their respective talents, by the general disposition to truck, barter, and exchange, being brought, as it were, into a common stock, where every man may purchase whatever part of the produce of other men's talents he has occasion for. . . .

THE ACCUMULATION OF CAPITAL AND THE INVISIBLE HAND

In that rude state of society in which there is no division of labor, in which exchanges are seldom made, and in which every man provides everything for himself, it is not necessary that any stock should be accumulated or stored up beforehand, in order to carry on the business of the society. Every man endeavors to supply by his own industry his own occasional wants as they occur. When he is hungry, he goes to the forest to hunt; when his coat is worn out, he clothes himself with the skin of the first large animal he kills; and when his hut begins to go to ruin, he repairs it, as well as he can, with the trees and the turf that are nearest it.

But when the division of labor has once been thoroughly introduced, the produce of a man's own labor can supply but a small part of his occasional wants. The far greater part of them are supplied by the produce of other men's labor, which he purchases with the produce, or what is the same thing, with the price of the produce of his own. But this purchase cannot be made till such time as the produce of his own labor has not only been completed but sold. A stock of goods of different kinds, therefore, must be stored up somewhere sufficient to maintain him, and to supply him with the materials and tools of his work, till such time, at least, as both these events can be brought about. A weaver cannot apply himself entirely to his peculiar business unless there is beforehand stored up somewhere, either in his own possession or in that of some other person, a stock sufficient to maintain him, and to supply him with the materials and tools of his work, till he has not only completed but sold his web. This accumulation must, evidently, be previous to his applying his industry for so long a time to such a peculiar business.

As the accumulation of stock must, in the nature of things, be previous to the division of labor, so labor can be more and more subdivided in proportion only as stock is previously more and more accumulated. . . .

Parsimony, and not industry, is the immediate cause of the increase of capital. Industry, indeed, provides the subject which parsimony accumulates. But whatever industry might acquire, if parsimony did not save and store up, the capital would never be the greater.

Parsimony, by increasing the fund which is destined for the maintenance of productive hands, tends to increase the number of those hands whose labor adds to the value of the subject upon which it is bestowed. It tends therefore to increase the exchangeable value of the annual produce of the land and labor of the country. It puts into motion an additional quantity of industry, which gives an additional value to the annual produce. . . .

. . . The capital employed in agriculture . . . not only puts into motion a greater quantity of productive labor than any equal capital employed in manufactures, but in proportion too to the quantity of productive labor which it employs, it adds a much greater value to the annual produce of the land and labor of the country, to the real wealth and revenue of its inhabitants. Of all the ways in which a capital can be employed, it is by far the most advantageous to the society. . . .

After agriculture, the capital employed in manufactures puts into motion the greatest quantity of productive labor, and adds the greatest value to the annual produce. That which is employed in the trade of exportation, has the least effect of any of the three. . . .

Every individual is continually exerting himself to find out the most advantageous employment for whatever capital he can command. It is his own advantage, indeed, and not that of society, which he has in view. But the study of his own advantage naturally or, rather, necessarily leads him to prefer that employment which is most advantageous to the society.

First, every individual endeavors to employ his capital as near home as he can and consequently as much as he can in the support of domestic industry, provided always that he can thereby obtain the ordinary or not a great deal less than the ordinary profits of stock. . . .

Secondly, every individual who employs his capital in the support of domestic industry necessarily endeavors so to direct that industry that its produce may be to the greatest possible value.

The produce of industry is what it adds to the subject or materials upon which it is employed. In proportion as the value of this produce is great or small, so will likewise be the profits of the employer.

But it is only for the sake of profit that any man employs a capital in the support of industry; and he will always, therefore, endeavor to employ it in the support of that industry of which the produce is likely to be of the greatest value, or to exchange for the greatest quantity either of money or of other goods.

But the annual revenue for every society is always precisely equal to the exchangeable value of the whole annual produce of its industry, or rather is precisely the same thing with that exchangeable value. As every individual, therefore, endeavors as much as he can both to employ his capital in the support of domestic industry, and so to direct that industry that its produce may be of the greatest value, every individual necessarily labors to render the annual revenue of the society as great as he can. He generally, indeed, neither intends to promote the public interest nor knows how much he is promoting it. By preferring the support of domestic to that of foreign industry, he intends only his own security; and by directing that industry in such a manner as its produce may be of the greatest value, he intends only his own gain, and he is in this, as in many other cases, led by an invisible hand to promote an end which was no part of his intention. Nor is it always the worse for the society that it was no part of it. By pursuing his own interest, he frequently promotes that of the society more effectually than when he really intends to promote it. I have never known much good done by those who affected to trade for the public good. It is an affectation, indeed, not very common among merchants, and very few words need be employed in dissuading them from it.

What is the species of domestic industry which his capital can employ, and of which the produce is likely to be of the greatest value, every individual, it is evident, can, in his local situation, judge much better than any statesman or law-giver can do for him. The statesman, who should attempt to direct private people in what manner they ought to employ their capitals, would not only load himself with a most unnecessary attention but assume an authority which could safely be trusted not only to no single person but to no council or senate whatever, and which would nowhere be so dangerous as in the hands of a man who had folly and presumption enough to fancy himself fit to exercise it. . . .

THE OPERATION OF THE MARKET

There is in every society or neighborhood an ordinary or average rate both of wages and profit in every different employment of labor and stock. This rate is naturally regulated, as I shall show hereafter, partly by the general circumstances of the society, their riches or poverty, their advancing, stationary or declining condition; and partly by the particular nature of each employment....

When the price of any commodity is neither more nor less than what is sufficient to pay the rent of the land, the wages of the labor, and the profits of the stock employed in raising, preparing, and bringing it to market, according to their natural rates, the commodity is then sold for what may be called its natural price.

The commodity is then sold precisely for what it is worth, or for what it really costs the person who brings it to market; for though in common language what is called the prime cost of any commodity does not comprehend the profit of the person who is to sell it again, yet if he sells it at a price which does not allow him the ordinary rate of profit in his neighborhood, he is evidently a loser by the trade, since by employing his stock in some other way he might have made that profit. His profit, besides, is his revenue, the proper fund of his subsistence. As, while he is preparing and bringing the goods to market, he advances to his workmen their wages, or their subsistence, so he advances to himself, in the same manner, his own subsistence, which is generally suitable to the profit which he may reasonably expect from the sale of his goods. Unless they yield him this profit, therefore, they do not repay him what they may very properly be said to have really cost him.

Though the price, therefore, which leaves him this profit is not always the lowest at which a dealer may sometimes sell his goods, it is the lowest at which he is likely to sell them for any considerable time; at least where there is perfect liberty, or where he may change his trade as often as he pleases.

The actual price at which any commodity is commonly sold is called its market price. It may either be above, or below, or exactly the same with its natural price.

The market price of every particular commodity is regulated by the proportion between the quanity which is actually brought to the market and the demand of those who are willing to pay the natural price of the commodity, or the whole value of the rent, labor, and profit which must be paid in order to bring it thither. Such people may be called the effectual demanders, and their demand the effectual demand, since it may be sufficient to effectuate the bringing of the commodity to market. . . .

When the quantity of any commodity which is brought to market falls short of the effectual demand, all those who are willing to pay the whole value of the rent, wages, and profit which must be paid in order to bring it thither cannot be supplied with the quantity which they want. Rather than want it altogether, some of them will be willing to give more. A competition will immediately begin among them, and the market price will rise more or less above the natural price, according as either the greatness of the deficiency or the wealth and wanton luxury of the competitors happen to animate more or less the eagerness of the competition. Among competitors of equal wealth and luxury the same deficiency will generally occasion a more or less eager competition, according as the acquisition of the commodity happens to be of more or less importance to them. Hence the exorbitant price of the necessaries of life during the blockade of a town or in a famine.

When the quantity brought to market exceeds the effectual demand, it cannot be all sold to those who are willing to pay the whole value of the rent, wages, and profit which must be paid in order to bring it thither. Some part must be sold to those who [will not buy unless they] pay less, and the low price which they give for it must reduce the price of the whole. The market price will sink more or less below the natural price, according as the greatness of the excess increases more or less the competition of the sellers, or according as it happens to be more or less important to them to get immediately rid of the commodity. The same excess in the importation of perishables will occasion a much greater competition than in that of durable commodities; in the importation of oranges, for example, than in that of old iron.

When the quantity brought to market is just sufficient to supply the effectual demand and no more, the market price naturally comes to be either exactly, or as nearly as can be judged of, the same with the natural price. The whole quantity upon hand can be disposed of for this price and cannot be disposed of for more. The competition of the different dealers obliges them all to accept of this price but does not oblige them to accept of less.

The quantity of every commodity brought to market naturally suits itself to the effectual demand. It is the interest of all those who employ their land, labor, or stock, in bringing any commodity to market, that the quantity never should exceed the effectual demand; and it is the interest of all other people that it never should fall short of that demand.

If at any time it exceeds the effectual demand, some of the component parts of its price must be paid below their natural rate. If it is rent, the interest of the landlords will immediately prompt them to withdraw a part of their land; and if it is wages or profit, the interest of the laborers in the one case, and of their employers in the other, will prompt them to withdraw a part of their labor or stock from this employment. The quantity brought to market will soon be no more than sufficient to supply the effectual demand. All the different parts of its price will rise to their natural rate, and the whole price to its natural price.

If, on the contrary, the quantity brought to market should at any time fall short of the effectual demand, some of the component parts of its price must rise above their natural rate. If it is rent, the interest of all other landlords will naturally prompt them to prepare more land for the raising of this commodity; if it is wages or profit, the interest of all other laborers and dealers will soon prompt them to employ more labor and stock in preparing and bringing it to market. The quantity brought thither will soon be sufficient to supply the effectual demand. All the different parts of its price will soon sink to their natural rate, and the whole price to its natural price.

The natural price, therefore, is, as it were, the central price, to which the prices of all commodities are continually gravitating. Different accidents may sometimes keep them suspended a good deal above it, and sometimes force them down even somewhat below it. But whatever may be the obstacles which hinder them from settling in this center of repose and continuance, they are constantly tending toward it.

The whole quantity of industry annually employed in order to bring any commodity to market naturally suits itself in this manner to the effectual demand. It naturally aims at bringing always that precise quantity thither which may be sufficient to supply, and no more than supply, that demand. . . .

When by an increase in the effectual demand, the market price of some particular commodity happens to rise a good deal above the natural price, those who employ their stocks in supplying that market are generally careful to conceal this change. If it was commonly known, their great profit would tempt so many new rivals to employ their stocks in the same way that, the effectual demand being fully supplied, the market price would soon be reduced to the natural price and perhaps for some time even below it. If the market is at a great distance from the residence of those who supply it, they may sometimes be able to keep the secret for several years together and may so long enjoy their extraordinary profits without any new rivals. Secrets of this kind, however, it must be acknowledged, can seldom be long kept; and the extraordinary profits can last very little longer than they are kept.

Secrets in manufactures are capable of being longer kept than secrets in trade. A dyer who has found the means of producing a particular color with materials which cost only half the price of those commonly made use of, may, with good management, enjoy the advantage of his discovery as long as he lives, and even leave it as a legacy to his posterity. His extraordinary gains arise from the high price which is paid for his private labor. They properly consist in the high wages of that labor. But as they are repeated upon every part of his stock, and as their whole amount bears, upon that account, a regular proportion to it, they are commonly considered as extraordinary profits of stock.

MONOPOLY, BUSINESSMEN, AND THE CONSUMER

A monopoly granted either to an individual or to a trading company has the same effect as a secret in trade or manufactures. The monopolists, by keeping the market constantly understocked, by never fully supplying the effectual demand, sell their commodities much above the natural price and raise their emoluments, whether they consist in wages or profit, greatly above their natural rate.

The price of monopoly is upon every occasion the highest which can be got. The natural price, or the price of free competition, on the contrary, is the lowest which can be taken, not upon every occasion indeed, but for any considerable time together. The one is upon every occasion the highest which can be squeezed out of the buyers, or which, it is supposed, they will consent to give; the other is the lowest which the sellers can commonly afford to take and at the same time continue their business.

The exclusive privileges of corporations, statutes of apprenticeship, and all those laws which restrain, in particular employments, the competition to a smaller number than might otherwise go into them have the same tendency, though in a less degree. They are a sort of enlarged monopolies and may frequently, for ages together and in whole classes of employments, keep up the market price of particular commodities above the natural price and maintain both the wages of the labor and the profits of the stock employed about them somewhat above their natural rate.

Such enhancements of the market price may last as long as the regulations of police which give occasion to them.

The market price of any particular commodity, though it may continue long above, can seldom continue long below, its natural price. Whatever part of it was paid below the natural rate, the persons whose interest it affected would immediately feel the loss and would immediately withdraw either so much land, or so much labor, or so much stock, from being employed about it that the quantity brought to market would soon be no more than sufficient to supply the effectual demand. Its market price, therefore, would soon rise to the natural price. This at least would be the case where there was perfect liberty.

. . . Merchants and master-manufacturers are . . . the two classes of people who commonly employ the largest capitals, and who by their wealth draw to themselves the greatest share of the public consideration. As during their whole lives they are engaged in plans and projects, they have frequently more acuteness of understanding than the greater part of country gentlemen. As their thoughts, however, are commonly exercised rather about the interest of their own particular branch of business than about that of the society, their judgment, even when given with the greatest candor (which it has not been upon every occasion), is much more to be depended upon with regard to the former of those two objects than with regard to the latter. Their superiority over the country gentlemen is not so much in their knowledge of the public interest as in their having a better knowledge of their own interest than he has of his. It is by this superior knowledge of their own interest that they have frequently imposed upon his generosity and persuaded him to give up both his own interest and that of the public from a very simple but honest conviction that their interest, and not his, was the interest of the public. The interest of the dealers, however, in any particular branch of trade or manufactures, is always in some respects different from, and even opposite to, that of the public. To widen the market and to narrow the competition is always the interest of the dealers. To widen the market may frequently be agreeable enough to the interest of the public; but to narrow the competition must always be against it and can serve only to enable the dealers, by raising their profits above what they naturally would be, to levy, for their own benefit, an absurd tax upon the rest of their fellow-citizens. The proposal of any new law or regulation of commerce which comes from this order ought always to be listened to with great precaution and ought never to be adopted till after having been long and carefully examined, not only with the most scrupulous, but with the most suspicious attention. It comes from an order of men whose interest is never exactly the same with that of the public, who have generally an interest to deceive and even to oppress the public, and who accordingly have, upon many occasions, both deceived and oppressed it. . . .

People of the same trade seldom meet together, even for merriment and diversion, but the conversation ends in a conspiracy against the public or in some contrivance to raise prices. It is impossible indeed to prevent such meetings, by any law which either could be executed, or would be consistent with liberty and justice. But though the law cannot hinder people of the same trade from sometimes assembling together, it ought to do nothing to facilitate such assemblies, much less to render them necessary.

Consumption is the sole end and purpose of all production, and the interest of the producer ought to be attended to only so far as it may be necessary for promoting that of the consumer. The maxim is so perfectly self-evident that it would be absurd to attempt to prove it. But in the mercantile system, the interest of the consumer is almost constantly sacrificed to that of the producer; and it seems to consider production, and not consumption, as the ultimate end and object of all industry and commerce.

In the restraints upon the importation of all foreign commodities which can come into competition with those of our own growth, or manufacture, the interest of the home consumer is evidently sacrificed to that of the producer. It is altogether for the benefit of the latter that the former is obliged to pay that enhancement of price which this monopoly almost always occasions.

It is altogether for the benefit of the producer that bounties are granted upon the exportation of some of his productions. The home consumer is obliged to pay, first, the tax which is necessary for paying the bounty and, secondly, the still greater tax which necessarily arises from the enhancement of the price of the commodity in the home market.

By the famous treaty of commerce with Portugal, the consumer is prevented by high duties from purchasing of a neighboring country a commodity which our own climate does not produce but is obliged to purchase it of a distant country, though it is acknowledged that the commodity of the distant country is of a worse quality than that of the near one. The home consumer is obliged to submit to this inconveniency, in order that the producer may import into the distant country some of his productions upon more advantageous terms that he would otherwise have been allowed to do. The consumer, too, is obliged to pay whatever enhancement in the price of those very productions this forced exportation may occasion in the home market.

But in the system of laws which has been established for the management of our American and West Indian colonies, the interest of the home consumer has been sacrificed to that of the producer with a more extravagant profusion than in all our other commercial regulations. A great empire has been established for the sole purpose of raising up a nation of customers who should be obliged to buy from the shops of our different producers all the goods with which these could supply them. For the sake of that little enhancement of price which this monopoly might afford our producers, the home consumers have been burdened with the whole expense of maintaining and defending that empire, For this purpose, and for this purpose only, in the two last wars, more than two hundred millions have been spent, and a new debt of more than a hundred and seventy millions has been contracted over and above all that had been expended for the same purpose in former wars. The interest of this debt alone is not only greater than the whole extraordinary profit, which, it ever could be pretended, was made by the monopoly of the colony trade, but than the whole value of that trade, or than the whole value of the goods, which at an average have been annually exported to the colonies.

It cannot be very difficult to determine who have been the contrivers of this whole mercantile system; not the consumers, we may believe, whose interest has been entirely neglected; but the producers, whose interest has been so carefully attended to; and among this latter class our merchants and manufacturers have been by far the principal architects. In the mercantile regulations, which have been taken notice of in this chapter, the interest of our manufacturers has been most peculiarly attended to; and the interest, not so much of the consumers, as that of some other sets of producers, has been sacrificed to it. . . .

THE GOVERNMENT'S ROLE

All systems either of preference or of restraint, therefore, being thus completely taken away, the obvious and simple system of natural liberty establishes itself of its own accord. Every man, as long as he does not violate the laws of justice, is left perfectly free to pursue his own interest his own way and to bring both his industry and capital into competition with those of any other man or order of men. The sovereign is completely discharged from a duty, in the attempting to perform which he must always be exposed to innumerable delusions, and for the proper performance of which no human wisdom or knowledge could ever be sufficient—the duty of superintending the industry of private people and of directing it toward the employments most suitable to the interest of the society. According to the system of natural liberty, the sovereign has only three duties to attend to; three duties of great importance, indeed, but plain and intelligible to common understandings: first, the duty of protecting the society from the violence and invasion of other independent societies; secondly, the duty of protecting, as far as possible, every member of the society from the injustice or oppression of every other member of it, or the duty of establishing an exact administration of justice; and, thirdly, the duty of erecting and maintaining certain public works and certain public institutions. . . .

. . . The first duty of the sovereign, that of protecting the society from the violence and invasion of other independent societies, can be performed only by means of a military force. . . .

The art of war in the progress of improvement necessarily becomes one of the most complicated of all arts. The state of the mechanical, as well as of some other arts, with which it is necessarily connected, determines the degree of perfection to which it is capable of being carried at any particular time. But in order to carry it to this degree of perfection, it is necessary that it should become the sole or principal occupation of a particular class of citizens, and the division of labor is as necessary for the improvement of this, as of every other art.

In these circumstances, there seem to be but two methods, by which the state can make any tolerable provision for the public defense.

It may either, first, by means of a very rigorous police, and in spite of the whole bent of the interest, genius and inclinations of the people, enforce the practice of military exercises, and oblige either all the citizens of the military age, or a certain number of them, to join in some measure the trade of a soldier to whatever other trade or profession they may happen to carry on.

Or secondly, by maintaining and employing a certain number of citizens in the constant practice of military exercises, it may render the trade of a soldier a particular trade, separate and distinct from all others.

If the state has recourse to the first of those expedients, its military force is said to consist in a militia; if to the second, it is said to consist in a standing army. The practice of military exercises is the sole or principal occupation of the soldiers of a standing army, and the maintenance or pay which the state affords them is the principal and ordinary fund of their subsistence. The practice of military exercises is only the occasional occupation of the soldiers of a militia, and they derive the principal and ordinary fund of their subsistence from some other occupation. In a militia, the character of the laborer, artificer, or tradesman, predominates over that of the soldier: in a standing army, that of the soldier predominates over every other character; and in this distinction seems to consist the essential difference between those two different species of military force.

The first duty of the sovereign, that of defending the society from the violence and injustice of other independent societies, grows gradually more and more expensive, as the society advances in civilization. The military force of the society, which originally cost the sovereign no expense either in time of peace or in time of war, must, in the progress of improvement, first be maintained by him in time of war, and afterwards even in time of peace. . . .

The second duty of the sovereign, that of protecting, as far as possible, every member of the society from the injustice or oppression of every other member of it, or the duty of establishing an exact administration of justice requires two very different degrees of expense in the different periods of society.

Among nations of hunters, as there is scarce any property, or at least none that exceeds the value of two or three days' labor; so there is seldom any established magistrate or any regular administration of justice. Men who have no property can injure one another only in their persons or reputations. But when one man kills, wounds, beats, or defames another, though he to whom the injury is done suffers, he who does it receives no benefit. It is otherwise with the injuries to property. The benefit of the person who does the injury is often equal to the loss of him who suffers it. Envy, malice, or resentment, are the only passions which can prompt one man to injure another in his person or reputation. But the greater part of men are not very frequently under the influence of those passions; and the very worst men are so only occasionally. As their gratification too, how agreeable soever it may be to certain characters, is not attended with any real or permanent advantage, it is in the greater part of men commonly restrained by prudential considerations. Men may live together in society with some tolerable degree of security, though there is no civil magistrate to protect them from the injustice of those passions. But avarice and ambition in the rich, in the poor the hatred of labor and the love of present ease and enjoyment, are the passions which prompt to invade property, passions much more steady in their operation, and much more universal in their influence. Wherever there is great property, there is great inequality. For one very rich man, there must be at least five hundred poor, and the affluence of the few supposes the indigence of the many. The affluence of the rich excites the indignation of the poor, who are often both driven by want, and prompted by envy, to invade his possessions. It is only under the shelter of the civil magistrate that the owner of that valuable property, which is acquired by the labor of many years, or perhaps of many successive generations, can sleep a single night in security. The acquisition of valuable and extensive property, therefore, necessarily requires the establishment of civil government. . . .

The third and last duty of the sovereign or commonwealth is that of erecting and maintaining those public institutions and those public works, which, though they may be in the highest degree advantageous to a great society, are, however, of such a nature, that the profit could never repay the expense to any individual or small number of individuals, and which it therefore cannot be expected that any individual or small number of individuals should erect or maintain. . . .

HENRY C. SIMONS

(1899–1946)

Henry C. Simons was a member of what is sometimes called the "Chicago School of Economists." The early members of the school included, along with Simons, University of Chicago economists Frank Knight and Jacob Viner. Today its banner is carried by Milton Friedman and George Stigler at Chicago and a growing number of economists throughout the country who associate themselves with the movement. Although differences of opinion exist among this group of classical liberals, they hold certain basic views in common. One writer has described the "Chicago economist" as distinguishable by

> the polar position that he occupies among economists as an adovcate of an individualistic market economy; the emphasis that he puts on the usefulness and relevance of neoclassical economic theory; the way in which he equates the actual and the ideal market; the way in which he sees and applies economics in and to every nook and cranny of life; and the emphasis that he puts on hypothesis-testing as a neglected element in the development of positive economics.[1]

When it comes to public policy these views translate themselves into support for the solution of economic and social problems via the market mechanism rather than through governmental action. Where government has a role to play, the school emphasizes the importance of placing rather strict restraints on that authority so as to limit discretionary action. Nowhere is this more evident than in their view toward monetary policy. Faith in the market and in neoclassical as opposed to Keynesian theory also shows itself in the belief that an economy with flexible wages and prices will consistently move toward full employment and that a government's attempt to speed the process along will only aggravate the problem. Underlying their overall disapproval of market manipulation is the fear that individual freedoms will be eroded in the process.

One of the best statements of the Chicago school's position was penned by Henry C. Simons as a reaction, or alternative plan of action, to Roosevelt's New Deal legislation. An edited version of that statement is reprinted here. It is understandable that a classical liberal would react against the policies of an era which was quickly abandoning hope in the viability of the free market by instituting greater controls over wages and prices and sanctioning price-fixing and market-sharing agreements. While New Deal legislation seemed to seek a cure for the depression by eliminating competition, Simons viewed lack of competition as a major reason for the depression.

Though most of Simons' proposals were presented as long-run solutions to the problems of capitalism, he did not lack for short-term solutions either. He agreed with Keynes that one cause of the depression was the uncertainty of investment opportunities and the resultant emphasis on saving over investment. Along with others at the University of Chicago, including economists Jacob Viner and Frank Knight, Simons sent a memorandum to Washington in 1932 which urged deficit spending through an expansion of the money supply as a means of stimulating the economy. During the 1930s the Chicago economists continued to urge Keynesian remedies for the depression. These recommendations, coming from a group considered to include some of the strongest advocates of free-market capitalism, helped pave the way for a change in the government's attitude on the desirability of continuously balanced budgets. But though Simons may have helped break down the barriers to the acceptance of some Keynesian ideas, he was critical of the long-run implications of the *General Theory*. He said of Keynes:

> [A]ttempting mischievous and salutary irritation of his peers . . . he may only succeed in becoming the academic idol of our worst cranks and charlatans—not to mention the possibilities of the book as the economic bible of a fascist movement.

Following the classical liberal tradition, Simons stressed the dangers to liberty inherent in a policy of governmental intervention as a permanent feature of capitalism. To him, reliance on the competitive market was the long-run answer to the need for protection of individual freedoms. Defenders of this viewpoint were not hard to find during the 1930s, but Simons' position differed from others in its stress on the positive role that government could play in maintaining a viable free market economy. Seeing a clear "division of labor" between political and market controls, he insisted that the primary role of the former was to provide a stable environment for the operation of competition. In the pamphlet reprinted here, he outlines several areas of action which he felt would provide that environment. In reading them, one is struck with their relevance to the economic scene of the 1970s, particularly in regard to taxation and price-control policies. Simons' concern with the adverse economic effects of large corporations and the whole merchandising effort is also superficially in accord with the radical approach, as we have classified it in this volume. Simons' proposals, of course, are intended to clear the decks so that the free market can be reestablished, not to replace that market with some system of central planning.

Central to Simons' plan for restructuring the economy was the elimination of corporate monopoly power. Relying on his preference for legal rather than regulatory power, he proposed that the federal government be given the exclusive right to charter corporations and that limitations on the size of firms and the amount of property they could own be written into their incorporation charters. In those cases where large size was necessary for efficiency, as perhaps in railroads and utilities, he favored government ownership. On this point his student Milton Friedman differs with him, calling for private monopoly of large industries rather than public regulation or ownership. In

1. H. Laurence Miller Jr., "On the Chicago School of Economics," *Journal of Political Economy* 70 (Feb. 1962): 65.

Capitalism and Freedom, Friedman says:

> If society were static so that the conditions which give rise to a technical monopoly were sure to remain, I would have little confidence in this solution. In a rapidly changing society, however, the conditions making for technical monopoly frequently change and I suspect that both public regulation and public monopoly are likely to be less responsive to such changes in conditions, to be less readily capable of elimination, than private monopoly.

The difference between Simons and Friedman on this point may be due to the fact that Friedman has had a longer time period over which to observe governmental behavior. However, it is also likely that he sees business operations in the actual market as closer to his ideal than Simons did. This would help explain why Friedman is less likely to criticize the power of business monopolies than the power of unions or government. Thus, while Friedman and Simons differ on the type and extent of governmental action necessary to promote competitive markets, they both agree that such an environment is essential for the preservation of a free democratic society.

R R

From

A POSITIVE PROGRAM FOR LAISSEZ-FAIRE

(1934)

SOME PROPOSALS FOR A LIBERAL ECONOMIC POLICY

This is frankly a propagandist tract—a defense of the thesis that traditional liberalism offers, at once, the best escape from the moral confusion of current political and economic thought, and the best basis or rationale for a program of economic reconstruction. This view has been widely ridiculed of late, by communists and fascists, by most of our "liberal" reformers and politically ambitious intellectuals. Old-fashioned liberals, and the more orthodox economists especially, have responded meagerly to the attack; only their position is inadequately represented in the welter of current controversy. Consequently, one is impelled to try, humbly but uncompromisingly, to state that position, and to indicate specifically how economic reconstruction might be achieved along lines dictated by a faith in liberty.

There is in America no important disagreement as to the proper objectives of economic policy—larger real income, greater regularity of production and employment, reduction of inequality, preservation of democratic institutions. The real issues have to do merely with means, not with ends (or intentions); but the future of our civilization hangs in balance as these issues are decided; and those whom the recent crisis has brought to positions of political and intellectual leadership seem to lack insight as to the

Reprinted from *A Positive Program for Laissez-Faire* by Henry C. Simons, by permission of the University of Chicago Press and the author.

nature of our economic ills or the effects of their own prescriptions. . . .

The real enemies of liberty in this country are the naïve advocates of managed economy or national planning; but with them we must agree on one vital point, namely, that there is now imperative need for a sound, positive program of economic legislation. Our economic organization is perilously near to disintegration and collapse. In earlier periods, it could be expected to become increasingly strong if only protected from undue political interference. Now, however, it has reached a condition where it can be saved only through adoption of the wisest measures by the state. Modern democracy arose under conditions which made only negligible demands for intelligence in economic legislation; it remains soon to be seen whether democracy can survive when those demands are very great. . . .

PART I

Much significance has been, and should be, attached to the simultaneous development of capitalism and democracy. Indeed, it seems clear that *none of the precious "freedoms" which our generation has inherited can be extended, or even maintained, apart from an essential freedom of enterprise—apart from a genuine "division of labor" between competitive and political controls.* The existence (and preservation) of a competitive situation in private industry makes possible a minimizing of the responsibilities of the sovereign state. It frees the state from the obligation of adjudicating endless, bitter disputes among persons as participants in different industries, and among owners of different kinds of productive services. In a word, it makes possible a political policy of laissez-faire.

This policy and the correlative political philosophy, nineteenth-century liberalism, have been subjected latterly to gross misrepresentation and to shallow satirical jibes in the "new economics." The representation of laissez-faire as a merely do-nothing policy is unfortunate and misleading. It is an obvious responsibility of the state under this policy to maintain the kind of legal and institutional framework within which competition can function effectively as an agency of control. The policy, therefore, should be defined positively, as one under which the state seeks to establish and maintain such conditions that it may avoid the necessity of regulating "the heart of the contract"—that is to say, the necessity of regulating relative prices. Thus, the state is charged, under this "division of labor," with heavy responsibilities and large "control" functions: the maintenance of competitive conditions in industry; the control of the currency (of the quantity and value of the effective money); the definition of the institution of property (especially with reference to fiscal practices)—not to mention the many social-welfare activities.

The great errors of economic policy in the past century may be defined—and many of our present difficulties explained—in terms of excessive political interference with relative prices, and in terms of disastrous neglect of the positive responsibilities of government under a free-enterprise system. Our governments have tinkered interminably with relative prices (witness the tariff). On the other hand, they have never really tried to maintain effectively competitive conditions in industry (witness the "rule of reason" and the absurd grants of powers to corporations). They have evaded—when they have not abused—their responsibility of controlling the currency (witness the growth of private banks which provide, and potentially can destroy, all but a small percentage of our total effective circulating media). Moreover, they have scarcely recognized the obligation, or the opportunities, of mitigating inequality through appropriate fiscal practices—that is to say, through appropriate definition of the institution of property. Consequently, the so-called failure of capitalism (of the free-enterprise system, of competition) may reasonably be interpreted as primarily a failure of the political state in the discharge of its minimum responsibilities under capitalism. This view may suggest reasons for skepticism with reference to currently popular schemes for curing our ills.

It seems clear, at all events, that there is an intimate connection between freedom of enterprise and freedom of discussion, and that political liberty can survive only within an effectively competitive economic system. Thus, *the great enemy of democracy is monopoly, in all its forms:* gigantic corporations, trade associations and other agencies for price control, trade unions—or, in general, organization and concentration of power within functional classes. Effectively organized functional groups possess tremendous power for exploiting the community at large and even for sabotaging the system. The existence of competition within such groups, on the other hand, serves to protect the community as a whole and to give an essential flexibility to the economy. The disappearance of competition would almost assure the wrecking of the system in the economic struggle of organized minorities; on the political side, it would present a hopeless dilemma. If the organized economic groups were left to exercise their monopoly powers without political restraint, the result would be a usurpation of sovereignty by these groups—and, perhaps, a domination of the state by them. On the other hand, if the state undertakes to tolerate (instead of destroying) such organizations and to regulate their regulations, it will have assumed tasks and responsibilities incompatible with its enduring in a democratic form. . . .

If popular government did for a time achieve that infinitely wise and effective control which would be necessary merely to prevent economic collapse, the system could not survive. Political determination of relative prices, of relative returns from investment in different industries, and of relative wages in different occupations, implies settlement by peaceful negotiation of conflicts too bitter and too irreconcilable for deliberate adjudication and compromise. The petty warfare of competition within groups can be kept on such a level that it protects and actually promotes the general welfare. The warfare among organized economic groups, on the other hand, is unlikely to be more controllable or less destructive than warfare among nations. Indeed, democratic governments would have hardly so good a chance of arbitrating these conflicts tolerably as have the League of Nations and the World Court in their field.

Suppression of the competitive struggle within economic groups, and their organization into collective fighting units, will create conditions such that only ruthless dictatorship can maintain the degree of order necessary to survival of the population in an economy of intricate division of labor. Under these circumstances, the distribution of power among nations is likely, by the way, to be altered drastically in favor of those people best disciplined to submission and least contaminated with dangerous notions about the rights of man. In the

Western world, the price of short-run security under such political arrangements is likely to be greater insecurity in the long run; for Western peoples will probably insist on changing dictators occasionally, even at the expense of catastrophic upheavals, disintegration of national units, and progressive political and economic separatism.

It seems nowise fantastic, indeed, to suggest that present developments point toward a historic era which will bear close resemblance at many points to the early Middle Ages. With the disappearance of the vestiges of free trade among nations will come intensification of imperialism and increasingly bitter and irreconcilable conflicts of interest internationally. With the disappearance of free trade within national areas will come endless, destructive conflict among organized economic groups—which should suffice, without assistance from international wars, for the destruction of Western civilization and its institutional heritage.

Thus, the increasing organization of interest groups (monopoly) and the resurgence of mercantilism ("planning")[1] promise an end of elaborate economic organization (of extensive division of labor, nationally and internationally), and an end of political freedom as well. If the situation is not yet hopeless because of the technical difficulties of turning back (and I refuse to believe it is), one finds abundant reason for despair in the fact that our sophisticated generation seems simply not to care. It has become unfashionable to reveal affection for democracy; and the meager curiosity about the future of our institutions leads only to the publication of our cheapest romantic literature in the guise of economics.

Competition and laissez-faire have not brought us to heaven. The severe depression, regarded as resulting from competition *instead of from the lack of it,* naturally produces an impairment of our affection for the system. But the widespread disposition to deprecate our institutional heritage seems explicable only in terms of general unwillingness and inability to consider seriously what the actual alternatives are—where new roads lead—or, whatever their destination, how much human suffering must be endured on the way. Few people are now interested in assessing the opportunities for remodelling the old system without destroying its foundations. Worst of all, perhaps, is the popular disposition to accept from zealous "uplifters" devices for salvaging our institutions which are, in fact, the most effective means for undermining them irreparably.

Let us consider now what circumstances are most inimical, within the old system, to production of a large social income (to economic efficiency). The effective functioning of our economic organization requires full utilization of existing resources, including labor, use of the best available technical methods, and, less obviously, economical allocation of resources among available, alternative uses. This latter aspect of the problem may well be emphasized here.

Any judgment of efficiency implies a standard or scale of values—merely physical efficiency is an absurd conception. For economic analysis, such a scale of values is available in the market values (prices) of commodities. These market values, being the result of competitive purchase by persons free to utilize

1. The reference here, of course, is merely to that kind of planning which, like mercantilism, implies elaborate regulation of trade, both foreign and domestic, and extensive political control of relative prices, relative wages, and investment.

purchasing power as they please, may be accepted as measuring roughly the relative importance (for the community) of physical units of different things. To be sure, these prices are the result of free disposition of purchasing power by individuals of widely different income-circumstances. But the problems of efficiency and of inequality may usefully be separated for purposes of discussion—and properly, if one accepts the view that the appropriate measures for improving efficiency and for mitigating inequality are, within fairly wide limits, distinct and independent.

Efficient utilization of resources implies an allocation such that units of every kind of productive service make equally important (valuable) contributions to the social product in all the different uses among which they are transferable. Such allocation will be approximated if, by virtue of highly competitive conditions, resources move freely from less productive (remunerative) to more productive employments. It is an essential object of monopoly, on the other hand, to maintain an area of abnormally high yield (productivity), and to prevent such influx of resources as would bring the monopolized industry down to the common level. Any effectively organized group may be relied upon to use to this end the power which organization brings.

Monopoly thus means the exclusion of available resources from uses which, on the market-value standard, are more important, and, therefore, means diversion of resources to less important uses. Every organized group, whether of employers or of workers, possesses great power, both for exploiting consumers and for injuring other groups of producers to whose industries resources are diverted by virtue of the monopoly restrictions. . . .

The gains from monopoly organization in general are likely, of course, to accrue predominantly to the strong and to be dervied at the expense of the weak. Among producers, organization is least expensive and most easily achieved, as well as most effective, within groups whose members were unusually large and prosperous at the outset. Among workers, the bias is not less striking. The most highly skilled and most highly remunerated trades are the trades where organization is least difficult and where the fighting strength of groups once organized is greatest. Little evidence, inductive or analytic, can be conjured up to support the popular conception of trade unionism as a device for raising incomes at the bottom of the scale. Its possibilities lie mainly in the improvement of the position of labor's aristocracy[2]—and largely at the expense of labor generally. Here as elsewhere the gains from monopoly are exploitative. The restriction of employment in the more remunerative occupations injures other laborers, both as consumers and as sellers of services rendered more abundant in other areas by the restriction.

Another major factor in the inefficient allocation of resources is to be found in government regulation and interference. . . .

While the tariff is the example par excellence of how the political process works in the control of relative prices, our experience with regulation of the so-called "natural monopolies" is also instructive. . . .

Public regulation of private monopoly would seem to be, at best, an anomalous arrangement, tolerable only as a temporary expedient. . . . Analysis of the problem, and examination of experience to date, would seem to indicate the wisdom of abandoning the existing scheme of things with respect to the railroads and utilities, rather than of extending the system to include other industries as well. Political control of utility charges is imperative, to be sure, for competition simply cannot function effectively as an agency of control. We may endure regulation for a time, on the dubious assumption that governments are more nearly competent to regulate than to operate. *In general, however, the state should face the necessity of actually taking over, owning, and managing directly, both the railroads and utilities, and all other industries in which it is impossible to maintain effectively competitive conditions.* For industries other than the utilities, there still remains a real alternative to socialization, namely, the establishment and preservation of competition as the regulative agency.

Turning now to questions of justice, of equitable distribution, we may suggest that equitable distribution is at least as important with respect to power as with reference to economic goods or income; also, that the cause of justice, perhaps in both directions, would be better served if well-intentioned reformers would reflect seriously on what their schemes imply with respect to the distribution of power. Surely there is something unlovely, to modern as against medieval minds, about marked inequality of either kind. A substantial measure of inequality may be unavoidable or essential for motivation; but it should be recognized as evil and tolerated only so far as the dictates of expediency are clear.

If we dislike extreme inequality of power, it is appropriate to view with especial misgivings the extension of political (and monopoly) control over relative prices and incomes. Either socialization or the mongrel system of "national planning" implies and requires extreme concentration of political power, under essentially undemocratic institutions. A system of democratic socialism is admittedly an attractive ideal; but, for the significant future, such a system is merely a romantic dream. On the other hand, it seems unlikely that any planners or controllers, with the peculiar talents requisite for obtaining dictatorial power, would be able to make decisions wise enough to keep an elaborate economic organization from falling apart. Even if one regards that prospect as not unpromising, the implied division of power between controllers and controllees would seem an intolerable price for increased efficiency.

An important factor in existing inequality, both of income and of power, is the gigantic corporation. We may recognize, in the almost unlimited grants of powers to corporate bodies, one of the greatest sins of governments against the free-enterprise system. There is simply no excuse, except with respect to a narrow and specialized class of enterprises, for allowing corporations to hold stock in other corporations—and no reasonable excuse (the utilities apart) for hundred-million-dollar corporations, no matter what form their property may take. Even if the much-advertised economies of gigantic financial combinations were real, sound policy would wisely sacrifice these economies to preservation of more economic freedom and equality.

Another cardinal sin of government against the free-enterprise system is manifest in the kind of institution of property which the state has inflicted upon that system. It has lain within the powers of the political state, in defining

2. It is, perhaps, easy, from this general viewpoint, to see both advantages and serious practical difficulties in the development of labor organization along industrial, as against occupational, lines.

rights of property and inheritance, to prevent the extreme inequality which now obtains; and the appropriate changes might still be effected without seriously impairing the efficiency of the system. In a practical sense, there is not much now wrong with the institution of property except our arrangements with respect to taxation. Instead of collecting their required revenues in such manner as to diminish the concentration of wealth and income, governments have relied on the whole upon systems of levies which actually aggravated inequality. Until recently (and the situation is not strikingly different now) governments have financed their activities largely by conglomerations of miscellaneous exactions which have drawn funds predominantly from the bottom of the income scale. Modern fiscal arrangements, like those of medieval barons, must be explained largely in terms of efforts to grab funds wherever they could be reached with least difficulty—to levy upon trade wherever tribute could most easily be exacted—and with almost no regard for consequences in terms of either economic efficiency or personal justice.[3]

The problem of stabilization, of maintaining reasonably full employment of resources, calls for emphasis mainly upon two factors, one of which again is monopoly. If all prices moved up and down with substantial uniformity, changes in the general level of prices would have only unimportant effects upon the volume of production or employment. A major factor in the cycle phenomenon is the quite unequal flexibility of different sets of prices and, more explicitly, the stickiness of prices which, for the bulk of industry, determine out-of-pocket, operating (marginal) costs. This stickiness of prices reflects, first, competition-restraining organization, and, second, a widespread disposition to sacrifice volume to price—which is the characteristic exercise of monopoly power. Decisively important in the total situation is the exceeding inflexibility of wages—the explanation of which would require attention to many factors, of which effective labor organization is but one. . . . At all events, the existence of extreme inflexibility in large areas of the price structure is one of the primary factors in the phenomenon of severe depression. This inflexibility increases the economic loss and human misery accompanying a given deflation, and it causes deflation itself to proceed much farther than it otherwise would.

The major responsibility for the severity of industrial fluctuations, however, falls directly upon the state. Tolerable functioning of a free-enterprise system presupposes effective performance of a fundamental function of government, namely, regulation of the circulating medium (money). We should characterize as insane a governmental policy of alternately expanding rapidly and contracting precipitously the quantity of paper currency in circulation—as a malevolent dictator easily could do, first issuing currency to cover fiscal deficits, and then retiring currency from surplus revenues. Yet that is essentially the kind of monetary policy which actually obtains, by virtue of usurpation by private institutions (deposit banks) of the basic state function of providing the medium of circulation (and of private "cash" reserves). It is no exaggeration to say that the major proximate factor in the present crisis is commercial banking. This is not to say that private bankers are to blame for our plight; they have only played the game (and not so unfairly, on the whole) under the preposterous rules laid down by governments–rules which mean evasion or repudiation by governments of one of their crucial responsibilities. Everywhere one hears assertions of the failure of competitive controls, of the chaos of unplanned economy, when the chaos arises from reliance by the state upon competitive controls in a field (currency) where they cannot possibly work. Laissez-faire, to repeat, implies a division of tasks between competitive and political controls; and the failure of the system, if it has failed, is properly to be regarded as a result of failure of the state, especially with respect to money, to do its part. . . .

Capitalism seems to retain remarkable vitality; but it can hardly survive the political rigors of another depression; and banking, with the able assistance of monopoly, seems certain to give us both bigger and better depressions hereafter–unless the state does reassume and discharge with some wisdom its responsibility for controlling the circulating medium.

PART II

. . . The main elements in a sound liberal program may be defined in terms of five proposals or objectives (in a descending scale of relative importance):

1. Elimination of private monopoly in all its forms
   a. Through drastic measures for establishing and maintaining effectively competitive conditions in all industries where competition can function as a regulative agency (as a means for insuring effective utilization of resources and for preventing exploitation), *and*
   b. Through gradual transition to direct government ownership and operation in the case of all industries where competition cannot be made to function effectively as an agency of control.
2. Establishment of more definite and adequate "rules of the game" with respect to money, through
   a. Abolition of private deposit banking on the basis of fractional reserves,[4]
   b. Establishment of a completely homogeneous, national circulating medium, *and*
   c. Creation of a system under which a federal monetary authority has a direct and inescapable responsibility for controlling (not with broad discretionary powers, but under simple, definite rules laid down in legislation) the quantity (or, through quantity, the value) of effective money.[5]
3. Drastic change in our whole tax system, with regard primarily for the

3. For the disillusioned economist-liberal, a certain bitter satisfaction may be found in the spectacle of capitalism, and the whole institution of property, collapsing under the feet of distinguished propertied gentlemen addressing their brethren on the remarkable virtues of the sales tax.

4. The essential practice of modern banking is that of maintaining obligations payable on demand, or on short notice, while holding "cash" amounting to only *a small fraction* of those obligations.

5. It should be clear that *the measures here proposed have no affinity whatever with schemes for socialization or nationalization of banking.* Indeed, they contemplate a financial system under which there would be the least danger and the least occasion for government control over the lending function, i.e., over the allocation of investment funds. One of the great faults of the present banking system is that it is peculiarly exposed to socialization, merely because of its instability. If we could isolate the lending and investment business from deposit banking, we might eliminate a real danger of government control or socialization in an area where it is most important to avoid it.

effects of taxation upon the distribution of wealth and income.
4. Gradual withdrawal of the enormous differential subsidies implicit in our present tariff system.
5. Limitation upon the squandering of our resources in advertising and selling activities. . . .

As a main feature of the program, *there must be a complete "new deal" with respect to the private corporation.* As many writers have pointed out, the corporation is simply running away with our economic (and political) system—by virtue merely of an absurd carelessness and extravagance on the part of the states in granting powers to these legal creatures. . . .

. . . Few of our gigantic corporations can be defended on the ground that their present size is necessary to reasonably full exploitation of production economies; their existence is to be explained in terms of opportunities for promoter profits, personal ambitions of industrial and financial "Napoleons," and advantages of monopoly power. We should look toward a situation in which the size of ownership units in every industry is limited by the minimum size of operating plant requisite to efficient, but highly specialized, production—and even more narrowly limited, if ever necessary to the maintenance of freedom of enterprise.[6]. . .

There must be outright dismantling of our gigantic corporations, and persistent prosecution of producers who organize, by whatever methods, for price maintenance or output limitation. There must be explicit and unqualified repudiation of the so-called "rule of reason." Legislation must prohibit, and administration effectively prevent, the acquisition by any private firm, or group of firms, of substantial monopoly power, regardless of how reasonably that power may appear to be exercised. The Federal Trade Commission must become perhaps the most powerful of our governmental agencies; and the highest standards must be maintained, both in the appointment of its members, and in the recruiting of its large technical staff. In short, restraint of trade must be treated as a major crime, and prosecuted unremittingly by a vigilant administrative body. . . .

Our proposal with reference to taxation is based on the view: (1) that reduction of inequality is per se immensely important; (2) that progressive taxation is both an effective means and, within the existing framework of institutions, the only effective means to that end; (3) that, in a world of competitive, invidious consumption, the gains at the bottom of the income scale can be realized without significant loss to persons of large income, so long as their rank in the income scale is unchanged; and (4) that drastic reduction of inequality through taxation is attainable without much loss of efficiency in the system, and without much impairing the attractiveness of the economic game.[7]

Taxation must affect the income distribution, whether we will it so or not. Actually, it has operated to increase inequality, except for a slight opposite effect at the upper extremes of the income scale. The proposal here is simply that tax systems be ordered in such a way as to diminish income differences all along the line; that the funds which governments require be obtained through a system of levies which is actually progressive throughout the income scale.

Such a policy requires the establishment of the personal-income tax as the predominant element in our whole fiscal system, and the rescue of inheritance taxation from its miserable failure. The following measures may be suggested as among the important steps in this direction:

1. Elimination of all exemptions of in-

come by kind, establishment of the tax as a purely personal levy, and clear recognition in the law that the tax is a tax upon persons according to their incomes, not a tax upon income as such.

a. Abolition of "tax-exempt securities," and inclusion of all interest and salary items in the calculation of taxable income, whether such items are received from governmental bodies or from private persons.

b. Elimination of all special treatment for "capital gains" (and for "capital losses"). . . .

c. Levy upon estates under the income tax with respect to all "unrealized" appreciation of investment assets–i.e., levy of income tax upon the estate just as though the decedent had sold all his property at the time of his death at the appraised value as of that date.[8]. . .

d. Effective provision against evasion of personal-income tax by stockholders with respect to the undis-

6. It will be necessary to revise notions commonly accepted (especially by courts) as to the maximum size of firm compatible with effective competition. The general rule and ultimate objective should be that of fixing in each industry a maximum size of firm such that the results of perfect competition would be approximated even if all firms attained the maximum size. One may suggest, tentatively, that in major industries no ownership unit should produce or control more than 5 per cent of the total output. Any such rule, of course, raises the difficult question of what is "a commodity"–of how industries or significant classes of commodities should be defined. A period of several years should be allowed for orderly readjustment, the full restrictions coming into effect only gradually. Special arrangements would be necessary, of course, in the case of new industries and new products.

7. Some students would justify the reduction of inequality on the ground that it is essential to the political stability of the system; others, on the ground that it is important for the reduction of unemployment and for the mitigation of industrial fluctuations. The former position, while tenable, involves an unhappy confusion of means and ends. The latter, in my opinion, is open to the same objection, and also to the characterization of completely spurious economics. Moreover, the methods proposed by exponents of this now widely accepted position (widespread unionization, reduction of hours, and increase of wage rates *in a depression)* are the immediate occasion for the assertion that progressive taxation is the only effective means for improving the distribution of income.

8. The adoption of this proposal should be accompanied by appropriate changes in the now inadequate and anomalous provisions regarding transfers of property by gift. Every transfer of property should be treated as a "realization" by the former owner; where property is given away, such transfer should be made the occasion for calculation of taxable gain or loss to the donor (as to the decedent's estate) for purposes of income tax. When property acquired by gift is disposed of by the donee, his gain or loss should be calculated on the basis of value at the time of acquisition.

Suppose that Jones, in 1935, buys 100 shares of common stock at $100 per share; that he transfers these 100 shares by gift to a relative named Smith in 1940, at which time the market price of the stock is $200; and that, in 1942, Smith sells the 100 shares at a price of $150. Now, under the arrangements here proposed, these transfers would give rise to the following reportings for personal income tax: by Jones, in 1940, a gain of $10,000 (value of stock when disposed of by gift *minus* original cost); by Smith, in 1940, $20,000 as income obtained by gift; and by Smith, in 1942, a loss of $5,000 (value of stock when received by gift *minus* amount realized from sale).

Under an income tax which employs the "realization criterion," property should never be allowed to pass out of the possession of an individual without a final reconciliation–without a final calculation of gain or loss to him (or to his estate). However, since the practical problem is that of preventing wholesale and deliberate tax avoidance, a good case can be made, on grounds of administrative simplification, for not allowing deduction of "paper losses" on property disposed of by gift, even though the corresponding "paper profits" are included in taxable income.

It should be noted that the adoption of the measures here proposed, regarding transfers of property by gift, inheritance, and bequest, would solve rather completely the problem of undistributed corporate earnings as a problem of personal income taxation–and would eliminate the need for the kind of measures suggested in the text.

tributed earnings of corporations. . . .

e. Provision for inclusion, in the calculation of taxable personal income, of the net use value of all real estate used by the owner for consumption purposes (residence, etc.). . . .

2. Treatment of all inheritances, bequests, and (large) gifts *inter vivos* as personal income of the recipient for the year in which received. . . .
3. Reservation of estate, inheritance, and personal-income taxes for levy exclusively by the federal government, but with provision for generous sharing of revenues with the states.

   (One may suggest, tentatively, the return of 50 per cent of the revenues to the states, on the basis of collections—i.e., on the basis of the residence of the individual taxpayers. Herein lies, perhaps, the only real opportunity for eliminating antiquated and regressive elements in our state and local tax systems.)
4. Drastic alteration in the rate structure of the personal-income tax, with more rapid progression, and above all with the introduction of really substantial levies upon the so-called middle and lower income brackets. . . .

On the expenditure side, we may look forward confidently to continued augmenting of the "free income" of the masses, in the form of commodities and services made available by government, either without charge or with considerable modification of prevailing price controls. There are remarkable opportunities for extending the range of socialized consumption (medical services, recreation, education, music, drama, etc.) and, especially, for extending the range of social-welfare activities. The prospects in these directions, however, must remain somewhat unattractive so long as the expenditures involved must be covered by the kind of taxes on which we have relied in the past—i.e., so long as what the government gives to the masses with one hand is largely taken away with the other. . . .

It is a commonplace that our vaunted efficiency in production is dissipated extravagantly in the wastes of merchandising. This economic system is one which offers rewards, both to those who direct resources into industries where the indirect pecuniary demand is greatest, and to those who divert pecuniary demand to commodities which they happen to be producing. Profits may be obtained, either by producing what consumers want, or by making consumers want what one is actually producing. The possibility of profitably utilizing resources to manipulate demand is, perhaps, the greatest source of diseconomy under the existing system. If present tendencies continue, we may soon reach a situation where most of our resources are utilized in persuading people to buy one thing rather than another, and only a minor fraction actually employed in creating things to be bought.

Firms must spend enormous sums on advertising, if only to counteract the expenditures of competitors; and, finally, all of them may end up with about the same volume of business as if none had advertised at all. Moreover, every producer must bribe merchants into pushing his product, by providing fantastic "mark-ups," merely because other producers are doing the same thing. Consumers must be prohibited access to wholesale markets and prices, in order to protect the "racket" of retailers whose co-operation the individual producer requires; and there follows inevitably the absurd proliferation of small retail establishments which spring up to exact on small volumes of trade the large percentage tribute which existing arrangements allow to those who can classify as dealers rather than as consumers. There appears to be no significant limit, along these lines, to the potential accumulation of economic waste; for every producer must at least keep up to the pace which others set. . . .

. . . Besides, advertising entrenches monopoly by setting up a financial barrier to the competition of new and small firms. Consequently, an appropriate remodeling of the system with respect to merchandising would do more than free wasted resources for useful employment; it might remove one of the main factors working to destroy real competition in industry. . . .

Enterprises like Consumers Research, Inc., may represent the beginnings of an almost revolutionary development. We may hope that such undertakings may flourish, and that their growth may be promoted through private endowment. (It is hard to imagine a more worthy philanthropy.) Perhaps we shall see the establishment of endowed, non-profit-making institutions, of unimpeachable disinterestedness, which will offer to manufacturers (freely or with moderate charges) the use of the institutions' certification or recommendation in the labeling of approved products. Ultimately, we may see the labeling and classification of the more staple goods on the basis of Bureau of Standards specifications, so that consumers may know (and insist on knowing) which brands of goods meet requirements for government purchase. Perhaps we may still hope for substantial development of consumer co-operatives, organized for collective research and consumer education.

Early correction of merchandising evils by restrictive legislation is perhaps impossible; and one resents the conviction that many proposed remedies would prove worse than the disease. The strongest case can be made for heavy taxation of advertising, provided rates can be made much higher than revenue considerations would dictate. There are interesting possibilities in progressive taxes on manufacturers and jobbers according to the percentage of selling expenses to total expenses. The important objective, however, is that of breaking down, first, competitive advertising and, second, the artificial separation between wholesale and retail markets. Consumers should be free to purchase commodities either with or without the services offered by existing retail establishments—just as they should be free to purchase milk, at substantially different prices, with or without doorstep delivery. . . .

The depression is essentially a problem (1) of relative inflexibility in those prices which largely determine costs, and (2) of contraction in the volume and velocity of effective money. The crucial characteristic of the situation is maladjustment between product prices and operating costs; and, given this condition, there is no necessary limit to the possible deflation and decline of employment. Sound policy will look, first, toward pulling the more sticky prices down and, second, toward pulling the flexible prices up, in order to create favorable prospects with respect to business earnings. Little can be accomplished quickly in the first direction; consequently, main reliance must be placed on "reflationary" government spending.

Inflationary fiscal policy is dangerous, to be sure—but not so dangerous as the alternatives. It should be undertaken with definite preliminary announcement of an objective, stated, perhaps, in terms of *moderate* increase in a specified price index. The program should be planned with an eye to maximum flexibility, for prompt attainment of the price-level objective, and to assure checking of the inflation within the limits designated. Measures of this kind must be undertaken, merely to keep running a system which banking and monopoly have brought to its present plight.[9]. . .

This tract is submitted in the hope of promoting a consensus of opinion within a group which might now perform an invaluable service in intellectual leadership. The precious measure of political and economic freedom which has been won through centuries may soon be lost irreparably; and it falls properly to economists, as custodians of the great liberal tradition out of which their discipline arose, to point the escape from the chaos of political and economic thought which warns of what impends.

9. There remains one point which has not been properly emphasized, namely that genuinely liberal reform must aim primarily at explicit changes in the rules of the economic game and must minimize reliance on control or regulation through nominally administrative bodies with large discretionary, policy-determining powers. The point has already been noted with respect to monetary and banking reform; but it is of decisive importance in many other fields. There is now profound significance in the distinction between a government of men and a government of rules; and to the extent that we move toward the former we are accepting or inviting fascism. One highroad to dictatorship lies in the creation of a large number of petty, specialized authorities in particular fields. For an old-fashioned liberal, it is terrifying to reflect on the amount of arbitrary power which has recently been delegated to the President, the Secretary of the Treasury, the N.R.A., the A.A.A., the R.F.C., the S.E.C., etc. However reasonable this expedient in an acute emergency, we must face the fact that emergency measures are unlikely to prove entirely temporary, and also the fact that we were making substantial strides in this direction long before the emergency arose.

A substantial measure of administrative discretion is obviously essential to good government; but it must be economized. If large latitude must often be allowed in the administration of new reform measures, we should seek afterward to reduce the powers of the administrative authorities as rapidly as experience provides the basis for more definitive legislative rules.

MILTON FRIEDMAN

Professor of Economics, University of Chicago.

Milton Friedman is without doubt the most prominent advocate of conservatism within the ranks of professional economists. He has uncompromisingly advocated a free market approach in dealing with a wide variety of domestic and international economic problems; his advice has been eagerly solicited by several conservative political figures, including Senator Goldwater.

The main thrust of Friedman's critique is quite simple: The use of Keynesian fiscal and monetary policy—raising or lowering taxes, government spending, and the money supply to offset fluctuations in the private sector—has exacerbated the country's economic difficulties. Moreover, a continual enlargement of the sphere of government activities tends, in Friedman's view, to destroy political freedom because it combines economic and political power. Friedman takes the position that economic freedom is a prerequisite for political freedom—a stand which is superficially in accord with that taken by the radicals. An important difference, however, stems from their differing definitions of economic freedom. Whereas the term connotes some degree of control by workers and (or) greater economic equality to the radical, Friedman employs the concept in a narrower perspective. To him, economic freedom means that each man can vote in a market for what he wants produced, choose how he will dispose of his labor, and enter into any business that he believes will promote his self-interest. Economic freedom is thus a buying and selling freedom. This definition clearly predisposes Friedman to arrive at the position that capitalism is the system most synonymous with individual freedom. To the radical, an important factor overlooked by Friedman is that even if one operates within the assumptions implied by the given institutional environment (for example, private property), economic freedom to the worker has meaning only in terms of available alternatives. If, for example, a labor surplus market exists, the worker's economic freedom, as measured by his ability to choose how he will dispose of his labor, is seriously compromised. Questionable also is the issue of whether there is a significant tendency for political freedom to be strengthened under capitalism, as Friedman implies. A society operating within a private enterprise framework appears to further the concentration of political power in a relatively small group. These questions are not directly considered in Friedman's simplified approach.

Friedman does, however, raise important and serious objections to the liberal's justifications of the government's countercyclical policy. He notes quite accurately that an increase in government expenditures relative to taxes is not necessarily expansionary (the "multiplier effect"), since this increase in the government sector may be offset by decreases in investment spending by private business. Further, he says that rising money incomes may be offset by rising prices, and claims that

> [i]n fiscal policy as in monetary policy, all political considerations aside, we simply do not know enough to be able to use deliberate changes in taxation or expenditures as a sensitive stabilizing mechanism. In the process of trying to do so, we almost surely make matters worse.

As an antidote to the liberal's optimism concerning the use of countercyclical weapons, Friedman's warning is quite useful even though his statistical confirmation is debatable.

Friedman has attempted to rebuild the Quantity Theory of Money (changes in the money supply are viewed as an important cause of changes in price and output) as a counter to Keynesian theory (a statement of this position follows). In this neo-orthodox treatment, stable prices are viewed as a key prerequisite for a viable free enterprise system. Emphasis is placed on the demand for money, which Friedman regards as stable over time. Instead of allowing the Federal Reserve system to expand or contract the money supply, which Friedman believes is a strong destabilizing force, it is more effective, he says, to provide for a steady growth in the money stock roughly proportional to the growth in output. Price stability and full employment can be maintained if the money stock is increased by the proper amount. Friedman places the blame for the prolonged great depression of the 1930s on the monetary authorities; they permitted a severe decline in the money supply—a fall of one-third from July 1929 to March 1933. "Had the money stock been kept from declining," says Friedman, "as it clearly could and should have been, the contraction would have been both shorter and far milder." His treatment contains no reference to the increasing inequality in the functional distribution of income in the late 1920s as evidenced by the rapidly growing gap between wages and propertied income. At the very least, these facts cast doubt on Friedman's purely monetary explanation of *the* major crisis in American economic history.

The problem of inequality disturbs Friedman much less than the problems of allocation of resources (efficiency) and the maintenance of market freedom. All are allegedly related because "much of actual inequality derives from imperfections of the market," many of which are, in Friedman's opinion, created by government actions. In addition to chance and differences in natural ability, Friedman stresses the role of personal or social preferences as determinants of the degree of inequality, rather than the initial unequal distribution of wealth and the accompanying lack of early opportunities for the lowest economic strata. His approach hearkens back to Malthus' theory that the poverty of the poor is essentially due to their own inferior choice making. His reasoning is that in a dynamically changing society with a strong tendency to engage in risky economic ventures, considerable inequality would (and perhaps should) be generated.

Closely related to this issue is Friedman's attempt to apply his competitive market model to such problems as education, discrimination, and welfare. He favors increased competition in the educational sector as a method of inducing higher quality. Parents, according to his scheme, would receive a voucher equal to a maximum sum per child per year which they would be free to spend on any "approved" educational service, private as well as public. "Our present school system" says Friedman, "far from equalizing opportunity, very likely does the opposite. It makes it all the harder for the exceptional few—and it is they who are the hope of the future—to rise above the poverty of their initial state." Although tinged with elitism, this approach is nondiscriminatory, at least on a formal level of analysis. According to Friedman, the judgment of the community ought to be the decisive determinant of what portion of their scarce resources to allocate to education, but he doesn't appear to be aware that community judgments are affected by class factors. Although it is likely that Friedman's market-oriented educational methods would promote diversity, allow more personal choice, and perhaps improve the quality of education in some areas, it is hardly likely that such methods would offer more than token aid in dealing with the mass educational needs of today's low-income areas, particularly the black ghettos.

Friedman deals with discrimination in a similar manner. He notes, in the following article, that minority groups have a considerable stake in strengthening competitive capitalism, since an "impersonal market . . . protects men from being discriminated against in their economic activities for reasons that are irrelevant to their productivity." Those who discriminate pay a price for so doing; their range of choice is limited and they pay higher prices or receive lower wages. This approach is oversimplified because, among other defects, it supports a narrowly technical instead of a broader political economy. A more realistic analysis would focus on the short-run and long-run gains, as well as losses, that accrue to the various groups in our society as a result of discrimination in the labor market. It would also deal with the intermeshing of economic and political elements.

Friedman almost studiously avoids an examination of the limitations of a system of free competition and individual freedom. The American experience lends weight to the view that an economy operated according to laissez-faire tenets produces major concentrations of economic power. It is doubtful whether an economy based on Friedman's rules of the game would experience less cyclical instability and less inequity even if one agreed with his unproved position that there would be more individual freedom. Despite the questionable quality of many of his laissez-faire proposals, Friedman should be given credit for aiding the thrust of economics toward better research techniques. His subtle and sophisticated questioning of Keynesian economics is also salutary, though an accurate appraisal of this critique is still forthcoming.

The mainstream of both liberal and radical thought tends to see Friedman's proposals as increasingly irrelevant for dealing with the crises of our twentieth-century industrial society, a society characterized by large power concentrations in both the business and the labor sectors and by price and wage structures that reflect this power. To many, Friedman has in the main structured elegant and logical models for a universe of limited applicability. Although they do not detract from his skills as an economist, his models do reflect political irrelevance.

M L

From

CAPITALISM AND FREEDOM

(1962)

INTRODUCTION

In a much quoted passage in his inaugural address, President Kennedy said, "Ask not what your country can do for you—ask what you can do for your country." It is a striking sign of the temper of our times that the controversy about this passage centered on its origin and not on its content. Neither half of the statement expresses a relation between the citizen and his government that is worthy of the ideals of free men in a free society. The paternalistic "what your country can do for you" implies that government is the patron, the citizen the ward, a view that is at odds with the free man's belief in his own responsibility for his own destiny. The organismic, "what you can do for your country" implies that government is the master or the deity, the citizen the servant or the votary. To the free man, the country is the collection of individuals who compose it, not something over and above them. He is proud of a common heritage and loyal to common traditions. But he regards government as a means, an instrumentality, neither a grantor of favors and gifts, nor a master or god to be blindly worshipped and served. He recognizes no national goal except as it is the consensus of the goals that the citizens severally serve. He recognizes no national purpose except as it is the consensus of the purposes for which the citizens severally strive.

The free man will ask neither what his country can do for him nor what he can do for his country. He will ask rather "What can I and my compatriots do through government" to help us discharge our individual responsibilities, to achieve our several goals and purposes, and above all, to protect our freedom? And he will accompany this question with another: How can we keep the government we create from becoming a Frankenstein that will destroy the very freedom we establish it to protect? Freedom is a rare and delicate plant. Our minds tell us, and history confirms, that the great threat to freedom is the concentration of power. Government is necessary to preserve our freedom, it is an instrument through which we can exercise our freedom; yet by concentrating power in political hands, it is also a threat to freedom. Even though the men who wield this power initially be of good will and even though they be not corrupted by the power they exercise, the power will both attract and form men of a different stamp.

How can we benefit from the promise of government while avoiding the threat to freedom? Two broad principles embodied in our Constitution give an answer that has preserved our freedom so far, though they have been violated repeatedly in practice while proclaimed as precept.

First, the scope of government must be limited. Its major function must be to protect our freedom both from the enemies outside our gates and from our fellow-citizens: to preserve law and order, to enforce private contracts, to foster competitive markets. Beyond this major function, government may enable us at times to accomplish jointly what we would find it more difficult or expensive to accomplish severally. However, any such use of government is fraught with danger. We should not and cannot avoid using government in this way. But there should be a clear and large balance of advantages before we do. By relying primarily on voluntary cooperation and private enterprise, in both economic and other activities, we can insure that the private sector is a check on the powers of the governmental sector and an effective protection of freedom of speech, of religion, and of thought.

The second broad principle is that government power must be dispersed. If government is to exercise power, better in the county than in the state, better in the state than in Washington. If I do not like what my local community does, be it in sewage disposal, or zoning, or schools, I can move to another local community, and though few may take this step, the mere possibility acts as a check. If I do not like what my state does, I can move to another. If I do not like what Washington imposes, I have few alternatives in this world of jealous nations.

The very difficulty of avoiding the enactments of the federal government is of course the great attraction of centralization to many of its proponents. It will enable them more effectively, they believe, to legislate programs that—as they see it—are in the interest of the public, whether it be the transfer of income from the rich to the poor or from private to governmental purposes. They are in a sense right. But this coin has two sides. The power to do good is also the power to do harm; those who control the power today may not tomorrow; and, more important, what one man regards as good, another may regard as harm. The great tragedy of the drive to centralization, as of the drive to extend the scope of government in general, is that it is mostly led by men of good will who will be the first to rue its consequences.

The preservation of freedom is the protective reason for limiting and decentralizing governmental power. But there is also a constructive reason. The great advances of civilization, whether in architecture or painting, in science or literature, in industry or agriculture, have never come from centralized government. Columbus did not set out to seek a new route to China in response to a majority directive of a parliament, though he was partly financed by an absolute monarch. Newton and Leibnitz; Einstein and Bohr; Shakespeare, Milton, and Pasternak; Whitney, McCormick, Edison, and Ford; Jane Addams, Florence Nightingale, and Albert Schweitzer; no one of these opened new frontiers in human knowledge and understanding, in literature, in technical possibilities, or in the relief of human misery in response to governmental directives. Their achievements were the product of individual genius, of strongly held minority views, of a social climate permitting variety and diversity.

Government can never duplicate the variety and diversity of individual action.

At any moment in time, by imposing uniform standards in housing, or nutrition, or clothing, government could undoubtedly improve the level of living of many individuals; by imposing uniform standards in schooling, road construction, or sanitation, central government could undoubtedly improve the level of performance in many local areas and perhaps even on the average of all communities. But in the process, government would replace progress by stagnation, it would substitute uniform mediocrity for the variety essential for that experimentation which can bring tomorrow's laggards above today's mean. . . .

It is extremely convenient to have a label for the political and economic viewpoint elaborated [here]. The rightful and proper label is liberalism. Unfortunately, "As a supreme, if unintended compliment, the enemies of the system of private enterprise have thought it wise to appropriate its label,"[1] so that liberalism has, in the United States, come to have a very different meaning than it did in the nineteenth century or does today over much of the Continent of Europe.

As it developed in the late eighteenth and early nineteenth centuries, the intellectual movement that went under the name of liberalism emphasized freedom as the ultimate goal and the individual as the ultimate entity in the society. It supported laissez-faire at home as a means of reducing the role of the state in economic affairs and thereby enlarging the role of the individual; it supported free trade abroad as a means of linking the nations of the world together peacefully and democratically. In political matters, it supported the development of representative government and of parliamentary institutions, reduction in the arbitrary power of the state, and protection of the civil freedoms of individuals.

Beginning in the late nineteenth century, and especially after 1930 in the United States, the term liberalism came to be associated with a very different emphasis, particularly in economic policy. It came to be associated with a readiness to rely primarily on the state rather than on private voluntary arrangements to achieve objectives regarded as desirable. The catchwords become welfare and equality rather than freedom. The nineteenth-century liberal regarded an extension of freedom as the most effective way to promote welfare and equality; the twentieth-century liberal regards welfare and equality as either prerequisites of or alternatives to freedom. In the name of welfare and equality, the twentieth-century liberal has come to favor a revival of the very policies of state intervention and paternalism against which classical liberalism fought. In the very act of turning the clock back to seventeenth-century mercantilism, he is fond of castigating true liberals as reactionary!

The change in the meaning attached to the term liberalism is more striking in economic matters than in political. The twentieth-century liberal, like the nineteenth-century liberal, favors parliamentary institutions, representative government, civil rights, and so on. Yet even in political matters, there is a notable difference. Jealous of liberty, and hence fearful of centralized power, whether in governmental or private hands, the nineteenth-century liberal favored political decentralization. Committed to action and confident of the beneficence of power so long as it is in the hands of a government ostensibly controlled by the electorate, the twentieth-century liberal favors centralized government. He will resolve any doubt about where power should be located in favor of the state instead of the city, of the federal government instead of the state, and of a world organization instead of a national government.

Because of the corruption of the term liberalism, the views that formerly went under that name are now often labeled conservatism. But this is not a satisfactory alternative. The nineteenth-century liberal was a radical, both in the etymological sense of going to the root of the matter, and in the political sense of favoring major changes in social institutions. So too must be his modern heir. We do not wish to conserve the state interventions that have interfered so greatly with our freedom, though, of course, we do wish to conserve those that have promoted it. Moreover, in practice, the term conservatism has come to cover so wide a range of views, and views so incompatible with one another, that we shall no doubt see the growth of hyphenated designations, such as libertarian-conservative and aristocratic-conservative.

Partly because of my reluctance to surrender the term to proponents of measures that would destroy liberty, partly because I cannot find a better alternative, I shall resolve these difficulties by using the word liberalism in its original sense—as the doctrines pertaining to a free man.

THE RELATION BETWEEN ECONOMIC FREEDOM AND POLITICAL FREEDOM

It is widely believed that politics and economics are separate and largely unconnected; that individual freedom is a political problem and material welfare an economic problem; and that any kind of political arrangements can be combined with any kind of economic arrangements. The chief contemporary manifestation of this idea is the advocacy of "democratic socialism" by many who condemn out of hand the restrictions on individual freedom imposed by "totalitarian socialism" in Russia, and who are persuaded that it is possible for a country to adopt the essential features of Russian economic arrangements and yet to ensure individual freedom through political arrangements. The thesis [here] is that such a view is a delusion, that there is an intimate connection between economics and politics, that only certain combinations of political and economic arrangements are possible, and that in particular, a society which is socialist cannot also be democratic, in the sense of guaranteeing individual freedom.

Economic arrangements play a dual role in the promotion of a free society. On the one hand, freedom in economic arrangements is itself a component of freedom broadly understood, so economic freedom is an end in itself. In the second place, economic freedom is also an indispensable means toward the achievement of political freedom.

The first of these roles of economic freedom needs special emphasis because intellectuals in particular have a strong bias against regarding this aspect of freedom as important. They tend to express contempt for what they regard as material aspects of life, and to regard their own pursuit of allegedly higher values as on a different plane of significance and as deserving of special attention. For most citizens of the country, however, if not for the intellectual, the direct importance of economic freedom is at least comparable in significance to the indirect importance of economic freedom as a means to political freedom.

The citizen of Great Britain, who after

1. Joseph Schumpeter, *History of Economic Analysis* (New York: Oxford University Press, 1954), p. 394.

World War II was not permitted to spend his vacation in the United States because of exchange control, was being deprived of an essential freedom no less than the citizen of the United States, who was denied the opportunity to spend his vacation in Russia because of his political views. The one was ostensibly an economic limitation on freedom and the other a political limitation, yet there is no essential difference between the two.

The citizen of the United States who is compelled by law to devote something like 10 per cent of his income to the purchase of a particular kind of retirement contract, administered by the government, is being deprived of a corresponding part of his personal freedom. How strongly this deprivation may be felt and its closeness to the deprivation of religious freedom, which all would regard as "civil" or "political" rather than "economic," were dramatized by an episode involving a group of farmers of the Amish sect. On grounds of principle, this group regarded compulsory federal old age programs as an infringement of their personal individual freedom and refused to pay taxes or accept benefits. As a result, some of their livestock were sold by auction in order to satisfy claims for social security levies. True, the number of citizens who regard compulsory old age insurance as a deprivation of freedom may be few, but the believer in freedom has never counted noses.

A citizen of the United States who under the laws of various states is not free to follow the occupation of his own choosing unless he can get a license for it, is likewise being deprived of an essential part of his freedom. So is the man who would like to exchange some of his goods with, say, a Swiss for a watch but is prevented from doing so by a quota. So also is the Californian who was thrown into jail for selling Alka-Seltzer at a price below that set by the manufacturer under so-called "fair trade" laws. So also is the farmer who cannot grow the amount of wheat he wants. And so on. Clearly, economic freedom, in and of itself, is an extremely important part of total freedom.

Viewed as a means to the end of political freedom, economic arrangements are important because of their effect on the concentration or dispersion of power. The kind of economic organization that provides economic freedom directly, namely, competitive capitalism, also promotes political freedom because it separates economic power from political power and in this way enables the one to offset the other.

Historical evidence speaks with a single voice on the relation between political freedom and a free market. I know of no example in time or place of a society that has been marked by a large measure of political freedom, and that has not also used something comparable to a free market to organize the bulk of economic activity.

Because we live in a largely free society, we tend to forget how limited is the span of time and the part of the globe for which there has ever been anything like political freedom: the typical state of mankind is tyranny, servitude, and misery. The nineteenth century and early twentieth century in the Western world stand out as striking exceptions to the general trend of historical development. Political freedom in this instance clearly came along with the free market and the development of capitalist institutions. So also did political freedom in the golden age of Greece and in the early days of the Roman era.

History suggests only that capitalism

is a necessary condition for political freedom. Clearly it is not a sufficient condition. Fascist Italy and Fascist Spain, Germany at various times in the last seventy years, Japan before World Wars I and II, tzarist Russia in the decades before World War I—are all societies that cannot conceivably be described as politically free. Yet, in each, private enterprise was the dominant form of economic organization. It is therefore clearly possible to have economic arrangements that are fundamentally capitalist and political arrangements that are not free.

Even in those societies, the citizenry had a good deal more freedom than citizens of a modern totalitarian state like Russia or Nazi Germany, in which economic totalitarianism is combined with political totalitarianism. Even in Russia under the Tzars, it was possible for some citizens, under some circumstances, to change their jobs without getting permission from political authority, because capitalism and the existence of private property provided some check to the centralized power of the state.

The relation between political and economic freedom is complex and by no means unilateral. In the early nineteenth century, Bentham and the Philosophical Radicals were inclined to regard political freedom as a means to economic freedom. They believed that the masses were being hampered by the restrictions that were being imposed upon them, and that if political reform gave the bulk of the people the vote, they would do what was good for them, which was to vote for laissez-faire. In retrospect, one cannot say that they were wrong. There was a large measure of political reform that was accompanied by economic reform in the direction of a great deal of laissez-faire. An enormous increase in the well-being of the masses followed this change in economic arrangements.

The triumph of Benthamite liberalism in nineteenth-century England was followed by a reaction toward increasing intervention by government in economic affairs. This tendency to collectivism was greatly accelerated, both in England and elsewhere, by the two World Wars. Welfare rather than freedom became the dominant note in democratic countries. Recognizing the implicit threat to individualism, the intellectual descendants of the Philosophical Radicals—Dicey, Mises, Hayek, and Simons, to mention only a few—feared that a continued movement toward centralized control of economic activity would prove *The Road to Serfdom,* as Hayek entitled his penetrating analysis of the process. Their emphasis was on economic freedom as a means toward political freedom. . . .

As liberals, we take freedom of the individual, or perhaps the family, as our ultimate goal in judging social arrangements. Freedom as a value in this sense has to do with the interrelations among people; it has no meaning whatsoever to a Robinson Crusoe on an isolated island (without his Man Friday). Robinson Crusoe on his island is subject to "constraint," he has limited "power," and he has only a limited number of alternatives, but there is no problem of freedom in the sense that is relevant to our discussion. Similarly, in a society freedom has nothing to say about what an individual does with his freedom; it is not an all-embracing ethic. Indeed, a major aim of the liberal is to leave the ethical problem for the individual to wrestle with. The "really" important ethical problems are those that face an individual in a free society—what he should do with his freedom. There are thus two sets of values that a liberal will emphasize—the values that are relevant to relations among people, which is the context in which he assigns first priority to freedom; and the values that are relevant to the individual in the exercise of his freedom, which is the realm of individual ethics and philosophy.

The liberal conceives of men as imperfect beings. He regards the problem of social organization to be as much a negative problem of preventing "bad" people from doing harm as of enabling "good" people to do good; and, of course, "bad" and "good" people may be the same people, depending on who is judging them.

The basic problem of social organization is how to coordinate the economic activities of large numbers of people. Even in relatively backward societies, extensive division of labor and specialization of function is required to make effective use of available resources. In advanced societies, the scale on which coordination is needed, to take full advantage of the opportunities offered by modern science and technology, is enormously greater. Literally millions of people are involved in providing one another with their daily bread, let alone with their yearly automobiles. The challenge to the believer in liberty is to reconcile this widespread interdependence with individual freedom.

Fundamentally, there are only two ways of coordinating the economic activities of millions. One is central direction involving the use of coercion—the technique of the army and of the modern totalitarian state. The other is voluntary cooperation of individuals—the technique of the market place.

The possibility of coordination through voluntary cooperation rests on the elementary—yet frequently denied—proposition that both parties to an economic transaction benefit from it, *provided the transaction is bilaterally voluntary and informed.*

Exchange can therefore bring about coordination without coercion. A working model of a society organized through voluntary exchange is a *free private enterprise exchange economy*—what we have been calling competitive capitalism.

In its simplest form, such a society consists of a number of independent households—a collection of Robinson Crusoes, as it were. Each household uses the resources it controls to produce goods and services that it exchanges for goods and services produced by other households, on terms mutually acceptable to the two parties to the bargain. It is thereby enabled to satisfy its wants indirectly by producing goods and services for others, rather than directly by producing goods for its own immediate use. The incentive for adopting this indirect route is, of course, the increased product made possible by division of labor and specialization of function. Since the household always has the alternative of producing directly for itself, it need not enter into any exchange unless it benefits from it. Hence, no exchange will take place unless both parties do benefit from it. Cooperation is thereby achieved without coercion.

Specialization of function and division of labor would not go far if the ultimate productive unit were the household. In a modern society, we have gone much farther. We have introduced enterprises which are intermediaries between individuals in their capacities as suppliers of service and as purchasers of goods. And similarly, specialization of function and division of labor could not go very far if we had to continue to rely on the barter of product for product. In consequence, money has been introduced as a means of facilitating exchange, and of enabling the acts of purchase and of sale to be separated into two parts.

Despite the important role of enterprises and of money in our actual economy, and despite the numerous and complex problems they raise, the central characteristic of the market technique of achieving coordination is fully displayed in the simple exchange economy that contains neither enterprises nor money. As in that simple model, so in the complex enterprise and money-exchange economy, cooperation is strictly individual and voluntary *provided:* (a) that enterprises are private, so that the ultimate contracting parties are individuals and (b) that individuals are effectively free to enter or not to enter into any particular exchange, so that every transaction is strictly voluntary.

It is far easier to state these provisos in general terms than to spell them out in detail, or to specify precisely the institutional arrangements most conducive to their maintenance. Indeed, much of technical economic literature is concerned with precisely these questions. The basic requisite is the maintenance of law and order to prevent physical coercion of one individual by another and to enforce contracts voluntarily entered into, thus giving substance to "private." Aside from this, perhaps the most difficult problems arise from monopoly–which inhibits effective freedom by denying individuals alternatives to the particular exchange–and from "neighborhood effects"–effects on third parties for which it is not feasible to charge or recompense them. . . .

So long as effective freedom of exchange is maintained, the central feature of the market organization of economic activity is that it prevents one person from interfering with another in respect of most of his activities. The consumer is protected from coercion by the seller because of the presence of other sellers with whom he can deal. The seller is protected from coercion by the consumer because of other consumers to whom he can sell. The employee is protected from coercion by the employer because of other employers for whom he can work, and so on. And the market does this impersonally and without centralized authority.

Indeed, a major source of objection to a free economy is precisely that it does this task so well. It gives people what they want instead of what a particular group thinks they ought to want. Underlying most arguments against the free market is a lack of belief in freedom itself.

The existence of a free market does not of course eliminate the need for government. On the contrary, government is essential both as a forum for determining the "rules of the game" and as an umpire to interpret and enforce the rules decided on. What the market does is to reduce greatly the range of issues that must be decided through political means, and thereby to minimize the extent to which government need participate directly in the game. The characteristic feature of action through political channels is that it tends to require or enforce substantial conformity. The great advantage of the market, on the other hand, is that it permits wide diversity. It is, in political terms, a system of proportional representation. Each man can vote, as it were, for the color of tie he wants and get it; he does not have to see what color the majority wants and then, if he is in the minority, submit.

It is this feature of the market that

we refer to when we say that the market provides economic freedom. But this characteristic also has implications that go far beyond the narrowly economic. Political freedom means the absence of coercion of a man by his fellow men. The fundamental threat to freedom is power to coerce, be it in the hands of a monarch, a dictator, an oligarchy, or a momentary majority. The preservation of freedom requires the elimination of such concentration of power to the fullest possible extent and the dispersal and distribution of whatever power cannot be eliminated–a system of checks and balances. By removing the organization of economic activity from the control of political authority, the market eliminates this source of coercive power. It enables economic strength to be a check to political power rather than a reinforcement.

Economic power can be widely dispersed. There is no law of conservation which forces the growth of new centers of economic strength to be at the expense of existing centers. Political power, on the other hand, is more difficult to decentralize. There can be numerous small independent governments. But it is far more difficult to maintain numerous equipotent small centers of political power in a single large government than it is to have numerous centers of economic strength in a single large economy. There can be many millionaires in one large economy. But can there be more than one really outstanding leader, one person on whom the energies and enthusiasms of his countrymen are centered? If the central government gains power, it is likely to be at the expense of local governments. There seems to be something like a fixed total of political power to be distributed. Consequently, if economic power is joined to political power, concentration seems almost inevitable. On the other hand, if economic power is kept in separate hands from political power, it can serve as a check and a counter to political power.

The force of this abstract argument can perhaps best be demonstrated by example. Let us consider first a hypothetical example that may help to bring out the principles involved, and then some actual examples from recent experience that illustrate the way in which the market works to preserve political freedom.

One feature of a free society is surely the freedom of individuals to advocate and propagandize openly for a radical change in the structure of the society–so long as the advocacy is restricted to persuasion and does not include force or other forms of coercion. It is a mark of the political freedom of a capitalist society that men can openly advocate and work for socialism. Equally, political freedom in a socialist society would require that men be free to advocate the introduction of capitalism. How could the freedom to advocate capitalism be preserved and protected in a socialist society?

In order for men to advocate anything, they must in the first place be able to earn a living. This already raises a problem in a socialist society, since all jobs are under the direct control of political authorities. It would take an act of self-denial whose difficulty is underlined by experience in the United States after World War II with the problem of "security" among Federal employees, for a socialist government to permit its employees to advocate policies directly contrary to official doctrine.

But let us suppose this act of self-denial to be achieved. For advocacy of capitalism to mean anything, the proponents must be able to finance their cause—to hold public meetings, publish pamphlets, buy radio time, issue newspapers and magazines, and so on. How could they raise the funds? There might and probably would be men in the socialist society with large incomes, perhaps even large capital sums in the form of government bonds and the like, but these would of necessity be high public officials. It is possible to conceive of a minor socialist official retaining his job although openly advocating capitalism. It strains credulity to imagine the socialist top brass financing such "subversive" activities.

The only recourse for funds would be to raise small amounts from a large number of minor officials. But this is no real answer. To tap these sources, many people would already have to be persuaded, and our whole problem is how to initiate and finance a campaign to do so. Radical movements in capitalist societies have never been financed this way. They have typically been supported by a few wealthy individuals who have become persuaded—by a Frederick Vanderbilt Field, or an Anita McCormick Blaine, or a Corliss Lamont, to mention a few names recently prominent, or by a Friedrich Engels, to go farther back. This is a role of inequality of wealth in preserving political freedom that is seldom noted—the role of the patron.

In a capitalist society, it is only necessary to convince a few wealthy people to get funds to launch any idea, however strange, and there are many such persons, many independent foci of support. And, indeed, it is not even necessary to persuade people or financial institutions with available funds of the soundness of the ideas to be propagated. It is only necessary to persuade them that the propagation can be financially successful; that the newspaper or magazine or book or other venture will be profitable. The competitive publisher, for example, cannot afford to publish only writing with which he personally agrees; his touchstone must be the likelihood that the market will be large enough to yield a satisfactory return on his investment.

In this way, the market breaks the vicious circle and makes it possible ultimately to finance such ventures by small amounts from many people without first persuading them. There are no such possibilities in the socialist society; there is only the all-powerful state.

Let us stretch our imagination and suppose that a socialist government is aware of this problem and is composed of people anxious to preserve freedom. Could it provide the funds? Perhaps, but it is difficult to see how. It could establish a bureau for subsidizing subversive propaganda. But how could it choose whom to support? If it gave to all who asked, it would shortly find itself out of funds, for socialism cannot repeal the elementary economic law that a sufficiently high price will call forth a large supply. Make the advocacy of radical causes sufficiently remunerative, and the supply of advocates will be unlimited.

Moreover, freedom to advocate unpopular causes does not require that such advocacy be without cost. On the contrary, no society could be stable if advocacy of radical change were costless, much less subsidized. It is entirely appropriate that men make sacrifices to advocate causes in which they deeply believe. Indeed, it is important to preserve freedom only for people who are willing to practice self-denial, for otherwise freedom degenerates into license and irresponsibility. What is essential is that the cost of advocating unpopular causes be tolerable and not prohibitive.

But we are not yet through. In a free market society, it is enough to have the funds. The suppliers of paper are as willing to sell it to the *Daily Worker* as to the *Wall Street Journal.* In a socialist society, it would not be enough to have the funds. The hypothetical supporter of capitalism would have to persuade a government factory making paper to sell to him, the government printing press to print his pamphlets, a government post office to distribute them among the people, a government agency to rent him a hall in which to talk, and so on.

Perhaps there is some way in which one could overcome these difficulties and preserve freedom in a socialist society. One cannot say it is utterly impossible. What is clear, however, is that there are very real difficulties in establishing institutions that will effectively preserve the possibility of dissent. So far as I know, none of the people who have been in favor of socialism and also in favor of freedom have really faced up to this issue, or made even a respectable start at developing the institutional arrangements that would permit freedom under socialism. By contrast, it is clear how a free market capitalist society fosters freedom.

A striking practical example of these abstract principles is the experience of Winston Churchill. From 1933 to the outbreak of World War II, Churchill was not permitted to talk over the British radio, which was, of course, a government monopoly administered by the British Broadcasting Corporation. Here was a leading citizen of his country, a Member of Parliament, a former cabinet minister, a man who was desperately trying by every device possible to persuade his countrymen to take steps to ward off the menace of Hitler's Germany. He was not permitted to talk over the radio to the British people because the BBC was a government monopoly and his position was too "controversial." . . .

[An] example of the role of the market in preserving political freedom was revealed in our experience with McCarthyism. Entirely aside from the substantive issues involved, and the merits of the charges made, what protection did individuals, and in particular government employees, have against irresponsible accusations and probings into matters that it went against their conscience to reveal? Their appeal to the Fifth Amendment would have been a hollow mockery without an alternative to government employment.

Their fundamental protection was the existence of a private-market economy in which they could earn a living. Here again, the protection was not absolute. Many potential private employers were, rightly or wrongly, averse to hiring those pilloried. It may well be that there was far less justification for the costs imposed on many of the people involved than for the costs generally imposed on people who advocate unpopular causes. But the important point is that the costs were limited and not prohibitive, as they would have been if government employment had been the only possibility.

It is of interest to note that a disproportionately large fraction of people involved apparently went into the most competitive sectors of the economy–small business, trade, farming–where the market approaches most closely the ideal free market. No one who buys bread knows whether the wheat from which it is made was grown by a Communist or a Republican, by a constitutionalist or a Fascist, or, for that matter, by a Negro or a white. This illustrates how an impersonal market separates economic activities from political views and protects men from being discriminated against in their economic activities for reasons that are irrelevant to their productivity—whether these reasons are associated with their views or their color.

As this example suggests, the groups in our society that have the most at stake in the preservation and strengthening of competitive capitalism are those minority groups which can most easily become the object of the distrust and enmity of the majority—the Negroes, the Jews, the foreign-born, to mention only the most obvious. Yet, paradoxically enough, the enemies of the free market—the Socialists and Communists—have been recruited in disproportionate measure from these groups. Instead of recognizing that the existence of the market has protected them from the attitudes of their fellow countrymen, they mistakenly attribute the residual discrimination to the market.

THE GOVERNMENT

Fiscal Policy

Ever since the New Deal, a primary excuse for the expansion of governmental activity at the federal level has been the supposed necessity for government spending to eliminate unemployment. The excuse has gone through several stages. At first, government spending was needed to "prime the pump." Temporary expenditures would set the economy going and the government could then step out of the picture.

When the initial expenditures failed to eliminate unemployment and were followed by a sharp economic contraction in 1937–38, the theory of "secular stagnation" developed to justify a permanently high level of government spending. The economy had become mature, it was argued. Opportunities for investment had been largely exploited and no substantial new opportunities were likely to arise. Yet individuals would still want to save. Hence, it was essential for government to spend and run a perpetual deficit. The securities issued to finance the deficit would provide individuals with a way to accumulate savings while the government expenditures provided employment. This view has been thoroughly discredited by theoretical analysis and even more by actual experience, including the emergence of wholly new lines for private investment not dreamed of by the secular stagnationists. Yet it has left its heritage. The idea may be accepted by none, but the government programs undertaken in its name, like some of those intended to prime the pump, are still with us and indeed account for ever-growing government expenditures.

More recently, the emphasis has been on government expenditures neither to prime the pump nor to hold in check the specter of secular stagnation but as a balance wheel. When private expenditures decline for any reason, it is said, governmental expenditures should rise to keep total expenditures stable; conversely, when private expenditures rise, governmental expenditures should decline. Unfortunately, the balance wheel is unbalanced. Each recession, however minor, sends a shudder through politically sensitive legislators and administrators with their ever present fear that perhaps it is the harbinger of another 1929–33. They hasten to enact federal spending programs of one kind or another. Many of the programs do not in fact come into effect until after the recession has passed. Hence, insofar as they do affect total expenditures, . . .

they tend to exacerbate the succeeding expansion rather than to mitigate the recession. The haste with which spending programs are approved is not matched by an equal haste to repeal them or to eliminate others when the recession is passed and expansion is under way. On the contrary, it is then argued that a "healthy" expansion must not be "jeopardized" by cuts in governmental expenditures. The chief harm done by the balance-wheel theory is therefore not that it has failed to offset recessions, which it has, and not that it has introduced an inflationary bias into governmental policy, which it has done too, but that it has continuously fostered an expansion in the range of governmental activities at the federal level and prevented a reduction in the burden of federal taxes. . . .

Even if one were to accept the view that the federal budget should be and can be used as a balance wheel, there is no necessity to use the expenditure side of the budget for this purpose. The tax side is equally available. . . .

How different matters might now be if the balance-wheel theory had been applied on the tax side instead of the expenditure side. Suppose each recession had seen a cut in taxes and suppose the political unpopularity of raising taxes in the succeeding expansion had led to resistance to newly proposed governmental expenditure programs and to curtailment of existing ones. We might now be in a position where federal expenditures would be absorbing a good deal less of a national income that would be larger because of the reduction in the depressing and inhibiting effects of taxes. . . .

If the balance-wheel theory has in practice been applied on the expenditure side, it has been because of the existence of other forces making for increased governmental expenditures; in particular, the widespread acceptance by intellectuals of the belief that government should play a larger role in economic and private affairs; the triumph, that is, of the philosophy of the welfare state. This philosophy has found a useful ally in the balance-wheel theory; it has enabled governmental intervention to proceed at a faster pace than would otherwise have been possible. . . .

Other Policies

In the 1920s and the 1930s, intellectuals in the United States were overwhelmingly persuaded that capitalism was a defective system inhibiting economic well-being and thereby freedom, and that the hope for the future lay in a greater measure of deliberate control by political authorities over economic affairs. The conversion of the intellectuals was not achieved by the example of any actual collectivist society, though it undoubtedly was much hastened by the establishment of a communist society in Russia and the glowing hopes placed in it. The conversion of the intellectuals was achieved by a comparison between the existing state of affairs, with all its injustices and defects, and a hypothetical state of affairs as it might be. The actual was compared with the ideal.

At the time, not much else was possible. True, mankind had experienced many epochs of centralized control, of detailed intervention by the state into economic affairs. But there had been a revolution in politics, in science, and in technology. Surely, it was argued, we can do far better with a democratic political structure, modern tools, and modern science than was possible in earlier ages.

The attitudes of that time are still with

us. There is still a tendency to regard any existing government intervention as desirable, to attribute all evils to the market, and to evaluate new proposals for government control in their ideal form, as they might work if run by able, disinterested men, free from the pressure of special interest groups. The proponents of limited government and free enterprise are still on the defensive.

Yet, conditions have changed. We now have several decades of experience with governmental intervention. It is no longer necessary to compare the market as it actually operates and government intervention as it ideally might operate. We can compare the actual with the actual.

If we do so, it is clear that the difference between the actual operation of the market and its ideal operation—great though it undoubtedly is—is as nothing compared to the difference between the actual effects of government intervention and their intended effects. Who can now see any great hope for the advancement of men's freedom and dignity in the massive tyranny and despotism that holds sway in Russia? Wrote Marx and Engels in *The Communist Manifesto:* "The proletarians have nothing to lose but their chains. They have a world to win." Who today can regard the chains of the proletarians in the Soviet Union as weaker than the chains of the proletarians in the United States, or Britain or France or Germany or any Western state?

Let us look closer to home. Which if any of the great "reforms" of past decades has achieved its objectives? Have the good intentions of the proponents of these reforms been realized?

Regulation of the railroads to protect the consumer quickly became an instrument whereby the railroads could protect themselves from the competition of newly emerging rivals—at the expense, of course, of the consumer.

An income tax initially enacted at low rates and later seized upon as a means to redistribute income in favor of the lower classes has become a façade, covering loopholes and special provisions that render rates that are highly graduated on paper largely ineffective. A flat rate of 23½ per cent on presently taxable income would yield as much revenue as the present rates graduated from 20 to 91 per cent.* An income tax intended to reduce inequality and promote the diffusion of wealth has in practice fostered reinvestment of corporate earnings, thereby favoring the growth of large corporations, inhibiting the operation of the capital market, and discouraging the establishment of new enterprises.

Monetary reforms, intended to promote stability in economic activity and prices, exacerbated inflation during and after World War I and fostered a higher degree of instability thereafter than had ever been experienced before. The monetary authorities they established bear primary responsibility for converting a serious economic contraction into the catastrophe of the Great Depression from 1929–33. A system established largely to prevent bank panics produced the most severe banking panic in American history.

An agricultural program intended to help impecunious farmers and to remove what were alleged to be basic dislocations in the organization of agriculture has become a national scandal that has wasted public funds, distorted the use of resources, riveted increasingly heavy

*Author's note: In 1972, the corresponding flat rate was 21½ percent, for rates presently graduated from 14 to 70 percent.

and detailed controls on farmers, interfered seriously with United States foreign policy, and withal has done little to help the impecunious farmer.

A housing program intended to improve the housing conditions of the poor, to reduce juvenile delinquency, and to contribute to the removal of urban slums, has worsened the housing conditions of the poor, contributed to juvenile delinquency, and spread urban blight.

In the 1930s, "labor" was synonymous with "labor union" to the intellectual community; faith in the purity and virtue of labor unions was on a par with faith in home and motherhood. Extensive legislation was enacted to favor labor unions and to foster "fair" labor relations. Labor unions waxed in strength. By the 1950s, "labor union" was almost a dirty word; it was no longer synonymous with "labor," no longer automatically to be taken for granted as on the side of the angels.

Social security measures were enacted to make receipt of assistance a matter of right, to eliminate the need for direct relief and assistance. Millions now receive social security benefits. Yet the relief rolls grow and the sums spent on direct assistance mount.

The list can easily be lengthened: the silver purchase program of the 1930s, public power projects, foreign aid programs of the postwar years, F.C.C., urban redevelopment programs, the stockpiling program—these and many more have had effects very different and generally quite opposite from those intended.

There have been some exceptions. The expressways crisscrossing the country, magnificent dams spanning great rivers, orbiting satellites are all tributes to the capacity of government to command great resources. The school system, with all its defects and problems, with all the possibility of improvement through bringing into more effective play the forces of the market, has widened the opportunities available to American youth and contributed to the extension of freedom. It is a testament to the public-spirited efforts of the many tens of thousands who have served on local school boards and to the willingness of the public to bear heavy taxes for what they regarded as a public purpose. The Sherman antitrust laws, with all their problems of detailed administration, have by their very existence fostered competition. Public health measures have contributed to the reduction of infectious disease. Assistance measures have relieved suffering and distress. Local authorities have often provided facilities essential to the life of communities. Law and order have been maintained, though in many a large city the performance of even this elementary function of government has been far from satisfactory. As a citizen of Chicago, I speak feelingly.

If a balance be struck, there can be little doubt that the record is dismal. The greater part of the new ventures undertaken by government in the past few decades have failed to achieve their objectives. The United States has continued to progress; its citizens have become better fed, better clothed, better housed, and better transported; class and social distinctions have narrowed; minority groups have become less disadvantaged; popular culture has advanced by leaps and bounds. All this has been the product of the initiative and drive of individuals cooperating through the free market. Government measures have hampered, not helped this development. We have been able to afford and surmount these measures only because of the extraordinary fecundity of the market. The invisible hand has been more potent for progress than the visible hand for retrogression.

Is it an accident that so many of the government reforms of recent decades have gone awry, that the bright hopes have turned to ashes? Is it simply because the programs are faulty in detail?

I believe the answer is clearly in the negative. The central defect of these measures is that they seek through government to force people to act against their own immediate interests in order to promote a supposedly general interest. They seek to resolve what is supposedly a conflict of interest, or a difference in view about interests, not by establishing a framework that will eliminate the conflict, or by persuading people to have different interests, but by forcing people to act against their own interest. They substitute the values of outsiders for the values of participants; either some telling others what is good for them, or the government taking from some to benefit others. These measures are therefore countered by one of the strongest and most creative forces known to man—the attempt by millions of individuals to promote their own interests, to live their lives by their own values. This is the major reason why the measures have so often had the opposite of the effects intended. It is also one of the major strengths of a free society and explains why governmental regulation does not strangle it.

The interests of which I speak are not simply narrow self-regarding interests. On the contrary, they include the whole range of values that men hold dear and for which they are willing to spend their fortunes and sacrifice their lives. The Germans who lost their lives opposing Adolf Hitler were pursuing their interests as they saw them. So also are the men and women who devote great effort and time to charitable, educational, and religious activities. Naturally, such interests are the major ones for few men. It is the virtue of a free society that it nonetheless permits these interests full scope and does not subordinate them to the narrow materialistic interests that dominate the bulk of mankind. That is why capitalist societies are less materialistic than collective societies. . . .

A government which maintained law and order, defined property rights, served as a means whereby we could modify property rights and other rules of the economic game, adjudicated disputes about the interpretation of the rules, enforced contracts, promoted competition, provided a monetary framework, engaged in activities to counter technical monopolies and to overcome neighborhood effects widely regarded as sufficiently important to justify government intervention, and which supplemented private charity and the private family in protecting the irresponsible, whether madman or child—such a government would clearly have important functions to perform. The consistent liberal is not an anarchist.

Yet is is also true that such a government would have clearly limited functions and would refrain from a host of activities that are now undertaken by federal and state governments in the United States and their counterparts in other Western countries. . . . [I]t may help to give a sense of proportion about the role that a liberal would assign government simply to list . . . some activities currently undertaken by government in the United States that cannot, so far as I can see, validly be justified . . . :

1. Parity price support programs for agriculture.
2. Tariffs on imports or restrictions on

exports, such as current oil import quotas, sugar quotas, etc.

3. Governmental control of output, such as through the farm program, or through proration of oil as is practiced by the Texas Railroad Commission.
4. Rent control, such as is still practiced in New York, or more general price and wage controls such as were imposed during and just after World War II.
5. Legal minimum-wage rates, or legal maximum prices, such as the legal maximum of zero on the rate of interest that can be paid on demand deposits by commercial banks, or the legally fixed maximum rates that can be paid on savings and time deposits.
6. Detailed regulation of industries, such as the regulation of transportation by the Interstate Commerce Commission. This had some justification on technical monopoly grounds when initially introduced for railroads; it has none now for any means of transport. Another example is detailed regulation of banking.
7. A similar example, but one which deserves special mention because of its implicit censorship and violation of free speech, is the control of radio and television by the Federal Communications Commission.
8. Present social security programs, especially the old-age and retirement programs compelling people in effect (a) to spend a specified fraction of their income on the purchase of retirement annuity, (b) to buy the annuity from a publicly operated enterprise.
9. Licensure provisions in various cities and states which restrict particular enterprises or occupations or professions to people who have a license, where the license is more than a receipt for a tax which anyone who wishes to enter the activity may buy.
10. So-called "public housing" and the host of other subsidy programs directed at fostering residential construction, such as FHA and VA guarantee of mortgage, and the like.
11. Conscription to man the military services in peacetime. The appropriate free market arrangement is volunteer military forces; which is to say, hiring men to serve. There is no justification for not paying whatever price is necessary to attract the required number of men. Present arrangements are inequitable and arbitrary, seriously interfere with the freedom of young men to shape their lives, and probably are even more costly than the market alternative. (Universal military training to provide a reserve for wartime is a different problem and may be justified on liberal grounds.)
12. National parks. . . .
13. The legal prohibition on the carrying of mail for profit.
14. Publicly owned and operated toll roads. . . .

This list is far from comprehensive. . . .

As Adam Smith once said, "There is much ruin in a nation." Our basic structure of values and the interwoven network of free institutions will withstand much. I believe that we shall be able to preserve and extend freedom despite the size of the military programs and despite the economic powers already concentrated in Washington. But we shall be able to do so only if we awake to the threat that we face, only if we persuade our fellow men that free institutions offer a surer, if perhaps at times a slower, route to the ends they seek than the coercive power of the state. The glimmerings of change that are already apparent in the intellectual climate are a hopeful augury.

MONEY AND ECONOMIC ACTIVITY

LONG-RUN MONEY-PRICE RELATIONS

There is perhaps no empirical regularity among economic phenomena that is based on so much evidence for so wide a range of circumstances as the connection between substantial changes in the stock of money and in the level of prices. To the best of my knowledge *there is no instance in which a substantial change in the stock of money per unit of output has occurred without a substantial change in the level of prices in the same direction.* Conversely, I know of no instance in which there has been a substantial change in the level of prices without a substantial change in the stock of money per unit of output in the same direction. And instances in which prices and the stock of money have moved together are recorded for many centuries of history, for countries in every part of the globe, and for a wide diversity of monetary arrangements.

There can be little doubt about this statistical connection. The statistical connection itself, however, tells nothing about direction of influence, and it is on this question that there has been the most controversy. It could be that a rise or fall in prices, occurring for whatever reasons, produces a corresponding rise or fall in the stock of money, so that the monetary changes are a passive consequence. Alternatively, it could be that changes in the stock of money produce changes in prices in the same direction, so that control of the stock of money would imply control of prices. The variety of monetary arrangements for which a connection between monetary and price movements has been observed supports strongly the second interpretation, namely, that substantial changes in the stock of money are both a necessary and a sufficient condition for substantial changes in the general level of prices. But of course this does not exclude a reflex influence of changes in prices on the stock of money. This reflex influence is often important, almost always complex, and, depending on the monetary arrangements, may be in either direction.

The relationship between changes in the stock of money and changes in prices, while close, is not of course precise or mechanically rigid. Two major factors produce discrepancies: changes in output, and changes in the amount of money that the public desires to hold relative to its income.

A wide range of empirical evidence suggests that the ratio which people desire to maintain between their cash bal-

From *The Relationship of Prices to Economic Stability and Growth,* 85th Cong., 2d sess., Joint Economic Committee Print, Washington, D.C.: U.S. Government Printing Office (1958).

ances and their income is relatively stable over fairly long periods of time aside from the effect of two major factors: (1) The level of real income per capita, or perhaps of real wealth per capita; (2) the cost of holding money.

The cost of holding cash balances depends mainly on the rate of interest that can be earned on alternative assets—thus if a bond yields 4 per cent while cash yields no return, this means that an individual gives up $4 a year if he holds $100 of cash instead of a bond—and on the rate of change of prices—if prices rise at 5 per cent per year, for example, $100 in cash will buy at the end of the year only as much as $95 at the beginning so that it has cost the individual $5 to hold $100 of cash instead of goods. The empirical evidence suggests that while the first factor—the interest rate—has a systematic effect on the amount of money held, the effect is rather small. The second factor, the rate of change of prices, has no discernible effect in ordinary times when price changes are small—on the order of a few per cent a year. On the other hand, it has a clearly discernible and major effect when price change is rapid and long continued, as during extreme inflations or deflations. A rapid inflation produces a sizable decline in the desired ratio of cash balances to income; a rapid deflation, a sizable rise.

SHORT-RUN MONEY-PRICE RELATIONS

Over the longer periods considered in the preceding sections, changes in the stock of money per unit of output tend to dominate price changes, allowance being made for the effect of the growth of real income per head. This is less so over the shorter periods involved in the fluctuations we term business cycles, though the general and average relationship is very similar. The reason for the looser connection in such periods presumably is that movements in both the stock of money and in prices are smaller. Over longer periods, these movements cumulate and tend to swamp any disturbance in the relation between desired cash balances, real income, and the cost of holding money; in the ordinary business cycle, the disturbances, though perhaps no more important in an absolute sense, are much more important relative to the movements in money and prices.

There can be little doubt on the basis of this evidence that there is a close link between monetary changes and price changes over the shorter periods within which business cycles run their course as well as over longer periods and during major wartime episodes. But important considerations must be borne in mind if this fact is not to be a misleading guide to policy. [One] has to do with the timing of the changes in the money supply and in income and prices. The generally upward trend in the money supply which accounts for its continuing to rise, though at a slower rate, during most contractions in economic activity as well as during expansions makes it difficult to judge timing relations from ups and downs in the money supply itself. For this and other reasons, we have found it most useful to examine instead the ups and downs in the rate at which the money supply is changing. The rate of change of the money supply shows well-marked cycles that match closely those in economic activity in general and precede the latter by a long interval. On the average, *the rate of change of the money supply has reached its peak nearly sixteen months before the peak in general business and has reached its trough over twelve months before the trough in general business.*

This is strong though not conclusive evidence for the independent influence of monetary change. But it also has a very different significance. It means that it must take a long time for the influence of monetary changes to make themselves felt—apparently what happens now to the rate of change of the money supply may not be reflected in prices or economic activity *for twelve to sixteen months, on the average.* Moreover, the timing varies considerably from cycle to cycle—since 1907, the shortest time span by which the money peak preceded the business cycle peak was thirteen months, the longest, twenty-four months; the corresponding range at troughs is five months to twenty-one months. From the point of view of scientific analysis directed at establishing economic regularities on the basis of the historical record—the purpose for which the measures were computed—this is highly consistent behavior; it justifies considerable confidence in the reliability of the averages cited and means that they cannot easily be attributed simply to the accident of chance variation. But *from the point of view of policy directed at controlling a particular movement such as the current recession, the timing differences are disturbingly large*—they mean that monetary action taken today may, on the basis of past experience, affect economic activity within six months or again perhaps not for over a year and six months; and of course past experience is not exhaustive; the particular episode may establish a new limit in either direction.

The long time lag has another important effect. It leads to misinterpretation and misconception about the effects of monetary policy, as well as to consequent mistakes in monetary policy. Because the effects of monetary change do not occur instantaneously, monetary policy is regarded as ineffective.

OUTPUT RELATIONS

Over the cycle, prices and output tend to move together—both tend to rise during expansions and to fall during contractions. Both are part of the cyclical process and anything, including a monetary change, that promotes a vigorous expansion is likely to promote a vigorous rise in both and conversely. Over the longer period, the relation between price changes and output changes is much less clear. Now this seems clearly valid, not only as an expository device but also as a first approximation to reality. What happens to a nation's output over long periods of time depends in the first instance on such basic factors as resources available, the industrial organization of the society, the growth of knowledge and technical skills, the growth of population, the accumulation of capital and so on. This is the stage on which money and price changes play their parts as the supporting cast.

One proposition about the effect of changes in the stock of money and in prices that is widely accepted and hardly controversial is that large and unexpected changes in prices are adverse to the growth of output—whether these changes are up or down. At one extreme, the kind of price rise that occurs during hyperinflation seriously distorts the effective use of resources.[1] At the other

1. However, even open hyperinflations are less damaging to output than suppressed inflations in which a wide range of prices are held well below the levels that would clear the market. The German

extreme, sharp price declines such as occurred from 1920 to 1921 and again from 1929 to 1933 certainly produce a widespread and tragic waste of resources.

So much is agreed. The more controversial issue is the effect of moderate change in prices. One view that is widely held is that slowly rising prices stimulate economic output and produce a more rapid rate of growth than would otherwise occur. A number of reasons have been offered in support of this view. (1) Prices, and particularly wages, are, it is said, sticky. In a market economy, the reallocation of resources necessitated by economic growth and development requires changes in relative prices and relative wages. It is much easier, it is argued, for these to come about without friction and resistance if they can occur through rises in some prices and wages without declines in others. If prices were stable, some changes in relative wages could still come about in this way, since economic growth means that wages tend to rise relative to prices, but changes in relative prices could not, and, of course, there would not be as much scope even for relative wage changes. (2) Costs, and in particular, wages, are, it is argued, stickier than selling prices. Hence generally rising prices will tend to raise profit margins, giving enterprises both a bigger incentive to raise output and to add to capital and the means to finance the capital needed. (3) The most recently popular variant of the preceding point is that costs are not only sticky against declines but in addition have a tendency to be pushed up with little reference to the state of demand as a result of strong trade unions. If the money stock is kept from rising, the result, it is claimed, will be unemployment as profit margins are cut, and also a higher level of prices, though not necessarily a rising level of prices. Gently rising prices, it is argued, will tend to offset this upward pressure by permitting money wages to rise without real wages doing so. (4) Interest rates are particularly slow to adapt to price rises. If prices are rising at, say, 3 per cent a year, a 6 per cent interest rate on a money loan is equivalent to a 3 per cent rate when prices are stable. If lenders adjusted fully to the price rise, this would simply mean that interest rates would be three percentage points higher in the first case than in the second. But in fact this does not happen, so that productive enterprises find the cost of borrowing to be relatively low, and again have a greater incentive than otherwise to invest, and the associated transfer from creditors to debtors gives them greater means to do so.

In opposition to this view, it has been argued that generally rising prices reduce the pressure on enterprises to be efficient, stimulate speculative relative to industrial activity, reduce the incentives for individuals to save, and make it more difficult to maintain the appropriate structure of relative prices, since individual prices have to change in order to stay the same relative to others. Furthermore, it is argued that once it becomes widely recognized that prices are rising, the advantages cited in the preceding paragraph will disappear: escalator clauses or their economic equivalent will eliminate the stickiness of prices and wages and the greater stickiness of wages than of prices; strong unions will increase still further their wage demands to allow for price increases; and interest rates will rise to allow for the price rise. If the advantages are to be obtained, the rate of price rise will have to be accelerated and there is no stopping place short of runaway inflation.

Historical evidence on the relation between price changes and output changes is mixed and gives no clear support to any of these positions. All in all, perhaps the only conclusion that is justified is that either rising prices or falling prices are consistent with rapid economic growth, provided that the price changes are fairly steady, moderate in size, and reasonably predictable. The mainsprings of growth are presumably to be sought elsewhere. But unpredictable and erratic changes of direction in prices are apparently as disturbing to economic growth as to economic stability.

POLICY IMPLICATIONS

Past experience suggests that something like a 3 to 5 percent per year increase in the stock of money is required for long-term price stability. For cyclical movements, a major problem is to prevent monetary changes from being a source of disturbance. If the stock of money can be kept growing at a relatively steady rate, without erratic fluctuations in short periods, it is highly unlikely if not impossible that we would experience either a sharp price rise—like that during World Wars I and II and after World War I—or a substantial price or output decline—like those experienced from 1920-21, 1929-33, 1937-38.

A steady rate of growth in the money supply will not mean perfect stability even though it would prevent the kind of wide fluctuations that we have experienced from time to time in the past. It is tempting to try to go farther and to use monetary changes to offset other factors making for expansion and contraction. The available evidence casts grave doubts on the possibility of producing any fine adjustments in economic activity by fine adjustments in monetary policy—at least in the present state of knowledge.

There are thus serious limitations to the possibility of a discretionary monetary policy and much danger that such a policy may make matters worse rather than better. Federal Reserve policy since 1951 has been distinctly superior to that followed during any earlier period since the establishment of the System, mainly because it has avoided wide fluctuations in the rate or growth of the money supply. At the same time, I am myself inclined to believe that in our present state of knowledge and with our present institutions, even this policy has been decidedly inferior to the much simpler policy of keeping the money supply growing at a predesignated rate month in and month out with allowance only for seasonal influences and with no attempt to adjust the rate of growth to monetary conditions.[2]

To avoid misunderstanding, it should be emphasized that the problems just discussed are in no way peculiar to monetary policy. Fiscal action also involves lags. Indeed the lag between the recognition of need for action and the taking of action is undoubtedly longer for discretionary fiscal than for discretionary monetary action: the monetary authorities can act promptly, fiscal action inevitably involves serious delays for congressional consideration. Hence the basic difficulties and limitations of monetary policy apply with equal force to fiscal policy.

hyperinflation after World War I never caused anything like the reduction of production that was produced in Germany from 1945 to the monetary reform of 1948 by the suppression of inflation. And the inflationary pressure suppressed in the second case was a small fraction of that manifested in the first.

2. The extensive empirical work that I have done has given me no reason to doubt that the simple policy suggested above would produce a very tolerable amount of stability. This evidence has persuaded me that the major problem is to prevent monetary changes from themselves contributing to instability rather than to use monetary changes to offset other forces.

Political pressures to "do something" in the face of either relatively mild price rises or relatively mild price and employment declines are clearly very strong indeed in the existing state of public attitudes. The main moral to be drawn from the two preceding points is that *yielding to these pressures may frequently do more harm than good.* The goal of an extremely high degree of economic stability is certainly a splendid one; our ability to attain it, however, is limited; we can surely avoid extreme fluctuations; we do not know enough to avoid minor fluctuations; the attempt to do more than we can will itself be a disturbance that may increase rather than reduce instability. But like all such injunctions, this one too must be taken in moderation. It is a plea for a sense of perspective and balance, not for irresponsibility in the face of major problems or for failure to correct past mistakes.

EDWARD C. BANFIELD

Kenan Professor of Public Policy Analysis and Political Science, University of Pennsylvania.

Edward C. Banfield is one of a relatively small number of conservatives specializing in problems of urban political economy. Like virtually all conservatives, he favors a social policy that would deemphasize the role of the Federal government in favor of increased state and local initiative, and reemphasize the importance of competitive markets in place of public sector activities. He is sufficiently realistic, however, to recognize that a program embracing this new direction is "incompatible with the nature of our political system, which is energized by the pressures that [private] interests exert to get things from government."

Unlike liberal tracts dealing with the twentieth-century overpopulated, drug-infested, violence-prone, racist-breeding urban areas, Banfield's *Unheavenly City* does not beat the drum, either softly or stridently, for massive commitments of money, materials, and morality to overturn this type of urban culture and set it on a more progressive path. Quite the contrary. He proclaims:

> The fundamental problem of the central cities is of such a nature that it cannot be "solved," or even much relieved, by government action at any level. . . . The government cannot eliminate slums, educate the slum child, train the unskilled worker, end chronic poverty, stop crime and delinquency and prevent riots. In the main these problems are not susceptible to solution.

Thus, Banfield sees welfare measures like minimum-wage legislation, compulsory high school attendance, subsidization of transportation, and home ownership as blunders that can only exacerbate urban problems. His reasoning is simply that lower-class culture produces (and reproduces) these intertwining problems and that government intervention weakens the positive effects of the operation of private enterprise. Luckily, according to Banfield, the pernicious effects of government welfare activities are ameliorated by "accidental forces" at work in the economy—economic growth (expected to more or less end poverty by 2000), demographic change (a future relative decline in the "troublesome" adolescent part of the population is expected to lessen the strain on our overburdened urban institutions), and a general uplifting of cultural standards over time. Banfield stresses, however, that these favorable "objective" features may be partially overcome by unfavorable "subjective" features, e.g., the fact that rising expectations sometimes lead deprived groups to demand more rapid change than is possible and to behave in a socially disruptive manner. Forceful demands by blacks for more massive government programs may, says Banfield, set in motion a "self-fulfilling prophecy of racial hatred." This amounts to saying that black misperceptions of "reality" have intensified white racism—Banfield's way of making the victims look responsible for their own plight. What actually upsets Banfield is that black resistance to the pace of socioeconomic "improvements" may threaten the social stability of the "essentially healthy" system that he so ardently wants to preserve.

Although there are racist overtones in Banfield's work, his explanation of the black's inferior economic and social position is closer to a class-based view (superficially resembling the radical stance) than a racial one.

> Today the Negro's main disadvantage is . . . that he is the most recent unskilled, and hence relatively low income immigrant to reach the city from a backward rural area. . . . Almost everything said about the problems of the Negro tends to exaggerate the purely racial aspects of the situation.

The complex interplay between class and race is not adequately explained by Banfield; it is, in fact, barely alluded to. In his dubious concept of class, a person's "orientation to the future" (i.e., willingness to make short-run sacrifices, like acquiring advanced education, to improve the chance of future gains), rather than income or wealth, determines that person's class position. To this subjectivist view, class is more a psychological state of mind than an objective set of conditions. Banfield skillfully uses this class definition to blame the poverty plight of the urban lower classes on their myopic "present orientation" (a kind of innate psychological defect), suggesting that altruistic government income redistribution and housing measures, however well-intentioned, cannot help the urban poor to overcome this plight. In suggesting that an inability to look ahead explains the ghetto dweller's poverty, Banfield misses the obvious point that the objective realities of widespread poverty and lack of political power in the ghetto *cause* many of its inhabitants to confine their perspective to the immediate present. This present orientation is, in fact, a rational rather than a pathological response to the survival struggle in today's ghettos. It is the overall political, economic, and social environments of the ghetto inhabitant, rather than some pervasive lower-class culture, that explain this response.

In outlining his theory, Banfield makes a telling criticism of altruistically inclined liberals: "Sympathy for the oppressed, indignation at the oppressor, and a wish to make amends for wrongs done by one's ancestors lead to a misrepresentation of the Negro as the near-helpless victim of 'white racism.' " Unfortunately, that theory also incorporates three fundamental errors:

1. His concept of class is a subjective rather than an objective one, and hence reflects judgmental biases.
2. Although a racial analysis is insufficient to explain the inferior position of the blacks, so is a purely class analysis (particularly the defective one used by Banfield). The oppression of the black on class lines is of primary importance, but the oppression along racial lines is also significant, particularly in the struggle for the basic economic and political rights whites take for granted. In other words, a synthesis of race and class analysis is a prerequisite for understanding the black problem in capitalist America.
3. It is the capitalist structure itself that tends to perpetuate urban poverty, with the accompanying problems of crime and violence—not, as Banfield would have it, some alleged psychological malfunctioning of the lower class.

Despite these limitations, Banfield's work deserves serious attention, since its advocated social policy of "benign neglect" seems to be finding considerable grass-roots support in several strata of White America.

M L

From

THE UNHEAVENLY CITY

(1970)

It is probable that at this time we are about to make great changes in our social system. The world is ripe for such changes and if they are not made in the direction of greater social liberality, the direction forward, they will almost of necessity be made in the direction backward, of a terrible social niggardliness. We all know which of those directions we want. But it is not enough to want it, not even enough to work for it–we must want it and work for it with intelligence. Which means that we must be aware of the dangers which lie in our most generous wishes.

LIONEL TRILLING

It is impossible to avoid the conclusion that the serious problems of the cities will continue to exist in something like their present form for another twenty years at least. Even on the most favorable assumptions we shall have large concentrations of the poor and the unskilled, and–what, to repeat, is by no means the same thing–the lower class in the central cities and the larger, older suburbs. The outward movement of industry and commerce is bound to continue, leaving ever-larger parts of the inner city blighted or semi-abandoned. Even if we could afford to throw the existing cities away and build new ones from scratch, matters would not be essentially different, for the people who moved into the new cities would take the same old problems with them. Eventually, the present problems of the cities will disappear or dwindle into relative unimportance; they will not, however, be "solved" by programs of the sort now being undertaken or contemplated. On the contrary, the tendency of these programs will be to prolong the problems and perhaps even make them worse.

For the most part, the problems in question have arisen from and are inseparably connected with developments that almost everyone welcomes: the growth and spread of affluence has enabled millions of people to move from congested cities to new and more spacious homes in the suburbs; the availability of a large stock of relatively good housing in the central cities and older suburbs has enabled the Negro to escape the semislavery of the rural South and, a century late, to move into industrial society; better public health measures and facilities have cut the death rate of the lower class; the war and postwar baby boom has left the city with more adolescents and youths than ever before; and a widespread and general movement upward on the class-cultural scale has made poverty, squalor, ignorance, and brutality–conditions that have always and everywhere been regarded as inevitable in the nature of things–appear as anomalies that should be removed entirely and at once.

What stands in the way of dealing effectively with these problems (insofar as their nature admits of their being dealt with) is mainly the virtues of the American political system and of the American character. It is because governmental power is widely distributed that organized interests are so often able to veto measures that would benefit large numbers of people. It is the generous and public-regarding impulses of voters and taxpayers that impel them to support measures—for example, the minimum wage and compulsory high school attendance—the ultimate effect of which is to make the poor poorer and more demoralized. Our devotion to the doctrine that all men are created equal discourages any explicit recognition of class-cultural differences and leads to "democratic"—and often misleading—formulations of problems: for example, poverty as lack of income and material resources (something external to the individual) rather than as inability or unwillingness to take account of the future or to control impulses (something internal). Sympathy for the oppressed, indignation at the oppressor, and a wish to make amends for wrongs done by one's ancestors lead to a misrepresentation of the Negro as the near-helpless victim of "white racism." Faith in the perfectibility of man and confidence that good intentions together with strenuous exertions will hasten his progress onward and upward lead to bold programs that promise to do what no one knows how to do and what perhaps cannot be done, and therefore ends in frustration, loss of mutual respect and trust, anger, and even coercion.

Even granting that in general the effect of government programs is to exacerbate the problems of the cities, it might perhaps be argued that they have a symbolic value that is more than redeeming. What economist Kenneth Boulding has said of national parks—that we seem to need them "as we seem to need a useless dome on the capitol, as a symbol of national identity and of that mutuality of concern and interest without which government would be naked coercion"—may possibly apply as well to Freedom Budgets, domestic Marshall Plans, and other such concoctions. That government programs do not succeed in reducing welfare dependency, preventing crime, and so on, is a rather minor objection to them if in fact without them the feeling that the society is "not worth saving" would be widespread. One would hope, however, that other and better means—a useless dome on the capitol, for example—would serve the symbolic need well enough. Moreover, there is an evident danger that the failure of urban programs to contribute to the attainment of our objectives will make them symbols not of national identity and mutual concern, but rather of national divisiveness, confusion, and unwisdom.

That government cannot solve the problems of the cities and is likely to make them worse by trying does not necessarily mean that calamity impends. Powerful accidental (by which is meant, nongovernmental and, more generally, nonorganizational) forces are at work that tend to alleviate and even to eliminate the problems. Hard as it may be for a nation of inveterate problem-solvers to believe, social problems sometimes disappear in the normal course of events.

One powerful accidental force at work is economic growth. Because capital tends to increase by geometric progression, a rich country becomes exceedingly rich in the space of a few years. If Americans in the future take no more of their income in the form of leisure than they do now, the national income should increase from $713 billion in 1968 to $2,628 billion in the year 2000. If there has meanwhile been no great amount of immigration by people who are slow to adapt to the ways of industrial society, the end of urban poverty, in the sense of hardship, will be at hand even if the pattern of income distribution remains substantially unchanged.

A second such force is demographic change. The presence of large numbers of adolescent boys is (along with the presence of a large lower class) mainly responsible for school, job, crime, and disorder problems. This troublesome part of the population is now increasing at an extraordinarily rapid rate (in the ten years ending in 1975 the number of males aged fifteen to twenty-four will increase from 15,540,000 to an estimated 20,296,000). The increase will almost stop before long, however (in 1985 there will be about 21,107,000 males in this age group), and the proportion of boys and young men in the population will be smaller than it is now. A decline in the relative importance of the young male part of the population will do more to relieve strain on city institutions, it is safe to say, than even the most "massive" of government programs.

A third such force—perhaps the most important of all—is the process of middle- and upper-class-ification. . . . [I]t does not seem likely that the lower class will be absorbed into the culture of the larger society. With this important exception, however, there will no doubt continue to be a general upward movement all along the class-cultural scale. This will mean a softening of manners, better performance in schools, less violence (but not necessarily less nonviolent crime and disorder), and a reduction in racial prejudice and discrimination.

The decline of prejudice and discrimination should proceed with gathering momentum because of the operation of what Gunnar Myrdal, in *An American Dilemma,* called "the principle of cumulation."

> White prejudice and discrimination keep the Negro low in standards of living, health, education, manners and morals. This, in turn, gives support to white prejudice. White prejudice and Negro standards thus mutually "cause" each other. . . . Such a static "accommodation" is, however, entirely accidental. If either of the factors changes, this will cause a change in the other factor, too, and start a process of interaction where the change in one factor will continuously be supported by the reaction of the other factor.

It is impossible to judge how much effect these accidental forces will have on the lower class. . . . [I]t makes a great deal of difference how much of the present-orientedness of that class is cognitive, how much situational, and how much volitional, but this is a question for which answers do not exist at present. If, as many social scientists want to believe, present-orientedness is mainly or even entirely situational, rapid economic growth may before long offer the lower class the incentives—especially job opportunities—needed to bring its members into normal culture. On the other hand, increasing affluence may have a contrary effect: overgenerous welfare programs may destroy more incentives to look ahead and provide for the future than improved job and other opportunities can provide. For this and other reasons that have already been discussed, an increase in the absolute (if not the relative) size of the lower class is by no means out of the question. Unless the increase were very large, however, it would not necessarily lead to a radical worsening of the situation or precipitate a crisis in the life of the nation.

Although the *objective* situation does not warrant the alarmist tone of much that is said and written about the city, the *subjective* one may. However much the accidental forces may reduce the *real* importance of the problems that have been under discussion, they may have no impact on their *seeming* importance. Indeed, this is likely to grow, for some of the very same factors that improve the objective situation also raise people's standards and expectations, thus leaving the subjective situation no better—and perhaps even worse—than it was to begin with. What people *think* a situation is may (as sociologist Robert K. Merton has pointed out) become an integral part of that situation, and therefore a factor in its subsequent development. A false public definition of the situation may, as Merton says, evoke new behavior that makes the originally false definition come true, thus perpetuating a "reign of error." In short, wrong public definitions of urban problems may lead to behavior that will make matters worse despite the ameliorating influence of the accidental forces.

This possibility is most painfully apparent in the case of the Negro. That racial prejudice has long been declining and may be expected to continue to decline at an accelerating rate counts for little if the Negro *thinks* that white racism is as pervasive as ever; that his opportunities to improve his position by acquiring skills are at last fairly good counts for little if he *thinks* that "massive" government welfare, housing, and other programs—and *only* these—can help him. If he misperceives the situation in these ways, he is likely to do things that are counterproductive (for example, to cut himself off from "white" schools, jobs, and politics and to enter the fantasy world of black separatism). Such a course, if carried far enough, may validate his original (false) hypothesis—that is, he may become in fact as dependent upon government programs as he (wrongly) supposed himself to be and may revive the fact of white prejudice by giving it some objective grounds to feed upon.

Nothing could be so tragic and ironic as the acceptance of a false public definition of the situation that proves to be a self-fulfilling prophecy of racial hatred. Even if nonracial factors had not in recent years superseded the racial ones as the Negro's main handicap, it would be well to pretend that they had, for a self-fulfilling prophecy of the unimportance of racial factors would be as great a blessing as its opposite would be a curse.

Except as they create, or reinforce, counterproductive public definitions of problems and thereby encourage a "reign of error," wrong governmental measures are not likely to lead to catastrophe or even to any very significant worsening of the situation. Most wrong measures will lead to nothing worse than some additional waste and delay, usually a trivial amount. (One gets a sense of how unimportant even "important" governmental actions may be from one economist's estimate that the elimination of monopoly in the United States in 1929 would have raised income by no more than 1/13 of 1 percent, and from the estimate of another that benefits attributable to better resource allocation by virtue of the Common Market would also be much less than 1 percent.) The governmental measures having the largest effect upon the city since the turn of the century are probably subsidization of truck and automobile transportation and subsidization of home ownership for the well-off; these measures certainly hastened the departure of the white middle class from the central city and, *a fortiori,* the entry of the poor—especially the black poor—on a large scale, but they did not significantly change the pattern of metropolitan growth; this was determined by accidental forces . . . demographic, technological, economic, and class-cultural imperatives. . . .

Although it is easy to exaggerate the importance, either for good or ill, of the measures that government has adopted or might adopt, there does appear to be a danger to the good health of the society in the tendency of the public to define so many situations as "critical problems"—a definition that implies (1) that "solutions" exist or can be found and (2) that unless they are found and applied at once, disaster will befall. The import of what has been said [here] is that although there are many difficulties to be coped with, dilemmas to be faced, and afflictions to be endured, there are very few problems that can be solved; it is also that although much is seriously wrong with the city, no disaster impends unless it be one that results from public misconceptions that are in the nature of self-fulfilling prophecies.

Insofar as delusory and counterproductive public definitions of the situation arise from biases that lie deep within the culture (for example, from the impulse to DO SOMETHING! and to DO GOOD!), they are likely to persist in the face of all experience. To exhort the upper classes to display more of the quality that Trilling calls moral realism would be to offer a problem-begging "solution," since the very want of moral realism that constitutes the problem would prevent their recognizing the need of it.

The biases of the culture limit the range of possibilities, but they do not determine fully how the public will define the situation. This definition is in large part the result of a process of opinion formation that goes on within a relatively small world of officials, leaders of civic associations and other interest groups, journalists, and social scientists, especially economists; from this small world, opinion is passed on to the public-at-large through the mass media, books, classroom instruction, campaign oratory, after-dinner speeches, and so on. Needless to say, a vast amount of misinformation, prejudice, and illogic enters into the process of opinion formation. (The agony of the cities, someone has remarked, is what the network executive and his fellow-commuters on the Long Island Railroad see out the window as they make their agonized way to and from their offices in Manhattan.) Within the past decade or two, developments have occurred that could make for a more realistic view of the urban situation—for example, the number of technically trained persons working on urban problems has increased greatly, their resources for gathering and manipulating data and the analytical apparatus that they can bring to bear upon policy questions are much improved, and what they have to say is taken much more seriously by politicians and administrators and therefore also by journalists. It would not be surprising if the conventional wisdom were to be very much revised in the next decade or two as a consequence of these developments. Turnover within the small world of opinion-makers is rapid, and the young newcomers in that world tend to be open to new ideas and even in search of them. Because communication within the small world and between it and the public-at-large is excellent, a new definition of the situation, once formulated, could catch on very quickly.

It would be pleasant to be able to end this discussion on that relatively optimistic note. Unfortunately, another side to the matter requires mention. Technically trained persons have their own characteristic biases, and if their view of the city is different from that of the commuter on the Long Island Railroad it is not necessarily more realistic. Moreover, as the technician comes to play a more important part in policy-making he is bound to come more and more under the discipline of large organizations, especially foundations and government agencies, whose maintenance and enhancement depends in some way upon the elaboration of an alarmist, or at any rate expansionist, public definition of the situation. That young newcomers to the small world of opinion-makers tend to be open to new ideas is not altogether reassuring either, for they may tend to accept new ideas *just because* they are new. To the pessimist, the prospect is that a new conventional wisdom about the problems of the city, the product of many millions of dollars' expenditure on research, cast in the language of systems analysis and the computer, will only compound the existing confusion. The optimist, however, will see reason to believe that facts, rational analysis, and deliberation about the nature of the public interest will play a somewhat larger part than hitherto in the formation of both opinion and policy.

NIXON, THE GREAT SOCIETY, AND THE FUTURE OF SOCIAL POLICY

(1973)

What follows are Banfield's responses to these questions:

1. *It is frequently said that the Great Society was a failure. Do you agree with this assessment? If not, to what particular features of the Johnson program would you attribute its success? If so, where would you place the blame? Was it insufficient financing? Was it the "services" approach?*
2. *It is also frequently said that Richard Nixon is leading a "counterrevolution" against the general trend of social policy of the last thirty or forty years. Do you agree with this characterization of the Nixon program? If so, toward what objectives would you say the "counter-revolution" is aimed? If not, how would you characterize the general thrust of the Nixon administration's policies, especially as reflected in the new budget?*

3. What, in your judgment, would constitute a sound program in the area of social policy? In the light of the experience of the past ten years, what do you think the possibilities are in the foreseeable future? What are the limits?

1. The Great Society was a Great Cornucopia overflowing with all sorts of goodies; civil-rights laws, the Office of Economic Opportunity (a cornucopia within a cornucopia), Model Cities (another cornucopia), manpower-training programs, compensatory-education programs, and so on—hundreds of items altogether. Their diversity resists any one-word verdict.

Many millions of dollars were spent monitoring and evaluating, but the products of these efforts are of little value for the present purpose. The evaluations are mostly of bits and pieces of certain programs—Community Action in some cities and from certain standpoints, for example. So far as I am aware, not a single program has been evaluated systematically and in detail. That would be impossible in most cases because of the vague and contradictory nature of the goals. Model Cities, for example, was intended to concentrate resources in order to make a "substantial impact" on poor neighborhoods, to improve decision-making procedures in the offices of mayors and city managers, and (among other things) to foster coordination, innovation, and institutional change. No one had, or has, any way of knowing exactly what was meant by such words and, apart from that, there was, and is, no way of judging how much of one goal (say, innovation) ought to have been sacrificed in order to secure more in terms of another (say, coordination).

It must be remembered, too, that much of what is associated in the public mind with the Great Society had long been in existence. When Secretary George Romney called the Federal Housing Administration programs "a $100-billion-dollar mistake" he was not referring to those of the Great Society: the national housing goal was set by Congress in 1949 and even at that time the principal housing programs were a decade old.

Despite these considerations, I believe it is possible to separate out the Great Society programs and pass judgment upon them collectively. The Great Society had two general goals. The more widely publicized was that of bringing incomes up to what came to be called the poverty line. The other, which was more important from the standpoint of most of the professionals who participated in the design of the programs, was to bring "culturally deprived" persons into the "mainstream." The chronically poor, especially the young among them, were to be given training in schools and work places so that they could get steady, high-paying jobs; their civil rights were to be protected and extended; and they were to be provided with better health, housing, and recreational facilities—all with "maximum feasible participation" on their part. This, it was thought, would reduce frustration and "alienation" and engender self-confidence, self-respect, and a healthy desire for political and economic independence.

Judged against these goals, almost all of the Great Society programs (the exceptions that I have in mind are the civil-rights laws) range from unsuccessful to counterproductive.

The number of the poor did, it is true,

decline by one-fourth between 1965 and 1970. Without any doubt the Great Society programs accounted for some of this (OEO alone spent nearly $10 billion), but the Social Security program established by the New Deal accounted for more (mostly old people whose incomes had not been much below the line to begin with) and there were others—no one seems to know how many—whose increase of income was due to the natural growth of the economy. Indeed, on the whole poverty seems to have decreased at a *slower* rate in the 1960's than before. Robert J. Lampman, in his valuable *Ends and Means of Reducing Income Poverty* (Markham, 1971), reports that the percentage of the total population in low-income status fell from 26 in 1947 to 19 in 1957 and to 12 in 1967. The principal factors affecting the rate of movement out of poverty are not the good intentions of legislators or the generosity of taxpayers: rather they are changes in the composition of the population, in occupations (especially farm versus non-farm), and in the size of the gross national product. According to Lampman and other economists, it is reasonable to expect that by 1980 no one will be below the existing poverty line. This would be the case no doubt even if the War on Poverty had never been declared.

There has also been progress toward the other goal of the Great Society programs—that of bringing the "culturally deprived" into the "mainstream." But here again most of it is not attributable to the programs. The income return to blacks who finished school in recent years is now about equal to that of whites; this has encouraged young blacks to want—and to get—somewhat more schooling than do whites of the same ability as measured by test performance. The Great Society's civil-rights laws deserve some of the credit for these developments, but surely the fundamental fact of the situation (accounting, among other things, for the passage of the laws) is that there has been a dramatic decline in white bigotry and insensitivity since the Second World War, resulting in vastly improved employment opportunities for the "culturally deprived" and making it possible for the motivated among them to find their way into the "mainstream." There is no evidence, so far as I have been able to discover, that the Community Action and other Great Society programs designed to stimulate upward mobility have succeeded in doing so. Where motivation developed it may have done so in spite of these programs rather than because of them. There is no doubt but that the injection of many billions of dollars of public funds benefited the black communities. The people who gained most, however, were middle class, not "culturally deprived."

That compensatory education programs have not worked and probably cannot be made to work is a conclusion now widely accepted even among those who expected most from them. Robert Levine, OEO's director of research in the Johnson administration, has written (in *The Poor Ye Need Not Have with You,* MIT Press, 1970) that in general ". . . the evaluation of educational programs shows that very little is known about what [will work] and even throws doubt on the importance of anything that might work. . . ." Much of the same has been said by others with respect to delinquency control, manpower training, community action, coordination, and most of the other programs. Indeed, in a paper presented in March at the annual meeting of the Southwestern Political Science Association, Professor Robert J. Leonard of the University of Evansville showed that anti-poverty expenditures (OEO, VISTA, Community Action, and Head Start) in 1968 had *no effect* on poverty, education, employment, and crime in the cities to which they went so far as could be judged by such crude but plausible measures as proportion of employed males per capita before and after.

Whatever judgment one makes as to the benefits of these programs, one must face the fact of their costs. These have been, and are still, very large. It has been estimated (by Charles Schultze and his collaborators of the Brookings Institution in *Setting National Priorities: The 1973 Budget)* that federal expenditures on the major Great Society programs increased from $1.7 billion in fiscal 1963 to $35.7 billion in fiscal 1973.

These money costs are far exceeded, in my judgment, by many other, more or less intangible, costs, especially the following: the multiplication of categorical-grant programs beyond the capacity of the executive branch to administer them, with the result being delay, confusion, waste and corruption, and the "elbowing aside" (as the President recently put it) of state and local governments and of the private sector and their further decline in vigor and capacity; the raising of expectations to unreasonable levels, leading to widespread disappointment and frustration and, on the part of quite a few, to the conclusion that this is a "sick" society "not worth saving"; the use of public funds in some cities to underwrite the "leadership" of known criminals, revolutionaries, and mountebanks who exploited–and in some instances terrorized and ultimately destroyed–neighborhoods and institutions over which they were enabled to gain control (for a case in point, see the account of the destruction of the Woodlawn area of Chicago in the winter 1973 issue of the *Public Interest);* and, finally, the co-optation of most of the young potential leaders of the poor neighborhoods and their subsequent neutralization and, in many instances, demoralization.

It was not for lack of money that the Great Society programs failed. Some of the principal efforts–Model Cities, for example–had more of it than they could spend. Others spent prodigally without measurable achievement. Federal aid to public schools, for example, increased from $19 to $52 billion in the 1960s, but the test scores of pupils, which had previously been rising, declined. (However, it should be remembered that in this decade the schools were holding more low-achieving pupils for longer periods; presumably they had some success with a considerable number of them.)

If an "income" (as opposed to "services") strategy means giving money to people rather than to governments, it is doubtful whether–except perhaps in the very long run–it would have succeeded any better in changing the style of life of those whose handicap was not simply, or even primarily, lack of income–that is, the "culturally deprived." In my opinion, putting millions more on welfare (which is what the "income strategy" seems to mean in practice) would permanently seal a great many people off from the world of work. I agree with the authors of *Work in America* (MIT Press, 1973) that "the key to reducing familial dependency on the government lies in the opportunity [I would add also the disposition to accept the opportunity] for the central provider to work full-time at a living wage."

It is a virtue of the "services strategy" that the conspicuous failure of a "service" makes it politically vulnerable. Not so with the "income strategy"; whatever ill effects *that* produced would probably pass unnoticed or, in any event, not be charged against it. Politically it would be unassailable. Thus we have recently been told by Joel Handler that the theory that "if enough people get on welfare it will be politically untenable to treat them as 'undeserving' . . ." is "both brilliant and humane" *(Reforming the Poor,* Basic Books, 1972).

2. President Nixon no doubt wishes that Americans would do more for themselves and expect less to be done for them by government. Nevertheless I do not think that he is in the least likely to lead a "counterrevolution" against the trend of social policy. He knows, better perhaps than any man alive, that it is an indispensable condition of the working of the American political system that it offer strong incentives to all sorts of interests to press for advantages (not always "selfish" ones of course) and that incentives exist only as there is expectation of at least partial and occasional successes. He knows, therefore, that unwise and even outrageous measures must frequently be adopted, and that if it were otherwise (if, say, Congress were somehow made "responsible") the result would be to deprive the system of the energy that makes it work. That he is himself a very strenuous exerter of influence is evidence that he knows how to act effectively within the system, not that he wants to change it.

Although he may deplore it, the President must also be fully aware that the volume of demands placed upon the government is bound to increase. As Americans become more affluent, schooled, and leisured they discover (and also invent) more and more "social problems" which (they fondly suppose) can be "solved" if the government "really cares" (that is, if it passes enough laws, hires enough officials, and spends enough money). That one whose business it is to come to terms with reality, and who has shown himself to be extraordinarily adept at this business, will lead a "counterrevolution" against so conspicuous a feature of reality seems most unlikely. The President is a politician, not a preacher. His task and talent are for making things work, not for changing them.

The view that I am taking is in no way contradicted by the current budget proposals. The President is trying to curb inflation, avoid increases in taxes, get rid of programs that almost everyone knows have not worked, consolidate others for better administration, and turn responsibility for a wide range of matters back to the states and cities. Even if his budget contained no new initiatives (in fact it contains several major ones), it could not reasonably be taken as a portent of "counterrevolution."

The President's efforts to shift responsibilities to the states and local governments might perhaps be judged "counterrevolutionary" if he were leaving it to them to finance the programs. But this is not what he is doing. The fact is—although one would never guess it from the howls of mayors and governors—that the 1974 budget proposes to give state and local government more federal aid than they received this year (to make the figures comparable one must take into account that in 1974 public assistance for the aged, blind, and disabled will go to them directly rather than via grants to the states) and about four-and one-half times what they received a decade ago. And this although state and local governments are presently enjoying an aggregate revenue surplus which, if they do not lower their tax rates, is expected to reach some $13 billion in 1975.

I see revenue sharing and the New Federalism in general as a sort of domestic Vietnamization strategy under which Washington will provide the "villagers" with material resources and technical advice while allowing them to fight the "war" in their own way. This is not necessarily a strategy for winding down the "war." It may merely represent a facing of the fact, obvious in the Johnson administration but not faced by it, that federal programs have become too many and too complex to be administered from Washington. Another possibility–I find this more probable, although I do not suppose that it is the President's wish–is that the new strategy is preparatory to an escalation of the "war" and the opening of vast new fronts (health seems to be the most likely one now that education and welfare are both stalemated).

3. In my judgment a sound program in the area of social policy would involve a radical devolution of federal activities to state and local government and, beyond that, of many public ones to competitive markets. Such a program is, however, incompatible with the nature of our political system, which is energized by the pressures that interests exert to get things from government. Since I believe that despite its evident faults this political system is vastly better than any practical alternative, I am in the awkward position of having to conclude that a sound program is really unsound. When constituents begin asking politicians, "What have you *un*done for me lately?" the situation will improve.

MURRAY ROTHBARD

Professor of Economics, Polytechnic Institute of Brooklyn.

Rothbard represents an extreme right-wing mini-faction whose critique of modern American society reveals astonishingly close kinship with many radicals, closer in fact than with his fellow conservatives. Although he is as strongly committed to a defense of laissez-faire as other conservative figures (including those represented in this reader), his support of black power and his characterization of American foreign policy as "imperialistic" correspond to the thinking of many writers usually associated with the political left.

A comparison with conservative philosopher and novelist Ayn Rand (see pp. 81–88) reveals the maverick quality of Rothbard's conservatism. Rand asserts that statism ("a system of institutionalized violence") is the root of war and that capitalism is "the only system fundamentally opposed to war." In addition, she believes that our massive foreign aid program—now widely viewed as a massive mistake—serves a benevolent function. She did oppose the American presence in Vietnam, but on somewhat unorthodox grounds: she attributed our intervention not to capitalism, with its military-industrial complex, but to statism, with its altruist ethics. Rothbard's critique is in striking contrast. He attacks cold war patriotism among the libertarian conservatives on the grounds that war accelerates the trend toward statism, the real enemy of liberty. He also claims that historically the big businessman has been "one of the main driving forces of the statist dynamics of twentieth-century America." He describes the American corporate state as a "tripartite rapproachement of big business, big unions, and big government." His view of the function of unions—to discipline the workers and integrate them into the burgeoning corporate state—is embraced only by the far left, as is his claim that the function of our foreign aid program is to subsidize both American business and the foreign clients of American business. This approach amounts to a broadside attack on both the liberal intelligentsia and conservatives as responsible for the combination welfare and warfare state that governs (and perhaps threatens) our lives.

Rothbard's closest intellectual kinship in the conservative ranks is with Adam Smith. Like Smith, his sympathy is directed toward the lower classes and his suspicions toward the privileged classes. Unlike Smith, however, he is writing in twentieth-century corporate, industrial America; and in his efforts to halt the tide that threatens to swamp the competitive vessel, he seems as presumptuous as the legendary King Canute, standing on a beach in ancient Britain commanding the waves to obey him.

ML

THE GREAT SOCIETY: A LIBERTARIAN CRITIQUE

(1967)

The Great Society is the lineal descendant and the intensification of those other pretentiously named polities of twentieth-century America: the Square Deal, the New Freedom, the New Era, the New Deal, the Fair Deal, and the New Frontier. All of these assorted Deals constitute a basic and fundamental shift in American life—a shift from a relatively laissez-faire economy and minimal state to a society in which the state is unquestionably king.[1] In the previous century, the government could safely have been ignored by almost everyone; now we have become a country in which the government is the great and unending source of power and privilege. Once a country in which each man could by and large make the decisions for his own life, we have become a land where the state holds and exercises life-and-death power over every person, group, and institution. The great Moloch government, once confined and cabined, has burst its feeble bonds to dominate us all.

The basic reason for this development is not difficult to fathom. It was best summed up by the great German sociologist Franz Oppenheimer; Oppenheimer wrote that there were fundamentally two, and only two, paths to the acquisition of wealth. One route is the production of a good or service and its voluntary exchange for the goods or services produced by others. This method—the method of the free market—Oppenheimer termed "the economic means" to wealth. The other path, which avoids the necessity for production and exchange, is for one or more persons to seize other people's products by the use of physical force. This method of robbing the fruits of another man's production was shrewdly named by Oppenheimer the "political means." Throughout history, men have been tempted to employ the "political means" of seizing wealth rather than expend effort in production and exchange. It should be clear that while the market process multiplies production, the political, exploitative means is parasitic and, as with all parasitic action, discourages and drains off production and output in society. To regularize and order a permanent system of predatory exploitation, men have created the state, which Oppenheimer brilliantly defined as "the organization of the political means."[2]

Every act of the state is necessarily an occasion for inflicting burdens and assigning subsidies and privileges. By seizing revenue by means of coercion and assigning rewards as it disburses the

1. Recent triumphal disclosures by economic historians that pure laissez-faire did not exist in nineteenth-century America are beside the point; no one ever claimed that it did. The point is that state power in society was minimal, relative to other times and countries, and that the general locus of decision making resided therefore in the individuals making up society rather than in the State. Cf. Robert Lively, "The American System," *Business History Review* 29 (1955): 81–96.

2. Franz Oppenheimer, *The State* (New York: 1926), pp. 24–27. Or, as Albert Jay Nock, heavily influenced by Oppenheimer's analysis, concluded: "The state claims and exercises the monopoly of crime" in its territorial area. Albert Jay Nock, *On Doing the Right Thing, and Other Essays* (New York: 1928), p.143.

funds, the state creates ruling and ruled "classes" or "castes"; for one example, classes of what Calhoun discerned as net "taxpayers" and "taxconsumers," those who live off taxation.[3] And since by its nature, predation can only be supported out of the surplus of production above subsistence, the ruling class must constitute a minority of the citizenry.

Since the state, nakedly observed, is a mighty engine of organized predation, state rule, throughout its many millennia of recorded history, could be preserved only by persuading the bulk of the public that its rule has not really been exploitative: that, on the contrary, it has been necessary, beneficent, even, as in the Oriental despotisms, divine. Promoting this ideology among the masses has ever been a prime function of intellectuals, a function that has created the basis for co-opting a corps of intellectuals into a secure and permanent berth in the state apparatus. In former centuries, these intellectuals formed a priestly caste that was able to wrap a cloak of mystery and quasi-divinity about the actions of the state for a credulous public; nowadays, the apologia for the state takes on more subtle and seemingly scientific forms. The process remains essentially the same.[4]

In the United States, a strong libertarian and antistatist tradition prevented the process of statization from taking hold at a very rapid pace. The major force in its propulsion has been that favorite theater of state expansionism, brilliantly identified by Randolph Bourne as "the health of the state": namely, war. For although in wartime various states find themselves in danger from one another, every state has found war a fertile field for spreading the myth among its subjects that they are the ones in deadly danger, from which their state is protecting them. In this way states have been able to dragoon their subjects into fighting and dying to save them under the pretext that the subjects were being saved from the dread Foreign Enemy. In the United States, the process of statization began in earnest under cover of the Civil War (conscription, military rule, income tax, excise taxes, high tariffs, national banking and credit expansion for favored businesses, paper money, land grants to railroads), and reached full flower as a result of World Wars I and II, to finally culminate in the Great Society.

The recently emerging group of "libertarian conservatives" in the United States have grasped a part of the recent picture of accelerated statism, but their analysis suffers from several fatal blind spots. One is their complete failure to realize that war, culminating in the present garrison state and military-industrial economy, has been the royal road to aggravated statism in America. On the contrary, the surge of reverent patriotism that war brings to conservative hearts, coupled with their eagerness to don buckler and armor against the "international Communist conspiracy," has made the conservatives the most eager and enthusiastic partisans of the Cold War. Hence their inability to see the enormous distortions and interventions imposed upon the economy by the enormous system of war contracts.[5]

Another conservative blind spot is their failure to identify which groups have been responsible for the burgeoning of statism in the United States. In the conservative demonology, the responsibility belongs only to liberal intellectuals, aided and abetted by trade unions and farmers. Big businessmen, on the other hand, are curiously exempt from blame (farmers are small enough businessmen, apparently, to be fair game for censure). How, then, do conservatives deal with the glaringly evident onrush of big businessmen to embrace Lyndon Johnson and the Great Society? Either by mass stupidity (failure to read the works of free-market economists), subversion by liberal intellectuals (e.g., the education of the Rockefeller brothers at Lincoln School), or craven cowardice (the failure to stand foursquare for free market principles in the face of governmental powers). Almost never is interest pinpointed as an overriding reason for statism among businessmen. This failure is all the more curious in the light of the fact that the laissez-faire liberals of the eighteenth and nineteenth centuries (e.g., the Philosophical Radicals in England, the Jacksonians in the United States) were never bashful about identifying and attacking the web of special privileges granted to businessmen in the mercantilism of their day.

In fact, one of the main driving forces of the statist dynamic of twentieth century America has been big businessmen, and this long before the Great Society. Gabriel Kolko, in his path-breaking *Triumph of Conservatism,*[6] has shown that the shift toward statism in the Progressive period was impelled by the very big business groups who were supposed, in the liberal mythology, to be defeated and regulated by the Progressive and New Freedom measures. Rather than a "people's movement" to check big business, the drive for regulatory measures, Kolko shows, stemmed from big businessmen whose attempts at monopoly had been defeated by the competitive market, and who then turned to the federal government as a device for compulsory cartellization. This drive for cartellization through government accelerated during the New Era of the 1920s and reached its apex in Franklin Roosevelt's NRA. Significantly, this exercise in cartellizing collectivism was put over by organized big business; after Herbert Hoover, who had done much to organize and cartellize the economy, had balked at an NRA as going too far toward an outright fascist economy, the U.S. Chamber of Commerce won a promise from FDR that he would adopt such a system. The original inspiration was the corporate state of Mussolini's Italy.[7]

3. See John C. Calhoun, *Disquisition on Government* . . . (Columbia, S.C.: 1850). On the distinction between this and the Marxian concept of the ruling class, see Ludwig von Mises, *Theory and History* (New Haven, Conn.: 1957), pp. 112 ff. Perhaps the earliest users of this kind of class analysis were the French libertarian writers of the Restoration period of the early nineteenth century, Charles Comte and Charles Dunoyer. Cf. Elie Halévy, *The Era of Tyrannies* (Garden City, N.Y.: 1965), pp. 23–34.

4. On various aspects of the alliance between intellectuals and the State, see George B. de Huszar, ed., *The Intellectuals* (Glencoe, Ill.: 1960); Joseph A. Schumpeter, *Capitalism, Socialism, and Democracy* (New York: 1942), pp. 143–55; Karl A. Wittfogel, *Oriental Despotism* (New Haven, Conn.: 1957); Howard K. Beale, "The Professional Historian: His Theory and Practice," *The Pacific Historical Review* (August, 1953), pp. 227–55; Martin Nicolaus, "The Professor, the Policeman and the Peasant," *Viet-Report* (June–July, 1966), pp. 15–19.

5. Thus, cf. H. L. Nieburg, *In the Name of Science* (Chicago: 1966); Seymour Melman, *Our Depleted Society* (New York: 1965); C. Wright Mills, *The Power Elite* (New York: 1956).

6. (New York: 1963). Also see Kolko's *Railroads and Regulation* (Princeton, N.J.: 1965). The laudatory reviews of the latter book by George W. Hilton *(American Economic Review)* and George W. Wilson *(Journal of Political Economy)* symbolize a potential alliance between "new left" and free-market historiography.

7. The National Recovery Administration, one of the most important creations of the early New Deal, was established by the National Industrial Recovery Act of June, 1933. It prescribed and imposed codes of "fair competition" upon industry. It was declared unconstitutional by the Supreme Court in 1935. For an analysis of the inception of the NRA, see my *America's Great Depression* (Princeton, N.J.: 1963).

The formal corporation of the NRA is long gone, but the Great Society retains much of its essence. The locus of social power has been emphatically assumed by the state apparatus. Furthermore, that apparatus is permanently governed by a coalition of big business, big labor groupings, groups that use the state to operate and manage the national economy. The usual tripartite rapprochement of big business, big unions, and big government symbolizes the organization of society by blocs, syndics, and corporations, regulated and privileged by the federal, state, and local governments. What this all amounts to in essence is the "corporate state," which during the 1920s served as a beacon light for big businessmen, big unions, and many liberal intellectuals as the economic system proper to a twentieth century industrial society.[8]

The indispensable intellectual role of engineering popular consent for state rule is played, for the Great Society, by the liberal intelligentsia, who provide the rationale of "general welfare," "humanity," and the "common good" (just as the conservative intellectuals work the other side of the Great Society street by offering the rationale of "national security" and "national interest"). The liberals, in short, push the "welfare" part of our omnipresent welfare-warfare state, while the conservatives stress the warfare side of the pie. This analysis of the role of the liberal intellectuals puts into more sophisticated perspective the seeming "sellout" of these intellectuals as compared to their role during the 1930s. Thus, among numerous other examples, there is the seemingly anomaly of A. A. Berle and David Lilienthal, cheered and damned as flaming progressives in the thirties, now writing tomes hailing the new reign of big business. Actually, their basic views have not changed in the least. In the thirties, these theoreticians of the New Deal were concerned with condemning as "reactionaries" those big businessmen who clung to older individualist ideals and failed to understand or adhere to the new monopoly system of the corporate state. But now, in the 1950s and 1960s, this battle has been won, big businessmen are all eager to be privileged monopolists in the new dispensation, and hence they can now be welcomed by such theorists as Berle and Lilienthal as "responsible" and "enlightened," their "selfish" individualism a relic of the past.

The cruellest myth fostered by the liberals is that the Great Society functions as a great boon and benefit to the poor; in reality, when we cut through the frothy appearances to the cold reality underneath, the poor are the major victims of the welfare state. The poor are the ones to be conscripted to fight and die at literally slave wages in the Great Society's imperial war. The poor are the ones to lose their homes to the bulldozer of urban renewal, that bulldozer that operates for the benefit of real estate and construction interests to pulverize available low-cost housing.[9] All this, of course, in the name of "clearing the slums" and helping the aesthetics of housing. The poor are the welfare clientele whose homes are unconstitutionally but regularly invaded by government agents to ferret out sin in the middle of the night. The poor (e.g., Negroes in the South) are the ones disemployed by rising minimum wage floors, put in for the benefit of employers and unions in higher-wage areas (e.g., the North) to prevent industry from moving to the low-wage areas. The poor are cruelly victimized by an income tax that left and right alike misconstrue as an egalitarian program to soak the rich; actually, various tricks and exemptions insure that it is the poor and the middle classes who are hit the hardest.[10] The poor are victimized too by a welfare state of which the cardinal macroeconomic tenet is perpetual if controlled inflation. The inflation and the heavy government spending favor the businesses of the military-industrial complex, while the poor and the retired, those on fixed pensions or Social Security, are hit the hardest. (Liberals have often scoffed at the anti-inflationists' stress on the "widows and orphans" as major victims of inflation, but these remain major victims nevertheless.) And the burgeoning of compulsory mass public education forces millions of unwilling youth off the labor market for many years, and into schools that serve more as houses of detention than as genuine centers of education.[11] Farm programs that supposedly aid poor farmers actually serve the large wealthy farmers at the expense of sharecropper and consumer alike; and commissions that regulate industry serve to cartellize it. The mass of workers is forced by governmental measures into trade unions that tame and integrate the labor force into the toils of the accelerating corporate state, there to be subjected to arbitrary wage "guidelines" and ultimate compulsory arbitration.

The role of the liberal intellectual and of liberal rhetoric is even more stark in foreign economic policy. Ostensibly designed to "help the underdeveloped countries," foreign aid has served as a gigantic subsidy by the American taxpayer of American export firms, a similar subsidy to American foreign investment through guarantees and subsidized government loans, an engine of inflation for the recipient country, and a form of massive subsidy to the friends and clients of U.S. imperialism in the recipient country.

The symbiosis between liberal intellectuals and despotic statism at home and abroad is, furthermore, no accident; for at the heart of the welfarist mentality is an enormous desire to "do good to" the mass of other people, and since people don't usually wish to be done good to, since they have their own ideas of what they wish to do, the liberal welfarist inevitably ends by reaching for the big stick with which to push the ungrateful masses around. Hence, the liberal ethos itself provides a powerful stimulant for the intellectuals to seek state power and ally themselves with the other rulers of the corporate state. The liberals thus become what Harry Elmer Barnes has aptly termed "totalitarian liberals." Or, as Isabel Paterson put it a generation ago:

> The humanitarian wishes to be a prime mover in the lives of others. He cannot admit either the divine or the natural order, by which men have the power to help themselves. The humanitarian puts himself in the place of God.
>
> But he is confronted by two awkward facts; first, that the competent do not need his assistance; and second, that the majority of people . . . positively do not want to be "done good" by the humanitarian. . . . Of course, what the humanitarian actually proposes is that he shall do what he thinks is good for everybody. It is at this point that the humanitarian sets up the guillotine.[12]

---

8. Part of this story has been told in John P. Diggins, "Flirtation with Fascism: American Pragmatic Liberals and Mussolini's Italy," *American Historical Review* 71 (January, 1966): 487–506.

9. See Martin Anderson, *The Federal Bulldozer* (Cambridge, Mass.: 1964).

10. Thus, see Gabriel Kolko, *Wealth and Power in America* (New York: 1962).

11. Thus, see Paul Goodman, *Compulsory Mis-Education and the Community of Scholars* (New York: Vintage Books, 1966).

12. Isabel Paterson, *The God of the Machine* (New York: 1943), p. 241.

The rhetorical role of welfarism in pushing people around may be seen clearly in the Vietnam War, where American liberal planning for alleged Vietnamese welfare has been particularly prominent, e.g., in the plans and actions of Wolf Ladejinsky, Joseph Buttinger, and the Michigan State group. And the result has been very much of an American-operated "guillotine" for the Vietnamese people, North and South.[13] And even *Fortune* magazine invokes the spirit of humanitarian "idealism" as the justification for the United States' falling "heir to the onerous task of policing these shattered colonies" of Western Europe, and exerting its might all over the world. The will to make this exertion to the uttermost, especially in Vietnam and perhaps China, constitutes for *Fortune,* "the unending test of American idealism."[14] This liberal-welfarist syndrome may also be seen in the very different area of civil rights, in the terribly pained indignation of white liberals at the recent determination of Negroes to take the lead in helping themselves, rather than to keep deferring to the Lords and Ladies Bountiful of white liberalism.

In sum, the most important fact about the Great Society under which we live is the enormous disparity between rhetoric and content. In rhetoric, America is the land of the free and the generous, enjoying the fused blessings of a free market tempered by and joined to accelerating social welfare, bountifully distributing its unstinting largesse to the less fortunate in the world. In actual practice, the free economy is virtually gone, replaced by an imperial corporate state Leviathan that organizes, commands, exploits the rest of society and, indeed, the rest of the world, for its own power and pelf. We have experienced, as Garet Garrett keenly pointed out over a decade ago, a "revolution within the form."[15] The old limited republic has been replaced by Empire, within and without our borders.

---

13. See John McDermott, "Welfare Imperialism in Vietnam," *The Nation* (July 25, 1966): 76–88. Cf. readings 32 and 34.

14. *Fortune* (August, 1965). As the right wing of the Great Society Establishment, *Fortune* presumably passes the Berle–Lilienthal test as spokesman for "enlightened" as opposed to narrowly "selfish" capitalism.

15. Garet Garrett, *The People's Pottage* (Caldwell, Idaho: 1953).

AYN RAND: LIBERTARIAN CONSERVATIVE*

Serious students of theoretical political economy or political sociology tend to scoff at Ayn Rand. Some of them, embarrassed that they were once "taken in" by *The Fountainhead* or *Atlas Shrugged* and those impassioned pleas for youth to man the barricades for individualism, pretend now that Rand, like Santa Claus, was a part of their childhood dreams. But Rand takes herself seriously, and she is right in doing so, for she has carved out a unique position in the ranks of modern conservatism. Virtually all her fellow conservatives stress either the economic or political aspects of their philosophy; Rand, by contrast, offers an all-embracing species of libertarian conservatism which she calls "objectivism."

Her essays and novels tirelessly depict capitalism as the *only* moral system. She sees the combination of freedom and controls in our present mixed economy as an untenable and unstable mixture and depicts the altruist ethics of a welfare-oriented society as a "cancerous growth" which must be sternly extirpated by "intellectual surgery." While actively defending capitalism on grounds of objective morality, Rand claims that soft-headed liberal pragmatism

> holds that there is no objective reality or permanent truth, that there are no absolute principles. . . . That anything may be tried by rule of thumb, that objectivity consists of collective subjectivism, that whatever people wish to be true, is true . . . provided a consensus says so.

For Rand, this liberal approach constitutes a weak philosophical foundation that is seriously eroding the ethical basis of capitalism.

Some of Rand's strongest barbs are directed at ostensible conservatives who have accepted some of the welfare premises of liberalism. She calls on them for a united front against liberalism. Rebuking those who might base their case for capitalism on faith in God, she says that this merely substitutes mysticism for rationality. The subordination of the secular to the sacred is tantamount to the abandonment of reason as a guide to human action. This antireligious stand is in marked contrast to most conservatives. Typical is a comment by M. Stanton Evans in the *New Individualist Review*, a leading conservative journal: "The maintenance of freedom is not, and cannot be, purely secular. . . . The profession of irreligious, relativist ethics is in the long run harmful to liberty." To Rand, however, capitalism must be actively defended on grounds of objective morality. Her arguments are couched in terms of "basic principles" and "ultimate consequences" rather than the market efficiency of an abstract competitive

*Editor's note: We had hoped to reprint a selection by Rand, but after reading an abridged version of the appraisal above, her representatives wrote that it "slandered" her beyond recognition and "categorically denied" permission to use her essay. To slander was surely not my intention. The reader may wish to examine some of Rand's writings, then judge whether this introduction depicts her position fairly.

model or a high standard of living, although both of these features characterize countries operating under a capitalist framework.

Crucial to Rand's system is the inviolability of private property. "Without property rights," says Rand, "no other rights can be practiced." Property rights are seen as implementing the right to life since man's nature as a rational being requires the opportunity to obtain property and to keep and dispose of the products of his efforts. Capitalism, defined by voluntary human relationships with the widest expression of individual rights, is the "only system based on an objective theory of values." These values are applied on a social level through the free market. Thus the law of supply and demand acquires a moral connotation, and, through a process of voluntary exchange, the economic value of a man's work is determined.

Government is seen as the single greatest potential threat to man's exercise of freedom because government necessarily possesses a legal monopoly on the use of physical force. Therefore, it is imperative to sharply limit and circumscribe its powers. Rand says, à la Adam Smith, that the only truly legitimate purpose of government is to protect individual rights and apply laws in settling disputes. Government ought to be an "impersonal robot," impartially administering a minimum of necessary laws. On this score, the American Constitution, particularly its system of checks and balances, is viewed as an "incomparable achievement" despite its partial erosion by advocates of a mixed economy. "The United States was the first moral society in history."

Although it is true that government under both private and public ownership may be oppressive, Rand's analysis is misleading, primarily because it completely avoids a consideration of class factors. If a widening web of government activities were indeed a roughly equal threat to all classes, Rand's position would have some validity. Government, in fact, has usually been significantly more responsive to demands from the business community than from the laboring community (particularly from racial minorities). The law seldom acts in the evenhanded, impartial way assumed by Rand, despite the rhetorical guarantee of equality before the law. This differential application of law is not a matter of mere happenstance or malevolence of particular officials; it is grounded in the nature of the system. Legality is defined in terms of a private-property-based system, and the operative norms of the system reflect this definition. A challenge to private property is thus presumed to be illegal.

Unlike Friedman, Rand does not favor government enforcement of antitrust laws, because these laws interfere with individual freedom and allegedly penalize business efficiency: "The concept of free competition enforced by law is a gross contradiction in terms." Businessmen are "the productive, creative, efficient, competent members of society," who, through their search for profits, protect the consumer more than any interventionist government. A businessman's success in a competitive environment depends on his acquiring a good reputation, a powerful incentive for acting reasonably and honestly. Rand's uncompromising faith in business ethics is not shared by the other conservatives presented in this book; they emphasize the crucial role of competition, even government-maintained, in bringing the businessman's self-interest into greater harmony with the public interest.

Rand's assertion that all human relationships are voluntary under capitalism may well have theoretical validity for businessmen and professionals, but it cannot be applied to the position of the average working man. For him, the voluntary nature of the exchange relationship is largely negated by the fact that he *must* sell his labor services (mental and physical) at the market price in order to survive.

Rand's claim that in a capitalist system, "Men are free to cooperate or not, to deal with one another or not, as their own individual judgments, convictions and interests dictate" has a naively archaic ring. That rationale was a benchmark of eighteenth- and early nineteenth-century commercial and small-scale manufacturing capitalism on the eve of the industrial revolution. Any relevance to our present corporate-dominated society is quite far-fetched.

Rand posits not only that capitalism has greatly enlarged the sphere of freedom and society's productive potential, but that these unique developments were "achieved by non-sacrificial means." In other words, capitalism, unlike all other previous or present systems, from its very beginnings raised the economic (as well as moral) standards of the entire nation. This position does not bear up well under closer scrutiny, conflicting with several crucial aspects of American history. For one, capitalism did not suddenly emerge in a late-nineteenth-century blaze of glory, eclipsing slavery and feudalism. Its growth was intimately connected with both of these earlier systems. Slave labor turned out the most valuable export products and was therefore a dominant factor in early American economic development. The ties between Northern commercial manufacturing interests and Southern plantation aristocrats were intimate and strong. Perhaps slavery is defensible on economic grounds, but it is surely indefensible in terms of the very moral precepts that Rand espouses. Her analysis of this subject oversimplifies the development of capitalism by viewing it as completely separate from other systems. In fact, it was built on a foundation of both slavery and feudalism. All systems contain vestiges of previous systems while foreshadowing, however dimly or sharply, the development of future systems.

Another oversimplification is involved in her assertion that private property is essential in order to preserve individual rights; she fails to perceive that the concept of justice is necessarily a social one, determined by the values and the power distribution in a given society. Infringing on private property, while clearly a denial of some of the property owner's rights, does not necessarily interfere with the social rights of the group. The fact that the unrestricted exercise of private property rights may create significant inequality which burdens some individuals of the next generation, and thus violates their individual rights to a substantial degree, is excluded from Rand's framework. Although many people may be guided by rational self-interest, their ability to *act* in a way that will promote their self-interest varies considerably depending on political, economic, and social factors.

In one of her essays, "The New Fascism: Rule of Consensus," Rand attempts to link liberalism (which champions the mixed economy) and pragmatism. She sees the present socioeconomic system as operating without the guidance of "objective truth." Policies are tried on a "rule-of-thumb" basis rather than a principled one; they are maintained as long as a consensus ("cult of compromise") dictates. This results in a society with an extremely fragile philosophical foundation, undermining the perfect morality of capitalism. With some validity, Rand characterizes a mixed economy as "rule by pressure groups," both business and labor. She disparagingly adds, however, "It is an amoral, institutionalized civil war of special interests and lobbies, all fighting to seize a momentary control of the legislative machinery, to extort some special privilege at one another's expense by an act of government, i.e., by force."

For Rand, as for the radicals, the crucial political issue of our age is capitalism versus socialism; she sees it as a war between freedom and statism. The liberal champions of a mixed economy have made the unpardonable error, from her point of view, of obfuscating this issue. "They do not want to accept the full meaning of their goal; they want to keep all the advantages and effects of capitalism, while destroying the cause, and they want to establish statism without its necessary effects." Fascism, Nazism, Communism, and Socialism (although differing in some important ways) are, according to Rand, merely variants of statism; the underlying moral theme of each is that the individual exists to serve the state, with the ugly result that national interest emerges as superior to individual interest. By neglecting the forms of ownership (private or social) while stressing the forms of control (democracy or totalitarianism), she is logically justified, according to her unique terminology, in labeling Fascism as "modified socialism" instead of its usual representation as "modified capitalism." But in dramatizing the differing political structures of fascism and democratic capitalism, she overlooks their common private property base, a parallel which suggests that democracy under private ownership may have a different impact than it would under social ownership.

Rand's analysis of the kinship between Keynesian reformism and fascism is a provocative one. She observes that many of the "collectivist" welfare measures advocated by Keynes and his fellow reformers were also part of the Nazi and fascist political program. Rand claims that liberalism (particularly in America), despite the idealistic intentions of its practitioners, has served as a foundation for fascism. The ever-increasing regulation and coercion of men's economic behavior that characterizes the welfare state of the mixed economy (as opposed to Rand's ideal of a free capitalist economy) is seen as a stepping-stone to statist totalitarianism. Although the mixed economy retains the façade of private property—Rand considers the separation of ownership and control as contradictory—the moral fiber of laissez-faire capitalism is being sapped by these developments. America, says Rand, "is moving by imperceptible degrees through ignorance, confusion, evasion, moral cowardice, and intellectual default not toward socialism or any mawkish altruistic ideal, but toward a plain, brutal, predatory, power-grubbing, de facto fascism. . . . We are a disintegrating, unsound, precariously unstable mixed economy, a random, mongrel mixture of socialistic schemes, communistic influences, fascist controls, and shrinking remnants of capitalism . . . rolling in the direction of a fascist state."

The possible danger of an American fascist movement is real enough. On this point, Rand is correct. Her reasoning, however, is questionable. Fascism is likely to emerge only under a particular confluence of circumstances: a collapsed economy, an authoritarian tradition, and a politically weak labor movement. Rand avoids most of these issues; her method involves linguistic subterfuge rather than substantive analysis. Business cycles and wars, for example, are attributed to government intervention in which capitalism plays no part. Therefore, if both these phenomena do, in fact, occur in present-day America, it is because we are no longer a "pure" capitalist society. In this manner Rand, in effect, defines away crucial aspects of a private-property-based system.

Rand sees the labor movement as still another force working to undermine capitalism, one of many pressure groups supplanting the free market. One doesn't have to be a Keynesian or a radical to recognize the exaggerated quality of these assertions. The irony of Rand's approach is that a society operated according to her stern rules could produce an elite that, under certain historical conditions, might institute the fascist system she herself abhors.

There is, however, a more rational sense in which liberalism can be considered a forerunner of fascism. Liberalism helps to raise aspirations that cannot be realized within the mixed economy advocated by so many liberal intellectuals and politicians. Although many liberals humanistically (or pragmatically) believe in the necessity for income redistribution, their modest efforts to achieve this through an enlarged public sector have not borne fruit because of what one writer calls their "overambitious multiplicity of goals." On a political level, the price of an expanded welfare program is that in order to ensure middle-class support, it has to include middle-class benefits (e.g., support to higher education, middle-income housing subsidies, farm-support measures, etc.). On an economic level, the result of this government spending coupled with tax benefits for desired social ends is, in effect, "to multiply the burden on the income tax while contracting the base." These contradictory tendencies make the system vulnerable to the kind of populist-fascism epitomized by the views of George Wallace. Many of his supporters (particularly low- or middle-income blue-collar white workers) believe, with considerable short-run justification, that their material economic interests (jobs, wages, taxes) are threatened by the thrust of the black toward political and economic equality. Thus, they welcome his hard-line approach to minorities and government spending—an example of liberalism inadvertently clearing the way for fascism.

Rand's discussion of racism reveals the limitations of her conservative bias and method of analysis. Like Friedman, she makes her personal beliefs on racism quite clear: "Racism is an evil, irrational, and morally contemptible doctrine. . . ." She ties it up with the replacement of individualism by collectivism and statism. Her train of logic is: (1) racism is a crude form of collectivism; (2) both involve a rejection of individual rights; (3) statism is the key feature of collectivism; and finally, (4) statism reinforces racism ("racism is a crucial element in every variant of the absolute state"). Racism, for Rand, is anchored in psychological factors—the racist's sense of inferiority—rather than conditions of production or the social relations between classes engaged in the productive process. This bypasses the question of the relationship between the ongoing system of capitalism and racism, except for a parenthetical rationalization. Acknowledging the current existence of racism, Rand says that it stems from our modifications of capitalism and not capitalism per se. Individualism and laissez-faire capitalism are, in fact, Rand's twin antidotes to racism: "It is only by his own individual ability and ambition that capitalism judges a man and rewards him accordingly.... Capitalism is the only system that functions in a way that rewards rationality and penalizes all forms of irrationality, including racism." This ideal is juxtaposed with "a mixed economy" that "disintegrates a country into an institutionalized civil war of pressure groups each fighting for legislative favors and special privileges at the expense of one another." Thus, a society stressing individual rights (pure capitalism) would have less racism than one stressing group rights (mixed economies, especially fascism and socialism).

Rand claims that racism is weakest in the free market economies as opposed to the controlled economies, and that the relative economic status of the blacks improved the most when our economy was loosest. She is certainly right in noting the key role of competing pressure groups in our "mixed economy," but she misses the point that most of this conflict consists of propertied groups fighting over the spoils. Although blacks, unions, and students may seem to be agitating for special favors, their objective is social gains for the group, where business pressure groups seek their own private gains. Despite these caveats, however, Rand's analysis of "institutionalized civil war" in present-day America has much merit—more, in fact, than many liberals are willing to acknowledge.

The alleged historical closeness between a free economy and great black economic gains is another of Rand's many unsupported assertions. In reality, the greatest black economic gains were made during war periods, hardly known for their free market operations. They were, in fact, periods of greatest divergence from the pure competitive free market model. In Rand's attack on the liberals' racial policies, one sees the juxtaposition of a subjective antiracist position with an objective proracist stand. She objects to all supramarket government activities against racial discrimination and would protect the private entrepreneur's inalienable right to discriminate. She states:

> The government has no right to discriminate for some citizens at the expense of others. It has no right to violate the rights of private property by prohibiting discrimination in privately owned establishments. . . . Doctrines [like racism] cannot be forbidden or prescribed by law. . . . We have to protect a racist's right to the use and disposal of his own property.

Rand sees black aid programs like racial job quotas, preferential black hiring, busing to achieve racial balance in the schools, tax aids to potential black capitalists, and civil rights legislation as infringements of private property rights—an expansion of the rights and opportunities of one group at the expense of another. Like Friedman, Rand concludes with regret that blacks who advocate using government to improve their economic and political position are a threat to the rights of nonblacks. She recognizes neither the bond between capitalism and discrimination nor the inherent contradictions in capitalist attempts to end discrimination.

The principle weakness in Rand's moralistic stance is her refusal to recognize that the nature of class and race conflict in a private property system ensures that advances by one person or group almost always occur at the expense of others. Freedom in our system is more apparent than real. For successful members of the propertied class, the freedom to own, protect, and increase their holdings has cumulative advantages; but for others, this freedom may be meaningless.

Rand, like other conservatives, avoids a rigorous examination of the "laws of motion" of capitalist society. Instead of seeing the growing concentration of economic and political power as part of this process, they either deny its existence as a permanent feature of capitalism, or simply claim that the benefits outweigh the costs of alternative systems. Despite historical evidence to the contrary, virtually all conservatives are convinced that power and privilege are continually eroded under capitalism and entrenched under socialism. Powerful individuals in either the capitalist or so-called socialist systems have not been self-perpetuating, although the privileged ruling and unprivileged subordinate class-caste structure has been a permanent feature of both societies. As in the case of Friedman, it is doubtful whether an economy operated according to Rand's rules would experience significantly less power concentration, cyclical instability, and economic inequity, even granting the scant possibility of increased individual freedom. This flaw in the conservatives' logic makes their analysis of the relationship of capitalism and discrimination highly suspect, and their advocated policy of individual protest tortuously slow and unacceptable to those suffering from racial injustice. Blacks justifiably view the conservative medicine as part and parcel of the racism disease, rather than a cure for it.

Conservative proposals appear increasingly irrelevant for dealing with the crises of our twentieth-century industrial society, characterized by large power concentrations in both business and labor sectors, inflation combined with unemployment, vast ecological destruction, and a spiraling racial problem that threatens to engulf the social order. In this crisis-jammed society, conservative proposals aimed at restoring pure laissez-faire capitalism have a hollow ring, and those aimed at preserving its modern variant sound almost as empty. The withering roots of conservatism stem from a bygone era, an era whose inequities far exceeded its virtues.

Rand is the staunchest defender of laissez-faire capitalism among the conservatives presented in this volume. She owes a considerable intellectual debt to Adam Smith, Herbert

Spencer, Ludwig Von Mises, and Friedrich Von Hayek, although she rarely refers to their works. Her writings reflect the two contradictory tendencies within the right wing: libertarianism and conservatism. Conservatism represents the quest for tradition, order, stability, religion, and fanatical anticommunism—in short, for the maintenance of cultural and class stratification—while the libertarian ideal is the maximization of individual freedom based on rational self-interest. The former group became dominant during the wave of anticommunist hysteria in the 1950s. The shift of conservatives to anticommunism helped to weaken, if not to destroy, the individualist ethic of the old right. Russell Kirk, William Buckley, and James Burnham (whose main historical antecedent was Edmund Burke) became the new guard of conservatism, while the libertarian message of older conservatives like Frank Chodorov, Albert Nock, and Dean Russell (whose historical influence was Adam Smith) was quietly forgotten, except for a small group of heretics like Murray Rothbard and Leonard Liggio (both associated with the libertarian journal *Left and Right*). Whereas conservatism drives society toward fascism, since the cultural and societal structure it extols can best be realized through a powerful state capitalist form, libertarianism points society toward the democratic left. Neither monopoly capitalism (the controlling form in today's developed countries) nor the Soviet version of socialism (the controlling form in today's post-capitalist societies) fits the libertarian ideal, since both forms require a strong state that serves to further the interests of a ruling elite. An irony of history is that in order to create a weak, decentralized state, it is first necessary to destroy the existing coercive one. Certainly the litmus-paper test of genuine socialism is whether or not it realizes the libertarian ideal of extending individual freedom to its outermost limits.

Rand is uneasily anchored between conservatism and libertarianism; her philosophy is libertarian while her embracing of big business inevitably leads to a symbiotic big business–big government relationship which negates her own libertarian tendencies. Her reaction to the Watergate affair—"It is not Big Business contributions that corrupt politicians, but the politicians' power to demand and *extort* such contributions, which work like a protection racket"—naively overlooks the mutual accommodation of the political and economic power centers.

Despite all of the internal inconsistencies and irrational assumptions in Rand's works, they do have the merit of focusing on the *political economy* of capitalism rather than on the narrower aspects of the system. Because of this larger frame of reference, she may well have developed the full-fledged implications of capitalism with more detail and precision than any other member of the conservative group. She deserves to be read and analyzed as a serious, thoughtful advocate of a philosophy with its roots in a bygone era, an era that promoted the welfare of a propertied elite while ignoring the general welfare. Although Rand does not objectively "prove" the case for capitalism, she does structure an elegant defense in its behalf.

ML

BIBLIOGRAPHY

In addition to the works included in the body of this section, the editors also recommend the following.

Buckley, William. Column in *The National Review*.

——. *Up from Liberalism*. New York: Honor Books, 1959.

Chamberlin, John. *The Roots of Capitalism*. Princeton, N.J.: D. Van Nostrand Co., 1959.

Friedman, Milton. Column in *Newsweek*.

Friedman, Milton, and Heller, Walter. *Monetary vs. Fiscal Policy*. New York: W. W. Norton & Co., 1969.

Goldwater, Barry. *The Conscience of a Conservative*. Shepherdsville, Ky.: Victor Publishing Co., 1960.

Hazlitt, Henry. *The Failure of the "New Economics": An Analysis of the Keynesian Fallacies*. Princeton, N.J.: D. Van Nostrand Co., 1959.

Kirk, Russell. *The Conservative Mind*. Chicago: H. Regnery & Co., Gateway Editions, 1960.

——. *A Program for Conservatives*. Chicago: H. Regnery & Co., 1954.

Knight, Frank. *Freedom and Reform*. New York: Harper & Row, 1947.

Rand, Ayn. *Capitalism: The Unknown Ideal*. New York: New American Library, Signet Books, 1967.

Ropke, Wilhelm. *The Humane Economy: The Social Framework of the Free Market*. Chicago: H. Regnery & Co., 1960.

Snyder, Carl. *Capitalism the Creator: The Economic Foundations of Modern Industrial Society*. New York: The Macmillan Co., 1940.

Tucille, Jerome. *Radical Libertarianism*. Indianapolis: Bobbs-Merrill, 1970.

Vierick, Peter. *Conservativism Revisited* and *The New Conservatives: What Went Wrong*. New York: Free Press, 1965.

Von Hayek, Friedrich. *The Road to Serfdom*. Chicago: University of Chicago Press, 1944.

——. *Studies in Philosophy, Politics, and Economics*. New York: Simon & Schuster, 1967.

Von Mises, Ludwig. *Human Action: A Treatise on Economics*. New Haven: Yale University Press, 1949.

——. *Socialism: An Economic and Sociological Analysis*. New Haven: Yale University Press, 1959.

Wallich, Henry C. *The Cost of Freedom*. New York: Collier Books, 1962.

THE LIBERAL VIEW

The term *liberalism,* as used in this section, does not refer to the nineteenth-century liberalism advocated by conservatives. It can be regarded, however, as a reaction to that laissez-faire philosophy. The political economists of Adam Smith's day were concerned with unleashing the productive potential of the economy. They felt that this could be best accomplished under laissez-faire capitalism. In such a system each individual would be able to follow his basic psychological drive: the pursuit of his own self-interest. A key element in the argument is that, in so doing, he would also maximize the welfare of society. The role of the government, according to this philosophy, would have to be kept to a minimum for fear that it might otherwise restrict individual freedom and thus the well-being of society. The idea of the existence of such a natural order in society, bolstered by the economic theories of Smith, Malthus, and Ricardo, took hold in England during the first half of the nineteenth century.

In the second half, however, the writings of John Stuart Mill projected a transition from this early philosophy of laissez-faire to one favoring a more aggressive role for government and other cooperative ventures in working to correct the ill effects of industrialization. In the long run, Mill felt, the competitive economy would force profit rates to such a low level that capital accumulation would cease, and the stationary state would ensue. As the article reprinted here shows, he did not view that prospect with apprehension, since he felt that within it the quality of life could be improved. While accepting the competitive market and its private-property base as necessary institutions during his own time, he foresaw a period when the wage-price system would give way to new social arrangements like profit-sharing and voluntary cooperatives. In this way, Mill thought, capitalism's more objectionable features might be eliminated.

While some nineteenth-century radicals, most notably Karl Marx, broke completely from traditional support of the laissez-faire system and predicted that its inherent contradictions would generate its downfall, Mill did not. He, along with other less extreme philosophers, defended the basic institutions of capitalism but realized that the system needed certain modifications. These men became the "liberal reformers," and it is in their writings that liberalism ceases to mean support of the laissez-faire system and comes to signify the correction of its abuses. In England this feeling manifested itself in the passage of the Factory Acts and other measures regulating business activities in the second half of the nineteenth century, and in the movement toward the welfare state in the twentieth century. In America, Progressivism, New Dealism, and the Great Society are all examples of reform liberalism aimed at ameliorating the social ills of the free market.

Because liberals maintain a pragmatic and, in their view, nonideological viewpoint, their principles are more difficult to itemize than those of the other two groups presented in this volume. Most accept, as conservatives do, the role of prices and profits in determining the allocation of our economic resources. Most would say that the public sector ought not to engage in tasks best accomplished by the private sector, and most do not favor public ownership of the means of production. Because liberals generally accept the basic capitalist institutions, radicals often see little difference between liberals and conservatives; and in fact, the difference is often one of degree only. The conservative almost always thinks that the market and individuals can move society along more effectively than the government, while the liberal is more apt to point out the shortcomings of the market and to argue for a greater role for the government in solving social and economic problems. Although liberals might be expected to waver between the use of the market and governmental power to solve particular problems, it must be admitted that on balance they have moved the economy away from laissez-faire. The result has been the development of a mixed economy where the government's role has been expanded to promote full employment, economic growth, a more equal distribution of income, and a variety of social welfare programs. While conservatives concentrate on questions of individual freedom and economic efficiency, the liberal is more apt to be concerned with equality and social justice. The article by Paul Samuelson, then, is atypical of most liberal economists (including him) in that it addresses the question of freedom in a mixed economy. It does reflect, however, the typical liberal view that in a complex industrial society government action can advance the interests of the individuals it represents, and can expand rather than contract their overall freedoms.

A major thrust toward increasing the government's role in the economy came with the acceptance of the Keynesian idea that business cycles could be brought under control with the skillful use of monetary and fiscal policies. Although these prescriptions seem to work best against unemployment or inflation which stem from problems with demand (either too little or too much spending), all liberals accept the role of the government as a stabilizing agent in the economy. The first article by J. M. Keynes in this section sets forth the liberal position that the government can help society realize the goals that it sets for itself, while the second tries to project what the problems of society will be 100 years hence. The latter article represents an interesting view on the future of capitalism, which can be compared with J. S. Mill's speculations on the fringe benefits of a stationary state.

The government's role in society is also examined in several other articles in this section. On the question of why the public sector has grown so large, the view most commonly held by liberals is the one expressed by Michael Reagan. It might be contrasted with the historical perspective of Rothbard or Fusfeld on the rise of the state in America. Galbraith's description of the role of the government, in his *New Industrial State,* has attracted more attention among radicals than among orthodox economists, but in the end he opts for a state that will hold the interests of the general population above those of the corporate sector. In Galbraith's view, technology has played a more important part than the government in moving the economy toward planning. The articles by Mill, Keynes, Schumpeter, and especially Heilbroner also assign technology an important role in shaping the institutional and social structure of society.

Another force which has helped direct the movement toward a mixed economy is the influence of intellectuals. Their role has been determined by the need for their technical expertise and by their ability to formulate programs that promise a better life without drastic changes in the social structure. An insider's view of this role is offered in Daniel Moynihan's article. The reader should also note the part that Schumpeter and Galbraith expect intellectuals to play in the future.

The article by Walter W. Rostow is reprinted here because it is one of the few non-Marxist works that examines the entire span of modern history in an attempt to search out common forces of change in the evolution of societies. It invites comparison with the historical perspectives of Marx, Engels, and Heilbroner in this volume.

The fact that the liberal section of this volume is longer than either the conservative or radical ones reflects the dominance of liberal voices in America today. There are signs, however, that those in the liberal camp are more divided on the means of attaining their goals than they were during the 1960s. Some have moved to the right, where the emphasis is on the importance of the market as a regulator, while others have moved toward greater governmental regulation and control. Most, however, probably vary their position depending upon the issue involved. The reason for this apparent split from the center, and the question of its duration, are still unresolved issues. Certainly many liberals became disillusioned with the failure of the '60s programs to eliminate or even substantially curb poverty, inflation, and other social and economic ills. Such failures force a reexamination process and often a shift in position on important questions. The liberal would no doubt claim that this pragmatic approach has always been a characteristic of his thinking, since he has never been tied to any ideological position. The future direction of liberalism is uncertain, but the road is not entirely strewn with failures, and it is unlikely that many within this group will move far enough to merge with the conservative or radical streams of opinion.

R R

JOHN STUART MILL

(1806–1873)

Brought up under the rigid standards of utilitarianism, which formed the psychological foundation of classical economic thought, John Stuart Mill later partially abandoned this faith in an attempt to effect a reconciliation between capitalism and socialism. On the one hand he was sympathetic to the cooperative, egalitarian ethic of a socialist society; he favored increasing land taxes as a step toward land nationalization, profit sharing as a step toward the formation of cooperative societies of producers, and severe limits on inheritance rights. On the other hand he saw considerable virtue in the competitive capitalist model; it supposedly tended to yield higher wages and lower prices for consumer goods than would otherwise prevail, and provided a stimulus for economic activity. In the selection presented here Mill expresses the overlapping convictions that make him a transitional figure in the shift from a laissez-faire economy to an interventionist government. Mill concluded that the socialist schemes developed during his time were "workable only by the elite of mankind. . . . However valuable as an ideal, and even as a prophecy of ultimate possibilities, [socialism] is not available as a present resource. . . . For a long period to come the principle of individual property will be in possession of the field."

Unlike the early classical economists, such as Smith, Ricardo, Say, and Malthus, Mill considered the right of private property as a qualified rather than an absolute one. Although the precise line of demarcation is unclear in Mill's writings, he apparently believed that if legislation reduced the initial level of inequality, the social evils associated with private property would be significantly lessened. Mill believed that there was considerable room for integrating gradualistic reform measures within the framework of the market system. Unlike Marx he did not view class conflict as a necessary feature of a capitalist system. Still less did he see this conflict as an engine of revolutionary change, believing that "where the rich are content with being rich and do not claim as such any political privileges, their interest and that of the poor are generally the same." This approach bypasses the important empirical question of whether in fact there has been a close connection between economic and political power. Most present-day liberals and radicals would answer in the affirmative.

Mill's popular economic treatise, *Principles of Political Economy,* reflected not only his importance as a transitional thinker, but also served to sum up the thinking of the classical school; this book went on to become the leading text for over twenty-five years. Like Smith's other followers, Mill saw that profits had a tendency to decline in a competitive economy. He believed, however, that there were certain circumstances which counteracted the downward tendency of profits. These included technological improvements, which provided an outlet for absorbing the savings of businessmen, and the export of capital to colonies or foreign countries to seek higher profits than could be obtained at home. Mill thought that the latter method was crucially important in arresting the decline of profits in England. As an original extension of classical thought, Mill foresaw the day when continued capital accumulation would force the rate of profit down to a minimum and create a stationary state. This development was inevitable, he believed, because technological change could not go on forever. Though most economists paled at the prospect of a stationary state, Mill considered it undesirable only in countries which had not fully realized their production potential. Elsewhere, it would accomplish the mental and moral improvement of the species through such innovations as a shortened workday and a decrease in mechanical drudgery. Mill did note, nevertheless, that birth control was a prerequisite for an improvement in the status of the working class because the wealthy would take advantage of an unlimited labor supply to maximize profits. Here Mill departs from the position of Adam Smith, who claimed that when a country attained a fully developed wealthy stage, competition would cause profits as well as wages to be very low.

In the excerpt presented here Mill describes the conditions that would exist under the stationary state. His projection of the future of capitalism is similar to that of Keynes in the next selection. Perhaps because of this projection, and his astute observation that the key economic problem faced by a country is related to its stage of development, Mill saw the distribution problem as coming more and more to the fore. "It is only in the backward countries of the world that increased production is still an important object; in those most advanced, what is economically needed is a better distribution. . . ."

Today it is interesting to note that, although Mill saw nineteenth-century England on the verge of pleasant stagnation, the ultimate limits of technological change do not seem to have been reached. In fact it is increasingly obvious that technological improvements grow at an exponential rate and that if capitalism does ultimately stagnate it is unlikely to do so for the lack of new technological frontiers.

M L

From

THE PRINCIPLES OF POLITICAL ECONOMY

(1848)

THE PROBABLE FUTURE OF THE LABORING CLASSES

. . . A people who have once adopted the large system of production, either in manufactures or in agriculture, are not likely to recede from it; and when population is kept in due proportion to the means of support, it is not desirable that they should. Labor is unquestionably more productive on the system of large industrial enterprises; the produce, if not greater absolutely, is greater in proportion to the labor employed: the same number of persons can be supported equally well with less toil and greater leisure; which will be wholly an advantage, as soon as civilization and improvement have so far advanced, that what is a benefit to the whole shall be a benefit to each individual composing it. And in the moral aspect of the question, which is still more important than the economical, something better should be aimed at as the goal of industrial improvement, than to disperse mankind over the earth in single families, each ruled internally, as families now are, by a patriarchal despot, and having scarcely any community of interest, or necessary mental communion, with other human beings. The domination of the head of the family over the other members, in this state of things, is absolute; while the effect on his own mind tends towards concentration of all interests in the family, considered as an expansion of self, and absorption of all passions in that of exclusive possession, of all cares in those of preservation and acquisition. As a step out of the merely animal state into the human, out of reckless abandonment to brute instincts into prudential foresight and self-government, this moral condition may be seen without displeasure. But if public spirit, generous sentiments, or true justice and equality are desired, association, not isolation, of interests, is the school in which these excellences are nurtured. The aim of improvement should be not solely to place human beings in a condition in which they will be able to do without one another, but to enable them to work with or for one another in relations not involving dependence. Hitherto there has been no alternative for those who lived by their labor, but that of laboring either each for himself alone, or for a master. But the civilizing and improving influences of association, and the efficiency and economy of production on a large scale, may be obtained without dividing the producers into two parties with hostile interests and feelings, the many who do the work being mere servants under the command of the one who supplies the funds, and having no interest of their own in the enterprise except to earn their wages with as little labor as possible. The speculations and discussions of the last fifty years, and the events of the last thirty, are abundantly conclusive on this point. If the improvement which even triumphant military depotism has only retarded, not stopped, shall continue its course, there can be little doubt that the *status* of hired laborers will gradually tend to confine itself to the description of workpeople whose low moral qualities render them unfit for anything more independent: and that the relation of masters and workpeople will be gradually superseded by partnership, in one of two forms: in some cases, association of the laborers with the capitalist; in others, and perhaps finally in all, association of laborers among themselves. . . .

The form of association, however, which if mankind continue to improve, must be expected in the end to predominate, is not that which can exist between a capitalist as chief, and work-people without a voice in the management, but the association of the laborers themselves on terms of equality, collectively owning the capital with which they carry on their operations, and working under managers elected and removable by themselves. . . .

When . . . cooperative societies shall have sufficiently multiplied, it is not probable that any but the least valuable work-people will any longer consent to work all their lives for wages merely; both private capitalists and associations will gradually find it necessary to make the entire body of laborers participants in profits. Eventually, and in perhaps a less remote future than may be supposed, we may, through the cooperative principle, see our way to a change in society, which would combine the freedom and independence of the individual, with the moral, intellectual, and economical advantages of aggregate production; and which, without violence or spoliation, or even any sudden disturbance of existing habits and expectations, would realize, at least in the industrial department, the best aspirations of the democratic spirit, by putting an end to the division of society into the industrious and the idle, and effacing all social distinctions but those fairly earned by personal services and exertions. Associations like those which we have described, by the very process of their success, are a course of education in those moral and active qualities by which alone success can be either deserved or attained. As associations multiplied, they would tend more and more to absorb all work-people, except those who have too little understanding, or too little virtue, to be capable of learning to act on any other system than that of narrow selfishness. As this change proceeded, owners of capital would gradually find it to their advantage, instead of maintaining the struggle of the old system with work-people of only the worst description, to lend their capital to the associations; to do this at a diminishing rate of interest, and at last, perhaps, even to exchange their capital for terminable annuities. In this or some such mode, the existing accumulations of capital might honestly, and by a kind of spontaneous process, become in the end the joint property of all who participate in their productive employment: a transformation which, thus effected, (and assuming of course that both sexes participate equally in the rights and in the government of the association), would be the nearest approach to social justice, and the most beneficial ordering of industrial affairs for the universal good, which it is possible at present to foresee.

I agree, then, with the Socialist writers in their conception of the form which industrial operations tend to assume in the advance of improvement; and I entirely share their opinion that the time is ripe for commencing this transformation, and that it should by all just and effectual means be aided and encouraged. But while I agree and sympathize with Socialists in this practical portion of their aims, I utterly dissent from the most conspicuous and vehement part of their teaching, their declamations against competition. With moral conceptions in many respects far ahead of the existing arrangements of society, they have in general very confused and erroneous notions of its actual working; and one of their greatest errors, as I conceive, is to charge upon competition all the economical evils which at present exist. They forget that wherever competition is not, monopoly is; and that monopoly, in all its forms, is the taxation of the industrious for the support of indolence, if not of plunder. They forget, too, that with the exception of competition among laborers, all other competition is for the benefit of the laborers, by cheapening the articles they consume; that competition even in the labor market is a source not of low but of high wages, wherever the competition *for* labor exceeds the competition *of* labor, as in America, in the colonies, and in the skilled trades; and never could be a cause of low wages, save by the overstocking of the labor market through the too great numbers of the laborer's families; while, if the supply of laborers is excessive, not even Socialism can prevent their remuneration from being low. Besides, if association were universal, there would be no competition between laborer and laborer; and that between association and association would be for the benefit of the consumers, that is, of the associations; of the industrious classes generally.

I do not pretend that there are no inconveniences in competition, or that the moral objections urged against it by Socialist writers, as a source of jealousy and hostility among those engaged in the same occupation, are altogether groundless. But if competition has its evils, it prevents greater evils. As M. Feugueray well says, "The deepest root of the evils and iniquities which fill the industrial world, is not competition, but the subjection of labor to capital, and the enormous share which the possessors of the instruments of industry are able to take from the produce. . . . If competition has great power for evil, it is no less fertile of good, especially in what regards the development of the individual faculties, and the success of innovations." It is the common error of Socialists to overlook the natural indolence of mankind; their tendency to be passive, to be the slaves of habit, to persist indefinitely in a course once chosen. Let them once attain any state of existence which they consider tolerable, and the danger to be apprehended is that they will thenceforth stagnate; will not exert themselves to improve, and by letting their faculties rust, will lose even the energy required to preserve them from deterioration. Competition may not be the best conceivable stimulus, but it is at present a necessary one, and no one can foresee the time when it will not be indispensable to progress. Even confining ourselves to the industrial department, in which, more than in any other, the majority may be supposed to be competent judges of improvements; it would be difficult to induce the general assembly of an association to submit to the trouble and inconvenience of altering their habits by adopting some new and promising invention, unless their knowledge of the existence of rival associations made them apprehend that what they would not consent to do, others would, and that they would be left behind in the race.

Instead of looking upon competition as the baneful and antisocial principle which it is held to be by the generality of Socialists, I conceive that, even in the present state of society and industry, every restriction of it is an evil, and every extension of it, even if for the time injuriously affecting some class of laborers, is always an ultimate good. To be protected against competition is to be protected in idleness, in mental dullness; to be saved the necessity of being as active and as intelligent as other people; and if it is also to be protected against being underbid for employment by a less highly paid class of laborers, this is only where old custom, or local and partial monopoly, has placed some particular class of artisans in a privileged position as compared with the rest; and the time has come when the interest of universal improvement is no longer promoted by prolonging the privileges of a few. If the slop-sellers and others of their class have lowered the wages of tailors, and some other artisans, by making them an affair of competition instead of custom, so much the better in the end. What is now required is not to bolster up old customs, whereby limited classes of laboring people obtain partial gains which interest them in keeping up the present organization of society, but to introduce new general practices beneficial to all; and there is reason to rejoice at whatever makes the privileged classes of skilled artisans feel that they have the same interests, and depend for their remuneration on the same general causes, and must resort for the improvement of their condition to the same remedies, as the less fortunately circumstanced and comparatively helpless multitude.

THE STATIONARY STATE

. . . In contemplating any progressive movement, not in its nature unlimited, the mind is not satisfied with merely tracing the laws of the movement; it cannot but ask the further question, to what goal? Towards what ultimate point is society tending by its industrial progress? When the progress ceases, in what condition are we to expect that it will leave mankind?

It must always have been seen, more or less distinctly, by political economists, that the increase of wealth is not boundless: that at the end of what they term the progressive state lies the stationary state, that all progress in wealth is but a postponement of this, and that each step in advance is an approach to it. We have now been led to recognize that this ultimate goal is at all times near enough to be fully in view; that we are always on the verge of it, and that if we have not reached it long ago, it is because the goal itself flies before us. The richest and most prosperous countries would very soon attain the stationary state, if no further improvements were made in the productive arts, and if there were a suspension of the overflow of capital from those countries into the uncultivated or ill-cultivated regions of the earth.

This impossibility of ultimately avoiding the stationary state—this irresistible necessity that the stream of human industry should finally spread itself out into an apparently stagnant sea—must have been, to the political economists of the last two generations, an unpleasing and discouraging prospect; for the tone and tendency of their speculations goes completely to identify all that is economically desirable with the progressive state, and with that alone. With Mr. M'Culloch, for example, prosperity does not mean a large production and a good distribution of wealth, but a rapid increase of it; his test of prosperity is high profits; and as the tendency of that very increase of wealth, which he calls prosperity, is towards low profits, economical progress, according to him, must tend to the extinction of prosperity. Adam Smith always assumes that the condition of the mass of the people, though it may not be positively distressed, must be pinched and stinted in a stationary condition of wealth, and can only be satisfactory in a progressive state. The doctrine that, to however distant a time incessant struggling may put off our doom, the progress of society must "end in shallows and in miseries," far from being, as many people still believe, a wicked invention of Mr. Malthus, was either expressly or tacitly affirmed by his most distinguished predecessors, and can only be successfully combated on his principles. Before attention had been directed to the principle of population as the active force in determining the remuneration of labor, the increase of mankind was virtually treated as a constant quantity; it was, at all events, assumed that in the natural and normal state of human affairs population must constantly increase, from which it followed that a constant increase of the means of support was essential to the physical comfort of the mass of mankind. The publication of Mr. Malthus' *Essay* is the era from which better views of this subject must be dated; and notwithstanding the acknowledged errors of his first edition, few writers have done more than himself, in the subsequent editions, to promote these juster and more helpful anticipations.

Even in a progressive state of capital,

in old countries, a conscientious or prudential restraint on population is indispensable, to prevent the increase of numbers from outstripping the increase of capital, and the condition of the classes who are at the bottom of society from being deteriorated. Where there is not, in the people, or in some very large proportion of them, a resolute resistance to this deterioration—a determination to preserve an established standard of comfort—the condition of the poorest class sinks, even in a progressive state, to the lowest point which they will consent to endure. The same determination would be equally effectual to keep up their condition in the stationary state, and would be quite as likely to exist. Indeed, even now, the countries in which the greatest prudence is manifested in the regulating of population are often those in which capital increases least rapidly. Where there is an indefinite prospect of employment for increased numbers, there is apt to appear less necessity for prudential restraint. If it were evident that a new hand could not obtain employment but by displacing, or succeeding to, one already employed, the combined influences of prudence and public opinion might in some measure be relied on for restricting the coming generation within the numbers necessary for replacing the present.

I cannot, therefore, regard the stationary state of capital and wealth with the unaffected aversion so generally manifested towards it by political economists of the old school. I am inclined to believe that it would be, on the whole, a very considerable improvement on our present condition. I confess I am not charmed with the ideal of life held out by those who think that the normal state of human beings is that of struggling to get on; that the trampling, crushing, elbowing, and treading on each other's heels, which form the existing type of social life, are the most desirable lot of human kind, or anything but the disagreeable symptoms of one of the phases of industrial progress. It may be a necessary stage in the progress of civilization, and those European nations which have hitherto been so fortunate as to be preserved from it, may have it yet to undergo. It is an incident of growth, not a mark of decline, for it is not necessarily destructive of the higher aspirations and the heroic virtues; as America, in her great civil war, has proved to the world, both by her conduct as a people and by numerous splendid individual examples, and as England, it is to be hoped, would also prove, on an equally trying and exciting occasion. But it is not a kind of social perfection which philanthropists to come will feel any very eager desire to assist in realizing. Most fitting, indeed, is it, that while riches are power, and to grow as rich as possible the universal object of ambition, the path to its attainment should be open to all, without favor or partiality. But the best state for human nature is that in which, while no one is poor, no one desires to be richer, nor has any reason to fear being thrust back by the efforts of others to push themselves forward.

That the energies of mankind should be kept in employment by the struggle for riches, as they were formerly by the struggle of war, until the better minds succeed in educating the others into better things, is undoubtedly more desirable than that they should rust and stagnate. While minds are coarse they require coarse stimuli, and let them have them. In the meantime, those who do not accept the present very early stage of human improvement as its ultimate type, may be excused for being comparatively indifferent to the kind of economical progress which excites the congratulations of ordinary politicians; the mere increase of production and accumulation. For the safety of national independence it is essential that a country should not fall much behind its neighbors in these things. But in themselves they are of little importance, so long as either the increase of population or anything else prevents the mass of the people from reaping any part of the benefit of them. I know not why it should be matter of congratulation that persons who are already richer than any one needs to be, should have doubled their means of consuming things which give little or no pleasure except as representative of wealth; or that numbers of individuals should pass over, every year, from the middle classes into a richer class, or from the class of the occupied rich to that of the unoccupied. It is only in the backward countries of the world that increased production is still an important object: in those most advanced, what is economically needed is a better distribution, of which one indispensable means is a stricter restraint on population. Levelling institutions, either of a just or of an unjust kind, cannot alone accomplish it; they may lower the heights of society, but they cannot, of themselves, permanently raise the depths.

On the other hand, we may suppose this better distribution of property attained, by the joint effect of the prudence and frugality of individuals, and of a system of legislation favoring equality of fortunes, so far as is consistent with the just claim of the individual to the fruits, whether great or small, of his or her own industry. We may suppose, for instance . . . a limitation of the sum which any one person may acquire by gift or inheritance to the amount sufficient to constitute a moderate independence. Under this twofold influence society would exhibit these leading features: a well-paid and affluent body of laborers; no enormous fortunes, except what were earned and accumulated during a single lifetime; but a much larger body of persons than at present, not only exempt from the coarser toils, but with sufficient leisure, both physical and mental, from mechanical details, to cultivate freely the graces of life, and afford examples of them to the classes less favorably circumstanced for their growth. This condition of society, so greatly preferable to the present, is not only perfectly compatible with the stationary state, but, it would seem, more naturally allied with that state than with any other.

There is room in the world, no doubt, and even in old countries, for a great increase of population, supposing the arts of life to go on improving, and capital to increase. But even if innocuous, I confess I see very little reason for desiring it. The density of population necessary to enable mankind to obtain, in the greatest degree, all the advantages both of cooperation and of social intercourse, has, in all the most populous countries, been attained. A population may be too crowded, though all be amply supplied with food and raiment. It is not good for man to be kept perforce at all times in the presence of his species. A world from which solitude is extirpated is a very poor ideal. Solitude, in the sense of being often alone, is essential to any depth of meditation or of character; and solitude in the presence of natural beauty and grandeur, is the cradle of thoughts and aspirations which are not only good for the individual, but which society could ill do without. Nor is there much satisfaction in contemplating the world with nothing left to the spontaneous activity of nature; with every rood of land brought into cultivation, which is capable of growing food for human beings; every flowery waste or natural pasture ploughed up, all quadrupeds or birds which are not domesticated for man's use exterminated as his rivals for food, every hedgerow or superfluous tree rooted out, and scarcely a place left where a wild shrub or flower could grow without being eradicated as a weed in the name of improved agriculture. If the earth must lose that great portion of its pleasantness which it owes to things that the unlimited increase of wealth and population would extirpate from it, for the mere purpose of enabling it to support a larger, but not a better or happier population, I sincerely hope, for the sake of posterity, that they will be content to be stationary, long before necessity compels them to it.

It is scarcely necessary to remark that a stationary condition of capital and population implies no stationary state of human improvement. There would be as much scope as ever for all kinds of mental culture, and moral and social progress; as much room for improving the Art of Living, and much more likelihood of its being improved, when minds ceased to be engrossed by the art of getting on. Even the industrial arts might be as earnestly and as successfully cultivated, with this sole difference, that instead of serving no purpose but the increase of wealth, industrial improvements would produce their legitimate effect, that of abridging labor. Hitherto [1848] it is questionable if all the mechanical inventions yet made have lightened the day's toil of any human being. They have enabled a greater population to live the same life of drudgery and imprisonment, and an increased number of manufacturers and others to make fortunes. They have increased the comforts of the middle classes. But they have not yet begun to effect those great changes in human destiny, which it is in their nature and in their futurity to accomplish. Only when, in addition to just institutions, the increase of mankind shall be under the deliberate guidance of judicious foresight, can the conquests made from the powers of nature by the intellect and energy of scientific discoverers become the common property of the species, and the means of improving and elevating the universal lot.

JOHN MAYNARD KEYNES

(1883–1946)

A sharp break with the neoclassicist tradition can be found in the works of John Maynard Keynes, undoubtedly the most influential economist of the twentieth century. His rejection of this tradition in his famous *General Theory of Employment, Interest and Money* was, of course, influenced by the deep and prolonged depression of the 1930s. Intellectual discoveries tend to make their appearance when the times are ripe, and this was a period of idle men, idle factories, and mass discontent. Mainstream theory yielded opinions that, at best, were insufficient and misleading. Keynes' revolutionary contribution was an explanation of how and why an economy could operate with no automatic mechanism for returning to full employment. He was responsible for redirecting the main thrust of economic thinking from a microlevel, where concern focused on cost and price phenomena, to a macrolevel, where concern focused on levels of national income and employment. Keynes correctly claimed that the microoriented neoclassical economists assumed away the problems of business cycles by viewing a capitalist society as tending toward a norm of full employment. Deviations from this state were acknowledged by traditional theory but were thought of as temporary aberrations.

Keynes posited the heretical view that equilibrium could exist at any level of employment, and that the effective demands of the businessman (as evidenced by his investment spending) and of the consumer (as indicated by his expenditures) determined the level of employment and income. In order to maintain any given level of income and employment, it was necessary to find investment outlets for the abundant savings generated by rising incomes. This logic suggests that Keynesian economics is considerably more applicable to the economic problems of an advanced, industrial corporate society than to those of the typical underdeveloped country (where the critical problem is to raise the supply of savings, thus creating the ability to overcome economic stagnation). The former society has a potential for either growth or instability depending on how effectively the large savings are utilized. Keynes observed that the most volatile element in a business enterprise society was private investment expenditures, determined primarily by profit expectations and secondarily by the cost of borrowing (the rate of interest). Periods of cyclical downturn are characterized by diminishing profit expectations and increased cash hoardings, which are difficult to overcome even with falling interest rates. Moreover, upward or downward fluctuations in investment (or consumer) spending and respending produce an intensified up-or-down effect on income and employment. The greater the tendency to spend out of any marginal increment of income, the greater will be the ultimate income created by the original spending.

Like Mill, Keynes asserted the possibility of falling profit rates and the stationary state. In addition, Keynes provided a rationale for rejecting laissez-faire in favor of a governmental interventionist approach. By demonstrating the small likelihood that unhampered private enterprise could sustain equilibrium at full employment, Keynes was able to show the importance of counter-cyclical government fiscal and monetary policy, aimed at offsetting undesirable fluctuations in the private sector. As a future projection, Keynes held that "a somewhat comprehensive socialization of investment [this would include all devices, including some public corporations, through which government investment projects would take place] will prove the only means of securing an approximation of full employment." Keynes was also aware that consumer spending could be used to close the gap between available savings and the part that the businessman does not invest. Recovery from a recession could be furthered by measures which stimulated consumer spending. For example, income distribution could be equalized to some extent, since lower income groups tend to have a higher propensity to spend. This policy, however, beyond a critical (and unpredictable) point, would infringe drastically on the very basis of the capitalist system, which presupposes an unequal distribution of income. Hence, Keynes, interested in streamlining the engine of private enterprise rather than abandoning it, emphasized government spending rather than income redistribution.

Despite many criticisms from both conservatives and radicals, this new school of Keynesian economics remains the mainstream of economic thought in economically-advanced countries today. Keynesians believed that the price of tinkering with the system to make it more viable, and perhaps less inequitable, was less than the price paid through excessive devotion to laissez-faire principles. Writing in a period of growing political protest, Keynes represented the farsighted liberal view that reformism was the strategic key for preserving the basic features of the status quo. Keynesian economists have successfully checked some of the illusions of their predecessors. They have shown that yearly balancing of the budget can have a destabilizing effect—exacerbating both the expansions and contractions through increasing expenditures and reducing taxes in periods of expansion, and decreasing expenditures and increasing taxes in periods of contraction. They also cast doubt on the efficacy of reducing wages to stimulate employment by stressing that wages are a source of purchasing power to the consumer as well as a cost to the businessman.

In general, Keynes searched for a method of reconciling individual initiative with the social controls that appeared to be necessary for dealing with actual problems. This is the hallmark of a pragmatist with a predilection for finding solutions within the framework of a market system. He said:

> I think that Capitalism, wisely managed, can probably be made more efficient for attaining economic ends than any alternative system yet in sight, but that in itself it is in many ways extremely objectionable. Our problem is to work out a social organization which shall be as efficient as possible without offending our notions of a satisfactory way of life.

One of the most important limitations of Keynesian analysis is the narrowness of its focus and assumptions. It is a short-run model which takes the level of technology as given. It is, therefore, not particularly well equipped for dealing with problems of economic development since changes in technology must be accounted for in treating such problems. While post-Keynesian theorists have extended the basic model to deal with the longer-run problems of economic growth in both developed and undeveloped countries, their attempt has been only partially successful. They focus primarily on technical economic growth factors while excluding the political economy of the development process—the distribution of wealth, the political and economic power of domestic and foreign capitalists, and above all the nature of the social system. Hence, the post-Keynesian models have greater manageability but less realism. Furthermore, the basic rationale of Keynesian-oriented government spending is presented in terms of countering cyclical effects rather than in terms of welfare considerations. Here again, modern economic thinking has attempted to extend Keynesian analysis beyond this point, but the results are still inconclusive.

There is little doubt that the ideas of Keynes have had a monumental influence on the science of economics and on governmental economic policy. In the hands of skilled writers, Keynesian economics has been meshed with neoclassical analysis and presented in a form that the layman can readily understand. Keynes deserves credit for vastly enlarging the economist's macroeconomic kit of tools, which is directly or indirectly responsible for the high level of precision that has been developed for dealing (albeit with limited success) with the crucial problem of instability in a market system.

ML

THE END OF LAISSEZ-FAIRE

(1926)

Let us clear from the ground the metaphysical or general principles upon which, from time to time, laissez-faire has been founded. It is *not* true that individuals possess a prescriptive "natural liberty" in their economic activities. There is *no* "compact" conferring perpetual rights on those who Have or on those who Acquire. The world is *not* so governed from above that private and social interest always coincide. It is *not* so managed here below that in practice they coincide. It is *not* a correct deduction from the Principle of Economics that enlightened self-interest always operates in the public interest. Nor is it true that self-interest generally *is* enlightened; more often individuals acting separately to promote their own ends are

Reprinted from John Maynard Keynes, *Essays in Persuasion* (New York: W. W. Norton, 1963).

too ignorant or too weak to attain even these. Experience does *not* show that individuals, when they make up a social unit, are always less clear-sighted than when they act separately.

We cannot, therefore, settle on abstract grounds, but must handle on its merits in detail, what Burke termed "one of the finest problems in legislation, namely, to determine what the State ought to take upon itself to direct by the public wisdom, and what it ought to leave, with as little interference as possible, to individual exertion." We have to discriminate between what Bentham, in his forgotten but useful nomenclature, used to term *Agenda* and *Non-Agenda,* and to do this without Bentham's prior presumption that interference is at the same time, "generally needless" and "generally pernicious."[1] Perhaps the chief task of Economists at this hour is to distinguish afresh the *Agenda* of Government from the *Non-Agenda;* and the companion task of Politics is to devise forms of Government within a Democracy which shall be capable of accomplishing the *Agenda.* I will illustrate what I have in mind by two examples.

(1) I believe that in many cases the ideal size for the unit of control and organization lies somewhere between the individual and the modern State. I suggest, therefore, that progress lies in the growth and the recognition of semi-autonomous bodies within the State—bodies whose criterion of action within their own field is solely the public good as they understand it, and from whose deliberations motives of private advantage are excluded, though some place it may still be necessary to leave, until the ambit of men's altruism grows wider, to the separate advantage of particular groups, classes, or faculties—bodies which in the ordinary course of affairs are mainly autonomous within their prescribed limitations, but are subject in the last resort to the sovereignty of the democracy expressed through Parliament.

I propose a return, it may be said, towards mediaeval conceptions of separate autonomies. But, in England at any rate, corporations are a mode of government which has never ceased to be important and is sympathetic to our institutions. It is easy to give examples, from what already exists, of separate autonomies which have attained or are approaching the mode I designate—the Universities, the Bank of England, the Port of London Authority, even perhaps the Railway Companies.

But more interesting than these is the trend of Joint Stock Institutions, when they have reached a certain age and size, to approximate to the status of public corporations rather than that of individualistic private enterprise. One of the most interesting and unnoticed developments of recent decades has been the tendency of big enterprise to socialize itself. A point arrives in the growth of a big institution—particularly a big railway or big public utility enterprise, but also a big bank or a big insurance company—at which the owners of the capital, i.e., the shareholders, are almost entirely dissociated from the management, with the result that the direct personal interest of the latter in the making of great profit becomes quite secondary. When this stage is reached, the general stability and reputation of the institution are more considered by the management than the maximum of profit for the shareholders. The shareholders must be satisfied by

1. Bentham's *Manual of Political Economy,* published posthumously, in Bowring's edition (1843).

conventionally adequate dividends; but once this is secured, the direct interest of the management often consists in avoiding criticism from the public and from the customers of the concern. This is particularly the case if their great size or semi-monopolistic position renders them conspicuous in the public eye and vulnerable to public attack. The extreme instance, perhaps, of this tendency in the case of an institution, theoretically the unrestricted property of private persons, is the Bank of England. It is almost true to say that there is no class of persons in the Kingdom of whom the Governor of the Bank of England thinks less when he decides on his policy than of his shareholders. Their rights, in excess of their conventional dividend, have already sunk to the neighborhood of zero. But the same thing is partly true of many other big institutions. They are, as time goes on, socializing themselves.

Not that this is unmixed gain. The same causes promote conservatism and a waning of enterprise. In fact, we already have in these cases many of the faults as well as the advantages of State Socialism. Nevertheless we see here, I think, a natural line of evolution. The battle of Socialism against unlimited private profit is being won in detail hour by hour. In these particular fields—it remains acute elsewhere—this is no longer the pressing problem. There is, for instance, no so-called important political question so really unimportant, so irrelevant to the reorganization of the economic life of Great Britain, as the Nationalization of the Railways.

It is true that many big undertakings, particularly public utility enterprises and other business requiring a large fixed capital, still need to be semi-socialized. But we must keep our minds flexible regarding the forms of this semi-socialism. We must take full advantage of the natural tendencies of the day, and we must probably prefer semi-autonomous corporations to organs of the Central Government for which Ministers of State are directly responsible.

I criticize doctrinaire State Socialism, not because it seeks to engage men's altruistic impulses in the service of Society, or because it departs from laissez-faire, or because it takes away from man's natural liberty to make a million, or because it has courage for bold experiments. All these things I applaud. I criticize it because it misses the significance of what is actually happening; because it is, in fact, little better than a dusty survival of a plan to meet the problems of fifty years ago, based on a misunderstanding of what someone said a hundred years ago. Nineteenth-century State Socialism sprang from Bentham, free competition, etc., and is in some respects a clearer, in some respects a more muddled, version of just the same philosophy as underlies nineteenth-century individualism. Both equally laid all their stress on freedom, the one negatively to avoid limitations on existing freedom, the other positively to destroy natural or acquired monopolies. They are different reactions to the same intellectual atmosphere.

(2) I come next to a criterion of *Agenda* which is particularly relevant to what it is urgent and desirable to do in the near future. We must aim at separating those services which are *technically social* from those which are *technically individual.* The most important *Agenda* of the State relate not to those activities which private individuals are already fulfilling, but to those functions which fall outside the sphere of the individual, to those decisions which are made by *no one* if the State does not make them.

The important thing for Government is not to do things which individuals are doing already, and to do them a little better or a little worse; but to do those things which at present are not done at all.

It is not within the scope of my purpose on this occasion to develop practical policies. I limit myself, therefore, to naming some instances of what I mean from amongst those problems about which I happen to have thought most.

Many of the greatest economic evils of our time are the fruits of risk, uncertainty, and ignorance. It is because particular individuals, fortunate in situation or in abilities, are able to take advantage of uncertainty and ignorance, and also because for the same reason big business is often a lottery, that great inequalities of wealth come about; and these same factors are also the cause of the Unemployment of Labor, or the disappointment of reasonable business expectations, and of the impairment of efficiency and production. Yet the cure lies outside the operations of individuals; it may even be to the interest of individuals to aggravate the disease. I believe that the cure for these things is partly to be sought in the deliberate control of the currency and of credit by a central institution, and partly in the collection and dissemination on a great scale of data relating to the business situation, including the full publicity, by law if necessary, of all business facts which it is useful to know. These measures would involve Society in exercising directive intelligence through some appropriate organ of action over many of the inner intricacies of private business, yet it would leave private initiative and enterprise unhindered. Even if these measures prove insufficient, nevertheless they will furnish us with better knowledge than we have now for taking the next step.

My second example relates to Savings and Investment. I believe that some coordinated act of intelligent judgment is required as to the scale on which it is desirable that the community as a whole should save, the scale on which these savings should go abroad in the form of foreign investments, and whether the present organization of the investment market distributes savings along the most nationally productive channels. I do not think that these matters should be left entirely to the chances of private judgement and private profits, as they are at present.

My third example concerns Population. The time has already come when each country needs a considered national policy about what size of Population, whether larger or smaller than at present or the same, is most expedient. And having settled this policy, we must take steps to carry it into operation. The time may arrive a little later when the community as a whole must pay attention to the innate quality as well as to the mere numbers of its future members.

These reflections have been directed towards possible improvements in the technique of modern Capitalism by the agency of collective action. There is nothing in them which is seriously incompatible with what seems to me to be the essential characteristic of capitalism, namely the dependence upon an intense appeal to the money-making and money-loving instincts of individuals as the main motive force of the economic machine. Nor must I, so near to my end, stray towards other fields. Nevertheless, I may do well to remind you, in conclusion, that the fiercest contests and the most deeply felt divisions of opinion are likely to be waged in the coming years not round technical questions, where the arguments on either side are mainly economic, but round those which, for want of better words, may be called psychological or, perhaps, moral.

In Europe, or at least in some parts of Europe—but not, I think, in the United States of America—there is a latent reaction, somewhat widespread, against basing Society to the extent that we do upon fostering, encouraging, and protecting the money-motives of individuals. A preference for arranging our affairs in such a way as to appeal to the money-motive as little as possible, rather than as much as possible, need not be entirely *a priori,* but may be based on the comparison of experiences. Different persons, according to their choice of profession, find the money-motive playing a large or a small part in their daily lives, and historians can tell us about other phases of social organization in which this motive has played a much smaller part than it does now. Most religions and most philosophies deprecate, to say the least of it, a way of life mainly influenced by considerations of personal money profit. On the other hand, most men today reject ascetic notions and do not doubt the real advantages of wealth. Moreover it seems obvious to them that one cannot do without the money-motive, and that, apart from certain admitted abuses, it does its job well. In the result the average man averts his attention from the problem, and has no clear idea what he really thinks and feels about the whole confounded matter.

Confusion of thought and feeling leads to confusion of speech. Many people, who are really objecting to Capitalism as a way of life, argue as though they were objecting to it on the ground of its inefficiency in attaining its own objects. Contrariwise, devotees of Capitalism are often unduly conservative, and reject reforms in its technique, which might really strengthen and preserve it, for fear that they may prove to be first steps away from Capitalism itself. Nevertheless a time may be coming when we shall get clearer than at present as to when we are talking about Capitalism as an efficient or inefficient technique, and when we are talking about it as desirable or objectionable in itself. For my part, I think that capitalism, wisely managed, can probably be made more efficient for attaining economic ends than any alternative system yet in sight, but that in itself it is in many ways extremely objectionable. Our problem is to work out a social organization which shall be as efficient as possible without offending our notions of a satisfactory way of life.

The next step forward must come, not from political agitation or premature experiments, but from thought. We need by an effort of the mind to elucidate our own feelings. At present our sympathy and our judgment are liable to be on different sides, which is a painful and paralyzing state of mind. In the field of action reformers will not be successful until they can steadily pursue a clear and definite object with their intellects and their feelings in tune. There is no party in the world at present which appears to me to be pursuing right aims by right methods. Material Poverty provides the incentive to change precisely in situations where there is very little margin for experiments. Material Prosperity removes the incentive just when it might be safe to take a chance. Europe lacks the means, America the will, to make a move. We need a new set of convictions which spring naturally from a candid examination of our own inner feelings in relation to the outside facts.

ECONOMIC POSSIBILITIES FOR OUR GRANDCHILDREN

(1930)

ONE

We are suffering just now from a bad attack of economic pessimism. It is common to hear people say that the epoch of enormous economic progress which characterized the nineteenth century is over; that the rapid improvement in the standard of life is now going to slow down—at any rate in Great Britain; that a decline in prosperity is more likely than an improvement in the decade which lies ahead of us.

I believe that this is a wildly mistaken interpretation of what is happening to us. We are suffering, not from the rheumatics of old age, but from the growing-pains of over-rapid changes, from the painfulness of readjustment between one economic period and another. The increase of technical efficiency has been taking place faster than we can deal with the problem of labor absorption; the improvement in the standard of life has been a little too quick; the banking and monetary system of the world has been preventing the rate of interest from falling as fast as equilibrium requires. . . .

The prevailing world depression, the enormous anomaly of unemployment in a world full of wants, the disastrous mistakes we have made, blind us to what is going on under the surface—to the true interpretation of the trend of things. For I predict that both of the two opposed errors of pessimism which now make so much noise in the world will be proved wrong in our own time—the pessimism of the revolutionaries who think that things are so bad that nothing can save us but violent change, and the pessimism of the reactionaries who consider the balance of our economic and social life so precarious that we must risk no experiments.

My purpose in this essay, however, is not to examine the present or the near future, but to disembarrass myself of short views and take wings into the future. What can we reasonably expect the level of our economic life to be a hundred years hence? What are the economic possibilities for our grandchildren?

From the earliest times of which we have record—back, say, to two thousand years before Christ—down to the beginning of the eighteenth century, there was no very great change in the standard of life of the average man living in the civilized centers of the earth. Ups and downs certainly. Visitations of plague, famine, and war. Golden intervals. But no progressive, violent change. Some periods perhaps 50 percent better than others—at the utmost 100 percent better—in the four thousand years which ended (say) in A.D. 1700.

This slow rate of progress, or lack of progress, was due to two reasons—to the remarkable absence of important technical improvements and to the failure of capital to accumulate.

The absence of important technical inventions between the prehistoric age and comparatively modern times is truly remarkable. Almost everything which really matters and which the world possessed at the commencement of the modern age was already known to man at the dawn of history. Language, fire, the same domestic animals which we have today, wheat, barley, the vine and the olive, the plough, the wheel, the oar, the

Reprinted from John Maynard Keynes, *Essays in Persuasion* (New York: W. W. Norton, 1963).

sail, leather, linen and cloth, bricks and pots, gold and silver, copper, tin, and lead—and iron was added to the list before 1000 B.C.—banking, statecraft, mathematics, astronomy, and religion. There is no record of when we first possessed these things.

At some epoch before the dawn of history—perhaps even in one of the comfortable intervals before the last ice age—there must have been an era of progress and invention comparable to that in which we live today. But through the greater part of recorded history there was nothing of the kind.

The modern age opened, I think, with the accumulation of capital which began in the sixteenth century. I believe—for reasons with which I must not encumber the present argument—that this was initially due to the rise of prices, and the profits to which that led, which resulted from the treasure of gold and silver which Spain brought from the New World into the Old. From that time until today the power of accumulation by compound interest, which seems to have been sleeping for many generations, was reborn and renewed its strength. And the power of compound interest over two hundred years is such as to stagger the imagination. . . .

From the sixteenth century, with a cumulative crescendo after the eighteenth, the great age of science and technical inventions began, which since the beginning of the nineteenth century has been in full flood—coal, steam, electricity, petrol, steel, rubber, cotton, the chemical industries, automatic machinery and the methods of mass production, wireless, printing, Newton, Darwin, and Einstein, and thousands of other things and men too famous and familiar to catalogue.

What is the result? In spite of an enormous growth in the population of the world, which it has been necessary to equip with houses and machines, the average standard of life in Europe and the United States has been raised, I think, about fourfold. The growth of capital has been on a scale which is far beyond a hundredfold of what any previous age had known. And from now on we need not expect so great an increase of population.

If capital increases, say, 2 percent per annum, the capital equipment of the world will have increased by a half in twenty years, and seven and a half times in a hundred years. Think of this in terms of material things—houses, transport, and the like.

At the same time technical improvements in manufacture and transport have been proceeding at a greater rate in the last ten years than ever before in history. In the United States factory output per head was 40 percent greater in 1925 than in 1919. In Europe we are held back by temporary obstacles, but even so it is safe to say that technical efficiency is increasing by more than 1 percent per annum compound. There is evidence that the revolutionary technical changes, which have so far chiefly affected industry, may soon be attacking agriculture. We may be on the eve of improvements in the efficiency of food production as great as those which have already taken place in mining, manufacture, and transport. In quite a few years—in our own lifetimes I mean—we may be able to perform all the operations of agriculture, mining, and manufacture with a quarter of the human effort to which we have been accustomed.

For the moment the very rapidity of these changes is hurting us and bringing difficult problems to solve. Those countries are suffering relatively which are not in the vanguard of progress. We are being afflicted with a new disease of which some readers may not yet have heard the name, but of which they will hear a great deal in the years to come—namely, *technological unemployment*. This means unemployment due to our discovery of means of economizing the use of labor outrunning the pace at which we can find new uses for labor.

But this is only a temporary phase of maladjustment. All this means in the long run *that mankind is solving its economic problem.* I would predict that the standard of life in progressive countries one hundred years hence will be between four and eight times as high as it is today. There would be nothing surprising in this even in the light of our present knowledge. It would not be foolish to contemplate the possibility of a far greater progress still.

TWO

Let us, for the sake of argument, suppose that a hundred years hence we are all of us, on the average, eight times better off in the economic sense than we are today. Assuredly there need be nothing here to surprise us.

Now it is true that the needs of human beings may seem to be insatiable. But they fall into two classes—those needs which are absolute in the sense that we feel them whatever the situation of our fellow human beings may be, and those which are relative in the sense that we feel them only if their satisfaction lifts us above, makes us feel superior to, our fellows. Needs of the second class, those which satisfy the desire for superiority, may indeed be insatiable; for the higher the general level, the higher still are they. But this is not so true of the absolute needs—a point may soon be reached, much sooner perhaps than we are all of us aware of, when these needs are satisfied in the sense that we prefer to devote our further energies to noneconomic purposes.

Now for my conclusion, which you will find, I think, to become more and more startling to the imagination the longer you think about it.

I draw the conclusion that, assuming no important wars and no important increase in population, the *economic problem* may be solved, or be at least within sight of solution, within a hundred years. This means that the economic problem is not—if we look into the future—*the permanent problem of the human race.*

Why, you may ask, is this so startling? It is startling because—if, instead of looking into the future, we look into the past—we find that the economic problem, the struggle for subsistence, always has been hitherto the primary, most pressing problem of the human race—not only of the human race, but of the whole of the biological kingdom from the beginnings of life in its most primitive forms.

Thus we have been expressly evolved by nature—with all our impulses and deepest instincts—for the purpose of solving the economic problem. If the economic problem is solved, mankind will be deprived of its traditional purpose.

Will this be a benefit? If one believes at all in the real values of life, the prospect at least opens up the possibility of benefit. Yet I think with dread of the readjustment of the habits and instincts of the ordinary man, bred into him for countless generations, which he may be asked to discard within a few decades.

To use the language of today—must we not expect a general "nervous breakdown"? We already have a little experience of what I mean—a nervous breakdown of the sort which is already common enough in England and the United States amongst the wives of the well-to-do classes, unfortunate women, many of them, who have been deprived by their wealth of their traditional tasks and occupations—who cannot find it sufficiently amusing, when deprived of the spur of economic necessity, to cook and clean and mend, yet are quite unable to find anything more amusing.

To those who sweat for their daily bread leisure is a longed-for sweet—until they get it.

There is the traditional epitaph written for herself by the old charwoman:—

Don't mourn for me, friends, don't weep for me never,
For I'm going to do nothing for ever and ever.

This was her heaven. Like others who look forward to leisure, she conceived how nice it would be to spend her time listening-in—for there was another couplet which occurred in her poem:—

With psalms and sweet music the heavens'll be ringing,
But I shall have nothing to do with the singing.

Yet it will only be for those who have to do with the singing that life will be tolerable—and how few of us can sing!

Thus for the first time since his creation man will be faced with his real, his permanent problem—how to use his freedom from pressing economic cares, how to occupy the leisure, which science and compound interest will have won for him, to live wisely and agreeably and well.

The strenuous purposeful money-makers may carry all of us along with them into the lap of economic abundance. But it will be those peoples, who can keep alive, and cultivate into a fuller perfection, the art of life itself and do not sell themselves for the means of life, who will be able to enjoy the abundance when it comes.

Yet there is no country and no people, I think, who can look forward to the age of leisure and of abundance without a dread. For we have been trained too long to strive and not to enjoy. It is a fearful problem for the ordinary person, with no special talents, to occupy himself, especially if he no longer has roots in the soil or in custom or in the beloved conventions of a traditional society. To judge from the behavior and the achievements of the wealthy classes today in any quarter of the world, the outlook is very depressing! For these are, so to speak, our advance guard—those who are spying out the promised land for the rest of us and pitching their camp there. For they have most of them failed disastrously, so it seems to me—those who have an independent income but no associations or duties or ties—to solve the problem which has been set them.

I feel sure that with a little more experience we shall use the new-found bounty of nature quite differently from the way in which the rich use it today, and will map out for ourselves a plan of life quite otherwise than theirs.

For many ages to come the old Adam will be so strong in us that everybody will need to do *some* work if he is to be contented. We shall do more things for ourselves than is usual with the rich today, only too glad to have small duties and tasks and routines. But beyond this, we shall endeavor to spread the bread thin on the butter—to make what work there is still to be done to be as widely shared as possible. Three-hour shifts or a fifteen-hour week may put off the problem for a great while. For three hours a day is quite enough to satisfy the old Adam in most of us!

There are changes in other spheres too which we must expect to come. When the accumulation of wealth is no longer of high social importance, there will be great changes in the code of morals. We shall be able to rid ourselves of many of the pseudo-moral principles which have hag-ridden us for two hundred years, by which we have exalted some of the most distasteful of human qualities into the position of the highest virtues. We shall be able to afford to dare to assess the money-motive at its true value. The love of money as a possession—as distinguished from the love of money as a means to the enjoyments and realities of life—will be recognized for what it is, a somewhat disgusting morbidity, one of those semi-criminal, semi-pathological propensities which one hands over with a shudder to the specialists in mental disease. All kinds of social customs and economic practices, affecting the distribution of wealth and of economic rewards and penalties, which we now maintain at all costs, however distasteful and unjust they may be in themselves, because they are tremendously useful in promoting the accumulation of capital, we shall then be free, at last, to discard.

Of course there will still be many people with intense, unsatisfied purposiveness who will blindly pursue wealth—unless they can find some plausible substitute. But the rest of us will no longer be under any obligation to applaud and encourage them. For we shall inquire more curiously than is safe today into the true character of this "purposiveness" with which in varying degrees nature has endowed almost all of us. For purposiveness means that we are more concerned with the remote future results of our actions than with their own quality or their immediate effects on our own environment. The "purposive" man is always trying to secure a spurious and delusive immortality for his acts by pushing his interest in them forward into time. He does not love his cat, but his cat's kittens; nor, in truth, the kittens, but only the kittens' kittens, and so on forward forever to the end of cat-dom. For him jam is not jam unless it is a case of jam tomorrow and never jam today. Thus by pushing his jam always forward into the future, he strives to secure for his act of boiling it an immortality.

Let us remind you of the Professor in *Sylvie and Bruno:*

> "Only the tailor, sir, with your little bill," said a meek voice outside the door.
>
> "Ah, well, I can soon settle *his* business," the Professor said to the children, "if you'll just wait a minute. How much is it, this year, my man?" The tailor had come in while he was speaking.
>
> "Well, it's been a-doubling so many years, you see," the tailor replied, a little gruffly, "and I think I'd like the money now. It's two thousand pound, it is!"
>
> "Oh, that's nothing!" the Professor carelessly remarked, feeling in his pocket, as if he always carried at least *that* amount about with him. "But wouldn't you like to wait just another year and make it *four* thousand? Just think how rich you'd be! Why, you might be a *king,* if you liked!"
>
> "I don't know as I'd care about being a king," the man said thoughtfully. "But it *dew* sound a powerful sight o' money! Well, I think I'll wait——"
>
> "Of course you will!" said the Professor. "There's good sense in *you,* I see. Good-day to you, my man!"
>
> "Will you ever have to pay him that four thousand pounds?" Sylvie asked as the door closed on the departing creditor.
>
> "*Never,* my child!" the Professor replied emphatically. "He'll go on doubling it till he dies. You see, it's *always* worth while waiting another year to get twice as much money!"

Perhaps it is not an accident that the race which did most to bring the promise of immortality into the heart and essence of our religions has also done most for the principle of compound interest and particularly loves this most purposive of human institutions.

I see us free, therefore, to return to some of the most sure and certain principles of religion and traditional virtue—that avarice is a vice, that the exaction of usury is a misdemeanor, and the love of money is detestable, that those walk most truly in the paths of virtue and sane wisdom who take least thought for the morrow. We shall once more value ends above means and prefer the good to the useful. We shall honor those who can teach us how to pluck the hour and the day virtuously and well, the delightful people who are capable of taking direct enjoyment in things, the lilies of the field who toil not, neither do they spin.

But beware! The time for all this is not yet. For at least another hundred years we must pretend to ourselves and to everyone that fair is foul and foul is fair; for foul is useful and fair is not. Avarice and usury and precaution must be our gods for a little longer still. For only they can lead us out of the tunnel of economic necessity into daylight.

I look forward, therefore, in days not so very remote, to the greatest change which has ever occurred in the material environment of life for human beings in the aggregate. But, of course, it will happen gradually, not as a catastrophe. Indeed, it has already begun. The course of affairs will simply be that there will be ever larger and larger classes and groups of people from whom problems of economic necessity have been practically removed. The critical difference will be realized when this condition has become so general that the nature of one's duty to one's neighbor is changed. For it will remain reasonable to be economically purposive for others after it has ceased to be reasonable for oneself.

The *pace* at which we can reach our destination of economic bliss will be governed by four things—our power to control population, our determination to avoid wars and civil dissensions, our willingness to entrust to science the direction of those matters which are properly the concern of science, and the rate of accumulation as fixed by the margin between our production and our consumption; of which the last will easily look after itself, given the first three.

Meanwhile there will be no harm in making mild preparations for our destiny, in encouraging, and experimenting in, the arts of life as well as the activities of purpose.

But, chiefly, do not let us overestimate the importance of the economic problem, or sacrifice to its supposed necessities other matters of greater and more permanent significance. It should be a matter for specialists—like dentistry. If economists could manage to get themselves thought of as humble, competent people, on a level with dentists, that would be splendid!

JOSEPH A. SCHUMPETER

(1883–1950)

It is difficult to place Schumpeter into any of the three categories utilized in this volume. He is classified as a liberal only because he seems to fit less comfortably into either of the other two categories. While he did not advocate laissez-faire, neither did he look forward to the transformation of capitalism into socialism, which he predicted would eventually occur. Schumpeter saw himself as an objective scientist who perceived the forces of change within capitalism and regretfully predicted its eventual demise. In doing so, he went beyond the bounds of pure economics and examined the long-run psychological and social changes involved in the evolutionary process of economic development. The difficulty of placing Schumpeter into any school of economic thought should serve to remind the reader that arbitrary categorization is unwise.

Even though Schumpeter tended to be critical of Keynesian economics and the reformist tinkerings with capitalism that it inspired, he had a great deal of influence over American liberal thinking. Part of this influence is evident in the work of John Kenneth Galbraith (see pp. 151–186). In the selection presented here, Schumpeter draws a correlation between large firms and technological change. To him the misallocation of resources resulting from highly concentrated industries in static equilibrium was offset by the competition (in terms of quality more than price) stimulated by product innovations in those industries. Galbraith reaffirmed this link between size and progressiveness in his *New Industrial State* and is sharply criticized by those who believe that certain economic and political dangers are inherent in this form of technological determinism. These critics point to studies that show that America's largest firms are not always the most efficient or innovative. Very often it is the smaller firms, trying to secure a share of the market from the giants and thus forcing several firms to compete against each other, that actually produce the most innovation. If this is the case, then breaking up many of the country's largest firms might be the best way to hasten technological change. And, these critics point out, even if one could prove that size is necessary for efficiency and innovation, it still might be limited on grounds that large and wealthy firms tend to wield an unacceptable amount of political influence. Although economists still debate the relationship between size and progressiveness, the evidence seems to be going against Schumpeter at the present time.

Perhaps Schumpeter's greatest achievement, however, is the rich insight he provides into the operation of capitalist institutions through his broad approach to economic problems. In the study of business cycles, for instance, Schumpeter shows how the three elements which he holds chiefly responsible for economic development (the entrepreneur, innovation, and credit) combine to cause fluctuations in economic activity. The key to the cyclical pattern of economic growth under capitalism has been the dynamic impact of technological change. Schumpeter believed that technological breakthroughs came in a series of clusters or waves. When a new discovery was made, a few entrepreneurs entered the market in search of profits, followed by a flood of imitators. Eventually this led to a secondary wave of innovations, based on opportunities, provided by the original discovery. Entrepreneurs financed the development of these innovations with private bank credit provided by the capitalist system. The combination of innovations, entrepreneurial ability, and credit expansion caused a rise in economic prosperity which eventually produced its own doom. This inevitable downswing stemmed from the expansion of credit and speculation associated with the previous upturn, and from the competititon among producers trying to displace each other's goods and services on the market (Schumpeter's process of "creative destruction"). Schumpeter believed that this instability was part of the nature of capitalism and was a price worth paying for economic growth. The fact that he saw the seeds of the downswing inherent in the expansion of business activity reflects his entire approach to the evolution of capitalism, an approach which parallels Marx's dialectical method.

Schumpeter's analysis led him to conclude that the role of the entrepreneur and the process of innovation were gradually being replaced by a "depersonalized" routine. Through this evolutionary process, he believed that capitalism was losing its dynamic spirit and thus giving way to some form of socialism. Although routine might lessen the instability of capitalism, it undermined the system's traditional built-in defenses. Thus, Schumpeter predicted the demise of capitalism, but unlike Marx he attributed this demise to the system's successes, rather than its failures.

In the article presented here he shows how the bulwarks of capitalism, including the aristocracy, the bourgeoisie family, and the small businessman, are breaking down while hostile forces gain in strength. Crucial among these forces is a class of idle intellectuals, critical of capitalist institutions, who infiltrate the labor union movement to form a solid base for political change. The energies of the government are thus directed toward anticapitalist goals such as the nationalization of industry.

If one accepts the contentions of Galbraith and others on the increasing socialization of industry, some of Schumpeter's predictions seem to be bearing fruit; however, as liberals have pointed out, this tendency is not likely to result in nationalization. It seems upon closer examination that Schumpeter has overstated the radical tendencies of the intellectuals and their influence within the labor movement. The opinions of those who influence the public are molded as much by corporate capitalism (à la Galbraith) as the general citizenry itself, and the American union movement seems to be void of ideology. However, modern socialists, such as Michael Harrington, still feel that hope for the future lies in a coalition of trade unions and intellectuals. The lack of such a movement is a painful reminder to socialists that America is a country which has thus far psychologically resisted such a coalition.

R R

From

CAPITALISM, SOCIALISM, AND DEMOCRACY

(1942)

PROLOGUE

Can capitalism survive? No. I do not think it can. . . .

. . . The thesis I shall endeavor to establish is that the actual and prospective performance of the capitalist system is such as to negative the idea of its breaking down under the weight of economic failure, but that its very success undermines the social institutions which protect it, and "inevitably" creates conditions in which it will not be able to live and which strongly point to socialism as the heir apparent. My final conclusion therefore does not differ, however much my argument may, from that of most socialist writers and in particular from that of all Marxists. But in order to accept it one does not need to be a socialist. Prognosis does not imply anything about the desirability of the course of events that one predicts. If a doctor predicts that his patient will die presently, this does not mean that he desires it. One may hate socialism or at least look upon it with cool criticism, and yet foresee its advent. Many conservatives did and do.

THE PROCESS OF CREATIVE DESTRUCTION

Capitalism . . . is by nature a form or method of economic change and not only never is but never can be stationary. And this evolutionary character of the capitalist process is not merely due to the fact that economic life goes on in a social and natural environment which changes and by its change alters the data of economic action; this fact is important and these changes (wars, revolutions and so on) often condition industrial change, but they are not its prime movers. Nor is this evolutionary character due to a quasi-automatic increase in population and capital or to the vagaries of monetary systems of which exactly the same thing holds true. The fundamental impulse that sets and keeps the capitalist engine in motion comes from the new consumers' goods, the new methods of production or transportation, the new markets, the new forms of industrial organization that capitalist enterprise creates.

. . . The contents of the laborer's budget, say from 1760 to 1940, did not simply grow on unchanging lines but they underwent a process of qualitative change. Similarly, the history of the productive apparatus of a typical farm, from the beginnings of the rationalization of crop rotation, plowing and fattening to the mechanized thing of today—linking up with elevators and railroads—is a history of revolutions. So is the history of the productive apparatus of the iron and steel industry from the charcoal furnace to our own type of furnace, or the history of the apparatus of power production from the overshot water wheel to the modern power plant, or the history of transportation from the mail-coach to the airplane. The opening up of new markets, foreign or domestic, and the organizational development from the craft shop and factory to such concerns

Abridged from pp. 61, 82, 83, 84, 85, 87, 88, 89, 90, 106, 132, 133, 134, 139, 140, 141–42, 143, 145, 147, 152, 153, 154, 156, 157, 158, 160, 161, 162 in *Capitalism, Socialism, and Democracy,* Third Edition, by Joseph A. Schumpeter.

as U.S. Steel illustrate the same process of industrial mutation—if I may use that biological term—that incessantly revolutionizes[1] the economic structure *from within,* incessantly destroying the old one, incessantly creating a new one. This process of Creative Destruction is the essential fact about capitalism. It is what capitalism consists in and what every capitalist concern has got to live in. . . .

. . . Economists are at long last emerging from the stage in which price competition was all they saw. As soon as quality competition and sales effort are admitted into the sacred precincts of theory, the price variable is ousted from its dominant position. However, it is still competition within a rigid pattern of invariant conditions, methods of production and forms of industrial organization in particular, that practically monopolizes attention. But in capitalist reality as distinguished from its textbook picture, it is not that kind of competition which counts but the competition from the new commodity, the new technology, the new source of supply, the new type of organization (the largest-scale unit of control for instance)—competition which commands a decisive cost or quality advantage and which strikes not at the margins of the profits and the outputs of the existing firms but at their foundations and their very lives. This kind of competition is as much more effective than the other as a bombardment is in comparison with forcing a door, and so much more important that it becomes a matter of comparative indifference whether competition in the ordinary sense functions more or less promptly; the powerful lever that in the long run expands output and brings down prices is in any case made of other stuff.

It is hardly necessary to point out that competition of the kind we now have in mind acts not only when in being but also when it is merely an ever-present threat. It disciplines before it attacks. The businessman feels himself to be in a competitive situation even if he is alone in his field or if, though not alone, he holds a position such that investigating government experts fail to see any effective competition between him and any other firms in the same or a neighboring field and in consequence conclude that his talk, under examination, about his competitive sorrows is all make-believe. In many cases, though not in all, this will in the long run enforce behavior very similar to the perfectly competitive pattern. . . .

MONOPOLISTIC PRACTICES

. . . We have . . . seen that, both as a fact and as a threat, the impact of new things—new technologies for instance—on the existing structure of an industry considerably reduces the long-run scope and importance of practices that aim, through restricting output, at conserving established positions and at maximizing the profits accruing from them. We must now recognize the further fact that restrictive practices of this kind, as far as they are effective, acquire a new significance in the perennial gale of creative destruction, a significance which they would not have in a stationary state or in a state of slow and balanced growth. In either of these cases restrictive strategy would produce no result other than an increase in profits at the expense of buyers except that, in the case of balanced advance, it might still prove to be the easiest and most effective way of collecting the means by which to finance additional investment. . . .

Practically any investment entails, as a necessary complement of entrepreneurial action, certain safeguarding activities such as insuring or hedging. Long-range investing under rapidly changing conditions, especially under conditions that change or may change at any moment under the impact of new commodities and technologies, is like shooting at a target that is not only indistinct but moving–and moving jerkily at that. Hence it becomes necessary to resort to such protecting devices as patents or temporary secrecy of processes or, in some cases, long-period contracts secured in advance. But these protecting devices which most economists accept as normal elements of rational management[2] are only special cases of a larger class comprising many others which most economists condemn although they do not differ fundamentally from the recognized ones. . . .

In analyzing such business strategy *ex visu* of a given point of time, the investigating economist or government agent sees price policies that seem to him predatory and restrictions of output that seem to him synonymous with loss of opportunities to produce. He does not see that restrictions of this type are, in the conditions of the perennial gale, incidents, often unavoidable incidents, of a long-run process of expansion which they protect rather than impede. There is no more of paradox in this than there is in saying that motorcars are traveling faster than they otherwise would *because* they are provided with brakes.

This stands out most clearly in the case of those sectors of the economy which at any time happen to embody the impact of new things and methods on the existing industrial structure. The best way of getting a vivid and realistic idea of industrial strategy is indeed to visualize the behavior of new concerns or industries that introduce new commodities or processes (such as the aluminum industry) or else reorganize a part or the whole of an industry (such as, for instance, the old Standard Oil Company).

As we have seen, such concerns are aggressors by nature and wield the really effective weapon of competition. Their intrusion can only in the rarest of cases fail to improve total output in quantity or quality, both through the new method itself–even if at no time used to full advantage–and through the pressure it exerts on the preexisting firms. But these aggressors are so circumstanced as to require, for purposes of attack and defense, also pieces of armor other than price and quality of their product which, moreover, must be strategically manipulated all along so that at any point of time they seem to be doing nothing but restricting their output and keeping prices high.

On the one hand, largest-scale plans could in many cases not materialize at all if it were not known from the outset that competition will be discouraged by heavy capital requirements or lack of experience, or that means are available to discourage or checkmate it so as to gain the time and space for further developments. Even the conquest of financial control over competing concerns in otherwise unassailable positions or the

1. Those revolutions are not strictly incessant; they occur in discrete rushes which are separated from each other by spans of comparative quiet. The process as a whole works incessantly, however, in the sense that there always is either revolution or absorption of the results of revolution, both together forming what are known as business cycles.

2. Some economists, however, consider that even those devices are obstructions to progress which, though perhaps necessary in capitalist society, would be absent in a socialist one. There is some truth in this. But that does not affect the proposition that the protection afforded by patents and so on is, in the conditions of a profit economy, on balance a propelling and not an inhibiting factor.

securing of advantages that run counter to the public's sense of fair play–railroad rebates–move, as far as long-run effects on total output alone are envisaged, into a different light; they *may* be methods for removing obstacles that the institution of private property puts in the path of progress. In a socialist society that time and space would be no less necessary. They would have to be secured by order of the central authority.

On the other hand, enterprise would in most cases be impossible if it were not known from the outset that exceptionally favorable situations are likely to arise which if exploited by price, quality and quantity manipulation will produce profits adequate to tide over exceptionally unfavorable situations provided these are similarly managed. Again this requires strategy that in the short run is often restrictive. In the majority of successful cases this strategy just manages to serve its purpose. In some cases, however, it is so successful as to yield profits far above what is necessary in order to induce the corresponding investment. These cases then provide the baits that lure capital on to untried trails. Their presence explains in part how it is possible for so large a section of the capitalist world to work for nothing: in the midst of the prosperous twenties just about half of the business corporations in the United States were run at a loss, at zero profits, or at profits which, if they had been foreseen, would have been inadequate to call forth the effort and expenditure involved.

Our argument however extends beyond the cases of new concerns, methods and industries. Old concerns and established industries, whether or not directly attacked, still live in the perennial gale. Situations emerge in the process of creative destruction in which many firms may have to perish that nevertheless would be able to live on vigorously and usefully if they could weather a particular storm. Short of such general crises or depressions, sectional situations arise in which the rapid change of data that is characteristic of that process so disorganizes an industry for the time being as to inflict functionless losses and to create avoidable unemployment. Finally, there is certainly no point in trying to conserve obsolescent industries indefinitely; but there is point in trying to avoid their coming down with a crash and in attempting to turn a rout, which may become a center of cumulative depressive effects, into orderly retreat. Correspondingly there is, in the case of industries that have sown their wild oats but are still gaining and not losing ground, such a thing as orderly advance. . . .

Thus it is not sufficient to argue that because perfect competition is impossible under modern industrial conditions–or because it always has been impossible–the large-scale establishment or unit of control must be accepted as a necessary evil inseparable from the economic progress which it is prevented from sabotaging by the forces inherent in its productive apparatus. What we have got to accept is that it has come to be the most powerful engine of that progress and in particular of the long-run expansion of total output not only in spite of, but to a considerable extent through, this strategy which looks so restrictive when viewed in the individual case and from the individual point of time. In this respect, perfect competition is not only impossible but inferior, and has no title to being set up as a model of ideal efficiency. It is hence a mistake to base the theory of government regulation of industry on the principle that big business should be made to work as the respective industry would work in perfect competition. And socialists should rely for their criticisms on the virtues of a socialist economy rather than on those of the competitive model.

CRUMBLING WALLS

The Obsolescence of the Entrepreneurial Function

. . . The function of entrepreneurs is to reform or revolutionize the pattern of production by exploiting an invention or, more generally, an untried technological possibility for producing a new commodity or producing an old one in a new way, by opening up a new source of supply of materials or a new outlet for products, by reorganizing an industry and so on. Railroad construction in its earlier stages, electrical power production before the First World War, steam and steel, the motorcar, colonial ventures afford spectacular instances of a large genus which comprises innumerable humbler ones—down to such things as making a success of a particular kind of sausage or toothbrush. This kind of activity is primarily responsible for the recurrent "prosperities" that revolutionize the economic organism and the recurrent "recessions" that are due to the disequilibrating impact of the new products or methods. To undertake such new things is difficult and constitutes a distinct economic function, first, because they lie outside of the routine tasks which everybody understands and, secondly, because the environment resists in many ways that vary, according to social conditions, from simple refusal either to finance or to buy a new thing, to physical attack on the man who tries to produce it. To act with confidence beyond the range of familiar beacons and to overcome that resistance requires aptitudes that are present in only a small fraction of the population and that define the entrepreneurial type as well as the entrepreneurial function. This function does not essentially consist in either inventing anything or otherwise creating the conditions which the enterprise exploits. It consists in getting things done.

This social function is already losing importance and is bound to lose it at an accelerating rate in the future even if the economic process itself of which entrepreneurship was the prime mover went on unabated. For, on the one hand, it is much easier now than it has been in the past to do things that lie outside familiar routine—innovation itself is being reduced to routine. Technological progress is increasingly becoming the business of teams of trained specialists who turn out what is required and make it work in predictable ways. The romance of earlier commercial adventure is rapidly wearing away, because so many more things can be strictly calculated that had of old to be visualized in a flash of genius.

On the other hand, personality and will power must count for less in environments which have become accustomed to economic change—best instanced by an incessant stream of new consumers' and producers' goods—and which, instead of resisting, accept it as a matter of course. The resistance which comes from interests threatened by an innovation in the productive process is not likely to die out as long as the capitalist order persists. It is, for instance, the great obstacle on the road toward mass production of cheap housing which presupposes radical mechanization and wholesale elimination of inefficient methods of work on the plot. But every other kind of resistance—the resistance, in particular, of consumers and producers to a new kind of thing because it is new—has well-nigh vanished already.

Thus, economic progress tends to become depersonalized and automatized. Bureau and committee work tends to replace individual action. . . .

. . . If capitalist evolution—"progress"—either ceases or becomes completely automatic, the economic basis of the industrial bourgeoisie will be reduced eventually to wages such as are paid for current administrative work excepting remnants of quasi-rents and monopoloid gains that may be expected to linger on for some time. Since capitalist enterprise, by its very achievements, tends to automatize progress, we conclude that it tends to make itself superfluous—to break to pieces under the pressure of its own success. The perfectly bureaucratized giant industrial unit not only ousts the small or medium-sized firm and "expropriates" its owners, but in the end it also ousts the entrepreneur and expropriates the bourgeoisie as a class which in the process stands to lose not only its income but also what is infinitely more important, its function. The true pacemakers of socialism were not the intellectuals or agitators who preached it but the Vanderbilts, Carnegies and Rockefellers. This result may not in every respect be to the taste of Marxian socialists, still less to the taste of socialists of a more popular (Marx would have said, vulgar) description. But so far as prognosis goes, it does not differ from theirs.

The Destruction of the Institutional Framework of Capitalist Society

. . . The capitalist process in much the same way in which it destroyed the institutional framework of feudal society also undermines its own. . . .

. . . The very success of capitalist enterprise paradoxically tends to impair the prestige or social weight of the class primarily associated with it and . . . the giant unit of control tends to oust the bourgeoisie from the function to which it owed that social weight. The corresponding change in the meaning, and the incidental loss in vitality, of the institutions of the bourgeois world and of its typical attitudes are easy to trace.

On the one hand, the capitalist process unavoidably attacks the economic standing ground of the small producer and trader. What it did to the pre-capitalist strata it also does—and by the same competitive mechanism—to the lower strata of capitalist industry. . . .

The political structure of a nation is profoundly affected by the elimination of a host of small and medium-sized firms the owner-managers of which, together with their dependents, henchmen and connections, count quantitatively at the polls and have a hold on what we may term the foreman class that no management of a large unit can ever have; the very foundation of private property and free contracting wears away in a nation in which its most vital, most concrete, most meaningful types disappear from the moral horizon of the people.

On the other hand, the capitalist process also attacks its own institutional framework—let us continue to visualize "property" and "free contracting" as *partes pro toto*—within the precincts of the big units. Excepting the cases that are still of considerable importance in which a corporation is practically owned by a single individual or family, the figure of the proprietor and with it the specifically proprietary interest have vanished from the picture. There are the salaried executives and all the salaried managers and submanagers. There are the big stockholders. And then there are the small stockholders. The first group tends to acquire the employee attitude and rarely if ever identifies itself with the stockholding interest even in the most favorable cases, i.e., in the cases in which it identifies itself with the interest of the concern as such. The second group, even if it considers its connection with the concern as permanent and even if it actually behaves as financial theory would have stockholders behave, is at one remove from both the functions and the attitudes of an owner. As to the third group, small stockholders often do not care much about what for most of them is but a minor source of income and, whether they care or not, they hardly ever bother, unless they or some representatives of theirs are out to exploit their nuisance value; being often very ill used and still more often thinking themselves ill used, they almost regularly drift into an attitude hostile to "their" corporations, to big business in general and, particularly when things look bad, to the capitalist order as such. No element of any of those three groups into which I schematized the typical situation unconditionally takes the attitude characteristic of that curious phenomenon, so full of meaning and so rapidly passing, that is covered by the term Property.

Freedom of contracting is in the same boat. In its full vitality it meant individual contracting regulated by individual possibilities. The stereotyped, unindividual, impersonal and bureaucratized dual, impersonal and bureaucratized contract of today—this applies much more generally, but *a potiori* we may fasten upon the labor contract—which presents but restricted freedom of choice and mostly turns on a *c'est à prendre ou à laisser,* has none of the old features the most important of which become impossible with giant concerns dealing with other giant concerns or impersonal masses of workmen or consumers. The void is being filled by a tropical growth of new legal structures—and a little reflection shows that this could hardly be otherwise.

Thus the capitalist process pushes into the background all those institutions, the institutions of property and free contracting in particular, that expressed the needs and ways of the truly "private" economic activity. Where it does not abolish them, as it already has abolished free contracting in the labor market, it attains the same end by shifting the relative importance of existing legal forms—the legal forms pertaining to corporate business for instance as against those pertaining to the partnership or individual firm—or by changing their contents or meanings. The capitalist process, by substituting a mere parcel of shares for the walls of and the machines in a factory, takes the life out of the idea of property. It loosens the grip that once was so strong—the grip in the sense of the legal right and the actual ability to do as one pleases with one's own; the grip also in the sense that the holder of the title loses the will to fight, economically, physically, politically, for "his" factory and his control over it, to die if necessary on its steps. And this evaporation of what we may term the material substance of property—its visible and touchable reality—affects not only the attitude of holders but also that of the workmen and of the public in general. Dematerialized, defunctionalized and absentee ownership does not impress and call forth moral allegiance as the vital form of property did. Eventually there will be *nobody* left who really cares to stand for it—nobody within and nobody without the precincts of the big concerns.

GROWING HOSTILITY

The Social Atmosphere of Capitalism

. . . The capitalist process, so we have seen, eventually decreases the importance of the function by which the capitalist class lives. We have also seen that it tends to wear away protective strata, to break down its own defenses, to disperse the garrisons of its entrenchments. And we have finally seen that capitalism creates a critical frame of mind which, after having destroyed the moral authority of so many other institutions, in the end turns against its own; the bourgeois finds to his amazement that the rationalist attitude does not stop at the credentials of kings and popes but goes on to attack private property and the whole scheme of bourgeois values.

The bourgeois fortress thus becomes politically defenseless. Defenseless fortresses invite aggression especially if there is rich booty in them. Aggressors will work themselves up into a state of rationalizing hostility[3]–aggressors always do. No doubt it is possible, for a time, to buy them off. But this last resource fails as soon as they discover that they can have all. In part, this explains what we are out to explain. So far as it goes–it does not go the whole way of course–this element of our theory is verified by the high correlation that exists historically between bourgeois defenselessness and hostility to the capitalist order: there was very little hostility on principle as long as the bourgeois position was safe, although there was then much more reason for it; it spread *pari passu* with the crumbling of the protecting walls. . . .

The Sociology of the Intellectual

. . . Neither the opportunity of attack nor real or fancied grievances are in themselves sufficient to produce, however strongly they may favor, the emergence of active hostility against a social order. For such an atmosphere to develop it is necessary that there be groups to whose interest it is to work up and organize resentment, to nurse it, to voice it and to lead it. . . .

. . . Intellectuals are in fact people who wield the power of the spoken and the written word, and one of the touches that distinguish them from other people who do the same is the absence of direct responsibility for practical affairs. This touch in general accounts for another–the absence of that first-hand knowledge of them which only actual experience can give. The critical attitude [arises] no less from the intellectual's situation as an onlooker–in most cases also as an outsider–than from the fact that his main chance of asserting himself lies in his actual or potential nuisance value. . . .

. . . One of the most important features of the later stages of capitalist civilization is the vigorous expansion of the educational apparatus and particularly of the facilities for higher education. This development was and is no less inevitable than the development of the largest-scale industrial unit,[4] but, unlike the latter, it has been and is being fostered by public opinion and public authority so as to go much further than it would have done under its own steam. Whatever we may think of this from other standpoints and whatever the precise causation, there are several consequences that bear upon the size and attitude of the intellectual group.

First, inasmuch as higher education thus increases the supply of services in professional, quasi-professional and in the end all "white collar" lines beyond the point determined by cost-return considerations, it may create a particularly important case of sectional unemployment.

Second, along with or in place of such unemployment, it creates unsatisfactory conditions of employment–employment in substandard work or at wages below those of the better-paid manual workers.

Third, it may create unemployability of a particularly disconcerting type. The man who has gone through a college or university easily becomes psychically unemployable in manual occupations without necessarily acquiring employability in, say, professional work. . . .

All those who are unemployed or unsatisfactorily employed or unemployable drift into the vocations in which standards are least definite or in which aptitudes and acquirements of a different order count. They swell the host of intellectuals in the strict sense of the term, whose numbers hence increase disproportionately. They enter it in a thoroughly discontented frame of mind. Discontent breeds resentment. And it often rationalizes itself into that social criticism which . . . is in any case the intellectual spectator's typical attitude toward men, classes and institutions especially in a rationalist and utilitarian civilization. Well, here we have numbers; a well-defined group situation of proletarian hue; and a group interest shaping a group attitude that will much more realistically account for hostility to the capitalist order than could the theory—itself a rationalization in the psychological sense—according to which the intellectual's righteous indignation about the wrongs of capitalism simply represents the logical inference from outrageous facts and which is no better than the theory of lovers that their feelings represent nothing but the logical inference from the virtues of the beloved.[5] Moreover our theory also accounts for the fact that this hostility increases, instead of diminishing, with every achievement of capitalist evolution.

Of course, the hostility of the intellectual group—amounting to moral disapproval of the capitalist order—is one thing, and the general hostile atmosphere which surrounds the capitalist engine is another thing. The latter is the really significant phenomenon; and it is not simply the product of the former but flows partly from independent sources: . . . so far as it does, it is raw material for the intellectual group to work on. There are give-and-take relations between the two which it would require more space to unravel than I can spare. The general contours of such an analysis are however sufficiently obvious and I think it safe to repeat that the role of the intellectual group consists primarily in stimulating, energizing, verbalizing and organizing this material and only secondarily in adding to it. Some particular aspects will illustrate the principle.

---

3. It is hoped that no confusion will arise from my using the verb "to rationalize" in two different meanings. An industrial plant is being "rationalized" when its productive efficiency per unit of expenditure is being increased. We "rationalize" an action of ours when we supply ourselves and others with reasons for it that satisfy our standard of values regardless of what our true impulses may be.

4. At present this development is viewed by most people from the standpoint of the ideal of making educational facilities of any type available to all who can be induced to use them. This ideal is so strongly held that any doubts about it are almost universally considered to be nothing short of indecent, a situation not improved by the comments, all too often flippant, of dissentients. Actually, we brush here against a set of extremely complex problems of the sociology of education and educational ideals which we cannot attack within the limits of this sketch. . . .

5. The reader will observe that any such theories would be unrealistic even if the facts of capitalism or the virtues of the beloved were actually all that the social critic or the lover believes them to be. It is also important to note that in the overwhelming majority of cases both critics and lovers are obviously sincere: neither psycho-sociological nor psycho-physical mechanisms enter as a rule into the limelight of the Ego, except in the mask of sublimations.

Capitalist evolution produces a labor movement which obviously is not the creation of the intellectual group. But it is not surprising that such an opportunity and the intellectual demiurge should find each other. Labor never craved intellectual leadership but intellectuals invaded labor politics. They had an important contribution to make: they verbalized the movement, supplied theories and slogans for it–class war is an excellent example–made it conscious of itself and in doing so changed its meaning. In solving this task from their own standpoint, they naturally radicalized it, eventually imparting a revolutionary bias to the most bourgeois trade-union practices, a bias most of the non-intellectual leaders at first greatly resented. But there was another reason for this. Listening to the intellectual, the workman is almost invariably conscious of an impassable gulf if not of downright distrust. In order to get hold of him and to compete with non-intellectual leaders, the intellectual is driven to courses entirely unnecessary for the latter who can afford to frown. Having no genuine authority and feeling always in danger of being unceremoniously told to mind his own business, he must flatter, promise and incite, nurse left wings and scowling minorities, sponsor doubtful or submarginal cases, appeal to fringe ends, profess himself ready to obey– in short, behave toward the masses as his predecessors behaved first toward their ecclesiastical superiors, later toward princes and other individual patrons, still later toward the collective master of bourgeois complexion. Thus, though intellectuals have not created the labor movement, they have yet worked it up into something that differs substantially from what it would be without them.

The social atmosphere, for the theory of which we have been gathering stones and mortar, explains why public policy grows more and more hostile to capitalist interests, eventually so much so as to refuse on principle to take account of the requirements of the capitalist engine and to become a serious impediment to its functioning. The intellectual group's activities have however a relation to anti-capitalist policies that is more direct than what is implied in their share in verbalizing them. Intellectuals rarely enter professional politics and still more rarely conquer responsible office. But they staff political bureaus, write party pamphlets and speeches, act as secretaries and advisers, make the individual politician's newspaper reputation which, though it is not everything, few men can afford to neglect. In doing these things they to some extent impress their mentality on almost everything that is being done. . . .

DECOMPOSITION

Faced by the increasing hostility of the environment and by the legislative, administrative and judicial practice born of that hostility, entrepreneurs and capitalists–in fact the whole stratum that accepts the bourgeois scheme of life–will eventually cease to function. Their standard aims are rapidly becoming unattainable, their efforts futile. The most glamorous of these bourgeois aims, the foundation of an industrial dynasty, has in most countries become unattainable already, and even more modest ones are so difficult to attain that they may cease to be thought worth the struggle as the permanence of these conditions is being increasingly realized.

Considering the role of bourgeois motivation in the explanation of the economic history of the last two or three centuries, its smothering by the unfavorable reactions of society or its weakening by disuse no doubt constitutes a factor adequate to explain a flop in the capitalist process—should we ever observe it as a permanent phenomenon—and one that is much more important than any of those that are presented by the Theory of Vanishing Investment Opportunity. It is hence interesting to observe that that motivation not only is threatened by forces external to the bourgeois mind but that it also tends to die out from internal causes. There is of course close interdependence between the two. But we cannot get at the true diagnosis unless we try to disentangle them.

One of those "internal causes" . . . I have dubbed Evaporation of the Substance of Property. We have seen that, normally, the modern businessman, whether entrepreneur or mere managing administrator, is of the executive type. From the logic of his position he acquires something of the psychology of the salaried employee working in a bureaucratic organization. Whether a stockholder or not, his will to fight and to hold on is not and cannot be what it was with the man who knew ownership and its responsibilities in the fullblooded sense of those words. His system of values and his conception of duty undergo a profound change. Mere stockholders of course have ceased to count at all—quite independently of the clipping of their share by a regulating and taxing state. Thus the modern corporation, although the product of the capitalist process, socializes the bourgeois mind; it relentlessly narrows the scope of capitalist motivation; not only that, it will eventually kill its roots.[6]

Still more important however is another "internal cause," viz., the disintegration of the bourgeois family. The facts to which I am referring are too well known to need explicit statement. To men and women in modern capitalist societies, family life and parenthood mean less than they meant before and hence are less powerful molders of behavior; the rebellious son or daughter who professes contempt for "Victorian" standards is, however incorrectly, expressing an undeniable truth. The weight of these facts is not impaired by our inability to measure them statistically. . . . If in our statistical age readers insist on a statistical measure, the proportion of marriages that produce no children or only one child, though still inadequate to quantify the phenomenon I mean, might come as near as we can hope to come to indicating its numerical importance. The phenomenon by now extends, more or less, to all classes. But it first appeared in the bourgeois (and intellectual) stratum and its symptomatic as well as casual value for our purposes lies entirely there. It is wholly attributable to the rationalization of everything in life, which we have seen is one of the effects of capitalist evolution. In fact, it is but one of the results of the spread of that rationalization to the sphere of private life. All the other factors which are usually adduced in explanation can be readily reduced to that one.

As soon as men and women learn the utilitarian lesson and refuse to take for granted the traditional arrangements that their social environment makes for them, as soon as they acquire the habit

---

6. Many people will deny this. This is due to the fact that they derive their impression from past history and from the slogans generated by past history during which the institutional change brought about by the big corporation had not yet asserted itself. Also they may think of the scope which corporate business used to give for illegal satisfactions of the capitalist motivation. But that would cut my way: the fact that personal gain beyond salary and bonus cannot, in corporate business, be reaped by executives except by illegal or semi-illegal practices shows precisely that the structural idea of the corporation is averse to it.

of weighing the individual advantages and disadvantages of any prospective course of action—or, as we might also put it, as soon as they introduce into their private life a sort of inarticulate system of cost accounting—they cannot fail to become aware of the heavy personal sacrifices that family ties and especially parenthood entail under modern conditions and of the fact that at the same time, excepting the cases of farmers and peasants, children cease to be economic assets. These sacrifices do not consist only of the items that come within the reach of the measuring rod of money but comprise in addition an indefinite amount of loss of comfort, of freedom from care, and opportunity to enjoy alternatives of increasing attractiveness and variety—alternatives to be compared with joys of parenthood that are being subjected to a critical analysis of increasing severity. . . .

While the capitalist process, by virtue of the psychic attitudes it creates, progressively dims the values of family life and removes the conscientious inhibitions that an old moral tradition would have put in the way toward a different scheme of life, it at the same time implements the new tastes. As regards childlessness, capitalist inventiveness produces contraceptive devices of ever-increasing efficiency that overcome the resistance which the strongest impulse of man would otherwise have put up. As regards the style of life, capitalist evolution decreases the desirability of, and provides alternatives to, the bourgeois family home. . . .

In order to realize what all this means for the efficiency of the capitalist engine of production we need only recall that the family and the family home used to be the mainspring of the typically bourgeois kind of profit motive. Economists have not always given due weight to this fact. When we look more closely at their idea of the self-interest of entrepreneurs and capitalists we cannot fail to discover that the results it was supposed to produce are really not at all what one would expect from the rational self-interest of the detached individual or the childless couple who no longer look at the world through the windows of a family home. Consciously or unconsciously they analyzed the behavior of the man whose views and motives are shaped by such a home and who means to work and to save primarily for wife *and children.* As soon as these fade out from the moral vision of the businessman, we have a different kind of *homo oeconomicus* before us who cares for different things and acts in different ways. For him and from the standpoint of his individualistic utilitarianism, the behavior of that old type would in fact be completely irrational. He loses the only sort of romance and heroism that is left in the unromantic and unheroic civilization of capitalism—the heroism of *navigare necesse est, vivere non necesse est.*[7] And he loses the capitalist ethics that enjoins working for the future irrespective of whether or not one is going to harvest the crop oneself.

The last point may be put more tellingly. . . . The capitalist order entrusts the long-run interests of society to the upper strata of the bourgeoisie. They are really entrusted to the family motive operative in those strata. The bourgeoisie worked primarily in order to invest, and it was not so much a standard of consumption as a standard of accumulation that the bourgeoisie struggled for and tried to defend against governments that took the short-run view.[8] With the decline of the driving power supplied by the family motive, the businessman's time-horizon shrinks, roughly, to his life expectation. And he might now be less willing than he was to fulfill that function of earning, saving and investing even if he saw no reason to fear that the results would but swell his tax bills. He drifts into an anti-saving frame of mind and accepts with an increasing readiness anti-saving *theories* that are indicative of a short-run *philosophy*.

But anti-saving theories are not all that he accepts. With a different attitude to the concern he works for and with a different scheme of private life he tends to acquire a different view of the values and standards of the capitalist order of things. Perhaps the most striking feature of the picture is the extent to which the bourgeoisie, besides educating its own enemies, allows itself in turn to be educated by them. It absorbs the slogans of current radicalism and seems quite willing to undergo a process of conversion to a creed hostile to its very existence. Haltingly and grudgingly it concedes in part the implications of that creed. This would be most astonishing and indeed very hard to explain were it not for the fact that the typical bourgeois is rapidly losing faith in his own creed. And this again becomes fully understandable as soon as we realize that the social conditions which account for its emergence are passing.

This is verified by the very characteristic manner in which particular capitalist interests and the bourgeoisie as a whole behave when facing direct attack. They talk and plead–or hire people to do it for them; they snatch at every chance of compromise; they are ever ready to give in; they never put up a fight under the flag of their own ideals and interests–in this country there was no real resistance anywhere against the imposition of crushing financial burdens during the last decade or against labor legislation incompatible with the effective management of industry. . . . I am far from overestimating the political power of either big business or the bourgeoisie in general. Moreover, I am prepared to make large allowances for cowardice. But still, means of defense were not entirely lacking as yet and history is full of examples of the success of small groups who, believing in their cause, were resolved to stand by their guns. The only explanation for the meekness we observe is that the bourgeois order no longer makes any sense to the bourgeoisie itself and that, when all is said and nothing is done, it does not really care.

Thus the same economic process that undermines the position of the bourgeoisie by decreasing the importance of the functions of entrepreneurs and capitalists, by breaking up protective strata and institutions, by creating an atmosphere of hostility, also decomposes the motor forces of capitalism from within. Nothing else shows so well that the capitalist order not only rests on props made of extra-capitalist material but also derives its energy from extra-capitalist patterns of behavior which at the same time it is bound to destroy.

7. "Seafaring is necessary, living is not necessary." Inscription on an old house in Bremen.

8. It has been said that in economic matters "the state can take the longer view." But excepting certain matters outside of party politics such as conservation of natural resources, it hardly ever does.

PAUL A. SAMUELSON

Institute Professor of Economics, Massachusetts Institute of Technology.

Paul Samuelson is one of the world's most respected economists. In 1970 he received the Nobel Prize in Economics for his theoretical contributions to the subject. In addition, thousands of college students have cut their teeth on his principles textbook (first published in 1948), which constitutes a readable synthesis of neoclassical and Keynesian theory.

The article reprinted here is a liberal's response to the proposition of Hayek and Friedman that competitive capitalism is a necessary condition for personal freedom. Friedman's position is stated in the excerpt from *Capitalism and Freedom* (1962) reprinted in the conservative section of this volume. Hayek's views are similar. His most influential work, *The Road to Serfdom* (1944), was written against the backdrop of the 1930s depression and the second world war, both of which greatly accelerated the pace of governmental planning in the economy. Hayek feared that the movement toward central planning would lead to totalitarianism. Even though the leading advocates of planning may be men of good will, he warned, "from the saintly and single-minded individual to the fanatic is often but a step." Hayek felt that even though limited planning might seem justified in some situations, it should be avoided because of the planners' irresistible tendency to extend its scope—the ultimate result being the complete loss of individual and political freedoms.

Both Friedman and Hayek draw on history to show the connection between capitalism and freedom. But the argument that economic freedom leads to political freedom is not solidly confirmed by historical evidence. It might, for instance, be claimed that some degree of political freedom (at least for some classes) permitted and facilitated the emergence of a capitalist market economy. In fact, in nineteenth-century England, as democracy spread to larger segments of the population, it began to place limits on economic freedom and ushered in the policies of the welfare state. Thus the converse of the conservative position might be true, i.e.: political freedom might be a necessary condition for economic freedom, or, as political freedom expands, market freedom contracts.

In the article that follows, Samuelson questions Hayek's contention that a reduction in economic freedom leads a country down the road to serfdom. Is the government more involved in economic life in Sweden and England than in America? Yes, says Samuelson. But does that mean that the political freedoms of Swedish and English citizens have been abridged? Evidently Samuelson does not think that this is the case. Like most liberals, he feels that it is possible to separate the economic and political spheres and to control the probable outcomes. Such a separation would make it possible to combine increased planning with democracy. The case for competition (or the market), then, in Samuelson's words, "rests on the technocratic level of efficiency, not on the ethical level of freedom and individualism." On the latter issues, he adds, one cannot avoid coercion in a modern urban society. It is just possible that the degree of coercion is lessened through the intervention of governments, since it is likely that in any society where large groups of people interact, the freedom of one man can infringe upon the freedom of others.

The questions raised by Samuelson and his protagonists, Friedman and Hayek, on the relationship between capitalism and freedom and the proper role of the government in a market economy are among the most perplexing facing the social scientist today. Perhaps this is because they do not easily encourage scientific analysis, or perhaps it is because they are questions that we do not ask often enough.

R R

From

PERSONAL FREEDOMS AND ECONOMIC FREEDOMS IN THE MIXED ECONOMY

(1964)

. . . As a prelude to discussing the empirical and analytical relations between business and personal freedoms (which is roughly the distinction between economic and political freedoms), I might usefully give some reflections on the nature of individualism, liberty, freedom, coercion, and the marketplace.[1]

HOW DIVINE THE NATURAL ORDER?

Adam Smith, our patron saint, was critical of state interference of the pre-nineteenth-century type. And make no mistake about it; Smith was right. Most of the interventions into economic life by the state were then harmful both to prosperity and freedom. What Smith said needed to be said. In fact, much of what Smith said still needs to be said; good intentions by government are not enough; acts have consequences that must be taken into account, if good is to follow.

One hundred percent individualists concentrate on the purple passage in Adam Smith, where he discerns an Invisible Hand that leads each selfish individual to contribute to the best public good. Smith had a point; but he could not have earned a passing mark in a Ph.D. oral examination by explaining just what that point was. Until this century, his followers—such as Bastiat—thought that the doctrine of the Invisible

1. Some of the following thoughts appeared in two recent lectures. Since I do not believe in elegant variations, some of the words that follow will be in the same sequence as is published elsewhere. I own to no sense of self-plagiarism since, as indicated there, many of those words were stolen from the present research investigation.

Hand meant (1) that it produced maximum feasible total satisfaction, somehow defined; or (2) that it showed that anything resulting from the voluntary agreements of uncoerced individuals must make them better (or best) off in some important sense.

Both of these interpretations, which are still held by many modern libertarians, are wrong. They neglect the axiom concerning the ethical merits of the preexisting distribution of land, property, and genetic and acquired utilities. This is not the place for a technical discussion of economic principles, so I shall be very brief and cryptic in showing this.

First, suppose that some ethical observer, such as Jesus, Buddha, or for that matter, John Dewey or Aldous Huxley, were to examine whether the total of social utility (as that ethical observer scores the deservingness of the poor and rich, saintly and sinning individuals) was actually maximized by 1860 or 1964 laissez-faire. He might decide that a tax placed upon yachts whose proceeds go to cheapen the price of insulin to the needy increased the total of utility. Could Adam Smith prove him wrong? Could Bastiat? I think not.

Of course, they might say that there is no point in trying to compare different individuals' utilities, because they are incommensurable and can no more be added together than can apples and oranges. But if recourse is made to this argument, then the doctrine that the Invisible Hand maximizes total utility of the universe has already been discarded. If they admit that the Invisible Hand will truly maximize total social utility *provided the state intervenes so as to make the initial distribution of dollar votes ethically proper,* then they have abandoned the libertarian's position that individuals are not to be coerced, even by taxation.

In connection with the second interpretation that anything resulting from voluntary agreements is in some sense, *ipso facto,* optimal, we can reply by pointing out that when I make a purchase from a monopolistic octopus, that is a voluntary act; I can always go without Alka Seltzer or aluminum or nylon or whatever product you think is produced by a monopolist. Mere voluntarism, therefore, is not the root merit of the doctrine of the Invisible Hand;[2] what is important about it is the system of checks and balances that prevails under perfect competition, and its measure of validity is at the technocratic level of efficiency, not at the ethical level of freedom and individualism. That this is so can be seen from the fact that such socialists as Oskar Lange and A. P. Lerner have advocated channeling the Invisible Hand to the task of organizing a socialistic society efficiently.

THE CASH NEXUS

Just as there is a sociology of family life and of politics, there is also a sociology of individualistic competition. It need not be a rich one. Ask not your neighbor's name; enquire only for his numerical schedules of supply and demand. Under perfect competition, no buyer need face a seller. Haggling in a Levantine bazaar is a sign of less-than-perfect competition.

These economic contacts between atomistic individuals may seem a little chilly or, to use the language of wine tasting, "dry." This impersonality has its good side. Negroes in the South learned long ago that their money was welcome in local department stores. Money can be liberating. It corrodes the cake of custom. It does talk. In the West Indies there is a saying, "Money whitens." Sociologists know that replacing the rule of status by the rule of contract loses something in warmth; it also gets rid of some of the bad fire of olden times.

Impersonality of market relations has another advantage, as was brought home to many "liberals" in the McCarthy era of American political life. Suppose it were efficient for the government to be the one big employer. Then if, for good or bad, a person becomes in bad odor with government, he is dropped from employment and is put on a black list. He really has no place to go then. The thought of such a dire fate must in the course of time discourage that freedom of expression of opinion that individualists most favor.[3]

Many of the people who were unjustly dropped by the federal government in that era were able to land jobs in small-scale private industry. I say small-scale industry, because large corporations are likely to be chary of hiring names that appear on anybody's black list. What

---

2. Milton Friedman, *Capitalism and Freedom,* University of Chicago Press, Chicago, 1962, Chapters 1 and 2 seem grossly defective in these matters. In the first chapter, he regards market behavior as optimal merely because it is voluntary, save for the single passage: ". . . perhaps the most difficult problems arise from monopoly—which inhibits effective freedom by denying individuals alternatives to the particular exchange" and promises to discuss this matter in more detail in the next chapter. It turns out there that "Exchange is truly voluntary only when nearly equivalent alternatives exist." Why this new element of alternatives? Because, as I point out, *perfect* competition is efficient in the Pareto-optimality sense, and it is this property that modern economists have *proved* optimal (and interesting) about such competition.

Libertarians, like Hayek and von Mises, would be annoyed to learn that their case stands or falls on its nearness to "perfect competition." Unlike George J. Stigler and Milton Friedman, neither of these two men has remotely the same views on perfect competition as do modern economists generally. What libertarians have in common is the hope that departures from perfect competition are not too extreme in our society; Friedman, himself, has apparently come full circle to the view that public regulation of "monopoly" and state regulation of "monopoly" are greater evils than letting well enough alone. I do not feel competent to report on the algebraic degree of his agreement with Stigler and others who put considerable emphasis on antitrust action. [There appears to me to be a technical flaw in the view of Friedman and A. P. Lerner that regulated or publicly owned monopolies should always (as a matter of principle as well as pragmatic expediency) be permitted to have competition from free entrants. The mathematics of the increasing-returns situation admits of no such theorem; it is simply false game theory and bilateral monopoly theory, which asserts that letting one more viable person in the game must lead to a "better" result in any of the conventional senses of better. To make the Scottish Airlines keep up unprofitable schedules and at the same time permit a free enterpriser to make a profit partially at the regulated lines' expense can easily result in dead-weight loss to society under the usual feasibility conditions. The crime of legally abolishing the Pony Express because it competed with the Post Office would have to be examined on all its complicated demerits.]

3. F. A. Hayek, *The Road to Serfdom,* University of Chicago Press, Chicago, 1944, p. 119, aptly presents the following quotations from Lenin (1917) and Trotsky (1937):

> The whole of society will have become a single office and a single factory with equality of work and equality of pay.
>
> In a country where the sole employer is the State, opposition means death by slow starvation. The old principle: who does not work shall not eat, has been replaced by a new one: who does not obey shall not eat.

M. A. Adelman in Freeman, *op. cit.,* p. 295, says:

> . . . It has probably become clearer in the last ten years that the chief objection to socialism is not strictly economics but lies rather in its startling resemblance to the old-fashioned mining town where the one employer was also the landlord, the government, the school, etc., with the vital difference that there was a world outside the town which afforded means of escape for a few and, in time, of release for all.

See also the valuable words on this matter in Friedman, *op. cit.,* pp. 20–21.

David McCord Wright, *Democracy and Progress,* Macmillan, New York, 1948, p. 41, has observed: "Main Street creates the very diffusion of authority which protected them [the intellectuals] from Main Street."

about people who were justly dropped as security risks or as members of political organizations now deemed to be criminally subversive? Many of them also found jobs in the anonymity of industry.

Many conservative people, who think that such men should not remain in sensitive government work or in public employ at all, will still feel that they should not be hounded into starvation. Few want for this country the equivalent of Czarist Russia's Siberia or Stalinist Russia's Siberia either. It is hard to tell on the Chicago Board of Trade the difference between the wheat produced by Republican or Democratic farmers, by teetotalers or drunkards, Theosophists or Logical Positivists. I must confess that this is a feature of a competitive system that I find attractive.

Still, I must not overstress this point. A mixed economy in a society where people are by custom *tolerant* of differences in opinion may provide greater personal freedom and security of expression than does a purer price economy where people are less tolerant. Thus, in Scandinavia and Great Britain civil servants have, in fact, not lost their jobs when parties with a new philosophy come into power. In 1953, the Eisenhower Administration "cleaned house" in many government departments for reasons unconnected with McCarthyism. In 1951, when the Tories came to power, they deliberately recruited Fabian socialists to the civil service! Business freedoms may be fewer in those countries, but an excommunist probably meets with more tolerance from employers there.

This raises a larger question. Why should there be a perverse empirical relation between the degree to which public opinion is, in fact, tolerant and the degree to which it relies on free markets? In our history, the days of most rugged individualism—the Gilded Age and the 1920's—seem to have been the ages least tolerant of dissenting opinion.[4]

FALLACY OF FREEDOM ALGEBRA

I must raise some questions about the notion that absence of government means increase in "freedom." Is freedom simply a quantifiable magnitude, as much libertarian discussion seems to presume? Traffic lights coerce me and limit my freedom. Yet in the midst of a traffic jam on the unopen road, was I really "free" before there were lights? And has the algebraic total of freedom, for me or the representative motorist or the group as a whole, been increased or decreased by the introduction of well-engineered stop lights? Stop lights, you know, are also go lights.

Whatever may have been true on Turner's frontier, the modern city is crowded. Individualism and anarchy will lead to friction. We now have to coordinate and cooperate. Where cooperation is not fully forthcoming, we must introduce upon ourselves coercion. When we introduce the traffic light, we have, although the arch individualist may not like the new order, by cooperation and coercion created for ourselves greater freedom.

The principle of unbridled freedom has been abandoned; it is now just a question of haggling about the terms. On the one hand, few will deny that it is a bad thing for one man, or a few men, to impose their wills on the vast majority of mankind, particularly when that involves terrible cruelty and terrible inefficiency. Yet where does one draw the line? At a 51 percent majority vote? Or, should there be no action taken that cannot command unanimous agreement—a position toward which such modern exponents of libertarian liberalism as Professor Milton Friedman are slowly evolving. Unanimous agreement? Well, virtually unanimous agreement, whatever that will come to mean.

The principle of unanimity is, of course, completely impractical. Aside from its practical inapplicability, the principle of unanimity is theoretically faulty. It leads to contradictory and intransitive decisions. By itself, it argues that just as society should not move from laissez-faire to planning because there will always be at least one objector, so society should never move from planning to freedom because there will always be at least one objector. Like standing friction, it sticks you where you are. It favors the status quo. And the status quo is certainly not to the liking of arch individualists. When you have painted yourself into a corner, what can you do? You can redefine the situation, and I predicted some years ago that there would come to be defined a privileged status quo, a set of natural rights involving individual freedoms, which alone requires unanimity before it can be departed from.[5]

At this point the logical game is up. The case for "complete freedom" has been begged, not deduced. So long as full disclosure is made, it is no crime to assume your ethical case. But will your product sell? Can you persuade others to accept your axiom, when it is in conflict with certain other desirable axioms?

PROPERTY AND HUMAN RIGHTS

Closely related to ethical evaluation of business activity for its own sake are ethical attitudes towards the rights of property. Today, demagogues never tire of emphasizing the primacy of human over property rights; this is not an accident but rather a recognition that such sentiments evoke an increasingly resonant response from modern public opinion.

Today when we defend the rights of property, we often do so in the name of the *individual* rights of those who own property or hope one day to do so. The tides of modern politics pay little regard to the older view that property in all its prerequisites is a natural right and that whenever the democratic action of even 99 44/100 percent of the electorate limits property rights in any degree, then an act of theft has taken place. Instead, the effective defense of property rights consists largely of specifying the inefficiencies that will result at the level of means

4. Years ago someone asked me, "Why is it that economists who are most libertarian in economic philosophy tend to be personally more intolerant than the average and less concerned with civil liberties and such matters?" I replied, "Is this true?" He said, "Look at the monolithic character of the three most libertarian departments of economics." I said, "The three departments most radical or anything else can hardly be expected to show average tolerance of differences." Our conversation broke off. However, in the last dozen years I have been alert to observe the attitudes and actions of economic libertarians in connection with nonmarket issues—teachers' oaths, passport squabbles, and the like. I am sorry to have to report that my friend had a point (although there are one or two persons who are residuals from his regression).

5. A friend of mine is a justly famous expert on law. He has participated in world conferences, here and behind the Iron Curtain, dealing with such weighty concepts as "the Rule of Law." Apparently, the Russians do not view the matter in quite his way. I am not sure I do. After listening to his view, an eminent judge asked him, "Was slavery in Virginia in 1859 contrary to your 'Rule of Law'?" My friend squirmed. Finally, he replied, "Yes, really. Because the law permitting slavery was essentially a *bad* law." I congratulated my friend on his good luck: how fortunate that he had happened to be born in just those few years of the globe's history when *the* Rule of Law (about equivalent to that approved by a conservative New-Deal type) happened to be in bloom. Libertarians like Hayek are on the same boat, but they want it to stop at a different port; Gladstone's age turns out to have been the nearest approach to *the* (I mean Hayek's) Rule of Law. F. A. Hayek, *op. cit.*, Chapter 6.

and mechanisms from their impairment—the paralysis of risk taking, the effects upon saving, efforts and incentives; the certain or uncertain ruin that must follow wherever taxation exceeds 10 (or 90) percent of national income.

All this may be true enough. But for some people it does not go far enough. It is a little like the saying: "Honesty is the best policy." Or, "The golden rule is good business." Beyond the level of expediency, there can be thought to be human property rights at the ethical level in the sense that the individual's property is to be taxed or affected by state action only in an orderly manner, within the framework of constitutional procedures and with "due process" being legally observed.

As a bulwark to historical property rights, this is not saying very much. To say that the electorate cannot arbitrarily do something to one millionaire without doing the same thing to another (essentially similar) millionaire provides little protection to the class of all millionaires, some of whom may even have amassed their millions at a time when it seemed reasonable *not* to anticipate policies of heavy income or capital taxation. Whether we approve or disapprove, we should face squarely the fact that neoclassical economic-welfare policies—which hold that after the ethically desirable distribution of income has been properly determined by democratic decision, a pricing system is to organize and allocate production in response to individuals' purchases—provide little protection to ancient property rights.

PERSONAL LIBERTIES AND RIGHTS

This makes it all the more important to study the question of the relation of property rights and market institutions to essential individual freedoms and liberties. These were enumerated by Lord Beveridge in his *Full Employment in a Free Society* as

> . . . freedom of worship, speech, writing, study and teaching; freedom of assembly and association for political and other purposes, including the bringing about of a peaceful change of the governing authority; freedom of a choice of occupation; and freedom in the management of a personal income . . . including freedom to decide to spend now and save so as to have the power of spending later . . . it being recognized that none of these freedoms can be exercised irresponsibly. . . .
>
> The list of essential liberties given above does not include liberty of a private citizen to own means of production and to employ other citizens in operating them at a wage. Whether private ownership of means of production to be operated by others is a good economic device or not, it must be judged *as a device.* [The italics are mine.][6]

To Americans this British view is interesting, because the distinction is made clear-cut between (1) human individual civil liberties or freedoms and (2) ethical evaluations of property rights and of business activity for their own sakes. So-called diehard conservatives will not alone be shocked by the distinction. At the extreme left, violent exception will also be taken to the view that "political democracy" can exist in the absence of what is called "economic or industrial democracy." Both extremes seem to argue that the essential human freedoms are inseparable from the institutional framework under which production is carried on. But, of course, they believe this in diametrically opposite senses; the extreme conservatives at the ethical level link human freedoms with relatively unhampered free enterprise, whereas the extreme radicals proclaim that human freedoms are empty and meaningless in the absence of "industrial democracy" (in one or another of the many senses in which the last two words are used).

From the standpoint of pure logic, I believe that the two concepts are conceptually distinct at the purely ethical level of ends. Moreover, whatever its pragmatic wisdom, there appears to be nothing inherently illogical (whatever its wisdom) in the ethical belief that individual human liberties have an ethical primacy over the freedoms associated with property and commercial activity.

However, this brings us to a quite different, but possibly important, question: "Granted that human rights are to be accorded ethical primacy over property rights, is it not true that human rights can only flourish and be preserved in a society that organizes its economic activity on the basis of relatively free private enterprise?" Many economic libertarians strongly proclaim an affirmative answer to this question. Friedrich Hayek's *The Road to Serfdom* (1944) is an eloquent attempt to read this same empirical law in the tea leaves of history. Frank Knight and Milton Friedman have enunciated interesting views along the same line. It is ironical, but not incriminating, that this is a conservative's variant of the strong Marxian doctrine that economic relationships allegedly determine political relationships.

As stated, this is not at all a philosophical question. Nor is it very much a question of economics. It is primarily a political, sociological, and anthropological question. Basically, it is an empirical question of inductive extrapolation or forecasting rather than one of consistent logical deduction from universally true *a priori* premises. And unfortunately, the patterns of history have not been optimally designed to perform the controlled experiments that would enable us to make either certainty or probability inferences on the hypothesis in question.

It will be plain that I have little confidence in emphatic generalizations concerning the empirical linkage of human political rights with any one economic system. Evidence—as I understand this term—is not at hand to validate strong inferences; and such evidence as may exist has not, to my knowledge, been carefully brought together anywhere and sifted to bring out the degree of our knowledge and lack of knowledge. In a world where economists cannot even accurately predict national income one year ahead or identify the demand elasticity for a single commodity, I find it somewhat *simpliste* to think that economists can arrive at confident answers to an infinitely more complex and important question, resting primarily on noneconomic data. Certainly the degree of confidence and emphasis with which judgments on this matter are proclaimed seems to weaken rather than strengthen one's trust in their validity. I may add as a digression that I greatly resent the prevailing tendency to regard the broad questions of social development as being too important to be left to mere judicious scholarly investigation and to handle them instead by the transcendental poetic talents of a Toynbee or Spengler.

THE LIMITED NATURE OF INDIVIDUAL POLITICAL LIBERTIES

The above discussion has left civil liberties almost completely emasculated of intrinsic economic content. The doctrine "a man's home is his castle" is to apply to rented as well as self-owned homes. But some of the methods and tools used

6. Norton, New York, 1945, pp. 21-23.

to analyze theoretical economic concepts do have an application in this field of political theory.

For one thing, basic civil rights of the individual are shot through with "external effects." The ideal frontier community never existed in which freedom for the individual meant that he could live on his acre of land exactly as he wished, leaving others to live as they chose on theirs. Certainly today, the right of one man to speak what he wishes conditions the rights of another man to listen to what he wishes. The right of one man to "fair" consideration for a job has implications for the right of another man to "discriminate" as to whom he shall hire. The right of one group to preach nondemocratic principles has effects on the future existence of democracy itself. In the pursuit of happiness, we all interact.

Once we have recognized these external aspects of individual rights, we must recognize that precious little is being said in the familiar qualification that people are free so long as they do not inhibit the freedom of others. Any degree of limitation on freedoms can be rationalized by this formula.

Dogmatic absolutes being thus ruled out, democratic society is left in the position of pragmatically attempting to choose among partial evils so as to preserve as much as possible of human liberties and freedoms. Nor is it only in time of war and siege that it may become necessary to sacrifice some aspects of democratic freedoms in order to prevent losing more important aspects. Those who abandon the unproved faith that democratic individualism *is by its nature viable under all conditions* must compromise with evil at every turn. And it is not at all unlikely that they will end up killing, in the name of its salvation, much of what they wish to save, perhaps in these "scorched earth" operations killing even more than realistically had to be sacrificed.

FINAL QUESTIONS

Consider the little that is known concerning the interrelations between human rights and the organization of economic activity in the U.S.A. (1870, 1920, 1964) and the U.K.; the German Empire, the Weimar Republic, and the Third Reich; Norway, Sweden, Denmark, Australia, and New Zealand; pre- and post-1917 Russia; Italy, Czechoslovakia, and the Balkans–to say nothing of China, Arabia, Fiji, and non-Western cultures. Then ask ourselves what simple truths can be confidently inferred.

For a quite different appraisal of these same matters consider, in the cited Friedman book, the first chapter, "The Relation Between Economic Freedom and Political Freedom." A few quotations cannot do him justice but can give the flavor of the divergence of his view from mine.

> The citizen of Great Britain, who after World War II was not permitted to spend his vacation in the United States because of exchange control, was being deprived of an *essential* freedom no less than the citizen of the United States, who was denied the opportunity to spend his vacation in Russia because of his political views. . . .
>
> The citizen of the United States who is compelled by law to devote something like 10 percent of *his* income to the purchase of a particular kind of retirement contract, administered by the government, is being deprived of a corresponding part of his personal freedom (page 8). [My italics.]
>
> So is the man who would like to exchange some of his goods with, say, a Swiss for a watch but is prevented from doing so by a quota. . . .
>
> Historical evidence speaks with a single voice on the relation between political free-

dom and a free market. I know of no example in time or place of a society that has been marked by a large measure of political freedom, and that has not also used something comparable to a free market to organize the bulk of economic activity (page 9).

Economists love diagrams. Figures 1 and 2 plot economic freedom (as if it were measurable as a scalar) on the horizontal axes, and political freedom (as if that too were separately measurable as a scalar) on the vertical axes. What I regard as the grossly oversimplified views are shown in Figure 1. Social reform (moving "west") inevitably plunges society ("southward") into serfdom. Hayek does not tell us what his predicted delay period is, but since he formulated his thesis as early as 1938 (and using the simplifying assumption that we are not unknowingly now in serfdom), the mechanism must involve lags of more than a quarter of a century. Friedman also believes in strong positive correlation between Y and X but indicates that economic freedom is a necessary but not a sufficient condition for political freedom. (Sidney and Beatrice Webb, particularly in their final honeymoon stage of infatuation with Stalin's Russia, would relabel the axes as X = Economic Democracy—whatever that means—and Y = Political Democracy. The U.K. and U.S.A. they would place up in the northwest and, except *in extremis* of infatuation, would put Russia in the southeast. As Fabians, they would maneuver the U.K. eastward.)

Figure 2 represents the more relevant question. Will a little more of the welfare state push the U.S.A. westward and necessarily southward? For years libertarians have been challenged to explain what appears to most observers to be the greater political freedoms and tolerances that prevail in Scandinavia than in America. In Norway, a professor may be a communist; a communist may sit by right on the Board of the Central Bank or as an Alternate Board member. The B.B.C. and Scandinavian airwaves seem, if anything, more catholic in their welcome to speakers of divergent views than was true in McCarthy America or is true now. In 1939, I was told that none of this would last; active government economic policy had to result in loss of civil liberties and personal freedoms. One still waits. Figure 2 does not represent my informed evaluation of the facts but merely poses the problem provocatively.

These are subjects that need serious empirical study, not strong *a priori* utterances or casual travelers' anecdotes.

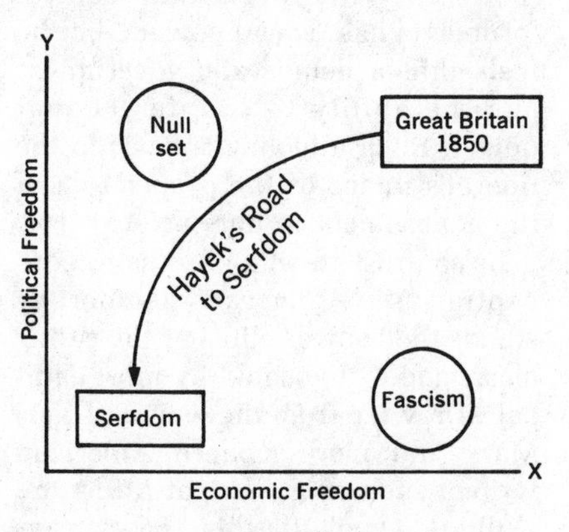

Figure 1.

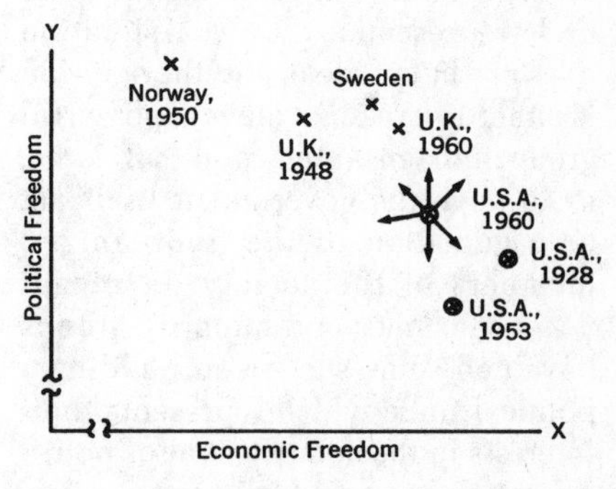

Figure 2.

MICHAEL D. REAGAN

Professor of Political Science, University of California at Riverside.

The article by Michael Reagan illustrates two important and interrelated liberal tenets. The first is that in a capitalist democracy it is possible to separate political affairs from the dominance of economic power, and that the actions of the government can thus be made to reflect the interest of the people. The second is that the government has expanded its role in the economy in the last few decades in order to fulfill those needs of society that the private sector could not or would not. The thrust for growth in the public sector thus emanates from the demands of a general population living in a changing social and economic climate.

The first point relates to the liberal's pluralistic conception of democracy. This model says that political decisions represent a compromise between various interest groups in the society. These groups compete with each other for power and press their demands upon federal, state, and local governments. Policymaking is thus seen as a democratic process in which all have a voice. If some interests are underrepresented, the actual situation does not fit the ideal, and the solution is either to organize the less powerful group into an active political force, or to have the government itself act as a guardian of the unorganized members of the society. In recent years consumer and minority groups have had some success in building a political force which represents their interests in the competition for political action (or possibly inaction). Presumably the greater the number of interests represented, the greater the degree of democracy.

The first section of Reagan's article presents one version of the pluralistic democracy in America. As he sees it, power resides in two broadly defined groups, one economic or property-based and the other based on the popular democratic power of the people. A basic assumption is that in a political democracy, the government represents the interests of the people, providing an avenue through which they can exercise their influence. If the power to shape society is left to the market (laissez-faire), then economic interests will dominate. However, democracy has the ability to overcome property-based power without resorting to the elimination of private ownership of the means of production. Reagan considers it "fortunate for American democracy that public allocation of 'privately owned' resources can serve the same social ends [as nationalization]." He seems to agree with Marx that capital [property] has "social power," but he feels that a democratic government has the ability to counteract that power. Such a feeling is basic to the liberal's image of the proper role of the government in our society.

In contrast to this pluralistic conception of American democracy stands the "power elite" or the ruling class model advocated by most radicals. Drawing from the works of Karl Marx and more modern American writers such as C. Wright Mills and William Domhoff, this theory says that in a capitalist society, government policy serves the interests of the propertied class or of its corporate elite. In the words of one of its proponents, David Gordon:

> The State, in the radical view, operates ultimately to serve the interests of the controlling class in a class society. Since the "capitalist class" fundamentally controls capitalist societies, the State functions in those societies to serve that class. It does so either directly, by directing services only to members of that class, or indirectly, by helping preserve the institutions which support and maintain the power of that class. In the United States, government subsidy of defense firms provides a clear example of the former, while government support of and control over an educational system which fundamentally supports the "system-defining" institutions illustrates the latter.[1]

The radical view of the State is expressed in the articles by Marx, Paul Baran and Paul Sweezy, and Daniel R. Fusfeld in this volume.

The second part of Reagan's article provides a liberal's explanation of why the public sector has grown in size and power during the twentieth century. As liberals see it, the economic policies of the government should be designed to strengthen the operation of market forces, where they produce desirable results, and to modify the operation of those forces where the results are deemed undesirable. The provision of a stable legal and social framework and the maintenance of competition through antitrust laws are examples of government activities that facilitate the operation of the market system. The establishment of social welfare programs, the production of public goods and services, the adjustment of prices to reflect social costs or benefits, and the controlling of inflation and unemployment are all examples of how the government has modified the operation of laissez-faire capitalism. Whether these policies have been at least moderately successful, whether they reflect the true needs of society, and whether they are activities that only the public sector can perform are issues that pervade the literature of all economists, conservative, radical, and liberal alike.

1. David M. Gordon, ed., *Problems in Political Economy: An Urban Perspective* (Lexington, Mass.: D. C. Heath & Co., 1971), p. 6.

R R

From

THE MANAGED ECONOMY

PROPERTY, POWER, AND THE PUBLIC ALLOCATION OF RESOURCES

If wealth and economic power were fairly evenly distributed among the population, the achievement of political equality would not require an attempt to disengage political from economic power. But, [has an] effective separation of the political and economic spheres . . . been achieved?

[Some flatly assert] that economic and political power cannot be separated. An equally strong assertion to the contrary has been made by E. E. Schattschneider: "American democracy was an early attempt to split the political power from the economic power. This is the great American experiment. . . . The divorce of the two power systems is perhaps the greatest American political achievement." The picture Schattschneider presents is of continuing tension between two power systems: the equalitarian, democratic system of politics, in which numbers are important, and the concentrated, unequal system of business, in which wealth is the important factor. The function of democracy, it follows, is to counterbalance the undemocratic force of industry. As Schattschneider sees it, we do not want the government-business conflict resolved; we want it perpetuated because "liberty is a by-product of competing power systems." Thus, it is not a case of the political force (voting strength) having become dominant over economic power, but of an equilibrium of two power systems. . . .

. . . While political democracy creates an opening for the exercise of popular power, it does not of itself bring about that exercise. The formal power of democracy was as great in 1880 as in 1936; the difference in effective power was tremendous. One way of expressing the reason behind the difference is to say that government had not yet, in the earlier period, taken on the function ascribed to it by Schattschneider: it had not yet used its power to countervail the economic power of business.

The nightwatchman, non-interventionist state left to economic power the decisions that shaped society. But this did not have to be, and, beginning with the Sherman Antitrust Act, the creation of the Interstate Commerce Commission, and the passage of the income tax amendment, there has been a sporadic, yet cumulative, development of the national government, and especially the Presidency, as the people's decision-maker. The limitations of market forces as a system of social control having become apparent, some decisions formerly left to the holders of economic power have been wrested away and placed in the hands of people accountable to the public. Slow and incomplete as this transfer of decisional power from the economic to the political arena has been, it has progressed far enough to make the size and scope of the public sector of economic control a leading issue of our time. The direct social power of property diminishes in direct ratio to the extent that this transfer takes place. As Daniel Bell has written, "In a managed economy, politics, not dollars, will determine what is to be produced, [and] the intervention of the government will not only sharpen pressure group identifications, but also force each to adopt an ideology which can justify its claims, and which can square with some concept of 'national interest.' " Within this framework, the outstanding political development of our time may have been the emergence in the 'thirties of a liberal-labor counter-ideology that provides continuing support for governmental action in the interests of the majority.

In the article just quoted, Bell speaks of the shift in decision-making from the market to politics as constituting a "basic and fundamental shift in the relations of economic power to political power." This is the kind of shift that socialist doctrine has long envisaged, yet Bell is not writing about a process of nationalization—that is, the government's taking legal title to factories—but of a process of public allocation of resources within an economy still having a private ownership framework. Although some British Laborites have blamed the failure of the postwar nationalization program to produce any basic change in social power on an insufficient amount of nationalization, Bell's analysis suggests that nationalization may be unnecessary. A combination of progressive taxes and public control over major investment and allocation decisions, might serve to strip private ownership of its social power just as effectively as compensated nationalization could ever do.

Because nationalization as such is so obviously anathema to the American ideology, while the exercise of popular political power is not, it is fortunate for American democracy that public allocation of "privately owned" resources can serve the same social ends. Let the self-appointed guardians of the free-enterprise way of life keep the familiar forms; that will simply make easier the task of infusing them with a new substantive meaning! The Employment Act of 1946 is a case in point: its avowal that government must keep the economy going constitutes a basic rejection of capitalist ideology's premise of automaticity. Yet, because it did not affect the legal bases of property ownership, it was assimilated into most businessmen's expectations without great difficulty. The same will be true with the next major step: the transfer from private to public hands of decisions that determine the rate of economic growth.

. . . We can then say that democracy's power to overcome property-based power rests on a tripod of which one leg is universal suffrage, the second is economic security obtained through collective bargaining and public policy, and the third is the developing transfer of economic decisions affecting the whole society from business to government control. Property itself may not be eliminated, but its social power can be circumscribed.

Thus, we have seen that property has not become unrelated to power—not by any means. But it is not the only variable in the equation of social power. Its inequalitarian tendency is forced to compete with the equalitarian thrust of political democracy, and the latter is not necessarily the weaker force in the long run. Laments for the Jeffersonian economic structure of the early 1800s are unnecessary and irrelevant. New forms of economic security are being and can be achieved, and the system is open to the demands of democracy. Our efforts should go less toward protesting against the inevitable and more toward creating an effective institutional base for democratic action to strengthen and concentrate popular power as the industrial corporation has done for property power.

THE MYTH OF LAISSEZ-FAIRE

Perhaps the greatest American economic myth is the belief that private enterprise is self-sustaining, that the only political requirement for a healthy economy is a policy of laissez-faire. It is small wonder, given this belief, that every increase in the scope of governmental economic activity is met with cries of alarm. Yet is is easily demonstrated that the freest economy imaginable would still require a considerable range of governmental actions and institutions, supporting as well as regulatory. As Wilbert E. Moore has written, "competition without rules is a contradiction in terms," and social controls are necessary "not only to maintain order in an economy which is only nominally self-regulating, but also to ensure the consistency of economic organization with such values as individual health and familial stability."

If government really left the economy alone, there would be no system of competition but Hobbes's war of each against all. Without governmental enforcement of contracts, businessmen would not dare to make them. If government did not protect property, each firm would have to hire its own police force—or even an army. Without a money system backed by government, we would be reduced to crude barter or constantly subjected to ruination by extreme fluctuations in the value of private money substitutes. Without governmental mechanisms for adjustment of disputes between employers and employees, our industrial relations would be patterned on the bloody model of the coal fields of 1900.

Government also provides organizational forms to fit business needs: proprietorships, partnerships, and the privilege of incorporation which vests the firm with immortality and the investor with limited liability. It develops procedures for bankruptcy and reorganizations, to minimize the economic and social losses of business failure. It rewards invention by giving it privileged economic status through the patent system. It collects and disseminates knowledge in support of business operations, as in research reports on technological developments and market opportunities, and it establishes standards essential to common exchange: weights and measures, grading, and labelling.

It is inconceivable that any economy could long endure in the absence of these governmentally provided supports. Certainly the modern, interdependent, complex industrialized economy could not. And businessmen recognize this, at least implicitly, for one does not hear them calling for repeal of the kinds of "intervention" mentioned to this point. What they object to is not intervention as such, but intervention which is regulatory rather than promotional. That is, it is not principle but self-interest which provides the rationale for their position.

The real question of government's role focuses on those activities which go beyond the provision of a legal framework. Undeniably, the extent of governmental involvement has vastly increased in this century. What are the causes of the more extensive role of government?

WHY GOVERNMENT'S ROLE HAS EXPANDED

The reasons for expanding governmental economic activity are a mixture of circumstantial development, increased knowledge of how an economy functions, and changing community values, each related to and reinforcing the others.

The rise of industrialization and its social corollary, urbanization, represent the circumstantial development. Perhaps the broadest effect of industrialization has been to substitute formal social controls for the informal ones of earlier society and to create new controls to handle problems that did not exist in the simpler and less interdependent technology of agricultural society.

As an example of new formal controls, we have the pure food and drug statutes and the Federal Trade Commission replacing the old attitude of *caveat emptor*. When consumer goods were largely limited to food and fiber products, "let the buyer beware" was not an impossible rule, for the consumer could easily be as knowledgeable as the seller regarding the desirable qualities in a vegetable or a pair of trousers made of natural fibers. But when industrialization and technological progress introduced a new and vastly extended range of products, complex in their mechanism and often artificial in their materials, common knowledge became a poor basis for purchase. The informal control by consumer information then required supplementation by formal protection. The

Pure Food and Drug Act established an agency and a set of rules to guard the hopeful and gullible consumer from harmful remedies and contaminated foods. Today we are moving toward additional protection: to ensure against the great economic waste and personal financial distress caused by purchase of products which are ineffective though innocuous, by requiring that the producer prove his remedy has beneficial effect. The Kefauver hearings on the drug industry, whatever they prove about profits, have certainly demonstrated the necessity to safeguard the consumer against medically meaningless though commercially profitable innovations in prescription and proprietary drugs. President Kennedy's 1962 consumer protection message to Congress and his establishment of a Consumer Advisory Council exemplify the increasing activities on the part of government in areas where lack of consumer knowledge needs to be compensated for by formal social control.

Or consider antimonopoly legislation. When production was agricultural and producers were many and small, the consumer was protected by the market mechanism itself, which enabled the retail distributor to have a choice of suppliers. With the rise of national markets and industrial producers, the maintenance of competition became a matter for conscious policy as concentration of production in a few firms came to typify the situation. It was not a change from no regulation to government regulation, but from market regulation to government regulation.

To illustrate the need for new controls where no controls previously existed, we can cite the development of traffic rules, motorcycle policemen, and traffic courts and, in quite another sphere, blue-sky laws and the Securities Exchange Commission. Also zoning and land-use regulations are the by-product of industrial urbanization, which makes my neighbor's use of his property a matter of economic, esthetic, and hygienic concern to me.

In addition to supplying the supporting framework for business, government in industrial society is also necessarily called upon to provide a supporting framework for individuals and families. This is not the result of an alleged loss of "moral fiber" in the people, but of the living pattern of urban culture and the specialization and interdependence of industrial employment. In the preindustrial society, people were literally more self-sufficient than it is possible for them to be today: the farm family grew its own food, made some of its own clothing and built its own house and outbuildings. Families were large, and children contributed economically by working in the fields or the house at an early age. Because there was a minimum of exchange and minimal use of cash, there was not the dependence upon cash income that there is today. The grandparents could be cared for within the home, and usually could continue to be useful members of the family, not a drain on their children's resources. When industrialism began to make some headway, and a son went off to the city to become a factory worker, it was still possible for him to return to the family farm if he lost his city job or became ill. Family responsibility for each member was then more feasible than it can be today.

Contrast with this picture the situation today, and the underlying causes for the expansion of economic welfare activities by government become quickly apparent. Production and consumption are divorced. The man does not work on his own farm but for an organization. He does not produce his own food, let alone clothing and housing, but performs a specialized task for a cash income, which he then exchanges for all of his family's needs. Loss of cash thus means loss of all sustenance. The family farm is no longer there to fall back on in rough times, nor would the urban-raised man know how to do farm work if it were available. Children in the city are economically unproductive; they cannot perform small tasks on their father's assembly line or in his office, as they could on the farm. Urban housing and the concentrated living patterns of the city do not easily accommodate three generations under one roof, so the grandparents require separate housing at separate expense. Furthermore, industrial employment is subject to fluctuations against which no individual can protect himself. Given the consequences of unemployment, and this inability to guard against it, income-support programs by government, such as unemployment compensation, disability compensation, health insurance, and old age pensions, can be seen as simply the modern equivalent of protections once, but no longer, provided by the socioeconomic system itself.

While agricultural societies had good and bad seasons, and incredible human suffering might be the price of the latter, they could still not have the complete collapse of economy that happened in 1933, when one-fourth of the work force was unemployed. The business cycle did not originate with industrialization, but its consequences were so vastly magnified that the price paid for a self-adjusting economy became intolerable. Hence changed circumstances called forth another whole area of governmental function: the stabilization of employment, production, and prices.

Yet it was not just changed circumstance, for when we say that a situation becomes intolerable we are making a value judgment, not just describing a situation. Community value changes were just as essential a part of the expanding economic role of government as changes in the objective situation. When unemployment was thought of, in Spencerian terms, as the justly deserved punishment of the shiftless and lazy, no one thought to provide governmental protection. When "the devil take the hindmost" and *caveat emptor* were the slogans of the day, the social and economic costs of the crude early brand of capitalism were ignored with good conscience—at least by those whose opinions counted politically. In short, when doctrines of individualism held a monopoly on the operative ideals of the community, collective economic action was by definition anathema. There were critics who posed more humane values—like Disraeli and Dickens in England, Lincoln Steffens and Ida M. Tarbell in the United States—but their impact was felt only belatedly.

Concepts of social justice began to receive more articulate support, and wider public awareness and acceptance around the turn of the century. The almost Marxian criticism of capitalism embedded in Pope Leo XIII's encyclical, *Rerum Novarum;* the growth of an industrial working class for whom the individualist precepts of the Horatio Alger literature had a distinctly hollow ring; the development of the Brandeis brief to break down with factual recitations of suffering and inequity the Supreme Court's dogmatic assumption of economic harmony under laissez-faire; and the beginnings of sociological analysis of power relationships—all these were forces undermining the Spencerian-Darwinian scheme of values.

Simultaneous change in conditions and in values provided the elemental forces necessary for development of new governmental roles; the catalytic agent was often a crisis or a catastrophe. The Triangle Shirt Waist Company fire in New York in 1911, in which 146 workers died, led to much factory legislation in 1912–14; ship losses led to radio requirements and legislation; and the depression of 1929–39 led to a whole range of programmatic and institutional innovations patterned on an industrially oriented scheme of values: the Securities and Exchange Commission, Home Owner's Loan Corporation, Old Age and Survivors Insurance, and the Council of Economic Advisers–just to list a few.

Nor is the conflict of values over yet. Roughly speaking, what Galbraith called the conventional wisdom and what Barry Goldwater and the NAM preach in the name of individualism represent vestiges of pre-industrial thinking, which are still quite lively, unfortunately. Such thinking contends for the power to shape public policy with what may be called the liberal-labor ideology, which accepts industrialization and recognizes its social imperatives–indeed, it overstresses them, say conservatives. The recent and continuing conflict over the means test versus the social-insurance approach to publicly provided medical care is a perfect case in point. The means test philosophy dates back hundreds of years. Its view of man is that his dignity counts only when he is self-supporting; its view of the economy is that no one ever lacks adequate means of support except through his own shiftlessness or inadequacy. The social-insurance approach emphasizes the technical concept of risk-sharing, the ethical concept that dignity resides in all humans, not just the fortunate ones, and the economic concept that social costs and benefits are not synonymous with private costs and benefits as measured by the market. Pictures of the situation and systems of values are thus fused into total approaches to socioeconomic problems, approaches with quite different implications for the range of public policy.

Two other developments were highly instrumental, and in some respects requisite, to expansion of government's economic role of social control. There was a recognition of social-economic institutions as man-made rather than divinely ordained, and, concurrently, the technical development of economic analysis as a social-scientific discipline. When social and economic systems were thought of as divinely ordained or as natural growths, it was popularly supposed that men neither could nor should make changes in the framework. If some men starved, it was regrettable; but nothing could be done in the face of "natural law." Although the early factory wage system reeked of injustice, one could not tamper with the "iron law of wages." Such crude doctrines of natural law, widely believed, for a long time effectively stopped social and economic reform measures, for "interference" with nature was immoral and, by definition, futile because "unnatural."

As the scientific spirit began to invade the sphere of moral philosophy and men began to doubt the finality of social institutions which showed great variation between cultures, it gradually came to be understood that social arrangements are what we make them, that within bounds set by resources and knowledge there are a great variety of ways in which goods production can be handled. And men began to demand that governments act as instigators of change to produce institutional patterns more in keeping with an enlightened humanist image of man. Although social science has become heavily self-conscious about its self-imposed role of analysis without prescription in recent years, its early growth came largely through men committed to engineering a better world. The draft of objectives circulated by Richard T. Ely in 1885 as a prospectus for an American Economics Association, for example, began with an explicit rejection of the laissez-faire doctrine: "We regard the state as an educational and ethical agency whose positive aid is an indispensable condition of human progress. . . . We hold that the doctrine of laissez-faire is unsafe in politics and unsound in morals." Not all the economists of that time agreed with Ely, yet a milder version of this statement was incorporated into the original constitution of the Association. And some men would have made the Association's role even more activist. Simon Patten, for example, felt that the Association membership "should give in some specific form our attitude on all the leading questions where State intervention is needed."

Use of governmental power to achieve reform objectives was made socially feasible by the social scientists' demonstration that economic and other institutions were not the immutable creations of nature but the conscious and unconscious creations of man. What once had to be accepted, though regretted, could now be attacked: men could be blamed and held responsible; their behavior could be required to conform to standards other than those enshrined in the market mechanism; and institutions could be reformed to accord with humanistic aims.

The best will in the world will accomplish little, however, if objective analysis of the problem is faulty or techniques have not been developed for directing social forces toward the desired goal. Advances in economic theory and in techniques of measuring performance of the economy were therefore prerequisite to the translation of humane ideals into programs of public economic policy. Concretely, the Keynesian revolution provided an essential key to understanding the nature of the business cycle and the failure of conventional budget-balancing economics to pull the economy out of a slump once begun. President Roosevelt's initial attempts to cut government spending are a leading example of the perils of action on the basis of faulty analysis. The development of the national income model and its accompanying analysis of the flow of funds and the relationships among savings, investment, and consumption are the intellectual basis for policies aimed at growth and full employment. While our understanding of economic behavior still appears to lag far behind our understanding of the physical world, and our institutional arrangements for using economic knowledge are about as well adapted to our needs as the old wagon trail would be to a high-speed automobile, we do know enough now to avoid the grosser fluctuations of the business cycle. In fact, these and similar technical developments in economic science have probably been themselves a causative factor in the change in values from acceptance of adversity as God-given to community demands that the economy be controlled in the interests of the general public.

For all of these reasons then, the economic role of government has been enlarged many times over in our day. The ubiquity of this development in all economically advanced or advancing nations is sufficient proof against the unenlightened conservative's easy explanation that it is all the fault of "that man in the White House," whether Roosevelt, Truman, Eisenhower, or Kennedy. And the nature of the forces catalogued suggests that the limits of essential intervention have not yet been reached.

JOHN K. GALBRAITH

Paul M. Warburg Professor of Economics, Harvard University.

John Kenneth Galbraith is an important figure in the political and intellectual establishment today, and is no doubt America's most popularly-read economist. Associating himself with the liberal wing of the Democratic party, Galbraith served as an advisor to President Kennedy and Ambassador to India from 1961 to 1963. Later, as Chairman of the Americans for Democratic Action, a liberal political organization, he was among the earliest critics of the Vietnam War. He campaigned actively for George McGovern in 1970 and is often reported as interested in running for national political office himself. During the late 1960s he was critical of President Nixon's handling of domestic problems and was one of the few economists who urged permanent wage and price controls as a means of controlling the inflationary spiral.

Galbraith's four major works, *American Capitalism* (1952), *The Affluent Society* (1958), *The New Industrial State* (1967), and *Economics and the Public Purpose* (1973) are all concerned with the balance of power in American capitalism and have earned Galbraith a reputation as one of America's most important social critics.

The first of these works attempts to show that even though the high concentration in manufacturing industries has broken down the competitive market as a regulating force, the allocation of resources is not as distorted as the traditional economic models would lead one to suspect. This is because a new self-regulating force, "countervailing power," has grown up. Galbraith sees the growth of large companies in the seller's market as breeding large power blocks on the opposite side of the market. Thus the big three of the automobile industry must deal with the big four of the tire industry or with the large labor unions in purchasing its inputs. These countervailing powers tend to neutralize the monopolist power of large sellers, with the resulting prices and wages more closely approximating those which would prevail under more traditional market conditions (same side of the market competition). This insight of Galbraith's does have some validity with regard to American capitalism; however, it also has a number of limitations. For one thing, this type of self-regulating force is not an inevitable offshoot of powerful industries, and even where it has the potential to operate, it tends to break down if any degree of collusion exists between the two opposing power blocks. In addition, Galbraith concedes that during periods of inflation, where high levels of aggregate demand are present, producers may be willing to capitulate to the high-wage demands of unions because the additional cost can be passed on to the consumer through higher product prices, without hurting sales. Also if firms are vertically integrated and supply their own inputs, or where reciprocal buying arrangements exist, countervailing forces tend to break down.

In *The Affluent Society* Galbraith shifts his attention from the balance of power among giant producers in the market to the allocation of resources between the public and private sectors of the economy. To Galbraith, business advertising, American unwillingness to increase taxes, and persistent inflation all tend to bring about an overproduction of private goods and an underproduction of public goods. This has created, according to Galbraith, a serious "social imbalance" in America. His book is a plea for an expansion of public services in order to improve the quality of life. In relation to public policy, the need for a better balance of public vs. private goods has led some liberals, including Galbraith, to favor increases in government spending over tax cuts as a means for countering business recessions. The acceptance of Galbraith's position necessitates a greater role for government in the economy.

The selection presented here contains the essential message of *The New Industrial State.*[1] In that work, Galbraith describes how the line between the public and private sectors of the economy has become blurred by the massive power of the giant corporations. In his view, a major segment of the American economy is planned, but the planning organization is the corporation rather than the state, and corporate sovereignty has replaced consumer sovereignty. According to Galbraith, "modern highly technical processes and products and [the] associated requirements of capital and time lead inevitably to planning–to the management of markets by those who supply them," and in order to carry out this planning, corporations must be large. Gone are the countervailing forces that, Galbraith once believed, kept monopolistic power in check, and in their absence both consumer and state are subject to the goals of the mature corporation and its ruling "technostructure." Galbraith is not entirely distressed by these developments, for he feels that they are the inevitable (and even desirable) result of the imperatives of modern technology. If society is to continue to advance, large corporations are necessary to achieve operational efficiency, innovation, and economic stability. It is on these points that Galbraith has been most severely criticized by economists. Many are not willing to accept his position that giant corporations are a necessary condition for efficiency and progress, or that technology destroys the usefulness of the competitive market. Indeed research has shown that in many industries the largest firms are not the most progressive and that competition is the primary force behind technical innovation.

As the following article shows, Galbraith often attacks traditional economists for rejecting his proposition that the market system is no longer viable for the largest part of the American economy. Coincidentally, some of Galbraith's peers regard him as a poor theoretician and a generalizer who cannot support his arguments with facts. Paul Samuelson once referred to him as "a noneconomist's economist." But criticism is not limited to the academic community; businessmen do not share his view that they make a practice of manipulating the market, and the public is suspicious of his seemingly ambitious programs which they see as increasing the tax burden. In fact Galbraith is an intellectual who is willing to go beyond the boundaries of traditional economics to try to arrive at a more realistic picture of the operation of American capitalism. He is a great admirer of American big business and demonstrates, both in his writings and in his personal actions, that he values the welfare of society above all else. What he dislikes about the system he describes is that the values of the industrial complex have become the values of our society at large.

In a review of the *New Industrial State,* his admirer Robert Heilbroner pointed out what he felt was Galbraith's greatest weakness: "[insufficient] courage to carry his theoretical model into the future, whatever its course." However, it may well have been concern for the future that prompted Galbraith to write his newest work, *Economics and the Public Purpose.* Here again, he stresses the inadequate balance between the public and private sectors and the growing dominance of the large corporate planning sector over the obsolete market and the values of society. But this time he proposes remedies for this imbalance of power. Among the actions suggested are:

1. nationalization of the weaker sectors of the market economy which provide basic services like transportation, housing, and medical care; also nationalization of defense contractors who rely on the government for 50 percent or more of their sales (e.g., Lockheed and General Dynamics);
2. government regulation of prices and encouragement of trade associations for small businesses to allow them to survive alongside the bigger firms in the planned sectors of the economy;
3. major increases in the minimum wage and a guaranteed income for those who cannot find work;
4. increased public support of the arts;
5. establishment of a public authority to coordinate activities within the private planning system.

Galbraith's suggestions, labeled "sensible radicalism" by *Newsweek,* show that he does not want the corporate planning sector to gain any more influence than it already has over the values and choices of society. What he calls for is the expansion of an alternate value system, promoted by a government which has emancipated itself from the grip of the corporate planning sector. This, of course, reflects the liberal doctrine that the interests of the political and economic sectors can be separated.

Galbraith's own feeling is that this separation of powers and interests might be achieved if the liberal elements of the Democratic Party come into power. Thus Galbraith manifests one side of the split among reform liberals in the 1970s. Reacting against the failure of many of the social and economic programs set up in the middle and late 1960s, part of the liberal camp has turned increasingly to the market for solutions, while another group has directed its efforts toward an expansion of government influence. It comes as no surprise that Galbraith, who felt all along that the market had outlived its usefulness, chose the path he did.

1. This article originally appeared in *The Atlantic Monthly* and is Galbraith's own condensation of his book.

From

THE NEW INDUSTRIAL STATE

(1967)

PLANNING AND THE MODERN CORPORATION

Few things so firmly establish one's grasp on the commonplace as to list the changes that have occurred in economic life in the last half century. Machines have, of course, extensively replaced crude manpower. Increasingly, one machine instructs other machines in the process called automation. Industrial corporations have become very, very large. They are no longer directed as a matter of right by their owners; they are guided impersonally by their management. They deploy large amounts of capital, much of which they derive from their own earnings. These earnings are now by far the most important source of savings–income that is needed for industrial expansion is no longer allowed to get into the hot and eager hands of those who might choose to use it for their personal consumption.

Economic well-being has also greatly increased–at least in the fortunate countries of Europe and North America. And the market has changed. In the world described by Alfred Marshall, the great English economist of the early decades of this century, prices were established, as he said, by the "higgling and bargaining" of the market after having been, as he also said, "tossed hither and thither like a shuttlecock." Now, in the world of the large corporation, they are set by the corporation, and they often remain fixed for long periods of time. These companies are also at considerable pains to persuade the customer on what he should buy. Everyone, including all economists, agrees on consumer sovereignty in principle, but no one wants to trust it unduly in practice.

Finally, even in countries such as the United States, where, as we all agree, faith in free enterprise is one of the minor branches of theology, the state plays a large and increasing role in economic affairs. It stabilizes purchasing power–what economists call aggregate demand; it underwrites expensive technology such as modern weaponry and the supersonic transports; it restrains, or anyhow seeks to restrain, wages and prices to prevent inflation; it educates the technical and specialized manpower that modern industry requires; and the state buys upwards of a fifth of all that the modern industrial community produces. In the presumptively capitalist economy of the United States, one is charmed to reflect, the state plays a very much larger role in almost every facet of economic activity than it does in the avowedly planned and socialist economy of, say, India.

I want to show . . . that the changes just mentioned are part of an interrelated complex, or matrix, as economists say. And I want to show also that the result is larger than the sum of the parts, that specifically there have been three great consequences. The first is rather comprehensive economic planning; which is to say, producers extensively manage the lives of those whom they are assumed to serve. And they must. By its nature, the modern industrial economy is a planned economy.

The second consequence is that there are strongly convergent tendencies, as there are in all industrial societies. This is despite their very different billing as capitalist or socialist or Communist by those who act as the custodians of our official ideology.

The third consequence is that to a far greater extent than we imagine, our beliefs and cultural attitudes are accommodated to the needs and goals of the industrial mechanism by which we are supplied. These serve the convenience of modern industry. Industrial societies differ not in the fact but in the method by which ideas are patterned to industrial convenience and need.

Let me begin by showing how technology, time, and capital shape the modern economy.

On June 15, 1903, after some months of preparation, the Ford Motor Company was formed in Detroit, Michigan, for the manufacture of automobiles. The first car reached the market that *same* October. The firm had an authorized capital of $150,000, although only $100,000 worth was issued and only $28,500 was for cash. Although it does not bear on the present discussion, the company made a handsome profit that year and did not fail to make a very large profit for many years thereafter. In 1903 Ford employed 125 men.

In the spring of 1964, the Ford Motor Company introduced what is now called a new automobile. In accordance with current fashion, it was named, one hopes inappropriately, a "Mustang"–a mustang is a very roughriding animal, as all close students of television are aware. Preparations for the Mustang required three and a half years. From late in the autumn of 1962, when the design was settled, until the spring of 1964, there was a fairly firm commitment to the particular car that eventually emerged. Engineering, "styling," and development costs were nearly $60 million.[1] In 1964, employment in the Ford Motor Company averaged 317,000 men. Assets in 1964 were approximately $6 billion.

Nearly all of the effects of industrial change are revealed in one way or another by these comparisons. Let me list them.

First. With increasingly sophisticated knowledge there is an increasing lapse of time between the beginning and the completion of a task. Technology means the systematic application of scientific or other organized knowledge to practical tasks. It is applied not to the manufacture of a car as a whole. It is brought to bear on very small elements of its manufacture–on the qualities of particular steels or the methods of machining a particular part. Then knowledge is applied to the combination of these parts, and then on assembly, and thus on to final completion. The process of manufacture stretches back in time as the root system of a plant stretches down into the ground, and the longest of these filaments, as it were, sets the total time required in production. The first Ford needed only ordinary steel, obtained from the warehouse in the morning and worked that afternoon. The provision of steel for the Mustang, in contrast, reached back to specifications prepared by the designers, to tests in the laboratory, then to design of the appropriate metalworking machinery, and to production and installation of these tools. Years thus elapse between the beginning of work on a car and its appearance.

1. I am grateful to Mr. Walter T. Murphy of the Ford Motor Company for providing these details. I have also drawn on earlier help from Robert McNamara which he gave when he was still an executive of Ford. Details on the early history of Ford are mostly from Allan Nevins, *Ford: The Times, the Man, the Company* (Charles Scribner's Sons, 1954).

Second. There is a great increase in the amount of capital that is committed to production. This is partly the result of the increased elapse of time, for that means increased investment in the work that is in process. But the knowledge which is applied to the various elements of the task also costs money. And so does machinery, which is the most characteristic manifestation of technology.

Only very simple machinery was used in the manufacture of the first Ford. No trained engineers were employed. The frame of the car was moved manually, and it could be lifted by two men. The modern auto factory, in contrast, is itself a complex and closely articulated machine. Nothing is done by muscular effort. Computers control the flow of parts and components to the assembly line. Only the recurrent hideousness of the product remains to remind one that human beings are involved. Thus (along with increased output, of course) the increase in capitalization of Ford to $6 billion.

Third. With increasing technology, time and capital tend to be committed ever more inflexibly to a particular task. Organized knowledge is used to improve the performance of a specific task. That task must be precisely defined before it is divided and subdivided into its component parts. Knowledge and equipment are then brought to bear on these fractions. But they are applied only to the fractions of the task as it was initially conceived. If that task is changed, new knowledge and new equipment will have to be mobilized for each part. So once a decision is made on what to produce, it is very difficult to alter it.

The engine and chassis of the original Ford were made by the Dodge Brothers (who eventually also made an automobile themselves). Their machine shop could have worked as well on bicycles, steam engines, or carriages, and in point of fact, it had been so employed. Had Ford and his associates decided at any point to shift from gasoline to steam power as a source of power for the vehicle, the machine shop could have accommodated itself to this considerable change by modern standards in a few hours.

By contrast, all parts of the Mustang, the tools and equipment that worked on these parts, and the steel and the other materials going into these parts were designed for this car and this car almost alone. The manufacture of a Barracuda, which differs mostly in having an even more bizarre name, would have required a very different tooling up. So would a "Serpent," a "Roach," or a "Locust" —if one may look ahead on automobile nomenclature.

Fourth. Technology requires specialized manpower. Not surprisingly, organized knowledge can be brought to bear only by those who possess such knowledge. However, technology is not the only thing that requires specialized manpower; so does the planning, which I will come to in a moment. And so does organization, for it takes specialists in organization to manage the organization which results from specialization.

This does not mean that the talent required for modern industry is necessarily more demanding, on some absolute scale of intelligence, than that of an earlier and technically less advanced era. Modern industrial man is not some species of superman; he must be helped to resist the temptation so to regard himself.

Indeed, the makers of the original Ford were men of considerable talent. The Dodge Brothers had previously invented a bicycle and a steam launch. Detroit legend also celebrated their remarkable exuberance when drunk.

James Couzens, who was Ford's partner and who almost certainly had more to do with the early success of the enterprise than Henry Ford himself, went on to be a police commissioner and mayor of Detroit and then to the Senate to become, as a Republican, a brilliant and undeviating supporter of Franklin D. Roosevelt. Not even Robert McNamara has shown more reach. What the members of the modern company do have is a much deeper knowledge of the specialized matters for which they are responsible. It is, like all others, a great assemblage of such specialists.

Fifth. Specialization obviously requires organization. Only thus is the work of specialists brought to a coherent result. It is obvious that if there are many specialists, this coordination will be a major task in itself. Next only to machinery, massive and complex organizations are the most visible manifestations of a world of advanced technology. Its manifestation in the case of Ford is the growth from 125 to 317,000 men.

Finally, from the time and capital that must be committed and the rigidity of these commitments comes the inevitability of planning. Tasks must be so performed that they are right not for the time that they are undertaken but for the time in the distant future when they are completed. Developments, occurring between the time of initiation and the time of accomplishment, must be anticipated. The effect, if adverse, must be neutralized. Or the events must be prevented.

In the early days of the Ford Motor Company, the future was very close at hand. What was raw material today would be a car next week. To fail to anticipate adverse contingencies was not fatal; anything that went unexpectedly wrong could be quickly remedied. Many things did go wrong. The earliest vehicles, as they came to the market, would have worried Ralph Nader. The cooling system did not always cool, the brakes did not reliably brake, and the carburetor did not always feed fuel to the engine. Once a Los Angeles dealer sent a message that when the cars he was receiving were steered, the "front wheels turn wrong." But these defects, though not minor, could be promptly remedied. Such faults in the Mustang would have been highly unpleasant and both time-consuming and costly to repair. Similarly, the original Ford used materials, labor, and components of a highly unspecialized character that were available in the open market. A shortage could be remedied by sending someone out to buy what was needed. A failure in delivery for the specialized machinery, materials, or components required for the modern vehicle would be subject to no such remedy. And the situation is the same with labor. In the days of the first Ford, an ordinary laborer or even a first-rate operative could be hired in the nearest saloon. A systems engineer cannot be so recruited. Nor can other specialized talent.

Here I come to a point of great importance. Technology—and associated change—not only requires planning, but also impairs and even destroys the usefulness of the market. Simple things can be bought and sold on the market. Complex things cannot. The farmer can find the things he needs for production in the next town. The automobile manufacturer cannot. There was an open market for muskets in their day. There is not, fortunately, for missiles. Orville Wright was able to buy most of what he needed for the first airplane in Dayton, Ohio. The market will not supply the materials, parts, systems, and engineering talent required for a modern spacecraft. These must be foreseen, and the supply and price arranged months and years in advance.

The modern automobile, by which I have illustrated the foregoing tendencies, is, by many standards, an elementary product. For more sophisticated products, time, capital, inflexibility of commitment, specialization, organization, and planning are all greatly increased. This is remarkably so for, among other things, modern weaponry.

When Philip II settled on the redemption of England at the end of March, 1587, he was not unduly troubled by the circumstance that Spain had no navy. Some men-of-war were available from newly conquered Portugal; but, in the main, merchant ships would suffice. In other words, a navy could be had from the market. At Cádiz three weeks later Sir Francis Drake destroyed quite a few of these vessels. But this was not a fatal blow; more could be bought or quickly built. Accordingly, and despite what historians have always described as unconscionable inefficiency, the Armada sailed in a strength of 130 ships a little over a year later on May 18, 1588. The cost, though it was certainly considerable, was well within the resources of the Spanish Empire.

To create a modern fleet of the numerical size of the Armada, comprising aircraft carriers and an appropriate complement of aircraft, nuclear submarines, Polaris missiles, destroyers, auxiliary and supporting craft, and bases and communications, would take a first-rate industrial power a minimum of twenty years. Though modern Spain is rich beyond the dreams of its monarchs in its most expansive age, it could not for a moment contemplate such an enterprise. In World War II, no combat plane that had not been substantially designed before the outbreak of hostilities saw actual service. Since then, the lead time for comparable weaponry has become very much greater. No one in late middle age stands in any danger of weapons now being designed; they are a menace to the unborn and the unconceived.

It is a commonplace of modern technology that we know that problems have solutions before there is knowledge of how they are to be solved. It is reasonably certain that a man can be landed on the moon within the next five years. However, numerous technical details of this journey remain to be worked out. It is known that air can be made breathable and water drinkable for those who must remain behind; but there is still much uncertainty as to the best methods of cleaning up the atmosphere and the lakes and streams.

If methods of performing a specified task have been fully worked out, the cost in time and money of bringing organized intelligence to bear on the task will be much less than if the methods are still uncertain. Uncertainty about the properties of the metal to be used for the skin of a supersonic transport, uncertainty therefore about the proper way of handling and working the metal, and uncertainty therefore about the character and design of the equipment required all can add extravagantly to the time and cost of obtaining such a vehicle. This problem-solving, with its high costs in time and money, is a recognized feature of modern technology. It graces all modern economic discussion under the cachet of industrial research and development.

The need for planning arises from the long period of time that elapses during the production process, the high investment that is involved, the inflexible commitment of that investment to the particular task, and the failure of the market when there is high technology. Where methods are unknown or uncertain, and where, accordingly, there must be this expenditure for research and development, planning is even more essential. It is also more demanding. The time that is involved, the money that is at risk, and the number of things, accordingly, that can go wrong and the magnitude of the possible ensuing disaster all increase. The cost and risk may be beyond the resources of a private firm.

An obvious solution is to have the state absorb the major risks under such circumstances. This is becoming established practice. It can guarantee a market for the weapon, airplane, or other similar technical product. Or it can underwrite the costs of development; if these increase beyond expectation, the firms will not have to carry them. The drift of this argument will be evident. Technology leads to planning. And in its higher manifestations, technology puts the problems of planning beyond the reach of the individual industrial firm. The compulsions of technology, not ideology or political wile, then require the firm to seek the help and the protection of the state. This is true under what has always been called capitalism. It is true, as a matter of course, in the formally planned and Communist economies. Technology and associated change require planning by the producing firm. Both impose a broadly similar role on the state.

But in the Western economies, it is a mistake to think of the state as the main planning instrument. Rather it is the large corporation. This is not without paradox. Large corporations, we were all taught from our prenatal days, are the very essence of unplanned capitalism.

A market economy is an arrangement by which people sally forth and by their purchases make clear what they want or do not want. Their market behavior, in turn, is an instruction to producers in regard to what they should or should not produce. The initiative lies with the individual. He is sovereign. There is something admirably libertarian and democratic about this process. It is not hard to understand why, among the devout, the market, no less than Christianity and Zen Buddhism, evokes such formidable spiritual feeling.

But in the case of the Mustang, the initiative came not from the consumer but the producer. It was not the consumer who established the price in the market. The price was set by the manufacturer. The consumer had no idea that he needed this blessing before it was unveiled, although indubitably he welcomed it thereafter. Nor was he left with a free choice of his purchase. On the contrary, considerable thought was given to the means of ensuring that he would want it and buy it.

When initiative lies with the consumer, we agree that we have a market economy. When it passes to the producer–and the consumer is accommodated to the needs and convenience of the producer–it is commonly and correctly said that we have a planned economy.

The planning may be imperfect. The consumer retains the right to resist persuasion or otherwise contract out of the management to which he or she is subject. There will be Edsels as well as Mustangs, and the latter may much exceed planned totals. Nevertheless, imperfect or otherwise, there is planning. The modern large corporation can be understood only as an adaptation to the needs of modern technology, related capital requirements, and of organization and the resulting planning.

Successful planning requires that the planning authority be able to control or sufficiently influence the various contingencies which bear upon the results it seeks. And it must not be subject to the power of those who might frustrate its plans either by ill-considered interference or even by carefully considered interference which reflects other and alien objectives. The modern large business corporation possesses the principal requisites of successful planning. What it cannot do is done by the state.

The modern corporation achieves much of the requisite authority merely by being very large. This enables it to possess and control large amounts of capital and to mobilize and direct the large number of specialists that modern technology requires. Also, if the firm is large, contingencies that cannot be perfectly controlled can be absorbed or offset. If planning for a particular product by General Motors or General Dynamics goes sour, there are other products to offset this misfortune.

A plausible consequence of these advantages of size is that the modern industrial enterprise will be very large. And so it is. In 1962 the five largest industrial corporations in the United States, with combined assets in excess of $36 billion, possessed over 12 percent, almost one eighth, of all the assets used by all companies in manufacturing. The 50 largest firms had over a third of all manufacturing resources. The 500 largest, a number whose presidents could be seated in a moderate-sized theater, had well over two thirds.[2] In the mid-nineteen-fifties, 23 corporations provided 15 percent of all the employment in manufacturing.

We have difficulty in thinking of the private firm as a planning instrument because we associate planning with the state. But the modern industrial enterprise operates on a scale that is far more nearly comparable with that of government than that of old-fashioned market-oriented activity. In 1965 three American industrial corporations, General Motors, Standard Oil of New Jersey, and Ford Motor Company, together had more gross income than all the farms in the United States. The income of General Motors alone about equaled that of the three million smallest farmers in the country. The gross revenues of each of these three corporations far exceeded those of any single state of the American Union. The revenues of General Motors in 1963 were fifty times those of the state of Nevada, eight times those of the state of New York, and slightly less than one-fifth those of the federal government.

Economists have anciently quarreled over the reason for the great size of the modern corporation. Is it because size is essential in order to reap the economies of modern large-scale production? Is it, more insidiously, because the big firm wishes to exercise monopoly power in its markets? There is a little truth in the answers to both of these shopworn questions. The firm must be large enough to carry the large capital commitments of modern technology. It must also be large enough to control its markets. But the modern firm is larger than either of these purposes requires. General Motors is not only large enough to afford the best size of automobile plant but is large enough to afford a dozen of the best size. And it is large enough, in addition, to produce a host of other things as diverse as aircraft engines and refrigerators. Why is this? And why, although it is large enough to have the market power associated with monopoly, do consumers not complain excessively about exploitation? We have here the answer. The great size of a modern corporation allows economies not possible for the small firm and permits the control of markets, to be sure; but its primary advantage lies in the service it renders to its planning. And for this planning–the control of supply, control of demand, control of capital supply, absorption of risk or minimization of risk where risk cannot be avoided–there is no clear upper limit to the desirable size. It could be that the bigger the better.

A prime requirement of the planning authority is control over its own decisions. This autonomy has, in fact, a double purpose. It is indispensable if the authority is to pursue the objectives of its planning. I shall have more to say on this later. It is also a vitally necessary aspect of decision-making under conditions of advanced technology. I must digress here for a special word about this.

As technology becomes increasingly sophisticated and as it leads on to specialization and planning, decisions in the business enterprise cease to come from individuals. They come necessarily, inescapably, from groups. The groups, as often informal as formal, and subject to constant change in composition, contain the men possessed of the information or with access to the information that bears on the particular decision. They contain also those whose skills consist in extracting and testing this information and obtaining a conclusion. It is through such groups that men act successfully on matters where no single person, however exalted or intelligent, has more than a fraction of the necessary knowledge. It is such groups that make modern business possible, and in other contexts, also make modern government possible.

Effective participation in such decision-making is not closely related to the individual's nominal rank in the formal hierarchy of the company or corporation. This is something that takes an effort of mind to grasp. Everyone is influenced by the stereotyped organization chart of the business enterprise. At the top is the board of directors, the chairman, the president, and the principal executive officer, thereafter the department or divisional heads. Power is assumed to pass down from this pinnacle. Those at the top give orders; those below relay them on or respond.

Power is employed in this way only in very simple organizations–in the peacetime drill of the National Guard or in a troop of Boy Scouts moving out on Saturday maneuvers. Elsewhere decisions require information, and some power will then pass to the person or persons who have this information. If this knowledge is highly particular to themselves, as in the case of sophisticated technology, their power becomes very great. At Los Alamos, New Mexico, during the development of the atomic bomb, Enrico Fermi rode a bicycle up the hill to his work; Major General Leslie Groves presided in grandeur over the entire Manhattan District. Fermi, in company with a handful of others, could, at various stages, have brought the entire enterprise to an end. They were also irreplaceable. No such power rested with General Groves at the top. At any moment he could have been replaced by any one of one hundred others without any loss.

When power is exercised in this fashion by a group, not only does it pass into the organization but it passes into

2. Data on the concentration of industrial activity in the hands of large firms, and especially any that seem to show an increase in concentration, sustain a controversy in the United States that at times reaches mildly pathological proportions. The reason is that much of the argument between those who see the market as a viable institution and those who feel that it is succumbing to monopolistic influences has long turned on these figures. These figures are defended or attacked according to predilection. However, the orders of magnitude given here are not subject to serious question.

the organization irrevocably. If an individual has taken a decision, he can be called before another individual, who is his superior in the hierarchy, and his information can be extracted and examined, and his decision can then be reversed by the greater wisdom or experience of the superior. But if the decision requires the combined information of a group, it cannot be safely reversed by another individual. The individual will have to get the judgment of other specialists. This returns the power once more to the organization.

The modern large business corporation is admirably equipped to protect the autonomy on which the group decision required by technology and planning so deeply depends. The corporate charter accords a large area of independent action to the firm in the conduct of its affairs. And this freedom of conduct is defended as a sacred right. In our business attitudes nothing is held to be so iniquitous as government interference in the internal affairs of the corporation. And attitudes in other countries are similar if somewhat less choleric. There is equally vehement resistance to any invasion by trade unions of the prerogatives of management.

But interference from those who own or supply capital would be equally damaging to the planning of the firm and to the quality of its decisions. The modern firm exempts itself from interference from those who supply current capital requirements first of all by having its own source of capital. The use of earnings returned from profits is wholly at the discretion of those who run the firm. If funds must come from a banker, his views must be treated with respect. He can also intervene. If he isn't needed and the funds aren't coming from him, only politeness is in order.

Few things have resulted in a greater shift in power than the ability of the large modern firm to supply itself with capital. Few things have more altered the character of capitalism. It is hardly surprising that retained earnings of corporations have become such an overwhelmingly important source of capital.

The stockholder too has been separated from all effective power in the large corporation. Many things have led to this result. With the passage of time and the ineluctable effects of distribution by inheritance, of estate taxes, of philanthropy, of alimony, and of the other enjoyments of nonfunctional heirs, even the largest holdings are dispersed. It is next to impossible to get any considerable number of stockholders together for an action in opposition to management. Instead, the board of directors meets in solemn conclave to select the management, which previously selected that board. The electoral rituals of the modern large company are among our most elaborate exercises in popular and self illusion.

But the exercise of authority by the modern enterprise is also protected by the technical complexity of its decisions. Some forty years ago it was discovered that Colonel Robert W. Stewart, who was then the head of the Standard Oil Company of Indiana, was transferring an appreciable share of the revenues of the company, at least temporarily, to his own pocket. With colleagues he had arranged to have the firm buy crude petroleum from a Canadian company, which he partly owned and which existed for the sole purpose of buying the oil in Texas and marking up the price to sell it to (among others) Colonel Stewart's firm. It was an admirable business. There were no costs at all, and Colonel Stewart got the profit. He later explained that he intended to return the bonds in which he put these profits to Standard Oil of Indiana, but had carelessly allowed them to remain in his safe-deposit box for many years and even more carelessly had clipped some of the coupons. The Rockefellers, who owned about 15 percent of the stock of the company, were able, though not without effort and expense, to throw the colonel out. It might not have been possible without the great prestige of John D. Rockefeller, Jr., and it was only possible because the colonel was engaged in a simple and very comprehensible form of skulduggery. Modern malfeasance or misfeasance would turn on some complicated problem of patents, procurement, royalties, government contracts, or the like in the technology of petrochemicals. It would not seem nearly so safe for outsiders to intervene in so difficult a matter, nor would the remedy be so unambiguous. I have said that modern group decision-making requires the exclusion of uninformed interference. This works both ways. The nature of the decision also excludes interference by owners.

One thing does make the autonomy of the modern corporation vulnerable. That is a failure of earnings. Then the corporation has no source of earnings, so it must turn to banks and other outside investors for savings. The latter, since the firm is doing badly, will have prying tendencies. And the stockholders who are not being rewarded may also be moved to do something about it. In modern times virtually all proxy battles in major companies have occurred when the firm was doing poorly. We may lay it down as a rule that a management which is making money is secure in its autonomy. One which is losing money is not. We should expect, as a final characteristic of the large corporation, that it would take care to protect its autonomy by always making money.

Here too our expectations are fulfilled. Economists have not yet noticed how completely they are fulfilled.

In the year 1957, a year of mild recession in the United States, not one of the hundred largest industrial corporations failed to return a profit. Only one of the largest two hundred finished the year in the red. Seven years later, in 1964, which was a prosperous year by general agreement, all of the first hundred again made money; only two among the first two hundred had losses, and only seven among the first five hundred. None of the fifty largest merchandising trading firms failed to return a profit. Nor did any one of the fifty largest utilities. And among the fifty largest transportation companies, only three railroads, together with the temporarily troubled Eastern Airlines, failed to make money.

Business liturgy has long intoned that profits and losses are symmetrical. One gets the profits at the price of risking losses. "The American competitive enterprise system is an acknowledged profit and loss system, the hope of profits being the incentive and the fear of loss being the spur." This is not true of that part of the economy in which the firm is able to protect its profits by planning. It isn't true of the United States Steel Corporation, author of the sentence just cited, which has not had losses for a quarter of a century.

Such is the corporation as a planning authority. It rivals in size the state itself. It has authority extending over and uniting the capital and organized talent that modern technology requires. Its authority extends on to its supply of capital. And its power is safely removed and protected from the extraneous or conflicting authority of either the state or its own owners or creditors.

[Next] I propose to examine how the corporation as a planning authority manages its environment—more especially, its prices and customers—and how it relates itself to the state.

MARKET PLANNING AND THE ROLE OF GOVERNMENT

In fact since Adam and as a matter of settled doctrine since Adam Smith, the businessman has been assumed to be subordinate to the market. . . . [I have shown that] modern highly technical processes and products and associated requirements of capital and time lead inevitably to planning—to the management of markets by those who supply them. It is technology, not ideology, that brings this result. The market serves admirably to supply simple things. But excellent as it may be on muskets, it is very bad on missiles. And not even the supply of components for the modern automobile can be trusted to the market; neither is it safe to assume that the market will absorb the necessary production at a remunerative price. There must be planning here as well.

The principal planning instrument in the modern economy is the large corporation. Within broad limits, it determines what the consumer shall have and at what price he shall have it. And it foresees the need for and arranges the necessary supply of capital, machinery, and materials.

The modern corporation is the direct descendant of the entrepreneur. This has kept us from seeing it in its new role. Had the corporation been an outgrowth of the state, which we readily associate with planning, we would not be in doubt. The modern corporation has, in fact, moved into a much closer association with the state than most of us imagine. And its planning activities are extensively and systematically supplemented by those of the state.

Let us consider first the regulation of prices in the modern economy and the means by which public behavior is accommodated to plan. Here, I should warn, we encounter some of the more deeply entrenched folk myths of our time, including a certain vested interest in error on the part of both economists and businessmen. If one takes faith in the market away from the economist, he is perilously barren of belief. So, he defends the market to defend his stock of knowledge. And the large corporate enterprise needs the concept of the market as a cover for the authority it exercises. It has great influence over our material existence and also our beliefs. But accepted doctrine holds that in all of its behavior it is subordinate to the market. It is merely an automation responding to instructions therefrom. Any complaint as to the use or misuse of power can be met by the answer that there is none.

Control of prices is an intrinsic feature of all planning. And it is made urgent by the special vagaries of the market for highly technical products. In the formally planned economies—that of the Soviet Union, for example—price control is a forthright function of the state, although there has been some tendency in recent times to allow some of the power over prices to devolve on the socialist firm. In the Western-type economies, comprehensive systems of price control have come about by evolution and adaptation. Nobody willed them. They were simply required by circumstance.

The power to set minimum industrial prices exists whenever a small number of firms share a market. The innocent at the universities have long been taught that small numbers of firms in the market—oligopoly, as it is known—accord to sellers the same power in imperfect form that has anciently been associated with monopoly. The principal difference is the imperfect nature of this monopoly power. It does not permit the exploitation of the consumer in quite such efficient fashion as was possible under the patents of monopoly accorded by the first Elizabeth to her favorites or by John D. Rockefeller to himself.

But in fact, the modern market shared by a few large firms is combined, in one of the more disconcerting contradictions of economic theory, with efficient production, expansive output, and prices that are generally thought rather favorable to the public. The consequences of oligopoly (few sellers) are greatly condemned in principle as being like those of monopoly but greatly approved in practice. Professor Paul Samuelson, the most distinguished of contemporary economists, warns in his famous textbook on economics that "to reduce the imperfections of competition" (by which he means markets consisting of a small number of large firms or oligopoly) "a nation must struggle perpetually and must ever maintain vigilance." Since American markets are now dominated by a very small number of large firms, the struggle, obviously, has been a losing one and is now lost. But the result is that the economy functions very well. Samuelson himself concludes that man-hour efficiency in the United States "can hardly help but grow at the rate of three percent or more, even if we do not rouse ourselves." A similar conflict between the inefficiency of oligopoly and the efficiency of an economy composed thereof is present in every well-regarded economic textbook. Samuelson agrees that technology and associated capital use are what improve efficiency. But these are precisely what require that there be planning and price control.

And here we have the answer. Prices in the modern economy are controlled not for the purposes of monopolistic exploitation. They are controlled for purposes of planning. This comes about as an effortless consequence of the development of that economy. Modern industrial planning both requires and rewards great size. This means, in turn, that a comparatively small number of large firms will divide the production of most (though not all) products. Each, as a matter of ordinary prudence, will act with full consideration of its own needs and of the common need. Each must have control of its own prices. Each will recognize this to be a requirement of others. Each will foreswear any action, and notably any sanguinary or competitive price-cutting, which would be prejudicial to the common interest in price control. This control is not difficult either to achieve or to maintain. Additionally, one firm's prices are another firm's costs. So, stability in prices means stability in costs.

The fact of control is far more important than the precise level at which prices are established. In 1964 in the United States, the big automobile companies had profits on their sales ranging from 5 percent to over 10 percent. There was security against collapse of prices and earnings for firms at either level. Planning was possible at either level of return. All firms could function satisfactorily. But none could have functioned had the price of a standard model fluctuated, depending on whim and reaction to the current novelties, from, say, $1800 to $3600, with steel, glass, chrome, plastics, paint, tires, stereo music, and labor moving over a similar range.

However, the level of prices is not unimportant. And from time to time, in response to major changes in cost—often when the renegotiation of a wage contract provides a common signal to all firms in the industry—prices must be changed. The prices so established will reflect generally the goals of those who guide the enterprise, not of the owners but of those who make the decisions. Security of earnings will be a prime objective. This is necessary for autonomy—for freedom from interference by shareholders and creditors. The next most important goal will be the growth of the firm. This is almost certainly more important than maximum profits. The professional managers and technicians who direct and guide the modern firm do not themselves get the profits. These accrue mainly to the shareholders. But the managers and technicians do get the benefits of expansion. This brings the prestige which is associated with a larger firm and which is associated with growth as such. And as a very practical matter, it opens up new executive jobs, new opportunities for promotion, and better excuses for higher pay.

Prices, accordingly, will be set with a view to attracting customers and expanding sales. When price control is put in the context of planning, the contradiction between expectation of monopolistic exploitation and expectation of efficiency, which pervades all textbook discussion, disappears. Planning calls for stability of prices and costs, security of return, and expansion. With none of these is the consumer at odds. Reality has, by its nature, advantages of internal consistency.

I must mention here one practical consequence of this argument, namely, its bearing on legal action against monopoly. There is a remarkable discrimination in which such measures, notably the antitrust laws, are now applied. A great corporation wielding vast power over its markets is substantially immune. It does not appear to misuse its power; accordingly, it is left alone. And in any case, to declare all large corporations illegal is, in effect, to declare the modern economy illegal. That is rather impractical—and would damage any President's consensus. But if two small firms making the same product seek to unite, this corporate union will be meticulously scrutinized. And very possibly, it will be forbidden. This may be so even though the merged firm is miniscule in size or market power as compared with the giant that is already a giant.

The explanation is that the modern antimonopoly and antitrust laws are substantially a charade. Their function is not to prevent exploitation of the public. If great size and great market power led to such exploitation, our case would long since have been hopeless. Their function is to persuade people, liberal economists in particular, that the market still exists, for here is the state vigilantly standing guard. It does so by exempting the larger firms and swatting those that seek to become larger.

The French, Germans, and Japanese either do not have or do not enforce such laws. That is because they are not impelled similarly to worship at the altar of the market. They quietly accept the logic of planning and its requirements in size for effective market control. There is no indication that they suffer in consequence.

When prices for a particular product are set by a few large firms, there is little danger of price-cutting. This part of the control is secure. There does remain a danger of uncontrolled price increases.

In particular, when a few large firms bargain with a strong union, conflict can be avoided by acceding to union demands. And there is not much incentive to resist. There is a common understanding among the firms that all will raise their prices to compensate for such a settlement. If demand is strong enough to keep the economy near full employment, it will be strong enough to make such price increases feasible. These price increases, in turn, set in motion demands for further wage increases. Thus, the familiar upward spiral of wages and prices proceeds. And this too is prejudicial to planning. The individual firm, moreover, cannot prevent such price increases; they are beyond its control as a planning unit.

So here, more and more we follow the practice of the formally planned economies. We rely on the state to set maximum wages and prices. In the United States as in Britain this is done with great caution, circumspection, and diffidence, somewhat in the manner of a Victorian spinster viewing an erotic statue. Such action is held to be unnatural and temporary. Economists accord it little or no standing in economic policy. They say it interferes with the market. Unions also dislike it: they say it interferes with free collective bargaining. Businessmen disapprove: they say it interferes with their natural freedom of decision on prices. And what everyone opposes in principle, all advanced countries end up doing in practice. The answer once more is clear. In a market economy, such ceilings would be unnecessary. But they are an indispensable counterpart of economic planning and of the minimum price control that already exists.

This price- and wage-setting by the state could be dispensed with by having such a shortage of demand that it would be impossible for firms to raise prices and unions to raise wages. That is to say, we could do without such controls by rehabilitating the market for labor and industrial products. It would not then be possible to raise wages in response to prices or prices in response to wages. But that would mean unemployment or greater uncertainty of employment, and it would mean greater market uncertainty for producers–for businessmen. Despite everyone's affection for the market, almost no one wants these results. So we have strong demand, small unemployment, reliable purchases, and the maximum price and wage controls that these require. And we try to avert our eyes from this result. It would be simpler were we to recognize that we have planning and that this control is an indispensable aspect.

This leads to another subject, the management of what people buy at the controlled prices.

The key to the management of demand is effective influence over the purchases of final consumers. The latter include both private individuals and the state. If all such purchases are under effective control, there will then be a reliable demand throughout the system for raw materials, parts, machinery, and other items going into the ultimate product. If the demand for its automobiles is secure, an automobile company can accord its suppliers the certainty of long-term contracts for *their* planning. And, even in the absence of such contracts, there will still be a reliable and predictable flow of orders. How, then, are the individual consumers managed?

As so often happens, change in modern industrial society has made possible what change requires. The need to control consumer behavior arises from the exigencies of planning. Planning, in turn, is made necessary by extensive use of advanced technology and the time and capital this requires. This is an efficient way of producing goods; the result is a very large volume of production. As a further consequence in the economically advanced countries, goods that serve elementary physical sensation—that prevent hunger, protect against cold, provide shelter, suppress pain—include only a small and diminishing part of what people consume. Only a few goods serve needs that are made known to the individual by the palpable discomfort or pain that is experienced in their absence. Most are enjoyed because of some psychic or aesthetic response to their possession or use. They give the individual a sense of personal achievement; they accord him a feeling of equality with his neighbors; they make him feel superior; or they divert his mind from thought or the absence of thought; or they promote or satisfy sexual aspiration; or they promise social acceptability; or they enhance his subjective feelings of health, well-being, and adequate peristalsis; or they are thought to contribute to personal beauty.

Thus it comes about that as the industrial system develops to where it has need for planning and the management of the consumer that this requires, we find it serving wants which are psychological in origin. And these are admirably subject to appeal to the psyche. Hence they can be managed. A man whose stomach is totally empty cannot be persuaded that his need is for entertainment. Physical discomfort will tell him he needs food more. But though a hungry man cannot be persuaded to choose between bread and a circus, a well-fed man can. And he can be persuaded to choose between different circuses and different foods.

By giving a man a ration card or distributing to him the specific commodities he is to consume, the individual can be required to consume in accordance with plan. But this is an onerous form of control, and is ill adapted to differences in personality. In advanced industrial societies, it is considered acceptable only in times of great stress or for the very poor. (Even in the formally planned economies—the Soviet Union and the Eastern European states—the ration card is a manifestation of failure.) It is easier, and if less precise, still sufficient, to manage people by persuasion rather than by fiat.

Though advertising will be thought of as the central feature of this persuasion, and is certainly important, it is but a part of a much larger apparatus for the management of demand. Nor does this consist alone in devising a sales strategy for a particular product. It often means devising a product, or features of a product, around which a sales strategy can be built. Product design, model change, packaging, and even performance reflect the need to provide what are called strong selling points. They are as much a part of the process of demand management as the advertising campaign.

The first step in this process, generally speaking, is to ensure a loyal or automatic corps of customers. This is known as building customer loyalty and brand recognition. If successful, it means that the firm has a stable body of customers who are secure against any large-scale defection. Being thus reliable and predictable, they allow planning.

A purely defensive strategy will not, however, suffice. In line with the goals of its directing organization, the firm will want to expand sales. And such effort is necessary to hold a given position. The same will be true of others. Out of these efforts, from firms that have the resources to play the game (another advantage of size), comes a crude equilibrating process which accords to each participant a reasonably reliable share of the market.

Specifically, when a firm is enjoying a steady patronage by its existing customers and recruiting new ones at what seems a satisfactory rate, the existing strategy for consumer management–advertising, selling methods, product design–will be considered satisfactory. The firm will not quarrel with success. However, if sales are stationary or slipping, this will call for a change in selling methods–in advertising, product design, or even in the product itself. Testing and experiment are possible. And sooner or later, a formula providing a suitable response is obtained. This will lead, in turn, to countering action by the firms that are then failing to make gains. And out of this process a rough but reliable equilibrium between the participants is achieved.

It does not always work. There are Edsels. But it is the everyday assumption of those who engage in management of demand that if sales of a product are slipping, a new selling formula can be found that will correct the situation. By and large, the assumption is justified. Means, in other words, can almost always be found to keep the exercise of consumer discretion within safe or planned limits.

Management of the consumer on the scale that I have just outlined requires that there be some comprehensive, repetitive, and compelling communication between the managers of demand and those who are managed. It must be possible to win the attention of those who are being managed for considerable periods of time without great effort on their part.

Technology, once again, solved the problem it created. Coincidentally with rising mass incomes came first radio and then television. In their capacity to hold effortless interest, their accessibility over the entire cultural spectrum, and their independence of any educational qualification, these were superbly suited to mass persuasion. Television was especially serviceable. Not since the invention of speech has any medium of communication appeared which is so readily accommodated to the whole spectrum of mental capacity.

There is an insistent tendency among social scientists, including economists, to think that any institution which features singing commercials, shows the human intestinal tract in full or impaired operation, equates the effortless elimination of human whiskers with the greatest happiness of man, and implies that exceptional but wholesome opportunities for seduction are associated with a particular make of automobile is inherently trivial. This is a great mistake. The modern industrial system is profoundly dependent on this art. What is called progress makes it increasingly so.

And the management of demand so provided is in all respects an admirably subtle arrangement in social design. It works not on the individual but on the mass. An individual of will and determination can, in principle, contract out from under its influence. This being the case, no individual compulsion in the purchase of any product can ever be established. To all who object there is a natural answer: You are at liberty to leave! Yet there is no danger that enough people will ever assert this choice–will ever leave–to impair the management of mass behavior.

In the nonsocialist economy, the modern large corporation is, to repeat, the basic planning unit. For some planning tasks, we see that it is exceedingly competent. It can fix minimum prices. It can sufficiently manage consumer wants. And it can extract from revenues the savings it needs for its own growth and expansion. But some things it cannot do. Though the modern corporation can set and maintain minimum prices, it cannot, we have seen, set maximum prices and wages; it cannot prevent wages from forcing up prices and prices from forcing up wages in the familiar spiral. And while it can manage the demand for individual products, it cannot control total demand—it cannot ensure that total purchasing power in the economy will be equal, or approximately equal, to the supply of goods that can be produced by the current working force.

There are two other planning tasks that the large corporation cannot perform. It cannot supply the specialized manpower that modern technology and complex organization and planning require. It can train, but on the whole, it cannot educate. And it cannot absorb the risks and costs that are associated with very advanced forms of scientific and technical development—with the development of atomic power, or supersonic air transports, or antimissile defenses, or weapons systems to pierce these defenses, or the like requirements of modern civilized living.

This leads to a conclusion of great importance. The shortcomings of the large corporation as a planning instrument define the role of the modern state in economic policy. Wherever the private corporation cannot plan, the state comes in and performs the required function. Wherever the modern corporation can do the job, as in setting minimum prices or managing consumer demand, the state must remain out, usually as a matter of principle. But the corporation cannot fix maximum prices, so we have the state establishing wage and price guideposts or otherwise limiting wage and price increases. The private firm cannot control aggregate demand, so the state comes in to manipulate taxes, public spending, and bank lending—to implement what we call modern Keynesian policy. The private firm cannot supply specialized manpower, so we have a great expansion in publicly supported education. Private firms cannot afford to underwrite supersonic aircraft. So governments—British, French, or American—come in to do so and with no taint of socialism.

Our attitudes on the proper role of the state are firmly fixed by what the private corporation can or cannot do. The latter can set minimum prices for cigarettes, persuade people to buy a new and implausible detergent, or develop a more drastic laxative. This being so, such planning activity is naturally held to be sacred to private enterprise.

The planning functions of the state are somewhat less sacred. Some still have an improvised or *ad hoc* aspect. Thus, restraints on wages and prices are perpetual emergency actions; though fully accepted. Keynesian regulation of aggregate demand is thought to be occasioned by the particular imperatives of full employment and growth; the expansion of education is regarded as a result of a new enlightenment following World War II; the underwriting of especially expensive technology is a pragmatic response to the urgent social need for faster travel, emigration to the moon, bigger explosions, and competition with the Soviet Union.

So to regard matters is to fail to see the nature of modern planning. It is to yield unduly to the desire to avert our eyes from the reality of economic life. The planning functions of the state are not *ad hoc* or separate developments. They are a closely articulated set of functions which supplement and fill the gaps in the planning of the modern large firm. Together these provide a comprehensive planning apparatus. It decides what people should have and then arranges that they will get it and that they will want it. Not the least of its achievements is in leaving them with the impression that the controlling decisions are all theirs.

The Keynesian regulation of aggregate demand also requires only a word. The need for it follows directly from modern industrial planning. As we have seen, corporations decide authoritatively what they will reserve from earnings for reinvestment and expansion. But in the non-Soviet economies, there is no mechanism that ensures that the amounts so withheld for investment will be matched in the economy as a whole by what is invested. So there must be direct action by the state to equate the two. This it does primarily by manipulating private investment (principally in housing) and public spending and taxation. The need to equate the planned savings and the planned investment of the large corporation is not, of course, the only reason for such action. Savings and investment elsewhere in the economy must also be matched. But savings and investment by the large planning corporations are by far the most important in the total.

The successful regulation of demand requires that the quantitative rôle of the state in the modern economy be relatively large. That is because demand is regulated primarily by increasing or decreasing the expenditures of the state or decreasing or increasing the taxes it collects. Only when the state is large and its revenues are substantial will these changes be large enough to serve. One effective way of ensuring the requisite scale of state activity is to have it underwrite modern technology, which is admirably expensive. Such is the case with modern weaponry, space exploration, even highway and airport design. Though technology helps destroy the market, it does make possible the planning that replaces the market.

The next function of the state is to provide the specialized and trained manpower which the industrial system cannot supply to itself. This has led in our time to a very great expansion in education, especially in higher education, as has been true in all of the advanced countries. In 1900, there were 24,000 teachers in colleges and universities in the United States; in 1920, there were 49,000; by 1970, three years hence, there will be 480,000. This is rarely pictured as an aspect of modern economic development; it is the vanity of educators that they consider themselves the moving force in a new enlightenment. But it may be significant that when industry, at a little earlier stage, required mostly unlettered proletarians, that is what the educational system supplied. As it has come to need engineers, sales executives, copywriters, computer programmers, personnel managers, information retrieval specialists, product planners, and executive panjandrums, these are what the educational system has come to provide.

Once the community or nation that wanted more industry gave first thought to its capital supply and how to reassure the bankers on its reliability. Now it gives first thought to its educational system.

We cannot be altogether happy about education that is so motivated. There is danger that it will be excessively vocational and that we shall have a race of men who are strong on telemetry and space communications but who cannot read anything but a blueprint or write anything but a computer program. There is currently some uneasiness about liberal education in the modern industrial society. But so far this has manifested itself only in speeches by university presidents. In this segment of society, unfortunately a solemn speech is regularly considered a substitute for action.

Much the most interesting of the planning functions of the state is the underwriting of expensive technology. Few changes in economic life have ever proceeded with such explosive rapidity. Few have so undermined conventional concepts of public and private enterprise. In 1962, the U.S. government spent an estimated $10.6 billion on research and development. This was more than its total dollar outlay for all purposes, military or civilian, before World War II. But this function also includes the underwriting of markets—the provision of a guaranteed demand for billions of dollars worth of highly technical products, from aircraft to missiles to electronic gear to space vehicles. Nearly all of this expenditure, some 80 to 85 percent, goes to the large corporation, which is to say that it is to the planned sector of the American economy. It also brings the modern large corporation into the most intimate association with the state. In the case of such public agencies as NASA, the Atomic Energy Commission, or the Air Force, and the corporations serving them, it is no longer easy to say where the public sector ends and the private sector begins. Individuals and organizations are intimately associated. The private sector becomes, in effect, an extended arm of the public bureaucracy. However, the banner of private enterprise can be quite aggressively flaunted by the firm that does 75 percent of its business with the government and yearns to do more.

In the past, Keynesians have argued that there is nothing very special about government business. Replying to standard Marxian charges that capitalism depends excessively on armaments, they have pointed out that spending for housing, theaters, automobiles, highways to allow more automobiles to exist, and for radios to supply more automobiles to amuse more people while they are sitting in the resulting traffic jams, and for other of the attributes of gracious living will serve to sustain demand just as well as spending on arms. This, we now see, is not the whole story. The expenditures I have just mentioned would not serve to underwrite technology. And this underwriting is beyond the reach of private planning. Replacement of military spending, with its emphasis on underwriting advanced technology, must be by other equally technical outlays if it is to serve the same purpose. Otherwise, technical development will have to be curtailed to that level where corporate planning units can underwrite on their own. And this curtailment under present circumstances would be very, very drastic.

This analysis makes a considerable case for the space race. It is not that exploring the moon, Mars, or even Saturn is of high social urgency. Rather, the space race allows for an extensive underwriting of advanced technology. And it does this in a field of activity where spending is large and where, in contrast with weapons and weapons systems, competition with the Soviets is comparatively safe and benign. At the same time, as in the case of competitive athletics, everyone can easily be persuaded that it is absolutely vital to win.

We now see the modern corporation, in the technological aspects of its activities, moving into a very close association with the state. The state is the principal customer for such technology and the underwriter of major risk. In the planning of tasks and missions, the mapping of development work, and the execution of contracts, there is nowadays a daily and intimate association between the bureaucracy and the large so-called private firm. But one thing, it will be said, keeps them apart. The state is in pursuit of broad national goals, whatever these may be. And the private firm seeks to make money–in the more solemn language of economics, to maximize profits. This difference in goals, it will be said, sufficiently differentiates the state from private enterprise.

But here again reality supplies that indispensable thread of consistency. For power . . . has passed from the owners of the corporation to the managers and scientists and technicians. The latter now exercise largely autonomous power, and not surprisingly, they exercise it in *their* own interest. And this interest differs from that of the owners. As noted, security of return is more important than the level of total earnings. When earnings fail, the autonomy of the decision-makers is threatened. And growth is more important to managers and technicians than maximum earnings.

But a further and important conclusion follows, for economic security and growth are also prime goals of the modern state. Nothing has been more emphasized in modern economic policy than the prevention of depression or recession. Politicians promise it automatically and without perceptible thought. And no test of social achievement is so completely and totally accepted as the rate of economic growth. It is the common measure of accomplishment of all the economic systems. Transcending political faith, religion, occupation, or all except eccentric philosophical persuasion, it is something on which Americans, Russians, Englishmen, Frenchmen, Germans, Italians, and Yugoslavs, and even Irishmen, all agree.

We have seen that as an aspect of its planning, the modern industrial enterprise accommodates the behavior and beliefs of the individual consumer to its needs. It is reasonable to assume that it has also accommodated our social objectives and associated beliefs to what it needs. In any case, there has been an interaction between state and firm which has brought a unity of goals.

A somber thought will occur to many here. We have seen that the state is necessary for underwriting the technology of modern industrial enterprise. Much of this it does within the framework of military expenditure. In the consumer goods economy, the wants and beliefs of the consumer, including his conviction that happiness is associated all but exclusively with the consumption of goods, are accommodated, in greater or less measure, to producer need. Is this true also of the state? Does it respond in its military procurement to what the supplying firms need to sell–and the technology that they wish to have underwritten? Are images of foreign policy in the planned industrial communities–in the United States, the Soviet Union, Western Europe–shaped by industrial need? Do we have an image of conflict because that serves technological and therewith planning need?

We cannot exclude that possibility; on the contrary, it is most plausible. It is a conclusion that was reached, perhaps a bit more intuitively, by President Eisenhower while he was President of the United States. In his famous valedictory, he warned of the influence on public policy resulting from the "conjunction of an immense military establishment and a large arms industry." This will not be an agreeable thought for those for whom the mind is an instrument for evading reality. Others will see the possibility of a two-way flow of influence. Presumably it will be true of any planned economy, East or West. The image of the foreign policy affects the demand of the state on industry. But the needs of economic planning expressed in the intimate association between industry and the state will affect the state's view of military requirements and of foreign policy. It is a matter where we had best be guided by reality. . . .

CAPITALISM, SOCIALISM, AND THE FUTURE OF THE INDUSTRIAL STATE

By its nature the direction of the modern large corporation is a collective, not an individual, function. Decisions are made by groups, not by individuals. That is because technology, planning, and organization all require specialized knowledge. The knowledge of specialists must be combined, and the result is collective authority. It is the authority of amorphous and changing combinations of specialized talent. . . . I want to look a little more broadly at this group authority, to show how it manifests itself not in the firm with capitalist antecedents but in the socialist enterprise. Is it inevitable there? And does it mean that under socialism or Communism one will tend to find the same general structure of organization as in the United States and Western Europe? And where, in this industrial development, are we headed?

We may agree at the outset that since technology and planning and organization are what accord power to the group as distinct from the individual, the group will have a decisive authority wherever technology, planning, and organization are features of the productive process. This is a technical matter; ideology is not involved. If decisions require the information of several or many people, power will pass to the several or many, whatever the proclaimed form of the system.

In the nonsocialist economies, as the firm develops, it becomes necessary to exclude uninformed authority. This, as I have shown in earlier articles, includes the owners. In the 1920s and 1930s and on into the war years, the first Henry Ford insisted on exercising his authority as the sole owner of the Ford Motor Company. It was disastrous. Losses were enormous; the firm very nearly failed. During the war there was discussion in Washington of having Ford taken over and managed by Studebaker. In the same period, Montgomery Ward suffered somewhat less severely from the similar effort of its chairman, Mr. Sewell Avery. And the creditors of TWA a few years ago made it a condition of their loans that Howard Hughes, the then owner, not exercise his prerogatives as owner. Ford, Avery, and Hughes were not notably stupid men; it was rather that all of these firms had reached the size and technical complexity where group decision-making had to be protected from such interference. Capitalism at its highest development requires there be no capitalist interference. One would expect that a public corporation of similar size and complexity would suffer from similar intervention by cabinet members, politicians, or bureaucrats. But if the latter must be excluded, it means that socialism, similarly, must be without social control. Experience bears out this expectation.

The British, who have a superior instinct for administration, have recognized the need for autonomy for the nationalized industries. These were considerably expanded in number by the Attlee government following World War II. A decisive issue was that of parliamentary questions and comment. If these were allowed on the decisions of nationalized industries, ministers would have to be informed of such decisions in advance. Otherwise they would confess ignorance and imply neglect of duty. But important decisions, those which Parliament would be most likely to be concerned with, turn on complex and technical information. So, if the minister were to exercise informed judgment, he would need the help of a technical staff. All this being so, responsibility would be removed from the nationalized firm to the ministry. The cost in delayed decision would also be high. So, only if parliamentary intervention were excluded could the firm, and therein the decision-making specialists, act responsibly on questions requiring specialized information. All important questions do. Coal, electricity, gas, road transport, the airlines, and the other publicly owned industries were, in consequence, all accorded such autonomy.

This autonomy is even more necessary for large decisions than for small. And it is large decisions that we call policy decisions. The choice between molecular and atomic reactions for the generation of electricity is a policy decision. It is also grounded in a variety of scientific, technical, economic, and planning judgments. Only a committee, or more precisely, a complex of committees, can combine the knowledge, training, and experience that such a decision requires. So also with the question of whether the North Atlantic should be flown by American or British aircraft. So, in only slightly less measure, the question of how wage scales are to be revised or the railways nationalized. These are the questions on which Parliament would most expect to be consulted. They are among the ones from which it is most decisively excluded. Some years ago Mr. C. A. R. Crosland, the economist and present Minister of Education in the Wilson government, observed that "the public corporation in Britain has not up to the present been in any real sense accountable to Parliament, whose function has been limited to fitful, fragmentary, and largely ineffective *ex post facto* criticism." This is as one would expect.

For most socialists the purpose of socialism is control of productive enterprise by the society. And for democratic socialists this means the legislature. None, or not many, seek socialism so that power can be exercised by an autonomous and untouchable corporation, and yet this is as it must be. It does not matter that the capitalist, the ancient target of the socialist, suffers from the same exclusion and must, like the Rockefellers, Kennedys, and Harrimans, go into politics in order to have power. Not all admit to this change in capitalism. They observe only how little difference nationalization of an industry seems to mean. As A. M. F. Palmer, a socialist commentator, referring to Britain put it a few years ago, "If an intelligent observer from Mars or Venus should come and examine all large contemporary industrial concerns—public or private—as *working enterprises,* he would notice, I suspect, only their overwhelming sameness."

One result is that a large number of socialists have come to feel that public corporations are, by their nature, and again in Mr. Crosland's words, "remote, irresponsible bodies, immune from public scrutiny or democratic control." And in further consequences, a considerable number have given up the fight for public ownership or accord it only lip service. They have agreed, though few have yet recognized it, that democratic socialism, like vintage capitalism, is the natural victim of modern technology and associated organization and planning.

There have been experiments with more aggressive public control which serve to show that this is not an alternative. In India and Ceylon, and also in some of the new African countries, public enterprises have not, as in Britain, been accorded autonomy. Here the democratic socialist prerogative had, in effect, been fully asserted. The right to examine budgets and expenditures, to review policies, and in particular, to question management through the responsible minister on all actions of the public corporation has been reserved to the legislature.

And here, as elsewhere, if the minister is to be questioned, he must have knowledge. He cannot plead that he is uninformed without admitting to being a nonentity, a common enough condition in the politics of all countries but one which can never be treated with candor. Technical personnel in these countries are less experienced than in the countries which were industrialized earlier. Organization is less mature. This leads to error, and it further suggests to parliamentarians and civil servants the need for careful review of decisions by higher and presumably wiser authority. India, in particular, as a legacy of colonial administration has an illusion of official omnipotence which extends to highly technical decisions. Moreover, poverty makes nepotism and favoritism in letting contracts both more tempting and more culpable than in the rich country where jobs are more plentiful and business is easier to come by. This also seems to call for further review. Rigid personnel and civil service requirements may prevent the easy constitution and reconstitution of groups with information relevant to changing problems.

The effect in these countries of this denial of autonomy has been exceedingly inefficient operations by the public firms. Delay occasioned by review of decisions has added its special dimensions of cost. In business operations a wrong decision can often be reversed at little cost when the error becomes evident. But the cost of a delayed decision—in terms of men and capital that stand idle awaiting the decision—can never be retrieved.

Social control naturally bears with particular effect on two decisions which are of great popular interest—on the prices to be charged to the public and the wages to be paid to workers. Its effect is to keep prices lower and wages higher than the more authoritarian corporations in the advanced countries would ever allow. This is no good fortune. It eliminates net earnings and therewith this source of savings. The poor country, which most needs capital, is thus denied the source of capital on which the rich countries most rely. In India and Ceylon nearly all publicly owned corporations operate at a loss. The situation is similar in other new countries. (One of the sometime exceptions, it is interesting to notice, is the publicly owned airline. It usually claims for itself an autonomy that other public corporations do not have. One possible reason is that public officials are among the principal clients and sense the personal danger in denying airline management the requisite autonomy.)

The poor showing of democratic socialism has, on the whole, been one of the great disappointments of these last years in countries where there has been a concern for industrial development. And the reason rests not with socialism as such, but with the effort to combine socialist industrial management with democracy. It is part of the modern faith that democracy is both good and omnipotent. Like the family, truth, and sound personal hygiene, it is always above doubt. But it cannot be brought to bear on the decisions of the modern large-scale industrial enterprise. By its nature, this is an autarchy of its managers and technicians.

If autonomy is necessary for the effective performance by the firm, it should be needed also in the Soviet-type economies. The requirement begins with the need to combine the specialized information of different men. This need, to repeat, cannot be dispensed with by any ideology.

The need for autonomy in the Soviet firm could, however, be somewhat less, for its functions are far fewer than those of an American enterprise of comparable size in a similar industry. That is because many of the planning functions performed by the American or European firm are, in the Soviet-type economy, performed by the state. The large American corporation sets its prices, organizes the demand for its products, establishes or negotiates prices for its raw materials and components, takes steps to ensure supply, and establishes or negotiates rates for various categories of trained and specialized employees. In the U.S.S.R. these tasks are all performed by the state planning apparatus. Production and investment targets, which are established by the American firm for itself, are also given to the Soviet firm, though with some flexibility in application, by the state.

In consequence, the organization of the Soviet firm is far simpler than that of its American or British counterpart. There are no comparable sales, merchandising, dealer relations, product planning, procurement planning, or industrial relations departments. Most of the top positions are held by engineers. This is in keeping with the much greater preoccupation of the Soviet Union with technical as distinct from planning functions.

Nonetheless, the Soviet firm sets considerable and increasing store by its autonomy. There are two major sources of outside interference in the Soviet Union—the state planning apparatus and the Communist Party.[3] Soviet economic literature recurrently warns against bureaucratic interference with the operations of the firm. As Professor Ely Devons, a noted British authority, concluded in an article in *The Listener* in 1957:

> The Russians have learnt by experience that you cannot have responsible and efficient action at the level of the firm with continuous intervention and instruction from numerous outside authorities. Conflicting instructions from outside give the manager innumerable excuses for failure; waste and inefficiency may result from a serious attempt to run the firm from a distance. Every argument for delegation, decentralization, and devolution used in discussions about business administration in the West is echoed, although in a different jargon, in Russia. And the case for such devolution has been pressed with increasing emphasis as Russian industry has grown and become more complex.

Soviet plant managers, from my own experience, do not hesitate to stress both their need for autonomy and also their past difficulties in this regard. And on the other side, managements, especially those of large firms, have often been condemned for excessive independence—for behaving as "feudal lords" above the law. In the Soviet Union the

3. I have drawn here not only on the vast literature of Soviet planning but on fairly extensive firsthand observation, in the spring of 1959 and more briefly in the summer of 1964. I am extensively grateful to Soviet economists and plant managers for help and hospitality.

most important medium of social comment after poetry is the novel; one of the half dozen most discussed works since World War II has been Vladimir Dudintsev's defense of the small, independent inventor against the mindless bureaucracy of the great metal *combinat* in his book *Not by Bread Alone.* The author's affections are in close harmony with those of the American who, in the tradition of Brandeis, argues for the genius of the small entrepreneur as against the solid, unimaginative behavior of the great corporation. Both have more support from humane instinct than reality. Neither sees that modern technology makes essential the machinery for mobilizing specialized knowledge. It might also be added that Dudintsev's inventor would never have got the Soviet astronauts into space.

The position of the Communist Party Secretary—the second source of interference—is also predictably difficult. This man enters the plant hierarchy horizontally, as a member of the staff or working force, and is still subject to the external authority of the Party. If he participates as a member of the decision-making group, he naturally becomes responsible for its decisions, and therefore he is no longer the independent agent of the Party. If he does not participate, he no longer knows what is going on. If he is too good a source of information, and here I quote from a distinguished authority, Professor Joseph S. Berliner, "He may be raised in party rank but . . . then he will not be able to find out what is going on in the plant. Nobody will have any confidence in him." Professor David Granick, another authority, concludes that the relationship of the party officials is "an uneasy compromise." Given the imperatives of group decision and the group's need to protect itself from outside intervention, we see that this is the plausible result.

So, it seems likely that the Soviet resolution of the problem of authority in the industrial enterprise is not so different from that in the West. Like that of the shareholder in the United States or Britain, the authority of the people and party is celebrated in public ritual. They are pictured as paramount, as the stockholder is with us. But in practice, as with us, extensive and increasing power of final decision is vested in the enterprise.

The trend to decentralization, so called, in the Soviet and other Eastern European countries reflects this growing autonomy. It accords to the firm greater authority over prices, individual wage rates, production targets, investment, and other uses of its earnings. Among the more eager or anxious friends of the price system in the United States, this trend has been widely hailed as reflecting a return to the market. The celebration is premature. The large Soviet firm is not being made subject to uncontrolled prices, unmanaged demand, or to the market prices for its labor or raw materials. Given the level of technology, the related commitment of time and capital, this would no more be possible in the U.S.S.R. than in the United States. The Soviet firm through decentralizations is being given some of the planning functions that Western corporations have long performed. This reflects the need of the Soviet firm to have more of the instruments for successful operation under its own authority. There is no tendency for the Soviet and the Western systems to converge under the authority of the market. Both have outgrown that. What exists is a very important convergence to the same form of planning under the authority of the business firm.

I want now to reflect on the meaning of this development—on the question, Where does all this lead?

For some of these consequences—the effect on government, education, urban life, the prospect for leisure and toil, the future of the unions, the evolution of what I have called the educational and scientific estate, and the effect of fewer workers and more educators on politics—I must refer the reader to *The New Industrial State*, . . . But though I cannot be exhaustive, I must sketch some broad conclusions here.

In the latter part of the last century and the early decades of this, no subject was more discussed than the future of capitalism. Economists, men of unspecific wisdom, political philosophers, knowledgeable ecclesiastics, and George Bernard Shaw all contributed their personal revelation. All agreed that the economic system was in a state of development and in time would transform itself into something hopefully better but certainly different. Socialists drew strength from the belief that theirs was the plausible next step in the natural process of change.

Now the future of the modern industrial economy is not much discussed. The prospect for agriculture is still subject to debate; it is assumed to be in a process of transition. So are the chances for the small businessman. But General Motors is an ultimate achievement. One does not wonder where he is going if he has already arrived. That there will be no further change in institutions that are themselves a result of such vast change is highly implausible. The future of the modern industrial system is not discussed, partly because of the influence it exercises over our belief. We agree that unions, the churches, airplanes, and the Congress lack absolute perfection. The modern corporation, however, is a perfected structure. So it has won exemption from speculation as to how it might be improved.

Additionally, to consider its future is to fix attention on where it already is. Among the least attractive phrases in the American business lexicon are planning, government control, and socialism. To consider the chance for these in the future is to bring home the extent to which they are already a fact. The government influences industrial prices and wages, regulates demand, supplies the decisive factor of production, which is trained manpower, underwrites much technology, and provides the markets for products of highest technical sophistication. In the formally planned economies of Eastern Europe, the role of the state is not startlingly different. And these things have arrived, at a minimum with the acquiescence, and at the maximum at the demand, of private enterprise itself.

The next step will be a general recognition of the convergent tendencies of modern industrial systems, even though differently billed as socialism or capitalism. And we must also assume that this is a good thing. In time it will dispose of the notion of inevitable conflict based on irreconcilable difference. This difference is still cherished by the ideologists on both sides. To Marxists, the evolution here described, and most notably the replacement of capitalist power by that of technical organization, is unacceptable. Marx did not foresee it, and Marx has always been required by his disciples to have had the supernatural power of foreseeing everything for all time—although some alterations are allowed on occasion in what he is thought to have seen. And ideologists in the West who speak for the unbridgeable gulf that divides the free from the Communist world are protected by a similar theology, supported in many cases by a rather proud immunity to intellectual influences. But these positions can survive the evidence only for a time. Men lose their resistance when they realize that they are coming to look retarded or old-fashioned. Vanity is a great force for intellectual modernization.

The modern planned economy requires that the state underwrite its more sophisticated and risky technology. The weapons competition provides the rationale for much of this underwriting at the present time. This competition depends, in its turn, on the notion of irreconcilable hostility based on irreconcilable difference between economic systems. But the fact is convergence. The conclusion follows and by no especially elaborate chain of reasoning. The difference between economic systems, from which the assumption of hostility and conflict derives, does not exist. What exists is an image adhered to on both sides that serves the underwriting of technology. And very obviously, there are other ways of underwriting technology.

To bring the weapons competition to an end will not be easy. But it contributes to this goal, one trusts, to realize that the economic premises on which it rests are not real. None of this disposes of different attitudes on intellectual and cultural freedom and the First Amendment. I set rather high store by these. But these have been thought to be partially derivative of the economic systems.

Private enterprise has anciently been so described because it was subordinate to the market and those in command derived their power from the ownership of private property. The modern corporation is no longer subordinate to the market; those who guide it no longer depend on ownership for their authority. They must have autonomy within a framework of goals. But this allows them to work intimately with the public bureaucracy and, indeed, to perform tasks for the bureaucracy that it cannot do, or cannot do as well, for itself. In consequence, for tasks of technical sophistication, there is a close fusion, as we have seen, of the modern industrial system with the state. As I have earlier observed, the line that now divides public from so-called private organization in military procurement, space exploration, and atomic energy is so indistinct as to be nearly imperceptible. Men move easily across the line. Technicians from government and corporations work constantly together. On retirement, admirals and generals and high civil servants go more or less automatically to government-related industries. Onc close and experienced observer, Professor Murray L. Weidenbaum, a former employee of Boeing, has called this the "seminationalized" branch of the economy.

He is speaking of firms which do all or a large share of their business with the government. But most large firms do a substantial share of their business with the state. And they are as dependent on the state as the weapons firms for the other supports to their planning. It requires no great exercise of imagination to suppose that the mature corporation, as it develops, will eventually become a part of the larger administrative complex with the state. In time the line between the two will largely disappear. Men will marvel at the thin line that once caused people to refer to General Electric, Westinghouse, or Boeing as *private* business.

Although this recognition will not be universally welcomed, it will be healthy. And if the mature corporation is recognized to be part of the state or some penumbra of the state, it cannot plead its inherently private character, or its subordination to the market, as cover for the pursuit of goals of primary interest to its own guiding organization. It can be expected to accept public goals in matters of aesthetics, health and safety, and general social tranquillity that are not inconsistent with its survival. The public bureaucracy has an unquestioned tendency to pursue its own goals and reflect its own interest and convenience. But it cannot plead this as a right. So with the corporation as its essentially public character comes to be accepted.

Other changes can be imagined. As the public character of the mature corporation comes to be recognized, attention will doubtless focus on the position of the shareholder. This is already anomalous. A shareholder is a passive and functionless figure, remarkable only in his capacity to participate, without effort or even, given the planning, without risk, in the gains of the growth by which the directing organization now measures its success. No grant of feudal privilege in history ever equaled, for effortless return, that of the American grandparent who thoughtfully endowed his descendants with a thousand shares each of General Motors and IBM. But I do not need to pursue these matters here. Questions of equity as between the accidentally rich have their own special expertise.

Some will insist that the world of the modern large firms is not the whole economy. At the opposite pole from General Motors and Standard Oil is the world of the independent shopkeeper, farmer, shoe repairman, bookmaker, narcotics peddler, pizza merchant, streetwalker, and owner of the car and dog laundry. Here prices are not controlled. Here the consumer is sovereign. Here pecuniary motivation is unimpaired. Here technology is simple, and there is no research or development to make it otherwise. Here there are no government contracts; independence from the state, the narcotics trade and prostitution possibly apart, is a reality. But one should cherish his critics and protect them where possible from foolish error. The tendency of the great corporation in the modern industrial system to become part of the administrative complex of the state cannot be refuted by appeal to the contrary tendencies of the miniscule enterprise.

The two questions most asked about an economic system are whether it serves man's physical needs and whether it is consistent with his liberty and general happiness. There is little doubt as to the ability of the modern industrial system to supply man with goods–it is able to manage consumer demand only because it supplies it so abundantly. Wants would not be subject to management or manipulation had they not been first dulled by sufficiency. In the United States, as in other advanced countries, there are many poor people. But they are not to be found within the part of the economy with which we are here concerned. That [this] article [does] not deal with poverty does not mean, incidentally, that I am unaware of its existence.

The prospect for liberty is far more interesting. It has always been imagined, especially by conservatives, that to associate all, or a large part, of economic activity with the state is to endanger freedom. The individual in one way or another will be sacrificed to the convenience of the political and economic power so conjoined. As the modern industrial system evolves into a penumbra of the state, the question of its relation to liberty thus arises in urgent form. In recent years in the Soviet Union and in the Soviet-type economies, there has been a poorly concealed conflict between the state and the intellectuals. It has been between those who speak for the needs of the state and its disciplines, as economic planner and producer of goods, and those who assert the higher claims of intellectual and artistic expression. Is this a warning to us?

The instinct which warns of dangers in this association of economic and public power is quite sound. Unhappily, those who warn look in the wrong place. They have feared that the state might reach out and destroy the vigorous moneymaking entrepreneur. They have not noticed that, all the while, the successors to this vintage hero have been uniting themselves ever more closely with the state and rejoicing in the result. With equal enthusiasm, they have been accepting drastic abridgement of their own freedom. This is partly the price of organized activity. But they were also losing freedom in the precise pattern of classical expectation. The officers of Republic Aviation, which does all of its business with the United States government, are no more likely in public to speak critically of some nonsense perpetrated by the Air Force than is the head of a Soviet *combinat* of the ministry to which he reports. No Ford executive will ever fight Washington as did Henry I. No head of Montgomery Ward will ever again breathe defiance of a President as did Sewell Avery in the age of Roosevelt. Manners may be involved here. But most would state the truth: "Too much is now at stake!"

But the problem is not the freedom of the businessman. It can be laid down as a general rule that those who speak most of liberty least use what they have. The businessman who praises it most is a disciplined organization man. The retired general who now lectures on the threat of Communist regimentation was invariably a martinet who relished an existence in accordance with military regulations. The Secretary of State who speaks most feelingly of the free world most admires the fine conformity of his own thought.

The greater danger is in the subordination of belief to the needs of the modern industrial system. As this persuades us on the goods we buy, and as it persuades us on the public policies that are necessary for its planning, so it also accommodates us to its goals and values. These are that technology is always good; that economic growth is always good; that firms must always expand; that consumption of goods is the principal source of happiness; that idleness is wicked; and that nothing should interfere with the priority we accord to technology, growth, and increased consumption.

If we continue to believe that the goals of the modern industrial system and the public policies that serve these goals are coordinate with all of life, then all of our lives will be in the service of these goals. What is consistent with these ends we shall have or be allowed; all else will be off limits. Our wants will be managed in accordance with the needs of the industrial system; the state in civilian and military policy will be heavily influenced by industrial need; education will be adapted to similar need; the discipline required by the industrial system will be the conventional morality of the community. All other goals will be made to seem precious, unimportant, or antisocial. We will be the mentally indentured servants of the industrial system. This will be the benign servitude of the household retainer who is taught to love her master and mistress and believe that their interests are her own. But it is not exactly freedom.

If, on the other hand, the industrial system is seen to be only a part, and as we grow wealthier, a diminishing part, of life, there is much less occasion for concern. Aesthetic goals will have pride of place; those who serve them will not be subject to the goals of the industrial system; the industrial system itself will be subordinate to the claims of larger dimensions of life. Intellectual preparation will be for its own sake and not merely for the better service to the industrial system. Men will not be entrapped by the belief that apart from the production of goods and income by progressively more advanced technical methods there is nothing much in life. Then, over time, we may come to see industrial society as a technical arrangement for providing convenient goods and services in adequate volume. Those who rise through its hierarchy will so see themselves. And the public consequences will be in keeping. For if economic goals are the only goals of the society, the goals of the industrial system will dominate the state. If industrial goals are not the only goals, other purposes will be pursued.

Central among these other purposes is the aesthetic dimension of life. It is outside the scope of the modern industrial system. And that is why the industrial system tends to dismiss aesthetic considerations as precious and impractical and to condemn their proponents as "aesthetes."

The conflict arises in three forms. First and simply, there is the conflict between beauty and industrial efficiency. It is cheaper to have power lines march across the fields; to have highways take the most direct route through countryside or villages or towns or cities; or to allow jet aircraft to ignore the tranquillity of those below; or to pour industrial refuse into the air or into the water.

Next, there is a conflict between the artist and organization. Scientists and engineers can specialize; artists cannot. Accordingly, the organization which accommodates the specialist, though right for the engineer or scientist, is wrong for the artist. The artist does badly as an organization man; the organization does badly by the artist. So the artist tends to stand outside the modern industrial system; and it responds, naturally enough, by minimizing the importance of the aesthetic concerns it cannot easily embrace.

Finally, some important forms of artistic expression require a framework of order. This is notably true of structural and landscape architecture and urban design. It is order rather than the intrinsic merit of their buildings which accounts for the charm of Georgetown or Bloomsbury or Haussman's boulevards. Not even the Taj Mahal would be terribly attractive between two gasoline stations and surrounded by neon signs. Individuals, nevertheless, could have served better their economic interest by rejecting Haussman's designs or by getting a Shell franchise adjacent to the Taj.

The need is to subordinate economic to aesthetic goals—to sacrifice efficiency, including the efficiency of organization, to beauty. Nor must there be any nonsense about beauty paying in the long run. It need not pay. The requisite order will also require strong action by the state. Because of the abdication of this function in the interest of economic goals, no city, some noncommercial capitals apart, built since the Industrial Revolution attracts any particular admiration. And millions flock to admire ancient and medieval cities where, as a matter of course, such order was provided. The liberalism which allowed every individual and every entrepreneur to build as he wished was faster, more adaptable, and more efficient, and accommodated site better to need, than anything that could be provided under a "controlled" environment. But the aesthetic effect was at best undistinguished, and more often it was ghastly.

The change in goals and values which is here required is aided by the fact that the modern industrial system is intellectually demanding. It brings into existence, to serve its technical and scientific and other intellectual needs, a very large community of educated men and women. Hopefully this community will, in turn, reject the monopoly of social purpose by the industrial system.

But the rewards of time and understanding can also be hastened and enlarged by energetic political action. It is through the state that the society must assert the superior claims of aesthetic over economic goals and particularly of environment over cost. It is to the state that we must look for freedom of individual choice as to toil; for a balance between liberal education and the technical training that primarily serves the industrial system; and it is for the state to reject images of international politics that underwrite technology but at the price of unacceptable danger. If the state is to serve these ends, the scientific and educational estate and larger intellectual community must be aware of their power and their opportunity and they must use them. There is no one else.

MANDATORY AND PERMANENT WAGE-PRICE CONTROLS

CONTROL OF THE WAGE-PRICE SPIRAL

A complete attack on inflation requires that both causes of inflation—both the *excess of demand,* or spending, and the *wage-price spiral* [cost-push]—be brought under control.

The line of attack on excess spending is obvious. It calls primarily for heavy—very heavy—taxation. It calls for intelligent economy in expenditures by government. It calls for postponement of business investment. It calls for increased voluntary saving. This means that Americans must be assured for the future, as they have so long been assured in the past, that their dollars are good. They must be assured that the dollar they save instead of spend and put in a bank account or government bonds will have as high a purchasing power in the future as in the present. Nothing will serve this end more effectively than evidence of a strong determination by the administration and the Congress to check inflation.

I should like to make one comment concerning taxes. We shall need higher personal-income taxes and higher corporate-income taxes. We shall certainly have to have more and higher excise taxes. But I especially hope that doctrinaire opposition to the idea of sales taxes will not prevent us from looking carefully at the possibilities of this tax. I would not be in favor of a flat across-the-board levy on food, clothing, and other essentials. I do feel that the sales tax has great possibilities if it is properly designed. The British made extremely effective use of the sales tax in World War II—they called it the purchase tax—as a way of taxing expensive or luxury goods. These are the goods which

From *Hearings before the Joint Committee on the Economic Report,* 82d Cong., 1st Sess., pp. 354–56.

place the greatest drain on scarce materials, labor, and skills and plant. A sales tax directed toward these goods—toward expensive lines of clothing, for example—can be actually helpful in keeping lower-priced lines of goods cheap and abundant. It can also raise a lot of revenue.

The defense against the wage-price spiral—the second of the inflationary forces which work in our economy—are the *direct controls over prices and wages.* These direct controls are not a substitute for a strong fiscal policy; they perform a different task. Taxes and other fiscal measures dry up the excess of purchasing power; wage and price controls keep wages from shoving up prices and prices from shoving up wages. We cannot, under conditions we now face, be sure that any tax or fiscal policy will control the wage-price spiral. No more can we look upon wage- and price-fixing as a defense, in itself, against inflation. *Both* lines of attack are necessary because each deals with a different cause of inflation.

Because the primary purpose of the direct controls is to check the wage-price spiral, the controls we invoke must accomplish that purpose. It is not necessary, however, assuming no one wants control for the sake of control, to do more than necessary to achieve this end. To tie down the wage-price spiral, with reasonable justice and equity, we need to do three things. They are:

1. Effectively *stabilize basic living costs.* This is necessary if wages are to be stabilized.
2. Maintain a *general ceiling on wages and prices* in that part of the economy where wages are determined by collective-bargaining contracts and where prices normally move in response to wage movements. I have reference here to what may properly be called the great industrial core of the American economy—the steel, automobile, electrical goods, construction, transport, and like industries.
3. As a contribution to overall stability, placing of firm *ceiling prices on basic raw materials.*

Had we approached the problem of controls with a view to having as few of them as possible (though as many as necessary) and had the action been timely, we would have started out along the above lines. It is a system of controls with which, if necessary, we could live for a long time. It would not require a large administrative or enforcement staff.

Stabilizing the wage-price spiral is the central task of the direct controls. Fixing *all* prices [including] a great many prices that do not need to be controlled provides no guaranty of stable living costs. There is danger that administrative energies will be dissipated over a large number of products when, in fact, the key danger to wage-price stability lies in a relatively *few*—in food, basic clothing, and rents. None of these latter is now securely controlled. While we managed, although not without difficulty, to keep such a general ceiling in effect throughout World War II and for a period thereafter, it is not the kind of regulation which is right for the long pull. In World War II we, in effect, improvised for a particular set of circumstances of *limited duration.* For those circumstances it was the thing to do. We now face a *long* period of inflationary tension. For that a different line of action is called for. Energies should now be concentrated on getting the kind of stabilization program with which we can live, if we must, for a long time. This requires that we control strongly where control is necessary and not at all where it isn't.

The first step is a fundamental attack on living costs. Apart from rent I do not see this as, primarily, a problem in price-fixing. The ceilings, which undoubtedly should be kept on basic clothing and on food, should be viewed as merely an adjunct to more fundamental action. In the case of clothing, for example, a far more effective approach than price-fixing would be to use government allocation powers to direct generous quantities of fiber and textiles into standard low-priced goods–into work clothing, household textiles, children's clothing, and the lower priced lines of men's and women's clothing. These should be made abundant, and so kept cheap. I would not worry if expensive lines of clothing became more expensive and scarce; freedom from ceilings on such clothing should readily be conceded in return for a substantial tax. If we rely on ceilings on clothing we will get too much expensive clothing and not enough of the cheap. We all remember during World War II when gay sports shirts were plentiful and ordinary ones not to be had.

The key to our problem is meat. I very much doubt if present ceilings, even when buttressed by slaughter controls, will hold meat prices even at their present astronomical levels. And even if they should, the attempt to meet the demand at these prices will place a heavy drain on our feed supplies. Rising feed prices will mean higher costs for dairy and poultry farmers, higher milk, poultry, and egg prices, and also more expensive cereals for direct consumption. Barring crop failure and full-scale war, our food position is strong. Could the demand for meat be effectively restrained, feed prices would be easier, and other animal products would be cheaper and more abundant. The necessary steps are not easy. It may be necessary to control here in order to have fewer controls elsewhere. And a policy of minimizing controls may well take more vigor and imagination than one which merely fixes ceilings and hopes for the best.

Action along these commodity lines in the cost-of-living area–coupled with the necessary fiscal policy–will lessen our reliance on price controls as such while greatly increasing our security against inflation. I should not want you to think I am arguing for a soft policy. I regard the threat of inflation as extremely grave. We are currently in much greater danger of demoralization of the economy as a result of inflation than we ever were from the great depression which the Russians were presumed to be counting upon to finish off American capitalism after World War II. It will take a stronger and more sure-footed policy to minimize reliance on ceilings than to multiply them.

DANIEL P. MOYNIHAN

Formerly Harvard University and Massachusetts Institute of Technology urbanologist.

Daniel P. Moynihan, along with John K. Galbraith and Arthur Schlesinger, Jr., established himself as a leading member of America's eastern liberal establishment during the early 1960s. On leave from academic positions, these three men rallied to the support of President Kennedy and became part of the inner circle that was to guide American foreign and domestic policies until his death. Only Moynihan managed to stay on to help direct President Johnson's Great Society programs. Later he became Nixon's special assistant for urban affairs and then served as his Ambassador to India. Clearly, Moynihan is in a good position to describe the inner philosophy of the vast bureaucracy which operates the social and economic programs of the federal government.

In the article reprinted here, he describes the movement toward the professionalization of reform within this bureaucracy. Although the modern reform movement, according to Moynihan, lacks the outside ideological push of past eras, meaningful progress can still be made because the internal structure of the government has developed a direction of its own. Bolstered by the vast amount of statistical data collected by governmental agencies, and the theoretical work of the academic community, the professionals within the government initiate programs to attack America's social and economic problems. Thus external pressure groups, such as the labor unions, need no longer be relied upon to provide leadership for reforms; this new bureaucracy with a social conscience means to use government power to correct the misallocations of the market system. Although Moynihan states that there is always the danger of creating a too-powerful government, he is quick to assure us that the new style of reform provides a "promise of social sanity and stability" for the future.

This article reflects the optimistic feeling among liberals during the early 1960s that new federal programs were the best means of attacking the nation's social problems. The funds for these programs, as Moynihan explains, were to come from a fiscal dividend, based on the tendency of government tax revenues to increase at a faster rate than government expenditures for current programs during periods of economic growth. As the frequency of business cycles lessened, the professional decision-makers could calculate how great a dividend the tax system would produce and arrange their social programs accordingly. One problem with this plan might be the chance that the hypothetical fiscal dividend would be drained off in military expenditures or returned to the private sector through tax reductions or subsidies. Despite the need to finance new programs, politicians might well find it more expedient to dispose of fiscal dividends by cutting taxes, especially in a period of recession, than by increasing the government's social expenditures. Galbraith has labeled this use of Keynesian economics as "reactionary," because he believes it would decrease already-inadequate social welfare expenditures and thus aggravate the existing social imbalance.

When the tax dividend did not appear in the late 1960s, policymakers started looking toward the revenue surplus that American withdrawal from Vietnam was supposed to produce to finance new domestic programs. Again the dividends did not materialize. The fact is that these growth and peace dividends, once thought of as primary revenue sources for new high-priority programs, had been preempted by the built-in expenditures of programs already underway. Almost 75 percent of federal expenditures are now in the "relatively uncontrollable" category, and the rising costs of maintaining current programs, in part mandated by legislation, have exceeded whatever dividends the tax system has generated. Perhaps this is one reason that Moynihan's enthusiasm for federal programs diminished during his tenure in Washington, although he also became more and more convinced that the programs would not work even if they were instituted. Many liberals have come to realize that such social welfare programs are an expensive way to redistribute income because of the costly bureaucracies needed to run them. In addition, as the War on Poverty showed, transmitting plans from the federal to the local level is difficult and often distorts the intent of social legislation. An alternative to providing income-in-kind to the poor is to give direct cash payments. This method has been recommended by conservatives like Friedman for years and has now been taken over by liberals who are disenchanted with the services approach to welfare. Over the long pull, however, it seems unlikely that the taxpayers will be willing to support significant direct-income transfers because of their fear that the poor would use the subsidy in the "wrong" way. The Nixon cutback of services to the poor, then, represents only a temporary interruption in the expansion of such income transfers, for as Moynihan shows, institutionalized planning in these areas has become a significant freature of American capitalism.

R R

THE PROFESSIONALIZATION OF REFORM

(1965)

Our best hope for the future lies in the extension to social organization of the methods that we already employ in our most progressive fields of effort. In science and in industry . . . we do not wait for catastrophe to force new ways upon us. . . . We rely, and with success, upon quantitative analysis to point the way; and we advance because we are constantly improving and applying such analysis.

The passage above, as succinct a case for social planning as could be made, is not a product of either the thought or the institutions of the liberal left. It

Reprinted from Daniel P. Moynihan, "The Professionalization of Reform," *The Public Interest,* No. 1 (Fall 1965), 6–16. © 1965 by National Affairs, Inc. Reprinted by permission of The Public Interest and the author.

is, rather, a statement by the late mathematical economist Wesley C. Mitchell. And it has recently been approvingly reprinted at the beginning of a report on "The Concept of Poverty" published by—the Chamber of Commerce of the United States.

The report itself, the work of businessmen and scholars, is perhaps the most competent commentary on the government's antipoverty program yet to appear. It is replete with citations of articles in *Social Research* and *Land Economics,* and the data from *The Statistical Abstract of the United States;* the perspective ranges from friendly references to the works of Friedrich Engels, to more detached assessments of contemporary tracts. ("Michael Harrington, author of a widely read book on poverty, *The Other America,* has written, 'Any gain for America's minorities will immediately be translated into an advance for all the unskilled workers. One cannot raise the bottom of society without benefiting everyone above.' This is almost precisely wrong.") But the report is less significant for what it says than for what it is: an example of the evolving technique and style of reform in the profoundly new society developing in the United States. Lacking a better term, it might be described as the professionalization of reform.

Writing for the British journal, *The New Society,* just prior to the assassination of President Kennedy, Nathan Glazer described the process:

> Without benefit of anything like the Beveridge report to spark and focus public discussion and concern, the United States is passing through a stage of enormous expansion in the size and scope of what we may loosely call the social services—the public programs designed to help people adapt to an increasingly complex and unmanageable society. While Congress has been painfully and hesitantly trying to deal with two great measures—tax reform and a civil rights bill—and its deliberations on both have been closely covered by the mass media, it has also been working with much less publicity on a number of bills which will contribute at least as much to changing the shape of American society.

The vast Mental Retardation Facilities and Community Mental Health Centers Construction Act had just become law. The no less enormous vocational education bill was moving steadily through the Congress. The Kennedy Administration had earlier obtained such measures as the Area Redevelopment Act, the Manpower Development and Training Act, and the Public Welfare Amendments of 1962. "Waiting in the wings" were a domestic peace corps and an ambitious youth conservation corps, while the community action programs developed by the President's Committee on Juvenile Delinquency and Youth Crime, established in 1961, were scheduled for new and expanded funding.

It is a special mind that can as much as keep the titles of these programs straight. But the most interesting thing about all this sudden expansion of social services was that it had behind it, as Glazer noted, "nothing like the powerful political pressure and long-sustained intellectual support that produced the great welfare measures of the New Deal—Social Security, Unemployment Insurance, Public Welfare, Public Housing." The "massive political support and intellectual leadership that produced the reforms of the thirties" simply did not exist; yet the reforms were moving forward.

Glazer accounted for this in terms of the emergence of a large body of professional persons and professional organizations that had taken on themselves the concern for the 20 to 30 percent of the population that was outside the mainstream of American prosperity. Intellectuals knew little about the subject, and were not much interested. Organized labor, while both concerned and knowledgeable, had had but limited success in involving its membership in such efforts. As a result

> the fate of the poor is in the hands of the administrators and the professional organizations of doctors, teachers, social workers, therapists, counselors and so forth. It is these, who, in a situation where the legislation and programs become ever more complex, spend the time to find out—or rather have brought home to them—through their work the effects of certain kinds of measures and programs, and who propose ever more complex programs which Congress deliberates upon in the absence of any major public interest. When Congress argues these programs, the chief pressures upon it are not the people, but the organized professional interests that work with that segment of the problem, and those who will benefit from or be hurt by the legislation.

The antipoverty program that was being developed even as Glazer wrote is far the best instance of the professionalization of reform yet to appear. In its genesis, its development, and now its operation, it is a prototype of the social technique of action that will almost certainly become more common in the future. It is a technique that will not appeal to everyone, and in which many will perceive the not altogether imaginary danger of a too-powerful government. But it is also a technique that offers a profound promise of social sanity and stability in time to come.

There are two aspects of the poverty program which distinguish it from earlier movements of its kind: The initiative came largely from within. The case for action was based on essentially esoteric information about the past and probable future course of events.

The most distinctive break with the past is with regard to initiative. War on poverty was not declared at the behest of the poor. Just the opposite. The poor were not only invisible, as Michael Harrington described them, they were also for the most part silent. John F. Kennedy ventured into Appalachia searching for Protestant votes, not for poverty. There he encountered the incredible pauperization of the mountain people, most particularly the soft coal miners, an industrial work force whose numbers had been reduced by nearly two-thirds in the course of a decade—but with hardly a sound of protest. The miners were desperately poor, shockingly unemployed, but neither radical nor in any significant way restive. It may be noted that in 1964, in the face of the historic Democratic sweep, Harlan County, Kentucky, returned a freshman Republican Congressman.

True, the civil rights movement was well established and highly effective during this period, but it was primarily concerned with just that: the demand for the recognition of the civil rights of the Negro American. While the movement would clearly in time turn to the problem of poverty and of the economic position of the Negro, it had only begun to do so, as in the March on Washington in August 1963, and its economic demands were still general and essentially traditional, as for example, an increased minimum wage.

Apart from the always faithful labor movement, the only major lobbies working for any of the programs that came together to form the War on Poverty were the conservationists supporting the youth conservation camps, and the National Committee on the Employment of Youth, an organization representing a variety of groups in the social welfare field. The essential fact is that the main pressure for a massive government assault on poverty developed within the Kennedy-Johnson Administration, among officials whose responsibilities were to think about just such matters. These men now exist, they are well paid, have competent staffs, and have access to the President. (Many of these officials, of course, were originally brought to Washington by the New Deal: they are by no means all *nuovi uomini.)* Most importantly, they have at their command an increasing fund of information about social conditions in the United States.

Almost all this information is public, but the art of interpreting it is, in a sense, private. Anyone is free to analyze income statistics, or employment data, or demographic trends to his heart's content. But very few persons in the beginning years of the present decade were able to perceive in those statistics the gradual settling of a poverty class in America. A number of officials in the Federal government (mostly academicians on leave) were. Leaving aside the question of whether or not they were right—a question which must always be open—it is clear that the judgment they reached was quite at variance, almost poles apart, from the general public understanding of the time.

Whereas the public, both high and low in the intellectual hierarchy, saw income distribution steadily compressing, saw the Negro American more and more winning his rightful place in society, saw prosperity spreading through the land, the men in the government saw something quite different: an income distribution gap that had not budged since the end of the war, and had in fact worsened sharply for Negroes, a rising measure of social disorganization among poor families and poor communities, a widening gap between the prospects of the poor and those of the middle class.

In President Johnson these officials found a chief executive who knew a good deal about poverty, and seemingly everything about politics. In a matter of weeks from the time he assumed office, the array of programs and bills Glazer had described as "waiting in the wings" were mustered into a coherent legislative program, reinforced by some entirely new ideas, and moved out under the banner of War on Poverty. It was an issue that united rather than divided, and the ranks of its supporters if anything swelled as it moved through the legislative process.

There is nothing, as such, startling about these developments. They have been foreseen, with either hope or fear, by many persons for many years. However, in recent times a number of events have occurred which very much hasten the process, and make it of greater moment. These have to do with the almost sudden emergence of the fact that the industrial nations of the world seem finally about to learn how to manage their economies, with the professionalization of the middle class, and with the exponential growth of knowledge.

THE ECONOMIC REVOLUTION

Recent years, with the steady advance of technology, have given birth to a good number of neo-apocalyptic views of the future of the American economy, most of them associated with the concept of automation. No one should doubt there is something called automation going on, and that it does change things. However, there is no evidence whatever that it is in fact transforming American society, or any other society. It is simply the newest phase in a process that has been under way for at least two centuries, and will presumably go on and on, past any immediate concern of this age or the next.

At the same time, there is a good deal of evidence, if that is the term for what are little more than everyday impressions, that in the area of economic policy there has occurred a genuine discontinuity, a true break with the past: Men are learning how to make an industrial economy work.

What is involved is something more permanent than simply a run of good luck, or specially refined intuitions on the part of persons responsible for the economic affairs of one nation, or a group of nations. Rather it is the fact that for two decades now, since the end of World War II, the industrial democracies of the world have been able to operate their economies on a high and steadily expanding level of production and employment. Nothing like it has ever happened before in history. It is perhaps the central fact of world politics today. The briefest recollection of what happened to those economies in the two decades that followed World War I will suggest why.

Moreover, it is a development that has all the markings of a scientific event, of a profound advance in knowledge, as well as of an improvement in statecraft.

In the beginning was the theory. With but little data either to support or confound them, economic theories multiplied and conflicted. But gradually more and better data accumulated: progress begins on social problems when it becomes possible to measure them. As the data accumulated and technology made it possible to calculate more rapidly, the theories gradually became able to explain more, and these in turn led to the improvement in the data. John Maynard Keynes at King's College, Cambridge, and Wesley C. Mitchell at the National Bureau of Economic Research in New York, are supremely good symbols of the two processes that ended up in a deeply symbiotic relationship. And then one day it all more or less hangs together and the world is different, although of course not quite aware of the change. Governments promise full employment—and then produce it. (In 1964 unemployment, adjusted to conform more or less to United States' definitions, was 2.9 percent in Italy, 2.5 percent in France and Britain, and 0.4 percent in Germany. Consider the contrast with post-World War I.) Governments undertake to expand their economy at a steady rate—and do so. (In 1961 the members of the Organization for Economic Cooperation and Development, which grew out of the Marshall Plan, undertook to increase their output by 50 percent during the decade of the 1960s. The United States at all events is right on schedule.)

The ability to predict events, as against controlling them, has developed even more impressively—the Council of Economic Advisers' forecast of GNP for 1964 was off by only $400 million in a total of $623 billion; the unemployment forecast was on the nose.

There is a temptation, of course, to go too far in presuming what can be done with the economy. The international exchange system is primitive, and at the moment menacing. The stock market can be wildly irrational. There are, as Hyman Lewis points out, competing theories of investment which could bring us unsettling dilemmas. We in the United States have not achieved full employment. We have accepted the use of federal taxing and spending powers as a means of social adjustment, but so far only in pleasant formulations. Our willingness to raise taxes, for example, is yet to be tested. In general, the political component of political economy remains very much uncertain. Thus the British, again to cite Lewis, have the best economists, but one of the less successful economies. But the fact remains that economics is approaching the status of an applied science.

In the long run this econometric revolution, assuming it works itself out, is bound to have profound effects on the domestic politics of all the nations involved. The central political issue of most industrial nations over the past century and a half has been how to make an economy work. Almost every conceivable nostrum, from the nationalization of the means of production, distribution, and exchange, to the free coinage of silver, has been proposed, and most have been tried. Usually without success. In the United States, for one administration after another, economic failure has led to political failure. But if henceforth the business cycle has a longer sweep, and fewer abrupt downturns, the rise and fall of political fortunes may follow the same pattern. Once in power, a party may be much more likely to remain so. Or in any event, the issues that elect or defeat governments could be significantly different from those of the past.

The more immediate impact of this econometric revolution in the United States is that the federal government will be endowed, more often than not, with a substantial, and within limits predictable, rise in revenues available for social purposes. Significantly, the War on Poverty began in the same year of the great tax cut. The President was not forced to choose between the measures; he was able to proceed with both. In that sense, the War on Poverty began not because it was necessary (which it was), but because it was possible.

The singular nature of the new situation in which the federal government finds itself is that the immediate *supply* of resources available for social purposes might actually outrun the immediate *demand* of established programs. Federal expenditures under existing programs rise at a fairly predictable rate. But, under conditions of economic growth, revenues rise faster. This has given birth to the phenomenon of the "fiscal drag"—the idea that unless the federal government disposes of this annual increment, either by cutting taxes or adding programs, the money taken out of circulation by taxes will slow down economic growth, and could, of course, at a certain point stop it altogether.

Thus, assuming the continued progress of the economy in something like the pattern of recent years, there is likely to be $4–5 billion in additional, unobligated revenue coming in each year. *But* this increment will only continue to come on conditions that it is disposed of. Therefore one of the important tasks to which an Administration must address itself is that of devising new and responsible programs for expending public funds in the public interest.

This is precisely the type of decision making that is suited to the techniques of modern organizations, and which ends up in the hands of persons who make a profession of it. They are less and less political decisions, more and more administrative ones. They are decisions that can be reached by consensus rather than conflict.

THE PROFESSIONALIZATION OF THE MIDDLE CLASS

"Everywhere in American life," Kenneth S. Lynn reports, "the professions are triumphant." The period since the G.I. Bill has witnessed an extraordinary expansion of higher education. In the United States, a quarter of the teenage population now goes on to some kind of college, and among specific class and ethnic groups the proportion is as high as three quarters. The trend is unmistakable and probably irresistible: In the course of the coming decades some form of higher education will become near to universal. But most importantly, for more and more persons the form of education will involve professional training. This is not the same thing as traditional higher education; it does not produce the same types of persons.

The difference has been most succinctly stated by Everett C. Hughes: "Professionals *profess.* They profess to know better than others the nature of certain matters, and to know better than their clients what ails them or their affairs." And he continues:

> Lawyers not only give advice to clients and plead their cases for them; they also develop a philosophy of law—of its nature and its functions, and of the proper way in which to administer justice. Physicians consider it their prerogative to define the nature of disease and of health, and to determine how medical services ought to be distributed and paid for. Social workers are not content to develop a technique of casework; they concern themselves with social legislation. Every profession considers itself the proper body to set the terms in which some aspect of society, life or nature is to be thought of, and to define the general lines, or even the details, of public policy concerning it.

As the number of professionals increase, so also do the number of professions, or neo-professions. More and more, middle-class persons are attracted by the independence of judgment, esoteric knowledge, and immunity to outside criticism that characterize professionals. As Everett Hughes puts it: "The YMCA secretary wants his occupation recognized not merely as that of offering young men from the country a pleasant road to Protestant righteousness in the city, but as a more universal one of dealing with groups of young people. All that is learned of adolescence, of behavior in small groups, of the nature and organization of community life is considered the intellectual basis of his work."

There are now an extraordinary number of such persons in America. Those Americans classified as professional and technical workers have just passed the nine million mark—more than the number of "managers, officials, and proprietors," more than the craftsmen and foremen. And of this group, an enormous number is involved in various aspects of social welfare and reform. Through sheer numbers they would tend to have their way; but as professionals in a professionalizing society, they are increasingly *entitled* to have their way. That is how the system works.

One of the more powerful demonstrations of the influence of professional thinking on programs of social reform is the provision of the Economic Opportunity Act that community action programs be carried out with the "maximum feasible participation" of the poor themselves. This is one of the most important and pioneering aspects of the entire antipoverty program. But typically this demand was inserted in the legislation not because of any demand of the poor, but because the intellectual leaders of the social reform profession had come to the conclusion that this was indispensable to effective social action. Typically also, the literature describes the process in terms of the use of the "indigenous nonprofessional"—persons identified by the fact that they are *not* professional. A somewhat ironical turn of events in this area is the role the community action programs are playing in recreating the ethnic political-social organizations of the big city slums—the dismantling of which was for so long the object of political and social reformers in the United States!

The prospect of large-scale opposition to the new professions is, for the moment at least, limited because the professionalization of the middle class has led to a no less extraordinary opening up of careers to talent. The time when any considerable number of persons of great ability and ambition have found their way out of poverty blocked by their inability to obtain an education has all but passed. (There are still many, many persons whose natural abilities are stunted by poverty, but that is another matter.) A nationwide survey of 1960 high school graduates, Project Talent, found that about 97 percent of those in the top 1 percent of aptitude and 93 percent of those in the top 5 percent, entered college within a year. Among the next 5 percent (the 90th to 94th percentile) 86 percent did so. As a general proposition, ability is recognized and rewarded in America today as at no time in history. (Michael Young's forecast of the revolt of the lower quartile against the ultimate injustice of a society based on merit may not be discounted, but it is not on the other hand scheduled until 2031.)

It is possible that this process, just because it is successful in drawing up talent from lower economic and social groups, will deprive those groups of much of their natural leadership, and make them all the more dependent on professionals. Kenneth Clark has noted that the degree of recruitment of civil rights leaders into "establishment" organizations verges on raiding—and has raised suspicions of hidden motives! On the other hand, there is rather a pronounced tendency for persons from such groups, when they do rise to the middle class, to settle into professions which involve work with the very groups they left behind. Thus, in a certain sense the poor are not so much losing their natural leaders as obtaining them through different routes.

THE EXPONENTIAL GROWTH OF KNOWLEDGE

Among the complexities of life is the fact that the American business community, in a period when it was fiercely opposed to the idea of economic or social planning, nonetheless supported, even pressed for, the development of a national statistical system which has become the best in the world and which now makes certain types of planning and regulation—although quite different from the collective proposals of earlier eras—both feasible and in a measure inevitable. Much as mountains are climbed, so statistics are used if they are there. As an example, trade union wage settlements in recent years have been profoundly influenced by the wage-price guidelines set by the federal government. This could not possibly have occurred on an essentially voluntary basis were it not that the Bureau of Labor Statistics has developed the technique of measuring productivity—and has done so, accompanied, step by step, by the business and labor advisory committees that work with the bureau. A measure of the near quantum change that has only recently occurred in the information available for social planning in the United States (the development work began long ago, but the pay-off has been rather recent) may be suggested by the fact that the nation went through the great depression of the 1930s without ever really knowing what the rate of unemployment was! This was then a measurement taken but once every ten years, by the census. Today, of course, employment and unemployment data are collected monthly, and debated in terms of the decimal points. Similarly, the census has been quietly transformed from a ten-times-a-century proceeding to a system of current accounts on a vast range of social data.

Most of the information that went into the development of the antipoverty program was essentially economic, but the social data available to the President's task force was of singular importance in shaping the program, and in turn the program will greatly stimulate the collection of more such. The nation is clearly on the verge of developing a system of social statistics comparable to the now highly developed system of economic statistics.

The use of all such statistics is developing also. A vast "industry of discovery," to use William Haber's description of events in the physical sciences, is developing in the social sciences as well. Computer technology has greatly enhanced the possible use of such data. Just as the effort to stimulate the American economy is now well advanced, the simulation of social processes, particularly in decision making, is also begun, and may be expected to produce important, if not indeed revolutionary insights. Such prospects tend to stir some alarm in thoughtful persons, but it may be noted the public has accepted with calm, even relish, the fact that the outcome of elections is now predicted with surpassing accuracy. If that most solemn of democratic rituals may be simulated without protest, there is not likely to be much outcry against the simulation of various strategies of housing integration, or techniques of conflict resolution, or patterns of child rearing.

Expenditure for social science research was somewhere between $500 and $600 million in 1964. This was only 10 percent of the $6 billion spent in the same year on the life and physical sciences (including psychology), and much less a proportion of the $19 billion spent on research and development altogether. Nonetheless it represents a sixfold growth in a decade. There is, moreover, some indication that social scientists are not yet thinking in the money terms that are in fact available to them. Angus Campbell suggested recently that social scientists still think in budgets of thousands of dollars when they should be thinking of millions. "The prevailing format for social research is still the exploitation of opportunities which are close at hand, easily manageable, and inexpensive." But, he adds, "there are a good many social scientists who know very well how to study social change on a broad scale and are intensely interested in going about it." The Survey Research Center at the University of Michigan, which Campbell directs, has, for example, under way a year-long panel survey of the impact of the 1964 tax cut on the nation's taxpayers, a specific example of the use of social science techniques in the development of economic policy.

All in all, the prospect is for a still wider expansion of knowledge available to governments as to how people behave. This will be accompanied by further improvement of the now well-developed techniques of determining what they think. Public opinion polls are already a daily instrument of government decision-making (a fact which has clearly affected the role of the legislature). In combination, these two systems of information make it possible for a government to respond intelligently and in time to the changing needs and desires of the electorate. The day when mile-long petitions and mass rallies were required to persuade a government that a popular demand existed that things be done differently is clearly drawing to a close.

Indeed, the very existence of such petitions and rallies may in time become a sign that what is being demanded is *not yet* a popular demand.

THE PERILS OF PROGRESS

The professionalization of reform will proceed, regardless of the perils it presents. Even in the face of economic catastrophe, which is certainly conceivable if not probable, the response will be vastly more systematic and informed than any of the past.

A certain price will be paid, and a considerable risk will be incurred. The price will be a decline in the moral exhilaration of public affairs at the domestic level. It has been well said that the civil rights movement of the present time has at last provided the youth of America with a moral equivalent of war. The more general effect of the civil rights movement has been a much heightened public concern for human dignity and welfare. This kind of passion could seep out of the life of the nation, and we would be the less for it.

The risk is a combination of enlightenment, resources, and skill which in the long run, to use Harold D. Laswell's phrase, becomes a "monocracy of power."

But the potential rewards are not less great. The creation of a society that can put an end to the "animal miseries" and stupid controversies that afflict most peoples would be an extraordinary achievement of the human spirit. The argument may be made, for example, that had the processes described in this article not progressed as far as they had by 1961, the response of the federal government to the civil rights revolution would have been thoroughly inadequate: that instead of joining with and helping to direct the movement, the national government would have trailed behind with grudging, uncomprehending, and increasingly inadequate concessions that could have resulted in the problem of the Negro American becoming insoluble in terms of existing American society.

The prospect that the more primitive social issues of American politics are at last to be resolved need only mean that we may now turn to issues more demanding of human ingenuity than that of how to put an end to poverty in the richest nation in the world. Many such issues might be in the area of foreign affairs, where the enormity of difficulty and the proximity of disaster is sufficient to keep the citizens and political parties of the nation fully occupied. And there is also the problem of perfecting, to the highest degree possible, the *quality* of our lives and of our civilization. We may not be accustomed to giving political priority to such questions. But no one can say they will be boring or trivial!

WALTER W. ROSTOW

Professor of Economics and of History, University of Texas at Austin.

Walter W. Rostow's *Stages of Economic Growth* (1960) has undoubtedly been one of the leading anti-Marxist polemics in the arsenal of mainstream liberalism. Rostow makes no attempt to hide this point; the subtitle of his book is, in fact, *A Non-Communist Manifesto,* and Marxism is referred to as "a monstrous guide to public policy."

Although dissimilar in many fundamental ways, both Marxian and Rostovian models contain a heady mixture of economic and political aspects of the development process. The universal stages of growth postulated by Rostow (which he claims are more flexible, less deterministic, and more all-encompassing than Marx's growth theory) are:

1. "traditional society," where growth is limited by a combination of primitive technology, social values, and a centralized power structure;
2. "the preconditions for takeoff," where changes in technology and the social structure "unhinge" the traditional society and result in a buildup of social overhead capital, increased productivity in agriculture, and the ascendency of an active entrepreneurial group;
3. "the takeoff" (about twenty years in duration), in which the annual investment rate rises to approximately 10 percent and self-sustaining growth becomes a "normal" condition;
4. "the drive to maturity" (roughly sixty years), in which modern technology is extended throughout a wide range of the economy, accompanied by increasing urbanization of the labor force, and far-sighted industrial leaders play a crucial role;
5. "the age of high mass consumption," during which a technologically mature society makes the deliberate choice of reallocating a significant part of its resources to consumer durables and social welfare services.

Rostow's basic political message to the undeveloped third-world countries rings out clearly: Since Western democratic capitalist countries as well as the Soviet communist society both pass through similar stages of growth at approximately the same rate, there is little, if anything, to be gained by the undeveloped countries in choosing the "peculiarly inhumane" Communist option over "the more humane process that Western values would suggest." Both, in time, follow the same path from poverty to affluence, shedding one stage while somehow acquiring the characteristics of the next.

Unfortunately, Rostow's "series of stages" approach does not contain a sufficiently thorough explanation of the mechanism by which particular societies acquire these successive sets of characteristics. Thus, his method has a heavy, mechanistic cast rather than a creative, innovative one, capable of explaining the connective links between the stages. While it is undoubtedly true that there are some universal technical problems to be overcome in achieving economic growth, e.g., availability of physical and human resources, generation of savings for capital accumulation, and some sort of control that coordinates different sectors of the economy, different types of socioeconomic systems solve these problems differently. To say, as Rostow does, that preconditions for the acceleration of growth can be developed in a number of ways, and that development proceeds unevenly rather than according to an established pattern, is too obvious a formulation to provide insight into the complex dynamics of development and decline—what Marx calls society's "laws of motion." Contrary to Rostow's claim that his method has "an inner logic and continuity . . . rooted in a dynamic theory of production," it is merely a descriptive device which abstracts from the all-important question of the social system.

In a skillful attempt at inverting the Marxian schema, Rostow depicts the Soviet alternative as primarily (but not uniquely) effective in the transition period *before* the "takeoff." With reference to Russia's own historical experience—which admittedly does not conform to Marx's prediction that capitalism would break down sooner in developed than in undeveloped countries—he suggests that if a given country has not succumbed to Communism by the "takeoff" or initial phase of the "drive for maturity" stage, it is likely to remain "invulnerable to Communism." This naive assumption of the permanence (as well as beneficence) of capitalism pervades Rostow's analysis.

There are many shortcomings in Rostow's basic conceptions, reflected in the historical applications he chooses to make. His views that the Russian economy entered a self-sustained takeoff after 1890, that "the progress of (Russian) industry, after takeoff, was remarkably similar" to that of the U.S., and that the gap between Soviet Russia's industrial growth and that in the U.S. (between 1870 and 1955) has not appreciably narrowed, are based on a combination of faulty historical understanding and clever statistical maneuvering. Although Russian industry in the pre-Bolshevik period had a few developed sectors (primarily oil and textiles), it did not possess a self-sustaining character. The commanding heights of the economy (including banks) were foreign-owned, while the primitive agricultural sector embraced the overwhelming part of the population, and the capital and consumer goods industries were very weak. Like many of today's undeveloped countries, Russia's early pattern of growth reflected its subordination to the advanced Western capitalist countries. Rostow's suggestion that the Soviet's "drive to maturity" was merely adding to the earlier Czarist "takeoff" bypasses the fundamental differences between the institutional framework of Czarist Russia and the Soviet Union. The statistics showing the continued lag of Soviet industry behind the U.S. are based to a large extent on the inclusion of the Civil and World War years, in which Russia's incredible losses pulled down her growth rate while the wars boomed the American economy. Eliminate these years from the comparison, and the superiority of the Soviet planning system as an engine of growth becomes more evident. A planning system that consciously subjects the resources of society to human control has a growth potential considerably greater than a private-enterprise, market-oriented society, even one in which a powerful state intervenes at many levels of operation and the giant corporation has replaced the weaker competitive business firm.

Rostow's method of analysis overlooks the dual growth effects of colonialism or imperialism on the economically advanced and backward countries. It is the colonial-imperialist relationship that explains the enormous contribution of the undeveloped world to Europe's "takeoff." Certainly the surplus earned from slave-based operations in North America provided an important part of the fuel for Europe's nineteenth-century Industrial Revolution. Similarly, some degree of control (imperfect though it may be) over energy reserves in the Middle East and Latin America is essential to the viability of twentieth-century advanced capitalist countries, increasingly dependant on external sources of supply.

America continues to pump a considerable surplus out of the undeveloped countries, thus stunting their growth pattern even while providing a thin veneer of development. Magdoff, in his *Age of Imperialism,* cites a net dollar inflow from Latin America to the United States of $7.5 billion between 1950 and 1965. The pattern of foreign investment in these undeveloped countries is geared to the industrial needs of the advanced countries; very little of the wealth generated in the former trickles down to the masses, who remain concentrated in the low-productivity subsistence sector. Periods of temporarily high raw material export prices create the illusion of growth until the bubble bursts. When the structure of world prices does not favor undeveloped countries, as during cyclical downturns in the industrial countries, the fragile base of their development is revealed. It becomes a severe strain to maintain interest payments to investors in the advanced countries, or to the international aid agencies they control, in this period of adversity. The small capital-intensive export sector stands in marked contrast to the labor-intensive domestic sector. The maldistribution of wealth, stemming in part from the lopsided pattern of foreign investment in undeveloped countries, results in a weak domestic market structure incapable of sustaining an economic "takeoff."

The growing income inequality between developed and undeveloped countries is inexplicable in terms of Rostow's optimistic growth model. As Paul Baran, A. G. Frank, and others have shown, the lack of structural development in third-world countries is directly or indirectly related to the imperialist chain binding them to advanced capitalist societies. And Rostow has not demonstrated that these undeveloped countries (comprising a majority of the world's population) are on the path to self-sustained growth. Their Western capitalist "option," in fact, ensures their continued economic stagnation.

It is worth noting that when Rostow temporarily transferred from academia to a leading role in the Johnson administration, his influence as a leading cold warrior led him to *impose* a western "option" on the Vietnamese. One is tempted to ask Rostow, "If there is a natural convergence of all systems, as you claim, what justification is there for a policy of forced intervention in Southeast Asia?" The answer, of course, is that Rostow tends to favor the extension of American (i.e., capitalist) power and control by whatever means are deemed necessary at any given time. In judging the validity of his "stages of growth" doctrine, some weight should be attached to this bias.

ML

THE STAGES OF ECONOMIC GROWTH

(1959)

This article summarizes a way of generalizing the sweep of modern economic history. The form of this generalization is a set of stages of growth, which can be designated as follows: the traditional society; the preconditions for takeoff; the takeoff; the drive to maturity; the age of high mass consumption. Beyond the age of high mass consumption lie the problems which are beginning to arise in a few societies, and which may arise generally when diminishing relative marginal utility sets in for real income itself.

These descriptive categories are rooted in certain dynamic propositions about supply, demand, and the pattern of production; and before indicating the historical content of the categories I shall briefly state the underlying propositions.

A DYNAMIC THEORY OF PRODUCTION

The classical theory of production is formulated under essentially static assumptions which freeze—or permit only once-over change—in the variables most relevant to the process of economic growth. As modern economists have sought to merge classical production theory with Keynesian income analysis, they have introduced the dynamic variables: population, technology, entrepreneurship, etc. But they have tended to do so in forms so rigid and general that their models cannot grip the essential phenomena of growth, as they appear to an economic historian. We require a dynamic theory of production which isolates not only the distribution of income between consumption, saving, and investment (and the balance of production between consumers and capital goods) but which focuses directly and in some detail on the composition of investment and on developments within particular sectors of the economy. The argument that follows is based on such a flexible, disaggregated theory of production.

When the conventional limits on the theory of production are widened, it is possible to define theoretical equilibrium positions not only for output, investment, and consumption as a whole, but for each sector of the economy.[1] Within the framework set by forces de-

1. W. W. Rostow, *The Process of Economic Growth* (Oxford, 1953), especially Ch. 4. Also "Trends in the Allocation of Resources in Secular Growth," Ch. 15 in *Economic Progress*, ed. Leon H. Dupriez, with the assistance of Douglas C. Hague (Louvain, 1955); also, "The Takeoff into Self-Sustained Growth," *Economic Journal* (March 1956).

Reprinted by permission from *The Economic History Review*, August 1959, by permission of the Economic History Review and the author.

termining the total level of output, sectoral optimum positions are determined, on the side of demand, by the levels of income and of population, and by the character of tastes; on the side of supply, by the state of technology and the quality of entrepreneurship, as the latter determines the proportion of technically available and potentially profitable innovations actually incorporated in the capital stock.[2] In addition, one must introduce an extremely significant empirical hypothesis; namely, that deceleration is the normal optimum path of a sector, due to a variety of factors operating on it, from the side of both supply and demand.[3] The equilibria which emerge from the application of these criteria are a set of sectoral paths, from which flows, as first derivatives, a sequence of optimum patterns of investment.

Historical patterns of investment did not, of course, exactly follow these optimum patterns. They were distorted by imperfections in the private investment process; by the policies of governments; and by the impact of wars. Wars temporarily altered the profitable directions of investment by setting up arbitrary demands and by changing the conditions of supply; they destroyed capital; and, occasionally, they accelerated the development of new technology relevant to the peacetime economy and shifted the political and social framework in ways conducive to peacetime growth.[4] The historical sequence of business cycles and trend periods results from these deviations of actual from optimal patterns; and such fluctuations, along with the impact of wars, yield historical paths of growth which differ from those which the optima, calculated before the event, would have yielded. Nevertheless, the economic history of growing societies takes a part of its rude shape from the effort of societies to approximate the optimum sectoral paths.

At any period of time, the rate of growth in the sectors will vary greatly; and it is possible to isolate empirically certain leading sectors at early stages of their evolution, whose rapid rate of expansion plays an essential direct and indirect role in maintaining the overall momentum of the economy.[5] For some purposes it is useful to characterize an economy in terms of its leading sectors; and a part of the technical basis for the stages of growth lies in the changing sequence of leading sectors. In essence it is the fact that sectors tend to have a rapid growth phase early in their life, that makes it possible and useful to regard economic history as a sequence of stages rather than merely as a continuum, within which nature never makes a jump.

The stages of growth also require, however, that elasticities of demand be taken into account, and that this familiar concept be widened; for these rapid growth phases in the sectors derive not merely from the discontinuity of production functions but also from high price or income elasticities of demand. Leading sectors are determined not merely by the changing flow of technology and the changing willingness of entrepreneurs to accept available innovations: they are also partially determined by those types of demand which have exhibited high elasticity with respect to price, income, or both.

The demand for resources has resulted, however, not merely from demands set up by private taste and choice, but also from social decisions and from the policies of governments—whether democratically responsive or not. It is necessary, therefore, to look at the choices made by societies in the disposition of their resources in terms which transcend conventional market processes. It is necessary to look at their welfare functions, in the widest sense, including the noneconomic processes which determined them.

The course of birthrates, for example, represents one form of welfare choice made by societies, as income has changed; and population curves reflect (in addition to changing death rates) how the calculus about family size was made in the various stages; from the usual (but not universal) decline in birthrates, during or soon after the takeoff, as urbanization took hold and progress became a palpable possibility, to the recent rise, as Americans (and others in societies marked by high mass consumption) have appeared to seek in larger families values beyond those afforded by economic security and by an ample supply of durable consumers goods and services.

And there are other decisions as well that societies have made as the choices open to them have been altered by the unfolding process of economic growth; and these broad collective decisions, determined by many factors–deep in history, culture, and the active political process–outside the market place, have interplayed with the dynamics of market demand, risk-taking, technology, and entrepreneurship to determine the specific content of the stages of growth for each society.

How, for example, should the traditional society react to the intrusion of a more advanced power: with cohesion, promptness, and vigor, like the Japanese; by making a virtue of fecklessness, like the oppressed Irish of the eighteenth century; by slowly and reluctantly altering the traditional society like the Chinese? When independent modern nationhood was achieved, how should the national energies be disposed: in external aggression, to right old wrongs or to exploit newly created or perceived possibilities for enlarged national power; in completing and refining the political victory of the new national government over old regional interests; or in modernizing the economy?

Once growth is under way, with the takeoff, to what extent should the requirements of diffusing modern technology and maximizing the rate of growth be moderated by the desire to increase consumption per capita and to increase welfare?

When technological maturity is reached, and the nation has at its command a modernized and differentiated industrial machine, to what ends should it be put, and in what proportions: to increase social security, through the welfare state; to expand mass consumption into the range of durable consumers goods and services; to increase the nation's stature and power on the world scene; or to increase leisure? And then the further question, where history offers us only fragments: what to do when the increase in real income itself loses its charm? Babies; boredom; three-day weekends; the moon; or the creation of new inner, human frontiers in substitution for the imperatives of scarcity?

In surveying now the broad contours of each stage of growth, we are examining, then, not merely the sectoral struc-

---

2. In a closed model, a dynamic theory of production must account for changing stocks of basic and applied science, as sectoral aspects of investment, which is done in *The Process of Economic Growth, op. cit.*, especially pp. 22–25.

3. *Ibid.*, pp. 96–103.

4. *Ibid.*, Ch. 7, especially pp. 164–167.

5. For a discussion of the leading sectors, their direct and indirect consequences, and the diverse routes of their impact, see "Trends in the Allocation of Resources in Secular Growth," *op. cit.*

ture of economies, as they transformed themselves for growth, and grew; we are also examining a succession of strategic choices made by various societies concerning the disposition of their resources, which include but transcend the income and price elasticities of demand.

THE TRADITIONAL SOCIETY

The central economic fact about traditional societies is that they evolved within limited production functions. Both in the more distant past and in recent times the story of traditional societies is a story of endless change, reflected in the scale and patterns of trade, the level of agricultural output and productivity, the scale of manufactures, fluctuations in population and real income. But limitations of technology decreed a ceiling beyond which they could not penetrate. They did not lack inventiveness and innovations, some of high productivity. But they did lack a systematic understanding of their physical environment capable of making invention a more or less regular current flow, rather than a stock of *ad hoc* achievements inherited from the past. They lacked, in short, the tools and the outlook toward the physical world of the post-Newtonian era.

It followed from this productivity ceiling that food production absorbed 75 percent or more of the working force and that a high proportion of income above minimum consumption levels was spent in nonproductive or low productivity outlays: religious and other monuments; wars; high living for those who controlled land rents; and for poorer folk, there was a beggar-thy-neighbor struggle for land or the dissipation of the occasional surplus in an expensive wedding or funeral. Social values were geared to the limited horizons which men could perceive to be open to them; and social structures tended to hierarchy, although the traditional societies never wholly lacked paths for vertical mobility. The center of gravity of political power tended to reside in the regions, with the landowners, despite a fluctuating tension with those who—along with their soldiers and civil servants—exercised a degree of central authority.

THE PRECONDITIONS FOR TAKEOFF

The initial preconditions for takeoff were created in Western Europe out of two characteristics of the post-medieval world which interacted and reinforced each other: the gradual evolution of modern science and the modern scientific attitude; and the lateral innovation that came with the discovery of new lands and the rediscovery of old, converging with the impulse to create new technology at certain strategic points. The widening of the market—both within Europe and overseas—brought not only trade, but increased specialization of production, increased interregional and international dependence, enlarged institutions of finance, and increased market incentives to create new production functions. The whole process was heightened by the extension to trade and colonies of the old dynastic competition for control over European territories, inherited from the world of traditional societies.[6]

Britain was the first of the European nations to move from the stage of preconditions into takeoff, a fact capable of various explanations but certainly influenced by these circumstances: its achievement of a political and religious settlement by 1688; the area of social latitude and the limited but powerful incentives offered to nonconformists, who played a remarkable role in the process of industrial innovation; its naval and, thus, trading advantages, partly determined by a greater freedom from commitments to land warfare than the French; an endowment in industrial raw materials superior to the Dutch.

The existence of the British takeoff from, say, 1783, set in motion a series of positive and negative demonstration effects which progressively unhinged other traditional societies or accelerated the creation of the preconditions for takeoff, where the preconditions process was already under way.[7] Before examining the manner in which these demonstration effects were communicated, however, the structural characteristics of the preconditions period should be defined.

Technically, the preconditions for sustained industrialization have generally required radical change in three nonindustrial sectors. First, a buildup of social overhead capital, notably in transport. This buildup was necessary not merely to permit an economical national market to be created and to allow natural resources to be productively exploited, but also to permit the national government effectively to rule. Second, a technological revolution in agriculture. The processes at work during the preconditions generally yielded both a general rise in population and a disproportionate rise in urban populations. Increased productivity in agriculture has been generally a necessary condition for preventing the process of modernization from being throttled. Third, an expansion in imports financed by the more efficient production and marketing of some natural resources plus, where possible, capital imports. Such increased access to foreign exchange was required to permit the less advanced region or nation to increase the supply of the equipment and industrial raw materials it could not then itself supply, as well as to preserve the level of real income while social overhead capital of long gestation period was being created. Framed by these three forms of sectoral development, yielding both new markets and new inputs for industry, the initially small enclaves of modern industrial activity could begin to expand, and then sustain expansion, mainly by the plowback of profits.

These technical developments required, in turn, prior or concurrent changes in the noneconomic dimensions of the traditional society: a willingness of the agricultural community to accept new techniques and to respond to the possibilities of the widened commercial markets; the existence and freedom to operate of a new group of industrial entrepreneurs; and, above all, a national government capable not only of providing a setting of peaceful order which encouraged the new modernizing activities but also capable and willing to take a degree of direct responsibility for the buildup of social overhead capital (in-

---

6. This analysis shares with Schumpeter's the view that the ultimate causes of war were inherited from traditional societies, and were not a consequence of the more or less rational pursuit of direct economic interests. But, whereas Schumpeter tends to emphasize the persistence of irrational and romantic nationalist attitudes, this analysis would underline the structural fact that, once national sovereignty was accepted as a rule of the world arena, nations found themselves gripped in an almost inescapable oligopolistic struggle for power, which did have elements of noneconomic rationality.

7. This article will not examine the preconditions process in the nations which, in Louis Hartz's phrase, were "born free" of traditional societies, mainly deriving from a British society already well advanced in the preconditions process or in regular growth. I refer to the United States, Canada, New Zealand, Australia, etc.

cluding its finance); for an appropriate trade policy; and often, as well, for the diffusion of new agricultural and industrial techniques.

THE TAKEOFF

As I have suggested in an earlier article,[8] the takeoff consists, in essence, of the achievement of rapid growth in a limited group of sectors, where modern industrial techniques are applied. Historically, the leading sectors in takeoff have ranged from cotton textiles (Britain and New England); to railroads (the United States, France, Germany, Canada, Russia); to modern timber cutting and railroads (Sweden). In addition, agricultural processing, oil, import substitution industries, shipbuilding, and rapid expansions in military output have helped to provide the initial industrial surge.

The takeoff is distinguished from earlier industrial surges by the fact that prior and concurrent developments make the application of modern industrial techniques a self-sustained rather than an abortive process. Not only must the momentum in the three key sectors of the preconditions be maintained but the corps of entrepreneurs and technicians must be enlarged, and the sources of capital must be institutionalized in such a way as to permit the economy to suffer structural shocks; to redispose its investment resources; and to resume growth. It is the requirement that the economy exhibit this resilience that justifies defining the takeoff as embracing an interval of about two decades.

A result—and one key manifestation—of takeoff is the ability of the society to sustain an annual rate of net investment of the order of, at least, 10 percent. This familiar (but essentially tautological) way of defining the takeoff should not conceal the full range of transformations required before growth becomes a built-in feature of a society's habits and institutions.

In noneconomic terms, the takeoff usually witnesses a definitive social, political, and cultural victory of those who would modernize the economy over those who would either cling to the traditional society or seek other goals; but—because nationalism can be a social solvent as well as a diversionary force—the victory can assume forms of mutual accommodation, rather than the destruction of the traditional groups by the more modern; see, for example, the role of the Junkers in nascent industrial Germany, the persistence of much of traditional Japan beyond 1880. By and large, the maintenance of momentum for a generation persuades the society to persist and to concentrate its efforts on extending the tricks of modern technology out beyond the sectors modernized during takeoff.

THE DRIVE TO MATURITY

After takeoff there follows, then, what might be called the drive to maturity. There are a variety of ways a stage of economic maturity might be defined; but for these purposes it is defined as the period when a society has effectively applied the range of (then) modern technology to the bulk of its resources.

During the drive to maturity the industrial process is differentiated, with new leading sectors gathering momentum to supplant the older leading sectors of the takeoff, where deceleration has increasingly slowed the pace of expansion. After the railway takeoffs of the third quarter of the nineteenth century—with coal, iron, and heavy engineering at the center of the growth process—it is steel, the new ships, chemicals, electricity, and the products of the modern machine tool that come to dominate the economy and sustain the overall rate of growth. This is also, essentially, the case with the later Russian drive to maturity, after 1929. But in Sweden after 1890 it was the evolution from timber to wood pulp and paper; from ore to high-grade steel and finely machined metal products. The leading sectors in the drive to maturity will be determined, then, not merely by the pool of technology but by the nature of resource endowments; and it may be shaped to a degree, as well, by the policies of governments. Although much further detailed analysis would be required to apply this definition rigorously, I would offer the following sample as rough symbolic dates for technological maturity.[9]

Great Britain	1850
United States	1900
Germany	1910
France	1910
Sweden	1930
Japan	1940
Russia	1950
Canada	1950

The meaning of this technological definition of maturity—and its limits—may be better perceived by considering briefly a few specific problems posed by these particular dates.

Is France for example, on the eve of World War I, to be regarded as technologically mature, despite its large, comfortable, but technologically backward peasantry and its tendency to export large amounts of capital, despite certain technologically lagging industrial sectors? The case can, of course, be argued either way; but it does dramatize the need to allow, within the present definition, for regions of a nation or sectors of the economy to resist—for whatever reason—the full application of the range of modern technology. And this turns out to be generally true of nations which, by and large, one would judge mature. The United States of 1900 contained, after all, the South, whose takeoff can only be dated from the 1930s; and contemporary mature Canada contains the still lagging province of Quebec. The technological definition of maturity must, then, be an approximation, when applied to a whole national society. . . .

What about contemporary Russia, with more than 40 percent of the working force still in agriculture and much modern technology still unapplied in consumers-goods industries? Here again, the present definition of maturity would not predetermine how a society chooses to allocate its technological capabilities. By and large contemporary Russia is to be judged a mature economy despite the fact that its leaders have chosen for political reasons to bear the costs of a low productivity agriculture and have chosen to concentrate capital and technology in sectors other than manufactured consumption goods. Put another way, the obstacles to full modernization of the Russian economic structure do not lie in the supply of capital, entrepreneurial administrators, or technicians.

Finally, there is the case of Britain, mature on this definition as early, say,

8. "The Takeoff into Self-Sustained Growth," *op. cit.*

9. An oddity is to be noted. These dates, independently derived, come more or less sixty years after the dates established, on quite different criteria, for the beginning of takeoff. There is no body of argument or evidence I can now offer to make rational such a uniformity. But it may be that when we explore the implications of some six decades of compound interest applied to the capital stock, in combination with three generations of men living under an environment of growth, elements of rationality will emerge.

as the Crystal Palace Exhibition. How is one to deal with the long interval between the stage of its maturity, in terms of the effective application of mid-nineteenth-century technology, and the next stage of growth: the age of high mass consumption, when the radical improvements in housing and durable consumers goods and services become the economy's leading sectors? The reasons for the gap in the British sequence lie in the nature of this next stage. The age of high mass consumption represents a direction of development a society may choose when it has achieved both technological maturity and a certain level of real income per head. Although income per head—and usually consumption per head—will rise in the drive to maturity, it is evident that there is no fixed connection between technological maturity and any particular level of real consumption per head. The course of these variables after takeoff will depend primarily on the society's population-resource balance and on its income-distribution policy. The process of growth, by definition, raises income per head, but it does not necessarily lead to uniformity of per capita income among nations or, even, among regions within nations. There are—and there are likely to be—technologically mature societies that are, so to speak, both rich and poor. When historical data on national income are developed to permit systematic comparison, we are likely to find that incomes per head, at maturity, vary over a considerable range. Midcentury Britain would, presumably, stand low in that range. The improvements in real income and consumption per head that occurred in the second half of the nineteenth century took the form of improvements in diet, housing, and urban overhead capital which, while substantial, did not create within Britain new leading industrial sectors—at least down to the bicycle boom of the 1890s. . . .

As societies move to technological maturity, the structure and quality of the working force change. The proportion of the population in agriculture and rural life decreases; and within the urban population the proportion of semiskilled and white-collar workers increases.[10] This emergent working force is not only likely to organize itself with increasing effectiveness in the labor markets, but also to perceive that the industrial civilization of which it is a part can offer levels and types of consumption not previously regarded as a realistic possibility on a mass basis. And the rise in real income per head is likely to make these new tastes effective. Further, the new working force, increasingly born to the city rather than transferred from the lower margins of rural life, is likely to perceive that it can bring its weight to bear on the political process in such ways as to make the government increasingly provide measures of social and economic security. Moreover, the character of leadership in industry begins to change as well. The takeoff is usually managed by relatively modest, creative men with an insight as to how output in their sector can be radically expanded: the Boultons and Lowells. In the drive to maturity men take over with more grandiose visions, with a more acute sense of scale and of power: Although there are vast differences between post-Civil War United States and Stalin's Russia, there is, nevertheless, a distant family resemblance between some of the great entrepreneurs of the American drive to maturity and the men who administered the Five-Year Plans between, say, 1929 and 1953. At maturity, however, the professional managers become more important: the nameless, comfortable, cautious committeemen who inherit and manage large sectors of the economy, while the society begins to seek objectives which include but transcend the application of modern technology to resources. . . .

THE AGE OF HIGH MASS CONSUMPTION

There have been, essentially, three directions in which the mature economy could be turned once the society ceased to accept the extension of modern technology as a primary, if not overriding objective: to offer, by public measures, increased security, welfare, and, perhaps, leisure to the working force; to provide enlarged private consumption—including single family homes and durable consumers goods and services—on a mass basis; to seek enlarged power for the mature nation on the world scene. A good deal of the history of the first half of the twentieth century can be told in terms of the pattern and succession of choices made by various mature societies as among these three alternatives.

After a brief and superficial flirtation with the attractions of world power at the turn of the century and after imposing a set of mild measures of social reform, during the progressive period, the United States opted wholeheartedly in the 1920s for the second choice.[11] The boom of that decade was built squarely on the migration to suburbia, the mass extension of the automobile, and the household gadgetry which modern industry could provide. And these decisions to relocate the population and provide it with mobility, brought in their train not only new leading sectors—housing, automobiles, petroleum, rubber, electric-powered household devices, etc.—but also vast commitments to build new social overhead capital and commercial centers.

Down to 1914 Britain and Western Europe opted more substantially for public measures of social security, influenced perhaps by the higher proportions of urban population and by the greater power of socialist thought and political influence than in the United States. In addition, Germany was more seriously tempted than the United States to translate industrial maturity into enlarged world power; and in the inherently oligopolistic circumstances of the European arena of power, this decision led to a greater relative enlargement of military expenditures in Europe as a whole than in pre-1914 United States.

During the 1920s Britain, in effect, took its favorable terms of trade in the form of chronic unemployment in the export industries. Only in the 1930s did a pervasive recovery occur. This phase did begin to exhibit a shift into the age of high mass consumption: Suburban housing, automobiles, and durable consumers goods began to assert themselves more strongly as leading sectors. But rearmament and war postponed the immediate fruition of this trend.

Although the post-1920 terms of trade problem struck the Continent with less force than Britain, there too the return to relative prosperity, of 1925–1929, did not move the economies far beyond pre-1914 patterns. France, on the whole,

10. Although Colin Clark's categories—of primary, secondary, and tertiary activity—do not fit precisely this analysis, his pioneer compilations suggest that considerable uniformities in the structure of the working force of mature economies exist.

11. The time lag in the United States between the achievement of technological maturity in, say, 1900, and the high mass consumption boom of the 1920s is to be accounted for in part by the relative stagnation of industrial real wages in the pre-1914 trend period, due to rising living costs (*Process of Economic Growth,* Ch. 6). The more protracted lag of Western Europe is partly a consequence of the economic impact of World War I and of the public policies and dominant social attitudes of the interwar years.

continued to stagnate down to World War II, and German recovery, while reflecting certain symptoms of the new phase, was dominated by rearmament.

Svennilson presents calculations of motor-vehicle production (private and commercial) which suggest the relative movements of the United States and Western Europe between the wars. In 1929 the four major European nations (Great Britain, Germany, France, and Italy) produced 702,000 vehicles; the United States, 5.4 million. After a decade of protracted depression in the United States (marked by a compensatory turn to the welfare state), and a considerably greater degree of European recovery, the European figure was 1.1 million in 1938; the American, 2.5 million.[12]

In the decade 1946–1956 the United States resumed a pattern of recovery and growth markedly similar to that of the 1920s: the migration to suburbia, and the extension of the automobile and the standard mix of durable consumers household gadgets to 75 percent or more of American families. And, after an interval of postwar reconstruction, Western Europe resumed with force the similar but more laggard development of the 1930s. By the late 1950s Western European growth was based on the fact that this region had at last fully entered the age of durable consumers goods and services, experiencing a version of the American 1920s. The patterns of consumption, as among the various European countries, emerge as largely explicable in terms of income and price elasticities of demand. And in Russia, as well, the inexorable attraction of the sewing machine, washing machine, refrigerator, and television was beginning to assert itself; and the first satellite town was under construction. It was evident, however, from the pattern of future plans that the Soviet government was not yet prepared to give the vast hostages to fortune that follow a society's commitment to the mass automobile.

BEYOND CONSUMPTION

While Western Europe (and to a degree, also, Japan) were entering the era of high mass consumption and the Soviet Union was dallying on its fringes, an important new element entered the world economic system in the form of a quite unexpected tendency of birthrates to rise in rich societies. Although the tendency can be observed in a number of countries, it is most marked in the United States. During the years of World War II the American birthrate rose from 18 to about 22 per 1000. This was judged at the time, and to a large degree it certainly was, a phenomenon of resumed full employment and early wartime marriages. In the postwar years, however, it moved up and has stayed at about 25 per 1000. An official forecast in 1946 estimated that the American population would reach 165 million in 1990; an official forecast of 1958 estimated that the figure might be of the order of 240 million by 1980.

The human motivations and social processes which have yielded this extraordinary result are not yet well understood; but Americans have behaved as if diminishing relative marginal utility set in to the expansion of real income along the old paths. They have opted at the margin for larger families; and this trend may be related to the high rate of expansion in family trips to national parks, motorboats, do-it-yourself implements, and, even, to a widely noted tendency to turn away from the pursuit of income and authority within the large-scale bureaucratic establishments where a high proportion of the population do their work.

Whatever the motivation, however, an

expansion of population on this scale will set up requirements for the lateral extension of the society's resources, including its requirements of social overhead capital. These requirements in any case had been enlarged by the consequences of the previous phase of extension in automobile ownership and suburban housing. There is a vast American backlog of investment to be carried out in roads and in the reconstruction of old depopulated urban centers. Finally, a quite significant change in the dependency ratio is under way. After falling for about a century, the number of persons under twenty and over sixty-five in the American population supported by each 100 members of the working force had reached 74 in 1935; by 1955 the figure was 81; and if present population patterns persist it is estimated that the figure will rise to 98 by 1975.

The pattern of American economic growth over the next several decades is likely to differ, then, from that of either the 1920s or the 1946–1956 decade; and it is likely to be based on somewhat different leading sectors. In any case, it is clear that American society, by its quiet collective decision about birthrates, has postponed the problems of a time of true affluence, when the full utilization of resources would not much matter.

The somewhat strenuous choice made by Americans as they pushed high mass consumption to a kind of logical conclusion, in the first decade after World War II, need not prove to be universal: The income elasticity of demand for children may vary. It is evident, however, that the march of compound interest is bringing some societies close to the point where the pursuit of food, shelter, clothing, as well as durable consumers goods and public and private services, may no longer dominate their lives. A new and revolutionary set of choices is being confronted, or is a mere generation or so over the horizon.

---

12. Ingvar Svennilson, *Growth and Stagnation in the European Economy* (Geneva: United Nations, 1954), pp. 144–152. I am inclined to believe that the length of the American depression and its intractibility in the 1930s stems from the character of leading sectors in the age of high mass consumption. The diffusion of single-family housing, the automobile, etc. requires expanding levels of private income and, in effect, full employment. Moreover, until the diffusion process is actively under way certain major forms of investment are likely to be slack, because of idle capacity. Full employment is needed, in a sense, to maintain full employment when the leading sectors are consumption sectors. This was not true before 1914 when, even with unemployment high and incomes low, it might well pay to press on with railroadization, steel ships, etc. where the high expected rate of return over costs derived primarily from lowered costs. Put another way, in the age of high mass consumption a higher proportion of investment becomes endogenous, rather than exogenous, when the latter term is used to embrace investment stimulated by new technological possibilites.

ROBERT L. HEILBRONER

Professor of Economics, New School for Social Research.

Operating within a Modified Keynesian framework, Heilbroner starts his analysis in the following article with the assumption that capitalism will be maintained as the dominant socio-economic organization for the next several generations. Whether or not this assumption of the semipermanence of capitalism is a reasonable one is, of course, a moot point. Unless the existing system is beset by innumerable and obvious contradictions, it always appears more reasonable to assume continuity rather than a rupture of the status quo. This was as true of long periods under slavery and feudalism as it is now under the present modified capitalist system.

Heilbroner is concerned with exploring the limits of change within the bounds of capitalism. He recognizes that in America a system of privilege is grounded in capitalist institutions and is therefore a source of resistance to social and economic change. Although aware of many aspects of Marxian analysis, Heilbroner eschews its theory of history based on class conflict and replaces it with a technological deterministic theory of social change, in which the strategic group in society is the technological elite rather than powerful wealth holders or a proletariat. The latter group, in fact, nowhere appears as an active agent in Heilbroner's scheme. Rather he stresses the continuing tension between the former two groups as the dominant shaper of history. Heilbroner believes that the new elite, whose organized knowledge and scientific technology is geared to social control and planning, must ultimately subvert the capitalist order, since their mentality and outlook are geared to social control and planning. In the short run, however, he admits that the skills of this elite are used to buttress the capitalist order; and he fails to explain how the "technocracy" which supports capitalist institutions in the short run is antagonistic to these same institutions in the long run. His position is, at best, a questionable one. Although it is quite possible that individual members of the scientific elite may feel an ideological incompatibility with the materialistic and nationalistic aims of the social system, the overwhelming number show every evidence of being willingly co-opted into business and government where they occupy a privileged position. To claim that important historical changes are to be engineered by these groups is to adopt an elitist view of history in which the masses are passively moved by forces they neither understand nor control. Although Heilbroner's approving comment that "conscious social control in more and more areas of life will be a marked feature of society in the future" would appear to transcend liberalism, it is belied by his elitist frame of reference.

The merit of Heilbroner is that he, like Galbraith, has assiduously tried to make economics more socially relevant by directing its focus on how capitalism actually operates rather than spinning imaginary theories about an imaginary competitive market model. He notes with considerable acumen that the dominant corporate sector attempts through planning to insulate itself against disruptive market forces, and is more and more prone to accept a government with widespread supervisory and regulatory powers. His claim that considerable economic planning on a governmental level is compatible with a capitalist structure, and that technology creates a need for more societal organization, places Heilbroner on the left end of the liberal spectrum. Heilbroner believes that the capitalist system, preserved according to Keynesian ideals, is capable of maintaining effective demand at high employment levels, gradually redistributing income sufficiently to end poverty, utilizing technology without serious disruptive effects in the short run, and achieving a peaceful accord with Russia—although Heilbroner acknowledges the presence of a "semimilitarized economy" in the United States and predicts the likelihood of Communist expansion in undeveloped countries during the next decade. One has to admire Heilbroner's courage in the hazardous game of crystal-ball gazing. It remains to be seen whether or not the capitalist model is capable of delivering all that he optimistically claims for it. His view of the long-run demise of capitalism because of the sapping of its ideological underpinnings is in marked contrast to his short-run forecasts.

M L

THE FUTURE OF CAPITALISM

(1966)

For roughly the last century and a half the dominant system of economic organization in most of the West has been that of capitalism. In all likelihood, barring the advent of a catastrophic war, capitalism will continue as the dominant system of the Western world during the remainder of this century and well into the next. Although it will inevitably change, will likely suffer considerable duress over the next decades, and in the longer run will gradually give way to a very different kind of social order, for our lives and for those of our children, capitalism bids fair to confront us as the prevailing form of social organization in those nations where it is now solidly entrenched.

It seems to me that all serious social analysis and prediction must start from some such premise. At any rate, it is my premise, and I propose to explore—with all the uncertainties and risks inherent in such an enterprise—the social changes available to us within the limits of capitalism in the future.

But how can we establish these "limits"? Perhaps we can shed an initial light on the question if we imagine asking some perceptive observer in, say, thirteenth-century France what were the

 This essay was included in somewhat different form in Heilbroner's book, *The Limits of American Capitalism*, New York: Harper & Row, 1966.

limits of feudalism. Our observer might be hard put to find an answer, particularly if he looked about him at the striking variety of forms that feudalism assumed in the various domains of Europe. Yet undoubtedly we could have suggested an answer to him that would have sounded reasonable. It is that certain kinds of economic and social change were unimaginable—indeed impossible—in thirteenth-century France because they would have implied the establishment of some totally different form of social organization. To take a central instance, it would have been impossible to have replaced the traditional ties, established customs, and fixed obligations by which the manorial economy hung together with some radically different system, such as the cash markets that were already disrupting the settled tenor of feudal economic life, because a change of this dimension would have critically undermined the power of the lord, elevated out of all proportion that of the parvenu class of merchants, and thereby destroyed the fixed hierarchy of status that was the very backbone of the feudal social structure. Thus, one meaning we can give to the idea of "limits" in a society is very simple: It is those boundaries of change that would so alter the functional base of a society, or the structure of privilege built on that base, as to displace a given social order by a new one.

In terms of the immediate subject of our essay, this draws the broad limits of American capitalism in the last third of the twentieth century with reasonable fixity. To take a few examples: It is certainly beyond the present limits of capitalism to replace the guiding principle of production for profit by that of production for use; it is impossible to nationalize the great corporations or to end the private ownership of the means of mass communication; and it is impossible to end the concentration of wealth in private hands. One can debate whether all or any of these changes are desirable, but there is little point in debating whether they are realizable. Barring only some disaster that would throw open the gates to a radical reconstruction of society, they are not.

What we have established thus far, however, is only the first and most obvious answer to the question of what we mean by the "limits" of social change. For if we now return to the thirteenth century, we could imagine suggesting to our medieval observer another approach to the idea of feudal limits. Rather than pointing out to him the contemporary incompatibility of the market system, we might be able to show him the immense long-term historical momentum of the emergent forces of the monetized economy. Indeed, we might even be able to bring him to see that by the end of another four or five centuries, feudalism would have virtually disappeared, and that an economic organization of society once incompatible with feudalism would have triumphed over it.

From such a perspective, the task of delineating the limits of feudalism becomes a different one. It is no longer to discover what cannot be done in the short run, but to explore what *can* be done, and how, in doing it, the social structure may slowly and subtly alter, making possible still further change in the future.

It need hardly be said that one cannot project such a long evolutionary—or possibly revolutionary—advance in close detail. The precise route to be taken, the pace of progress, the roadblocks where the invading forces of a new society may be temporarily halted or even thrown back—all this surpasses any power of analysis we now have. But the grand line of march is not beyond our ability to foresee. Looking back at thirteenth-century France, we can see how defenseless were its castle walls against the insinuating influence of the market system. In similar fashion, it should be possible to explore the limits of capitalism in America, not alone in terms of changes that cannot now be accommodated by the business system, but in terms of those forces that are altering capitalism, like feudalism in an earlier day, in ways that will eventually cause its social and economic structure to be displaced by another.

We cannot, however, explore change until we answer a prior question: Why do societies resist change? A full explanation of social inertia must reach deep into the psychological and technical underpinnings of the human community. But in the process of gradual social adjustment it is clear enough where to look for the main sources of the resistance to change. They are to be found in the structure of privilege inherent in all social systems.

Privilege is not an attribute we are accustomed to stress when we consider the construction of *our* social order. When pressed, we are, of course, aware of its core institutions in capitalism—the right to reap private benefits from the use of the means of production and the right to utilize the dynamic forces of the marketplace for private enrichment. The element of privilege in these institutions, however—that is, their operative result in favoring certain individuals and classes—is usually passed over in silence in favor of their purely functional aspects. Thus, private property is ordinarily explained as being no more than a convenient instrumentality for the efficient operation of an economic system, or the market elements of Land, Labor, and Capital as purely neutral "factors of production."

Now these institutions and relationships do indeed fulfill the purposes for which they are advertised. But this is not the only use they have. Land, Labor, and Capital are not just functional parts of a mechanism but are categories of social existence that bring vast differences in life chances with them. It is not just Labor on the one hand, and Land or Capital on the other; it is the Bronx on the one hand and Park Avenue on the other. Similarly, private property is not merely a pragmatic arrangement devised for the facilitation of production, but a social institution that brings to some members of the community a style of life qualitatively different from that afforded to the rest. In a word, the operation of capitalism as a *functional* system results in a structure of wealth and income characteristic of capitalism as a *system of privilege*—a structure in which the top 2 percent of American families own between two-thirds and three-quarters of all corporate stock, and enjoy incomes roughly ten times larger than the average received within the nation as a whole.

The mere presence of these concentrations of wealth or large disparities of income does not in itself differentiate the system of privilege under capitalism from those of most other societies in history. Rather, what marks off our system is that wealth and income within capitalism are not mainly derived from noneconomic activity, such as war, plunder, extortionate taxation, etc., but arise from the activity of marketers or the use of property by its owners.

This mixture of the functional and the privileged aspects of capitalism has a curious but important political consequence. It is that privilege under capitalism is much less "visible," especially to the favored groups, than privilege under other systems. The upper classes in feudalism were keenly alive to the gulf that separated them from the lower classes, and perfectly open about the need for preserving it. The upper groups under capitalism, on the other hand, are typically unaware that the advantages accruing to them from following the paths of the market economy constitute in any sense or fashion a privilege.

This lack of self-awareness is rendered even more acute by virtue of another differentiating characteristic of privilege under capitalism. It is that privilege is limited to the advantages inherent in the economic structure of society. That is, the same civil and criminal law, the same duties in war and peace, apply to both economically privileged and unprivileged. It would be a mistake to concentrate on obvious differences in the application of the law as being of the essence. Rather, one must contrast the single system of law and obligation under capitalism—however one-sidedly administered—with the *differing* systems that apply to privileged and unprivileged in other societies.

The divorce of economic from political or social privilege brings up the obvious fact that, at least in democratic societies like America, the privileged distribution of economic rewards is exposed to the corrective efforts of the democratic electorate. The question is, however, why the structure of privilege has remained relatively intact, despite so long an exposure to the potentially leveling influences of the majority.

In part, we can trace the answer to the very "invisibility" of privilege we have just described. Furthermore, in all stable societies the structure of privilege appears to the general public not as a special dispensation, but as the natural order of things, with which their own interests and sentiments are identified. This is especially true under capitalism, where the privileges of wealth are open, at least in theory, and to some extent in practice, to all comers. Finally, the overall results of capitalism, particularly in America during the entire twentieth century and recently in Europe as well, have been sufficiently rewarding to hold anticapitalist sentiment to a relatively small segment of the population.

That the defense of privilege is the active source of resistance to social and economic change may appear so obvious as scarcely to be worth emphasizing. Obvious or not, it is a fact too often passed over in silence. It seems to me impossible to analyze the nature of the opposition to change without stressing the vulgar but central fact that every person who is rich under capitalism is a beneficiary of its inherent privileges. Taking the American system as it now exists, it seems fair to assert that the chance to own and acquire wealth constitutes a primary—perhaps even a dominating—social motivation for most men, and that those who enjoy or aspire to these privileges will not readily acquiesce in changes that will substantially lessen their chances of maintaining or gaining them.

The touchstone of privilege provides an indispensable key when we now return to our main theme. If it does not give us an exact calculus by which to compute what changes will and will not be acceptable, it does give us an angle of entry, a point of view, without which attempts to cope with the problem of social change are apt to have no relevance at all.

Take, for example, the problem of the poverty that now afflicts some 30 or 40 million Americans. Our alleged cause of this poverty has always directly stressed the privileges of capitalism. This is the view that poverty under capitalism is largely ascribable to wage exploitation. There is clearly an element of truth here, in that the affluence of the favored groups in capitalism does indeed stem from institutions that divert income from the community at large into the channels of dividends, interest, rent, monoply returns, etc. It is by no means clear, however, that the amount of this diversion, if redistributed among the masses, would spell the difference between their poverty and their well-being. On the contrary, it is now generally acknowledged that the level of wages reflects workers' productivity more than any other single factor, and that this productivity in turn is primarily determined by the quantity and the quality of the capital equipment of the economic system.

Certainly, the productivity of the great mass of workers under capitalism has steadily increased, and so have their real wages. Today, for example, industrial workers in America cannot be classified as "poor" by prevailing absolute standards, if we take $4,000 a year as defining a level of minimum adequacy for a small family. Although wage poverty is clearly present in capitalism, it is primarily restricted to the agricultural areas and to the lowest categories of skills in the service trades. No small part of it is accounted for by discrimination against Negroes, and by the really shocking levels of income of Negro farm and service labor. On the other hand, the proportion of the labor force that is afflicted with this poverty is steadily diminishing. Farmers, farm managers, and farm laborers together will probably constitute only 5 percent of the labor force within a decade. The low-paid non-farm common laborer, who constituted over 12 percent of the working force in 1900, makes up only 5 percent of it today and will be a smaller percentage tomorrow.

There remains, nevertheless, the question of how much the existing level of wages could be increased if the categories of capitalist privilege did not exist. Since it is difficult to estimate accurately the total amount of "privileged" income under capitalism, let us take as its convenient representation the sum total of all corporate profits before tax. In the mid 1960s, these profits exceeded $70 billion a year. If this sum were distributed equally among the 70 million members of the work force, the average share would be $1,000. For the lowest-paid workers, such as migrant farm laborers, this would represent an increase in annual incomes of 100 percent or more—an immense gain. For the average industrial worker, however, the gain would be in the neighborhood of 20–25 percent, certainly a large increase but not one that would fundamentally alter his living standards.

Thus, insofar as the institutions of capitalism constitute a drain upon non-privileged groups, it can be fairly said that they are only marginally responsible for any inadequacy in the prevailing general level of income. Individual companies may indeed be capable of vastly improving the lot of their workers—General Motors makes nearly as much gross profit on a car as it pays out in wages, and "could," therefore, virtually double its wages. But for the economy as a whole, no such large margin of redistribution is possible. So long, then, as the defense of these privileges does not result in substantially *increasing* the share of national income accruing to the privileged elements of the nation, it seems fair to conclude that the level of material well-being under capitalism is limited mainly by the levels of productivity it can reach. If the trend of growth of the past century is continued, the average level of real wages for industrial labor should double in another two to three decades. This would bring average earnings to a level of about $10,000 and would effectively spell the abolition of wage poverty, under any definition.

This conclusion does not close our investigation into the relationship between poverty and privilege, but rather directs it toward what is now revealed as the principal cause of poverty. This is the fact that large groups within the population—the aged, the handicapped, the sick, the unemployed, the castaways in rural backwaters—have no active tie into the market economy and must therefore subsist at the very meager levels to which non-participants in the work process are consigned. There is only one way that their condition can be quickly alleviated, but that one way would be very effective indeed. This is to redistribute to them enough income earned or received by more favored members of the community to bring them to levels of economic decency. A program with this objective would require some $10 to $12 billion above the public assistance that the poor now receive in this country. Such a sum would amount to approximately a seventh of corporate profits before tax. Alternatively, shared among the 11 or 12 million consumer units who constitute the top 20 percent of the nation's income receivers, it would require an average additional tax of roughly $1,000 on incomes that average $16,000.

In both cases, in other words, a program to eliminate sheer need among the poor would constitute a sizable incursion into the incomes enjoyed by favored groups, although hardly such an invasion as to constitute the elimination of these privileges. Thus, the failure to carry out such a program cannot be laid to the "objective" or functional difference that such a redistribution would entail, but simply to the general unwillingness of those who enjoy higher incomes to share their good fortune with those who do not. As Adam Walinsky has very aptly put it, "The middle class knows that the economists are right when they say that poverty could be eliminated if we only will it; they simply do not will it."

To what extent does that conclusion, then, lead to the prospect of alleviating poverty within the next generation or so? In the short run the outlook is not very hopeful. Given the temptations of luxury consumption and the general lack of deep concern in a nation lulled by middle-class images of itself, it is doubtful that very effective programs of social rescue can be launched within the next decade or two. Yet, of all the problems confronting capitalism, poverty seems the least likely to be blocked permanently by the resistance of privilege. Tax receipts are now growing at the rate of some $6 billion a year simply as a consequence of the growth of the level of output, and this flow of funds to the government will increase over the future. It may be that these receipts will be used for larger arms expenditures for some years, but assuming that full-scale war will be averted, sooner or later the arms budget must level off. Thereafter the funds will become available for use either in the form of tax reductions—an operation which normally favors the well-to-do—or as the wherewithal for a major assault on the slums, etc. In this choice between the claims of privilege and those of social reform, the balance is apt to be tipped by the emerging new national elites, especially from government. In addition, a gradual liberalization of the prevailing business ideology is likely to ease opposition to measures that clearly promise to improve the quality of society without substantially affecting its basic institutions of privilege.

It is idle to predict when Harlem will be reconstructed and Appalachia reborn, since so much depends on the turn of events in the international arena. Yet it seems to me that the general dimensions of the problem make it possible to envisage the substantial alleviation—perhaps even the virtual elimination—of massive poverty within the limits of capitalism three or four decades hence, or possibly even sooner.

The elimination of poverty is, however, only part of a larger problem within capitalism—the problem of income distribution. Hence, we might now look to the chances that capitalism will alter the moral anomalies of wealth as well as those of poverty.

Here it is not so easy to foresee a change in the operational results of the system of privilege. Since the 1930s, the political intent of the public has clearly been to bring about some lessening of the concentration of income that goes to the very rich, and some diminution of the enclaves of family wealth that have passed intact from one generation to the next. Thus, we have seen the introduction of estate taxes that levy imposts of about one-third on net estates of only $1 million, and of fully half on net estates of $5 million; and these rates have been supplemented by measures to prevent the tax-free passage of wealth before death by gift.

Since the enactment of these taxes, a full generation has passed, and we would therefore expect to see some impact of the legislation in a significant lowering of the concentration of wealth among the top families. Instead, we find that the share held by the top families has decreased only slightly—from 33 percent of all personal wealth in 1922, to 29 percent in 1953 (the last year for which such calculations exist). Concentration of stock—the single most important medium for the investment of large wealth—has shown no tendency to decline since 1922. Equally recalcitrant before egalitarian measures is the flow of income to topmost groups. Legal tax rates on top incomes have risen from 54 percent under President Hoover to over 90 percent in the 1940s and early 1950s, and to 72 percent in the mid 1960s. The presumed higher incidence of taxes at the peak of the income pyramid has, however, been subverted by innumerable stratagems of trusts, family sharing of income, capital gains, deferred compensation, or other means of tax avoidance or outright tax evasion.

There is no indication that this resistive capacity of the system of privilege is likely to weaken, at least within the time span of a generation. Nor is there any sign that the "natural workings" of the system will lessen the flow of income to the top. The statistics of income distribution clearly show a slow but regular drift of income *toward* the upper end of the spectrum. Three percent of all income was received by income receivers in the $15,000-and-up brackets in 1947; in 1963, in terms of constant dollars, this fraction had grown to eight. This determined self-perpetuation of large concentrations of private wealth is likely to continue—afflicting the social order with that peculiar irresponsibility that is the unhappy hallmark of the system. The power of wealth is by no means the only source of power in America and may, in fact, be expected to decline. But the voice of money still speaks very loudly, and the capacity of wealth to surmount the half-acquiescent opposition of a democratic political system promises that it will continue to resound in America for a long while to come.

The maldistribution of income and the social problems that spring from it can no longer be said to threaten the viability—although it may seriously jeopardize the social peace—of capitalism. This cannot be said, however, of a second problem—the economic malfunction that has periodically racked capitalism over the last hundred years and that nearly caused its demise in the 1930s.

The persistent breakdowns of the capitalist economy can all be traced to a single underlying cause: the anarchic or planless character of capitalist production. So long as the output of individual firms is guided solely by the profitable opportunities open to each, without regard to the state of the market as a whole, economic short-circuits must result whenever the output of all firms fails to dovetail with the structure of demand, or when the production plans of the business community as a whole are not adequate to cope with the independently formulated savings plans of the community at large. In a milieu of huge enterprises and enormous fixed investments, such miscalculations or imbalances carry the potential of a major disruptive impact.

Hence, it is not surprising that reformers have long advocated planning as the remedy for capitalist depressions or stagnation. The trouble has been, however, that much of the planning which its partisans have urged upon it has been incompatible with the institutions of capitalism. For example, proposals to nationalize the core of heavy industry or to convert the biggest corporations into quasi-public utilities, may have much to recommend them along strictly economic lines, but they all infringe the preserves of private property or of the market to a degree intolerable to the American business community.

This does not mean, however, that planning is therefore ruled out. On the contrary, a great deal of planning is virtually inevitable over the coming decades, but it is likely to be used in support of the main institutions of capitalism rather than as a means of replacing them.

One such planning instrument is certain to be the reliance on the government's fiscal powers to maintain aggregate demand. Although we are still only in the early stages of experience with public demand-creation, there is little doubt that a bold use of fiscal mechanisms can virtually guarantee a steady or rising level of total expenditure. Moreover, since demand-creation involves little or no interference with individual markets or business, it impinges little, if at all, on the preserves of privilege. Tax cuts, for example, are certain to be welcomed by business and upper-income groups. Additional spending, so long as it is within the established areas of public concern—arms, roads, schools, rivers and harbors, conservation, and perhaps now social welfare—is also welcomed as a source of new business.

There remains, to be sure, a body of ideological resistance to the use of fiscal measures of a compensatory sort, compounded of an ignorance of public finance and a shrewd foreboding that the assumption of public economic responsibility, no matter how useful at the moment, is freighted with serious long-term implications. Yet it seems likely that this is a view of dwindling importance. A very considerable segment of business backed the controversial Kennedy tax cut, and the undoubted success of that policy should pave the way for further measures of the same kind. In addition, the non-business elites, especially from the academic and government establishments, are strongly in favor of fiscal controls to buoy up the system, and their influence in securing the bold use of these measures may be very important or even decisive. Thus, there seems a reasonable expectation that measures to safeguard the economy against the collapse of effective demand lie well within the ambit of capitalism today.

What is more difficult to judge is the extent to which capitalism will be able to go beyond general fiscal planning into planning on a more detailed basis for the achievement of broad welfare objectives. Here the experience of Europe since the war is relevant. In nearly every nation of Europe we have seen the formulation of planning techniques that go considerably beyond the mere application of fiscal leverage, to the conscious "design" of the economic future. The very fact that European capitalism has taken this turn puts it beyond argument that a considerable amount of indirect planning is compatible with the main institutions of capitalism.

On the other hand, the growth of European planning owes much to the particular traditions of European capitalism, including the more or less formalized structures of employers' federations and the pronounced *"étatist"* tradition in many states. The absence of comparable institutions and history makes doubtful the possibility of a wholesale transplantation of European forms of planning to America. Furthermore, unlike its sister capitalisms across the Atlantic, the United States has not become accustomed to the public ownership of transportation or utilities, or to a large public-housing sector, or to the development of a strong system of public welfare.

As a result, the United States has always entertained an exaggerated suspicion of all invasions by the public authority into private terrain. Hence the extent and speed with which American capitalism may evolve in the direction of detailed economic planning would seem to depend primarily on whether circumstances arise that require such techniques. If, for example, the continued incursion of technology, coupled with a very large inflow of young people into the labor market, should create an employment crisis during the next decade, some form of industrial planning would quite possibly emerge as an instrument of social policy. In that case, policies designed deliberately to create employment through a substantial enlargement of public activities at state or local levels, or—looking farther ahead—the designation of a civil sector, such as the rebuilding of the cities, as the peacetime equivalent of the military sector, might well show up as part of the practicable social agenda.

Capitalism, then, can achieve considerable change within the boundaries imposed by its market mechanisms and privileges of private property. But there are also important limits beyond which it cannot go—at least within the foreseeable future. Primary among these is the continuing requirement that the economic participants in a capitalist world—even in a planned capitalist world—behave in the manner that is required of them if the market mechanism is to work. That is, they must act as "economic men," buying cheap and selling dear, allowing relative remunerations to weigh heavily in their choices of occupations or employment, setting acquisitive aims high in the hierarchy of life goals. These marketing traits are not merely pervasive private idiosyncrasies that can be dispensed with if they are no longer esteemed. They are integral to, and necessary for, the successful operation of a market system. In a setting of bare subsistence and newly-risen entrepreneurs there is little difficulty in adducing the acquisitive behavior required to run a capitalist economy. But in a more advanced and affluent society, where the primary drives of self-preservation begin to fail, the necessary marketing behavior must be sustained by supplementary motives of emulation and competitive striving. Thus, the endless and relentless exacerbation of economic appetites in advanced capitalism is not merely a surface aberration, but a deeply-rooted functional necessity to provide the motivations on which the market system depends.

This thralldom to an overweening economic imperative of sales and profits and its accompanying worship of a calculus of income are features of capitalism that cannot be eliminated by planning. A planned capitalism of the future, however rid of its gross malfunctions, will nonetheless be one in which men are subservient to the economic demands of a market environment.

Nowhere is this apt to pose a more serious problem than along the extended frontier where technology interacts with society. This interaction takes two forms. One, which we may call the *direct effect,* is revealed as the immediate change in the environment brought about by the application of a new technique such as the computerized control of production, or the use of a new product such as a jet transport. This effect, as we know from experience, may bring radical changes into economic or social life, but these changes have, at least, been consciously introduced into society (although often with inadequate appreciation of their immediate impact).

But there is as well an *indirect effect* of technology that diffuses throughout society as the secondary consequences of new machinery or new processes. Thus, the indirect effect of the new technology of automation is unemployment; the indirect effect of the new technology of medicine and health is an aging population; the indirect effect of the technology of war is the creation of a military-industrial economic sector. Not least we find, as a general indirect effect of all modern technology, an increasing complexity, size, and hierarchical organization of production, which gives rise in turn to a growing need for public intervention into the economic process itself.

Against this tremendous invasion of technology, a market economy offers but one instrument of control—the profit or loss stemming from the direct effect of a particular technology. As to its side effects, the market mechanism proper has no controls whatsoever. As a result, the invasion of technology becomes an essentially disruptive force, continuously upsetting the patterns of life in a haphazard manner. Under a system that abdicates as much decision-making as possible to the rule of profit, the possibilities for a rational restraint over this force that rearranges our lives thus shrinks to a minimum. Capitalism is essentially defenseless before the revolutionizing impact of its technical drive. Of all the limits to which capitalism is subject, this is the most unyielding—although, as we shall see, it is this very helplessness of the system before the technological onslaught that holds out the most important promise for the long-term remaking of capitalism itself.

Our next concern lies with the reach and inhibitions of what we might call the *capitalist imagination.*

The quality of this imagination is most clearly revealed if we think for a moment of the "visionary" glimpse of the future often spelled out for us by business spokesmen—a future of enormous affluence, technical marvels, widespread leisure, etc. There is, in these vistas, much that is genuinely new and rich with possibilities for material betterment. But there is also something inherent in all these visions that remains unmentioned. It is that these imagined societies of the future still depend on "workers," however well off, who work for "businessmen," however enlightened, in a system motivated and directed by the commercial impulse, however tempered or refined. A society in which there were no workers or businessmen as we understand the terms; or in which the categories of privilege had been fundamentally altered; or where the pressures of the marketplace had been replaced by some other means of assuring economic continuity—all these possibilities are absent from the capitalist imagination. More than that, they are dismissed as "utopian."

Albeit unwittingly, this is set forth all too clearly in the peroration of a recent book by Frederick R. Kappel, President of A.T.&T.:

> We are involved in one of the great ideological struggles of all times. Essentially it is a contest between two quite basic concepts. One is that men are capable of faith in ideas that lift their minds and hearts, ideas that raise their sights and give them hope, energy, and enthusiasm. Opposing this is the belief that the pursuit of material ends is all that life on this earth is about.

The words are eloquent enough, but alas, what do they reveal? Which side, ours or theirs, is the side of "ideas that lift minds and hearts," which the side that believes "the pursuit of material ends is all that life on this earth is about"? In the breathtaking ambiguity of this intended affirmation of business faith, the unseeing confusion of identities meant to be so clearly polarized, lies an all too clear exposition of the weakness that inhabits the very center of the capitalist imagination.

We cannot be sure what effects such a constricted view of the future may have on the aspirations and attitudes of most American citizens. It is likely that for the majority who are understandably concerned with their material lot, it would make no difference whatsoever. But for a not unimportant minority—I think of college youth and of the intellectual community—the absence of any transcendent secular goal is apt to present an oppressive limitation to thought and spirit. Indeed, in my opinion the present anarchic mood of youth may well be due to just such a lack of a visionary future to which to bend its hopes and efforts.

Whatever the ultimate effect of this stifling at home, there is another area where the limitations of the capitalist imagination are likely to be of very great importance. This is in the contest with Communism for the guidance of future world society.

It is hardly necessary to speak of the power of Communism as a force bearing on American capitalism. Yet in appraising that force, we often fail to articulate that which is most threatening about it to ourselves as members or protagonists of the capitalist way of life. This is the presence of Communism as a viable social system that has dispensed with our institutions of privilege, and that therefore faces capitalism with the living refutation of their necessity. In this fundamental sense, Communism puts capitalism on trial before the bar of history. In this trial it matters not that Communism has its own system of privilege, in some ways more primitive than our own. Nor does it count for much that capitalist performance on many fronts is manifestly superior to that of Communism. What matters is that Communism has demonstrated the mutability and historic transiency of our particular social order, and that that social order can never again feel entirely secure in its claims to permanence and legitimacy.

I believe it is this sense of historic unease that lies behind the deep, uncritical, and often unreasoning hostility of America toward Communism. The reasons we cite for our fear and hatred—the undeniable acts of cruelty and repression, of aggression and intolerance, of intrigue and untrustworthiness—can be duplicated in many non-Communist countries: in Portugal, in Spain, in the Union of South Africa, in various Latin American dictatorships, past and present. There, however, they have never roused in us the fervor or revulsion they do when discovered in the Communist world. In part, this is no doubt because these other nations are small and weak and do not constitute centers of national power comparable to Russia or China (although hardly Cuba); in part, because they do not seek to export their particular world views. But more deeply, especially among the conservative interests of this country, I think it is because the existence of Communism frightens American capitalism, as the existence of Protestantism once frightened the Catholic Church; or the French Revolution the English aristocracy.

The fundamental threat of Communism is not likely to decline over the next generation. Rather, it is apt to grow. In Russia, the prospect is clearly for substantial economic expansion; for the gradual improvement of the still dreary life of its people; for a continuation of its massive scientific advances; for further intellectual, and perhaps political, liberalization. For China, no such sanguine assurances can be given, but its continuing emergence as the unquestioned leader of Asia seems hardly likely to be reversed. In Latin America and Africa, the outlook can only be for political turmoil as the aspirations of excited masses outdistance any conceivable pace of progress. In the ensuing unrest, radical leaders are bound to emerge, and it would be a miracle if they were not inclined, to some degree, toward Communism or some kind of national collectivism.

This tendency is apt to be reinforced by the very ideological limitations of capitalism we have been concerned with. If we look to the developing nations, we find in nearly all of them a yearning, not alone for material progress, but for a great social and political, even spiritual, transformation. However millennial these hopes, however certain to be dashed, they are not to be lightly disregarded. The leaders and elites of the young nations, like those of our own youth, are looking for a model of a society that will fire them to great efforts, and it is unlikely that they will find this model in the market-based and wealth-protecting philosophy of capitalism.

All these considerations point to the very great likelihood that Communism or radical national collectivism will make substantial inroads during the coming generation or two, perhaps by conquest or subversion, but more probably by the decay of existing orders unable to handle the terrible demands of political awakening and economic reformation.

Given this grave outlook, what would be its impact on America?

We have already witnessed the initial impact in the substantial militarization of American capitalism. The so-called military-industrial complex (to which should be added "political" as an equal partner) today contributes between 8 and

10 percent to the Gross National Product. In the 1960s, military expenditure has regularly exceeded the sum total of all personal income taxes, has accounted for one-fourth of all federal public works, has directly employed some 3.2 million workers in defense industries and another 1.1 million as civilian employees of the Defense Department and the services, has subsidized about one-third of all research in the United States; and not least, has come to be accepted as a normal and permanent fixture of American life by all groups, including the academic. The fact is that American capitalism is now a semi-militarized economy and will very probably become even more so during the next decade.

In this dangerous situation, it is important for us to clarify the specific influence over the direction of events that can be ascribed to the business interest in society. According to Marxism—or more properly Leninism—the business structure itself inherently presses the state toward armed conflict. The fierce economic conflicts of capitalist nations prior to World War II, the long history of capitalist suppression of colonials continuing down to the present in some parts of Africa, the huge and jealously guarded interests of the United States and other capitalist nations in the oil regions of the Near East or Latin America—all make it impossible to dismiss such a picture of a belligerent capitalist imperialism. At the same time, even a cursory review of the nations initiating aggressive actions since 1945 should raise doubts as to the exclusive capitalist predisposition to war. More important, an analysis of the roots of belligerency in the more warlike capitalisms, specifically pre-war Germany or Japan, must emphasize the leading role played by purely military or lingering feudal elements, and the largely passive, although not always reluctant, part taken by capitalist groups.

On somewhat more Marxian lines, Victor Perlo has made a determination of the direct economic interest of the top American corporations in war or peace. He concludes that the economic self-interest of the biggest corporations is more or less evenly divided, with half profiting from a defense economy, and half—including such giants as General Motors and U.S. Steel—being penalized by it. Assuming that big businessmen would be motivated to oppose or support disarmament on such grounds, it is important to note that nothing like a monolithic "pro-war" economic interest can be said to exist within American capitalism.

Further, the imperialist thrust that increased both the chances and the causes of war in the late nineteenth century seems to be giving way to less dangerous forms of international relationship. Property interests that once had to be defended by force of arms are now protected by government insurance. International relationships that formerly allowed large capitalist enterprises to intervene directly into the economic and political life of colonial nations have been succeeded by relationships in which the independence of action of foreign companies is severely restricted. In a word, the politics of nationalism has asserted its preeminence over the economics of imperialism, with the salutary consequence of a diminution in the role of business as the active initiator of foreign economic policy.

Thus, the role of business proper in the struggle for world power does not seem intrinsically warlike. Unfortunately, that does not mean the chances for conflict are therefore small. Business is not the only power center within capitalist societies, and in America the military and the civil branches of government contain more than their share of belligerent-minded leaders who are in a position to influence foreign policy. Then, too, we must reckon with the generalized hatred of Communism among the lower and middle classes, a hatred that may originally have been implanted but that now flourishes as a self-maintaining source of aggression.

In this situation, given the reciprocal posture of the other side, it is difficult to see how a major conflict could be avoided, were not the consequences of all-out warfare so terrifying. On both sides, only the instinct of self-preservation—fortunately the single most powerful instinct—holds back the military-minded, the fundamentalist, the ambitious, or simply the self-righteous. As a result, the most probable outlook becomes a continuation of the military-political struggle on the scale of Korea or Vietnam. The danger is that a succession of such involvements may encourage the rise of a strict garrison state, one that is marked by an atmosphere of internal repression and external belligerence.

The grave possibility may well be the single most dangerous eventuality during the next decade or two, when the chances of Communist "take-overs" will be greatest. But the longer-term future is far from foreclosed along such lines. On both sides of the great divide, forces are at work that can lessen the intensity of hostilities. One of these is the enhanced prospect for international stabilization, once the worst is over and those nations that are going to go Communist or national-collectivist have done so. A second hopeful possibility is the growth of a greater degree of isolationism in American politics—or perhaps one should say a lesser degree of interventionism—compounded in part of disillusion, in part of fear, and in part of a more realistic appreciation of our inability to affect the unruly tides of world history. Yet another force for peaceful accommodation is the possibility that the specter of Communist "world domination" will be dispelled by the sight of Communist nations in intense rivalry, just as the Communist world may be relieved by the continuing evidence of inter-capitalist frictions.

And finally, we can hope that within a generation or so, new concerns posed by enormous world populations, interlocked global technical devices for communications, transport, power, and other uses, vanishing fossil fuel supplies, a worldwide polluted atmosphere, etc., will cause the present ideological fervor to subside under more pressing problems, just as did the great religious animosities of the past.

Not all the preconditions for such a turn of events lie in our own hands. Much depends on the continuation of the present trend toward the fragmentation and gradual liberalization of the Communist world. But given this opportunity, there seems at least a reasonable chance that American and European capitalism can find a *modus vivendi* with the other side. There again, I believe, the critical determination of direction is apt to reside with the new elites rising within capitalism. Indeed, if there are limits to the adaptability of capitalism before the untoward development of world events, these limits appear to reside, more than is the case with the other challenges before the system, in the quality of the "new men" who are rising to positions of power within it.

It is time to revert to the question we set ourselves at the outset. What limits, we asked, were inherent in the capitalist system as such? The answer at which we have arrived is necessarily of a speculative nature. Yet, it does not appear entirely fanciful. What seems possible is to bring about social change that stops short of a direct assault on the economic machinery of privilege that all elites—indeed, that even the general public—in a capitalist society are normally eager to protect. This enables us to draw the general boundaries of short-term evolution for capitalism. The distribution of wealth can be corrected at the bottom, albeit showly, but not at the top. The control over output can be improved very greatly but the essential commercial character of a market system, with its surrender to the acquisitive impulse, is incorrigible. A considerable accommodation can be made with the non-capitalist world, but the imagination of that world cannot be captured by a basically conservative outlook. There are, in a word, deep-seated attributes to the quality of life that constitute an impregnable inner keep of the system of American capitalism as we know it.

And yet, if we now recall our earlier concern with feudalism, we will recall that despite the seeming impregnability of its institutions in the thirteenth century, by the eighteenth century, somehow, the system had nonetheless changed out of all recognition. How did feudalism expire? It gave way to capitalism as part of a subversive process of historic change in which a newly emerging attribute of daily life proved to be as irresistibly attractive to the privileged orders of feudalism as it was to be ultimately destructive of them. This subversive influence was the gradual infiltration of commercial relationships and cash exchanges into the everyday round of feudal life, each act of marketing binding men more fully into the cash nexus and weakening by that degree the traditional duties and relationships on which feudalism was based. Against this progressive monetization the old order struggled in vain, for the temptations and pleasures of the cash economy were greater than the erosion of privileges that went with it.

Could there be in our day an equivalent of that powerfully disintegrative and yet constitutive force—a force sufficiently overwhelming to render impotent the citadel of capitalism, and yet as irresistibly attractive to it as the earlier current of change was to feudalism? I think there is such a force, and that it already bulks very large within our world. This revolutionary power is the veritable explosion of organized knowledge, and its applied counterpart, scientific technology.

The extraordinary rate of expansion of this explosion is sufficiently familiar to require only a word of exposition. There is, for instance, the often-quoted but still astonishing statement that of all the scientists who have ever lived in all of history, half are alive today. There is the equally startling calculation that the volume of scientific publication during the last ten to fifteen years is as large as, or larger than, that of all previous ages. Such examples serve accurately enough to convey the notion of the exponential growth of scientific inquiry in our day. As to the equally phenomenal growth of the powers of the technology, if that needs any demonstration, there is the contrast cited by Kenneth Boulding between the centuries needed to recuperate from the physical destruction that accompanied the collapse of the Roman Empire, and the scant twenty years in which the shattered and burned cities of modern Europe and Japan were rebuilt after the Second World War.

This explosion of science and technology is often thought of as a product of capitalism, insofar as it arose in an age dominated by capitalism. Yet the association was far more one of coexistence than of causal interrelation. At best we can say that the secular air of bourgeois culture was compatible with, perhaps even conducive to, scientific investigation, but we can hardly credit the acceleration of scientific activities around the middle of the nineteenth century to the direct stimulus or patronage of capitalism itself.

Even scientific technology exhibits but little debt to the existence of capitalism. The technology on which capitalism began its long course of growth was strictly of a pragmatic, intuitive, prescientific kind. Watt, for example, invented the steam engine over fifty years before the basic formulation of the law of thermodynamics. The English textile, iron and steel, or chemical industries were founded and prospered with no "scientific" underpinnings at all. The same is true for the young railroad industry, for canal building, or road-laying. The deliberate employment of scientific investigation to create or refine the technology of production was considerably delayed in arriving. In this country the first private industrial laboratory was not built until 1900 by the General Electric company, and organized research and development on a large scale did not really get under way until 1913.

Thus, we find the flowering of science and the application of science to technology–the very hallmarks of the modern era–to be currents that arose *within* capitalism, but that do not owe their existence directly to capitalism. Rather, science and its technology emerge as a great underground river whose tortuous course has finally reached the surface during the age of capitalism, but which springs from far distant sources. Having now surfaced, that river must cut its own channels through the existing social landscape. Indeed, if we ask what force in our day might in time be strong enough to undercut the bastions of privilege of capitalism and to create its own institutions and social structures in their place, the answer must surely be the one force that dominates our age–the power of science and of scientific technology.

There is, I suspect, little to argue about as to the commanding pressure of science in modern times. What is likely to be a good deal less readily accepted, however, is the contention that this force will cause drastic modifications in, or even the eventual supersession of, capitalism. For at first glance this new current of history seems to have imparted an immense momentum to capitalism by providing it with a virtually inexhaustible source of invention and innovation to insure its economic growth. Merely to review in our minds the broad areas of investment and economic output that owe their existence *entirely* to the laboratory work of the last three decades–the nuclear and space establishments, electronics, the computerization of industry, the creation of new materials such as plastics–is to reveal the breadth of this new gulf stream of economic nourishment.

Yet, like the attractions of the cash market for the feudal lord, the near-term advantages of science and technology conceal long-term conflicts and incompatibilities between this new force of history and its host society. Indeed, the insinuation of science and technology into the interstices of business enterprise promises to alter the fundamental working arrangements of capitalism.

At least one of these alterations is already familiar to us. This is the tendency of technology to create social problems that require public controls to correct or forestall. In part, these agencies of control are contained and concealed *within* the centers of production themselves, where they show up as rising echelons of corporate administration and supervision. In part, the controls show up in the familiar bureaus of government that cope, with greater or lesser success, with the social repercussions of transportation, nuclear energy, drugs, air pollution, etc. In still a different aspect, the controls invade areas of social life rather than production, as in the astonishing network of government required solely to manage the automobile (an effort that requires the labor of one out of every ten persons employed by all state and local governments). Meanwhile, in the background of the social system the controls are manifest as the growing apparatus of regulation over wages and prices, and over the total flow of economic activity–all ultimately traceable to the need to intervene more closely into an economy of increasing technological disruption.

Not that the disruptive effect of technology is itself a new phenomenon. The dislocations of the technology of the pre-scientific age–say the spinning jenny–were quite as great as those of the modern age. The difference is that in an earlier age the repair of technological disturbances was largely consigned to the adaptive powers of the individual and his family, to the ameliorative efforts of small-scale local government, and to the annealing powers of the market itself. Today, however, these traditional agencies of social repair can no longer cope effectively with the entrance of technology. The individual, now typically a member of a small urban family rather than of a large extended rural family, is much less capable of withstanding economic displacement without external assistance. The local community, faced with large-scale problems of unemployment or ecological maladjustment brought about by technical change, has no recourse but to turn to the financial help and expertise available only from larger government units. The market, which no longer "clears" when the marketers are enormous firms rather than atomistic business units, also discovers that the only antidote to grave economic disjunction is the countervailing influence or *force majeur* of the central governing authority. In a word, technology seems to be exerting a steady push from many levels and areas of the economy in the direction of a society of *organization.*

To this well-known effect of technical progress we must now add another–the capacity of technology to render redundant the physical energies of man. That is, machines do man's work for him, thereby freeing him from the bonds of toil and, not less important in the context of our inquiry, from the hegemony of the market process.

We see this disemployment effect most dramatically in the case of agriculture. But equally startling is the labor-displacing effect of modern technology in that congeries of activities associated with the extraction of basic materials from nature and their fabrication, assembly, conversion, or transport to point of sale. Since 1900, science and technology have given us a stupendous array of new products, each requiring large quantities of human effort–the automobile, the whole range of consumer durables, the communications industry, office machinery, new metals, fabrics, and materials of all kinds, to name but a few. Yet at the end of that period, the total requirements on the labor force for all these goods-centered industries had risen by only *two percentage points.* During the era of the greatest increase in factory production ever known, virtually no increase in the distribution of labor in favor of the goods sector was needed—indeed, since the hours of work fell, there was actually a *relatively decreased* need for human effort in the output of these goods.

Today we stand at the threshold of a new stage in the application of scientific technology to human activities: automation. What is most threatening about this technology is that it has begun to invade a sanctuary of hitherto relatively unmechanized work—the vast numbers of jobs in the office, administrative, and service occupations. By 1960, more than half the labor force was in these jobs. And now, into this varied group of occupations, technology is starting to penetrate in the form of machines as complex as those that can read and sort checks, or as relatively simple as those that dispense coffee and sandwiches.

This is not to maintain that no new areas of employment exist. Certainly there remain very large and still untapped possibilities for work in the reconstruction of the cities; the provision of education; the improvement of health and recreation facilities; the counseling of the young and the care of the aged; the beautification of the environment. Provided only that demand can be marshaled for these activities, there is surely no dearth of job prospects for the coming generation.

But that is precisely the point. The incursion of technology has pushed the frontiers of work into a spectrum of jobs whose common denominator is that they require *public action and public funds* for their initiation and support. The employment-upsetting characteristics of technology thus act to speed capitalism along the general path of planning and control down which it is simultaneously impelled by the direct environment-upsetting impact of technological change.

If we look further ahead, the necessity for planning is apt to become still more pressing. The day of a "fully automated" society is by no means a fantasy, although its realization may well require another century, or more. That is to say, we can, without too much difficulty, imagine a time when as small a proportion of the labor force as now suffices to overprovide us with food, will serve to turn out the manufactured staples, the houses, the transportation, the retail services, even the governmental supervision that will be required.

What the leisured fraction of the population will then do with itself is an interesting and important question. It may possibly find avenues of remuneration that are resistive to mechanical duplication, so that instead of taking in one another's wash, we buy one another's paintings. But even in this best outcome, the underlying process of production, now enormously mechanized and intricately interconnected, would require some form of coordination other than the play of market forces. If we think of the network of controls over output and disposal that now characterize the agricultural sector, we catch some idea of the controls required to operate an economy where manpower requirements generally would have been reduced to a level comparable to that of farming today. And, if the leisured population does not find adequate remuneration in unmechanizable private employments, it will have to be given the direct right to share in society's output—another vital infringement on the market's function.

But the erosion of the market goes deeper yet. For the introduction of technology has one last effect whose ultimate implications for the metamorphosis of capitalism are perhaps greatest of all. This is the effect of technology in steadily raising the average level of well-being, thereby gradually bringing to an end the condition of material need as an effective stimulus for human behavior.

Everyone recognizes that the end to want would represent the passage over an historic watershed for mankind. But it must be equally clear that such a passage will also represent a basic revision of the existential situation that has hitherto provided the main impetus for work. As needs diminish, the traditional stimuli of capitalism begin to lose their force, occupations become valued for their intrinsic pleasures rather than for their extrinsic rewards. The very decision to work or not becomes a matter of personal preference rather than of economic necessity. More telling, the drive for profit—the nuclear core of capitalist energy—becomes blunted, as the purchasable distinctions of wealth decline. In a society of the imaginable wealth implicit in another hundred years of technical progress, who will wish to be the rich man's servant at any price?

All this is no doubt a gain in human dignity. But that is not an end to it. As a result of this inestimable gain in personal freedom, a fundamental assurance for social viability also vanishes, for the market stimuli that bring about social provisioning are no longer met with obedient responses. One has but to imagine employees in an industry of central importance going on strike, not with the slim backing of unemployment insurance and a small union supplement, as today, but with liquid assets sufficient to maintain them, if need be, for a year or more, to envisage the potential for social disorder inherent in the attainment of a genuinely widespread and substantial affluence.

Yet is is precisely such an affluence that is within clear sight, provided that the impetus of science and technology continue to propel the economy for another century. In this impasse there is but one possible solution. *Some authority other than the market must be entrusted with the allocation of men to the essential posts of society, should they lack for applicants.*

We have concerned ourselves so far only with the curious two-edged effect of science and technology on the functional aspects of capitalism. Now we must pay heed to a second and perhaps even more critical effect, the conquest of the capitalist imagination by science and scientific technology.

I think it is fair to say that capitalism as an *idea* has never garnered much enthusiasm. All efforts to raise money-making to the level of a positive virtue have failed. The self-interest of the butcher and the baker to which Adam Smith appealed in lieu of their benevolence may serve as powerful sources of social energy, but not as powerful avatars of the social imagination.

By way of contrast, I think it is also fair to say that science *is* the burning idea of the twentieth century, comparable in its impact on men's minds to the flush of democratic enthusiasm of the late eighteenth century or to the political commitment won by Communism in the early twentieth. The altruism of science, its "purity," the awesome vistas it opens and the venerable path it has followed, have won from all groups exactly that passionate interest and conviction that is egregiously lacking to capitalism as a way of life.

It is not alone that science carries a near-religious ethos of conviction and even sacrifice. Within Communism as within capitalism, the new elites arising within the framework of the old society owe their ascendancy and their allegiance in large part to science. The scientific cadres proper, the social scientists, the government administrative personnel—even the military—look to science not merely as the vehicle of their expertise, but as the magnetic North of their compass of values. These new elites have not as yet divorced their social goals from those of the society to which they are still glad to pay allegiance, and no more than the thirteenth-century merchants huddled under the walls of a castle, do they see themselves as the potential architects and lords of a society built around their own functions. But as with the merchants, we can expect that such notions will in time emerge and assert their primacy over the aims of the existing order.

What sorts of notions are these apt to be?

One general direction of thought will surely be the primacy of scientific discovery as a central purpose of society, a *raison d'être* for its existence, perhaps even a vehicle for its religious impulses. No doubt the distribution of social resources and of privileges will reflect this basic orientation toward scientific exploration and application. Not less characteristic will be an emphasis on rational solutions to social problems. The key word of the new society is apt to be *control.* Not alone economic affairs (which should become of secondary importance), but the numbers and location of the population and its genetic quality, the manner of social domestication of children, the choice of life-work—even the very duration of life itself—are all apt to become subjects for scientific investigation and direction.

It is tempting, but idle, to venture beyond these few suggestions. What manner of life, what institutions, what ideologies may serve the purposes of a society dedicated to the accumulation of scientific knowledge and power, we cannot foretell; variations may well be as great as those observable in societies dedicated to the accumulation of material wealth. Nor does there seem to be much point in attempting to foresee by what precise strategems the elites and ideas of the future may finally assert their claims. Historic projection is rarely, if ever, a matter of simple extrapolation from the present and recent past. Should there arise radical parties in America, broadly-based and aimed at a rational reorganization of economic affairs, the pace of transition would be quicker. Should there not, changes will still occur, but more slowly. Veblen was too impatient for his engineers to take over; Schumpeter, more realistic when he advised the intelligentsia to be prepared to wait in the wings for possibly a century, a "short run" in affairs of this kind, he said.

So, too, the examples of the past discourage us from attempting to prophesy the manner of demise of the system to be superseded. The new protagonists of social and economic control will lack for some time an articulate conception of a purposively constituted and consciously directed social system. The old ideas of the proper primacy of economic aims will linger side-by-side with newer ideas of the priority of scientific interests. And no doubt the privileges of the older order will endure side-by-side with those of the new, just as titles of nobility exist to this very day. It is conceivable that violence may attend the transfer of power and responsibility from one elite to another, but more probably the transfer will be imperceptible; managed by the sons of the old elite entering the profession of the new.

All these are the merest speculations, difficult to avoid entirely, not to be taken too literally. Only one thing is certain. It is the profound incompatibility between the new idea of the active use of science within society and the idea of capitalism.

The conflict lies in the ideas that ultimately inform both worlds. The world of science as it is applied to society is committed to the idea of man as a being who shapes his collective destiny; the world of capitalism to an idea of man as one who permits his common social destination to take care of itself. The essential idea of a society built on scientific engineering is to impose human will on the social universe; that of capitalism to allow the social universe to unfold as if it were beyond human interference.

Before the activist philosophy of science as a social instrument, this inherent social passivity of capitalism becomes archaic, and eventually intolerable. The "self-regulating" economy that is its highest social achievement stands condemned by its absence of meaning and intelligence, and each small step taken to correct its deficiencies only advertises the inhibitions placed on the potential exercise of purposeful thought and action by its remaining barriers of ideology and privilege. In the end, capitalism is weighed in the scale of science and found wanting, not alone as a system but as a philosophy.

That an ascendant science, impatient to substitute reason for blind obedience, inquiry for ideology, represents a great step forward for mankind, I do not doubt. Yet it seems necessary to end on a cautionary note. Just as the prescient medievalist might have foreseen in capitalism the possibilities for the deformation of human life as well as for its immense improvement, so the approaching world of scientific predominance has its darker sides. There lurks a dangerous collectivist tinge in the prospect of controls designed for the enlargement of man but inherently capable of his confinement as well. But beyond that, there is, in the vista of scientific quest grimly pursued for its own sake, a chilling reminder of a world where economic gains are relentlessly pursued for their own sake. Science is a majestic driving force from which to draw social energy and inspiration, but its very impersonality, its "value-free" criteria, may make its tutelary elites as remote and unconcerned as the principles in whose name they govern.

Against these cold and depersonalizing tendencies of a scientifically organized world, humanity will have to struggle in the future, as it has had to contend against not dissimilar excesses of economic involvement in this painful–but also liberating–stage of human development. Thus, if the dawn of an age of science opens larger possibilities for mankind than it has enjoyed heretofore, it does not yet promise a society in which the overriding aim of mankind will be the cultivation and enrichment of all human beings, in all their diversity, complexity and profundity. That is the struggle for the very distant future, which must be begun, nonetheless, today.

BIBLIOGRAPHY

In addition to the works included in the body of this section, the editors also recommend the following.

Berle, Adolf A. *The Twentieth Century Capitalist Revolution*. New York: Harcourt Brace Jovanovich, 1954.

Clark, John M. *Alternative to Serfdom*. New York: Vintage Books, 1960.

———. *Social Control of Business*. New York: McGraw-Hill, 1939.

Finer, Herman. *Road to Reaction.* Chicago: Quadrangle Books, 1963.
Galbraith, John Kenneth. *The Affluent Society.* Boston: Houghton Mifflin Co., 1971.
———. *American Capitalism: The Concept of Countervailing Power.* Boston: Houghton Mifflin Co., 1956.
———. *Economics and the Public Purpose.* Boston: Houghton Mifflin Co., 1973.
Hansen, Alvin. *The American Economy.* New York: McGraw-Hill, 1957.
Harris, Seymour E. *Economics of the Kennedy Years and a Look Ahead.* New York: Harper & Row, 1964.
Heller, Walter W. *New Dimensions of Political Economy.* New York: W. W. Norton & Co., 1967.
Lekachman, Robert. *The Age of Keynes.* New York: Random House, 1966.
Moynihan, Daniel P. *Capitalism and Democracy: Schumpeter Revisited.* New York: New York University Press, 1972.
Myrdal, Gunnar. *Beyond the Welfare State.* New Haven: Yale University Press, 1960.
Okun, Arthur M. *The Political Economy of Prosperity.* New York: W. W. Norton Co., 1970.
Rostow, Walter W. *The Stages of Economic Growth.* London: Cambridge University Press, 1960.
Samuelson, Paul. Column in *Newsweek.*
Schlesinger, Arthur M., Jr. *The Crisis of Confidence: Ideas, Power and Violence in America.* Boston: Houghton Mifflin Co., 1969.
Shonfield, Andrew. *Modern Capitalism: The Changing Balance of Public and Private Power.* New York: Oxford University Press, 1965.

THE RADICAL VIEW

What is a radical? One could say that anyone who does not support the status quo might be considered a radical—hence Ayn Rand's claim that she is a "radical for capitalism." But the changes Rand desires place her on the far right of the political spectrum; and "radical," as the term is used here, applies only to those thinkers whose approach to change places them on the left. Whereas modern conservatives, like Rand and Milton Friedman, urge a return to a purer form of capitalism (laissez-faire), radicals would like to see basic capitalist institutions eliminated altogether. Both groups are concerned with maximizing individual freedom, and the conflict between the two often boils down to the issue of capitalism versus socialism. To modern conservatives, maximum economic efficiency and a high degree of individual freedom are best achieved under a system of competitive capitalism. To radicals, capitalism is incapable of delivering a future that is just and equitable. They view the profit-driven market system with its base of private property and privilege as anathema to the emergence of such a society. Even liberal attempts to "patch up" capitalism may be viewed with disdain, because as most radicals see it, the abuses of capitalism are an inherent part of the system itself, and only the replacement of that system will eliminate them. In contrast, then, to the conservative's desire for a purer form of capitalism, most radicals want to see the existing capitalist system structurally transformed into some kind of socialism.

The words "most" and "may be" in the paragraph above indicate that a wide range of opinions can be found within the radical camp. However, the modern radical paradigm, as opposed to the liberal one, has a consistent and identifiable ideology, because it draws much of its inspiration and methodology from a single source, the work of Karl Marx. The radical critique of capitalism, then, generally includes some of the following ideas:

1. The institutional framework under which production takes place molds the social, economic, political, and moral attitudes, problems, and policies of the society.
2. Private ownership of the means of production and the impersonal relations of the market subordinate human needs to the needs of profit and irrational materialism.
3. The competitive atmosphere of capitalism results in class and racial conflicts between the workers and the owners of capital, and among the workers themselves.
4. Capitalist societies are run by a wealthy class which uses the power of the state to further its own selfish ends.
5. The elimination of capitalism would result in a more democratic and humanistic society which would use its resources for the benefit of all and which would free men and women to develop their individuality in an atmosphere of cooperation and brotherhood, consistent with the "true nature of man."

Like the other schools of thought we have discussed, this one includes a group of subordinate philosophies, ranging from left to right within the limits of the radical spectrum. On the right are those who see the possibility of democratic socialism evolving out of the present social structure, and even within the present political party system. Michael Harrington, for instance, pushes for a worker-intellectual coalition to take over the Democratic party, to free the government from the grip of big business, and to institute a system of national planning that will expand the welfare state. At the other end of the spectrum, revolutionary groups see no chance of a peaceful evolution to socialism, although most also admit the unlikelihood of a mass uprising in America.

The readings presented in this section do not exhaust the range of views that one might find within the radical group. Because the ideas of Marx and Engels have been very influential for most radicals, a long selection is reprinted from their works. Paul Baran and Paul Sweezy update Marx's treatment of the structure and irrationalities of capitalism by attempting to demonstrate, among other things, the crucial functions of imperialism, militarism, and other forms of wasteful expenditures in maintaining a viable economy. While no less revolutionary than Marx himself, these two modern American Marxists place the center of revolution in the less-developed areas of the world rather than in the advanced capitalist countries.

The other articles, with the exception of Veblen's, tend to be more issue-oriented. Herbert Gintis concentrates on alienation, Daniel R. Fusfeld on the rise of the Fascist state, and Herbert Marcuse on the nature of capitalist man. The works of Marcuse, in particular, have had an important influence on the New Left movement. Although this group lacks a coherent ideology, most of its members argue against both the competitive market and the government as the ideal allocator of resources. They seem to favor a system of production something like John Stuart Mill's voluntary cooperatives. Such a system incorporates the decentralized, nonhierarchical power structure which they see as a more democratic form of control.

The one important work in this section that does not fit either the Marxist or the New Left mold is that of Thorstein Veblen, a man once described by *Fortune* magazine as "America's most brilliant and influential critic of modern business and the values of a business civilization." While seeing the downfall of capitalism as inevitable, Veblen did not make clear his preferences for any alternative system. He emphasized that the basic conflicting elements within capitalism are the efficiency of modern technology in producing goods and the attempts of businessmen to restrict output in order to increase profits. Like the other radicals presented here, Veblen is very critical of the goals of the modern corporation, claiming that they are inconsistent with the goals of society. To him, contradictions and conflicts grow from the fact that conservative business institutions tend to be incompatible with the dynamic machine technology. Unlike Marx, Veblen was not a revolutionary socialist; he believed that the replacement of the capitalist system would be an evolutionary process. Marx, of course, is also concerned with the evolution of economic systems and views capitalism as merely a stage in this evolution. For Marx the course of history is shaped by the economic pressures the changing forces of production exert on the class structure. In contrast to Veblen, Marx sees an end to this evolutionary process in the establishment of a communist society (characterized by the ultimate disappearance of the state) and is willing to help speed the process along through revolution. The *Communist Manifesto* is a call to action toward this end.

George Stigler, a well-known modern economist, has claimed that the study of economics makes people politically conservative. In general, the writers in this section would surely reject this position in favor of the view that as one matures he realizes that only radical activism can bring about meaningful change. The future of capitalism may depend on what position the majority of its citizens take on this issue. Given the present state of affairs, the radical must conclude that thus far the American people have been lulled into a shortsighted position.

R R

KARL MARX (1818–1883)

FRIEDRICH ENGELS (1820–1895)

Marxian theory represents an intellectual reaction to the social, political, and economic conditions of nineteenth-century Europe, the period historians refer to as the Industrial Revolution. The transformation of society during this process of industrialization was truly a revolutionary one. With the movement from the self-sufficient rural areas to the mushrooming urban factory areas, the workers were made dependent on the sale of their labor services for survival, since they no longer owned the means of production. The social disorganization caused by the early capitalistic process of industrialization was unparalleled. Under the new rigid discipline of the machine, labor power became a commodity to be bought and sold like any other commodity. Long hours of labor under barbarian working conditions, at little more than subsistence-level wages, resulted in what many saw as exploitation of the working masses. Against this background, Marx set his savage pen. He explained the origins of capitalism in the sixteenth century in terms of the brute force used to create a laboring class, instead of the popularly accepted idea of a frugal, enterprising elite starting the process of "primitive accumulation." The English Enclosure Acts, in effect, removed the free peasant proprietors from the land by denying them the use of the common land.[1] This forced development of the working class forms the prelude to capitalist exploitation.

The general shape of any given era was set, in Marx's view, by the mode of production of the material means of subsistence, since this "conditions the social, political, and spiritual life-process in general." Although Marx and Engels were not economic determinists, as often alleged by their bourgeois detractors, they did hold that economic factors were "ulti-

1. Under the English feudal system, lord, freeman, and serf were all subject to the general village policy regarding cultivation of the "common field," the total agricultural land of a given manor. Starting in the sixteenth century, the practice of enclosure—surrounding open land with permanent walls and fences, creating compact farms and hedged fields—made a landless laborer of the small man who could not prove a legal claim to the rights he exercised on the common. His right to keep cows or geese there, or to farm one or two strips of land, was sometimes compensated with a small sum; but that would not suffice to set him up as a capitalist farmer or pay for the hedging of "his" plot. In addition, enclosure deprived the agricultural laborer of the village industries previously conducted by his wife and children, which had provided up to half his income. [G. M. Trevelyan, *History of England* (New York: Longmans, Green and Co., 1928), pp. 283–87.] During the reign of George III (1760–1820), the partial enclosures of Tudor and Stuart times gave way to wholesale enclosures, with a series of Acts of Parliament that carved much of England into the "chessboard" of fields it is today. Even Arthur Young, one of the prime movers behind these Enclosure Acts, acknowledged in 1801 that "By nineteen out of twenty Enclosure Bills the poor are injured and most grossly." (Trevelyan, pp. 609–12.)

mately decisive" in determining the political, juridical, and cultural superstructure.

The kernel of Marxist thought is the idea that capitalism is merely a stage in the historical progress of mankind, having been successively preceded by primitive communism, slavery, and feudalism. Marx was interested in examining the dynamic development of capitalism ("the laws of motion") and the human and class relationships that accompany the process of production. From this historically-oriented study, using a method he referred to as dialectical materialism, Marx attempted to prove that the economic structure of capitalism had developed out of the previous feudal structure, and that in turn it would be replaced by a higher socialist order. This analytic technique represented a considerable improvement over previous schools of economic thought. With the partial exception of John Stuart Mill, earlier economists assumed the eternal nature of capitalism, and viewed this system, moreover, as continually tending toward a norm of full employment.

The core of the capitalist system, according to Marx, is found in the necessity for the propertyless proletariat to sell its labor power to those who have accumulated capital. It is this need that prompts Marx to view capital as a "social power" in addition to its usual technical definition. Exploitation of the worker occurred because the capitalists derived a surplus through the worker's creation of commodities whose value was greater than the value the workers received for their labor services (under normal conditions and in the long run). This surplus value is the key to the entire growth process, since the capitalist is under unremitting pressure to invest and reinvest his surplus. Whenever it was profitable to do so, the capitalist introduced technological improvements into the production process, in the form of laborsaving devices. Technologically-displaced labor became, according to Marx, part of the "reserve army" of unemployed. The existence of this surplus pool of labor competing for the available jobs kept wages close to a social subsistence level. The consequence of this exploitation and unemployment, as Marx saw it, was that the consuming power of the working class was held down. At the same time, the capitalists restricted their own present consumption so as to accumulate more capital (i.e., they saved part of their income and invested it in labor-saving machinery, steel mills, mines, buildings, etc. that would facilitate the production of still more goods in the future). Accumulating more and more capital therefore means adding to society's productive capacity and subsequently to its "reserve army" of unemployed. One Marxist economist has commented that capitalism embodies the paradox of stepping on the brake as far as consumption is concerned and on the accelerator as far as production is concerned. Another result of this pattern is the disruption of the intricate relationship between the capital goods and the consumer goods sectors.

These basic internal economic contradictions in the capitalist system, according to Marx, lead inevitably to depressions, imperialism, wars, and a class struggle of ever-increasing severity. Eventually, the bourgeoisie will be overthrown by a politically-organized, class-conscious proletariat constantly growing in size and importance, who will establish a system based on common ownership of the means of production and distribution. It is the very process of capitalist development which undermines the system. The concentration of capital (increasing the scale of production) and its centralization (the expropriation of many smaller capitalists by a few larger ones) unites and disciplines the working class, the only class with power at the point of production. Combining the passion of the activist with the measured tones of the intellectual, Marx stridently proclaimed:

> Centralization of the means of production and socialization of labor at last reach a point where they become incompatible with their capitalist integument [i.e., shell]. This integument is burst asunder. The knell of capitalist private property sounds. The expropriators are expropriated.

In brief, this is the Marxian system, including the theory of social change that emerges from its operation.

A proper assessment of the Marxian system involves an analysis of its predictive ability. On the one hand, Marx insightfully predicted the rise of monopoly capital and a mass labor movement at a time when world events offered only a dim foreshadowing of such developments. On the other, he proved to be an incorrect prophet in several important areas:

1. He expected capitalism to break down in the most advanced industrial countries rather than the less-developed nations. In this regard, he stated, "No social formation ever disappears before all the productive forces are developed for which it has room, and new higher relations of production never appear before the material conditions of their existence are matured in the womb of the old society." In point of fact, the system under the stress of war broke at its weakest link—Czarist Russia—and not at its strongest points—England, Germany, and the United States.
2. Growth of labor unions led to somewhat more equal bargaining power with management, and the State, under pressure, was able and willing to introduce a wide variety of reformist programs. Both these factors created much less class-consciousness among the workers than Marx anticipated.
3. In a similar fashion, nationalism and racial discrimination served to divide the workers, thus weakening still further their revolutionary potential on both a national and an international level.

These developments were reinforced by limited improvements in the economic status of the workers in industrially advanced countries by the latter decades of the Victorian era. The savings and capital formation of the early industrialization period made possible a greater output of consumer goods, which helped to raise the masses' standard of living despite recurring business cycles and a lopsided distribution of wealth and income. Marxists still believe that the "stability" of capitalism is more temporary than permanent, more apparent than real. They assert that the contradictions besetting capitalism, both abroad and at home, are growing in intensity, and thus it is only a question of time before the gathering revolutionary forces yield the expected Marxian results. They also note that the gap between the rich nations and poor nations continues to widen.

There has been a degree of revival of interest in Marxism in recent years (perhaps triggered by the growing ideological competition between capitalism and socialism in the third world) and a growing amount of dialogue between Marxists and non-Marxists (such as Joan Robinson, C. Wright Mills, William A. Williams, and Robert Heilbroner). This is a fruitful development that hopefully will strengthen the trend towards more realism and analytical rigor in the social sciences. Marxism has several unique contributions to make, particularly concerning the dynamic relationship between class conflict and economic development, and recognition of this fact is slowly asserting itself in intellectual circles.

M L

From

A CONTRIBUTION TO THE CRITIQUE OF POLITICAL ECONOMY

(Marx, 1859)

I [Marx] was led by my studies to the conclusion that legal relations as well as forms of state could neither be understood by themselves, nor explained by the so-called general progress of the human mind, but that they are rooted in the material conditions of life, which are summed up by Hegel after the fashion of the English and French of the eighteenth century under the name "civic society;" the anatomy of that civic society is to be sought in political economy. . . . The general conclusion at which I arrived and which, once reached, continued to serve as the leading thread in my studies, may be briefly summed up as follows.

In the social production which men carry on they enter into definite relations that are indispensable and independent of their will; these relations of production correspond to a definite stage of development of their material powers of production. The sum total of these relations of production constitutes the economic structure of society—the real foundation, on which rise legal and political superstructures and to which correspond definite forms of social consciousness. The mode of production in material life determines the general character of the social, political and spiritual processes of life. It is not the consciousness of men that determines their existence, but, on the contrary, their social existence determines their consciousness. At a certain stage of their development, the material forces of production in society come in conflict with the existing relations of production, or—what is but a legal expression for the same thing—with the property relations within which they had been at work before. From forms of development of the forces of production these relations turn into their fetters. Then comes the period of social revolution. With the change of the economic foundation the

From Karl Marx, *A Contribution to the Critique of Political Economy* (Chicago, 1904), pp. 11–13. First published 1859.

entire immense superstructure is more or less rapidly transformed. In considering such transformations the distinction should always be made between the material transformation of the economic conditions of production which can be determined with the precision of natural science, and the legal, political, religious, esthetic or philosophic—in short ideological forms in which men become conscious of this conflict and fight it out. Just as our opinion of an individual is not based on what he thinks of himself, so can we not judge of such a period of transformation by its own consciousness; on the contrary, this consciousness must rather be explained from the contradictions of material life, from the existing conflict between the social forces of production and the relations of production. No social order ever disappears before all the productive forces, for which there is room in it, have been developed; and new higher relations of production never appear before the material conditions of their existence have matured in the womb of the old society. Therefore, mankind always takes up only such problems as it can solve; since, looking at the matter more closely, we will always find that the problem itself arises only when the material conditions necessary for its solution already exist or are at least in the process of formation. In broad outlines we can designate the Asiatic, the ancient, the feudal, and the modern bourgeois methods of production as so many epochs in the progress of the economic formation of society. The bourgeois relations of production are the last antagonistic form of the social process of production—antagonistic not in the sense of individual antagonism, but of one arising from conditions surrounding the life of individuals in society; at the same time the productive forces developing in the womb of bourgeois society create the material conditions for the solution of that antagonism. This social formation constitutes, therefore, the closing chapter of the prehistoric stage of human society. . . .

From

SOCIALISM: SCIENTIFIC AND UTOPIAN

(Engels, 1887)

THE RISE OF CAPITALISM AND THE WORKING CLASS

The materialist conception of history starts from the proposition that the production of the means to support human life and, next to production, the exchange of things produced, is the basis of all social structure; that in every society that has appeared in history, the manner in which wealth is distributed and society divided into classes or orders is dependent upon what is produced, how it is produced, and how the products are exchanged. From this point of view the final causes of all social changes and political revolutions are to be sought, not in men's brains, not in men's better insight into eternal truth and justice, but in changes in the modes of production and exchange. They are to be sought not in the *philosophy*, but in the *economics* of each particular epoch. The growing

Friedrich Engels, from *Socialism: Scientific and Utopian* (1887).

perception that existing social institutions are unreasonable and unjust, that reason has become unreason and right wrong, is only proof that in the modes of production and exchange changes have silently taken place with which the social order, adapted to earlier economic conditions, is no longer in keeping. From this it also follows that the means of getting rid of the incongruities that have been brought to light must also be present, in a more or less developed condition, within the changed modes of production themselves. These means are not to be invented by deduction from fundamental principles, but are to be discovered in the stubborn facts of the existing system of production.

What is, then, the position of modern socialism in this connection?

The present structure of society—this is now pretty generally conceded—is the creation of the ruling class of today, of the bourgeoisie. The mode of production peculiar to the bourgeoisie, known, since Marx, as the capitalist mode of production, was incompatible with the feudal system, with the privileges it conferred upon individuals, entire social ranks, and local corporations, as well as with the hereditary ties of subordination which constituted the framework of its social organization. The bourgeoisie broke up the feudal system and built upon its ruins the capitalist order of society, the kingdom of free competition, of personal liberty, of the equality, before the law, of all commodity owners, of all the rest of the capitalist blessings. Thenceforward the capitalist mode of production could develop in freedom. Since steam, machinery, and the making of machines by machinery transformed the older manufacture into modern industry, the productive forces evolved under the guidance of the bourgeoisie developed with a rapidity and in a degree unheard of before. But just as the older manufacture, in its time, and handicraft, becoming more developed under its influence, had come into collision with the feudal trammels of the guilds, so now modern industry, in its more complete development, comes into collision with the bounds within which the capitalistic mode of production holds it confined. The new productive forces have already outgrown the capitalistic mode of using them. And this conflict between productive forces and modes of production is not a conflict engendered in the mind of man, like that between original sin and divine justice. It exists, in fact, objectively, outside us, independently of the will and actions even of the men that have brought it on. Modern socialism is nothing but the reflex, in thought, of this conflict in fact; its ideal reflection in the minds, first, of the class directly suffering under it, the working class.

Now, in what does this conflict consist?

Before capitalistic production, i.e., in the Middle Ages, the system of petty industry obtained generally, based upon the private property of the laborers in their means of production; in the country, the agriculture of the small peasant, freeman, or serf; in the towns, the handicrafts organized in guilds. The instruments of labor—land, agricultural implements, the workshop, the tool—were the instruments of labor of single individuals, adapted for the use of one worker, and, therefore, of necessity, small, dwarfish, circumscribed. But, for this very reason they belonged, as a rule, to the producer himself. To concentrate these scattered, limited means of production, to enlarge them, to turn them into the powerful levers of production of the present day—this was precisely the historic role of capitalist production and of its upholder, the bourgeoisie. In the fourth section of *Capital,* Marx has explained in detail, how since the fifteenth century this has been historically worked out through the three phases of simple cooperation, manufacture, and modern industry. But the bourgeoisie, as is also shown there, could not transform these puny means of production into mighty productive forces without transforming them, at the same time, from means of production of the individual into *social* means of production, only workable by a collectivity of men. The spinning wheel, the hand loom, the blacksmith's hammer, were replaced by the spinning machine, the power loom, the steam hammer; the individual workshop, by the factory implying the cooperation of hundreds and thousands of workmen. In like manner, production itself changed from a series of individual into a series of social acts, and the products from individual to social products. The yarn, the cloth, the metal articles that now came out of the factory, were the joint product of many workers, through whose hands they had successively to pass before they were ready. No one person could say of them: "I made that; this is *my* product."

But where, in a given society, the fundamental form of production is that spontaneous division of labor which creeps in gradually and not upon any preconceived plan, there the products take on the form of *commodities,* whose mutual exchange, buying and selling, enable the individual producers to satisfy their manifold wants. And this was the case in the Middle Ages. The peasant, for instance, sold to the artisan agricultural products and bought from him the products of handicraft. Into this society of individual producers, of commodity producers, the new mode of production thrust itself. In the midst of the old division of labor, grown up spontaneously, and upon *no definite plan,* which had governed the whole of society, now arose division of labor upon a *definite plan,* as organized in the factory; side by side with *individual* production appeared *social* production. The products of both were sold in the same market, and, therefore, at prices at least approximately equal. But organization upon a definite plan was stronger than spontaneous division of labor. The factories working with the combined social forces of a collectivity of individuals produced their commodities far more cheaply than the individual small producers. Individual production succumbed in one department after another. Socialized production revolutionized all the old methods of production. But its revolutionary character was, at the same time, so little recognized that it was, on the contrary, introduced as a means of increasing and developing the production of commodities. When it arose, it found ready-made, and made liberal use of, certain machinery for the production and exchange of commodities: merchants' capital, handicraft, wage labor. Socialized production thus introducing itself as a new form of the production of commodities, it was a matter of course that under it the old forms of appropriation remained in full swing, and were applied to its products as well.

In the medieval stage of evolution of the production of commodities, the question as to the owner of the product of labor could not arise. The individual producer, as a rule, had, from raw material belonging to himself, and generally his own handiwork, produced it with his own tools, by the labor of his own hands or of his family. There was no need for him to appropriate the new product. It belonged wholly to him, as a matter of course. His property in the product was, therefore, based *upon his own labor.* Even where external help was used, this was, as a rule, of little importance, and very generally was compensated by something other than wages. The apprentices and journeymen of the guilds worked less for board and wages than for education, in order that they might become master craftsmen themselves.

Then came the concentration of the means of production and of the producers in large workshops and manufactories, their transformation into actual socialized means of production and socialized producers. But the socialized producers and means of production and their products were still treated, after this change, just as they had been before, i.e., as the means of production and the products of individuals. Hitherto, the owner of the instruments of labor had himself appropriated the product, because, as a rule, it was his own product and the assistance of others was the exception. Now the owner of the instruments of labor always appropriated to himself the product, although it was no longer *his* product but exclusively the product of the *labor of others.* Thus, the products now produced socially were not appropriated by those who had actually set in motion the means of production and actually produced the commodities, but by the *capitalists.* The means of production, and production itself, had become in essence socialized. But they were subjected to a form of appropriation which presupposes the private production of individuals, under which therefore, everyone owns his own product and brings it to market. The mode of production is subjected to this form of appropriation, although it abolishes the conditions upon which the latter rests.[1]

This contradiction, which gives to the new mode of production its capitalistic character, *contains the germ of the whole of the social antagonisms of today.* The greater the mastery obtained by the new mode of production over all important fields of production and in all manufacturing countries, the more it reduced individual production to an insignificant residuum, *the more clearly was brought out the incompatibility of socialized production with capitalistic appropriation.*

The first capitalists found, as we have said, alongside of other forms of labor, wage labor ready-made for them on the market. But it was exceptional, complementary, accessory, transitory wage labor. The agricultural laborer, though, upon occasion, he hired himself out by the day, had a few acres of his own land on which he could at all events live at a pinch. The guilds were so organized that the journeyman of today became the master of tomorrow. But all this changed, as soon as the means of production became socialized and concentrated in the hands of capitalists. The means of production, as well as the product, of the individual producer became more and more worthless; there was nothing left for him but to turn wage worker under the capitalist. Wage labor, aforetime the exception and accessory, now became the rule and basis of all production; aforetime complementary, it now became the sole remaining function of the worker. The wage worker for a time became a wage worker for life. The number of these permanent wage workers was further enormously increased by the breaking up of the feudal system that occurred at the same time, by the disbanding of the retainers of the feudal lords, the eviction of the peasants from their homesteads, etc. The separation was made complete between the means of production concentrated in the hands of the capitalists, on the one side, and the producers, possessing nothing but their labor power, on the other. *The contradiction between socialized production and capitalistic appropriation manifested itself as the antagonism of proletariat and bourgeoisie.*

We have seen that the capitalistic

mode of production thrust its way into a society of commodity producers, of individual producers, whose social bond was the exchange of their products. But every society based upon the production of commodities has this peculiarity: that the producers have lost control over their own social interrelations. Each man produces for himself with such means of production as he may happen to have and for such exchange as he may require to satisfy his remaining wants. No one knows how much of his particular article is coming on the market, nor how much of it will be wanted. No one knows whether his individual product will meet an actual demand, whether he will be able to make good his costs of production or even to sell his commodity at all. Anarchy reigns in socialized production.

But the production of commodities, like every other form of production, has its peculiar, inherent laws inseparable from it; and these laws work, despite anarchy, in and through anarchy. They reveal themselves in the only persistent form of social interrelations, i.e., in exchange, and here they affect the individual producers as compulsory laws of competition. They are, at first, unknown to these producers themselves and have to be discovered by them gradually and as the result of experience. They work themselves out, therefore, independently of the producers, and in antagonism to them, as inexorable natural laws of their particular form of production. The product governs the producers.

In medieval society, especially in the earlier centuries, production was essentially directed towards satisfying the wants of the individual. It satisfied, in the main, only the wants of the producer and his family. Where relations of personal dependence existed, as in the country, it also helped to satisfy the wants of the feudal lord. In all this there was, therefore, no exchange; the products, consequently, did not assume the character of commodities. The family of the peasant produced almost everything they wanted: clothes and furniture, as well as means of subsistence. Only when it began to produce more than was sufficient to supply its own wants and the payments in kind to the feudal lord, only then did it also produce commodities. This surplus, thrown into socialized exchange and offered for sale, became commodities.

The artisans of the towns, it is true, had from the first to produce for exchange. But they, also, themselves supplied the greatest part of their own individual wants. They had gardens and plots of land. They turned their cattle out into the communal forest, which, also, yielded them timber and firing. The women spun flax, wool, and so forth. Production for the purpose of exchange, production of commodities, was only in its infancy. Hence, exchange was restricted, the market narrow, the methods of production stable; there was local exclusiveness without, local unity within; the mark in the country; in the town, the guild.

But with the extension of the production of commodities, and especially with the introduction of the capitalist mode of production, the laws of commodity production, hitherto latent, came into

---

1. It is hardly necessary in this connection to point out that, even if the *form* of appropriation remains the same, the *character* of the appropriation is just as much revolutionized as production is by the changes described above. It is, of course, a very different matter whether I appropriate to myself my own product or that of another. Note in passing that wage labor, which contains the whole capitalistic mode of production in embryo, is very ancient; in a sporadic, scattered form it existed for centuries alongside of slave labor. But the embryo could duly develop into the capitalistic mode of production only when the necessary historical preconditions had been furnished. [Note by Engels.]

action more openly and with greater force. The old bonds were loosened, the old exclusive limits broken through, the producers were more and more turned into independent, isolated producers of commodities. It became apparent that the production of society at large was ruled by absence of plan, by accident, by anarchy; and this anarchy grew to greater and greater height. But the chief means by aid of which the capitalist mode of production intensified this anarchy of socialized production was the exact opposite of anarchy. It was the increasing organization of production, upon a social basis, in every individual productive establishment. By this, the old, peaceful, stable condition of things was ended. Wherever this organization of production was introduced into a branch of industry, it brooked no other method of production by its side. The field of labor became a battleground. The great geographical discoveries, and the colonization following upon them, multiplied markets and quickened the transformation of handicraft into manufacture. The war did not simply break out between the individual producers of particular localities. The local struggles begot in their turn national conflicts, the commercial wars of the seventeenth and the eighteenth centuries.

Finally, modern industry and the opening of the world market made the struggle universal, and at the same time gave it an unheard-of virulence. Advantages in natural or artificial conditions of production now decide the existence or nonexistence of individual capitalists, as well as of whole industries and countries. He that falls is remorselessly cast aside. It is the Darwinian struggle of the individual for existence transferred from nature to society with intensified violence. The conditions of existence natural to the animal appear as the final term of human development. The contradiction between socialized production and capitalistic appropriation now presents itself as *an antagonism between the organization of production in the individual workshop and the anarchy of production in society generally.*

The capitalistic mode of production moves in these two forms of the antagonism immanent to it from its very origin. It is never able to get out of that "vicious circle" which Fourier had already discovered. What Fourier could not, indeed, see in his time is that this circle is gradually narrowing; that the movement becomes more and more a spiral, and must come to an end, like the movement of the planets, by collision with the center. It is the compelling force of anarchy in the production of society at large that more and more completely turns the great majority of men into proletarians; and it is the masses of the proletariat again who will finally put an end to anarchy in production. It is the compelling force of anarchy in social production that turns the limitless perfectibility of machinery under modern industry into a compulsory law by which every individual industrial capitalist must perfect his machinery more and more, under penalty of ruin.

But the perfecting of machinery is making human labor superfluous. If the introduction and increase of machinery means the displacement of millions of manual by a few machine workers, improvement in machinery means the displacement of more and more of the machine workers themselves. It means, in the last instance, the production of a number of available wage workers in excess of the average needs of capital, the formation of a complete industrial reserve army, as I called it in 1845,[2] available at the times when industry is working at high pressure, to be cast upon the street when the inevitable crash comes, a constant dead weight upon the limbs of the working class in its struggle for existence with capital, a regulator for the keeping of wages down to the low level that suits the interests of capital. Thus it comes about, to quote Marx, that machinery becomes the most powerful weapon in the war of capital against the working class; that the instruments of labor constantly tear the means of subsistence out of the hands of the laborer; that the very product of the worker is turned into an instrument for his subjugation. Thus it comes about that the economizing of the instruments of labor becomes at the same time, from the outset, the most reckless waste of labor power, and robbery based upon the normal conditions under which labor functions; that machinery, "the most powerful instrument for shortening labor time, becomes the most unfailing means for placing every moment of the laborer's time and that of his family at the disposal of the capitalist for the purpose of expanding the value of his capital." (Marx, *Capital.*) Thus it comes about that the overwork of some becomes the preliminary condition for the idleness of others, and that modern industry, which hunts after new consumers over the whole world, forces the consumption of the masses at home down to a starvation minimum, and in doing thus destroys its own home market. "The law that always equilibrates the relative surplus population, or industrial reserve army, to the extent and energy of accumulation, this law rivets the laborer to capital more firmly than the wedges of Vulcan did Prometheus to the rock. It establishes an accumulation of misery, corresponding with accumulation of capital. Accumulation of wealth at one pole is, therefore, at the same time, accumulation of misery, agony of toil slavery, ignorance, brutality, mental degradation, at the opposite pole, i.e., on the side of the class that produces *its own product in the form of capital.*" (Marx, *Capital.*) And to expect any other division of the products from the capitalistic mode of production is the same as expecting the electrodes of a battery not to decompose acidulated water, not to liberate oxygen at the positive, hydrogen at the negative pole, so long as they are connected with the battery.

We have seen that the ever-increasing perfectibility of modern machinery is, by the anarchy of social production, turned into a compulsory law that forces the individual industrial capitalist always to improve his machinery, always to increase its productive force. The bare possibility of extending the field of production is transformed for him into a similar compulsory law. The enormous expansive force of modern industry, compared with which that of gases is mere child's play, appears to us now as a *necessity* for expansion, both qualitative and quantitative, that laughs at all resistance. Such resistance is offered by consumption, by sales, by the markets for the products of modern industry. But the capacity for extension, extensive and intensive, of the markets is primarily governed by quite different laws that work much less energetically. The extension of the markets cannot keep pace with the extension of production. The collision becomes inevitable, and as this cannot produce any real solution so long as it does not break in pieces the capitalist mode of production, the collisions become periodic. Capitalist production has begotten another "vicious circle."

As a matter of fact, since 1825, when the first general crisis broke out, the whole industrial and commercial world, production and exchange among all civilized peoples and their more or less barbaric hangers-on, are thrown out of joint about once every ten years. Com-

2. In *The Condition of the Working Class in England.*

merce is at a standstill, the markets are glutted, products accumulate, as multitudinous as they are unsaleable, hard cash disappears, credit vanishes, factories are closed, the mass of the workers are in want of the means of subsistence, because they have produced too much of the means of subsistence; bankruptcy follows upon bankruptcy, execution upon execution. The stagnation lasts for years; productive forces and products are wasted and destroyed wholesale, until the accumulated mass of commodities finally filters off, more or less depreciated in value, until production and exchange gradually begin to move again. Little by little the pace quickens. It becomes a trot. The industrial trot breaks into a canter, the canter in turn grows into the headlong gallop of a perfect steeplechase of industry, commercial credit, and speculation which finally, after breakneck leaps, ends where it began—in the ditch of a crisis: And so over and over again. We have now, since the year 1825, gone through this five times, and at the present moment we are going through it for the sixth time. And the character of these crises is so clearly defined that Fourier hit all of them off when he described the first as *"crise pléthorique,"* a crisis from plethora.

In these crises, the contradiction between socialized production and capitalist appropriation ends in a violent explosion. The circulation of commodities is, for the time being, stopped. Money, the means of circulation, becomes a hindrance to circulation. All the laws of production and circulation of commodities are turned upside down. The economic collision has reached its apogee. *The mode of production is in rebellion against the mode of exchange.*

The fact that the socialized organization of production within the factory has developed so far that it has become incompatible with the anarchy of production in society, which exists side by side with and dominates it, is brought home to the capitalists themselves by the violent concentration of capital that occurs during crises, through the ruin of many large, and a still greater number of small, capitalists. The whole mechanism of the capitalist mode of production breaks down under the pressure of the productive forces, its own creations. It is no longer able to turn all this mass of means of production into capital. They lie fallow, and for that very reason the industrial reserve army must also lie fallow. Means of production, means of subsistence, available laborers, all the elements of production and of general wealth, are present in abundance. But "abundance becomes the source of distress and want" (Fourier), because it is the very thing that prevents the transformation of the means of production and subsistence into capital. For in capitalistic society the means of production can only function when they have undergone a preliminary transformation into capital, into the means of exploiting human labor power. The necessity of this transformation into capital of the means of production and subsistence stands like a ghost between these and the workers. It alone prevents the coming together of the material and personal levers of production; it alone forbids the means of production to function, the workers to work and live. On the one hand, therefore, the capitalistic mode of production stands convicted of its own incapacity to further direct these productive forces. On the other, these productive forces themselves, with increasing energy, press forward to the removal of the existing contradiction, to the abolition of their quality as capital, to the *practical recognition of their character as social productive forces.*

The rebellion of the productive forces, as they grow more and more powerful, against their quality as capital, this stronger and stronger command that their social character shall be recognized, forces the capitalist class itself to treat them more and more as social productive forces, so far as this is possible under capitalist conditions. The period of industrial high pressure, with its unbounded inflation of credit, not less than the crash itself, by the collapse of great capitalist establishments, tends to bring about that form of the socialization of great masses of means of production which we meet with in the different kinds of joint-stock companies. Many of these means of production and of distribution are, from the outset, so colossal that, like the railways, they exclude all other forms of capitalistic exploitation. At a further stage of evolution this form also becomes insufficient. The producers on a large scale in a particular branch of industry in a particular country unite in a trust, a union for the purpose of regulating production. They determine the total amount to be produced, parcel it out among themselves, and thus enforce the selling price fixed beforehand. But trusts of this kind, as soon as business becomes bad, are generally liable to break up, and on this very account compel a yet greater concentration of association. The whole of the particular industry is turned into one gigantic joint-stock company; internal competition gives place to the internal monopoly of this one company. This has happened in 1890 with the English alkali production, which is now, after the fusion of 48 large works, in the hands of one company, conducted upon a single plan, and with a capital of £6,000,000.

In the trusts, freedom of competition changes into its very opposite—into monopoly; and the production without any definite plan of capitalistic society capitulates to the production upon a definite plan of the invading socialist society. Certainly this is so far still to the benefit and advantage of the capitalists. But in this case the exploitation is so palpable that it must break down. No nation will put up with production conducted by trusts, with so barefaced an exploitation of the community by a small band of dividend mongers.

In any case, with trusts or without the official representative of capitalist society—the state—will ultimately have to undertake the direction of production.[3]

3. I say "have to." For only when the means of production and distribution have *actually* outgrown the form of management by joint-stock companies, and when, therefore, the taking them over by the state has become *economically* inevitable, only then—even if it is the state of today that effects this—there is an economic advance, the attainment of another step preliminary to the taking over of all productive forces by society itself. But of late, since Bismarck went in for state ownership of industrial establishments, a kind of spurious socialism has arisen, degenerating, now and again, into something of flunkeyism, that without more ado declares *all* state ownership, even of the Bismarckian sort, to be socialistic. Certainly, if the taking over by the state of the tobacco industry is socialistic, then Napoleon and Metternich must be numbered among the founders of socialism. If the Belgian state, for quite ordinary political and financial reasons, itself constructed its chief railway lines; if Bismarck, not under any economic compulsion, took over for the state the chief Prussian lines, simply to be the better able to have them in hand in case of war, to bring up the railway employees as voting cattle for the government, and especially to create for himself a new source of income independent of parliamentary votes—this was, in no sense, a socialistic measure, directly or indirectly, consciously or unconsciously. Otherwise, the Royal Maritime Company, the Royal porcelain manufacture, and even the regimental tailor shops of the Army would also be socialistic institutions, or even, as was seriously proposed by a sly dog in Frederick William III's reign, the taking over by the state of the brothels. [Note by Engels.]

This necessity for conversion into state property is felt first in the great institutions for intercourse and communication—the post office, the telegraphs, the railways.

If the crises demonstrate the incapacity of the bourgeoisie for managing any longer modern productive forces, the transformation of the great establishments for production and distribution into joint-stock companies, trusts, and state property shows how unnecessary the bourgeoisie are for that purpose. All the social functions of the capitalist are now performed by salaried employees. The capitalist has no further social function than that of pocketing dividends, tearing off coupons, and gambling on the Stock Exchange, where the different capitalists despoil one another of their capital. At first the capitalistic mode of production forces out the workers. Now it forces out the capitalists and reduces them, just as it reduced the workers, to the ranks of the surplus population, although not immediately into those of the industrial reserve army.

But the transformation, either into joint-stock companies and trusts or into state ownership, does not do away with the capitalistic nature of the productive forces. In the joint-stock companies and trusts this is obvious. And the modern state, again, is only the organization that bourgeois society takes on in order to support the external conditions of the capitalist mode of production against the encroachments as well of the workers as of individual capitalists. The modern state, no matter what its form, is essentially a capitalist machine, the state of the capitalists, the ideal personification of the total national capital. The more it proceeds to the taking over of productive forces, the more does it actually become the national capitalist, the more citizens does it exploit. The workers remain wage workers—proletarians. The capitalist relation is not done away with. It is rather brought to a head. But, brought to a head, it topples over. State ownership of the productive forces is not the solution of the conflict, but concealed within it are the technical conditions that form the elements of that solution.

This solution can only consist in the practical recognition of the social nature of the modern forces of production, and therefore in the harmonizing of the modes of production, appropriation, and exchange with the socialized character of the means of production. And this can only come about by society openly and directly taking possession of the productive forces which have outgrown all control except that of society as a whole. The social character of the means of production and of the products today reacts against the producers, periodically disrupts all production and exchange, acts only like a law of nature working blindly, forcibly, destructively. But with the taking over by society of the productive forces, the social character of the means of production and of the products will be utilized by the producers with a perfect understanding of its nature, and instead of being a source of disturbance and periodical collapse, will become the most powerful lever of production itself.

Active social forces work exactly like natural forces: blindly, forcibly, destructively, so long as we do not understand, and reckon with, them. But when once we understand them, when once we grasp their action, their direction, their effects, it depends only upon ourselves to subject them more and more to our own will, and by means of them to reach our own ends. And this holds quite especially of the mighty productive forces of today. As long as we obstinately refuse to understand the nature and the character of these social means of action—and this understanding goes against the grain of the capitalist mode of production and its defenders—so long these forces are at work in spite of us, in opposition to us, so long they master us, as we have shown above in detail.

But when once their nature is understood, they can, in the hands of the producers working together, be transformed from master demons into willing servants. The difference is as that between the destructive force of electricity in the lightning of the storm, and electricity under command in the telegraph and the voltaic arc; the difference between a conflagration, and fire working in the service of man. With this recognition, at last, of the real nature of the productive forces of today, the social anarchy of production gives place to a social regulation of production upon a definite plan, according to the needs of the community and of each individual. Then the capitalist mode of appropriation, in which the product enslaves first the producer and then the appropriator, is replaced by the mode of appropriation of the products that is based upon the nature of the modern means of production: upon the one hand, direct social appropriation, as means to the maintenance and extension of production; on the other, direct individual appropriation, as means of subsistence and of enjoyment.

Whilst the capitalist mode of production more and more completely transforms the great majority of the population into proletarians, it creates the power which under penalty of its own destruction, is forced to accomplish this revolution. Whilst it forces on more and more the transformation of the vast means of production, already socialized, into state property, it shows itself the way to accomplishing this revolution. *The proletariat seizes political power and turns the means of production into state property.*

But, in doing this, it abolishes itself as proletariat, abolishes all class distinctions and class antagonisms, abolishes also the state as state. Society thus far, based upon class antagonisms, had need of the state. That is, of an organization of the particular class which was *pro tempore* the exploiting class, an organization for the purpose of preventing any interference from without with the existing conditions of production, and, therefore, especially, for the purpose of forcibly keeping the exploited classes in the condition of oppression corresponding with the given mode of production (slavery, serfdom, wage labor). The state was the official representative of society as a whole; the gathering of it together into a visible embodiment. But it was this only insofar as it was the state of that class which itself represented, for the time being, society as a whole: in ancient times, the state of slaveowning citizens; in the Middle Ages, the feudal lords; in our own time, the bourgeoisie. When at last it becomes the real representative of the whole of society, it renders itself unnecessary. As soon as there is no longer any social class to be held in subjection; as soon as class rule, and the individual struggle for existence based upon our present anarchy in production, with the collisions and excesses arising from these, are removed, nothing more remains to be repressed, and a special repressive force, a state, is no longer necessary. The first act by virtue of which the state really constitutes itself the representative of the whole of society—the taking possession of the means of production in the name of society—this is, at the same time, its last independent act as a state. State interference in social relations becomes, in one domain after another, superfluous, and then dies out of itself; the government of persons is replaced by the administration of things and by the conduct of processes of production. The state is not "abolished." *It dies out.* This gives the measure of the value of the phrase *"a free state,"* both as to its justifiable use at times by agitators and as to its ultimate scientific insufficiency; and also of the demands of the so-called anarchists for the abolition of the state out of hand.

Since the historical appearance of the capitalist mode of production, the appropriation by society of all the means of production has often been dreamed of, more or less vaguely, by individuals, as well as by sects, as the ideal of the future. But it could become possible, could become a historical necessity, only when the actual conditions for its realization were there. Like every other social advance, it becomes practicable, not by men understanding that the existence of classes is in contradiction to justice, equality, etc., not by the mere willingness to abolish these classes, but by virtue of certain new economic conditions. The separation of society into an exploiting and an exploited class, a ruling and an oppressed class, was the necessary consequence of the deficient and restricted development of production in former times. So long as the total social labor only yields a produce which but slightly exceeds that barely necessary for the existence of all; so long, therefore, as labor engages all or almost all the time of the great majority of the members of society—so long, of necessity, this society is divided into classes. Side by side with the great majority, exclusively bond slaves to labor, arises a class freed from directly productive labor, which looks after the general affairs of society: the direction of labor, state business, law, science, art, etc. It is, therefore, the law of division of labor that lies at the basis of the division into classes. But this does not prevent this division into classes from being carried out by means of violence and robbery, trickery and fraud. It does not prevent the ruling class, once having the upper hand, from consolidating its power at the expense of the working class, from turning its social leadership into an intensified exploitation of the masses.

But if, upon this showing, division into classes has a certain historical justification, it has this only for a given period, only under given social conditions. It was based upon the insufficiency of production. It will be swept away by the complete development of modern productive forces. And, in fact, the abolition of classes in society presupposes a degree of historical evolution at which the existence, not simply of this or that particular ruling class, but of any ruling class at all, and, therefore, the existence of class distinction itself has become an obsolete anachronism. It presupposes, therefore, the development of production carried out to a degree at which appropriation of the means of production and of the products, and, with this, of political domination, of the monopoly of culture, and of intellectual leadership by a particular class of society, has become not only superfluous but economically, politically, intellectually, a hindrance to development. . . .

From

THE COMMUNIST MANIFESTO

(1848)

A spectre is haunting Europe—the spectre of Communism. All the powers of old Europe have entered into a holy alliance to exorcise this spectre: Pope and Czar, Metternich and Guizot, French Radicals and German police-spies.

Where is the party in opposition that has not been decried as communistic by its opponents in power? Where the Opposition that has not hurled back the branding reproach of Communism, against the more advanced opposition parties, as well as against its reactionary adversaries?

Two things result from this fact:

1. Communism is already acknowledged by all European powers to be itself a power.
2. It is high time that Communists should openly, in the face of the whole world, publish their views, their aims, their tendencies, and meet this nursery tale of the spectre of Communism with a manifesto of the party itself.

To this end, Communists of various nationalities have assembled in London, and sketched the following manifesto, to be published in the English, French, German, Italian, Flemish, and Danish languages.

BOURGEOIS AND PROLETARIANS

The history of all hitherto existing society is the history of class struggles.

Freeman and slave, patrician and plebian, lord and serf, guild-master and journeyman, in a word, oppressor and oppressed, stood in constant opposition to one another, carried on an uninterrupted, now hidden, now open fight, a fight that each time ended, either in a revolutionary reconstitution of society at large, or in the common ruin of the contending classes.

In the earlier epochs of history, we find almost everywhere a complicated arrangement of society into various orders, a manifold gradation of social rank. In ancient Rome we have patricians, knights, plebeians, slaves; in the Middle Ages, feudal lords, vassals, guild-masters, journeymen, apprentices, serfs; in almost all of these classes, again, subordinate gradations.

The modern bourgeois society that has sprouted from the ruins of feudal society, has not done away with class antagonisms. It has but established new classes, new conditions of oppression, new forms of struggle in place of the old ones.

Our epoch, the epoch of the bourgeoisie, possesses, however, this distinctive feature: It has simplified the class antagonisms. Society as a whole is more and more splitting up into two great hostile camps, into two great classes directly facing each other—bourgeoisie and proletariat.

From the serfs of the Middle Ages sprang the chartered burghers of the earliest towns. From these burgesses the first elements of the bourgeoisie were developed.

The discovery of America, the rounding of the Cape, opened up fresh ground for the rising bourgeoisie. The East-Indian and Chinese markets, the colonization of America, trade with the colonies, the increase in the means of

From Karl Marx and Friedrich Engels, *Manifesto of the Communist Party*. First published 1848.

exchange and in commodities generally, gave to commerce, to navigation, to industry, an impulse never before known, and thereby, to the revolutionary element in the tottering feudal society, a rapid development.

The feudal system of industry, in which industrial production was monopolized by closed guilds, now no longer sufficed for the growing wants of the new markets. The manufacturing system took its place. The guild-masters were pushed aside by the manufacturing middle class; division of labor between the different corporate guilds vanished in the face of division of labor in each single workshop.

Meantime the markets kept ever growing, the demand ever rising. Even manufacture no longer sufficed. Thereupon, steam and machinery revolutionized industrial production. The place of manufacture was taken by the giant, modern industry, the place of the industrial middle class, by industrial millionaires—the leaders of whole industrial armies, the modern bourgeois.

Modern industry has established the world market, for which the discovery of America paved the way. This market has given an immense development to commerce, to navigation, to communication by land. This development has, in its turn, reacted on the extension of industry; and in proportion as industry, commerce, navigation, railways extended, in the same proportion the bourgeoisie developed, increased its capital, and pushed into the background every class handed down from the Middle Ages.

We see, therefore, how the modern bourgeoisie is itself the product of a long course of development, of a series of revolutions in the modes of production and of exchange.

Each step in the development of the bourgeoisie was accompanied by a corresponding political advance of that class. An oppressed class under the sway of the feudal nobility, it became an armed and self-governing association in the medieval commune; here independent urban republic (as in Italy and Germany), there taxable "third estate" of the monarchy (as in France); afterwards, in the period of manufacture proper, serving either the semi-feudal or the absolute monarchy as a counterpoise against the nobility, and, in fact, cornerstone of the great monarchies in general—the bourgeoisie has at last, since the establishment of modern industry and of the world market, conquered for itself, in the modern representative state, exclusive political sway. The executive of the modern state is but a committee for managing the common affairs of the whole bourgeoisie.

The bourgeoisie has played a most revolutionary role in history.

The bourgeoisie, wherever it has got the upper hand, has put an end to all feudal, patriarchal, idyllic relations. It has pitilessly torn asunder the motley feudal ties that bound man to his "natural superiors," and has left no other bond between man and man than naked self-interest, than callous "cash payment." It has drowned the most heavenly ectasies of religious fervor, of chivalrous enthusiasm, of philistine sentimentalism, in the icy water of egotistical calculation. It has resolved personal worth into exchange value, and in place of the numberless indefeasible chartered freedoms, has set up that single, unconscionable freedom—Free Trade. In one word, for exploitation, veiled by religious and political illusions, it has substituted naked, shameless, direct, brutal exploitation.

The bourgeoisie has stripped of its

halo every occupation hitherto honored and looked up to with reverent awe. It has converted the physician, the lawyer, the priest, the poet, the man of science, into its paid wage-laborers.

The bourgeoisie has torn away from the family its sentimental veil, and has reduced the family relation to a mere money relation.

The bourgeoisie has disclosed how it came to pass that the brutal display of vigor in the Middle Ages, which reactionaries so much admire, found its fitting complement in the most slothful indolence. It has been the first to show what man's activity can bring about. It has accomplished wonders far surpassing Egyptian pyramids, Roman aqueducts, and Gothic cathedrals; it has conducted expeditions that put in shade all former migrations of nations and crusades.

The bourgeoisie cannot exist without constantly revolutionizing the instruments of production, and thereby the relations of production, and with them the whole relations of society. Conservation of the old modes of production in unaltered form, was, on the contrary, the first condition of existence for all earlier industrial classes. Constant revolutionizing of production, uninterrupted disturbance of all social conditions, everlasting uncertainty and agitation distinguish the bourgeois epoch from all earlier ones. All fixed, fast-frozen relations, with their train of ancient and venerable prejudices and opinions, are swept away, all new-formed ones become antiquated before they can ossify. All that is solid melts into air, all that is holy is profaned, and man is at last compelled to face with sober senses his real conditions of life and his relations with his kind.

The need of a constantly expanding market for its products chases the bourgeoisie over the whole surface of the globe. It must nestle everywhere, settle everywhere, establish connections everywhere.

The bourgeoisie has through its exploitation of the world market given a cosmopolitan character to production and consumption in every country. To the great chagrin of reactionaries, it has drawn from under the feet of industry the national ground on which it stood. All old established national industries have been destroyed or are daily being destroyed. They are dislodged by new industries, whose introduction becomes a life and death question for all civilized nations, by industries that no longer work up indigenous raw material, but raw material drawn from the remotest zones; industries whose products are consumed, not only at home, but in every quarter of the globe. In place of the old wants, satisfied by the production of the country, we find new wants, requiring for their satisfaction the products of distant lands and climes. In place of the old local and national seclusion and self-sufficiency, we have intercourse in every direction, universal interdependence of nations. And as in material, so also in intellectual production. The intellectual creations of individual nations become common property. National one-sidedness and narrow-mindedness become more and more impossible, and from the numerous national and local literatures there arises a world literature.

The bourgeoisie, by the rapid improvement of all instruments of production, by the immensely facilitated means of communication, draws all nations, even the most barbarian, into civilization. The cheap prices of its commodities are the heavy artillery with which it batters down all Chinese walls, with which it forces the barbarians' intensely obstinate hatred of foreigners to capitulate. It compels all nations, on pain of extinction, to adopt the bourgeois mode of production; it compels them to introduce what it calls civilization into their midst, i.e., to become bourgeois themselves. In a word, it creates a world after its own image.

The bourgeoisie has subjected the country to the rule of the towns. It has created enormous cities, has greatly increased the urban population as compared with the rural, and has thus rescued a considerable part of the population from the idiocy of rural life. Just as it has made the country dependent on the towns, so it has made barbarian and semi-barbarian countries dependent on the civilized ones, nations of peasants on nations of bourgeois, the East on the West.

More and more the bourgeois keeps doing away with the scattered state of the population, of the means of production, and of property. It has agglomerated population, centralized means of production, and has concentrated property in a few hands. The necessary consequence of this was political centralization. Independent, or but loosely connected provinces, with separate interests, laws, governments and systems of taxation, became lumped together into one nation, with one government, one code of laws, one national class interest, one frontier and one customs tariff.

The bourgeoisie, during its rule of scarce one hundred years, has created more massive and more colossal productive forces than have all preceding generations together. Subjection of nature's forces to man, machinery, application of chemistry to industry and agriculture, steam navigation, railways, electric telegraphs, clearing of whole continents for cultivation, canalization of rivers, whole populations conjured out of the ground–what earlier century had even a presentiment that such productive forces slumbered in the lap of social labor?

We see then that the means of production and of exchange, which served as the foundation for the growth of the bourgeoisie, were generated in feudal society. At a certain stage in the development of these means of production and of exchange, the conditions under which feudal society produced and exchanged, the feudal organization of agriculture and manufacturing industry, in a word, the feudal relations of property became no longer compatible with the already developed productive forces; they became so many fetters. They had to be burst asunder; they were burst asunder.

Into their place stepped free competition, accompanied by a social and political constitution adapted to it, and by the economic and political sway of the bourgeois class.

A similar movement is going on before our own eyes. Modern bourgeois society with its relations of production, of exchange and of property, a society that has conjured up such gigantic means of production and of exchange, is like the sorcerer who is no longer able to control the powers of the nether world whom he has called up by his spells. For many a decade past, the history of industry and commerce is but the history of the revolt of modern productive forces against modern conditions of production, against the property relations that are the conditions for the existence of the bourgeoisie and of its rule. It is enough to mention the commercial crises that by their periodical return put the existence of the entire bourgeois society on trial, each time more threateningly. In these crises a great part not only of the existing products, but also of the previously created productive forces, are periodically destroyed. In these crises there breaks out an epidemic that, in all earlier epochs, would have seemed an absurdity—the epidemic of overproduction. Society suddenly finds itself put back into a state of momentary barbarism; it appears as if a famine, a universal war of devastation had cut off the supply of every means of subsistence; industry and commerce seem to be destroyed. And why? Because there is too much civilization, too much means of subsistence, too much industry, too much commerce. The productive forces at the disposal of society no longer tend to further the development of the conditions of bourgeois property; on the contrary, they have become too powerful for these conditions, by which they are fettered, and no sooner do they overcome these fetters than they bring disorder into the whole of bourgeois society, endanger the existence of bourgeois property. The conditions of bourgeois society are too narrow to comprise the wealth created by them. And how does the bourgeoisie get over these crises? On the one hand by enforced destruction of a mass of productive forces; on the other, by the conquest of new markets, and by the more thorough exploitation of the old ones. That is to say, by paving the way for more extensive and more destructive crises, and by diminishing the means whereby crises are prevented.

The weapons with which the bourgeoisie felled feudalism to the ground are now turned against the bourgeoisie itself.

But not only has the bourgeoisie forged the weapons that bring death to itself; it has also called into existence the men who are to wield those weapons—the modern working class—the proletarians.

In proportion as the bourgeoisie, i.e., capital, is developed, in the same proportion is the proletariat, the modern working class, developed—a class of laborers, who live only so long as they find work, and who find work only so long as their labor increases capital. These laborers, who must sell themselves piecemeal, are a commodity, like every other article of commerce, and are consequently exposed to all the vicissitudes of competition, to all the fluctuations of the market.

Owing to the extensive use of machinery and to division of labor, the work of the proletarians has lost all individual character, and, consequently, all charm for the workman. He becomes an appendage of the machine and it is only the most simple, most monotonous, and most easily acquired knack, that is required of him. Hence, the cost of production of a workman is restricted, almost entirely, to the means of subsistence that he requires for his maintenance, and for the propagation of his race. But the price of a commodity, and therefore also of labor, is equal to its cost of production. In proportion, therefore, as the repulsiveness of the work increases, the wage decreases. Nay more, in proportion as the use of machinery and division of labor increases, in the same proportion the burden of toil also increases, whether by prolongation of the working hours, by increase of the work exacted in a given time, or by increased speed of the machinery, etc.

Modern industry has converted the little workshop of the patriarchal master into the great factory of the industrial capitalist. Masses of laborers, crowded into the factory, are organized like soldiers. As privates of the industrial army they are placed under the command of a perfect hierarchy of officers and sergeants. Not only are they slaves of the bourgeois class, and of the bourgeois state; they are daily and hourly enslaved by the machine, by the overlooker, and, above all, by the individual bourgeois manufacturer himself. The more openly this despotism proclaims gain to be its end and aim, the more petty, the more hateful and the more embittering it is.

The less the skill and exertion of strength implied in manual labor, in other words, the more modern industry develops, the more is the labor of men superseded by that of women. Differences of age and sex have no longer any distinctive social validity for the working class. All are instruments of labor, more or less expensive to use, according to their age and sex.

No sooner has the laborer received his wages in cash, for the moment escaping exploitation by the manufacturer, than he is set upon by the other portions of the bourgeoisie, the landlord, the shopkeeper, the pawnbroker, etc.

The lower strata of the middle class—the small tradespeople, shopkeepers, and retired tradesmen generally, the handicraftsmen and peasants—all these sink gradually into the proletariat, partly because their diminutive capital does not suffice for the scale on which modern industry is carried on, and is swamped in the competition with the large capitalists, partly because their specialized skill is rendered worthless by new methods of production. Thus the proletariat is recruited from all classes of the population.

The proletariat goes through various stages of development. With its birth begins its struggle with the bourgeoisie. At first the contest is carried on by individual laborers, then by the work people of a factory, then by the operatives of one trade, in one locality, against the individual bourgeois who directly exploits them. They direct their attacks not against the bourgeois conditions of production, but against the instruments of production themselves; they destroy imported wares that compete with their labor, they smash machinery to pieces, they set factories ablaze, they seek to restore by force the vanished status of the workman of the Middle Ages.

At this stage the laborers still form an incoherent mass scattered over the whole country, and broken up by their mutual competition. If anywhere they unite to form more compact bodies, this is not yet the consequence of their own active union, but of the union of the bourgeoisie, which class, in order to attain its own political ends, is compelled to set the whole proletariat in motion, and is moreover still able to do so for a time. At this stage, therefore, the proletarians do not fight their enemies, but the enemies of their enemies, the remnants of absolute monarchy, the landowners, the nonindustrial bourgeois, the petty bourgeoisie. Thus the whole historical movement is concentrated in the hands of the bourgeoisie; every victory so obtained is a victory for the bourgeoisie.

But with the development of industry the proletariat not only increases in numbers; it becomes concentrated in greater masses, its strength grows, and it feels that strength more. The various interests and conditions of life within the ranks of the proletariat are more and more equalized, in proportion as machinery obliterates all distinctions of labor and nearly everywhere reduces wages to the same low level. The growing competition among the bourgeois, and the resulting commercial crises, make the wages of the workers ever more fluctuating. The unceasing improvement of machinery, ever more rapidly developing, makes their livelihood more and more precarious; the collisions between individual workmen and individual bourgeois take more and more the character of collisions between two classes. Thereupon the workers begin to form combinations (trade unions) against the bourgeoisie; they club together in order to keep up the rate of wages; they found permanent associations in order to make provision beforehand for these occasional revolts. Here and there the contest breaks out into riots.

Now and then the workers are victorious, but only for a time. The real fruit of their battles lies, not in the immediate result, but in the ever-expanding union of the workers. This union is furthered by the improved means of communication which are created by modern industry, and which place the workers of different localities in contact with one another. It was just this contact that was needed to centralize the numerous local struggles, all of the same character, into one national struggle between classes. But every class struggle is a political struggle. And that union, to attain which the burghers of the Middle Ages, with their miserable highways, required centuries, the modern proletarians, thanks to railways, achieve in a few years.

This organization of the proletarians into a class, and consequently into a political party, is continually being upset again by the competition between the workers themselves. But it ever rises up again, stronger, firmer, mightier. It compels legislative recognition of particular interests of the workers, by taking advantage of the divisions among the bourgeoisie itself. Thus the ten-hour bill in England was carried.

Altogether, collisions between the classes of the old society further the course of development of the proletariat in many ways. The bourgeoisie finds itself involved in a constant battle. At first with the aristocracy; later on, with those portions of the bourgeoisie itself whose interests have become antagonistic to the progress of industry; at all times with the bourgeoisie of foreign countries. In all these battles it sees itself compelled to appeal to the proletariat, to ask for its help, and thus, to drag it into the political arena. The bourgeoisie itself, therefore, supplies the proletariat with its own elements of political and general education, in other words, it furnishes the proletariat with weapons for fighting the bourgeoisie.

Further, as we have already seen, entire sections of the ruling classes are, by the advance of industry, precipitated into the proletariat, or are at least threatened in their conditions of existence. These also supply the proletariat with fresh elements of enlightenment and progress.

Finally, in times when the class struggle nears the decisive hour, the process of dissolution going on within the ruling class, in fact within the whole range of old society, assumes such a violent, glaring character, that a small section of the ruling class cuts itself adrift, and joins the revolutionary class, the class that holds the future in its hands. Just as, therefore, at an earlier period, a section of the nobility went over to the bourgeoisie, so now a portion of the bourgeoisie goes over to the proletariat, and in particular, a portion of the bourgeois ideologists, who have raised themselves to the level of comprehending theoretically the historical movement as a whole.

Of all the classes that stand face to face with the bourgeoisie today, the proletariat alone is a really revolutionary class. The other classes decay and finally disappear in the face of modern industry; the proletariat is its special and essential product.

The lower middle class, the small

manufacturer, the shopkeeper, the artisan, the peasant, all these fight against the bourgeoisie, to save from extinction their existence as fractions of the middle class. They are therefore not revolutionary, but conservative. Nay more, they are reactionary, for they try to roll back the wheel of history. If by chance they are revolutionary, they are so only in view of their impending transfer into the proletariat; they thus defend not their present, but their future interests; they desert their own standpoint to adopt that of the proletariat.

The "dangerous class," the social scum *(Lumpenproletariat),* that passively rotting mass thrown off by the lowest layers of old society, may, here and there, be swept into the movement by a proletarian revolution; its conditions of life, however, prepare it far more for the part of a bribed tool of reactionary intrigue.

The social conditions of the old society no longer exist for the proletariat. The proletarian is without property; his relation to his wife and children has no longer anything in common with bourgeois family relations; modern industrial labor, modern subjection to capital, the same in England as in France, in America as in Germany, has stripped him of every trace of national character. Law, morality, religion, are to him so many bourgeois prejudices, behind which lurk in ambush just as many bourgeois interests.

All the preceding classes that got the upper hand, sought to fortify their already acquired status by subjecting society at large to their conditions of appropriation. The proletarians cannot become masters of the productive forces of society, except by abolishing their own previous mode of appropriation, and thereby also every other previous mode of appropriation. They have nothing of their own to secure and to fortify; their mission is to destroy all previous securities for, and insurances of, individual property.

All previous historical movements were movements of minorities, or in the interest of minorities. The proletarian movement is the self-conscious, independent movement of the immense majority, in the interest of the immense majority. The proletariat, the lowest stratum of our present society, cannot stir, cannot raise itself up, without the whole superincumbent strata of official society being sprung into the air.

Though not in substance, yet in form, the struggle of the proletariat with the bourgeoisie is at first a national struggle. The proletariat of each country must, of course, first of all settle matters with its own bourgeoisie.

In depicting the most general phases of the development of the proletariat, we traced the more or less veiled civil war, raging within existing society, up to the point where that war breaks out into open revolution, and where the violent overthrow of the bourgeoisie lays the foundation for the sway of the proletariat.

Hitherto, every form of society has been based, as we have already seen, on the antagonism of oppressing and oppressed classes. But in order to oppress a class, certain conditions must be assured to it under which it can, at least, continue its slavish existence. The serf, in the period of serfdom, raised himself to membership in the commune, just as the petty bourgeois, under the yoke of feudal absolutism, managed to develop into a bourgeois. The modern laborer, on the contrary, instead of rising with the progress of industry, sinks deeper and deeper below the conditions of existence of his own class. He becomes a pauper, and pauperism develops more rapidly than population and wealth. And here it becomes evident, that the bourgeoisie is unfit any longer to be the ruling class in society, and to impose its conditions of existence upon society as an overriding law. It is unfit to rule because it is incompetent to assure an existence to its slave within his slavery, because it cannot help letting him sink into such a state, that it has to feed him, instead of being fed by him. Society can no longer live under this bourgeoisie, in other words, its existence is no longer compatible with society.

The essential condition for the existence and sway of the bourgeois class, is the formation and augmentation of capital; the condition for capital is wage-labor. Wage-labor rests exclusively on competition between the laborers. The advance of industry, whose involuntary promoter is the bourgeoisie, replaces the isolation of the laborers, due to competition, by their revolutionary combination, due to association. The development of modern industry, therefore, cuts from under its feet the very foundation on which the bourgeoisie produces and appropriates products. What the bourgeoisie therefore produces, above all, are its own gravediggers. Its fall and the victory of the proletariat are equally inevitable.

PROLETARIANS AND COMMUNISTS

In what relation do the Communists stand to the proletarians as a whole?

The Communists do not form a separate party opposed to other working-class parties.

They have no interests separate and apart from those of the proletariat as a whole.

They do not set up any sectarian principles of their own, by which to shape and mold the proletarian movement.

The Communists are distinguished from the other working-class parties by this only:

1. In the national struggles of the proletarians of the different countries, they point out and bring to the front the common interests of the entire proletariat, independently of all nationality.
2. In the various stages of development which the struggle of the working class against the bourgeoisie has to pass through, they always and everywhere represent the interests of the movement as a whole.

The Communists, therefore, are on the one hand, practically, the most advanced and resolute section of the working class parties of every country, that section which pushes forward all others; on the other hand, theoretically, they have over the great mass of the proletariat the advantage of clearly understanding the line of march, the conditions, and the ultimate general results of the proletarian movement.

The immediate aim of the Communists is the same as that of all the other proletarian parties: formation of the proletariat into a class, overthrow of bourgeois supremacy, conquest of political power by the proletariat.

The theoretical conclusions of the Communists are in no way based on ideas or principles that have been invented, or discovered, by this or that would-be universal reformer.

They merely express, in general terms, actual relations springing from an existing class struggle, from a historical movement going on under our very eyes. The abolition of existing property relations is not at all a distinctive feature of Communism.

All property relations in the past have

continually been subject to historical change consequent upon the change in historical conditions.

The French Revolution, for example, abolished feudal property in favor of bourgeois property.

The distinguishing feature of Communism is not the abolition of property generally, but the abolition of bourgeois property. But modern bourgeois private property is the final and most complete expression of the system of producing and appropriating products that is based on class antagonisms, on the exploitation of the many by the few.

In this sense, the theory of the Communists may be summed up in the single sentence: Abolition of private property.

We Communists have been reproached with the desire of abolishing the right of personally acquiring property as the fruit of a man's own labor, which property is alleged to be the groundwork of all personal freedom, activity, and independence.

Hard-won, self-acquired, self-earned property! Do you mean the property of the petty artisan and of the small peasant, a form of property that preceded the bourgeois form? There is no need to abolish that; the development of industry has to a great extent already destroyed it, and is still destroying it daily.

Or do you mean modern bourgeois private property?

But does wage-labor create any property for the laborer? Not a bit. It creates capital, i.e., that kind of property which exploits wage-labor, and which cannot increase except upon condition of begetting a new supply of wage-labor for fresh exploitation. Property, in its present form, is based on the antagonism of capital and wage-labor. Let us examine both sides of this antagonism.

To be a capitalist, is to have not only a purely personal, but a social *status* in production. Capital is a collective product, and only by the united action of many members, nay, in the last resort, only by the united action of all members of society, can it be set in motion.

Capital is therefore not a personal, it is a social, power.

When, therefore, capital is converted into common property, into the property of all members of society, personal property is not thereby transformed into social property. It is only the social character of the property that is changed. It loses its class character.

Let us now take wage-labor.

The average price of wage-labor is the minimum wage, i.e., that quantum of the means of subsistence which is absolutely requisite to keep the laborer in bare existence as a laborer. What, therefore, the wage-laborer appropriates by means of his labor, merely suffices to prolong and reproduce a bare existence. We by no means intend to abolish this personal appropriation of the products of labor, an appropriation that is made for the maintenance and reproduction of human life, and that leaves no surplus wherewith to command the labor of others. All that we want to do away with is the miserable character of this appropriation, under which the laborer lives merely to increase capital, and is allowed to live only insofar as the interest of the ruling class requires it.

In bourgeois society, living labor is but a means to increase accumulated labor. In Communist society, accumulated labor is but a means to widen, to enrich, to promote the existence of the laborer.

In bourgeois society, therefore, the past dominates the present; in Communist society, the present dominates the past. In bourgeois society capital is independent and has individuality, while the living person is dependent and has no individuality.

And the abolition of this state of things is called by the bourgeois, abolition of individuality and freedom! And rightly so. The abolition of bourgeois individuality, bourgeois independence, and bourgeois freedom is undoubtedly aimed at.

By freedom is meant, under the present bourgeois conditions of production, free trade, free selling and buying.

But if selling and buying disappears, free selling and buying disappears also. This talk about free selling and buying, and all the other "brave words" of our bourgeoisie about freedom in general, have a meaning, if any, only in contrast with restricted selling and buying, with the fettered traders of the Middle Ages, but have no meaning when opposed to the Communist abolition of buying and selling, of the bourgeois conditions of production, and of the bourgeoisie itself.

You are horrified at our intending to do away with private property. But in your existing society, private property is already done away with for nine-tenths of the population; its existence for the few is solely due to its nonexistence in the hands of those nine-tenths. You reproach us, therefore, with intending to do away with a form of property, the necessary condition for whose existence is the nonexistence of any property for the immense majority of society.

In a word, you reproach us with intending to do away with your property. Precisely so; that is just what we intend.

From the moment when labor can no longer be converted into capital, money, or rent, into a social power capable of being monopolized, i.e., from the moment when individual property can no longer be transformed into bourgeois property, into capital, from that moment, you say, individuality vanishes.

You must, therefore, confess that by "individual" you mean no other person than the bourgeois, than the middle-class owner of property. This person must, indeed, be swept out of the way, and made impossible.

Communism deprives no man of the power to appropriate the products of society; all that it does is to deprive him of the power to subjugate the labor of others by means of such appropriation.

It has been objected, that upon the abolition of private property all work will cease, and universal laziness will overtake us.

According to this, bourgeois society ought long ago to have gone to the dogs through sheer idleness; for those of its members who work, acquire nothing, and those who acquire anything, do not work. The whole of this objection is but another expression of the tautology: There can no longer be any wage-labor when there is no longer any capital.

All objections urged against the Communist mode of producing and appropriating material products, have, in the same way, been urged against the Communist modes of producing and appropriating intellectual products. Just as, to the bourgeois, the disappearance of class property is the disappearance of production itself, so the disappearance of class culture is to him identical with the disappearance of all culture.

That culture, the loss of which he laments, is, for the enormous majority, a mere training to act as a machine.

But don't wrangle with us so long as you apply, to our intended abolition of bourgeois property, the standard of your bourgeois notions of freedom, culture, law, etc. Your very ideas are but the outgrowth of the conditions of your bourgeois production and bourgeois property, just as your jurisprudence is but the will of your class made into a law for all, a will whose essential character and direction are determined by the economic conditions of existence of your class.

The selfish misconception that induces you to transform into eternal laws of nature and of reason, the social forms springing from your present mode of production and form of property—historical relations that rise and disappear in the progress of production—this misconception you share with every ruling class that has preceded you. What you see clearly in the case of ancient property, what you admit in the case of feudal property, you are of course forbidden to admit in the case of your own bourgeois form of property.

Abolition of the family! Even the most radical flare up at this infamous proposal of the Communists.

On what foundation is the present family, the bourgeois family, based? On capital, on private gain. In its completely developed form this family exists only among the bourgeoisie. But this state of things finds its complement in the practical absence of the family among the proletarians, and in public prostitution.

The bourgeois family will vanish as a matter of course when its complement vanishes, and both will vanish with the vanishing of capital.

Do you charge us with wanting to stop the exploitation of children by their parents? To this crime we plead guilty.

But, you will say, we destroy the most hallowed of relations, when we replace home education by social.

And your education! Is not that also social, and determined by the social conditions under which you educate, by the intervention of society, direct or indirect, by means of schools, etc.? The Communists have not invented the intervention of society in education; they do but seek to alter the character of that intervention, and to rescue education from the influence of the ruling class.

The bourgeois claptrap about the family and education, about the hallowed co-relation of parent and child, becomes all the more disgusting, the more, by the action of modern industry, all family ties among the proletarians are torn asunder, and their children transformed into simple articles of commerce and instruments of labor.

But you Communists would introduce community of women, screams the whole bourgeoisie in chorus.

The bourgeois sees in his wife a mere instrument of production. He hears that the instruments of production are to be exploited in common, and, naturally, can come to no other conclusion than that the lot of being common to all will likewise fall to the women.

He has not even a suspicion that the real point aimed at is to do away with the status of women as mere instruments of production.

For the rest, nothing is more ridiculous than the virtuous indignation of our bourgeois at the community of women which, they pretend, is to be openly and officially established by the Communists. The Communists have no need to introduce community of women; it has existed almost from time immemorial.

Our bourgeois, not content with having the wives and daughters of their proletarians at their disposal, not to speak of common prostitutes, take the greatest pleasure in seducing each other's wives.

Bourgeois marriage is in reality a system of wives in common and thus, at the most, what the Communists might possibly be reproached with is that they desire to introduce, in substitution for a hypocritically concealed, an openly legalized community of women. For the rest, it is self-evident, that the abolition of the present system of production must bring with it the abolition of the community of women springing from that system, i.e., of prostitution both public and private.

The Communists are further reproached with desiring to abolish countries and nationality.

The workingmen have no country. We cannot take from them what they have not got. Since the proletariat must first of all acquire political supremacy, must rise to be the leading class of the nation, must constitute itself *the* nation, it is, so far, itself national, though not in the bourgeois sense of the word.

National differences and antagonisms between peoples are vanishing gradually from day to day, owing to the development of the bourgeoisie, to freedom of commerce, to the world market, to uniformity in the mode of production and in the conditions of life corresponding thereto.

The supremacy of the proletariat will cause them to vanish still faster. United action, of the leading civilized countries at least, is one of the first conditions for the emancipation of the proletariat.

In proportion as the exploitation of one individual by another is put an end to, the exploitation of one nation by another will also be put an end to. In proportion as the antagonism between classes within the nation vanishes, the hostility of one nation to another will come to an end.

The charges against Communism made from a religious, a philosophical, and, generally, from an ideological standpoint, are not deserving of serious examination.

Does it require deep intuition to comprehend that man's ideas, views, and conceptions, in one word, man's consciousness, changes with every change in the conditions of his material existence, in his social relations, and in his social life?

What else does the history of ideas prove, than that intellectual production changes its character in proportion as material production is changed? The ruling ideas of each age have ever been the ideas of its ruling class.

When people speak of ideas that revolutionize society, they do but express the fact that within the old society the elements of a new one have been created, and that the dissolution of the old ideas keeps even pace with the dissolution of the old conditions of existence.

When the ancient world was in its last throes, the ancient religions were overcome by Christianity. When Christian ideas succumbed in the eighteenth century to rationalist ideas, feudal society fought its death battle with the then revolutionary bourgeoisie. The ideas of religious liberty and freedom of conscience, merely gave expression to the sway of free competition within the domain of knowledge.

"Undoubtedly," it will be said, "religious, moral, philosophical and juridical ideas have been modified in the course of historical development. But religion, morality, philosophy, political science, and law, constantly survived this change.

"There are, besides, eternal truths, such as Freedom, Justice, etc., that are common to all states of society. But Communism abolishes eternal truths, it abolishes all religion, and all morality, instead of constituting them on a new basis; it therefore acts in contradiction to all past historical experience."

What does this accusation reduce itself to? The history of all past society has consisted in the development of class antagonisms, antagonisms that assumed different forms at different epochs.

But whatever form they may have taken, one fact is common to all past ages, viz., the exploitation of one part of society by the other. No wonder, then, that the social consciousness of past ages, despite all the multiplicity and variety it displays, moves within certain common forms, or general ideas, which cannot completely vanish except with the total disappearance of class antagonisms.

The Communist revolution is the most radical rupture with traditional property relations; no wonder that its development involves the most radical rupture with traditional ideas.

But let us have done with the bourgeois objections to Communism.

We have seen above, that the first step in the revolution by the working class, is to raise the proletariat to the position of ruling class, to establish democracy.

The proletariat will use its political supremacy to wrest, by degrees, all capital from the bourgeoisie, to centralize all instruments of production in the hands of the state, i.e., of the proletariat organized as the ruling class; and to increase the total of productive forces as rapidly as possible.

Of course, in the beginning, this cannot be effected except by means of despotic inroads on the rights of property, and on the conditions of bourgeois production; by means of measures, therefore, which appear economically insufficient and untenable, but which, in the course of the movement, outstrip themselves, necessitate further inroads upon the old social order, and are unavoidable as a means of entirely revolutionizing the mode of production.

These measures will of course be different in different countries.

Nevertheless in the most advanced countries, the following will be pretty generally applicable.

1. Abolition of property in land and application of all rents of land to public purposes.
2. A heavy progressive or graduated income tax.
3. Abolition of all right of inheritance.
4. Confiscation of the property of all emigrants and rebels.
5. Centralization of credit in the hands of the state, by means of a national bank with state capital and an exclusive monopoly.
6. Centralization of the means of communication and transport in the hands of the state.
7. Extension of factories and instruments of production owned by the state; the bringing into cultivation of waste lands, and the improvement of the soil generally in accordance with a common plan.
8. Equal obligation of all to work. Establishment of industrial armies, especially for agriculture.
9. Combination of agriculture with manufacturing industries; gradual abolition of the distinction between town and country, by a more equable distribution of the population over the country.
10. Free education for all children in public schools. Abolition of child factory labor in its present form. Combination of education with industrial production, etc.

When, in the course of development, class distinctions have disappeared, and all production has been concentrated in the hands of a vast association of the whole nation, the public power will lose its political character. Political power, properly so called, is merely the organized power of one class for oppressing another. If the proletariat during its contest with the bourgeoisie is compelled, by the force of circumstances, to organize itself as a class; if, by means of a revolution, it makes itself the ruling class, and, as such, sweeps away by force the old conditions of production, then it will, along with these conditions, have swept away the conditions for the existence of class antagonisms, and of classes generally, and will thereby have abolished its own supremacy as a class.

In place of the old bourgeois society, with its classes and class antagonisms, we shall have an association, in which the free development of each is the condition for the free development of all. . . .

From

CAPITAL

(Marx, 1867)

PRIMITIVE ACCUMULATION

. . . Through capital surplus-value is made, and from surplus-value more capital. But the accumulation of capital presupposes surplus-value; surplus-value presupposes capitalistic production; capitalistic production presupposes the pre-existence of considerable masses of capital and of labor power in the hands of producers of commodities. The whole movement, therefore, seems to turn in a vicious circle, out of which we can only get by supposing a primitive accumulation preceding capitalistic accumulation; an accumulation not the result of the capitalist mode of production, but its starting point.

Political Economy explains the origin of this primitive accumulation as an anecdote of the past. In times long gone by there were two sorts of people: one, the diligent, intelligent, and above all, frugal élite; the other, lazy rascals, spending their substance, and more, in riotous living. Thus it came to pass that the former sort accumulated wealth, and the latter sort had at last nothing to sell except their own skins. And from this original sin dates the poverty of the great majority that, despite all its labor, has up to now nothing to sell but itself, and the wealth of the few that increases constantly although they have long ceased to work. In actual history it is notorious that conquest, enslavement, robbery, murder, briefly force, play the great part. In the tender annals of Political Economy, the idyllic reigns from time immemorial. Right and "labor" were from all time the sole means of enrichment, the present year of course always excepted. As a matter of fact, the methods of primitive accumulation are anything but idyllic.

The capitalist system presupposes the complete separation of the laborers from all property in the means by which they can realize their labor. As soon as capitalist production is once on its own legs, it not only maintains this separation, but reproduces it on a continually extending scale. The process, therefore, that clears the way for the capitalist system, can be none other than the process which takes away from the laborer the possession of his means of production. The so-called primitive accumulation, therefore, is nothing else than the historical process of divorcing the producer from the means of production.

The economic structure of capitalistic society has grown out of the economic structure of feudal society. The dissolution of the latter set free the elements of the former.

The laborer could only dispose of his

From Karl Marx, *Capital*, Vol. 1. First published 1867.

own person after he had ceased to be attached to the soil and ceased to be the slave, serf, or bondman of another. To become a free seller of labor power, who carries his commodity wherever he finds a market, he must further have escaped from the regime of the guilds, their rules for apprentices and journeymen, and the impediments of their labor regulations. Hence, the historical movement which changes the producers into wageworkers, appears, on the one hand, as their emancipation from serfdom and from the fetters of the guilds, and this side alone exists for our bourgeois historians. But, on the other hand, these new freemen became sellers of themselves only after they had been robbed of all their own means of production, and of all the guarantees of existence afforded by the old feudal arrangements. And the history of this, their expropriation, is written in the annals of mankind in letters of blood and fire.

The industrial capitalists, these new potentates, had on their part not only to displace the guild-masters of handicrafts, but also the feudal lords, the possessors of the sources of wealth. In this respect their conquest of social power appears as the fruit of a victorious struggle both against feudal lordship and its revolting prerogatives, and against the guilds and the fetters they laid on the free development of production and the free exploitation of man by man. The *chevaliers d'industrie,* however, only succeeded in supplanting the knights of the sword by making use of events of which they themselves were wholly innocent. They have risen by means as vile as those by which the Roman freedman once on a time made himself the master of his *patronus.*

The starting point of the development that gave rise to the wage-laborer as well as to the capitalist, was the servitude of the laborer. The advance consisted in a change of form of this servitude, in the transformation of feudal exploitation into capitalist exploitation. To understand its march, we need not go back very far. Although we come across the first beginnings of capitalist production as early as the fourteenth or fifteenth century, sporadically, in certain towns of the Mediterranean, the capitalist era dates from the sixteenth century. Wherever it appears, the abolition of serfdom has been long effected, and the highest development of the middle ages, the existence of sovereign towns, has been long on the wane.

In the history of primitive accumulation, those moments are particularly important, when great masses of men are suddenly and forcibly torn from their means of subsistence, and hurled as free and "unattached" proletarians on the labor market. The expropriation of the peasant from the soil, is the basis of the whole process. . . .

WHAT CAPITALIST ACCUMULATION LEADS TO

What does the primitive accumulation of capital, i.e., its historical genesis, resolve itself into? Insofar as it is not immediate transformation of slaves and serfs into wage-laborers, and therefore a mere change of form, it only means the expropriation of the immediate producers, i.e., the dissolution of private property based on the labor of its owner.

The private property of the laborer in his means of production is the foundation of petty industry; petty industry, again, is an essential condition for the development of social production and of the free individuality of the laborer himself. Of course, this petty mode of production exists also under slavery, serfdom, and other states of dependence.

But it flourishes, it lets loose its whole energy, only where the laborer is the private owner of his own means of labor set in action by himself: the peasant of the land which he cultivates, the artisan of the tool which he handles as a virtuoso. This mode of production presupposes parcelling of the soil, and scattering of the other means of production. As it excludes the concentration of these means of production, so also it excludes cooperation, division of labor within each separate process of production, the control over and the productive application of the forces of nature by society, and the free development of the social productive powers. It is compatible only with a system of production, and a society, moving within narrow and more or less primitive bounds. To perpetuate it, would be to decree universal mediocrity. At a certain stage of development it brings forth the material agencies for its own dissolution. From that moment new forces and new passions spring up in the bosom of society; but the old social organization fetters them and keeps them down. It must be annihilated; it is annihilated.

Its annihilation, the transformation of the individualized and scattered means of production into socially concentrated ones, of the pigmy property of the many into the huge property of the few, the expropriation of the great mass of the people from the soil, from the means of subsistence and from the means of labor, this fearful and painful expropriation of the mass of people forms the prelude to the history of capital. Self-earned private property, that is based, so to say, on the fusing together of the isolated, independent laborer with the conditions of his labor, is supplanted by capitalistic private property, which rests on exploitation of the nominally free labor of others, i.e., on wage-labor.

As soon as the process of transformation has sufficiently decomposed the old society from top to bottom, as soon as the laborers are turned into proletarians, their means of labor into capital, as soon as the capitalist mode of production stands on its own feet, then the further socialization of labor and the further transformation of the land and other means of production, as well as the further expropriation of private proprietors, takes a new form. That which is now to be expropriated is no longer the laborer working for himself, but the capitalist exploiting many laborers. This expropriation is accomplished by the action of the immanent laws of capitalistic production itself, by the centralization of capital. One capitalist always kills many.

Hand in hand with this centralization, or this expropriation of many capitalists by few, develops, on an ever-extending scale, the cooperative form of the labor process, the conscious technical application of science, the economizing of all means of production by combined, socialized labor, the entanglement of all peoples in the net of the world market, and with this, the international character of the capitalistic regime.

Along with the constantly diminishing number of the magnates of capital, who usurp and monopolize all advantages of this process of transformation, grows the mass of misery, oppressions, slavery, degradation, exploitation; but with this too grows the revolt of the working class, always increasing in numbers, and disciplined, united, organized by the very mechanism of the process of capitalist production itself. The monopoly of capital becomes a fetter upon the mode of production, which has sprung up and flourished along with, and under it. Centralizations of the means of production and socialization of labor at last reach a point where they become incompatible with their capitalist integument. This integument is burst asunder. The knell of capitalist private property sounds. The expropriators are expropriated.

The capitalist mode of appropriation, the result of the capitalist mode of production, capitalist private property, is the first negation of individual private property, as founded on the labor of the proprietor. But capitalist production begets, with the inexorability of a law of nature, its own negation. This does not re-establish private property, but individual property based on the acquisitions of the capitalist era: i.e., on cooperation and the possession in common of the land and of the means of production produced by labor itself.

The transformation of scattered private property, arising from individual labor, into capitalist private property was, naturally, a process incomparably more protracted, violent, and difficult, than the transformation of capitalistic private property, already practically resting on socialized production, into socialized property. In the former case, we had the expropriation of the mass of the people by a few usurpers; in the latter, we have the expropriation of a few usurpers by the mass of the people.

THORSTEIN VEBLEN

(1857–1929)

Thorstein Veblen was the ideological father of the institutionalist school in American economic thought. Whereas his followers (like Wesley Mitchell and John R. Commons) were inclined to champion the accumulation of empirical data and the shifting forms of social control necessary to deal with the limited problems of a developing market society, Veblen's critique of American capitalism was uncompromising and revolutionary. Yet unfortunately, the satirical, elliptical style that so delighted or enraged sophisticated scholars was his undoing, in the sense that he all too often missed the very audience (workers and engineers) who could have benefited from his pungent criticism. His caustic judgment of society's most cherished institutions, e.g., the utter wastefulness and acquisitiveness of the leisured propertied class or religious officialdom, helped to make his academic career a stormy and unstable one.

Veblen wrote against a background of rising social discontent. Around the turn of the twentieth century, the rapid thrust toward capitalist development was accompanied by the first wave of business mergers, engineered by a rising class of investment bankers, scandalous corruption of public officials linked to a business elite, prolonged depression in agriculture, and boom-bust cycles in industry. In addition, violence against labor unions and radicals questioning the merits of rampaging capitalism was officially condoned. Federal troops and court injunctions were used to break strikes and protests against unemployment by the working class, while predatory business practices were considered as American as the proverbial apple pie. The captains of industry and finance became American folk heroes.

With immense erudition at his command, Veblen fearlessly crossed the boundaries of specific intellectual disciplines. His writings embraced economics, history, philosophy, political theory, anthropology, psychology, and even the natural sciences. This unique range of learning and interest sets Veblen apart from the overwhelming majority of his contemporaries. Veblen reacted strongly against the marginalist school of economics, firmly entrenched in academia at that time. The thrust of his critique was that orthodox economics was overly concerned with value and price phenomena instead of the more important evolutionary considerations of the cumulative growth of changing institutions. Furthermore, the marginalist theory was based on a questionable psychological base—hedonism—in which man's actions are attributed to an alleged pleasure-pain calculus. Veblen, by contrast, held that man's activities were influenced not only by this pecuniary drive, but also by an instinct of workmanship (need for purposeful or useful work), parental bent (concern for continuity of the group), and idle curiosity (desire for systematic knowledge). Man, to Veblen, thus appears as a multi-dimensioned animal operating in a dynamic social universe, as opposed to the orthodox concept of the "economic man" in a static personal universe. Veblen was more like a modern social behaviorist developing a theory of complex and often conflicting human behavior patterns than a traditional economist building an exacting mathematical theory based on one-dimensional, oversimplified assumptions of the "free market" man. In his famous study, *The Theory of Business Enterprise* (1904), Veblen claimed that the industrial process subjects the worker to an unremitting machine discipline which inculcates new "habits of thought." These thoughts, oriented to mechanical efficiency, have a "materialistic . . . impersonal cause-and-effect" cast. The machine process in a private enterprise system "compels the adaptation of the workman to his work, rather than the adaptation of the work to the workman." The result is a potential for either alienation or radicalization.

Fundamental to Veblen's attempt to discover the laws of change within capitalism is his assertion that the two basic institutions of American society are the business enterprise system and technology. Unlike the neoclassical economists, who continued to structure their models in terms of pure competition even as this competition was rapidly disappearing, Veblen saw these institutions as fundamentally opposed to one another. While the businessmen were concerned with maximization of private profit, the engineers and technicians operating the machine technology were concerned with the most efficient utilization of resources. Veblen's writings in this area foreshadow later work on imperfect competition and welfare economics. He contrasted the community need for maximum productivity—greater output at lower cost—with the consistent business practice of restricting output to increase profits. Under capitalism, according to Veblen, the interests of industry and community welfare were sacrificed in favor of business interests. This was Veblen's way of saying that our vast accumulation of knowledge and technology, which ought to be the common heritage of all men, was being misused to further the economic interests of a small propertied class. He noted, furthermore—the first American social scientist to do so—that business enterprise had become international in the scope of its activities, and that the full power of the state was available to further its interests. In language strikingly reminiscent of the modern left, Veblen said:

> In this international competition the machinery and policy of the state are in a peculiar degree drawn into the service of the larger business units. . . . Armaments . . . are similarly useful in extending and maintaining business enterprise and privileges in the outlying regions of the earth. . . . The objective end of warlike endeavor is the peace and security necessary to an orderly development of business.

According to Veblen, a possible but not inevitable result of the conflict between "business" and "industry"—akin to that between the predatory and productive classes in society—was that industry control would shift from businessmen (concerned solely with profitability) to engineers and technicians (concerned with serviceability). The question was whether or not changing technology would affect man's thinking enough to accomplish this shift in control. In *Engineers and the Price System* (1921), Veblen says our complex, interdependent industrial system requires a "general staff of industrial experts" in order to maintain a balanced, efficient operation. He viewed the businessman as a manipulator, inhibiting technological advance and wasting much of society's productive capacity, and the corporate financier as "no better than an idle wheel in the economic mechanism." Veblen believed that the younger members of the industrial general staff, realizing that the profit-driven capitalists were distorting their work, were gradually developing "class consciousness" in the sense of rebelling against the social wastefulness of the capitalists. Although Veblen's provocative thesis about the greater rationality of this technical elite is undoubtedly exaggerated, his depiction of the dualism in capitalism—between technology per se and the business uses it serves—is a valuable and original insight.

Unlike Marx, Veblen did not view the conflict between labor and capital as the key to a revolutionary transformation; to him, their wage negotiations were just another business transaction. Only a general strike by an aroused group of indispensable, strategically situated technological specialists could sweep away the old order and end the "sabotage" of industry by the capitalist owners. While Veblen himself clearly favored placing control of industry in the hands of the engineers, he saw them as only a distant threat to the vested interests. Veblen applauded the Bolshevik revolutionists for abolishing private property and substituting production for use in place of production for profit, but he died before the Stalinist degeneration of the isolated socialist experiment set in. Although he was not fully in favor of any alternative socioeconomic system, Veblen was without doubt hostile to capitalism; it was wasteful, predatory, prone toward economic crises, and based on drives he considered irrational, such as religion, salesmanship, and patriotism.

Although few Marxists have embraced Veblen, there is much in common in their critiques of capitalist society. Both Marx and Veblen had a "materialist" conception of history with the stress on technology (Marx uses the term *forces of production)* as the prime agent in the evolution of institutions. They both held that capitalism could not permanently coexist with advanced technology. Noneconomic factors affected the pace and direction of social change, but the economic organization was viewed as decisive by both. Veblen, however, was more aware of the importance of noneconomic factors in guiding man's thinking and action; instead of turning to socialism, the masses could be coopted into the pursuit of "conspicuous consumption," "devout observances," "sportsmanship," and "chauvinism." There is less inevitability in Veblen's evolutionary approach than in Marx's. This reflects Darwin's influence on Veblen. Unlike Marx, he views history as a "scheme of blindly cumulative causation, in which there is no trend, no final term, no consummation." Both philosophers, however, agree that the capitalist regime is a temporary phase. For Veblen the economic pressure which shapes the course of history is the disciplinary effect of changing technology on prevailing social habits; for Marx, the key economic pressure is the effect of changing production conditions on social classes. Veblen was a reporter of the social scene, standing apart from the events he described, while Marx was both a reporter and an active participant, determined to speed up the evolutionary process toward socialism.

ML

From

THE THEORY OF BUSINESS ENTERPRISE

(1904)

The material framework of modern civilization is the industrial system, and the directing force which animates this framework is business enterprise. To a greater extent than any other known phase of culture, modern Christendom takes its complexion from its economic organization. This modern economic organization is the "Capitalistic System" or "Modern Industrial System," so called. Its characteristic features, and at the same time the forces by virtue of which it dominates modern culture, are the machine process and investment for a profit.

The scope and method of modern industry are given by the machine. This may not seem to hold true for all industries, perhaps not for the greater part of industry as rated by the bulk of the output or by the aggregate volume of labor expended. But it holds true to such an extent and in such a pervasive manner that a modern industrial community cannot go on except by the help of the accepted mechanical appliances and processes. The machine industries—those portions of the industrial system in which the machine process is paramount—are in a dominant position; they set the pace for the rest of the industrial system. In this sense the present is the age of the machine process. This dominance of the machine process in industry marks off the present industrial situation from all else of its kind.

In a like sense the present is the age of business enterprise. Not that all industrial activity is carried on by the rule of investment for profits, but an effective majority of the industrial forces are organized on that basis. There are many items of great volume and consequence that do not fall within the immediate scope of these business principles. The housewife's work, e.g., as well as some appreciable portion of the work on farms and in some handicrafts, can scarcely be classed as business enterprise. But those elements in the industrial world that take the initiative and exert a far-reaching coercive guidance in matters of industry go to their work with a view to profits on investment, and are guided by the principles and exigencies of business. The businessman, especially the businessman of wide and authoritative discretion, has become a controlling force in industry, because, through the mechanism of investments and markets, he controls the plants and processes, and these set the pace and determine the direction of movement for the rest. His control in those portions of the field that are not immediately under his hand is, no doubt, somewhat loose and uncer-

From Thorstein Veblen, *The Theory of Business Enterprise.* First published 1904, Agustus M. Kelley, Publishers.

tain; but in the long run his discretion is in great measure decisive even for these outlying portions of the field, for he is the only large self-directing economic factor. . . . [A]s near as it may be said of any human power in modern times, the large businessman controls the exigencies of life under which the community lives. . . .

For a theoretical inquiry into the course of civilized life as it runs in the immediate present, therefore, and as it is running into the proximate future, no single factor in the cultural situation has an importance equal to that of the businessman and his work.

This of course applies with peculiar force to an inquiry into the economic life of a modern community. Insofar as the theorist aims to explain the specifically modern economic phenomena, his line of approach must be from the businessman's standpoint, since it is from that standpoint that the course of these phenomena is directed. . . .

BUSINESS ENTERPRISE

The motive of business is pecuniary gain, the method is essentially purchase and sale. The aim and usual outcome is an accumulation of wealth. Men whose aim is not increase of possessions do not go into business, particularly not on an independent footing.

. . . The aim [of this study is to offer] a theory of such business enterprise in outline sufficiently full to show in what manner business methods and business principles, in conjunction with the mechanical industry, influence the modern cultural situation. . . .

In early modern times, before the regime of the machine industry set in, business enterprise on any appreciable scale commonly took the form of commercial business—some form of merchandising or banking. Shipping was the only considerable line of business which involved an investment in or management of extensive mechanical appliances and processes, comparable with the facts of the modern mechanical industry. And shipping was commonly combined with merchandising. . . . Under these circumstances the work of the businessman was rather to take advantage of the conjunctures offered by the course of the seasons and the fluctuations of demand and supply than to adapt the course of affairs to his own ends. The large businessman was more of a speculative buyer and seller and less of a financiering strategist than he has since become.

Since the advent of the machine age the situation has changed. The methods of business have, of course, not changed fundamentally, whatever may be true of the methods of industry; for they are, as they had been, conditioned by the facts of ownership. But instead of investing in the goods as they pass between producer and consumer, as the merchant does, the businessman now invests in the processes of industry; and instead of staking his values on the dimly foreseen conjunctures of the seasons and the act of God, he turns to the conjunctures arising from the interplay of the industrial processes, which are in great measure under the control of businessmen.

So long as the machine processes were but slightly developed, scattered, relatively isolated, and independent of one another industrially, and so long as they were carried on on a small scale for a relatively narrow market, so long the management of them was conditioned by circumstances in many respects similar to those which conditioned the English domestic industry of the eighteenth century. It was under the conditions of this inchoate phase of the machine age that the earlier generation of economists worked out their theory of the businessman's part in industry. It was then still true, in great measure, that the undertaker was the owner of the industrial equipment, and that he kept an immediate oversight of the mechanical processes as well as of the pecuniary transactions in which his enterprise was engaged; and it was also true, with relatively infrequent exceptions, that an unsophisticated productive efficiency was the prime element of business success. A further feature of that pre-capitalistic business situation is that business, whether handicraft or trade, was customarily managed with a view to earning a livelihood rather than with a view to profits on investment.

In proportion as the machine industry gained ground, and as the modern concatenation of industrial processes and of markets developed, the conjunctures of business grew more varied and of larger scope at the same time that they became more amenable to shrewd manipulation. The pecuniary side of the enterprise came to require more unremitting attention, as the chances for gain or loss through business relations simply, aside from mere industrial efficiency, grew greater in number and magnitude. The same circumstances also provoked a spirit of business enterprise, and brought on a systematic investment for gain. With a fuller development of the modern close-knit and comprehensive industrial system, the point of chief attention for the businessman has shifted from the old-fashioned surveillance and regulation of a given industrial process, with which his livelihood was once bound up, to an alert redistribution of investments from less to more gainful ventures, and to a strategic control of the conjunctures of business through shrewd investments and coalitions with other businessmen.

As shown above, the modern industrial system is a concatenation of processes which has much of the character of a single, comprehensive, balanced mechanical process. A disturbance of the balance at any point means a differential advantage (or disadvantage) to one or more of the owners of the sub-processes between which the disturbance falls; and it may also frequently mean gain or loss to many remoter members in the concatenation of processes, for the balance throughout the sequence is a delicate one, and the transmission of a disturbance often goes far. It may even take on a cumulative character, and may thereby seriously cripple or accelerate branches of industry that are out of direct touch with those members of the concatenation upon which the initial disturbance falls. Such is the case, for instance, in an industrial crisis, when an apparently slight initial disturbance may become the occasion of a widespread derangement. . . .

The keeping of the industrial balance, therefore, and adjusting the several industrial processes to one another's work and needs, is a matter of grave and far-reaching consequence in any modern community. . . . The channel by which disturbances are transmitted from member to member of the comprehensive industrial system is the business relations between the several members of the system. . . . Hard times or prosperity spread through the system by means of business relations, and are in their primary expression phenomena of the business situation simply. It is only secondarily that the disturbances in question show themselves as alterations in the character or magnitude of the mechanical processes involved. Industry is carried on for the sake of business, and not conversely; and the progress and activity of industry are conditioned by the outlook of the market, which means the presumptive chance of business profits. . . . The adjustments of industry take place through the mediation of pecuniary transactions, and these transactions take place at the hands of the businessmen and are carried on by them for business ends, not for industrial ends in the narrower meaning of the phrase.

The economic welfare of the community at large is best served by a facile and uninterrupted interplay of the various processes which make up the industrial system at large; but the pecuniary interests of the businessmen in whose hands lies the discretion in the matter are not necessarily best served by an unbroken maintenance of the industrial balance. Especially is this true as regards those greater businessmen whose interests are very extensive. The pecuniary operations of these latter are of large scope, and their fortunes commonly are not permanently bound up with the smooth working of a given sub-process in the industrial system. Their fortunes are rather related to the larger conjunctures of the industrial system as a whole, the interstitial adjustments, or to conjunctures affecting large ramifications of the system. Nor is it at all uniformly to their interest to enhance the smooth working of the industrial system at large insofar as they are related to it. Gain may come to them from a given disturbance of the system whether the disturbance makes for heightened facility or for widespread hardship, very much as a speculator in grain futures may be either a bull or a bear. To the businessman who aims at a differential gain arising out of interstitial adjustments or disturbances of the industrial system, it is not a material question whether his operations have an immediate furthering or hindering effect upon the system at large. The end is pecuniary gain, the means is disturbance of the industrial system. . . . The point immediately in question is the part which the businessman plays in what are here called the interstitial adjustments of the industrial system; and so far as touches his transactions in this field it is, by and large, a matter of indifference to him whether his traffic affects the system advantageously or disastrously. His gains (or losses) are related to the magnitude of the disturbances that take place, rather than to their bearing upon the welfare of the community.

The outcome of this management of industrial affairs through pecuniary transactions, therefore, has been to dissociate the interests of those men who exercise the discretion from the interests of the community. . . .

In current discussion of business, indeed ever since the relation of businessmen to the industrial system has seriously engaged the attention of economists, the point to which attention has chiefly been directed is the businessman's work as an organizer of comprehensive industrial processes. During the later decades of the nineteenth century, particularly, has much interest centered, as there has been much provocation for its doing, on the formation of large industrial consolidations; and the evident good effects of this work in the way of heightened serviceability and economies of production are pointed to as the chief and characteristic end of this work of reorganization. So obvious are these good results and so well and widely has the matter been expounded, theoretically, that it is not only permissible, but it is a point of conscience, to shorten this tale by passing over these good effects as a matter of common notoriety. But there are other features of the case, less obtrusive and less attractive to the theoreticians, which need more detailed attention than they have commonly received.

The circumstances which condition the work of consolidation in industry and which decide whether a given move in the direction of a closer and wider organization of industrial processes will be practicable and will result in economies of production–these circumstances are of a mechanical nature. They are facts of the comprehensive machine process. The conditions favorable to industrial consolidation on these grounds are not created by the businessmen. They are matters of "the state of the industrial arts," and are the outcome of the work of those men who are engaged in the industrial employments rather than of those who are occupied with business affairs. The inventors, engineers, experts, or whatever name be applied to the comprehensive class that does the intellectual work involved in the modern machine industry, must prepare the way for the man of pecuniary affairs by making possible and putting in evidence the economies and other advantages that will follow from a prospective consolidation.

But it is not enough that the businessman should see a chance to effect economies of production and to heighten the efficiency of industry by a new combination. Conditions favorable to consolidation on these grounds must be visible to him before he can make the decisive business arrangements; but these conditions, taken by themselves, do not move him. The motives of the businessman are pecuniary motives, inducements in the way of pecuniary gain to him or to the business enterprise with which he is identified. The end of his endeavors is, not simply to effect an industrially advantageous consolidation, but to effect it under such circumstances of ownership as will give him control of large business forces or bring him the largest possible gain. The ulterior end sought is an increase of ownership, not industrial serviceability. His aim is to contrive a consolidation in which he will be at an advantage, and to effect it on the terms most favorable to his own interest. . . .

It is notorious, beyond the need of specific citation, that the great business coalitions and industrial combinations which have characterized the situation of the last few years have commonly been the outcome of a long-drawn struggle, in which the industrial ends, as contrasted with business ends, have not been seriously considered, and in which great shrewdness and tenacity have commonly been shown in the staving off of a settlement for years in the hope of more advantageous terms. The like is true as regards further coalitions, further consolidations of industrial processes which have not been effected, but which are known to be feasible and desirable so far as regards the mechanical circumstances of the case. The difficulties in the way are difficulties of ownership, of business interest, not of mechanical feasibility.

. . . [B]usiness interests and maneuvers commonly delay consolidations, combinations, correlations of the several plants and processes, for some appreciable time after such measures have become patently advisable on industrial grounds. In the meantime the negotiators are working at cross purposes and endeavoring to put their rivals in as disadvantageous a light as may be, with the result that there is chronic derangement, duplication, and misdirected growth of the industrial equipment while the strategy is going forward, and expensive maladjustment to be overcome when the negotiations are brought to a close.

Serviceability, industrial advisability, is not the decisive point. The decisive point is business expediency and business pressure. In the normal course of business touching this matter of industrial consolidation, therefore, the captain of industry works against, as well as for, a new and more efficient organization. He inhibits as well as furthers the higher organization of industry. Broadly, it may be said that industrial consolidations and the working arrangements made for the more economical utilization of resources and mechanical contrivances are allowed to go into effect only after they are long overdue.

In current economic theory the businessman is spoken of under the name of "entrepreneur" or "undertaker," and his function is held to be the coordinating of industrial processes with a view to economies of production and heightened serviceability. The soundness of this view need not be questioned. It has a great sentimental value and is useful in many ways. There is also a modicum of truth in it as an account of facts. In common with other men, the businessman is moved by ideals of serviceability and an aspiration to make the way of life easier for his fellows. Like other men, he has something of the instinct of workmanship. No doubt such aspirations move the great businessman less urgently than many others, who are, on that account, less successful in business affairs. Motives of this kind detract from business efficiency, and an undue yielding to them on the part of businessmen is to be deprecated as an infirmity. Still, throughout men's dealings with one another and with the interests of the community there runs a sense of equity, fair dealing, and workmanlike integrity; and in an uncertain degree this bent discountenances gain that is got at an undue cost to others, or without rendering some colorable equivalent. Businessmen are also, in a measure, guided by the ambition to effect a creditable improvement in the industrial processes which their business traffic touches. These sentimental factors in business exercise something of a constraint, varying greatly from one person to another, but not measurable in its aggregate results. The careers of most of the illustrious businessmen show the presence of some salutary constraint of this kind. Not infrequently an excessive sensitiveness of this kind leads to a withdrawal from business, or from certain forms of business which may appeal to a vivid fancy as peculiarly dishonest or peculiarly detrimental to the community.... Probably in many cases the business strategist, infected with this human infirmity, reaches an agreement with his rivals and his neighbors in the industrial system without exacting the last concession that a ruthless business strategy might entitle him to. The result is, probably, a speedier conclusion and a smoother working of the large coalitions than would follow from the unmitigated sway of business principles.

But the sentiment which in this way acts in constraint of business traffic proceeds on such grounds of equity and fair dealing as are afforded by current business ethics; it acts within the range of business principles, not in contravention of them; it acts as a conventional restraint upon pecuniary advantage, not in abrogation of it. This code of business ethics consists, after all, of mitigations of the maxim, *Caveat emptor*. It touches primarily the dealings of man with man, and only less directly and less searchingly inculcates temperance and circumspection as regards the ulterior interests of the community at large. . . .

Great and many are the items of service to be set down to the businessman's account in connection with the organization of the industrial system, but when all is said, it is still to be kept in mind that his work in the correlation of industrial processes is chiefly of a permissive kind. His furtherance of industry is at the second remove, and is chiefly of a negative character. In his capacity as businessman he does not go creatively into the work of perfecting mechanical processes and turning the means at hand to new or larger uses. That is the work of the men who have in hand the devising and oversight of mechanical processes. The men in industry must first create the mechanical possibility of such new and more efficient methods and correlations, before the businessman sees the chance, makes the necessary business arrangements, and gives general directions that the contemplated industrial advance shall go into effect. The period between the time of earliest practicability and the effectual completion of a given consolidation in industry marks the interval by which the businessman retards the advance of industry. Against this are to be offset the cases, comparatively slight and infrequent, where the businessmen in control push the advance of industry into new fields and prompt the men concerned with the mechanics of the case to experiment and exploration in new fields of mechanical process.

When the recital is made, therefore, of how the large consolidations take place at the initiative of the businessmen who are in control, it should be added that the fact of their being in control precludes industrial correlations from taking place except by their advice and consent. The industrial system is organized on business principles and for pecuniary ends. The businessman is at the center, he holds the discretion and he exercises it freely, and his choice falls out now on one side, now on the other. The retardation as well as the advance is to be set down to his account.

As regards the economies in cost of production effected by these consolidations, there is a further characteristic feature to be noted, a feature of some significance for any theory of modern business. In great measure the saving effected is a saving of the costs of business management and of the competitive costs of marketing products and services, rather than a saving in the prime costs of production. The heightened facility and efficiency of the new and larger business combinations primarily affect the expenses of office work and sales, and it is in great part only indirectly that this curtailment and consolidation of business management has an effect upon the methods and aims of industry proper. It touches the pecuniary processes immediately, and the mechanical processes indirectly and in an uncertain degree. . . . [B]usiness management involves waste wherever a greater number of men or transactions are involved than are necessary to the effective direction of the mechanical processes employed. The amount of "business" that has to be transacted per unit of product is much greater where the various related industrial processes are managed in severalty than where several of them are brought under one business management. . . . Business transactions have to do with ownership and changes of ownership. The greater the parcelment in point of ownership, the greater the amount of business work that has to be done in connection with a given output of goods or services, and the slower, less facile, and less accurate, on the whole, is the work. This applies both to the work of bargain and contract, wherein pecuniary initiative and discretion are chiefly exercised, and to the routine work of accounting, and of gathering and applying information and misinformation. . . .

But apart from this remoter and larger guidance of the course of industry, the businessmen also, and more persistently and pervasively, exercise a guidance over the course of industry in detail. The production of goods and services is carried on for gain, and the output of goods is controlled by businessmen with a view to gain. Commonly, in ordinary routine business, the gains come from this output of goods and services. By the sale of the output the businessman in industry "realizes" his gains. To "realize" means to convert salable goods into money values. The sale is the last step in the process and the end of the businessman's endeavor. When he has disposed of the output, and so has converted his holdings of consumable articles into money values, his gains are as nearly secure and definitive as the circumstances of modern life admit. It is in terms of price that he keeps his accounts, and in the same terms he computes his output of products. The vital point of production with him is the vendibility of the output, its convertibility into money values, not its serviceability for the needs of mankind. A modicum of serviceability, for some purpose or other, the output must have if it is to be salable. But it does not follow that the highest serviceability gives the largest gains to the businessman in terms of money, nor does it follow that the output need in all cases have other than a factitious serviceability. There is, on the one hand, such a possibility as overstocking the market with any given line of goods, to the detriment of the businessman concerned, but not necessarily to the immediate disadvantage of the body of consumers. And there are, on the other hand, certain lines of industry, such as many advertising enterprises, the output of which may be highly effective for its purpose but of quite equivocal use to the community. . . .

In the older days, when handicraft was the rule of the industrial system, the personal contact between the producer and his customer was somewhat close and lasting. Under these circumstances the factor of personal esteem and disesteem had a considerable play in controlling the purveyors of goods and services. This factor of personal contact counted in two divergent ways: (1) producers were careful of their reputation for workmanship, even apart from the gains which such a reputation might bring; and (2) a degree of irritation and ill will would arise in many cases, leading to petty trade quarrels and discriminations on other grounds than the gains to be got, at the same time that the detail character of dealings between producer and consumer admitted a degree of petty knavery and huckstering that is no longer practicable in the current large-scale business dealings. Of these two divergent effects resulting from close personal relations between producer and consumer the former seems on the whole to have been of preponderant consequence. Under the system of handicraft and neighborhood industry, the adage that "Honesty is the best policy" seems on the whole to have been accepted and to have been true. This adage has come down from the days before the machine's regime and before modern business enterprise.

Under modern circumstances, where industry is carried on on a large scale, the discretionary head of an industrial enterprise is commonly removed from all personal contact with the body of customers for whom the industrial process under his control purveys goods or services. The mitigating effect which personal contact may have in dealings between man and man is therefore in great measure eliminated. The whole takes on something of an impersonal character. One can with an easier conscience and with less of a sense of meanness take advantage of the necessities of people whom one knows of only as an indiscriminate aggregate of consumers. . . . Under these circumstances the adage cited above loses much of its axiomatic force. Business management has a chance to proceed on a temperate and sagacious calculation of profit and loss, untroubled by sentimental considerations of human kindness or irritation or of honesty.

The broad principle which guides producers and merchants, large and small, in fixing the prices at which they offer their wares and services is what is known in the language of the railroads as "charging what the traffic will bear." Where a given enterprise has a strict monopoly of the supply of a given article or of a given class of services this principle applies in the unqualified form in which it has been understood among those who discuss railway charges. But where the monopoly is less strict, where there are competitors, there the competition that has to be met is one of the factors to be taken account of in determining what the traffic will bear; competition may even become the most serious factor in the case if the enterprise in question has little or none of the character of a monopoly. But it is very doubtful if there are any successful business ventures within the range of the modern industries from which the monopoly element is wholly absent. . . .

Work that is, on the whole, useless or detrimental to the community at large may be as gainful to the businessman and to the workmen whom he employs as work that contributes substantially to the aggregate livelihood. This seems to be peculiarly true of the bolder flights of business enterprise. Insofar as its results are not detrimental to human life at large, such unproductive work directed to securing an income may seem to be an idle matter in which the rest of the community has no substantial interests. Such is not the case. Insofar as the gains of these unproductive occupations are of a substantial character, they come out of the aggregate product of the other occupations in which the various classes of the community engage. The aggregate profits of the business, whatever its character, are drawn from the aggregate output of goods and services; and whatever goes to the maintenance of the profits of those who contribute nothing substantial to the output is, of course, deducted from the income of the others, whose work tells substantially.

There are, therefore, limits to the growth of the industrially parasitic lines of business just spoken of. A disproportionate growth of parasitic industries, such as most advertising and much of the other efforts that go into competitive selling, as well as warlike expenditure and other industries directed to turning out goods for conspicuously wasteful consumption, would lower the effective vitality of the community to such a degree as to jeopardize its chances of advance or even its life. The limits which the circumstances of life impose in this respect are of a selective character, in the last resort. A persistent excess of parasitic and wasteful efforts over productive industry must bring on a decline. But owing to the very high productive efficiency of the modern mechanical industry, the margin available for wasteful occupations and wasteful expenditures is very great. The requirements of the aggregate livelihood are so far short of the possible output of goods by modern methods as to leave a very wide margin for waste and parasitic income. . . .

While it is in the nature of things unavoidable that the management of industry by modern business methods should involve a large misdirection of effort and a very large waste of goods and services, it is also true that the aims and ideals to which this manner of economic life gives effect act forcibly to offset all this incidental futility. These pecuniary aims and ideals have a very great effect, for instance, in making men work hard and unremittingly, so that on this ground alone the business system probably compensates for any wastes involved in its working. . . . It makes up for its wastefulness by the added strain which it throws upon those engaged in the productive work.

BUSINESS PRINCIPLES

The physical basis of modern business traffic is the machine process. . . . The spiritual ground of business enterprise, on the other hand, is given by the institution of ownership. "Business principles" are corollaries under the main proposition of ownership; they are principles of property—pecuniary principles. These principles are of older date than the machine industry, although their full development belongs within the machine era. As the machine process conditions the growth and scope of industry, and as its discipline inculcates habits of thought suitable to the industrial technology, so the exigencies of ownership condition the growth and aims of business, and the discipline of ownership and its management inculcates views and principles (habits of thought) suitable to the work of business traffic.

The discipline of the machine process enforces a standardization of conduct and of knowledge in terms of quantitative precision, and inculcates a habit of apprehending and explaining facts in terms of material cause and effect. It involves a valuation of facts, things, relations, and even personal capacity, in terms of force. Its metaphysics is materialism and its point of view is that of causal sequence. Such a habit of mind conduces to industrial efficiency, and the wide prevalence of such a habit is indispensable to a high degree of industrial efficiency under modern conditions. This habit of mind prevails most widely and with least faltering in those communities that have achieved great things in the machine industry, being both a cause and an effect of the machine process.

Other norms of standardization, more or less alien to this one, and other grounds for the valuation of facts, have prevailed elsewhere, as well as in the earlier phases of the Western culture. Much of this older standardization still stands over, in varying degrees of vigor or decay, in that current scheme of knowledge and conduct that now characterizes the Western culture. Many of these ancient norms of thought which have come down from the discipline of remote and relatively primitive phases of the cultural past are still strong in the affections of men, although most of them have lost greatly in their power of constraint. . . .

These ancient norms differ from the modern norms given by the machine in that they rest on conventional, ultimately sentimental grounds; they are of a putative nature. Such are, e.g., the principles of (primitive) blood relationship, clan solidarity, paternal descent, Levitical cleanness, divine guidance, allegiance, nationality. In their time and under the circumstances which favored their growth these were, all and several, powerful factors in controlling human conduct and shaping the course of events. . . . As time has brought change of circumstances, the facts of life have gradually escaped from the constraint of these ancient principles; so that the dominion which they now hold over the life of civilized men is relatively slight and shifty.

It is among these transmitted institutional habits of thought that the ownership of property belongs. It rests on the like general basis of use and wont. The binding relation of property to its owner is of a conventional, putative character. . . .

In absolute terms the institution of ownership is ancient, no doubt; but it is young compared with blood relationship, the state, or the immortal gods. Especially is it true that its fuller development is relatively late. Not until a comparatively late date in West European history has ownership come to be emancipated from all restrictions of a non-pecuniary character and to stand in a wholly impersonal position, without admixture of personal responsibility or class prerogative. Freedom and inviolability of contract has not until recently been the unbroken rule. Indeed, it has not even yet been accepted without qualification and extended to all items owned. . . . Ownership is not all-prevading and all-dominant, but it prevades and dominates the affairs of civilized peoples more freely and widely than any other single ground of action, and more than it has ever done before. The range and number of relations and duties that are habitually disposed of on a pecuniary footing are greater than in the past, and a pecuniary settlement is final to a degree unknown in the past. The pecuniary norm has invaded the domain of the older institutions, such as blood relationship, citizenship, or the church, so that obligations belonging under the one or the other of these may now be assessed and fulfilled in terms of a money payment, although the notion of a pecuniary liquidation seems to have been wholly remote from the range of ideas—habits of thought—on which these relations and duties were originally based.

BUSINESS IN LAW AND POLITICS

. . . Representative government means, chiefly, representation of business interests. The government commonly works in the interest of the businessmen with a fairly consistent singleness of purpose. And in its solicitude for the businessmen's interests it is borne out by current public sentiment, for there is a naïve, unquestioning persuasion abroad among the body of the people to the effect that, in some occult way, the material interests of the populace coincide with the pecuniary interests of those businessmen who live within the scope of the same set of governmental contrivances. This persuasion is an article of popular metaphysics, in that it rests on an uncritically assumed solidarity of interests, rather than on an insight into the relation of business enterprise to the material welfare of those classes who are not primarily businessmen. This persuasion is particularly secure among the more conservative portion of the community, the businessmen, superior and subordinate, together with the professional classes, as contrasted with those vulgar portions of the community who are tainted with socialistic or anarchistic notions. But since the conservative element comprises the citizens of substance and weight, and indeed the effective majority of law-abiding citizens, it follows that, with the sanction of the great body of the people, even including those who have no pecuniary interests to serve in the matter, constitutional government has, in the main, become a department of the business organization and is guided by the advice of the businessmen. The government has, of course, much else to do besides administering the general affairs of the business community; but in most of its work, even in what is not ostensibly directed to business ends, it is under the surveillance of the business interests. It seldom happens, if at all, that the government of a civilized nation will persist in a course of action detrimental or not ostensibly subservient to the interests of the more conspicuous body of the community's businessmen. The degree in which a government fails to adapt its policy to these business exigencies is the measure of its senility.

The ground of sentiment on which rests the popular approval of a government for business ends may be summed up under two heads: patriotism and property. Both of these terms stand for institutional facts that have come down out of a past which differed substantially from the present situation. The substance of both is of the nature of unreasoning sentiment, in the sense that both are insisted on as a matter of course, as self-legitimating grounds of action which, it is felt, not only give expedient rules of conduct, but admit of no question as to their ulterior consequences or their value for the life-purposes of the community. The former of these fundamental institutional habits of thought (perhaps better, habits of mind) runs back to the discipline of early barbarism, through the feudal days of fealty to the earlier days of clan life and clannish animosity. It has therefore the deep-rooted strength given by an extremely protracted discipline of predation and servitude. Under modern conditions it is to be rated as essentially an institutional survival. . . .

By force of this happy knack of clannish fancy the common man is enabled to feel that he has some sort of metaphysical share in the gains which accrue to the businessmen who are citizens of the same "commonwealth"; so that whatever policy furthers the commercial gains of those businessmen whose domicile is within the national boundaries is felt to be beneficial to all the rest of the population.

The second institutional support of business politics, viz. property, is similarly an outgrowth of the discipline of the past. . . . In the form in which it prevails in the current popular animus, the principle of ownership comes down from the days of handicraft industry and petty trade. . . . As it is of less ancient and less unbroken descent, so it seems also to be a less secure cultural heritage than the sense of patriotic solidarity. It says that the ownership of property is the material foundation of human well-being, and that this natural right of ownership is sacred, after the manner in which individual life, and more especially national life, is sacred. The habits of life and thought inculcated by joint work under the manorial system and by joint rules under the handicraft system have apparently contributed much to the notion of a solidarity of economic interests, having given the notion such a degree of consistency as has enabled it to persist in the face of a visible discrepancy of interests in later, capitalistic times. Under this current, business regime, business gains are the basis of individual wealth. . . . The institutional animus of ownership, as it took shape under the discipline of early modern handicraft, awards the ownership of property to the workman who has produced it. By a dialectical conversion of the terms, this metaphysical dictum is made to fit the circumstances of later competitive business by construing acquisition of property to mean production of wealth; so that a businessman is looked upon as the putative producer of whatever wealth he acquires. By force of this sophistication the acquisition of property by any person is held to be, not only expedient for the owner, but meritorious as an action serving the common good. Failure to bargain shrewdly or to accumulate more goods than one has produced by the work of one's own hands is looked upon with a feeling of annoyance, as a neglect, not only of opportunity, but of duty. . . . [I]t is felt that he best serves the common good who, other things equal, diverts the larger share of the aggregate wealth to his own possession. His acquiring a defensible title to it makes him the putative producer of it. . . .

. . . Modern business is competitive, emulative, and the direction of business enterprise is in the hands of men who are single-minded in their competitive conduct of affairs. They neither are inclined, nor will business competition permit them, to neglect or overlook any expedient that may further their own advantage or hinder the advantage of their rivals. Under the modern situation, as it has taken shape since the industrial revolution, business competition has become international, covering the range of what is called the world market. In this international competition the machinery and policy of the state are in a peculiar degree drawn into the service of the larger business interests; so that, both in commerce and industrial enterprise, the businessmen of one nation are pitted against those of another and swing the forces of the state, legislative, diplomatic, and military, against one another in the strategic game of pecuniary advantage. . . .

. . . It is a favorite maxim of modern politics that trade follows the flag. This is the businessman's valuation of national policy and of the ends of national life. So stated, the maxim probably inverts the sequence of facts, but it is nonetheless a fair expression of the close relation there is between business endeavor and the modern military policies. Diplomacy, if it is to be effective for whatever end, must be backed by a show of force and of a readiness to use it. . . .

Armaments serve trade not only in the making of general terms of purchase and sale between the businessmen of civilized countries, but they are similarly useful in extending and maintaining business enterprise and privileges in the outlying regions of the earth. . . . There is commonly a handsome margin of profit in doing business with these pecuniarily unregenerate populations, particularly when the traffic is adequately backed with force. But, also commonly, these peoples do not enter willingly into lasting business relations with civilized mankind. It is therefore necessary, for the purposes of trade and culture, that they be firmly held up to such civilized rules of conduct as will make trade easy and lucrative. To this end armament is indispensable. . . .

Insofar as it is guided by the exigencies of trade, the objective end of warlike endeavor is the peace and security necessary to an orderly development of business. International business relations, it is well said, make for peace; in the sense, of course, that they enforce the pacification of recalcitrant barbarians and lead to contention between civilized nations for a revision of the peace terms. When a modern government goes to war for trade purposes, it does so with a view to reestablishing peace on terms more lucrative to its businessmen. . . .

. . . One after another, the states that have offered some show of peaceable inclinations have been drawn into the international game of competitive armaments, as they have one after another become ambitious to push the enterprises of their businessmen in the international markets. . . .

. . . War and preoccupation with warlike enterprise breed a warlike animus in the community, as well as a habit of arbitrary, autocratic rule on the part of those in authority and an unquestioning, enthusiastic subservience on the part of the subjects. National animosity and national pride demand more and more of military standing, at the same time that the growing official class needs increasing emoluments and a larger field of employment and display. The cultural effects of the discipline of warfare and armament are much the same whether it is undertaken for dynastic or for business ends: . . . The objective end of protracted warlike endeavor necessarily shifts from business advantage to dynastic ascendancy and courtly honor. Business interests fall to the position of fiscal ways and means, and business traffic becomes subservient to higher ends, with a fair chance of ultimate exhaustion or collapse through the bankruptcy of the state.

. . . The machine process pervades the modern life and dominates it in a mechanical sense. Its dominance is seen in the enforcement of precise mechanical measurements and adjustment and the reduction of all manner of things, purposes and acts, necessities, conveniences, and amenities of life, to standard units. . . . The point of immediate interest here is the further bearing of the machine process upon the growth of culture—the disciplinary effect which this movement for standardization and mechanical equivalence has upon the human material.

This discipline falls more immediately on the workmen engaged in the mechanical industries, and only less immediately on the rest of the community which lives in contact with this sweeping machine process. Wherever the machine process extends, it sets the pace for the workmen, great and small. . . . He now does this work as a factor involved in a mechanical process whose movement controls his motions. It remains true, of course, as it always has been true, that he is the intelligent agent concerned in the process, while the machine, furnace, roadway, or retort are inanimate structures devised by man and subject to the workman's supervision. But the process comprises him and his intelligent motions, and it is by virtue of his necessarily taking an intelligent part in what is going forward that the mechanical process has its chief effect upon him. The process standardizes his supervision and guidance of the machine. . . .

There results a standardization of the workman's intellectual life in terms of mechanical process, which is more unmitigated and precise the more comprehensive and consummate the industrial process in which he plays a part. . . . [T]he intelligence required and inculcated in the machine industry is of a peculiar character. The machine process is a severe and insistent disciplinarian in point of intelligence. It requires close and unremitting thought, but it is thought which runs in standard terms of quantitative precision. Broadly, other intelligence on the part of the workman is useless; it is even worse than useless, for a habit of thinking in other than quantitative terms blurs the workman's quantitative apprehension of the facts with which he has to do.

Insofar as he is a rightly gifted and fully disciplined workman, the final term of his *habitual* thinking is mechanical efficiency, understanding "mechanical" in the sense in which it is used above. But mechanical efficiency is a matter of precisely adjusted cause and effect. What the discipline of the machine industry inculcates, therefore, in the habits of life and of thought of the workman, is regularity of sequence and mechanical precision; and the intellectual outcome is an habitual resort to terms of measurable cause and effect, together with a relative neglect and disparagement of such exercise of the intellectual faculties as does not run on these lines. . . .

The machine process compels a more or less unremitting attention to phenomena of an impersonal character and to sequences and correlations not dependent for their force upon human predilection nor created by habit and custom. The machine throws out anthropomorphic habits of thought. It compels the adaptation of the workman to his work, rather than the adaptation of the work to the workman. The machine technology rests on a knowledge of impersonal, material cause and effect, not on the dexterity, diligence, or personal force of the workman, still less on the habits and propensities of the workman's superiors. Within the range of this machine-guided work, and within the range of modern life so far as it is guided by the machine process, the course of things is given mechanically, impersonally, and the resultant discipline is a discipline in the handling of impersonal facts for mechanical effect. It inculcates thinking in terms of opaque, impersonal cause and effect, to the neglect of those norms of validity that rest on usage and on the conventional standards handed down by usage. Usage counts for little in shaping the processes of work of this kind or in shaping the modes of thought induced by work of this kind.

The machine process gives no insight into questions of good and evil, merit and demerit, except in point of material causation, nor into the foundations or the constraining force of law and order, except such mechanically enforced law and order as may be stated in terms of pressure, temperature, velocity, tensile strength, etc. . . . Its scheme of knowledge and of inference is based on the laws of material causation, not on those of immemorial custom, authenticity, or authoritative enactment. . . .

The discipline exercised by the mechanical occupations, insofar as it is in question here, is a discipline of the habits of thought. It is, therefore, as processes of thought, methods of apperception, and sequences of reasoning, that these occupations are of interest for the present purpose; it is as such that they have whatever cultural value belongs to them. They have such a value, therefore, somewhat in proportion as they tax the mental faculties of those employed; and the largest effects are to be looked for among those industrial classes who are required to comprehend and guide the processes, rather than among those who serve merely as mechanical auxiliaries of the machine process. Not that the latter are exempt from the machine's discipline, but it falls upon them blindly and enforces an uncritical acceptance of opaque results, rather than a theoretical insight into the causal sequences which make up the machine process. The higher degree of training in such matter-of-fact habits of thought is accordingly to be looked for among the higher ranks of skilled mechanics, and perhaps still more decisively among those who stand in an engineering or supervisory relation to the processes. It counts more forcibly and farthest among those who are required to exercise what may be called a mechanical discretion in the guidance of the industrial process, who, as one might say, are required to administer the laws of causal sequence that run through material phenomena, who therefore must learn to think in the terms in which the machine processes work. The metaphysical ground, the assumption, on which such thinking proceeds must be such as will hold good for the sequence of material phenomena; that is to say, it is the metaphysical assumptions of modern material science—the law of cause and effect, cumulative causation, conservation of energy, persistence of quantity, or whatever phrase be chosen to cover the concept. The men occupied with the modern material sciences are, accordingly, for the purpose in hand, in somewhat the same case as the higher ranks of those employed in mechanical industry.

Leaving aside the archaic vocations of war, politics, fashion, and religion, the employments in which men are engaged may be distinguished as pecuniary or business employments on the one hand, and industrial or mechanical employments on the other hand. In earlier times, and indeed until an uncertain point in the nineteenth century, such a distinction between employments would not to any great extent have coincided with a difference between occupations. But gradually, as time has passed and production for a market has come to be the rule in industry, there has supervened a differentiation of occupations, or a division of labor, whereby one class of men have taken over the work of purchase and sale and of husbanding a store of accumulated values. Concomitantly, of course, the rest, who may, for lack of means or of pecuniary aptitude, have been less well fitted for pecuniary pursuits, have been relieved of the cares of business and have with increasing specialization given their attention to the mechanical processes involved in this production for a market. In this way the distinction between pecuniary and industrial activities or employments has come to coincide more and more nearly with a difference between occupations. Not that the specialization has even yet gone so far as to exempt any class from all pecuniary care; for even those whose daily occupation is mechanical work still habitually bargain with their employers for their wages and with others for their supplies. So that none of the active classes in modern life is fully exempt from pecuniary work.

But the need of attention to pecuniary matters is less and less exacting, even in the matter of wages and supplies. The scale of wages, for instance, is, for the body of workmen, and also for what may be called the engineering force, becoming more and more a matter of routine, thereby lessening at least the constancy with which occasions for detail bargaining in this respect recur. . . .

Conversely, as regards the men in the pecuniary occupations, the businessmen. Their exemption from taking thought of mechanical facts and processes is likewise only relative. Even those businessmen whose business is in a peculiar degree remote from the handling of tools or goods, and from the oversight of mechanical processes, as, for example, bankers, lawyers, brokers, and the like, have still, at the best, to take some cognizance of the mechanical apparatus of everyday life. . . . Whereas those businessmen whose business is more immediately concerned with industry commonly have some knowledge and take some thought of the processes of industry; to some appreciable extent they habitually think in mechanical terms. . . . [T]he beginning and end of their more serious thinking is of a pecuniary kind, but it always takes in some general features of the mechanical process along the way. Their exemption from mechanical thinking, from thinking in terms of cause and effect, is, therefore, materially qualified.

But after all qualifications have been made, the fact still is apparent that the everyday life of those classes which are engaged in business differs materially in the respect cited from the life of the classes engaged in industry proper. There is an appreciable and widening difference between the habits of life of the two classes; and this carries with it a widening difference in the discipline to which the two classes are subjected. It induces a difference in the habits of thought and the habitual grounds and methods of reasoning resorted to by each class. There results a difference in the point of view, in the facts dwelt upon, in the methods of argument, in the grounds of validity appealed to; and this difference gains in magnitude and consistency as the differentiation of occupations goes on. So that the two classes come to have an increasing difficulty in understanding one another and appreciating one another's convictions, ideals, capacities, and shortcomings.

The ultimate ground of validity for the thinking of the business classes is the natural-rights ground of property—a conventional, anthropomorphic fact having an institutional validity, rather than a matter-of-fact validity such as can be formulated in terms of material cause and effect; while the classes engaged in the machine industry are habitually occupied with matters of causal sequence, which do not lend themselves to statement in anthropomorphic terms of natural rights and which afford no guidance in questions of institutional right and wrong, or of conventional reason and consequence. Arguments which proceed on material cause and effect cannot be met with arguments from conventional precedent or dialectically sufficient reason, and conversely.

The thinking required by the pecuniary occupations proceeds on grounds of conventionality, whereas that involved in the industrial occupations runs, in the main, on grounds of mechanical sequence or causation, to the neglect of conventionality. The institution (habit of thought) of ownership or property is a conventional fact; and the logic of pecuniary thinking—that is to say, of thinking on matters of ownership—is a working out of the implications of this postulate, this concept of ownership or property. The characteristic habits of thought given by such work are habits of recourse to conventional grounds of finality or validity, to anthropomorphism, to explanations of phenomena in terms of human relation, discretion, authenticity, and choice. The final ground of certainty in inquiries on this natural-rights plane is always a ground of authenticity, of precedent, or accepted decision. The argument is an argument *de jure,* not *de facto,* and the training given lends facility and certainty in the pursuit of *de jure* distinctions and generalizations, rather than in the pursuit or the assimilation of a *de facto* knowledge of impersonal phenomena. The end of such reasoning is the interpretation of new facts in terms of accredited precedents, rather than a revision of the knowledge drawn from past experience in the matter-of-fact light of new phenomena. The endeavor is to make facts conform to law, not to make the law or general rule conform to facts. . . .

The ubiquitous presence of the machine, with its spiritual concomitant—workday ideals and skepticism of what is only conventionally valid—is the unequivocal mark of the Western culture of today as contrasted with the culture of other times and places. It pervades all classes and strata in a varying degree, but on an average in a greater degree than at any time in the past, and most potently in the advanced industrial communities and in the classes immediately in contact with the mechanical occupations. As the comprehensive mechanical organization of the material side of life has gone on, a heightening of this cultural effect throughout the community has also supervened, and with a farther and faster movement in the same direction a farther accentuation of this "modern" complexion of culture is fairly to be looked for, unless some remedy be found. And as the concomitant differentiation and specialization of occupations goes on, a still more unmitigated discipline falls upon ever widening classes of the population, resulting in an ever weakening sense of conviction, allegiance, or piety toward the received institutions. . . .

The conditions of life imposed upon the working population by the machine industry discourage thrift. But after allowance has been made for this almost physical restraint upon the acquisition of property by the working classes, something is apparently left over, to be ascribed to the moral effect of the machine technology. The industrial classes appear to be losing the instinct of individual ownership. The acquisition of property is ceasing to appeal to them as a natural, self-evident source of comfort and strength. The natural right of property no longer means so much to them as it once did.

A like weakening of the natural-rights animus is visible at another point in the current frame of mind of these classes. The growth of trade unionism and of what is called the trade-union spirit is a concomitant of industry organized after the manner of a machine process. . . . Particularly, experience seems to say that it is not feasible to introduce the trade-union spirit or the trade-union rules into any community until the machine industry has had time extensively to standardize the scheme of work and of life for the working classes on mechanical lines. Workmen do not take to full-blown trade-union ideals abruptly on the introduction of those modern business methods which make trade-union action advisable for the working class. A certain interval elapses between the time when business conditions first make trade-union action feasible, as a business proposition, and the time when the body of workmen are ready to act in the spirit of trade unionism and along the lines which the union animus presently accepts as normal for men in the mechanically organized industries. An interval of discipline in the ways of the mechanically standardized industry, more or less protracted and severe, seems necessary to bring such a proportion of the workmen into line as will give a consensus of sentiment and opinion favorable to trade-union action.

The pervading characteristic of the trade-union animus is the denial of the received natural-rights dogmas wherever the mechanical standardization of modern industry traverses the working of these received natural rights. Recent court decisions in America, as well as decisions in analogous cases in England at that earlier period when the British development was at about the same stage of maturity as the current American situation, testify unequivocally that the common run of trade-union action is at variance with the natural-rights foundation of the common law. Trade-unionism denies individual freedom of contract to the workman, as well as free discretion to the employer to carry on his business as may suit his own ends. Many pious phrases have been invented to disguise this iconoclastic trend of trade-union aims and endeavors; but the courts, standing on a secure and familiar natural-rights footing, have commonly made short work of the shifty sophistications which trade-union advocates have offered for their consideration. They have struck at the root of the matter in declaring trade-union regulations inimical to the natural rights of workman and employer alike, in that they hamper individual liberty and act in restraint of trade. The regulations, therefore, violate that system of law and order which rests on natural rights, although they may be enforced by that *de facto* law and order which is embodied in the mechanical standardization of the industrial processes. . . .

When unionism takes an attitude of overt hostility to the natural-rights institutions of property and free contract, it ceases to be unionism simply and passes over into something else, which may be called socialism for want of a better term. Such an extreme iconoclastic position, which would overtly assert the mechanical standardization of industry as against the common-law standardization of business, seems to be the logical outcome to which the trade-union animus tends, and to which some approach has latterly been made by more than one trade-unionist body, but which is, on the whole, yet in the future, if, indeed, it is to be reached at all. . . .

. . . [W]orkmen who make up the trade-union element take the course indicated simply because their selfish interest urges them to this course; that their common necessities and common weakness constrains them to stand together and to act collectively in dealing with their employers; while the fact that their demands have no standing in court constrains them to seek their ends by extra-legal means of coercion. But this objection is little else than another way of saying that the exigencies forced upon the workmen by the mechanically standardized industrial system are extra-legal exigencies—exigencies which do not run in business terms and therefore are not amenable to the natural-rights principles of property and contract that underlie business relations; that they can therefore not be met on common-law ground; and that they therefore compel the workmen to see them from another point of view and seek to dispose of them by an appeal to other principles than those afforded by the common-law standpoint. That is to say, in other words, these exigencies which compel the trade unionists to take thought of their case in other terms than those afforded by existing legal institutions are the means whereby the discipline of the machine industry is enforced and made effective for recasting the habits of thought of the workmen. The harsh discipline of these exigencies of livelihood drives home the new point of view and holds the workmen consistently to it. But that is not all that the mechanical standardization of industry does in the case; it also furnishes the new terms in which the revised scheme of economic life takes form. The revision of the scheme aimed at by trade-union action runs, not in terms of natural liberty, individual property rights, individual discretion, but in terms of standardized livelihood and mechanical necessity; it is formulated, not in terms of business expediency, but in terms of industrial, technological standard units and standard relations. . . .

The point primarily had in view in entering on this characterization of trade unionism was that under the discipline of the mechanically standardized industry certain natural rights, particularly those of property and free contract, are in a degree falling into abeyance among those classes who are most immediately subjected to this discipline. It may be added that other classes also, to an uncertain extent, sympathize with the trade unionists and are affected with a similar (mild and equivocal) distrust of the principles of natural liberty. When distrust of business principles rises to such a pitch as to become intolerant of all pecuniary institutions, and leads to a demand for the abrogation of property rights rather than a limitation of them, it is spoken of as "socialism" or "anarchism." This socialistic disaffection is widespread among the advanced industrial peoples. No other cultural phenomenon is so threatening to the received economic and political structure; none is so unprecedented or so perplexing for practical men of affairs to deal with. The immediate point of danger in the socialistic disaffection is a growing disloyalty to the natural-rights institution of property, but this is backed by a similar failure of regard for other articles of the institutional furniture handed down from the past. The classes affected with socialistic vagaries protest against the existing economic organization, but they are not necessarily averse to a somewhat rigorous economic organization on new lines of their own choosing. They demand an organization on industrial as contrasted with business lines. Their sense of economic solidarity does not seem to be defective, indeed it seems to many of their critics to be unnecessarily pronounced; but it runs on lines of industrial coherence and mechanical constraint, not on lines given by pecuniary conjunctures and conventional principles of economic right and wrong.

There is little agreement among socialists as to a program for the future. Their constructive proposals are ill-defined and inconsistent and almost entirely negative. The negative character of the socialistic propaganda has been made a point of disparagement by its critics, perhaps justly. But their predilection for shifty iconoclasm, as well as the vagueness and inconsistency of their constructive proposals, are in the present connection to be taken as evidence that the attitude of the socialists cannot be expressed in positive terms given by the institutions at present in force. It may also be evidence of the untenability of the socialistic ideals; but the merits of the socialist contentions do not concern the present inquiry. The question here is as to the nature and causes of the socialist disaffection; it does not concern the profounder and more delicate point, as to the validity of the socialist contentions. Current socialism is an animus of dissent from received traditions. The degree and the direction of this dissent varies greatly, but it is, within the socialist scheme of thought, agreed that the institutional forms of the past are unfit for the work of the future. . . .

. . . [T]he machine technology not only trains the workmen into materialistic iconoclasm; it has also a selective effect. Persons endowed with propensities and aptitudes of a materialistic, matter-of-fact kind are drafted into the mechanical employments, and such are also peculiarly available socialistic material. Aptitude for the matter-of-fact work of the machine technology means, in a general way, ineptitude for an uncritical acceptance of institutional truths. It is probable, therefore, that the apparent facility with which the mechanical employments (and the material sciences) induce a socialistic or iconoclastic bent is to be set down in part to the fact that the human material in these employments is picked material, peculiarly amenable to this discipline. There is a sifting of the working classes, whereby the socialistic and mechanically capable are roughly segregated out from the rest and subjected to the iconoclastic discipline of the mechanical employments and matter-of-fact thinking; while the residue, which is on the whole made up of the persons that are relatively least capable of revolutionary socialism, is at the same time less exposed to the discipline that might fit them for the socialistic movement. This sifting is, of course, a rough one, and leaves many exceptions both ways.

In the light of this consideration, then, it is to be noted: (1) that the dominance of the machine process in modern industry is not so potent a factor for the inculcation of socialistic notions—it does not so irresistibly shape men's habit of mind in the socialistic sense—as the first survey of the facts would suggest; and (2) that the differentiation of occupations involved in modern industrial methods selectively bunches the socialistic elements together, and so heightens their sense of class solidarity and acts to accentuate their bias, gives consistency to their ideals, and induces that boldness of conviction and action which is to be had only in a compact body of men.

But in either case, whether the visible outcome is chiefly due to their selective or to their disciplinary effect, the bearing of the industrial occupations upon the growth of socialism seems equally close and undeniable. The two modes of influence seem to converge to the outcome indicated above, and for the purpose of the present inquiry a detailed tracing out of the two strands of sequence in the case neither can nor need be undertaken.

With such generality as commonly holds in statements of this kind, it may be said that the modern socialistic disaffection is loosely bound up with the machine industry—spreading where this industry spreads and flourishing where this industry gives the dominant note of life. The correlation between the two phenomena is of such a kind as to leave no doubt that they are causally connected; which means either that the machine industry, directly or indirectly, gives rise to socialism, or that the two are expressions of the same complex of causes. The former statement probably expresses the truth of the case in great part, but the latter need not therefore be false. Wherever and insofar as the increase and diffusion of knowledge has made the machine process and the mechanical technology the tone-giving factor in men's scheme of thought, there modern socialistic iconoclasm follows by easy consequence. . . .

In the nature of the case the cultural growth dominated by the machine industry is of a skeptical, matter-of-fact complexion, materialistic, unmoral, unpatriotic, undevout. The growth of habits of thought, in the industrial regions and centers particularly, runs in this direction; but hitherto there has enough of the ancient norms of Western Christendom remained intact to make a very respectable protest against that deterioration of the cultural tissues which the ferment of the machine industry unremittingly pushes on. The machine discipline, however, touches wider and wider circles of the population, and touches them in an increasingly intimate and coercive manner. In the nature of the case, therefore, the resistance opposed to this cultural trend given by the machine discipline on grounds of received conventions weakens with the passage of time. The spread of materialistic, matter-of-fact preconceptions takes place at a cumulatively accelerating rate, except insofar as some other cultural factor, alien to the machine discipline, comes in to inhibit its spread and keep its disintegrating influence within bounds.

THE NATURAL DECAY OF BUSINESS ENTERPRISE

Broadly, the machine discipline acts to disintegrate the institutional heritage, of all degrees of antiquity and authenticity—whether it be the institutions that embody the principles of natural liberty or those that comprise the residue of more archaic principles of conduct still current in civilized life. It thereby cuts away that ground of law and order on which business enterprise is founded. The further cultural bearing of this disintegration of the received order is no doubt sufficiently serious and far-reaching, but it does not directly concern the present inquiry. It comes in question here only insofar as such a deterioration of the general cultural tissues involves a setback to the continued vigor of business enterprise. But the future of business enterprise is bound up with the future of civilization, since the cultural scheme is, after all, a single one, comprising many interlocking elements, no one of which can be greatly disturbed without disturbing the working of all the rest.

In its bearing on the question in hand, the "social problem" at large presents this singular situation. The growth of business enterprise rests on the machine technology as its material foundation. The machine industry is indispensable to it; it cannot get along without the machine process. But the discipline of the machine process cuts away the spiritual, institutional foundations of business enterprise; the machine industry is incompatible with its continued growth; it cannot, in the long run, get along with the machine process. In their struggle against the cultural effects of the machine process, therefore, business principles cannot win in the long run; since an effectual mutilation or inhibition of the machine system would gradually push business enterprise to the wall; whereas with a free growth of the machine system business principles would presently fall into abeyance.

The institutional basis of business enterprise—the system of natural rights—appears to be a peculiarly unstable affair. There is no way of retaining it under changing circumstances, and there is no way of returning to it after circumstances have changed. It is a hybrid growth, a blend of personal freedom and equality on the one hand and of prescriptive rights on the other hand. The institutions and points of law under the natural-rights scheme appear to be of an essentially provisional character. There is relatively great flexibility and possibility of growth and change; natural rights are singularly insecure under any change of circumstances. The maxim is well approved that eternal vigilance is the price of (natural) liberty. When, as now, this system is endangered by socialistic or anarchistic disaffection there is no recourse that will carry the institutional apparatus back to a secure natural-rights basis. The system of natural liberty was the product of a peaceful regime of handicraft and petty trade; but continued peace and industry presently carried the cultural growth beyond the phase of natural rights by giving rise to the machine process and the large business; and these are breaking down the structure of natural rights by making these rights nugatory on the one hand and by cutting away the spiritual foundations of them on the other hand. Natural rights being a by-product of peaceful industry, they cannot be reinstated by a recourse to warlike habits and a coercive government, since warlike habits and coercion are alien to the natural-rights spirit. Nor can they be reinstated by a recourse to settled peace and freedom, since an era of settled peace and freedom would push on the dominance of the machine process and the large business, which break down the system of natural liberty.

When the question is cast up as to what will come of this conflict of institutional forces—called the Social Problem—it is commonly made a question of remedies: What can be done to save civilized mankind from the vulgarization and disintegration wrought by the machine industry?

Now, business enterprise and the machine process are the two prime movers in modern culture; and the only recourse that holds a promise of being effective, therefore, is a recourse to the workings of business traffic. And this is a question, not of what is conceivably, ideally, idyllically possible for the business community to do if they will take thought and act advisedly and concertedly toward a chosen cultural outcome, but of what is the probable cultural outcome to be achieved through business traffic carried on for business ends, not for cultural ends. It is a question not of what ought to be done, but of what is to take place. . . .

Nothing can serve as a corrective of the cultural trend given by the machine discipline except what can be put in the form of a business proposition. . . . [D]iscretion rests with the businessmen, not with the moralists, and the businessmen's discretion is bounded by the exigencies of business enterprise. Even the businessmen cannot allow themselves to play fast and loose with business principles in response to a call from humanitarian motives. The question, therefore, remains, on the whole, a question of what the businessmen may be expected to do for cultural growth on the motive of profits.

Something they are doing, as others are, from motives of benevolence, with a well-advised endeavor to maintain the cultural gains of the past and to make the way of life smoother for mankind in the future. But the more secure and substantial results to be looked for in this direction are those that follow incidentally, as by-products of business enterprise, because these are not dependent on the vagaries of personal preference, tastes, and prejudices, but rest on a broad institutional basis.

The effects of business enterprise upon the habits and temper of the people, and so upon institutional growth, are chiefly of the nature of sequelae. . . . [T]he discipline of business employments is of a conservative nature, tending to sustain the conventions that rest on natural-rights dogma, because these employments train the men engaged in them to think in terms of natural rights. . . . [I]n its severer, more unmitigated form, this discipline in pecuniary habits of thought falls on a gradually lessening proportion of the population. . . . The number of men in business pursuits, in proportion to the population, is . . . apparently not decreasing; but within the business employments a larger proportion are occupied with office routine, and so are withdrawn from the more effectual training given by business management proper. . . .

This business discipline is somewhat closely limited both in scope and range. (1) It acts to conserve, or to rehabilitate, a certain restricted line of institutional habits of thought, viz. those preconceptions of natural rights which have to do with property. What it conserves, therefore, is the bourgeois virtues of solvency, thrift, and dissimulation. The nobler and more spectacular aristocratic virtues, with their correlative institutional furniture, are not in any sensible degree fortified by the habits of business life. Business life does not further the growth of manners and breeding, pride of caste, punctilios of "honor," or even religious fervor. (2) The salutary discipline of business life touches the bulk of the population, the working classes, in a progressively less intimate and less exacting manner. It can, therefore, not serve to correct or even greatly to mitigate the matter-of-fact bias given these classes by the discipline of the machine process.

As a direct disciplinary factor the machine process holds over the business employments, in that it touches larger classes of the community and inculcates its characteristic habits of thought more unremittingly. And any return to more archaic methods of industry, such as is sometimes advocated on artistic grounds, seems hopeless, since business interests do not countenance a discontinuance of machine methods. The machine methods that are corrupting the hearts and manners of the workmen are profitable to the businessmen, and that fact seems to be decisive on the point. A direct, advised return to handicraft, or any similar discontinuance of the machine industry, is out of the question; although something in the way of a partial return to more primitive methods of industry need not be impracticable as a remote and indirect consequence of the working of business enterprise. . . .

The indirect or incidental cultural bearing of business principles and business practice is wide-reaching and forceful. Business principles . . . have permeated the educational system, thoroughly and intimately. Their presence, as an element of common sense, in the counsels of the "educators" shows itself in a naïve insistence on the "practical" whenever the scheme of instruction is under advisement. "Practical" means useful for private gain . . . ; which results in a progressive, though not wholly consistent, narrowing of instruction to such learning as is designed to give a ready application of results rather than a systematic organization of knowledge. The primary test is usefulness for getting an income. . . .

The largest and most promising factor of cultural discipline—most promising as a corrective of iconoclastic vagaries—over which business principles rule is national politics. The purposes and the material effects of business politics have already been spoken of above, but in the present connection their incidental, disciplinary effects are no less important. Business interests urge an aggressive national policy and businessmen direct it. Such a policy is warlike as well as patriotic. The direct cultural value of a warlike business policy is unequivocal. It makes for a conservative animus on the part of the populace. During wartime, and within the military organization at all times, under martial law, civil rights are in abeyance; and the more warfare and armament the more abeyance. Military training is a training in ceremonial precedence, arbitrary command, and unquestioning obedience. A military organization is essentially a servile organization. Insubordination is the deadly sin. The more consistent and the more comprehensive this military training, the more effectually will the members of the community be trained into habits of subordination and away from that growing propensity to make light of personal authority that is the chief infirmity of democracy. This applies first and most decidedly, of course, to the soldiery, but it applies only in a less degree to the rest of the population. They learn to think in warlike terms of rank, authority, and subordination, and so grow progressively more patient of encroachments upon their civil rights. . . .

The modern warlike policies are entered upon for the sake of peace, with a view to the orderly pursuit of business. In their initial motive they differ from the warlike dynastic politics of the sixteenth, seventeenth, and eighteenth centuries. But the disciplinary effects of warlike pursuits and of warlike preoccupations are much the same whatever may be their initial motive or ulterior aim. The end sought in the one case was warlike mastery and high repute in the matter of ceremonial precedence; in the other, the modern case, it is pecuniary mastery and high repute in the matter of commercial solvency. But in both cases alike the pomp and circumstance of war and armaments, and the sensational appeals to patriotic pride and animosity made by victories, defeats, or comparisons of military and naval strength, act to rehabilitate lost ideals and weakened convictions of the chauvinistic or dynastic order. At the same stroke they direct the popular interest to other, nobler, institutionally less hazardous matters than the unequal distribution of wealth or of creature comforts. Warlike and patriotic preoccupations fortify the barbarian virtues of subordination and prescriptive authority. Habituation to a warlike, predatory scheme of life is the strongest disciplinary factor that can be brought to counteract the vulgarization of modern life wrought by peaceful industry and the machine process, and to rehabilitate the decaying sense of status and differential dignity. Warfare, with the stress on subordination and mastery and the insistence on gradations of dignity and honor incident to a militant organization, has always proved an effective school in barbarian methods of thought.

In this direction, evidently, lies the hope of a corrective for "social unrest" and similar disorders of civilized life. There can, indeed, be no serious question but that a consistent return to the ancient virtues of allegiance, piety, servility, graded dignity, class prerogative, and prescriptive authority would greatly conduce to popular content and to the facile management of affairs. Such is the promise held out by a strenuous national policy.

The reversional trend given by warlike experience and warlike preoccupations, it is plain, does not set backward to the regime of natural liberty. Modern business principles and the modern scheme of civil rights and constitutional government rest on natural-rights ground. But the system of natural rights is a halfway house. The warlike culture takes back to a more archaic situation that preceded the scheme of natural rights, viz. the system of absolute government, dynastic politics, devolution of rights and honors, ecclesiastical authority, and popular submission and squalor. It makes not for a reinstatement of the Natural Rights of Man but for a reversion to the Grace of God.

The barbarian virtues of fealty and patriotism run on national or dynastic exploit and aggrandizement, and these archaic virtues are not dead. In those modern communities whose hearts beat with the pulsations of the world market they find expression in an enthusiasm for the commercial aggrandizement of the nation's businessmen. But when once the policy of warlike enterprise has been entered upon for business ends, these loyal affections gradually shift from the business interests to the warlike and dynastic interests, as witness the history of imperialism in Germany and England. The eventual outcome should be a rehabilitation of the ancient patriotic animosity and dynastic loyalty, to the relative neglect of business interests. This may easily be carried so far as to sacrifice the profits of the businessmen to the exigencies of the higher politics.

The disciplinary effect of war and armaments and imperialist politics is complicated with a selective effect. War not only affords a salutary training, but it also acts to eliminate certain elements of the population. . . . But in the more advanced industrial communities, of which the English and American are typical, the service is a volunteer service; which means that those who go to the wars seek this employment by their own choice. That is to say, the human material so drawn off is automatically selected on the basis of a peculiar spiritual fitness for this predatory employment; they are, on the whole, of a more malevolent and vagabond temper, have more of the ancient barbarian animus, than those who are left at home to carry on the work of the home community and propagate the home population. And since the troops and ships are officered by the younger sons of the conservative leisure class and by the buccaneering scions of the class of professional politicians, a natural selection of the same character takes effect also as regards the officers. There results a gradual selective elimination of that old-fashioned element of the population that is by temperament best suited for the old-fashioned institutional system of status and servile organization.

This selective elimination of conservative elements would in the long run leave each succeeding generation of the community less predatory and less emulative in temper, less well endowed for carrying on its life under the servile institutions proper to a militant regime. But, for the present and the nearer future, there can be little doubt but that this selective shaping of the community's animus is greatly outweighed by the contrary trend given by the discipline of warlike preoccupations. What helps to keep the balance in favor of the reversional trend is the cultural leaven carried back into the home community by the veterans. These presumptive past masters in the archaic virtues keep themselves well in the public eye and serve as exemplars to the impressionable members of the community, particularly to the less mature.

The net outcome of the latter-day return to warlike enterprise is, no doubt, securely to be rated as fostering a reversion to national ideals of servile status and to institutions of a despotic character. On the whole and for the present, it makes for conservatism, ultimately for reversion.

The quest of profits leads to a predatory national policy. The resulting large fortunes call for a massive government apparatus to secure the accumulations, on the one hand, and for large and conspicuous opportunities to spend the resulting income, on the other hand; which means a militant, coercive home administration and something in the way of an imperial court life—a dynastic fountain of honor and a courtly bureau of ceremonial amenities. Such an ideal is not simply a moralist's daydream; it is a sound business proposition, in that it lies on the line of policy along which the business interests are moving in their own behalf. If national (that is to say dynastic) ambitions and warlike aims, achievements, spectacles, and discipline be given a large place in the community's life, together with the concomitant coercive police surveillance, then there is a fair hope that the disintegrating trend of the machine discipline may be corrected. The regime of status, fealty, prerogative, and arbitrary command would guide the institutional growth back into the archaic conventional ways and give the cultural structure something of that secure dignity and stability which it had before the times, not only of socialistic vapors, but of natural rights as well. Then, too, the rest of the spiritual furniture of the ancient regime shall presumably be reinstated; materialistic skepticism may yield the ground to a romantic philosophy, and the populace and the scientists alike may regain something of that devoutness and faith in preternatural agencies which they have recently been losing. As the discipline of prowess again comes to its own, conviction and contentment with whatever is authentic may return to distracted Christendom, and may once more give something of a sacramental serenity to men's outlook on the present and the future.

But authenticity and sacramental dignity belong neither with the machine technology, nor with modern science, nor with business traffic. Insofar as the aggressive politics and the aristocratic ideals currently furthered by the business community are worked out freely, their logical outcome is an abatement of those cultural features that distinguish modern times from what went before, including a decline of business enterprise itself.

How imminent such a consummation is to be accounted is a question of how far the unbusinesslike and unscientific discipline brought in by aggressive politics may be expected to prevail over the discipline of the machine industry. It is difficult to believe that the machine technology and the pursuit of the material sciences will be definitively superseded, for the reason, among others, that any community which loses these elements of its culture thereby loses that brute material force that gives it strength against its rivals. And it is equally difficult to imagine how any one of the communities of Christendom can avoid entering the funnel of business and dynastic politics, and so running through the process whereby the materialistic animus is eliminated. Which of the two antagonistic factors may prove the stronger in the long run is something of a blind guess; but the calculable future seems to belong to the one or the other. It seems possible to say this much, that the full dominion of business enterprise is necessarily a transitory dominion. It stands to lose in the end whether the one or the other of the two divergent cultural tendencies wins, because it is incompatible with the ascendancy of either.

PAUL BARAN

Former professor at Stanford University.
(Died in 1964.)

PAUL SWEEZY

Editor of the independent socialist magazine Monthly Review.

Paul Sweezy is the most prominent modern American Marxist economist. His collaborator in the following selection, the late Paul Baran, was one of the few avowed Marxists in academic circles. Their book *Monopoly Capital* is without a doubt the most important addition to Marxist economic thought in the last generation. It attempts to remedy an important deficiency in Marx's economic writings; while Marx foreshadowed important aspects of the transition from competitive capitalism to monopoly capitalism, he did not develop a full-fledged theory of monopoly capitalism. Although their analysis has a general Marxist character (the class struggle is the underlying theme), Baran and Sweezy make several important modifications of Marxist doctrine.

To begin with, they conclude that the center of revolution has shifted from developed to undeveloped countries and that the key revolutionary agents are the peasantry and a thin stratum of workers in the latter, rather than the industrial working class in the former. The material basis for the loss of revolutionary élan among the advanced industrial labor force, according to Baran and Sweezy, is the trickling down of the economic benefits of colonialism and imperialism to the white working class in the Western capitalist countries.

Baran and Sweezy also modify Marx's doctrine that an important factor causing a secular decline of capitalism was a tendency toward a falling profit rate. They present an alternative formulation: The secular tendency for economic surplus (they discard Marx's term "surplus value") to rise is rooted in the cost and pricing policies of a regime increasingly dominated by monopoly capital. Economic surplus refers to "the difference between total social output and the socially necessary costs of producing it." This surplus has to be absorbed in order to maintain economic stability. The methods employed in our "irrational system," according to Baran and Sweezy, are the capitalists' consumption and investment, the sales effort, civilian government spending, and, increasingly, militarism and imperialism. The latter two forms are seen as necessary rather than merely possible features of monopoly capitalism.

The authors predict increasing military intervention by our corporate-dominated society to stem the world-wide tide of revolutionary protest. It is worth noting that many people view the method, and perhaps the purpose, of the Russian noncapitalist society's intervention in Czechoslovakia as strikingly similar to the American capitalist society's intervention in Vietnam. It is not unreasonable to suppose that there are powerful economic and/or political groups in both societies that stand to gain through a militaristic stance and attempt to develop governmental policies to carry out their own interests. It is also becoming increasingly clear that the relationship between the United States and Russia is not as clashing as Baran and Sweezy viewed it when they wrote *Monopoly Capital.* In fact the "bourgeoisification" of Russia (which involves containing rather than unleashing world revolutionary forces) may indirectly help maintain the stability of American capitalism by providing an important outlet for surplus American capital. In the terms of Baran-Sweezy's method of analysis, such investment aids the absorption of output, thus supporting a higher level of output.

Baran and Sweezy assign the supersize corporation to the same commanding post as do Galbraith, Heilbroner, and Schumpeter, although Baran and Sweezy are considerably less sympathetic to this institution than are their liberal colleagues. A comparison is revealing: Baran and Sweezy reject the liberal argument that the modern corporation is less profit-oriented since corporate management has become increasingly socialized. They state that, "The big corporation, if not more profit-oriented than the individual entrepreneur, is at any rate better equipped to follow a policy of profit maximization. . . . The economy of large corporations is more, not less, dominated by the logic of profit-making than the economy of small entrepreneurs ever was." Many liberals, particularly Galbraith, stress the separation of ownership and control in the modern corporation as well as the difference in interests between owners and managers. Baran and Sweezy claim that this dichotomy is only valid on a technical level. "Because of the strategic positions they [the managers] occupy, they function as the protectors and spokesmen for all large-scale property. Far from being a separate class, they constitute in reality the leading echelon of the property-owning class." Another important point of divergence can be observed in the relationship of corporate planning to economic stability. Galbraith suggests that technology necessitates the superseding of the market place and the institutionalization of economic planning by the large-scale corporations, aided by governmental policies that closely reflect the needs of these corporations. While Baran and Sweezy would very willingly agree that a tightly-knit bond unites the government and the leading corporations, their adherence to the Marxist position is seen in their statement, "The function of the State is to serve the interests of monopoly capital." They would not agree that capitalism has been made more stable by corporate economic planning. They conclude that although the individual large-scale enterprise (particularly the conglomerate) may have become more stable than smaller business units, the system as a whole remains vulnerable, unstable, and dependent on a war economy: "Except in war and periods of war-related prosperity, stagnation is now the normal state of the United States economy." This dismal picture of an "intolerable social order" which progressively dehumanizes man is presented in sharp contrast to a growing world revolutionary movement aimed at overthrowing it and establishing a humane, planned society. Whether this vision of the limited potential of a capitalist order and the limitless potential of a post-capitalist order is a correct projection remains to be seen.

The socialist critique of Baran and Sweezy stands in marked contrast to that of traditional economic theorists. The great weakness of the latter is their inability or unwillingness to probe to the heart of the system. As James Tobin, a leading liberal economist (and former advisor to John F. Kennedy), admitted:

> Most contemporary economists feel ill at ease with respect to big topics—national economic organization, interpretation of economic history, relations of economic and political power, origins and functions of economic institutions. The terrain is unsuitable for our tools. We find it hard to frame meaningful questions, much less to answer them.

More often than not, orthodox economists perform highly sophisticated operations for dealing with problems of second-order importance.

The crucial contribution of contemporary Marxists, particularly skilled and subtle thinkers like Baran and Sweezy, has been to redirect the main line of inquiry to the broad, highly relevant question of the continually changing relationship between the economic and political structures of capitalism. To the extent that they succeed, not only will the scientific character of the social sciences be improved, but their relevance to the real world will be immeasurably heightened.

M L

From

MONOPOLY CAPITAL

(1966)

THE GIANT CORPORATION

One

Scientific understanding proceeds by way of constructing and analyzing "models" of the segments or aspects of reality under study. The purpose of these models is not to give a mirror image of reality, not to include all its elements in their exact sizes and proportions, but rather to single out and make available for intensive investigation those elements which are decisive. We abstract from nonessentials, we blot out the unimportant to get an unobstructed view of the important, we magnify in order to improve the range and accuracy of our observation. A model is, and must be, unrealistic in the sense in which the word is most commonly used. Nevertheless, and in a sense paradoxically, if it is a good model it provides the key to understanding reality.

There are no rules for model building, and, as the literature of economics attests, it is much easier to build a bad one than a good one—a bad model being one which abstracts from essentials and therefore leads to neither insight nor understanding.[1] Nor are there any simple *a priori* tests by which a model can be judged. The proof of the pudding is in the eating. We can only start with certain hypotheses and ideas; we can use them to separate the unimportant from the important; out of the residue of the important we can shape what look like the parts and elements of a system; we can assemble the parts and elements, refining and polishing as we proceed. When we finally get our model, there is one test to which we must subject it: does it help to make sense of the real world? Or, to put the matter in another way, does it help us to see connections to which we were previously blind, to relate effects to causes, to replace the arbitrary and the accidental by the regular and the necessary? In a word, does it help us to understand the world and act in it intelligently and effectively?

These are the general ideas and aims by which we have been guided in constructing a model of the monopoly capitalist economy. It is intended to put at the center of the stage and play the spotlight on those features which, despite all diversity and underneath whatever overlay of detail, make the system what it is. And in order to accomplish this, we start . . . with an analysis of the typical unit of Big Business, the modern giant corporation.

Once again: we are not interested in realism of a photographic kind. There undoubtedly are corporations which correspond closely to the "ideal type"—to use Max Weber's expression—with which we shall be concerned, but the analysis would lose none of its relevance even if there were not. The point is that the decisive units of the economy are unmistakably moving toward a definite, recognizable pattern, and this pattern itself is much more important than any of the concrete approximations to it. A model of which the major component parts are corporations of the ideal type will display with sharpness and clarity what may appear in everyday economic life in a disguised form, difficult to recognize and easy to misinterpret.

Two

The corporate paradigm on which we wish to focus attention has a number of characteristic features, of which we may single out the following:

1. Control rests in the hands of management, that is to say, the board of directors plus the chief executive officers. Outside interests are often (but not always) represented on the board to facilitate the harmonization of the interests and policies of the corporation with those of customers, suppliers, bankers, etc.; but real power is held by the insiders, those who devote full time to the corporation and whose interests and careers are tied to its fortunes.
2. Management is a self-perpetuating group. Responsibility to the body of stockholders is for all practical purposes a dead letter. Each generation of managers recruits its own successors and trains, grooms, and promotes them according to its own standards and values. The corporate career recognizes two characteristic forms of advance: rising from lower to higher positions within a given company, and moving from a smaller company to a larger one. The acme of success is the presidency or board chairmanship of one of the biggest corporations.
3. Each corporation aims at and normally achieves financial independence through the internal generation of funds which remain at the disposal

of management. The corporation may still, as a matter of policy, borrow from or through financial institutions, but it is not normally forced to do so and hence is able to avoid the kind of subjection to financial control which was so common in the world of Big Business fifty years ago.

Before we investigate the behavior of giant corporations of this type, a few words of explanation and clarification may be useful.

In the first place, there is no implication in our description of the corporate paradigm that great wealth, or family connections, or large personal or family stockholdings are unimportant in the recruiting and promotion of management personnel–that, for example, the chances of a David Rockefeller's getting a job at the Chase Manhattan Bank and rising to the top position are the same as those of anyone else with similar personal and intellectual attributes. On the contrary, wealth and connections are of the utmost importance, and it may indeed be taken for granted that they are normally decisive. What we are implying is something quite different: that stock ownership, wealth, connections, etc., do not as a rule enable a man to control or exercise great influence on a giant corporation from the outside. They are rather tickets of admission to the inside, where real corporate power is wielded. Mills put the essential point in a nutshell:

> Not great fortunes, but great corporations are the important units of wealth, to which individuals of property are variously attached. The corporation is the source of, and the basis of the continued power and privilege of wealth. All the men and the families of great wealth are now identified with large corporations in which their property is seated.[2]

What needs to be emphasized is that the location of power inside rather than outside the typical giant corporation renders obsolete the conception of the "interest group" as a fundamental unit in the structure of capitalist society. In traditional usage, an interest group is a number of corporations under common control, the locus of power being normally an investment or commercial bank or a great family fortune.[3] Thus a Morgan company was one under the control of the investment banking firm of J. P. Morgan and Company, a Rockefeller company one under the control of the Rockefeller family, and so on. The members of an interest group would naturally coordinate their policies; and in the case of conflicts, the interests of the controlling power (or of the whole group as interpreted by the controlling power) would prevail.

A whole series of developments have loosened or broken the ties that formerly bound the great interest groups together. The power of the investment banker was based on the urgent need of the early corporate giants, at the time of foundation and in the first stages of growth, for outside financing. Later this need declined in importance or disappeared altogether as the giants, reaping a rich

1. As Duesenberry rightly says: "Knowing how to simplify one's description of reality without neglecting anything essential is the most important part of the economist's art." James S. Duesenberry, *Business Cycles and Economic Growth,* New York, 1958, pp. 14–15.

2. C. Wright Mills, *The Power Elite,* New York, 1956, p. 116.

3. An analysis of interest groups in the American economy as of the mid-1930s will be found in Appendix 13 to Part 1 of the National Resources Committee's well-known report *The Structure of the American Economy,* Washington, 1939 (reprinted in Paul M. Sweezy, *The Present as History,* New York, 1953, Chapter 12).

harvest of monopoly profits, found themselves increasingly able to take care of their financial needs from internally generated funds. At the same time, the domineering founders of family fortunes were dying off, leaving their stockholdings to numerous heirs, foundations, charities, trust funds, and the like, so that the ownership unit which once exercised absolute control over many enterprises became increasingly amorphous and leaderless. Thus the larger corporations gradually won more and more independence from both bankers and dominant stockholders, and their policies accordingly were geared to an ever greater extent each to its own interests rather than being subordinated to the interests of a group.

We are not of course maintaining that interest groups have disappeared or are no longer of any importance in the United States economy. We do hold that they are of rapidly diminishing importance and that an appropriate model of the economy no longer needs to take account of them. . . .

Three

What pattern of behavior can we expect from huge, management-controlled, financially independent corporations?

Formal economic theory has largely ignored this question, continuing to operate with the assumption of the profit-maximizing individual entrepreneur who has occupied the central role in theories of the capitalist system since well before the time of Adam Smith. Retaining this assumption amounts in effect to making another: that in all respects that matter to the functioning of the system the corporation acts like an individual entrepreneur.

If one stops to think about it, this seems unlikely on the face of it. Furthermore, while economic theorists have largely ignored the corporation, other social scientists have devoted much time and energy to its study. So far as we know, none of them has ever supported the proposition that the modern corporation is merely an enlarged version of the classical entrepreneur. On the other hand, there is a voluminous literature dating back to the turn of the century and reaching its culmination in the famous work of Berle and Means which argues most emphatically that the modern corporation represents a qualitative break with the older form of individual enterprise and that radically different types of behavior are to be expected from it. According to Berle and Means:

> It is conceivable—indeed it seems almost inevitable if the corporate system is to survive—that the "control" of the great corporations should develop into a purely neutral technocracy, balancing a variety of claims by various groups in the community and assigning to each a portion of the income stream on the basis of public policy rather than private cupidity.[4]

What Berle and Means described as "conceivable" a quarter of a century ago is taken for granted as an accomplished fact by many present-day observers of the business scene. Thus Carl Kaysen, in a paper delivered at the 1956 annual meeting of the American Economic Association, speaks of "the wide-ranging scope of responsibility assumed by management" as one of the "characteristic features of behavior" of the modern corporation, and proceeds as follows:

> No longer the agent of proprietorship seeking to maximize return on investment, management sees itself as responsible to stockholders, employees, customers, the general public, and, perhaps most important, the firm itself as an institution. . . . From one point of view, this behavior can be termed responsible: there is

no display of greed or graspingness; there is no attempt to push off onto workers or the community at large part of the social costs of the enterprise. The modern corporation is a soulful corporation.[5]

According to this view, which is certainly very widespread nowadays, the maximization of profits has ceased to be the guiding principle of business enterprise. Corporate managements, being self-appointed and responsible to no outside group, are free to choose their aims and in the typical case are assumed to subordinate the old-fashioned hunt for profits to a variety of other, quantitatively less precise but qualitatively more worthy, objectives.

The implications of this doctrine of the "soulful corporation" are far-reaching. The truth is that if it is accepted, the whole corpus of traditional economic theory must be abandoned and the time-honored justification of the existing social order in terms of economic efficiency, justice, etc., simply falls to the ground. This has been most effectively pointed out by Edward S. Mason:

> But if profit maximization is not the directing agent, how are resources allocated to their most productive uses, what relation have prices to relative scarcities, and how do factors get remunerated in accordance with their contribution to output? Assume an economy composed of a few hundred large corporations, each enjoying substantial market power and all directed by managements with a "conscience." Each management wants to do the best it can for society consistent, of course, with doing the best it can for labor, customers, suppliers, and owners. How do prices get determined in such an economy? How are factors remunerated, and what relation is there between remuneration and performance? What is the mechanism, if any, that assures effective resource use, and how can corporate managements "do right by" labor, suppliers, customers, and owners while simultaneously serving the public interests?[6]

Economists have made no attempt to answer these questions, and indeed it is doubtful whether it even makes sense to ask them in relation to an economy such as Mason postulates, that is to say, one made up of or dominated by a few hundred soulful corporations. Prices and incomes would be indeterminate, and there would be no theoretically definable tendencies toward equilibrium. To be sure, economic life in such a society might settle down into routines and patterns which could be analyzed by historians, sociologists, and statisticians, but it seems reasonably clear that today's economic theorists would be out of a job.

One school of thought, associated especially with the name of Herbert A. Simon of Carnegie Institute of Technology, seems already to have drawn these conclusions and is attempting to study the big corporation and its implications by means of what Simon calls "organization theory." According to this theory, corporations do not try to maximize anything but merely to achieve "satisfactory" results. Thus, to the maximizing behavior which was assumed to characterize the old-fashioned entrepreneur, Simon contrasts what he calls the "satisficing" behavior of modern corporate

---

4. *The Modern Corporation and Private Property*, New York, 1932, p. 356.

5. Carl Kaysen, "The Social Significance of the Modern Corporation," *American Economic Review*, May 1957, pp. 313–314. See also M. J. Rathbone, President of Standard Oil of New Jersey, in the *Saturday Review*, April 16, 1960: "Managements of large companies must harmonize a wide span of obligations: to investors, customers, suppliers, employees, communities and the national interest. Thus the large organization may actually have a narrower range for its decision-making than the small, closely held corporation which is not so much in the public eye and hence not so exposed to criticism."

6. Edward S. Mason, "The Apologetics of 'Managerialism,'" *The Journal of Business*, January 1958, p. 7.

managements. At the annual meetings of the American Economic Association in 1956, a paper by Simon expounding this view was answered by James Earley of the University of Wisconsin who had been engaged for a number of years on a study of the management policies of a sample of large and successful American corporations. Summing up a wealth of carefully collected and analyzed empirical material, Earley had little difficulty in disposing of Simon's theory; what is more significant from our point of view is that he went on to give a most useful and illuminating description of how modern corporate managements really behave. This statement is so good that it seems worthwhile to rescue large parts of it from the untitled obscurity of the Economic Association's *Papers and Proceedings.* After noting some points of agreement and others of minor disagreement with Simon, Earley proceeds as follows:

I have more serious reservations concerning what appears to be the major economic theorem Simon arrives at; namely, that the business enterprise looks for merely satisfactory solutions of its problems and specifically seeks merely satisfactory profits. That his approach has led so directly to this conclusion is one of the facts that makes me especially doubt that it is a satisfactory one. Whatever may be true of individuals or of other types of organization, I cannot square Simon's "satisficing" behavior with the behavior of the large-scale American business firm. I agree that the conventional notion of profit maximization and of general "optimization" must be modified. I contend this is carrying the change much too far. Let me briefly catalogue the main types of evidence that lead me to reject the "satisficing" postulate.

(1) As a part of my research, I have made a study of recent management literature, both general and specialized, one of my hypotheses in doing so being that this literature will reveal the frames of reference and mores of advanced business management. A striking characteristic of this literature (except where public relations is an evident objective) is its systematic focus on cost reduction, the expansion of revenue, and the increase of profits. There is, of course, much reference to standards and to the need of remedying unsatisfactory situations. The drive is always toward the better and frequently the best, not just the good. Like Samuel Gompers' ideal union leader, the exemplary man of management seems to have "More!" for at least one of his mottoes.

(2) Secondly, my questionnaire studies of the practices and policies of leading so-called "excellently managed" companies lead me toward generally similar conclusions. I have published the major results of the first of these studies and will not review them here.[7]

(3) The third fact that makes me doubt Simon's postulate as applied to the firm is the rapidly growing use of economists, market analysts, other types of specialists, and management consultants by our larger businesses. The main function of most of these people is to help the firm reduce costs, find superior methods, choose the most profitable alternatives, and uncover new profit opportunities. As these sophisticated gentlemen gain in influence in business councils—and I confidently believe they will—profit-oriented rationality is likely to be more and more representative of business behavior.

(4) Most of all I am impressed by the rapid development of analytical and managerial techniques that both stimulate and assist the business firms to find the least costly ways of doing things and the most profitable things to do. Operations research and mathematical programming are only the more fancy of this growing genus. There are also greatly improved forms of accounting and budgeting, improved methods of market analysis, refinements in business forecasting, and interesting types of nonmathematical programming. The unifying character of these new techniques is that they seek to apply the principles of rational problem solving to business planning and decision making.

Let me conclude by briefly sketching the notion of business behavior that seems to be emerging from my own studies. It falls somewhere between the old postulate of profit maximization and Simon's "satisfactory profit." It fully recognizes the limited informational and computational resources of the firm. It also incorporates his suggested concept of the "aspiration level" and a modified principle of "viability." My behavioral postulate could best be briefly described as "a systematic temporal search for highest practicable profits."

The theory underlying it runs, very briefly, as follows:

The major goals of modern large-scale business are high managerial incomes, good profits, a strong competitive position, and growth. Modern management does not view these goals as seriously inconsistent but rather, indeed, as necessary, one to the other. Competitive strength and even survival, management believes, require large innovative and substantial growth expenditures in the rapidly changing technical and market conditions of the present day. Since growth by merger is hazardous and frequently impossible, large and more or less continuous capital expenditures are necessary. For well-recognized reasons, management wishes to minimize outside financing, so the funds for most of these expenditures must be internally generated. This requires high and growing profits above dividend levels. So, too, do high managerial rewards. High and rising profits are hence an instrument as well as a direct goal of great importance.

With these goals and needs in view, advanced management plans for profit through time, using coordinated programs stretching as far ahead as practicable. The profit targets incorporated in these programs are sufficient to finance not only good dividends but also desired innovative and growth expenditures. The programs are revised frequently, as experience accrues and new opportunities are discovered.

The tendency toward profit maximization (i.e., highest practicable profit) appears in this system along several dimensions. In the process of revising and reformulating programs, more expensive and less profitable activities are pruned or dropped and cheaper or more profitable ones are added. Less costly processes and the more profitable product and market sectors serve as the standards toward which others are expected to converge or be replaced. By steadily selecting those methods and sectors that promise better returns, these standards are kept high and, if possible, rising. Finally, the overall profit and growth targets of the enterprise as a whole are raised through time, unless adversity prevents.

These goals and programs and standards, it is true, represent at any time certain "aspiration levels," and the efforts to satisfy them receive prime attention. But the two major points about them are that (1) they are likely to be hard to reach and (2) they will ordinarily recede (i.e., grow larger) through time. Even in good times the firm's aspiration levels, therefore, are fairly taut, and they are highly elastic upward. On the other hand, there is great resistance to adjusting profit and other standards downward, so that in bad times the business firm tries even harder to make the highest practicable profits.

I readily agree that I have sketched the behavior of what might be called the "exemplary firm" rather than the firm that is quantitatively representative of the present business population. But my main point is that the management techniques and the *expertise* that can validate my notion are developing rapidly, are increasingly being made available to business, and are being rapidly adopted by leading firms. Consequently, I suspect, the exemplary firm will be the representative firm of the future. If so, its behavior will be more rather than less appropriately analyzed by some of our time-honored theoretical notions, such as profit maximization. . . .[8]

Two aspects of this admirable statement call for comment. First, it introduces a healthy corrective to what Earley calls "the conventional notion of profit

7. The author's reference here is to James S. Earley, "Marginal Policies of 'Excellently Managed' Companies," *The American Economic Review,* March 1956.

8. *American Economic Review,* May 1957, pp. 333–335.

maximization and general 'optimization.'" This conventional notion has been tied to a more or less explicitly stated assumption that the maximizing entrepreneur has complete knowledge of all alternatives open to him and of the consequences of choosing any combination of them. Given this assumption, he can always select the combination of alternatives which yields an absolute maximum. Further, if it is assumed that his knowledge remains equally complete in the face of changing conditions, it follows logically that he can always make instantaneous and appropriate adjustments to new circumstances. What is involved here is an assumption of omniscience on the part of the entrepreneur, which, far from being a useful abstraction, is of course an absurdity. In practice, to be sure, economists have usually given a more sensible meaning to the maximization principle, but by failing expressly to repudiate the omniscience postulate, by failing to spell out what is and what is not involved in the assumption of profit maximization, they have left themselves vulnerable to attacks of the kind mounted by Simon. It is therefore valuable to have Earley's carefully considered statement. By stressing the "limited informational and computational resources of the firm," he makes clear that no assumption of complete knowledge is involved, and his entire argument is based on the rejection of any idea of an absolute maximum or optimum. The firm (whether individual entrepreneur or corporation makes no difference) always finds itself in a given historical situation, with limited knowledge of changing conditions. In this context it can never do more than improve its profit position. In practice, the search for "maximum" profits can only be the search for the greatest *increase* in profits which is possible in the given situation, subject of course to the elementary proviso that the exploitation of today's profit opportunities must not ruin tomorrow's. This is all there is to the profit maximization principle, but it also happens to be all that is necessary to validate the "economizing" behavior patterns which have been the very backbone of all serious economic theory for the last two centuries.

The second aspect of Earley's statement which we want to emphasize, and the one most relevant to our present purpose, is the convincing demonstration that the big corporation, if not more profit-oriented than the individual entrepreneur (he quite properly leaves this question open), is at any rate better equipped to pursue a policy of profit maximization. The result is much the same: the economy of large corporations is more, not less, dominated by the logic of profit-making than the economy of small entrepreneurs ever was.

It might be thought that this is enough to dispose of the soulful corporation and at the same time to justify the procedure of those economists who have altogether ignored the rise of the corporate form of enterprise and continued to reason in terms of the individual entrepreneur. This is not so, however, and for two reasons: First, the alleged soulfulness of the corporation relates not only to its attitude toward the acquisition of profits but also to its attitude toward the utilization of profits, and there is still much to be said on the latter subject. Second, there are undoubtedly differences between individual enterprise and corporate enterprise which have little to do with the goal of profit maximization but which still are of great importance for economic theory. . . . [Let] us probe somewhat more deeply into the motivational and behavioral patterns of corporate management. . . .

Four

Big corporations are run by company men. What kind of people are they? What do they want and why? What position do they hold in the class structure of American society?

There is a widespread impression, and much literature to support and propagate it, that the managements of big corporations form some sort of separate, independent, or "neutral" social class. This view we have already encountered in an elementary form in the "neutral technocracy" of Berle and Means and the "soulful corporation" of Carl Kaysen; it is developed more elaborately in such works as James Burnham's *The Managerial Revolution* and Berle's *The 20th-Century Capitalist Revolution.* Most of the variants of this theory have interesting and enlightening insights to contribute, but in our view they all share a common defect: the basic idea is wrong.

The fact is that the managerial stratum is the most active and influential part of the propertied class. All studies show that its members are largely recruited from the middle and upper reaches of the class structure; they overlap with what C. Wright Mills calls the "very rich"; with few and negligible exceptions, they are wealthy men in their own right, quite apart from the large incomes and extensive privileges which they derive from their corporate connections.[9] It is of course true, as we have emphasized, that in the typical big corporation the management is not subject to stockholder control, and in this sense the "separation of ownership from control" is a fact. But there is no justification for concluding from this that managements in general are divorced from ownership in general. Quite the contrary, managers are among the biggest owners; and because of the strategic positions they occupy, they function as the protectors and spokesmen for all large-scale property. Far from being a separate class, they constitute in reality the leading echelon of the property-owning class.

This is not to argue that managers have no distinctive interests *qua* managers. Like other segments of the propertied class, they do. But the conflicts of interest that arise in this way are between managers and small property owners rather than between managers and large property owners. The clearest case in point has to do with dividend policy.

It is generally assumed that the desire of managers to generate the largest feasible volume of internal corporate funds leads to an interest in a low dividend payout rate, while stockholders' concern to maximize their disposable cash income leads to an interest in a high payout rate. Actually, this is much too simple. Most managers are themselves big owners of stock (in their own and other companies) and as such have the same interest in dividends as other big stockholders. This interest is neither in a minimum nor a maximum payout rate but somewhere in between: stockholdings should yield a reasonable cash income (for managers this is particularly important as a guarantee of family security after they retire or die); on the other hand, they should also steadily appreciate in value. The first requirement calls for dividends, the second for plowing back of earnings. Nevertheless, the special managerial interest in a low payout rate does exist and is undoubtedly important. But the point to be emphasized is that this makes managers the allies

9. By far the best treatment of these subjects will be found in C. Wright Mills, *The Power Elite,* especially Chapters 6, 7, and 8.

of the very largest stockholders for whom a minimum payout rate is also a desideratum. The reason of course is that the very rich save a large part of their incomes in any case, and it is to their advantage for the corporations in which they own stock to do the saving for them rather than pay out dividends from which to do their own saving. Corporate saving results in an increase in the value of their stocks. If at any time they need the cash, either to spend or for some other investment, they can sell part or all of their shares, realizing the increment of value in the form of a capital gain taxable at the maximum rate of 25 percent. On the other hand, if they receive more in the form of dividends they have to pay taxes at the much higher rates applicable to their brackets, which of course cuts down their effective rate of saving.

Pressure for higher payout rates generally comes from small stockholders. Only rarely is it effectively exerted on managements via the formal corporate voting machinery, but this does not mean that the small stockholder is without influence. Socially the seven million or so small stockholders in the United States are an important group: they are quite likely to be solid citizens, leaders of public opinion with local political influence. Since the tiny upper echelon of the propertied class (including its leading element, the managers of the big corporations) is always politically vulnerable, it naturally wants to have the support and loyalty of the small stockholder. A moderate, and perhaps even more important a steady, dividend policy is the most effective way of insuring this support.

In practice, dividend policies are the outcome of a compromise between the desire of managements and large stockholders for a low payout rate and the desire of small stockholders for a high rate. Moreover, as would be expected, there is considerable variation from one company to another. Those which are largely owned by a few rich individuals or families tend to have the lowest payout rates; while the highest rates of all are likely to be paid by companies which both have a large number of small stockholders and are also situated in what may be called "public-relations-sensitive" areas of the economy. As would also be expected, managements as a rule hold the upper hand in determining the terms of the compromise, maintaining payout rates of 50 percent or less in most management-controlled industrial corporations. When profits rise, moreover, managements deliberately delay the adjustment of dividends to the new profit level, so that in time of prosperity the actual as distinct from the target payout rate tends to decline.[10] All of which testifies to the combined power of management and the very rich: the two are in fact integrated into a harmonious interest group at the top of the economic pyramid.

Five

The company man is dedicated to the advancement of his company. This does not mean, however, that he is any more or less *homo economicus,* any more or less selfish, any more or less altruistic than either the tycoon or the individual owner-entrepreneur before him. . . .

To be a going concern, a social order must instill in its members the ambition to be a success in its own terms. Under capitalism the highest form of success is business success, and under monopoly capitalism the highest form of business is the big corporation. In this system the normal procedure for an ambitious young man must be to work himself up to as near the top as possible of as big a corporation as possible. Once he enters a given corporation, he devotes himself to two ends: ascending the managerial ladder and advancing the relative status of his company in the corporate world. In practice these two ends are indistinguishable: the young man's rise in the company depends on his contribution to improving the position of the company. This is the crux of the matter, and this is why we can say without qualification that the company man is dedicated to the advancement of his company: he is dedicated to the advancement of his company precisely to the extent that he is dedicated to advancing himself.

This remains true even after he has reached the top of a given company. If he makes a good record, he may be "called" to a larger company. And even if he is not, or has no hope of being, he is still just as much interested in improving the position of the company he heads; for standing, prestige, and power in the business world are not personal attributes but rather are conferred on the individual businessman by the standing, prestige, and power of his company and by his position in that company. . . .

. . . Size is not the only index of corporate status: this is an oversimplification. Other important indexes are rate of growth and "strength" as measured by such standards as credit rating and the price of a company's securities. Thus, assuming equal size, one company will rank ahead of others if it is stronger and growing more rapidly; and strength and rapid growth may even offset a big size differential if the larger company is stagnant or declining. The primary objectives of corporate policy—which are at the same time and inevitably the personal objectives of the corporate managers—are thus strength, rate of growth, and size. There is no general formula for quantifying or combining these objectives—nor is there any need for one. For they are reducible to the single common denominator of profitability. Profits provide the internal funds for expansion. Profits are the sinew and muscle of strength, which in turn gives access to outside funds if and when they are needed. Internal expansion, acquisition, and merger are the ways in which corporations grow, and growth is the road to size. Thus profits, even though not the ultimate goal, are the necessary means to all ultimate goals. As such, they become the immediate, unique, unifying, quantitative aim of corporate policies, the touchstone of corporate rationality, the measure of corporate success. Here is the real—the socio-structural as distinct from individual-psychological—explanation of the kind of profit maximizing behavior so ably described by Earley. . . .

To sum up: Business is an ordered system which selects and rewards according to well understood criteria. The guiding principle is to get as near as possible to the top inside a corporation which is as near as possible to the top among corporations. Hence the need for maximum profits. Hence the need to devote profits once acquired to enhancing financial strength and speeding up growth. These things become the subjective aims and values of the business world because they are the objective requirements of the system. The character of the system determines the psychology of its members, not vice versa. . . .

. . . The real capitalist today is not the individual businessman but the cor-

10. For more complete quantitative data, see the excellent study of John Lintner, "Distribution of Incomes of Corporations among Dividends, Retained Earnings, and Taxes," *American Economic Review*, May 1956.

poration. What the businessman does in his private life, his attitude toward the getting and spending of his personal income—these are essentially irrelevant to the functioning of the system. What counts is what he does in his company life and his attitude toward the getting and spending of the company's income. And here there can be no doubt that the making and accumulating of profits hold as dominant a position today as they ever did. . . .

The replacement of the individual capitalist by the corporate capitalist constitutes an institutionalization of the capitalist function. The heart and core of the capitalist function is accumulation: accumulation has always been the prime mover of the system, the locus of its conflicts, the source of both its triumphs and its disasters. . . .

Six

We have tried to show that the giant corporation of today is an engine for maximizing profits and accumulating capital to at least as great an extent as the individual enterprise of an earlier period. But it is not merely an enlarged and institutionalized version of the personal capitalist. There are major differences between these types of business enterprise, and at least two of them are of key importance to a general theory of monopoly capitalism: the corporation has a longer time horizon than the individual capitalist, and it is a more rational calculator. Both differences are fundamentally related to the incomparably larger scale of the corporation's operations. . . .

The long corporate time horizon and the rationalization of management generate certain characteristic attitudes and modes of behavior. Of these perhaps the most important are (1) a systematic avoidance of risk-taking, and (2) an attitude of live-and-let-live toward other members of the corporate world. In both respects the change from the old-fashioned individual enterprise is so great in quantity as to amount to a change in quality. . . .

. . . In the early days when Big Business was emerging from the jungle of small-scale competition, corespective behavior was rare indeed. Even the railroads had to go through a series of exhausting rate wars before they finally got it into their corporate heads that roadbeds and tracks and locomotives and cars would go on being used to carry passengers and freight whatever might happen to security owners or rival managements. The original tycoons, faced with the consequences of cutthroat competition, sought a way out through a policy of ruthless monopolization. The victims of this drive, however, were numerous and not without influence. By entering into a temporary alliance with dissatisfied farmers and workers, they succeeded in getting the antitrust laws passed, which, though far from achieving their avowed aim of preserving (or restoring) free competition, nevertheless put very real roadblocks in the way of full monopolization. For this reason, as well as others of a technological and economic nature, there were few cases in which one corporation or even one financial interest group succeeded in establishing effective control over an entire market.

It was under these circumstances that Big Businessmen began to learn the virtues of corespective behavior. The process of learning was hastened as the highly individualistic tycoon passed from the scene and the company man gradually took his place as the typical representative of corporate business. Today there are probably fewer genuine monopolies than there were at the turn of the century, but there is also infinitely less cutthroat competition. . . .

THE TENDENCY OF SURPLUS* TO RISE

One

Monopoly capitalism is a system made up of giant corporations. This is not to say that there are no other elements in the system or that it is useful to study monopoly capitalism by abstracting from everything except giant corporations. It is both more realistic and more enlightening to proceed from the outset by including, alongside the corporate-monopoly sector, a more or less extensive smaller-business sector, the reason being that smaller business enters in many ways into the calculations and strategies of Big Business. To abstract from smaller business would be to exclude from the field of investigation some of the determinants of Big Business behavior.

One must, however, be careful not to fall into the trap of assuming that Big Business and smaller business are qualitatively equal or of coordinate importance for the *modus operandi* of the system. The dominant element, the prime mover, is Big Business organized in giant corporations. These corporations are profit maximizers and capital accumulators. They are managed by company men whose fortunes are identified with the corporations' success or failure. They—and here the pronoun stands for both the corporations and the men—look ahead and calculate with care. It is their initiative that sets the economy in motion, their power that keeps it moving, their policies that get it into difficulties and crises. Smaller business is on the receiving end, reacting to the pressures of Big Business, to a certain extent shaping and channeling them, but without effective power to counter them and still less to exercise an independent initiative of its own. From the point of view of a theory of monopoly capitalism, smaller business should properly be treated as a part of the environment within which Big Business operates rather than as an actor on the stage.

Within the corporation, relations are direct, hierarchical, bureaucratic. Here genuine planning holds sway, with directives flowing from the top down and responsibility from the bottom up. For the system as a whole, however, such relations are absent. Not even the largest corporations produce more than a very small fraction of society's total output. Take General Motors, for example, which, measured in terms of sales, is the biggest industrial corporation in the country. In 1957, GM's total of wages, overhead costs, and profits, which corresponds closely to the company's contribution to the Gross National Product, amounted to just over $4 billion, about 1 percent of GNP for that year. It is of course true that several giant corporations often act in concert, but they do so for the purpose of serving their own ends rather than for the purpose of influencing, not to say controlling, the functioning of the system as a whole.

Overall, monopoly capitalism is as unplanned as its competitive predecessor. The big corporations relate to each other, to consumers, to labor, to smaller business primarily through the market. The way the system works is still the unintended outcome of the self-regard-

*[The difference between total output and the socially necessary costs of producing total output.]

ing actions of the numerous units that compose it. And since market relations are essentially price relations, the study of monopoly capitalism, like that of competitive capitalism, must begin with the workings of the price mechanism.

The crucial difference between the two is well known and can be summed up in the proposition that under competitive capitalism the individual enterprise is a "price taker," while under monopoly capitalism the big corporation is a "price maker." When we say that giant corporations are price makers, we mean that they can and do choose what prices to charge for their products. The typical giant corporation, however, is one of several corporations producing commodities which are more or less adequate substitutes for each other. When one of them varies its price, the effect will immediately by felt by others. . . . A wrong guess about rivals' reactions would throw the whole calculation off and necessitate readjustments which in turn would provoke further moves by rivals, and so on, the whole process quite possibly degenerating into mutually destructive price warfare.

Unstable market situations of this sort were very common in the earlier phases of monopoly capitalism, and still occur from time to time, but they are not typical of present-day monopoly capitalism. And clearly they are anathema to the big corporations with their penchant for looking ahead, planning carefully, and betting only on the sure thing. To avoid such situations therefore becomes the first concern of corporate policy, the *sine qua non* of orderly and profitable business operations.

This objective is achieved by the simple expedient of banning price cutting as a legitimate weapon of economic warfare. . . . With price competition banned, sellers of a given commodity or of close substitutes have an interest in seeing that the price or prices established are such as to maximize the profits of the group as a whole. . . . And it means that the appropriate general price theory for an economy dominated by such corporations is the traditional monopoly price theory of classical and neo-classical economies. What economists have hitherto treated as a special case turns out to be, under conditions of monopoly capitalism, the general case. . . . [Since] prices tend to be stickier on the downward side than on the upward side, this fact introduces a significant upward bias into the general price level in a monopoly capitalist economy. . . .

Two

Now under monopoly capitalism it is true as it was in Marx's day that "the executive power of the . . . state is simply a committee for managing the common affairs of the entire bourgeois class."[11] And the common affairs of the entire bourgeois class include a concern that no industries which play an important role in the economy and in which large property interests are involved should be either too profitable or too unprofitable. Extra-large profits are gained not only at the expense of consumers but also of other capitalists (electric power and telephone service, for example, are basic costs of all industries), and in addition they may, and at times of political instability do, provoke demands for genuinely effective antimonopoly action. Abnormally low profits in a major branch of the economy such as agriculture, on the other hand, damage the interests of a large and politically powerful group of property owners who are able through pressure and bargaining with the other capitalists to enlist the necessary support for remedial action. It therefore becomes a state responsibility under monopoly capitalism to insure, as far as possible, that prices and profit margins in the deviant industries are brought within the range prevailing among the general run of giant corporations.

This is the background and explanation of the innumerable regulatory schemes and mechanisms which characterize the American economy today—commission regulation of public utilities, prorationing of oil production, price supports and acreage controls in agriculture, and so on. In each case of course some worthy purpose is supposed to be served—to protect consumers, to conserve natural resources, to save the family-size farm—but only the naïve believe that these fine-sounding aims have any more to do with the case than the flowers that bloom in the spring. There is in fact a vast literature, based for the most part on official documents and statistics, to prove that regulatory commissions protect investors rather than consumers, that oil prorationing wastes rather than conserves natural resources, that the family-size farm is declining faster than in any previous period of American history.[12] All of this is fully understandable once the basic principle is grasped that under monopoly capitalism the function of the state is to serve the interests of monopoly capital. As two champions of free competition have so truthfully said: "With every advance of monopoly toward greater economic power and more general social acceptance the federal government becomes more subservient to it, more dependent on it, more disposed to favor it with grants of privilege, protection, and subsidy."[13]

Consequently the effect of government intervention into the market mechanisms of the economy, whatever its ostensible purpose, is to make the system work more, not less, like one made up exclusively of giant corporations acting and interacting in the manner analyzed [previously].

Three

Strengthening monopoly and regularizing its operations is of course not the only function of the state under monopoly capitalism.... The state, through its taxing and spending activities and through its policies toward the rest of the world, plays a decisive role in the way the system operates. The question therefore arises: Would it not be better to adopt from the outset terminology which calls attention to and emphasizes the role of the state in this social system? There is ample precedent for doing so. In *State and Revolution* (1917) Lenin spoke of "the epoch of the development of monopoly capitalism into state monopoly capitalism," and it is now the accepted view in the Communist world that the advanced capitalist countries have long since passed through this transitional stage and entered that of state monopoly capitalism.

We have chosen not to follow this precedent but rather to use the terms "monopoly capital" and "monopoly capitalism" without qualification for two reasons. In the first place, the state has always played a crucial role in the development of capitalism, and while this role has certainly increased quantitatively we find the evidence of a qualitative change in recent decades unconvincing. Under the circumstances, to lay special emphasis on the role of the state in the present stage of monopoly capitalism

11. *Communist Manifesto,* Part 1, paragraph 12.

12. A considerable body of the relevant material is conveniently assembled and summarized in Walter Adams and Horace M. Gray, *Monopoly in America: The Government as Promoter,* New York, 1955.

13. *Ibid.*, p. 1.

may only mislead people into assuming that it was of negligible importance in the earlier history of capitalism. Even more important is the fact that terms like "state capitalism" and "state monopoly capitalism" almost inevitably carry the connotation that the state is somehow an *independent* social force, coordinate with private business, and that the functioning of the system is determined not only by the cooperation of these two forces but also by their antagonisms and conflicts. This seems to us a seriously misleading view—in reality, what appear to be conflicts between business and government are reflections of conflict within the ruling class—and we think it desirable to avoid terminology which tends to give it currency.

Four

The abandonment of price competition does not mean the end of all competition: it takes new forms and rages on with ever increasing intensity. Most of these new forms of competition come under the heading of what we call the sales effort . . . [and are] those forms of competition which have a direct bearing on costs of production and hence on the magnitude of the surplus.

If it is true, as we have argued, that oligopolies succeed in attaining a close approximation to the theoretical monopoly price and if their never-ceasing efforts to cut costs, so much stressed by James Earley, are generally successful, then it follows with inescapable logic that surplus must have a strong and persistent tendency to rise. But before this conclusion can be accepted, we must ask whether the *system* of oligopolies generates pressures which force corporate managers to cut costs and improve efficiency. We know that this is the case in the competitive system: as Marx expressed it, "competition makes the immanent laws of capitalist production to be felt by each individual capitalist as external coercive laws."[14] Is this true of the kind of competition that exists among giant corporations? Or must we say about them what Adam Smith said about joint stock companies, which he identified with monopoly: "Monopoly is a great enemy to good management, which can never be universally established but in consequence of that free and universal competition which forces everybody to have recourse to it for the sake of self-defense."[15]

These are extremely important questions for an understanding of monopoly capitalism, and we must be careful in answering them not to take at face value the literature which emanates from the corporate establishment itself. We know that the managers of giant corporations and their spokesmen have every interest in projecting an image of technological progressiveness and organizational efficiency. We also know that such images are often mere rationalizing ideologies. What needs to be determined is not what corporate managements want us to believe but what modes of behavior are imposed upon them by the workings of the system itself.

There are, it seems to us, two aspects of non-price competition which are of decisive importance here. The first has to do with what may be called the dynamics of market sharing. The second has to do with the particular form which the sales effort assumes in the producer goods industries.

To begin with, the firm with lower costs and higher profits enjoys a variety of advantages over higher-cost rivals in the struggle for market shares. (This fact seems to have been largely overlooked by economists,[16] but it is perfectly clear to businessmen.) The firm with the lowest costs holds the whip hand; it can afford to be aggressive even to the point of threatening, and in the limiting case precipitating, a price war. It can get away with tactics (special discounts, favorable credit terms, etc.) which if adopted by a weak firm would provoke retaliation. It can afford the advertising, research, development of new product varieties, extra services, and so on, which are the usual means of fighting for market shares and which tend to yield results in proportion to the amounts spent on them. Other less tangible factors are involved which tend to elude the economist's net but which play an important part in the business world. The lower-cost, higher-profit company acquires a special reputation which enables it to attract and hold customers, bid promising executive personnel away from rival firms, and recruit the ablest graduates of engineering and business schools. For all these reasons, there is a strong positive incentive for the large corporation in an oligopolistic industry not only to seek continuously to cut its costs but to do so faster than its rivals.

Here is where the self-defense factor considered so crucial by Adam Smith comes into play. Any company which falls behind in the race to cut costs is soon in trouble. Its power to fight back against attack is undermined, its freedom of maneuver curtailed, its ability to use the normal weapons of the competitive struggle weakened. Playing a more and more passive role, it finds its position progressively deteriorating, and eventually it is faced with some unpleasant but unavoidable alternatives: it can merge, on unfavorable terms of course, with a stronger firm; it can attempt a reorganization and comeback, usually under new management and with new capital; or it can give up the ghost and leave the field to its more successful rivals. This sort of thing happens very often in the business world, and every manager knows of numerous cases and lives in constant fear that a similar fate will overtake him if his company falls behind in the cost race. The stick of failure thus complements the carrot of success in an oligopolistic system no less than in a competitive one.

There is an additional reason, in our judgment as important as it is neglected, why a tendency for costs of production to fall is endemic to the entire monopoly capitalist economy, even including those areas which if left to themselves would stagnate technologically. It stems from the exigencies of non-price competition in the producer goods industries. Here, as in industries producing consumer goods, sellers must be forever seeking to put something new on the market. But they are not dealing with buyers whose primary interest is the latest fashion or keeping up with the Joneses. They are dealing with sophisticated buyers whose concern is to increase profits. Hence the new products offered to the prospective buyers must be designed to help them increase their profits, which in general means to help them reduce their costs. If the manufacturer can convince his customers that his new instrument or material or machine will save them money, the sale will follow almost automatically.

Probably the clearest example of the cost-reducing effects of the innovating activity of manufacturers of producer goods is to be found in agriculture. As Galbraith has pointed out, "there would be little technical development and not much progress in agriculture were it not

14. *Capital,* Volume 1, Chapter 22, Section 3.

15. *The Wealth of Nations,* Book 1, Chapter 11, Part 1.

16. Duesenberry is an exception; see his *Business Cycles and Economic Growth,* especially pp. 124–125.

for government-supported research supplemented by the research of the corporations which devise and sell products to the farmer."[17] No doubt, as this statement implies, government research has been the main factor behind the spectacular reduction in agricultural costs during the last two decades, but the sales-hungry manufacturers of farm machinery, fertilizers, pesticides, etc., have also played an important part in the process. Similarly, producers of machine tools, computers and computer systems, business machines, automatic control equipment, loading and transfer machinery, new plastics and metal alloys, and a thousand and one other kinds of producer goods are busy developing new products which will enable their customers–comprising literally the entire business world–to produce more cheaply and hence to make more profits. In a word: producers of producer goods make more profits by helping others to make more profits. The process is self-reinforcing and cumulative, and goes far toward explaining the extraordinarily rapid advance of technology and labor productivity which characterizes the developed monopoly capitalist economy.

We conclude, then, that with regard to the cost discipline which it imposes on its members the monopoly capitalist economy is no less severe than its competitive predecessor, and that in addition it generates new and powerful impulses to innovation. There can therefore be no doubt about the downward trend of production costs under monopoly capitalism.

On the face of it this would seem to be an argument for monopoly capitalism's being considered a rational and progressive system. And if its cost-reducing proclivities could somehow be disentangled from monopoly pricing and a way could be found to utilize the fruits of increasing productivity for the benefit of society as a whole, the argument would indeed be a powerful one. But of course this is just what cannot be done. The whole motivation of cost reduction is to increase profits, and the monopolistic structure of markets enables the corporations to appropriate the lion's share of the fruits of increasing productivity directly in the form of higher profits. This means that under monopoly capitalism, declining costs imply continuously widening profit margins. And continuously widening profit margins in turn imply aggregate profits which rise not only absolutely but as a share of national product. If we provisionally equate aggregate profits with society's economic surplus, we can formulate as a law of monopoly capitalism that the surplus tends to rise both absolutely and relatively as the system develops.[18]

This law immediately invites comparison, as it should, with the classical-Marxian law of the falling tendency of the rate of profit. Without entering into an analysis of the different versions of the latter, we can say that they all presuppose a competitive system. By substituting the law of rising surplus for the law of falling profit, we are therefore not rejecting or revising a time-honored theorem of political economy: we are simply taking account of the undoubted fact that the structure of the capitalist economy has undergone a fundamental change since that theorem was formulated. What is most essential about the structural change from competitive to monopoly capitalism finds its theoretical expression in this substitution. . . .

. . . The persistent rise in the unemployment rate in recent years lends strong support to the view that the problem of realizing surplus value is indeed more chronic today that it was in Marx's time. The truth would seem to be that except in war and periods of war-related prosperity stagnation is now the normal state of the United States economy.

THE ABSORPTION OF SURPLUS

One

. . . Under monopoly capitalism, owing to the nature of the price and cost policies of the giant corporations, there is a strong and systematic tendency for surplus to rise, both absolutely and as a share of total output. We now come to the problem of the absorption or utilization of the surplus.

In general, surplus can be absorbed in the following ways: (1) it can be consumed, (2) it can be invested, and (3) it can be wasted. . . .

Two

To the extent that surplus is consumed by capitalists, the amount available for investment is correspondingly reduced. . . . The question therefore [is]: does capitalists' consumption tend to rise as a share of surplus? If not, the investment-seeking part of surplus must rise relatively to total income [in order to absorb the surplus].

Let us assume that capitalists consume the entire amount of distributed profits. This is not true, of course, but if it can be shown that even in this case capitalists' consumption does not tend to rise as a share of surplus, then the conclusion which follows will hold *a fortiori* for cases in which capitalists save out of their distributed profits.

The problem is now quite simply whether there is in fact a tendency for the distributed share of surplus (dividends) to rise, remain constant, or fall as surplus itself expands. And here the evidence leaves no doubt about the answer.

. . . Most large companies have a target dividend payout rate which remains remarkably constant over long periods of time (50 percent seems to be the most common figure). When profits rise, however, they do not immediately adjust dividends to maintain the target rate. For example, if a company has been earning $2 a share for some time and is paying a dividend of $1, and if earnings then rise to $4, the dividend will be raised to $2 not in one year but over a period of several years. In the meantime, the actual payout rate will lag behind the target rate. If this pattern is adhered to—and there is every indication that it is a deeply rooted aspect of corporate behavior—it follows that a continuous rise in earnings would be accompanied by an equally continuous decline in the payout rate.

Under these circumstances, capitalists' consumption would increase absolutely, which of course is to be expected, but it would decline as a proportion of surplus and even more as a proportion to total income. Since these conclusions hold *a fortiori* to the extent that capitalists save out of their dividend incomes,

17. J. K. Galbraith, *American Capitalism*, Boston, 1952, pp. 95–96.

18. As a matter of fact, statistically-recorded profits are far from comprising the entire economic surplus. Interest and rent are also forms of surplus; and under monopoly capitalism still other forms assume decisive importance. Up to this point, however, we have used the term "profits" to mean simply the difference between sales revenue and costs of production, and the aggregate of profits in this sense is a legitimate first approximation to a fully developed concept of the economic surplus.

it is clear that no solution of the problem of surplus absorption can be expected from this quarter.

Three

Not only surplus, then, but also the investment-seeking part of surplus tends to rise as a proportion of total income. Whether this tendency will be realized, however, is another question. In attempting to answer it, we must first determine whether the system normally provides investment outlets large enough to absorb a rising share of a rising surplus.

The logic of the situation is as follows: if total income grows at an accelerating rate, then a larger and larger share has to be devoted to investment; and, conversely, if a larger and larger share is devoted to investment, total income must grow at an accelerating rate.[19] What this implies, however, is nonsensical from an economic standpoint. It means that a larger and larger volume of producer goods would have to be turned out for the sole purpose of producing a still larger and larger volume of producer goods in the future. Consumption would be a diminishing proportion of output, and the growth of the capital stock would have no relation to the actual or potential expansion of consumption.[20]

Quite apart from the fact that such an explosive growth process would sooner or later exceed the physical potentialities of any conceivable economy, there is simply no reason to assume that anything like it has ever occurred or is likely to occur in the real world. Manufacturers of producer goods do not provide each other with an infinitely expanding market for each others' output, and they know it. In particular, it is sheer fantasy to imagine the cautious, calculating giant corporations of monopoly capitalism planning and carrying out the kind of snowballing expansion programs which this case presupposes.

If accelerating growth is ruled out as totally unrealistic, one is left with the inescapable conclusion that the actual investment of an amount of surplus which rises relatively to income must mean that the economy's capacity to produce grows more rapidly than its output. Such an investment pattern is certainly not impossible; indeed, it has frequently been observed in the history of capitalism. But what is impossible is that it should persist indefinitely. Sooner or later, excess capacity grows so large that it discourages further investment. When investment declines, so do income and employment and hence also surplus itself. In other words, this investment pattern is self-limiting and ends in an economic downturn—the beginning of a recession or depression. . . .

. . . On the other hand, if the economy moves up from a position of less-than-capacity production, both surplus and the investment-seeking segment of surplus swell absolutely and relatively. . . . Surplus swells when capacity is fully utilized and surplus rapidly shrinks when investment outlets fail and aggregate demand declines. As surplus shrinks, the investment-seeking part of it shrinks more than in proportion. On the downswing, in other words, the ratio of consumption to both surplus and total output rises, and this sooner or later puts a stop to the contraction. The lower turning point is reached when the amount of surplus seeking investment is exactly absorbed by available investment outlets. At this point, a temporary equilibrium is reached which is characterized by the existence of excess productive capacity and unemployed workers. The reverse side of the coin is that an upswing, however initiated, generates a similar rapid absolute and relative increase of surplus. As soon as the investment-seeking part of surplus exceeds available investment outlets, the expansion comes to an end. And it should be remembered that this upper turning point may be reached long before full utilization of capacity or full employment of labor is achieved. . . .

We have seen that . . . mechanisms tend to generate a steady rising supply of investment-seeking surplus, but that in the nature of the case they cannot generate a corresponding rise in the magnitude of investment outlets. . . .

Four

. . . A large part of investment over the years has been embodied in improved or altogether new types of producer goods. Does this mean that technological progress automatically provides outlets for investment-seeking surplus and that any shortage of outlets could in principle be overcome by an appropriate increase in the rate of technological progress? . . .

. . . Under monopoly capitalism there is no necessary correlation, as there is in a competitive system, between the rate of technological progress and the volume of investment outlets. Technological progress tends to determine the *form* which investment takes at any given time rather than its amount.[21]

This is not a rigid rule to which there are no exceptions. Particularly in the case of new products, as distinct from new versions of existing products, there may be a rush to get into the market first in order to enjoy for a time an unchallenged monopoly position. A "key feature of new products," says [a] McGraw-Hill survey, "is that they usually carry very high profit margins. When a company is first in the field, it can set a relatively high price . . . and hope to earn a high return—far higher, in most cases, than on standard products for which markets are intensively competitive. There is, therefore, every incentive to take quick advantage of new product developments by the construction of new plant capacity.[22] The importance of this point should not be exaggerated, however, for the same study, in discussing the lag between scientific discovery and economic application, indicates that there are also factors which work in the

19. See Evsey Domar, *Essays in the Theory of Economic Growth,* New York, 1957, pp. 127–128.

20. This is essentially the case analyzed by Tugan-Baranowsky in his well-known attempt to refute all underconsumption theories of economic crisis. For the relevant references, as well as a discussion of Tugan's theory, see Paul M. Sweezy, *The Theory of Capitalist Development,* New York, 1942, Chapter 10, Section 2.

21. It is one of Steindl's great merits to have seen this relationship clearly [*Maturity and Stagnation in American Capitalism* (1952), p. 133], but he made the mistake of formulating it as a general proposition applicable to all stages of capitalism. That it is true under oligopoly is recognized and emphasized by Paolo Sylos Labini in his stimulating work, *Oligopoly and Technical Progress,* Cambridge, Massachusetts, 1962, especially pp. 148–149.

22. Dexter M. Keezer and others, *New Forces in American Business,* New York, 1958, p. 34. Just how profitable a new product can be is well illustrated by the success story of the Xerox Corporation. In an article devoted to Xerox and its products, *Newsweek* (September 9, 1964) speaks of "the breathtaking profit potential of what has amounted to a monopoly in electrostatic copiers. A 914, for instance, costs something less than $2,500 to manufacture. Yet Xerox leases most of them, recovers even the manufacturing cost through depreciation—and each leased machine is returning an average of at least $4,000 a year. If a customer wants to buy, the price is $29,500. Even Wilson [President of Xerox] has remarked: 'I keep asking myself when I am going to wake up.' The indicated profit margin of over 1000 percent on sales must be something like a record.

opposite direction, inhibiting bursts of investment associated with the introduction of new products:

> Capital investment particularly tends to lag because the expenditures required to begin output of a *new product* are usually quite small. Often existing facilities, or a part of them, can be converted to turn out trial quantities of the new product. And the really heavy expenditures required to build a complete new plant are not made until a year or two later. Similarly, expenditures to introduce a *new process* are not usually made until there is a relatively large production volume to justify these outlays. Especially in our heavy industries, new processes tend to be introduced (and, in fact, designed) as the low-cost way of adding new capacity. [In other words, they merely determine the form of investment which would have been made anyway.] Therefore, capital outlays for both new products and new processes tend to be delayed beyond the time of strictly scientific development, until sales prospects justify the building of large-scale facilities.[23]

To the extent that this argument applies, there is little reason to distinguish between new products and new processes: both tend to be introduced in a controlled fashion and to determine the form which investment takes rather than its magnitude. The new product takes the place of the old, just as the new process takes the place of the old; there is little of that "creative destruction" which Schumpeter saw as the chief dynamic force of the capitalist economy. . . .

. . . Where the amount of depreciation is very large, as in present-day monopoly capitalism, it is quite possible that business can finance from this source alone all the investment it considers profitable to make in innovations (both new products and new processes), leaving no "innovational" outlets to help absorb investment-seeking surplus. Technological progress may, in other words, do little more than shape the most profitable uses for funds made available to corporate managements through their own "generous" depreciation policies. To the extent that this is so, technological progress makes no contribution at all to solving the problem of outlets for the "visible" part of investment-seeking surplus: whatever investment may be required to embody available innovations may well be less than enough to absorb the rising tide of depreciation allowances. . . .

Our conclusion is that technological progress is no more likely than population growth to make a significant contribution to solving the problem of surplus absorption. . . .

Twist and turn as one will, there is no way to avoid the conclusion that monopoly capitalism is a self-contradictory system. It tends to generate ever more surplus, yet it fails to provide the consumption and investment outlets required for the absorption of a rising surplus and hence for the smooth working of the system. Since surplus which cannot be absorbed will not be produced, it follows that the *normal* state of the monopoly capitalist economy is stagnation. With a given stock of capital and a given cost and price structure, the system's operating rate cannot rise above the point at which the amount of surplus produced can find the necessary outlets. And this means chronic underutilization of available human and material resources. . . .

Five

Counteracting forces do exist. If they did not, the system would indeed long since have fallen of its own weight. It therefore becomes a matter of the greatest importance to understand the nature and implications of these counteracting forces. . . .

The self-contradictory character of monopoly capitalism–its chronic inability to absorb as much surplus as it is capable of producing–impresses itself on the ordinary citizen in a characteristic way. To him, the economic problem appears to be the very opposite of what the textbooks say it is: not how best to utilize scarce resources but how to dispose of the products of superabundant resources. And this holds regardless of his wealth or position in society. If he is a worker, the ubiquitous fact of unemployment teaches him that the supply of labor is always greater than the demand. If he is a farmer, he struggles to stay afloat in a sea of surpluses. If he is a businessman, his sales persistently fall short of what he could profitably produce. Always too much, never too little.

This condition of affairs is peculiar to monopoly capitalism. The very notion of "too much" would have been inconceivable to all pre-capitalist forms of society; and even in the competitive stage of capitalism, it described a temporary derangement, not a normal condition. In a rationally ordered socialist society, no matter how richly endowed it might be with natural resources and technology and human skills, "too much" could only be a welcome signal to shift attention to an area of "too little." Only under monopoly capitalism does "too much" appear as a pervasive problem affecting everyone at all times.

From this source stem a whole series of attitudes and interests of crucial importance for the character and functioning of monopoly capitalist society. On the one hand, there is a stubborn spirit of restrictionism which pervades the institutional structure.[24] Union featherbedding and Henry Wallace's plowing under of little pigs are only the best publicized examples of practices which are all but universal in business and government: the most primitive reaction to an excess of supply is simply to cut back. During the 1930s, when "too much" took on the dimensions of a universal disaster, primitive restrictionism acquired, in the National Industrial Recovery Act and the National Recovery Administration, the dignity and sanction of official national policy.

But cutting back as a remedy for "too much," even if beneficial to particular groups or individuals, only aggravates the situation as a whole. A secondary and more sophisticated set of attitudes and policies therefore emerges, gropingly and slowly at first but with increasing purposefulness and momentum as monopoly capitalism develops. Their rationale derives from the simple fact that the obverse of "too much" on the supply side is "too little" on the demand side; instead of cutting back supply they aim at stimulating demand.

The stimulation of demand–the creation and expansion of markets–thus becomes to an ever greater degree the leitmotif of business and government policies under monopoly capitalism. But this statement, true as it is, can easily be misleading. There are many conceivable ways of stimulating demand. If a socialist society, for example, should find that through some planning error more consumer goods were being produced than could be sold, given the existing structure of prices and incomes, the simplest and most direct remedy would

23. *New Forces in American Business,* p. 62n.

24. This is what the French, by a somewhat attenuated logic, call Malthusianism.

clearly be to cut prices.[25] This would reduce the amount of surplus at the disposal of the planning authorities and correspondingly raise the purchasing power of consumers. The threatened glut could be quickly and painlessly averted: everyone would be better off, no one worse off. Such a course of action is obviously not open to a monopoly capitalist society, in which the determination of prices is the jealously guarded prerogative of the giant corporations. Each makes its own decisions with a view to maximizing its own private profit. Except for short periods of all-out war, when inflationary pressures threaten the entire economic and social fabric, there is no agency charged with controlling prices. Moreover, every attempt to maintain or establish such an agency in peacetime has resulted either in ignominious failure (witness the fiasco of price control after the Second World War) or in the thinly disguised legalization of monopoly pricing practices in "regulated" industries. The plain fact is that the pricing process is controlled by the most powerful vested interests in monopoly capitalist society. To imagine that it could possibly be regulated in the public interest would be to imagine away the very characteristics of that society which make it what it is.

If stimulation of demand through price reduction is impossible within the framework of monopoly capitalism, this cannot be said of other possible methods. Take, for example, advertising and related forms of salesmanship. . . . Every giant corporation is driven by the logic of its situation to devote more and more attention and resources to the sales effort. And monopoly capitalist society as a whole has every interest in promoting rather than restricting and controlling this method of creating new markets and expanding old ones.

Just as with price cutting and salesmanship, other forms of stimulating demand either are or are not compatible with the pattern of interests, the structure of power, the web of ideology that constitute the essence of monopoly capitalist society. Those which are compatible will be fostered and promoted; those which are incompatible will be ignored or inhibited. The question for monopoly capitalism is not whether to stimulate demand. It must, on pain of death.

The question is how to stimulate demand. And here . . . the system has its own built-in selective mechanisms which have the most far-reaching consequences for every aspect of life in monopoly capitalist society. . . .

Six

. . . With the law of rising surplus replacing the law of the falling tendency of the rate of profit, and with normal modes of surplus utilization patently unable to absorb a rising surplus, the question of other modes of surplus utilization assumes crucial importance. That they should be there in large and growing volume becomes a life-and-death issue for the system. And as they grow relative to capitalists' consumption and accumulation, they increasingly dominate the composition of social output, the rate of economic growth, and the quality of society itself.

One of these alternative modes of utilization we call the sales effort. . . . In its impact on the economy, it is outranked only by militarism. In all other aspects of social existence, its all-pervasive influence is second to none.

The tremendous growth of the sales effort and the spectacular intensification of its sway stem from its having undergone a far-reaching qualitative change. Price competition has largely receded as a means of attracting the public's custom, and has yielded to new ways of sales promotion: advertising, variation of the products' appearance and packaging, "planned obsolescence," model changes, credit schemes, and the like.

In an economic system in which competition is fierce and relentless and in which the fewness of the rivals rules out price cutting, advertising becomes to an ever increasing extent the principal weapon of the competitive struggle. . . .

Seven

. . . What indeed would happen to a market continually plagued by insufficient demand? And what would happen to an economic system suffering from chronic underconsumption, underinvestment, and underemployment? For the economic importance of advertising lies not primarily in its causing a reallocation of consumers' expenditures among different commodities but in its effect on the magnitude of aggregate effective demand and thus on the level of income and employment. This has been readily grasped by professors of marketing and advertising as well as by business journalists, but with few exceptions it has been ignored by economic theorists. . . .

The direct impact of the sales effort on the income and output structure of the economy is therefore similar to that of government spending financed by tax revenue. This impact, measured by what has come to be called in economic literature the "balanced budget multiplier," is to expand aggregate income and output by an amount as large as the original revenue (and outlay). And of course the expansion of aggregate income is associated with higher employment of unproductive workers in advertising agencies, advertising media, and the like. . . . The function of advertising, perhaps its dominant function today, thus becomes that of waging, on behalf of the producers and sellers of consumer goods, a relentless war against saving and in favor of consumption. And the principal means of carrying out this task are to induce changes in fashion, create new wants, set new standards of status, enforce new norms of propriety. The unquestioned success of advertising in achieving these aims has greatly strengthened its role as a force counteracting monopoly capitalism's tendency to stagnation and at the same time marked it as the chief architect of the famous "American Way of Life."

. . . Just as advertising, product differentiation, artificial obsolescence, model changing, and all the other devices of the sales effort do in fact promote and increase sales, and thus act as indispensable props to the level of income and employment, so the entire apparatus of "finance, insurance, and real estate" is essential to the normal functioning of the corporate system and another no less indispensable prop to the level of income and employment. The prodigious volume of resources absorbed in all these activities does in fact constitute necessary costs of capitalist production. What should be crystal clear is that an economic system in which *such* costs are socially necessary has long ceased to be a socially necessary economic system. . . .

Eight

In the preceding [paragraphs] it was shown that the sales effort absorbs, directly and indirectly, a large amount of surplus which otherwise would not have been produced. . . .

Under monopoly capitalism . . . the normal condition is less than capacity

25. See Kalecki, *Theory of Economic Dynamics,* London, 1954, pp. 62–63.

production. The system simply does not generate enough "effective demand" (to use the Keynesian term) to insure full utilization of either labor or productive facilities. If these idle resources can be put to work, they can produce not only necessary means of subsistence for the producers but also additional amounts of surplus. Hence if government creates more effective demand, it can increase its command over goods and services without encroaching on the incomes of its citizens. This creation of effective demand can take the form of direct government purchases of goods and services, or of "transfer payments" to groups which can somehow make good their claims for special treatment (subsidies to businessmen and farmers, doles to the unemployed, pensions to the aged, and so on). . . .

. . . The vast and growing amounts of surplus absorbed by government in recent decades are not, we repeat, deductions from what would otherwise be available to corporations and individuals for their private purposes. The structure of the monopoly capitalist economy is such that a continually mounting volume of surplus simply could not be absorbed through private channels; if no other outlets were available, it would not be produced at all. What government absorbs is in addition to, not subtracted from, private surplus. Even more: since a larger volume of government spending pushes the economy nearer to capacity operation, and since up to this point surplus grows more rapidly than effective demand as a whole, it follows that both the government and the private segments of surplus can and indeed typically do grow simultaneously. It is only when government absorption continues to expand even after full utilization has been reached, as during the later years of the Second World War, that private surplus is encroached upon. . . .

The American ruling class, at any rate its leading echelon of managers of giant corporations, has learned these lessons through the rich experience of three decades of depression, war, and Cold War. And its attitude toward taxation and government spending has undergone a fundamental change. The older hostility to any expansion of government activities has not of course disappeared. In the realm of ideology, deeply rooted attitudes never disappear quickly. Moreover, in some sections of the ruling class—especially rentiers and smaller businessmen—hatred of the tax collector dominates feelings about the role of government. But the modern Big Businessman, though he sometimes speaks the traditional language, no longer takes it so seriously as his ancestors. To him, government spending means more effective demand, and he senses that he can shift most of the associated taxes forward onto consumers or backward onto workers. In addition—and this point is of great importance in understanding the subjective attitudes of Big Businessmen—the intricacies of the tax system, specially tailored to fit the needs of all sorts of special interests, open up endless opportunities for speculative and windfall gains. . . .

Nine

During the interval 1929–1957, total government spending increased from roughly one tenth to one quarter of GNP, most of the difference representing absorption of surplus which would otherwise not have been produced. . . .

It is of course in the area of defense purchases that most of the expansion has taken place—from less than 1 percent of

GNP to more than 10 percent, accounting for about two thirds of the total expansion of government spending relative to GNP since the 1920s. This massive absorption of surplus in military preparations has been the key fact of postwar American economic history. Some six or seven million workers, more than 9 percent of the labor force, are now dependent for jobs on the arms budget. If military spending were reduced once again to pre-Second World War proportions, the nation's economy would return to a state of profound depression, characterized by unemployment rates of 15 percent and up, such as prevailed during the 1930s. . . .

The New Deal managed to push government spending up by more than 70 percent, but this was nowhere near enough to bring the economy to a level at which human and material resources were fully employed. Resistance of the oligarchy to further expansion in civilian spending hardened and held with unemployment still well above 15 percent of the labor force. By 1939 it was becoming increasingly clear that liberal reform had sadly failed to rescue United States monopoly capitalism from its own self-destructive tendencies. As Roosevelt's second term approached its end, a profound sense of frustration and uneasiness crept over the country.

Then came the war, and with it salvation. Government spending soared and unemployment plummeted. . . .

. . . The need of the American oligarchy for a large and growing military machine is a logical corollary of its purpose to contain, compress, and eventually destroy the rival world socialist system. . . .

. . . What really interests the giant multinational corporations which dominate American policy? What they want is *monopolistic control* over foreign sources of supply and foreign markets, enabling them to buy and sell on specially privileged terms, to shift orders from one subsidiary to another, to favor this country or that depending on which has the most advantageous tax, labor, and other policies—in a word, they want to do business on their own terms and wherever they choose. And for this what they need is not trading partners but "allies" and clients willing to adjust their laws and policies to the requirements of American Big Business. . . .

It would be misleading to leave the impression that only the oligarchy has favored the steady increase in military spending during these years. If one assumes the permanence of monopoly capitalism, with its proved incapacity to make rational use for peaceful and humane ends of its enormous productive potential, one must decide whether one prefers the mass unemployment and hopelessness characteristic of the Great Depression or the relative job security and material well-being provided by the huge military budgets of the 1940s and 1950s. Since most Americans, workers included, still do assume without question the permanence of the system, it is only natural that they should prefer the situation which is personally and privately more advantageous. And in order to rationalize this preference, they have accepted the official ideology of anti-Communism which appears to justify an unlimited expansion of the military establishment as essential to national survival.

Ten

. . . The real battlefields between capitalism and socialism have for years now been in Asia, Africa, and Latin America—in Korea, Vietnam, Algeria, Cuba, the Congo. The United States has been directly and militarily involved in most of these battles, and there is every reason to think that the leaders of the American oligarchy expect to go on being involved on an increasing scale in the future. This is the plain meaning of the increasing emphasis within the American military establishment on conventional arms, on building up so-called "counterinsurgency" and "special" forces, on the type of military planning and deployment of troops and supplies. . . .

These activities will continue and grow. They will undoubtedly lead to a long series of catastrophes, crises, and confrontations–of a kind with which we are already all too familiar. What does not seem likely is that they can provide any substitute for the nuclear arms race as an object for military spending. The fateful question "on what?" to which monopoly capitalism can find no answer in the realm of civilian spending has crept subversively into the military establishment itself. From all present indications there is no answer there either.

THE IRRATIONAL SYSTEM

It is of the essence of capitalism that both goods and labor power are typically bought and sold on the market. In such a society relations among individuals are dominated by the principle of the exchange of equivalents, of *quid pro quo,* not only in economic matters but in all other aspects of life as well.

Not that the principle of equivalent exchange is or ever has been universally practiced in capitalist society. As Marx showed so convincingly in the closing chapters of the first volume of *Capital,* the primary accumulation of capital was effected through violence and plunder, and the same methods continue in daily use throughout capitalism's dependent colonies and semi-colonies. Nevertheless the ideological sway of *quid pro quo* became all but absolute. In their relations with each other and in what they teach those over whom they rule, capitalists are fully committed to the principle of *quid pro quo,* both as a guide to action and as a standard of morality.

This commitment reflected an important step forward in the development of the forces of production and in the evolution of human consciousness. Only on the basis of equivalent exchange was it possible to realize the more rational utilization of human and material resources which has been the central achievement of capitalism. At the same time, it must never be forgotten that the rationality of *quid pro quo* is specifically capitalist rationality which at a certain stage of development becomes incompatible with the underlying forces and relations of production. To ignore this and to treat *quid pro quo* as a universal maxim of rational conduct is in itself an aspect of bourgeois ideology, just as the radical-sounding assertion that under socialism exchange of equivalents can be immediately dispensed with betrays a utopian view of the nature of the economic problems faced by a socialist society.

But even during the life span of capitalism itself, *quid pro quo* breaks down as a rational principle of economic and social organization. The giant corporation withdraws from the sphere of the market large segments of economic activity and subjects them to scientifically designed administration. This change represents a continuous increase in the rationality of the parts of the system, but it is not accompanied by any rationalization of the whole. On the contrary, with commodities being priced not according to their costs of production but to yield the maximum possible profit, the principle of *quid pro quo* turns into the opposite of a promoter of rational economic organization and instead becomes a formula for maintaining scarcity in the midst of potential plenty. Human and material resources remain idle because there is in the market no *quid* to exchange against the *quo* of their potential output. And this is true even though the real cost of such output would be nil. In the most advanced capitalist country a large part of the population lives in abysmal poverty while in the underdeveloped countries hundreds of millions suffer from disease and starvation because there is no mechanism for effecting an exchange of what they could produce for what they so desperately need. Insistence on the inviolability of equivalent exchange when what is to be exchanged costs nothing, strict economizing of resources when a large proportion of them goes to waste—these are obviously the very denial of the rationality which the concept of value and the principle of *quid pro quo* originally expressed.

The obsolescence of such central categories of bourgeois thought is but one symptom of the profoundly contradictory nature of monopoly capitalism, of the ever sharpening conflict between the rapidly advancing rationalization of the actual processes of production and the undiminished *elementality* of the system as a whole. This conflict affects all aspects of society. While rationality has been conquering ever new areas of consciousness, the inability of bourgeois thought to comprehend the development of society as a whole has remained essentially unchanged, a faithful mirror of the continuing elementality and irrationality of the capitalist order itself.

Social reality is therefore conceived in outlived, topsy-turvy, and fetishistic terms. Powerless to justify an irrational and inhuman social order and unable to answer the increasingly urgent questions which it poses, bourgeois ideology clings to concepts that are anachronistic and moribund. Its bankruptcy manifests itself not so much in the generation of new fetishes and half-truths as in the stubborn upholding of old fetishes and half-truths which now turn into blatant lies. And the more these old fetishes and half-truths lose whatever truth content they once possessed the more insistently they are hammered, like advertising slogans, into the popular consciousness.

The claim that the United States economy is a "free enterprise" system is a case in point. At no time was enterprise really free in the sense that anyone who wanted to could start a business of his own. Still the concept conveyed an important aspect of the truth by pointing up the difference between the relative freedom of competitive capitalism on the one hand and the restrictions imposed by the guild system and the mercantilist state on the other. Having long ago lost this limited claim to truthfulness and referring as it now does to the freedom of giant corporations to exercise undisturbed their vast monopoly powers, "free enterprise" has turned into a shibboleth devoid of all descriptive or explanatory validity.

Of a similar nature is the incessant repetition that the political regime in the United States today is a democracy. In the United States, as in all other capitalist countries, the propertyless masses have never been in a position to determine the conditions of their lives or the policies of the nation's government. Nevertheless as long as democracy meant the overthrow of monarchial despotism and the ascent to power of a relatively numerous bourgeoisie, the term focused attention on a major change in the life of society. But what is left of this truth content in a society in which a tiny oligarchy resting on vast economic power and in full control of society's political and cultural apparatus makes all the important political decisions? Clearly the claim that such a society is democratic serves to conceal, not to reveal, the truth. . . .

Adam Smith saw in the division of labor the key to the wealth of nations, and he was of course right. Many before and after him saw a darker side, and they were right too. In Marx's words, "the division of labor seizes upon not only the economic but every other sphere of society and everywhere lays the foundation of that all-engrossing system of specializing and sorting men, that development in a man of one single faculty at the expense of all other faculties which caused A. Ferguson, the master of Adam Smith, to exclaim: 'We make a nation of helots and have no free citizens.' " . . .

Marx thought that such a high degree of labor productivity could be realized only in a "higher stage of communist society." We can now see that this was an illusion, that from the point of view of raising the productivity of labor, capitalism had a much greater potential than Marx, or for that matter contemporary bourgeois social scientists, imagined. The giant corporation has proved to be an unprecedentedly effective instrument for promoting science and technology and for harnessing them to the production of goods and services. In the United States today the means already exist for overcoming poverty, for supplying everyone with the necessities and conveniences of life, for giving to all a genuinely rounded education and the free time to develop their faculties to the full—in a word for escaping from that all-engrossing system of specializing and sorting men of which Marx wrote.

In fact, of course, nothing of the sort has happened. Men are still being specialized and sorted, imprisoned in the narrow cells prepared for them by the division of labor, their faculties stunted and their minds diminished. And a threat to their security and peace of mind which already loomed large in Marx's day has grown in direct proportion to the spreading incidence and accelerated speed of technological change under monopoly capitalism. . . .

"There is," Paul Goodman writes, " 'nearly full employment' (with highly significant exceptions), but there get to be fewer jobs that are necessary and unquestionably useful; that require energy and draw on some of one's best capacities; and that can be done keeping one's honor and dignity." Goodman is certainly right to stress that this "simple objective fact" is important in explaining the troubles of young people in this society. But it is more than that: it is important in explaining the alienation from work, the cynicism, the corruption which permeate every nook and cranny of monopoly capitalism and which anyone with a sense of history cannot fail to recognize as characteristic features of a society in full decline.

Asked if he liked his job, one of John Updike's characters replied, "Hell, it wouldn't be a job if I liked it." All but a tiny minority of specially lucky or privileged workers would undoubtedly agree. There is nothing inherently interesting about most of the narrowly subdivided tasks which workers are obliged to perform; and with the purpose of the job at best obscure and at worst humanly degrading, the worker can find no satisfaction in what his efforts accomplish. As far as he is concerned, the one justification is the paycheck.

The paycheck is the key to whatever gratifications are allowed to working people in this society: such self-respect, status, and recognition by one's fellows as can be achieved depend primarily on the possession of material objects. The worker's house, the model of his automobile, his wife's clothes–all assume major significance as indexes of success or failure. And yet within the existing social framework these objects of consumption increasingly lose their capacity to satisfy. Forces similar to those which destroy the workers' identification with his work lead to the erosion of his self-identification as a consumer. With goods being sought for their status-bearing qualities, the drive to substitute the newer and more expensive for the older and cheaper ceases to be related to the serviceability of the goods and becomes a means of climbing up a rung on the social ladder.

In this way consumption becomes a sort of extension and continuation of the process of earning a livelihood. Just as the worker is always under pressure to get ahead at the expense of his fellows at the shop or office, so the consumer pursues the same goals at the expense of his neighbors after work. Neither worker nor consumer is ever really satisfied; they are always on the lookout for a new job, always wanting to move to a better neighborhood. Work and consumption thus share the same ambiguity: while fulfilling the basic needs of survival, they increasingly lose their inner content and meaning.

Nor are matters any better when it comes to another aspect of the worker's non-work life–the expenditure of leisure time. Leisure has traditionally been thought of as serving the purpose of "recreation," that is to say the revival and refocusing of mental and psychic energies from their compulsory commitment to work to genuinely interesting pursuits. Now, however, the function of leisure undergoes a change. As Erich Fromm has observed, leisure becomes a synonym of time spent in passivity, of idleness. It no longer signifies doing what a person *wants* to do, as distinct from doing, at work, what he *must* do; to an ever-increasing extent it means simply doing nothing. And the reason for doing nothing is partly that there is so little that is humanly interesting to do, but perhaps even more because the emptiness and purposelessness of life in capitalist society stifles the desire to do anything.

This propensity to do nothing has had a decisive part in determining the kinds of entertainment which are supplied to fill the leisure hour–in the evenings, on weekends and holidays, during vacations. The basic principle is that whatever is presented–reading matter, movies, radio and TV programs–must not make undue demands on the intellectual and emotional resources of the recipients: the purpose is to provide *"fun"* "relaxation," a "good time"–in short, passively absorbable amusement. Even the form and organization of the material is affected. The show is continuous, the movie theater can be entered at any time; the book can be read from front to back or from back to front; skipping a few installments of a serial does not matter; the TV can be switched from channel to channel without loss of coherence or comprehensions.

Other forms of "killing time"–what a revealing expression!–are hardly more exacting. Being a sports fan does not involve participation in any activity or acquiring any skill. Events are provided for all seasons, and it is not even necessary to attend in person since giant corporations find it a profitable form of advertising to sponsor radio and TV broadcasts of games and matches. Elaborate statistical records are compiled and regularly published in specialized books and periodicals, enabling even fans who have never played a game in their lives to discuss the various teams and players with all the assurance of experts. Being interested at different times of the year in the sports appropriate to the season turns into something people have in common. Like the largely imaginary good and bad points of different makes and models of automobiles, the strengths and weaknesses of teams and players become topics of conversation which the inherent triviality of the theme transforms into mere chatter. . . .

With the increasing specialization and rationalization of the part processes of the capitalist economy, calculation has come to pervade all aspects of life. The individual is pressed from the very beginning into one of the available prefabricated molds—depending on the social class and stratum to which he, or rather his family, belongs—and the normal outcome is a standardized, rationalized human product systematically checked by means of statistical quality controls administered by innumerable testing services from nursery school on. This "product's" reactions and responses become increasingly automatic and predictable. Smiling is to be expected from receptionists and airline hostesses, from sales clerks and gas station attendants—regardless of their mood, their physical condition, their attitude toward the other party. A sustained display of cheerfulness is a necessity in dealing with workers and employees, suppliers and customers—equally regardless of the content and meaning of these dealings as such. Similarly, whether a person, a landscape, a musical composition is judged beautiful depends not on its specific characteristics but on its market success, relation to the latest fad, cost, newness, its capacity to purvey "fun" and "relaxation." . . .

. . . Behind the emptiness, the degradation, and the suffering which poison human existence in this society lies the profound irrationality and moral bankruptcy of monopoly capitalism itself. No outraged protests, no reforms within the monopoly capitalist framework can arrest the decay of the whole. And as becomes clearer every day, this decay makes increasingly problematical the rationality of even the most spectacular advances in scientific knowledge and technical and organizational skills. Improvements in the means of mass communication merely hasten the degeneration of popular culture. The utmost perfection in the manufacture of weapons of destruction does not make their production rational. The irrationality of the end negates all improvements of the means. Rationality itself becomes irrational. We have reached a point where the only true rationality lies in action to overthrow what has become a hopelessly irrational system.

Will such action be forthcoming in sufficient volume and intensity to accomplish its purpose? The future of the United States and of monopoly capitalism obviously depends on the answer. So also, though more indirectly, does the future of mankind itself for a long time to come.

The answer of traditional Marxian orthodoxy—that the industrial proletariat must eventually rise in revolution against its capitalist oppressors—no longer carries conviction. Industrial workers are a diminishing minority of the American working class, and their organized cores in the basic industries have to a large extent been integrated into the system as consumers and ideologically conditioned members of the society. They are not, as the industrial workers were in Marx's day, the system's special victims, although they suffer from its elementality and irrationality along with all other classes and strata—more than some, less than others.

The system of course has its special victims. They are the unemployed and the unemployable, the migrant farm workers, the inhabitants of the big city ghettos, the school dropouts, the aged subsisting on meager pensions—in a word, the outsiders, those who because of their limited command over purchasing power are unable to avail themselves of the gratifications, such as they are, of consumption. But these groups, despite their impressive numbers, are too heterogeneous, too scattered and fragmented, to constitute a coherent force in society. And the oligarchy knows how, through doles and handouts, to keep them divided and to prevent their becoming a lumpen-proletariat of desperate starvelings.[26]

If we confine attention to the inner dynamics of advanced monopoly capitalism, it is hard to avoid the conclusion that the prospect of effective revolutionary action to overthrow the system is slim. Viewed from this angle, the more likely course of development would seem to be a continuation of the present process of decay, with the contradiction between the compulsions of the system and the elementary needs of human nature becoming ever more insupportable. The logical outcome would be the spread of increasingly severe psychic disorders leading to the impairment and eventual breakdown of the system's ability to function even on its own terms.[27]

. . . Advanced monopoly capitalism does not exist in isolation, and any speculation about its future which takes account only of its inner laws and tendencies is certain to be misleading. The United States dominates and exploits to one extent or another all the countries and territories of the so-called "free world" and correspondingly meets with varying degrees of resistance. The highest form of resistance is revolutionary war aimed at withdrawal from the world capitalist system and the initiation of social and economic reconstruction on a socialist basis. Such warfare has never been absent since the Second World War, and the revolutionary peoples have achieved a series of historic victories in Vietnam, China, Korea, Cuba, and Algeria. These victories, taken together with the increasingly obvious inability of the underdeveloped countries to solve their problems within the framework of the world capitalist system, have sown the seeds of revolution throughout the continents of Asia, Africa, and Latin America. Some of these seeds will sprout and ripen rapidly, others slowly, still others perhaps not until after a long period of germination. What seems in any case clear is that they are now implanted beyond any prospect of extirpation. It is no longer mere rhetoric to speak of the world revolution: the term

---

26. These are of course the objectives of the Johnson administration's so-called war on poverty.

27. That we may already be entering such a stage is suggested by the findings of the so-called Midtown Manhattan Study, by far the most thorough investigation yet undertaken of the mental health of a large population sample. Based on eight years of research in a relatively well-to-do, all-white area in New York City, and referring only to adults between ages 20 and 59, this Study found that only 18.5 percent of the sample could be classified as Well, i.e., free from significant symptoms. The Mild and Moderate levels of symptom formation accounted for 36.3 and 21.8 percent of the sample respectively. The Marked, Severe, and Incapacitated were 13.2, 7.5, and 2.7 percent respectively. Thus over four fifths of the sample were found to be suffering from some identifiable form of mental disturbance, and nearly a quarter were "in the impaired range of the mental health continuum." Leo Srole and others, *Mental Health in the Metropolis: The Midtown Manhattan Study*, New York, Toronto, London, 1962, p. 342.

describes what is already a reality and is certain to become increasingly the dominant characteristic of the historical epoch in which we live.

The implications of this fact for the future of monopoly capitalism are only beginning to become apparent. The ruling class of the United States understands, instinctively and through experience, that every advance of the world revolution is a defeat—economic, political and moral—for itself. It is determined to resist such advances wherever they may threaten, by whatever means may be available; and it counts on its enormous superiority in the technology of warfare to bring it victory. But the truth is that in this struggle there can be no real victories for the counter-revolutionary side. Underlying the revolutionary upsurge are real economic, social, and demographic problems; and it is the very nature of counterrevolution to prevent these problems from being rationally attacked, let alone solved. Counterrevolution may win, indeed already has won, many battles, but the war goes on and inexorably spreads to new peoples and new regions. And as it spreads so does the involvement of the United States.

No one can now foresee all the consequences for the United States of this increasing commitment to the cause of world counterrevolution, but equally no one can doubt that it will profoundly affect the inner as well as the outer course of events. In the long run its main impact may well be on the youth of the nation. The need for military manpower seems certain to rise sharply; it may soon be normal for young Americans to spend several years of their lives, if they are lucky enough to survive, fighting in the jungles and mountains of Asia, Africa, and Latin America. The psychic stress and physical suffering experienced by them and their families will add a new dimension to the agony inflicted by an anti-human social order. Will the effect be merely to hasten the process of decay already so far advanced? Will the shock perhaps awaken more and more people to the urgent need for basic change? Or will, as some believe, the increasingly evident hopelessness of its cause lead the American ruling class to the ultimate irrationality of unleashing nuclear holocaust?

That no one can now answer these questions means that all the options are not foreclosed, that action aimed at altering the course of events has a chance to succeed. There are even indications, especially in the Negro freedom movement in the South, in the uprisings of the urban ghettos, and in the academic community's mounting protest against the war in Vietnam, that significant segments of the American people are ready to join an active struggle against what is being cumulatively revealed as an intolerable social order. If this is so, who can set limits to the numbers who may join them in the future?

But even if the present protest movements should suffer defeat or prove abortive, that would be no reason to write off permanently the possibility of a real revolutionary movement in the United States. As the world revolution spreads and as the socialist countries show by their example that it is possible to use man's mastery over the forces of nature to build a rational society satisfying the human needs of human beings, more and more Americans are bound to question the necessity of what they now take for granted. And once that happens on a mass scale, the most powerful supports of the present irrational system will crumble and the problem of creating anew will impose itself as a sheer necessity. This will not happen in five years or ten, perhaps not in the present century: few great historical dramas run their course in so short a time. But perhaps even fewer, once they are fairly started, change their nature or reverse their direction until all their potentialities have been revealed. The drama of our time is the world revolution; it can never come to an end until it has encompassed the whole world.

In the meantime, what we in the United States need is historical perspective, courage to face the facts, and faith in mankind and its future. Having these, we can recognize our moral obligation to devote ourselves to fighting against an evil and destructive system which maims, oppresses, and dishonors those who live under it, and which threatens devastation and death to millions of others around the globe.

HERBERT MARCUSE

Formerly Professor of Philosophy, University of California at San Diego.

The following article by Herbert Marcuse, the widely-read German social and economic philosopher, is excerpted from his short book *An Essay on Liberation*. In this work, according to his publisher,

> Marcuse . . . argues that the time for utopian speculation has come, . . . the traditional conceptions of human freedom have been rendered obsolete by the development of advanced industrial society. Social theory can no longer content itself with repeating the formula, "from each according to his ability, to each according to his needs," but must now investigate the nature of human needs themselves. Marcuse's claim is that even if production were controlled and determined by the workers society would still be repressive—unless the workers themselves had the needs and aspirations of free men.

It is clear that, for Marcuse, the transition of social control from capitalists to workers will not suffice to liberate man from domination and exploitation. He must still contend with the tendency of his technological society to mold a "one-dimensional man": a man whose mind is culturally manipulated to repress his drive for freedom. As Marcuse puts it, modern society (especially but not exclusively the capitalist variety) actively whittles down "the inner dimensions of the mind in which opposition to the status quo can take root." Because of this, Marcuse sees capitalism as a totalitarian society:

> For "totalitarian" is not only a terroristic political coordination of society, but also a non-terroristic economic-technical coordination which operates through the manipulation of needs by vested interests.

Marcuse thinks modern technology has the potential to liberate man from a good deal of his physical toil and from material deprivation. But a truly free and democratic society depends upon the emergence of a new morality, a new sensitivity, a new level of consciousness that opposes the "false needs" of the established society. Marcuse sees several groups in America that could act as the catalysts for rebellion against the system and radicalize the working classes, if the system becomes economically and socially unstable. These small and weakly organized agents of change are not defined along Marxian class lines, but can be found among the nonconformist youth, the young middle-class intelligentsia, and the ghetto populations.

The feeling that man's violent and competitive nature is a product of the society in which he lives is a characteristic theme of utopian socialist literature of both the Marxist and non-Marxist varieties. The idea that deep in the libido there exist life instincts that "strive for the unification and enhancement of life" also reflects the Freudian idea that hostility to an existing culture may arise from "the primitive roots of the personality still unfettered by civilizing influences." In Marcuse one certainly does see a combination of Marxian and Freudian influences. But unlike Marx, he concentrates on the cultural rather than the economic structure of society as the one that needs transformation. He does not deny that capitalism has internal contradictions, but he feels "that in the present period [it] has been able to manage these contradictions." Although he is pessimistic about the possibility of establishing the utopian society which he desires, he seems to feel that capitalism might break down if its "moral fiber" wears thin enough:

> The result would be a spread, not only of discontent and mental sickness, but also of inefficiency, resistance to work, refusal to perform, negligence, indifference—factors of dysfunction which would hit a highly centralized and coordinated apparatus, where breakdown at one point may easily affect larger sections of the whole.

Marcuse's argument that the contradictions and irrationalities of advanced capitalism could manifest themselves in society's psychological makeup parallels that of Baran and Sweezy in the preceding article.

It seems, in reviewing Marcuse's critique of capitalism, that he believes a radical transformation of values is taking place, although at a slow and uneven pace. In more recent writings, he attempts to search out other potential agents of change and points to the possible development of a new level of consciousness. In a comment on the Watergate affair in a 1973 article in the *New York Times,* he said:

> The student movement has been broken up; the opposition has retreated. Temporarily, because the spirit of 1968–70 lives on, all over the nation, and not only among the young and the intelligentsia. . . . This opposition does not come from the left: it comes from those conservative and liberal forces which are still committed to the progressive ideas of the Republic.

R R

From

AN ESSAY ON LIBERATION

(1969)

A BIOLOGICAL FOUNDATION FOR SOCIALISM

In the affluent society, capitalism comes into its own. The two mainsprings of its dynamic—the escalation of commodity production and productive exploitation—join and permeate all dimensions of private and public existence. The available material and intellectual resources (the potential of liberation) have so much outgrown the established institutions that only the systematic increase in waste, destruction, and management keeps the system going. The opposition which escapes suppression by the police, the courts, the representatives of the people, and the people themselves, finds expression in the diffused rebellion among the youth and the intelligentsia, and in the daily struggle of the persecuted minorities. The armed class struggle is waged outside: by the wretched of the earth who fight the affluent monster.

The critical analysis of this society

calls for new categories: moral, political, aesthetic. I shall try to develop them in the course of the discussion. The category of obscenity will serve as an introduction.

This society is obscene in producing and indecently exposing a stifling abundance of wares while depriving its victims abroad of the necessities of life; obscene in stuffing itself and its garbage cans while poisoning and burning the scarce foodstuffs in the fields of its aggression; obscene in the words and smiles of its politicians and entertainers; in its prayers, in its ignorance, and in the wisdom of its kept intellectuals.

Obscenity is a moral concept in the verbal arsenal of the Establishment, which abuses the term by applying it, not to expressions of its own morality but to those of another. Obscene is not the picture of a naked woman who exposes her pubic hair but that of a fully clad general who exposes his medals rewarded in a war of aggression; obscene is not the ritual of the Hippies but the declaration of a high dignitary of the Church that war is necessary for peace. Linguistic therapy–that is, the effort to free words (and thereby concepts) from the all but total distortion of their meanings by the Establishment–demands the transfer of moral standards (and of their validation) from the Establishment to the revolt against it. Similarly, the sociological and political vocabulary must be radically reshaped: it must be stripped of its false neutrality; it must be methodically and provocatively "moralized" in terms of the Refusal. Morality is not necessarily and not primarily ideological. In the face of an amoral society, it becomes a political weapon, an effective force which drives people to burn their draft cards, to ridicule national leaders, to demonstrate in the streets, and to unfold signs saying, "Thou shalt not kill," in the nation's churches.

The reaction to obscenity is shame, usually interpreted as the physiological manifestation of the sense of guilt accompanying the transgression of a taboo. The obscene exposures of the affluent society normally provoke neither shame nor a sense of guilt, although this society violates some of the most fundamental moral taboos of civilization. The term obscenity belongs to the sexual sphere; shame and the sense of guilt arise in the Oedipal situation. If in this respect social morality is rooted in sexual morality, then the shamelessness of the affluent society and its effective repression of the sense of guilt would indicate a decline of shame and guilt feeling in the sexual sphere. And indeed, the exposure of the (for all practical purposes) naked body is permitted and even encouraged, and the taboos on pre- and extramarital intercourse are considerably relaxed. Thus we are faced with the contradiction that the liberalization of sexuality provides an instinctual basis for the repressive and aggressive power of the affluent society.

This contradiction can be resolved if we understand that the liberalization of the Establishment's own morality takes place within the framework of effective controls; kept within this framework, the liberalization strengthens the cohesion of the whole. The relaxation of taboos alleviates the sense of guilt and binds (though with considerable ambivalence) the "free" individuals libidinally to the institutionalized fathers. They are powerful but also tolerant fathers, whose management of the nation and its economy delivers and protects the liberties of the citizens. On the other hand, if the violation of taboos transcends the sexual sphere and leads to refusal and rebellion, the sense of guilt is not alleviated and repressed but rather transferred: not we, but the fathers, are guilty; they are not tolerant but false; they want to redeem their own guilt by making us, the sons, guilty; they have created a world of hypocrisy and violence in which we do not wish to live. Instinctual revolt turns into political rebellion, and against this union, the Establishment mobilizes its full force.

This union provokes such a response because it reveals the prospective scope of social change at this stage of development, the extent to which the radical political practice involves a cultural subversion. The refusal with which the opposition confronts the existing society is affirmative in that it envisages a new culture which fulfills the humanistic promises betrayed by the old culture. Political radicalism thus implies moral radicalism: the emergence of a morality which might precondition man for freedom. This radicalism activates the elementary, organic foundation of morality in the human being. Prior to all ethical behavior in accordance with specific social standards, prior to all ideological expression, morality is a "disposition" of the organism, perhaps rooted in the erotic drive to counter aggressiveness, to create and preserve "ever greater unities" of life. We would then have, this side of all "values," an instinctual foundation for solidarity among human beings—a solidarity which has been effectively repressed in line with the requirements of class society but which now appears as a precondition for liberation.

To the degree to which this foundation is itself historical and the malleability of "human nature" reaches into the depth of man's instinctual structure, changes in morality may "sink down" into the "biological"[1] dimension and modify organic behavior. Once a specific morality is firmly established as a norm of social behavior, it is not only introjected—it also operates as a norm of "organic" behavior: the organism receives and reacts to certain stimuli and "ignores" and repels others in accord with the introjected morality, which is thus promoting or impeding the function of the organism as a living cell in the respective society. In this way, a society constantly re-creates, this side of consciousness and ideology, patterns of behavior and aspiration as part of the "nature" of its people, and unless the revolt reaches into this "second" nature, into these ingrown patterns, social change will remain "incomplete," even self-defeating.

The so-called consumer economy and the politics of corporate capitalism have created a second nature of man which ties him libidinally and aggressively to the commodity form. The need for possessing, consuming, handling, and constantly renewing the gadgets, devices, instruments, engines, offered to and imposed upon the people, for using these wares even at the danger of one's own destruction, has become a "biological" need in the sense just defined. The second nature of man thus militates against any change that would disrupt and perhaps even abolish this dependence of

1. I use the terms "biological" and "biology" not in the sense of the scientific discipline, but in order to designate the process and the dimension in which inclinations, behavior patterns, and aspirations become vital needs which, if not satisfied, would cause dysfunction of the organism. Conversely, socially induced needs and aspirations may result in a more pleasurable organic behavior. If biological needs are defined as those which must be satisfied and for which no adequate substitute can be provided, certain cultural needs can "sink down" into the biology of man. We could then speak, for example, of the biological need of freedom, or of some aesthetic needs as having taken root in the organic structure of man, in his "nature," or rather "second nature." This usage of the term "biological" does not imply or assume anything as to the way in which needs are physiologically expressed and transmitted.

man on a market ever more densely filled with merchandise—abolish his existence as a consumer consuming himself in buying and selling. The needs generated by this system are thus eminently stabilizing, conservative needs: the counterrevolution anchored in the instinctual structure.

The market has always been one of exploitation and thereby of domination, insuring the class structure of society. However, the productive process of advanced capitalism has altered the form of domination: the technological veil covers the brute presence and the operation of the class interest in the merchandise. Is it still necessary to state that not technology, not technique, not the machine are the engines of repression, but the presence, in them, of the masters who determine their number, their life span, their power, their place in life, and the need for them? Is it still necessary to repeat that science and technology are the great vehicles of liberation, and that it is only their use and restriction in the repressive society which makes them into vehicles of domination?

Not the automobile is repressive, not the television set is repressive, not the household gadgets are repressive, but the automobile, the television, the gadgets which, produced in accordance with the requirements of profitable exchange, have become part and parcel of the people's own existence, own "actualization." Thus they have to buy part and parcel of their own existence on the market; this existence is the realization of capital. The naked class interest builds the unsafe and obsolescent automobiles, and through them promotes destructive energy; the class interest employs the mass media for the advertising of violence and stupidity, for the creation of captive audiences. In doing so, the masters only obey the demand of the public, of the masses; the famous law of supply and demand establishes the harmony between the rulers and the ruled. This harmony is indeed preestablished to the degree to which the masters have created the public which asks for their wares, and asks for them more insistently if it can release, in and through the wares, its frustration and the aggressiveness resulting from this frustration. Self-determination, the autonomy of the individual, asserts itself in the right to race his automobile, to handle his power tools, to buy a gun, to communicate to mass audiences his opinion, no matter how ignorant, how aggressive, it may be. Organized capitalism has sublimated and turned to socially productive use frustration and primary aggressiveness on an unprecedented scale—unprecedented not in terms of the quality of violence but rather in terms of its capacity to produce long-range contentment and satisfaction, to reproduce the "voluntary servitude." To be sure, frustration, unhappiness, and sickness remain the basis of this sublimation, but the productivity and the brute power of the system still keep the basis well under control. The achievements justify the system of domination. The established values become the people's own values: adaptation turns into spontaneity, autonomy; and the choice between social necessities appears as freedom. In this sense, the continuing exploitation is not only hidden behind the technological veil, but actually "transfigured." The capitalist production relations are responsible not only for the servitude and toil but also for the greater happiness and fun available to the majority of the population—and they deliver more goods than before.

Neither its vastly increased capacity to produce the commodities of satisfaction nor the peaceful management of class conflicts rendered possible by this capacity cancels the essential features of capitalism, namely, the private appropriation of surplus value (steered but not abolished by government intervention) and its realization in the corporate interest. Capitalism reproduces itself by transforming itself, and this transformation is mainly in the improvement of exploitation. Do exploitation and domination cease to be what they are and what they do to man if they are no longer suffered, if they are "compensated" by previously unknown comforts? Does labor cease to be debilitating if mental energy increasingly replaces physical energy in producing the goods and services which sustain a system that makes hell of large areas of the globe? An affirmative answer would justify any form of oppression which keeps the populace calm and content; while a negative answer would deprive the individual of being the judge of his own happiness.

The notion that happiness is an objective condition which demands more than subjective feelings has been effectively obscured; its validity depends on the real solidarity of the species "man," which a society divided into antagonistic classes and nations cannot achieve. As long as this is the history of mankind, the "state of nature," no matter how refined, prevails: a civilized *bellum omnium contra omnes,* in which the happiness of the ones must coexist with the suffering of the others. The First International was the last attempt to realize the solidarity of the species by grounding it in that social class in which the subjective and objective interest, the particular and the universal, coincided (the International is the late concretization of the abstract philosophical concept of "man as man," human being, *"Gattungswesen,"* which plays such a decisive role in Marx' and Engels' early writings). Then, the Spanish civil war aroused this solidarity, which is the driving power of liberation, in the unforgettable, hopeless fight of a tiny minority against the combined forces of fascist and liberal capitalism. Here, in the international brigades which, with their poor weapons, withstood overwhelming technical superiority, was the union of young intellectuals and workers—the union which has become the desperate goal of today's radical opposition.

Attainment of this goal is thwarted by the integration of the organized (and not only the organized) laboring class into the system of advanced capitalism. Under its impact, the distinction between the real and the immediate interest of the exploited has collapsed. This distinction, far from being an abstract idea, was guiding the strategy of the Marxist movements; it expressed the necessity transcending the economic struggle of the laboring classes, to extend wage demands and demands for the improvement of working conditions to the political arena, to drive the class struggle to the point at which the system itself would be at stake, to make foreign as well as domestic policy, the national as well as the class interest, the target of this struggle. The real interest, the attainment of conditions in which man could shape his own life, was that of no longer subordinating his life to the requirements of profitable production, to an apparatus controlled by forces beyond his control. And the attainment of such conditions meant the abolition of capitalism.

It is not simply the higher standard of living, the illusory bridging of the consumer gap between the rulers and the ruled, which has obscured the distinction between the real and the immediate interest of the ruled. Marxian theory soon recognized that impoverishment does not necessarily provide the soil for revolution, that a highly developed consciousness and imagination may generate a vital need for radical change in advanced material conditions. The power of corporate capitalism has stifled the emergence of such a consciousness and imagination; its mass media have adjusted the rational and emotional faculties to its market and its policies and steered them to defense of its dominion. The narrowing of the consumption gap has rendered possible the mental and instinctual coordination of the laboring classes: the majority of organized labor shares the stabilizing, counterrevolutionary needs of the middle classes, as evidenced by their behavior as consumers of the material and cultural merchandise, by their emotional revulsion against the nonconformist intelligentsia. Conversely, where the consumer gap is still wide, where the capitalist culture has not yet reached into every house or hut, the system of stabilizing needs has its limits; the glaring contrast between the privileged class and the exploited leads to a radicalization of the underprivileged. This is the case of the ghetto population and the unemployed in the United States; this is also the case of the laboring classes in the more backward capitalist countries.

By virtue of its basic position in the production process, by virtue of its numerical weight and the weight of exploitation, the working class is still the historical agent of revolution; by virtue of its sharing the stabilizing needs of the system, it has become a conservative, even counterrevolutionary force. Objectively, "in-itself," labor still is the potentially revolutionary class; subjectively, "for-itself," it is not. This theoretical conception has concrete significance in the prevailing situation, in which the working class may help to circumscribe the scope and the targets of political practice.

In the advanced capitalist countries, the radicalization of the working classes is counteracted by a socially engineered arrest of consciousness, and by the development and satisfaction of needs which perpetuate the servitude of the exploited. A vested interest in the existing system is thus fostered in the instinctual structure of the exploited, and the rupture with the continuum of repression—a necessary precondition of liberation—does not occur. It follows that the radical change which is to transform the existing society into a free society must reach into a dimension of the human existence hardly considered in Marxian theory—the "biological" dimension in which the vital, imperative needs and satisfactions of man assert themselves. Inasmuch as these needs and satisfactions reproduce a life in servitude, liberation presupposes changes in this biological dimension, that is to say, different instinctual needs, different reactions of the body as well as the mind.

The qualitative difference between the existing societies and a free society affects all needs and satisfactions beyond the animal level, that is to say, all those which are essential to the *human* species, man as rational animal. All these needs and satisfactions are permeated with the exigencies of profit and exploitation. The entire realm of competitive performances and standardized fun, all the symbols of status, prestige, power, of advertised virility and charm, of commercialized beauty—this entire realm kills in its citizens the very disposition, the organs, for the alternative: freedom without exploitation.

Triumph and end of introjection: the stage where the people cannot reject the system of domination without rejecting themselves, their own repressive instinctual needs and values. We would have to conclude that liberation would mean subversion against the will and against the prevailing interests of the great majority of the people. In this false identification of social and individual needs, in this deep-rooted, "organic" adaptation of the people to a terrible but profitably functioning society, lie the limits of democratic persuasion and evolution. On the overcoming of these limits depends the establishment of democracy.

It is precisely this excessive adaptability of the human organism which propels the perpetuation and extension of the commodity form and, with it, the perpetuation and extension of the social controls over behavior and satisfaction.

> The ever-increasing complexity of the social structure will make some form of regimentation unavoidable, freedom and privacy may come to constitute antisocial luxuries and their attainment to involve real hardships. In consequence, there may emerge by selection a stock of human beings suited genetically to accept as a matter of course a regimented and sheltered way of life in a teeming and polluted world, from which all wilderness and fantasy of nature will have disappeared. The domesticated farm animal and the laboratory rodent on a controlled regimen in a controlled environment will then become true models for the study of man.
>
> Thus, it is apparent that food, natural resources, supplies of power, and other elements involved in the operation of the body machine and of the individual establishment are not the only factors to be considered in determining the optimum number of people that can live on earth. Just as important for maintaining the *human qualities* of life is an environment in which it is possible to satisfy the longing for quiet, privacy, independence, initiative, and some open space. . . .[2]

Capitalist progress thus not only reduces the environment of freedom, the "open space" of the human existence, but also the "longing," the need for such an environment. And in doing so, quantitative progress militates against qualitative change even if the institutional barriers against radical education and action are surmounted. This is the vicious circle: the rupture with the self-propelling conservative continuum of needs must *precede* the revolution which is to usher in a free society, but such rupture itself can be envisaged only in a revolution—a revolution which would be driven by the vital need to be freed from the administered comforts and the destructive productivity of the exploitative society, freed from smooth heteronomy, a revolution which, by virtue of this "biological" foundation, would have the chance of turning quantitative technical progress into qualitatively different ways of life—precisely because it would be a revolution occurring at a high level of material and intellectual development, one which would enable man to conquer scarcity and poverty. If this idea of a radical transformation is to be more than idle speculation, it must have an objective foundation in the production process of advanced industrial society, in its technical capabilities and their use.

For freedom indeed depends largely on technical progress, on the advancement of science. But this fact easily obscures the essential precondition: in order to become vehicles of freedom, science and technology would have to change their present direction and goals; they would have to be reconstructed in accord with a new sensibility—the demands of the life instincts. Then one could speak of a technology of liberation, product of a scientific imagination free to project and design the forms of a human universe without exploitation and toil. But this *gaya scienza* is conceivable only after the historical break in the continuum of

2. René Dubos, *Man Adapting* (New Haven and London: Yale University Press, 1965), pp. 313–314.

domination—as expressive of the needs of a new type of man.[3]

The idea of a new type of man as the member (though not as the builder) of a socialist society appears in Marx and Engels in the concept of the "all-round individual," free to engage in the most varying activities. In the socialist society corresponding to this idea, the free development of individual faculties would replace the subjection of the individual to the division of labor. But no matter what activities the all-round individual would choose, they would be activities which are bound to lose the quality of freedom if exercised "en masse"—and they would be "en masse," for even the most authentic socialist society would inherit the population growth and the mass basis of advanced capitalism. The early Marxian example of the free individuals alternating between hunting, fishing, criticizing, and so on, had a joking-ironical sound from the beginning, indicative of the impossibility anticipating the ways in which liberated human beings would use their freedom. However, the embarrassingly ridiculous sound may also indicate the degree to which this vision has become obsolete and pertains to a stage of the development of the productive forces which has been surpassed. The later Marxian concept implies the continued separation between the realm of necessity and the realm of freedom, between labor and leisure—not only in time, but also in such a manner that the same subject lives a different life in the two realms. According to this Marxian conception, the realm of necessity would continue under socialism to such an extent that real human freedom would prevail only outside the entire sphere of socially necessary labor. Marx rejects the idea that work can ever become play.[4] Alienation would be reduced with the progressive reduction of the working day, but the latter would remain a day of unfreedom, rational but not free. However, the development of the productive forces beyond their capitalist organization suggest the possibility of freedom *within* the realm of necessity. The quantitative reduction of necessary labor could turn into quality (freedom), not in proportion to the reduction but rather to the transformation of the working day, a transformation in which the stupefying, enervating, pseudo-automatic jobs of capitalist progress would be abolished. But the construction of such a society presupposes a type of man with a different sensitivity as well as consciousness: men who would speak a different language, have different gestures, follow different impulses; men who have developed an instinctual barrier against cruelty, brutality, ugliness. Such an instinctual transformation is conceivable as a factor of social change only if it enters the social division of labor, the production relations themselves. They would be shaped by men and women who have the good conscience of being human, tender, sensuous, who are no longer ashamed of themselves—for "the token of freedom attained, that is, no longer being ashamed of ourselves" (Nietzsche, *Die Fröhliche Wissenschaft,* Book III, 275). The imagination of such men and women would fashion their reason and tend to make the process of production a process of creation. This is the utopian concept of socialism which envisages the ingression of freedom into the realm of necessity, and the union between causality by necessity and causality by freedom. The first would mean passing from Marx to Fourier; the second from realism to surrealism.

A utopian conception? It has been the great, real, transcending force, the *"idée neuve,"* in the first powerful rebellion against the whole of the existing society, the rebellion for the total transvaluation of values, for qualitatively different ways of life: the May rebellion in France. The graffiti of the *"jeunesse en colère"* joined Karl Marx and André Breton; the slogan *"l'imagination au pouvoir"* went well with *"les comités (soviets) partout"*; the piano with the jazz player stood well between the barricades; the red flag well fitted the statue of the author of *Les Misérables;* and striking students in Toulouse demanded the revival of the language of the Troubadours, the Albigensians. The new sensibility has become a political force. It crosses the frontier between the capitalist and the communist orbit; it is contagious because the atmosphere, the climate of the established societies, carries the virus.

---

3. The critique of the prevailing scientific establishment as ideological, and the idea of a science which has really come into its own, was expressed in a manifesto issued by the militant students of Paris in May 1968 as follows:

"Refusons aussi la division de la *science* et de *l'idéologie,* la plus pernicieuse de toutes puisqu'elle est sécrétée par nous-mêmes. Nous ne voulons pas plus être gouvernés passivement par les lois de la *science* que par celle de l'économie ou les *impératifs* de la technique. La science est un art dont l'originalité est d'avoir des applications possibles hors d'elle-même.

"Elle ne peut cependant être normative que pour elle-même. Refusons son impérialisme mystifiant, caution de tous les abus et reculs, y compris en son sein, et remplaçons-le par un choix réel parmi les possibles qu'elle nous offre" *(Quelle Université? Quelle Société?* Textes réunis par le centre de regroupement des informations universitaires. Paris: Editions du Seuil, 1968, p. 148).

[Let us also reject the division of science and ideology, the most harmful of all since we ourselves tend to protect it. We no longer wish to be passively governed by the laws of science, any more than those of economics or technology. Science is an art whose special quality lies in the applications it may have in other areas.

Science, however, can establish norms only for itself. Let us cast off its mystic imperialism—the reason for all its inherent abuses—and replace it with a real choice from the possible alternatives it offers us.]

4. For a far more "utopian" conception see the by now familiar passage in the *Grundrisse der Kritik der Politischen Oekonomie* (Berlin: Dietz, 1953), pp. 596 ff.

DANIEL R. FUSFELD

Professor of Economics, University of Michigan.

Fusfeld's writings are in the radical, but not specifically Marxist, tradition; they call for a radical restructuring of society's main economic and political institutions, but lack an adequate understanding of how class conflict in the modern corporate setting might generate the momentum for this action. He assumes that, by and large, the American corporate state has operated successfully enough to satisfy the material and psychological aspirations of the great majority of people (at least in terms of those values the system has been able to transmit to its members), even though radical intellectuals, like Fusfeld himself, see the poignant need for such change. These intellectuals appear to be alone in their awareness that many of our national goals are "irrational," and that any attempt to preserve the existing social structure by imposing more government controls in the face of growing problems—inequality, militarization, racism—will lead to "full-blown fascism."

The working class nowhere appears as an active agent of revolutionary transformation. Its unions are, in fact, viewed as "junior partners" (with the universities) in the socioeconomic system, who engage in mutually advantageous collective bargaining with the "senior partners," or businessmen. "Reasonable" union leaders, in effect, discipline the rank and file, while "wise business management" passes the worker enough economic gains to keep him contented.

Although inflation has disturbed this "mutuality of interest," Fusfeld appears to think that increasing government economic planning—e.g., wage and price controls—will lessen disruptive pressures. In fact, inflation in the price-administered oligopolistic sector is seen as a "safety valve that eases the conflict between unions and management." In short, "as long as government stands ready to maintain aggregate demand at full employment levels, the burden is shifted to the general public, to the mutual benefit of workers and business firms." The inference is that the public rather than the working class is exploited (using the term in a general rather than specific way). Fusfeld has missed (or at least understated) the point that this mutuality of interest is at best partial and temporary. The history of business cycles reveals that gently rising inflation is nonsustainable in our private enterprise system, even though that system is aided and abetted by a strong and sympathetic government. Government planning within the parameters of this system is reactive rather than target planning; thus it cannot integrate the sectors well enough to maintain full employment with no more than modest inflation.

A similar limitation is found in Fusfeld's otherwise excellent discussion of the "symbiosis [mutual need] of big government and big business." In a manner strongly reminiscent of Galbraith's radical-liberalism, Fusfeld states:

> Big business needs big government and the services it performs. Modern macroeconomic policies provide the economic

growth that large corporations need to satisfy their own desires for growth. Full employment stability provides the security and makes possible the long time horizons that enable giant firms to carry out long-range plans.

Again the point is that these policies are not and cannot be continuously effective; a good deal of risk still exists *under* a regime of monopoly capitalism. Despite these caveats, the strength of Fusfeld's analysis lies in detailing the significance, on both the domestic and international level, of the intimate ties between the *positive state*—whose chief characteristic is government intervention in the self-adjusting market to improve efficiency, socialize risks, and lessen conflicts between different groups or classes—and the *supercorporation*. He shows that as the scope of the economy became more national, the "locus of power" shifted to the executive branch (especially the president and military-national security managers), since only they had a national constituency and could thus overcome particularist interests. Moreover, the merging of the public power of this executive-dominated positive state and the private economic power of the supercorporation (whose share of manufacturing assets has increased dramatically over time) created a power bloc whose influence has permeated the most distant quarters of the globe.

Fusfeld correctly points out that the military and political dominance of the United States in the post-World War II period gave American corporations easy access to world markets. It is the international arena that produces the greatest coincidence of big business and big government interests. Fusfeld stresses the unprecedented manner in which American capital penetrated the world economy, and continues to dominate it in terms of the value of world trade and as a supplier of capital. Although he alludes to the monetary collapse of the dollar in 1971 under the combined pressure of domestic inflation and high military spending abroad, Fusfeld does not see that the heyday of American economic domination in world trade is beset by growing contradictions.

When the United States engineered the economic recovery of German and Japanese capitalism following World War II in order to crush the incipient forces of revolution in those countries, we helped set in motion forces that would ultimately weaken the sway of American capitalism. Western Europe and Japan constitute important counter-centers to American hegemony in the world economy. This new state of affairs—neglected by Fusfeld—has important implications on domestic as well as international levels. History suggests that capitalism as a world system has been most stable when based in one truly dominant center with several satellites whose operations meshed with the needs of the center (interpreted, of course, by its leading classes). When the power of this center starts to erode, world capitalism enters an era of instability and vulnerability. Polarization, tension, and conflict characterize the behavior of individuals and major powers alike, caught between the warring forces supporting change or status quo. For better or worse, ours is such an era.

M L

THE RISE OF THE CORPORATE STATE IN AMERICA

(1972)

Every society contains within itself the forces that create its own future. The social order is always in the process of becoming, and the future inevitably must be different from the past. The processes of change are rooted in the past, operate in the present, and thrust into the future. Social scientists have to develop a triple vision; they must look backward to the world we came from, analyze the world in which we live, and try to discern the future into which we will inevitably be cast. The crisis that came upon the world in the mid-1960s–Black revolt, the youth culture, disaffection of the intellectuals, turmoil in Southeast Asia, continuing peasant revolts in many parts of the world, the breakdown of the international financial system–compels us to look for the sources of the crisis, and ask where are we going and what forces propel us. We must look at the past to understand the present and divine the future.

The thesis of this paper is that the United States has moved well down the path toward a corporate state. Economic power is concentrated in the hands of a relatively few supercorporations that are now moving toward a dominance in the world economy to match their position in the domestic economy. Political power has shifted heavily into the hands of the executive branch of the federal government as the positive state has taken on an increasingly significant role. These two centers of economic and political power have developed a growing symbiosis. The self-selecting elite of the supercorporation dominates the decision-making process, while lesser centers of power in labor unions and the universities are drawn into the system as junior partners by a variety of economic and political mechanisms. Because of the tremendous economic strength of the United States, these domestic developments have tremendous import for the rest of the world. They enable American economic and political power to be used in the world at large in the interests of those who manage the emerging American corporate state.

The corporate state in this country involves an economic and political compromise between those who hold power and those who do not. As long as the economic system provides an acceptable degree of security, growing material wealth, and opportunity for further increase for the next generation, the average American does not ask who is running things or what goals are being pursued. The system and those in power remain unchallenged as long as the material payoff is sustained. The elite is free to use the great wealth of America to preserve and extend its power, and to use its power to preserve and extend its wealth.

THREE LONG-TERM TRENDS

Three great long-term trends have dominated the development of American economic institutions in the twentieth century: the continuing growth of giant corporations, the rise of the positive state, and a move toward American dominance in the world economy. To-

Reprinted with permission from the *Journal of Economic Issues,* Vol. VI, No. 1, March 1972. Reprinted also by permission of the author. This paper was the presidential address presented at the Annual Meeting of the Association for Evolutionary Economics, New Orleans, Louisiana, 27–28 December 1971.

gether they converged in the quarter century after World War II to create the basic outlines of the emerging American corporate state.

The Giant Corporation

The chief outlines of the rise of the giant corporation to a position of dominance in the American economy are familiar to all. Three merger movements, at the turn of the century, in the 1920s, and after World War II, created the pattern of big enterprise oligopoly that dominates those sectors of the economy to which we look for the products and services of the affluent economy and the sinews of national power. In manufacturing, for example, the 100 largest firms in 1968 held a larger share of manufacturing assets than the 200 largest in 1950; the 200 largest in 1968 controlled as large a share as the 1,000 largest in 1941. This aggrandizement of the giants is matched by similar, but less well-documented, trends in other sectors of the economy where big enterprise finds its home.

Increased concentration is supplemented by ties that bind large corporations into communities of interest, based on stockholdings by wealthy families, interlocking directorates, and financial connections with large banks. The trust activities of banks and trust companies add another dimension to linkages within the corporate community and strengthen the strategic position of financial institutions. In addition, trade associations promote common policies in both economic and political activity, and strengthen the leadership of large firms within their industries.

Several aspects of the large corporation merit further exploration. First, giant international firms have appeared. The international corporation was made possible by advances in the technology of transportation and communication after World War II (jet aircraft and automatic data communication, for example). U.S. corporations were able to take advantage of the new technology much more readily than foreign corporations, in part because much of that technology was developed here, but chiefly because of the predominance of the United States in world trade and international finance. The result is that U.S.-based corporations dominate the population of giant international corporations and provide an organizational expansion of the U.S. economy that supplements its outward thrust of trade and finance.

Second, the internal organization of the giant corporation is authoritarian, hierarchical, and bureaucratic. It is run from the top by a management that is largely self-selecting. Separation of ownership from control may have spread ownership very widely, although that conclusion remains controversial, but it has enabled managements to free themselves from control by owners to a considerable degree. The chief force with which they must contend is the influence of financial institutions that dominate access to the capital markets. The combination of the rise of giant firms of an authoritarian nature with separation of ownership and control brought a self-selecting business elite whose influence over economic affairs increases with the growing dominance of the firms they manage.

Third, giant corporations become private governments, in the sense that their actions and policies govern the alternatives open to millions of people and thousands of communities. Prices, investment policy, product development, location of plants, wage and employment policies—the whole range of corporate policy—are decisions of national importance because of the size and significance of the organizations that make them. In that sense much of our life is governed by the decisions made by a small group of men who are responsible only to themselves, who select their successors, and whose organizations continue for an indefinite time. A pattern of economic decision-making has emerged that is only imperfectly controlled by market forces and which has questionable legitimacy and limited accountability.

The Positive State

The rise of the positive state is the second major trend that is transforming our economic institutions. Its distinguishing feature is new and expanded functions for the federal government. Starting with the Federal Reserve Act of 1914 and continuing through the Employment Act of 1946 to the full-scale adoption of Keynesian macroeconomic policy in the 1960s, the national government has taken on the function of stabilizing the economy and fostering full employment growth. Simultaneously, it has socialized many of the economic risks of a self-adjusting system of markets through unemployment insurance, workmen's compensation, old age and survivors' insurance, mortgage guarantee programs, guaranty of bank deposits, stabilization of farm prices, and a host of other programs that reduce or shift economic risks that formerly were borne by individuals and business firms. Resolution of conflicts between labor and management is the object of a series of laws related to labor relations. Another area of conflict, that between consumer and seller, has been the concern of legislation at both the federal and state level, starting decades ago with regulation of public utilities and expanding to other areas of regulation decade by decade. Governments at all levels foster the education and training needed to keep a complex economy functioning and growing. All of these measures share a common characteristic. By intervening in the mechanism of the self-adjusting market, they are designed to create a framework within which the modern economy can flourish. They are positive action to achieve designated goals by a positive state, in contrast to the laissez-faire state.

A shift in constitutional law accompanied the functional change taking place in the role of government. The laissez-faire state's constitutional framework of limited powers permitted the federal government to do only those things specifically designated in the Constitution. In a series of path-breaking decisions over a five-year period in the mid-1930s those limitations were set aside: the federal government was enabled to use its taxing and spending powers to further the general welfare, and the general welfare was to be defined by Congress. We moved from a constitution of limitations to a constitution of powers, to use Arthur Selwyn Miller's expressive phrase.

These functional and legal changes were accompanied by a shift in the locus of political power. The New Deal years, with their enlarged federal functions and increased federal budgets, initiated a long-term shift of power from local and state governments to Washington. Within the federal government power tended to shift from the legislative to the executive branch. This change occurred partly because the departments of the executive branch had more funds to spend; the ability to allocate and use those funds increased the power of the administrative bureaucracy. Congress lost control of many programs because they were set up on a continuing basis that seriously reduced the freedom of

Congress to restructure the budget. In addition, new programs or changes in old ones originated in the executive departments; they had the experts and the experience necessary to determine what was necessary to achieve policy goals. Finally, power shifted to the executive branch because the new programs were national in scope. The president and the executive departments had a national constituency, while Congress was an agglomeration of local constituencies. Initiatives for the solution of national problems were bound to come from those with a national political base.

During World War II the locus of power within Washington shifted further, to the military and the national security managers. They had vastly increased funds to spend; they had a technical competence in an area that was a *terra incognita* to most Americans; they had a near monopoly on information; and they held national survival as a hostage. After World War II, when military spending was sharply cut, it seemed as if the power of the national security managers was waning, but events quickly changed their position. The Cold War, the Korean War, McCarthyism and anticommunism, the missile gap of 1960, the rise of Fidel Castro in Cuba, and the Vietnam War pushed military and related spending to new heights. The militarization of America over the last two decades kept the military and the national security managers firmly in positions of great power.

Throughout this period the role of the chief executive also was growing. The president, not Congress, was responsible for the formation of economic policy under the Employment Act of 1946. In addition, foreign policy and international affairs became almost totally the responsibility of the president and the executive branch. As those issues came to dominate postwar federal policy, the president inevitably became the focus of government.

In this fashion, over a period of forty years the locus of power shifted to Washington, within Washington to the executive branch, and within the executive branch to the president and to those policy makers concerned primarily with military and national security affairs.

America and the World

Concurrently with the rise of the giant corporation and the positive state, the United States moved to a position of economic and political dominance in world affairs. It is now the largest single participant in world trade, accounting for over 6 percent of world exports and imports. It is the largest supplier of capital to the world economy, generating more than 50 percent of the world's savings. After decades of foreign investment and an outward flow of capital, the U.S. balance of payments shows an annual net income on private international investment of about $6.4 billion, as compared with about $1.6 billion for the nine next most important trading countries combined (1968 figures). U.S. economic growth and high living standards have made it the world's most important market and the most important source of capital in the world.

The U.S.-based international corporation is in a special position of prominence. In 1970, U.S. direct investment abroad reached $78 billion in book value, and is expected to total $85 billion in 1971. The market value is undoubtedly much greater. Sales from U.S.-owned overseas production facilities are about $68 billion, which is more than double total U.S. exports of about $27 billion. Profit rates earned by overseas facilities generally exceed those from U.S. facilities, which partially explains why foreign operations of U.S. concerns are expanding more rapidly than domestic investment. IBM, for example, earned more total profits in 1970 from its international operations than it did from those in the United States, while Dow Chemical expects its foreign sales to equal its domestic sales sometime during the 1970s.

American economic penetration of the world economy was strengthened by the international financial system established at Bretton Woods in 1944. Under that system each nation's central bank was required to maintain the value of its currency within 1 percent of par. That innocent provision, when combined with a persistent U.S. balance of payments deficit, resulted in an annual shift of assets from foreign to U.S. ownership of from $1 billion to $3 billion annually, which was financed not by U.S. savings, but by foreign central banks. It also created inflationary pressures abroad that had to be countered by macroeconomic policies which tended to restrain economic growth in the countries in which they were applied. Meanwhile, the flow of additional assets to American ownership aided the international growth of U.S. corporations and helped the U.S. government to pay for some of its military commitments abroad.

This system finally collapsed in 1971, under the impact of U.S. inflation and expanded military spending abroad. The inflation brought our seemingly permanent favorable balance of trade to an end, while the Vietnam War escalated our overseas military spending. When foreign central banks indicated unwillingness to finance the resulting $22 billion deficit in the U.S. balance of payments, we were forced to float and then devalue the dollar. The fundamental reality of U.S. economic power politics was revealed by Secretary of the Treasury Connolly, however, who told the Group of Ten at Geneva that the new currency relationships we sought would have to provide a favorable balance of trade for the United States of $13 billion annually, to finance our "normal" foreign investments and overseas military spending with $2 billion to spare for emergencies. He was proposing, in essence, that the contribution of foreigners to U.S. world dominance be shifted from the international financial system to the international trade system, and that it be made permanent rather than subject to the discretion of foreign central banks.

In passing, we should note that Connolly's proposal was equivalent to an annual tax of $13 billion on the U.S. economy, in real terms. Yet neither the public nor Congress were consulted on the American position, which illustrates how much power has shifted into the hands of the executive. We also should note that the agreements reached in mid-December of this year reconstitute the Bretton Woods system with a somewhat greater degree of flexibility, but leave it equally vulnerable to the same forces that brought its downfall.

American economic expansion had political allies. Economic predominance in Canada came from the flow of capital and proximity of markets. Those forces plus the Monroe Doctrine and military and diplomatic intervention brought Latin America under U.S. economic influence. The rest of the world was to be available to American economic interests through the Open Door policy, enunciated first with respect to the Congo in 1884 and later for China in 1895–1900. We even tried colonialism in the Philippines and Cuba, but those were aberrant experiments for a nation whose

Manifest Destiny lay in the pervasive spread of its financial strength and the attracting force of its great market. It is not necessary for the United States to have colonies, or even political spheres of influence, as long as its more than 200 million people consume more than half the world's production of raw materials and manufactured goods, and generate over half the world's savings. It is only necessary that the rest of the world be open.

World War II brought political and military predominance as well. American technology achieved an initial monopoly of nuclear weapons and methods for their delivery. The war had left no nation in Western Europe with the strength to counter the USSR, so we filled the vacuum with troops, economic aid, and military alliances. Liquidation of the British and French empires in Africa and southern Asia brought U.S. military and political power to predominance there. In the Far East our military victory over Japan left us in command. Aside from the Soviet Union, Eastern Europe, and China, world power lay in Washington.

The international thrust of American political and economic power is of the greatest significance for the rise of the American corporate state. The interests of big government and big business coincide most strongly in the international sphere, where the political and military strength of the one supports and is supported by the economic power of the other. For example, U.S. oil companies in North Africa and the Middle East produce crude oil essential to the economic life of Europe and Japan, and they profit accordingly. A U.S. fleet in the Mediterranean not only maintains U.S. power and supports our Western European allies, but also maintains the existing political situation in the area and helps to stabilize economic arrangements there. It is one of the clearest examples of the symbiotic relationships between U.S. political and economic positions around the world. As America moved toward military and political predominance in the years after World War II it finally was able to achieve an Open Door policy that gave U.S. trade and U.S. capital full access to the world.

THE MERGING OF PUBLIC AND PRIVATE POWER

Concentration of economic power and the emergence of executive power in a positive state were not independent of each other. There has been a growing tendency for them to merge. Economists are familiar with an early manifestation, the regulation of utilities and other industries "affected with the public interest." What began ostensibly as protection of the public was gradually transformed into protection of those presumably being regulated, with the power of the state united behind the economic power of industry.

The petroleum industry is the classic example of the cooperative use of public and private power for private gain. It is the second largest industry in the country and its fuel products are essential to a modern economy. The federal and state governments cooperate with the large integrated oil companies to maintain a complex system of market control. The domestic market is protected from foreign competition by federal legislation that restricts and licenses imports of crude oil. The states, under the Interstate Oil Compact Commission, regulate domestic output on the basis of quotas that, in effect, maintain current prices. The quotas are enforced by federal prohibition of transportation in interstate commerce of oil produced above the quotas. Control of crude oil pipelines by the industry giants, validated by an antitrust consent decree, enables large firms to profit from transporting the raw material of smaller competitors. Finally, the industry as a whole is given a favored tax position through its large depletion allowance. This system stabilizes prices and protects the existing firms. The industry charges prices that not only produce a normal profit, but also provide, in normal times, almost all the capital needed for expansion. Existing stockholders can monopolize the gains from economic growth and new technology rather than sharing those gains with suppliers of new capital. Capital for expansion comes from the taxpayer and from the consumer of the industry's products.

On a much larger scale the symbiosis of big business and big government encompasses the whole economy. Big business needs big government and the services it performs. Modern macroeconomic policies provide the economic growth that large corporations need to satisfy their own desires for growth. Full employment stability provides the security and makes possible the long time horizons that enable giant firms to carry out long-range plans. For example, in 1971 the automobile companies begin planning for the automobiles that will be marketed in 1978; they can be relatively secure in their expectations about total purchasing power and automobile demand because they know the federal government will assure relatively full employment. Assurance of full employment growth provides the lush economic environment in which the supercorporation flourishes.

Big business needs big government for a second reason. Socialization of risks, social insurance, and welfare programs resolve some of the personal problems inherent in a market economy. By bringing greater security to people these programs stabilize the social order. They give the ordinary man a stake in the status quo, and they allay some of the discontent that otherwise might lead to social and political change. A similar point might be made about labor legislation and resolution of the conflict between labor and management, but more about that in a moment.

Finally, big business needs big government to educate the technical and managerial cadres that staff big enterprise. Most of the investment in human capital required by the giant corporation is made by governments when not by individuals. Much of the basic scientific research that lays the groundwork for technological change is carried out under public auspices.

On the other side of the bargain, big government needs big business, particularly in a nation that has the position of world power of the United States. The technology of modern warfare is provided by giant firms. Modern weaponry implies such firms as Lockheed Corporation. Faced with this need, the Department of Defense consciously set out to create, foster, and succor such firms during and after World War II. The recent rescue operation for Lockheed is only the latest and largest example of many similar situations in the past. The military-industrial complex, with its intricate and interwoven relationships between public officials and private firms, between public needs and private gain, is the offspring of the dependence of national power upon the economic base provided by big business.

Big government needs big business in an even more fundamental sense. Giant corporations now are so important that government must preserve them in order to keep the economy functioning. The case of the Penn Central Railroad is instructive. That corporation occupies two strategic positions in the economic landscape. Its transportation function is essential for the proper functioning of the industrial economy of the northeastern states; remove the Penn Central and the entire economy must falter. In addition, the financial obligations of the railroad constitute an important share of the assets of many leading banks and insurance companies, and its debts are owed to many municipalities and industrial firms as well. A financial breakdown of the Penn Central could bring with it a succession of other bankruptcies. For these reasons the federal government had to intervene to keep the railroad operating and to enable it to pay its most pressing debts. The entire economy was the Penn Central's hostage, and the federal government responded accordingly.

The mutuality of interest and symbiotic relationship between big business and big government is assuming formal organization. The most recent step in this direction is the system of economic controls instituted by the Nixon administration in its effort to halt inflation. An organization combining representatives of business, labor, and the public, under the leadership of government officials, seeks to define national economic policy with respect to wages and prices, makes decisions that bring those policies into effect, and has the legal sanctions necessary to enforce its decisions.

Whatever one may think of the wisdom or effectiveness of the policies and their administration, we must recognize here both the philosophy and the mode of operation of the corporate state: individual interests are subordinated to the common good, which is determined by representatives of the chief economic interests affected, and the decisions are enforced by the state. It echoes the style pioneered by Fascist Italy and tried once before in this country by the NRA of the 1930s. We do not know what the ultimate pattern will be, but the chances are good that some form of incomes policy embodying those principles will emerge as a permanent feature of the American economic constitution.

Big Business and Big Labor

The emerging corporate state creates a subtle mutuality of interest between big business and big unions, despite the contest between the two in collective bargaining. The pattern of labor-management relations established under the umbrella of federal law helps to preserve and stabilize the positions of big business and big unions. Long-term contracts, industry-wide bargaining, grievance procedures and arbitration, even the process of collective bargaining itself, contribute to the security of both sides. If corporations gain uniform wage rates throughout the industry, one source of cost differences between firms is eliminated and maintenance of common prices in oligopolistic industries is facilitated. Long-term contracts assure large corporations of known wage costs over a period of one to three years, facilitating the planning that gives large firms an advantage over small. Firms protected against unauthorized strikes and work stoppages need not contend with disruption of production lines. As long as reasonable collective bargaining agreements are reached, the industry is protected against government intervention in determining wages and working conditions.

Unions as organizations also benefit. Exclusive bargaining agreements protect the union from having its membership raided by other unions. Grievance procedures and arbitration are means to channel members' discontent into agreed-upon settlement procedures, thereby reducing internal pressures. Even union dues often are collected by the firm and paid directly to the union. Finally, a wise business management will protect a "reasonable" union leadership by seeing to it that its constituents obtain sufficient economic gains to keep it contented with that leadership as well as with their jobs.

In recent years this growing mutuality of interest has been disturbed by the process of inflation. As long as the economy expands at a rate fast enough to maintain reasonably full employment, and government fiscal and monetary policies provide the necessary level of total spending, both unions and management can seek gains that promote inflationary price increases. As long as wage increases plus fringe benefits do not exceed productivity gains, there is no internal cost pressure on the business firm, but it is tempting for unions to push for greater gains, particularly in oligopolistic industries in which administered prices can be moved upward without damaging profits. As long as government stands ready to maintain aggregate demand at full employment levels, the burden is shifted to the general public, to the mutual benefit of workers and business firms. Inflation validated by macroeconomic policy can be a safety valve that eases the conflict between unions and management.

When inflation is caused by excessive aggregate demand, as during the escalation of the Vietnam War, and government imposes fiscal and monetary policies designed to halt the rising prices, the conflict between unions and management is intensified. Union members press for wage increases to compensate for the rapid rise in prices, while management is faced with both rising costs and government pressures to keep prices from going up. These were the conflicts, coming to a head in the summer of 1971, that forced the Nixon administration to take a further step toward the corporate state by imposing controls on prices and wages. It now seems that the controls will succeed in rescuing the corporate community from the pressures of union demands on the one side and deflationary macroeconomic policy on the other.

Clearly there are conflicts within the pattern of mutuality of interest. Inflation created by the state's thrust toward world power disrupts the tripartite relationship between state, corporation, and union. The problem is resolved by a greater dose of economic planning and further development of the corporate state.

The Universities

American universities long have functioned as training grounds for the business elite, particularly schools of law, engineering, and business administration. This function has grown steadily, as technology has become more complex, as the scope of the giant corporation has expanded, and as the legal niceties of corporate relations with government and labor have become more intricate. In recent decades a close relationship between universities and government has arisen to supplement the ties with business. The center of this new relationship was military needs and international affairs: universities did much of the basic and applied research on development of new weapons, and they trained the experts in overseas areas required by the nation's expanded international commitments.

Development of military technology involves a symbiotic relationship between government, universities, and military contractors. Government supports weapons research in the universities; the enterprise hires professors as consultants and sends its personnel into the university's classes; and everyone involved receives some kind of payoff. Roswell Gilpatric, then deputy secretary of defense, described an ideal relationship of this sort in a 1962 speech at South Bend, Indiana, to an audience of midwestern businessmen and university people.

> What Bendix has been doing in this field deserves mention. Bendix personnel, I am informed, have worked closely with the University of Michigan faculty, sharing the use of the University's nuclear reactor in significant research. The Bendix Systems Division, the University, and the Federal Government have been associated in joint meteorological programs in field tests.
>
> Bendix has employed consultants from the University faculty; Bendix technicians have given part-time service as faculty members; and Bendix personnel are encouraged to take advanced courses and to secure degrees from the University–with 30 percent of all company engineers having taken some courses.
>
> I am pleased, also, to learn that Bendix maintains contacts with other great educational institutions in this area, including Michigan State University, Wayne State University, and South Bend's own Notre Dame. These activities may help to explain why Bendix received $172 million of prime military contract awards in Fiscal 1961 and an even larger total in Fiscal 1962.

Sometimes research is done by university departments. Sometimes it centers in quasi-independent research units such as the Lawrence Laboratories (University of California), Willow Run Laboratories (University of Michigan), Lexington Laboratories (MIT), Applied Physics Laboratory (Johns Hopkins), Forrestal Laboratories (Princeton), and Aeronautical Research Laboratory (Cornell). This organizational device partially removes administration of military research from academic controls, and creates an academic vested interest in military programs.

Much university activity outside the sciences is also caught up in the military-industrial-academic complex. International programs and training of foreign language experts are funded heavily by federal fellowships or grants from foundations designed to promote the international interests of the federal government. For example, the Foreign Area Fellowship Program was originated by the Ford Foundation to help the State Department find expertise "required for the effective discharge of this country's increased international responsibilities." The National Defense Education Act also served to move the entire university community toward the goals of national policy.

THE MANAGERIAL ELITE

A self-selecting economic elite dominates the emerging corporate state. There always have been economic and political leaders, but in a world in which power is dispersed an elite is not possible. In modern America, however, power itself is concentrated, both in a relatively small number of giant corporations (200, 250, 500, 750?), and in a small number of executive positions in the federal government. The supercorporation and the positive state have created an institutional structure readily controllable from a small number of strategic positions. How many positions? Perhaps several thousand at the most. Certainly no more than ten thousand business and financial leaders, military men, and federal administrators constitute this power elite.

There have been enough studies of the American managerial elite to give us a rough idea of its nature and changing scope. As a group, it comes predominantly from an urban, white, Protestant, upper or upper-middle income background. Studies of the social and economic characteristics of post–World War II business leaders by W. Lloyd Warner, C. Wright Mills, and G. William Domhof, building on studies of earlier periods by Frank Taussig and William Miller, show very few immigrants or sons of immigrants, small numbers from farm, worker, or lower white-collar backgrounds, relatively few Catholics and Jews, and no Blacks. About 10 percent inherited their top positions by moving into family-dominated companies; about 5 percent are entrepreneurs who built their own companies; some 10–15 percent are professional men, mostly lawyers, who moved into top business positions after professional success. Some 70 percent, however, moved to top positions by working up through the business hierarchy, which is a much greater proportion than in the past. Seventy years ago the entrepreneurs and family-connected managers were far more important (68 percent), the career executive much less important (18 percent), and the proportion of lawyers and other professions was about the same.

These data suggest that the business elite is a relatively open one. It recruits from outside the existing group, and this tendency appears to be increasing. The major source of recruits is the system of higher education; the business elite always has had more education that the average, and today that is more true than ever. The educational system is a primary screening mechanism and partially explains why so many of the business elite are from upper and upper-middle income groups. They tend to be drawn heavily from the Ivy League colleges (where most of the managers from "old wealth" families graduate) and from the large state universities (where most of the career executives receive their educations).

This first level of screening is supplemented by executive training programs and on-the-job training. There the aspiring top manager is indoctrinated with the business point of view and the ideology of management, there he learns to fit in with those already at the top, and there he develops the good judgment that top management requires. Since advancement depends on the judgment of those already at the top, a premium is placed on development of the viewpoints and styles of life that prevail. As Mills put it, "in personal manner and political view, in social ways and business style, he must be like those who are already in, and upon whose judgments his own success rests."

The business elite is a self-perpetuating and self-selecting group which develops a common set of values, an accepted mode of behavior, and an unspoken but recognizable set of goals. The value system, in particular, stresses the desirability of wealth, both for the individual and the nation, and accepts as generally beneficent the institutions of private property and the national state. Indeed, strengthening and preservation of those institutions seems to be the fundamental point of agreement among the business elite, irrespective of their political persuasions. Their value system embraces the slogan of the Medici family in fifteenth-century Florence: "Money to get power, power to protect the money."

The business elite is supplemented by a group of military leaders whose socialization occurs in the military academies. There they learn the values of national power and respect for the status quo, attitudes that are reinforced by the selection process for high command within the military itself and by contact with the leadership of the industrial part of the military-industrial complex.

The managerial elite of the executive branch of the government is another matter. We tend to think of that group as having risen from the political ranks, moving into top governmental positions from governorships, mayoraltys, or other elected posts. While that is true for some, the great majority are drawn from the business world, as studies by the Brookings Institution, Gabriel Kolko, and Richard Barnet have amply shown. In particular, the national security managers of the federal government are drawn almost wholly from the executives of large corporations, large financial institutions, and the large law firms that do their legal business. A similar situation prevails throughout other branches of the federal government, but not to the same extent. Nevertheless, one of the close ties between the positive state and the supercorporation is the presence of a managerial group in government that is drawn in large part from the top ranks of business leadership itself.

Within the managerial elite a complex set of relationships oriented toward achieving a consensus in national policy is at work. Much of what is taken for pluralist determinination of policy by political scientists is, in effect, a pluralism of the managerial elite. A sketch of the process, which is quite familiar to all once we stop to think about it, will clarify the point.

Corporation managers, their bankers and lawyers, and the wealthy families associated with them dominate the boards of trustees of the great private universities scattered from Cambridge to Palo Alto. They also dominate the large foundations, which had their origins in the wealth of an earlier elite generation. The foundations, in turn, provide funds for the "think tanks" staffed by professors and researchers from the academic world and often affiliated with the private universities. The think tanks provide expert advice and advisors directly to government agencies, and also create an expertise used by a wide variety of policy planning groups dominated by foundations and corporate managerial elite, such as The American Assembly, the Committee for Economic Development, and the Council on Foreign Relations. Ideas and personnel from these organizations and think tanks flow to the federal government, particularly the executive branch, and to federal task forces, commissions, and working parties, composed in large part of the managerial elite and its expert advisors. These groups examine problems and make policy recommendations, with the result that national goals and federal policy strategies are derived from a pluralist consensus of the elite. Specific policy programs come from the political hurly-burly of Congress, but the goals of national policy are seldom determined there.

THE POLITICAL ECONOMY OF OUR TIME

The corporate state in America rests on a complex political economy. Its power base is the supercorporation and the executive branch of the positive state. Its goals are strongly oriented toward national power, partly as an end in itself, and partly to preserve the existing structure of wealth. It is directed by a self-selecting and self-perpetuating elite. Its military power and economic strength are used to create a world in which it flourishes.

The power base is narrow, however,

as any elite's must be. Control can be retained only by appeal for support, or at least acquiescence, to millions who do not share directly in either wealth or power. Two methods are used: the growing affluence derived from economic growth, and psychological appeals that seek support on emotional grounds.

First, affluence. Economic growth maintained at rates that exceed the growth of population provides rising real incomes for the great majority of Americans. As long as the system has a material payoff for the average person, little question is raised about who controls power or who has great wealth. This fundamental characteristic of our political economy helps to explain the great emphasis placed on full employment and economic growth as goals of national policy, why the principal representatives of big business embraced Keynesian economics in the 1950s, and why President Nixon could say in 1970, "I am a Keynesian." Keynesian macroeconomic policy is essential to the political compromise that enables an elite-managed corporate state to survive.

The vital importance of the materialist payoff to midde-income America is illustrated by the reaction of public opinion to the Vietnam War. The war brought taxes and inflation that gobbled up real income, and the military draft began to take sons and husbands. The American middle class first became restive and then opposed the war. The material payoff stopped, the political compromise was broken, and opposition spread. Opponents of U.S. expansionism recognized this strategic weakness of the American corporate state relatively early. Ché Guevarra, for example, called for "a thousand Vietnams" to put such great strain on the system that it could not continue.

The U.S. response to that threat is just emerging. Initially, we are Vietnamizing the war in Southeast Asia to reduce the loss of U.S. manpower and placate the suburbs. Inflation is being halted by controls. For the longer strategy, however, we are developing a new type of capital-intensive warfare using electronic sensing, automatically controlled weapons, saturation bombing, and new types of chemical warfare that are designed, with the help of Lockheed's famous C5A, to fight limited wars on a moment's notice in any part of the world with few men and a great deal of material. Simultaneously, we are moving to a volunteer army to eliminate the draft. In the future, wars like those in Vietnam will be hardly distinguishable from peacetime. In both war and peace there will be plenty of jobs in military production, and active warfare on a Vietnam scale will disturb us hardly more than our intervention in the Dominican Republic or Guatemala.

Second, psychological appeals. The corporate state needs more than neo-Keynesian economics and a capital-intensive military technology. It needs spirit, belief in its righteousness, enemies. They are provided. All Americans, rich or poor, are taught the trappings of nationalism from an early age. Much of the teaching of history in our primary and secondary schools performs that function. Stephen Decatur's toast, "My country, right or wrong," is part of our heritage. Lyndon Johnson could appeal to a sense of national honor to justify his Vietnam policy. We are trained from childhood to see national goals as our individual goals, psychologically to identify ourselves with the nation, to feel a warm, emotional attachment to Old Glory. If the conditioning is successful the national goals designed by an elite to advance their wealth and power become the individual goals of millions.

For those who need more we provide a messianic democracy, the idea that the United States has a unique political and economic system more beneficent than any other, and it is the duty of America and Americans to spread that system to less fortunate people around the globe. From this chauvinism springs not only our well-known feelings of superiority to the rest of the world, but also such programs as the Peace Corps, foreign aid, and a series of quasi-charitable efforts that appeal to liberals and reformers.

For the fearful there is anticommunism. It identifies a known enemy of unknown dimensions, an external and internal threat that can never be fully countered. Anticommunism provides an excuse for American world hegemony, a rationale for huge military expenditures and space adventures, reasons for going to war against peasant revolutionary movements in the Third World, and justification for internal surveillance, mass arrests, and political trials.

Every fascist nation developed emotional appeals designed to gain loyalty to the regime. Japan deified the emperor, hated the westerner, and asserted the superiority of the Japanese race. Germany used anticommunism and anti-Semitism in combination with the appeal of Aryan superiority. Spain advertised a "Catholic state," whatever that may be. All were emotional appeals, irrational in their content, to gain acceptance for national goals selected by an elite that were opposed to the best interests of the mass of the people. The corporate state in America follows in the same path.

What Is to Be Done?

The American corporate state is torn by conflict. A broad malaise affects a society in which the great majority of people do not control the decisions that structure their lives. The U.S. position in the world is not sustainable without huge military expenditures, and it leads us into periodic wars that stop the domestic payoff of material gains and break up the political compromise between the haves and have-nots. We have been unable to maintain growing affluence without suffering from inflations that unsettle both domestic and international economic relationships. We have captive nations in our midst, the minority groups we crowd into low-wage, menial, service occupations. Our national goals are seen by increasing numbers of young people and intellectuals as essentially irrational, however rationally we may pursue them.

Our conflicts demand order. A society in turmoil reacts by seeking to impose new systems of control. The only other alternative is drastic change in the structure of society and the locus of power. We face the classic dilemma of the industrial society of the twentieth century. Will we opt for preservation of the existing structure by imposing the controls that keep the system's turmoil in check? Down that path lies the continuing development of our emerging corporate state into a full-blown fascism, the Leviathan of the future.

At the present moment the tacit agreement between those who hold power and those who do not has broken down under the combined impact of the war in Vietnam, the turmoil in our cities, and recognition by many that American society is malign, not benign. The Nixon administration seeks to patch up the cracks and rebuild the political compromise; it seeks a return to the days when the goals of the managerial elite were not seriously questioned; it is doing so by moving closer to the formal organization of the corporate state.

The far more difficult task is to restructure our economic institutions in the direction of a humane society. We need more than prosperity, economic growth, and stable prices. We need a redistribution of wealth to achieve greater equality and freedom. We need a world at peace. Those goals will not be achieved unless we can take the guns away from the generals and power from the managerial elite. We must disperse economic power and governmental authority. We must move to nothing less than a revolutionary transformation of our economic and political institutions.

HERBERT GINTIS

Professor, Harvard Graduate School of Education.

Herbert Gintis' perceptive essay on alienation is in the Marxist tradition, combining as it does economics and political sociology. Gintis does not confine himself to the usual question of whether technology furthers man's alienation or his liberation, whether its main influence is dehumanizing or humanizing. He understands all too well that technology has a totally different thrust for the alienated than for the liberated man, while technology in and of itself is not responsible for either alienation or liberation. It can, in fact, reflect a free and creative consciousness as well as a repressed, alienated one. What is crucial is the kind of society—its values, social relationships, distribution of power and wealth, etc.—in which the technology is being utilized. In bourgeois society, where dominant relationships are on a buying-selling basis, man is necessarily entwined in a multi-tiered web of alienation: from other men, from his own activity, from the community, even from nature. Alienation, Gintis correctly suggests, is inextricably woven into capitalist institutions; the basic relationship of wage-labor and capital makes of man a means and not an end, a tool for the production of wealth rather than an active agent in the planning and organizing of society's human and physical resources:

> The market in labor means that the worker sells his services to the capitalist firm and essentially agrees to relinquish total control over his work activities, thus leaving the determination of work roles to those who control capital and technology. Both technology and work roles are essentially determined by the dictates of profit maximization or output maximization and maintenance of hierarchy.

Bureaucratic organization and hierarchal stratification, which characterize the work process under capitalism, combine to destroy pride in one's work, to impart a sense of powerlessness, to encourage psychic malfunctioning, and to structure social roles so they reflect market criteria while remaining "essentially independent of individual needs." The result is a deep and pervasive sense of alienation on all class or group levels, which Gintis expects to grow rather than diminish over time. Economic growth, moreover, will undermine the psychological foundation of capitalism instead of strengthening it. Social consciousness of alienation will intensify with the discovery that beyond a certain limit, increased output of material goods—a significant justification for capitalism—involves a high cost to society as well as the individual. "Economic growth" says Gintis, "is itself subject to a self-negating dialectic."

Unlike most liberals, Gintis sees the educational system as intensifying rather than ameliorating these alienation-producing factors. Since it is closely intertwined with the capitalist mode of production, including above all the social relations based on a private property system, the educational system will reflect "the impersonal and competitive relations of the community and the bureaucratic-authoritarian aspects of alienated work."

Although Gintis does not spell out the precise dimensions of a new, liberating form of society (and, in rejecting the old, lumps the existing state socialist societies with their capitalist counterparts), its socioeconomic basis is clearly visualized as a "system of direct worker and community control." Marx, in a similar humanistic spirit, stated in the *Communist Manifesto* over five generations ago: "In place of the old bourgeois society, with its classes and class antagonisms, we shall have an association in which the free development of each is the condition for the free development of all." He elaborated this vision of the most developed form of the future society in his later *Critique of the Gotha Program* (1870):

> In a higher phase of Communist [Marx used this term interchangeably with Socialist] society, after the enslaving subordination of individuals under the division of labor, and therefore also the antithesis between mental and physical labor has vanished; after labor from a mere means of life has of itself become the prime necessity of life; after the productive resources have also increased with the all-round development of the individual, and all the springs of cooperative wealth flow more abundantly—only then can the narrow horizon of bourgeois law be fully left behind and society inscribe on its banners: from each according to his ability, to each according to his needs.

The experience of the Soviet Union should serve to moderate the idealism projected by Marx as well as Gintis. True, some of the contradictions besetting capitalism have been overcome in Russia's state socialist society, particularly the one (emphasized by Marx) between the social basis of production and the private property basis of social relations. But alienation is all too obvious in a system where control over socially-owned property resides in a small bureaucracy, and political forms of individual expression are even more primitive than in modern bourgeois societies. The absence of worker participation in the management of production and distribution of resources and output means, in effect, that the State (or Communist Party) has replaced the capitalist as the main alienating force in society. In Stalinist times, this fundamental alienation was strengthened by a deliberate widening of income-status differentials and the imposition of a punitive police apparatus. As Predrag Vranicki, a Yugoslav philosopher, stated:

> Alienation is not the problem of bourgeois society, because that society may [I would say must] exist as an alienated society. Alienation becomes the central problem of socialism, since socialism may exist and develop only under the condition that it overcomes and eliminates alienation.

Just when and how this higher form of society will be attained is among the vital questions of the day. Gintis has performed a valuable service in analyzing the need for such a society within the context of the alienation problem.

ML

ALIENATION IN CAPITALIST SOCIETY

(1972)

SOME SNAPSHOTS

A young ex-marine, perched atop a twenty-story University of Texas building with rifle and rangefinder, topples several dozen unknown passersby. He is alienated—alienated from his fellow men in the strongest sense of the word.

A car salesman spends his waking hours foisting on families automobiles more expensive than they can afford, less useful than he leads them to believe, and so constructed that the customer must return two-and-one-half years later for yet another sale. The salesman is alienated from his fellow men in that less dramatic manner familiar to us all.

A clot of people on a crowded rush-hour street see a man stagger and fall to the ground unconscious. They walk on by, unbothered, not wanting "to get involved." A young woman is threatened, then stabbed to death in full view of her Queens, New York, neighbors. They do not intervene and they notify neither police nor ambulance. They are similarly alienated from their fellow man.

Showing her engagement ring to a friend, a girl said: "You know what did it? I prepared a home-cooked meal for him—in a bikini." She is alienated from her body, and the course of her life may consist in substituting her physical attributes for her true self—exchanging her body for affluence and security.

A man arrives home from a brutal day's work and sits before the television set watching football, hockey, boxing, baseball; he drinks beer and smokes cigarettes and never engages in sports or physical activity himself. He experiences the "humanity of his own body" only vicariously through a Hank Aaron, Joe Namath, or an Arnold Palmer, while he slowly kills himself. He is alienated from his body.

A teenager retreats to his room, liquifies twenty of his mother's diet pills, inserts the solution into a syringe, and finds a vein. He will be dead in three years. He is alienated from his body.

A junior sales and promotion executive has three Martinis for lunch at work—his wife does the same at her Bridge Club at home—and three more before dinner. Their common, non-working life is diffused with Scotch and experienced in an alcoholic haze. They succeed in muting their anxieties and in staving off the brute realization of their personal loneliness and isolation at the cost of destroying themselves. They are also alienated from their bodies.

A throng of furious blacks in Watts (or Harlem or Detroit or Baltimore or Washington, D.C. or . . .) riot, loot, and burn, destroying square blocks of ghetto "property." They realize their lack of control over their communities and lives. They are alienated from their community in a most overt form.

An old couple sits in a dingy room with yellowed papers and magazines collecting in ragged and dusty piles, visited only on Christmas by their children living in other cities, inconscient of, unaided by, and cut off from their neighbors, waiting to die. They are alienated from their community.

A ghetto resident does not bother to vote in the municipal elections because, as he correctly perceives, "the people don't have any say anyway."

The suburbanite, who commutes thirty miles to work each day, does not know even his next door neighbors beyond their daily opinions on the weather prospects; he joins forces with them only in the face of such "external threats" as higher property taxes, a teachers' strike for better schools and working conditions, the threat of teaching sex education in the schools, or the imminent entrance of a black family down the street. These suburbanites are alienated from their community.

Similarly, people are alienated from their work: Monday is the start of a long, boring, anxious, unfulfilled week; Monday is a woman serving her bleary-eyed husband coffee, saying, "What do you mean 'Won't this day ever end?' This is Breakfast!"

THE EXPERIENCE OF ALIENATION

As Robert Blauner explains in his book *Alienation and Freedom,*[1] the worker experiences alienation from work in the form of powerlessness, meaninglessness, isolation, and self-estrangement. He or she is *powerless* because bureaucratic organization is ruled from the top, through lines of hierarchical authority treating the workers as just another piece of machinery, more or less delicate and subject to breakdown, to be directed and dominated.

Work seems *meaningless* because it is divided into numberless fragmented tasks, and the worker has some expertise over only one of these tasks; consequently, his contribution to the final product is minimal, impersonal, and standardized. Work also seems meaningless because most workers realize only too well the limited extent to which their activities contribute to perceived social welfare. If he produces steel, his factory pollutes atmosphere and streams. If he makes automobiles, his product congests, smogs, kills, and, finally, after thirty months of "service," falls apart. If he processes cost accounts or his secretary types the corporation's plan to avoid paying taxes, they know their work is unrelated to satisfying anyone's real needs. If he sells insurance, he understands that his success depends only on his relative cunning and talent in duping his customer.

Moreover, the worker is supremely and uniquely *isolated* in work: fragmentation of tasks precludes true solidarity and cooperation; hierarchical authority lines effectively pit workers on different "levels" against one another; and since workers do not come together to determine through their social interaction the important decisions governing production, no true work community develops. Lastly, the powerless, meaningless, and isolated position of the worker leads him to treat work merely as an *instrument,* as a *means* toward the end of material security, rather than an end in itself. But work is so important to a person's self-definition and self-concept, that he then comes to view *himself* as an instrument, as a means, to some ulterior end. Hence develops his *self-estrangement.*

That a person may be self-estranged —alienated from himself, his essence, and his psyche—has been characterized as the focal point of the industrial workers' self-concept, be he blue-collar or white-collar. As Erich Fromm notes:[2]

> [A man] does not experience himself as an active agent, as the bearer of human powers. He is alienated from these powers, his aim is to sell himself successfully on the market. His sense of self does not stem from his activity as a loving and thinking individual, but from his socioeconomic role. . . . He experiences himself not as a man, with love, fear, convic-

tions, doubts, but as that abstraction, alienated from his real nature, which fulfills a certain function in the social system. His sense of value depends on his success: on whether he can make more of himself than he started out with, whether he is a success. His body, his mind, and his soul are his capital, and his task in life is to invest it favorably, to make a profit of himself. Human qualities like friendliness, courtesy, kindness, are transformed into commodities, into assets of the "personality package" conducive to a higher price on the personality market.

A PROBLEM POSED

That capitalist society is alienating is a central element in the radical critique of capitalism, and the term has even attained general public acknowledgement—bemoaned by politicians everywhere, trotted out as a catchall explanation of "youth unrest" by television commentators, and generally seen by youth themselves as characterizing their own condition. But exactly what alienation *is,* and the nature of its *causes,* remains shrouded in uncertainty and confusion.

The difficulty surrounding the concept of alienation arises from the fact that it comprises both subjective, psychological elements and objective, social elements. Before the rise of the New Left in the decade of the 1960s, alienation was treated as a purely subjective phenomenon, essentially independent of the structure of society. In the Silent Decades following World War II, alienation was proposed as a part of the "human condition" by noted French philosophers, among whom Sartre, Camus, and Beckett are the most widely read in the U.S. We personally encounter the phenomenon on this subjective level, and we respond most immediately to its manifestations in our own lives, in the Beatles' "Nowhere Man," Nichol's *The Graduate,* and Phillip Roth's *Portnoy's Complaint.* Yet the sources of alienation inhere in the social system itself. Alienation as a general phenomenon coincides with the rise of capitalism.

We now see the treatment of alienation as an element of human nature as merely symptomatic of the political quiescence of the Silent Decades. Indeed, the very *appearance* of the concept of alienation coincides with the breakdown of feudal society and the rise of capitalism, in the works of Hegel and Marx, and the literary works of Kafka and Doestoevsky.

Yet the growing awareness of the social basis of alienation—an awareness of quite recent vintage—still fails to achieve the proper analytical depth. This is due in part to the particular *form* in which this awareness in couched. Alienation is seen to arise directly from the nature of technology in "modern industrial society" and, hence, to remain independent of any particular set of economic institutions. This view is reinforced through our understanding of the historical development of capitalism's main competitor, state socialism in the Soviet Union and Eastern Europe. So-called "socialist man" seems to differ little from his capitalist counterpart, and so-called "socialist society" seems little better equipped to avoid the problems of Alienated Man and Alienated Woman than its avowed adversary.

This paper will try to show not only that alienation is a social rather than a psychological problem at its root but that it results from the structure of technology only in the most immediate and superficial sense, because the form that tech-

1. Robert Blauner. *Alienation and Freedom* (Chicago: University of Chicago Press, 1964), especially Chapter 1.

2. Erich Fromm, *The Sane Society* (New York: Rinehart and Winston, Inc., 1955), p. 142.

nological development takes is itself strongly influenced by the structure of economic institutions and their day-to-day operations. If capitalist and so-called socialist economies experience these same problems, it is due to some essential similarities of their basic economic institutions.

AN ANALYSIS

The root meaning of the verb "to alienate" is "to render alien" or, more concretely, "to separate from" (e.g., "She alienated my husband's affections" means "She separated my husband's affections from me"). We can use this root meaning to motivate a social definition of alienation: when your pocket is picked, you are "alienated" from your wallet; similarly, when the structure of society denies you access to life-giving and personally rewarding activities and relationships, you are alienated from your life. Alienation, on the subjective level, means that elements of personal and social life that should be meaningful and integral, become meaningless, fragmented, out of reach, and–if one has an existentialist bent–absurd. The alienated individual is powerless to control central aspects of his life, just as he cannot "control" the wallet snatched from him.

Alienation appears on many levels. Most of these can be explained in terms of *social roles.* A social role is a "slot" that people fit into, carrying with it characteristic duties and obligations, and defined by what other people expect of the person in that role. These expectations become institutionalized, so the same behavior is expected of any individual who occupies a particular role. For example, take the role of foreman. A foreman, no matter what particular individual happens to occupy the position, is expected to supervise his workers, remain somewhat aloof and above them, and in general be more responsive than are the workers to the company's interests in getting the work done. Butcher, baker, worker, soldier, capitalist, lover, husband, community member–all these are social roles.

The nature of these roles and their availability to the individual are quite as important as the distribution of material goods and power in assessing the value of a social system. Alienation occurs because the roles open to individuals do not satisfy their immediate needs in terms of their interpersonal activities in family, community, and work, and their requirements for healthy personal psychic development. Thus, we center on the role concept to emphasize the inherently *social* nature of alienation. To be alienated is to be separated in concrete and specific ways from "things" important to well-being; however, these "things" are not physical objects or natural resources but are types of collaboration with others, with society, and with nature. These "things" are social roles.

The structure of roles at a point in time, and the way they change and develop over time, depends on criteria and priorities laid down by basic social and economic institutions. This is not an obvious assertion, and its truth can only be ascertained through specific examples, to be presented below. But its truth allows us a particularly simple *causal* explanation of alienation under capitalism: alienation arises when the social criteria determining the structure and development of important social roles are *essentially independent of individual needs.* These conditions are precisely what occur under capitalism: the social roles involving participation in work process and community (and to a lesser extent family life) develop in accordance with market criteria and are essentially independent of individual needs. The result is alienation.

Decisions can be made either through institutions or, consciously, in a political manner. The bulk of decision mechanisms in capitalist society are institutionally organized. The distribution of income, the prices of factors of production, the historical development of technology, the organization of work activities, and the structure and development of communities are all basically directed through the impersonal operation of economic institutions and through the economic power they bestow on individuals.

The decisive nature of institutional decision making cannot be overemphasized, because it runs counter to our most immediate political experience. We *experience* the war in Vietnam—an inherently political decision—while the most important aspects of imperialism are effected through the normal operation of international commodity, factor, and financial markets. We *observe* the political battle over tax rates, minimum wage legislation, income redistribution, and welfare programs—all political decision mechanisms—while the fact that the income distribution is basically determined by supply and demand of privately owned factors of production, themselves derived from modes of productive organization, is so basic it remains unnoticed. We *observe* collective bargaining—again a political decision mechanism—when in fact the level of wages is determined by quite other forces, and the institutional context within which the wage bargain is fought sets the determining limits of its outcome. And so it is with the nature, development, and availability of social roles.

An institutional decision mechanism will be termed "alienated" when the criteria—implicit or explicit—that determine outcomes are substantially independent of the wills of individuals whom the outcome affects. Hence the *content* of these criteria are likely, if not inevitably, independent of the *needs* of affected individuals. Insofar as this is true, we shall say that individuals are "alienated" from the social object (be it a physical object; a social role as worker, citizen, consumer, soldier, etc.; another individual; an element of culture; or himself) that is the outcome of the institutional decision.

ALIENATION OF WORK PROCESS

To illustrate the alienating consequences of capitalist institutions, consider the organization of work activities. An individual's work is of utmost importance for his personal life. Work directly engages nearly half of one's active life and is potentially the single major outlet for initiative, creativity, and craft. Moreover, work roles are basic and formative in individual personality development. But are these considerations reflected in the actual social decisions determining the structure of work roles? For instance, is the factory workers' welfare considered when the capitalist decides to produce automobiles by routine and monotonous assembly-line operations? Are the secretary's needs considered when she is reduced to the full-time subservient role of typing, stenography, and stamp licking? The structure of work roles is essentially determined by a set of basic economic institutions that operate on quite different criteria. The market in labor means that the worker sells his services to the capitalist firm and essentially agrees to relinquish total control over his work activities, thus leaving the determination of work roles to those who control capital and technology. Both technology and work roles are essentially determined by the dictates of profit maximization or output maximization and maintenance of hierarchy.

Control of work activities through alienating institutions has implications on both subjective and objective levels. Subjectively, workers mostly experience their work activities as "alien"–as opposing rather than contributing to their personal well-being and psychic growth. This is understandable in that their own needs were peripheral in the decision process determining the nature of work roles–their work activities have been snatched from them.

Objectively, alienating control leads to predictable consequences. In the early stages of the Industrial Revolution, this control resulted in work activities that were brutal, unhealthy, boring and repetitive, and required long hours. More recently, it has taken the form of bureaucratic organization of production, where individual work roles are so fragmented and formalized that the worker finds his initiative and autonomy totally muffled by and subordinated to a mass of regulations and "operating procedures." Also, hierarchical stratification of workers along lines of status and authority subjugates some workers to the personal control of others, subjects all workers to the control of managers and capitalists, and precludes cooperation and equality as a condition of production. Hence, bureaucratic organization and hierarchical control are the concrete modern manifestations of the worker's alienation from his work activities.

Of course, there is a standard objection to the above analysis. Although we have attributed alienation from work activities to capitalist economic institutions, some argue that bureaucratic organization and hierarchical control are simply immutable aspects of "industrial technology"; that, in effect, any "advanced" society must experience alienated labor. There are major errors in this view. It is not true that bureaucratic organization is chosen by capitalists only because it is "efficient" and "modern." It is chosen as well (perhaps primarily) because it is the only means of maintaining and stabilizing control over the profit generated in production and of preventing workers from gaining enough general expertise and initiative to embark on cooperative production on their own. Technologies that potentially increase the breadth of collective and individual control of workers, however productive and efficient, must be avoided if the "stability" of the corporate enterprise is to be secured. The loss of control, even in minor areas, might get out of hand: workers collectives might voice "wild" and "unrealistic" demands in a sort of free-for-all; union and management alike might lose control over workers. I shall illustrate this through several empirical examples.

First, bureaucratized and routinized tasks do not flow from the nature of "technology" but from the needs of centralized control. As Vroom notes in his masterful survey of experimental literature in industrial social psychology:[3]

> [The evidence indicates that] decentralized structures have an advantage for tasks which are difficult, complex, or unusual, while centralized structures are more effective for those which are simple and routinized.

That is, given that the corporate unit is based on centralized control, the most efficient technologies will be those involving routinized, dull, and repetitive tasks. In a decentralized environment, the exact reverse would be true.

Second, workers do not like fragmented jobs. The experimental literature shows that job enlargement and decision-making control on the part of workers increase their satisfaction, while lowering absenteeism and turnover.[4] Nevertheless, managers have organized the normal bureaucratic diversion of tasks so that actual worker performance is *substantially independent of the worker's attitudes and satisfactions.* This startling, counterintuitive fact is one of the major results of fifty years of investigation by industrial psychologists.[5]

Third, this bureaucratic organization of production, while insuring managerial control and corporate security against the vagaries of worker morale, is by no means efficient in the wider sense. For even *moderate* worker participation in decisions and goal setting increases productivity.[6] The average quality of decisions made by a group is moreover greater than the average quality of individual decisions,[7] and the best results are obtained when individuals *think up* solutions individually and *evaluate and choose* among them as solidary team.[8]

Let us give some examples. The MIT-generated Scanlon Plan of "participatory management" has been tried in some ten U.S. plants. This plan gives workers unlimited power to organize and improve the work process and working conditions, and guarantees them a share in the proceeds of cost reduction. In these ten plants, the average yearly increase in productivity amounted to 23.1 percent, and in one company 408 out of the 513 innovative ideas were successfully implemented because they led to real improvements in the productive process. Clearly, a stable dialogue between workers, technicians, and planners would even increase this fertile activity.

These results are reproduced in many other individual studies. When workers are given control over decisions and goal setting, productivity rises dramatically.[9] As Blumberg concludes:

> There is scarcely a study in the entire literature which fails to demonstrate that satisfaction in work is enhanced or . . . productivity increases accrue from a genuine increase in worker's decision-making power. Findings of such consistency, I submit, are rare in social research. . . . The participative worker is an involved worker, for his job becomes an extension of himself and by his decisions he is creating his work, modifying and regulating it.[10]

But such instances of even moderate worker control are instituted only in marginal areas and in isolated firms fighting for survival. When the threat is over, there is a return to "normal operating procedure." The threat of worker escalation of demand for control is simply too great, and the usurpation of the prerogatives of hierarchical authority is quickly quashed. Hence, efficiency in the broader sense is subordinated to the needs of bureaucratic control.

Moreover, it is wrong to think of technology as a single unidimensional force of which an economy can only have "more" or "less," but whose substance and form are essentially independent of social decision. What technology is at a point in time is the sum total of the past

3. Victor H. Vroom, "Industrial Social Psychology," *The Handbook of Social Psychology* V, 2d ed., ed. Gardner Lindzey and Elliot Aronsen (Reading, Massachusetts: Addison-Wesley, 1969), p. 243.

4. *Ibid.*, pp. 199–201.

5. *Ibid.*, p. 199.

6. *Ibid.*, p. 228.

7. *Ibid.*, p. 230.

8. *Ibid.*, p. 232–33.

9. *Ibid.*, p. 234–36.

10. Paul Blumberg, *Industrial Democracy* (New York: Schocken Books, 1969).

decisions made as to what *forms of research* are undertaken and which *results of research* are embodied in actual production in factory and office. Technology is "alienating" in capitalist society (and its state-socialist imitators) in the first instance because it is developed and diffused on the sole criterion of profit, and it is locked into bureaucratic organization only because capitalist and managerial representatives will introduce no new technology that is incompatible with their maintenance of power. So liberated, integrated, and antihierarchical technologies will develop only when we replace capitalist economic institutions by a system of direct worker and community control. Workers are alienated from their work activities because they are powerless to determine, or even significantly affect, the nature of work roles that hold sway over their lives. Work is for the most part "meaningless," not because of the nature of technology and the division of labor, but because the institutions determining them are not tailored to workers' needs.

ALIENATION FROM COMMUNITY

The institutional basis of alienation from work activities is mirrored in other alienating forms. Individuals are also alienated from their community in capitalist society. The roles open to the individual allowing him to relate to his social community are among the most central to his welfare and personal development, and they define his contact with social life. Aside from his work and his basic living and consumption unit—be it nuclear family or more extended commune—social community is the most important potential contribution to his well-being. Yet when his community is ugly, vast, and impersonal and through its fragmented and impotent role structure it fails to provide adequate personal outlets, the individual becomes estranged from his community.

The community in capitalist society is molded by its economic institutions. Because land is controlled individually rather than communally, its use conforms to private as opposed to social interests. If this individual control were distributed equally throughout the population, possibly commonness of interest would lead owners to cooperate in the interests of all. But land and property are very unequally apportioned.

How do powerful owners of land and capital decide its use? Clearly the motive is to maximize their own benefit—that is, their profit. Here a basic economic institution enters in, the "free market in land," whereby each parcel of community property is allocated to the highest bidder for its most remunerative personal use. Traditional economic theory shows that free markets in factors of production and commodities insure, as did Adam Smith's famous "invisible hand," the amassing of labor and the allocation of land according to their most "efficient" use in individual commodity production. This maximal remuneration leads to gargantuan accumulation of individuals in "urban environments" and "sleeping suburbs" whose only purpose is to supply the labor needs of monolithic bureaucratic enterprise. Commercial land use conforms to profit criteria independent of community needs.

Since the community as an autonomous entity, aside from minor zoning and tax regulations, has no control over economic activity and patterns of land use, the basis of stable and solidary community relations withers and disappears. An architecturally and socially integrated community cannot thrive when the only power the community holds over the autonomous activities of profit-maximizing capitalists takes the form of crude constraints, on their creative, synthesizing enterprises and activities.

Rather, a true community must be *itself* a creative, initiating, and synthesizing agent, with the power to determine the architectural unity of its living and working spaces and their coordination, the power to allocate community property to social uses such as participatory child-care and community recreation centers, and the power to insure the preservation and development of its natural ecological environment. It is not surprising that capitalist "communities" evince so little and such apathetic support from their members. The individual estranged from his community is realistic in understanding his lack of control over major community decisions. Clearly, alienation from community corresponds to our general proposition: the institutions determining the role structure, the power structure, and the physical structure of a community operate apart from the needs of individuals.

ALIENATION EXTENDED: PRODUCT AND SELF

Alienation from work activities and community are the basis of the individual's estrangement from all aspects of social life. They lie, for one, at the root of his alienation from the product of his labor. When the individual feels that the good or service he helps produce neither reflects his personal contribution through its properties and attributes nor contributes to his welfare either personally or through those with whom he has bonds of community, the *goal* of his work activities becomes meaningless and absurd; he is alienated from his product. In an integrated society, workers control their activities and, hence, the attributes of their product, as true skilled craftsmen. The workers' attachment to his product results not only from his pride in the object of his labor, but also in the personal value he holds for the community it serves. But in capitalist society, both disappear. Since the free market in labor and capitalist control of production eliminate worker control, and since the free market in land and private control of resources fragment and impersonalize community, his product becomes impersonal and external.

According to this explanation, alienation is a form of deprivation—deprivation from important social roles. But this deprivation holds deep subjective implications because individual psychic development is controlled by social experience. Just as "individuals develop through their social relations of production" and become incomplete individuals when alienated from their work activities, so individuals develop through their roles relating to community, product, and other individuals. When deprived of these formative influences in healthy forms, they become "self-alienated." To continue a metaphor, society may alienate a man's psyche as much as a pickpocket his wallet. We are alienated from ourselves when we are not what we really could be—when we cannot love, play, run, work, spiritualize, relate, create, empathize, or aid as much as our potential allows.

Self-alienation in this sense is often seen as a personal rather than social problem, and the "afflicted" troop to counselors and psychiatrists (and drugs) in search of themselves. But the social base of even this most intimate form of alienation lies in the deprivation of social environments and relationships conducive to personal growth, and its cure is accordingly *social.* When one grows up alienated from others, he cannot love or relate; alienated from work, he cannot create; from community, he cannot mature as a social being. Capitalist economic institutions, by which decisions are made on the basis of profit rather than human need provide unrewarding social roles. So psychic growth is thwarted, much as vitamin deprivation inhibits physical development.

Individuals become alienated from themselves for yet another reason. To produce workers with the proper ideologies, values, and personalities to participate effectively in alienated social roles requires special attention on the part of those institutions that regulate the development of youth. Communications media, especially advertising, instill materialist values that hold meaningful work and community of no importance in comparison with individual consumption. They depersonalize and objectivize interpersonal, intersexual, interracial, and international relations, reducing them to brute power, competition, and ruse by equating the individual's success as lover, worker, or community member with what he possesses in the form of goods or status.

Similarly, by mirroring the impersonal and competitive relations of community and the bureaucratic-authoritarian aspects of alienated work, schools thwart the development of true initiative, independence, and creativity in their charges. As a result they tend to produce docile, unimaginative workers fitting the needs of hierarchical commodity production. The media and the schools are alienating but are not the true culprits; they merely serve an economic mechanism that shapes community and work in patterns alien to human needs.

ALIENATION AND SOCIAL CHANGE

The virtue of capitalism is its level of economic growth in individual—as opposed to social—commodities, and the system accomplishes this at the expense of destruction in other social realms. Capitalism "delivers the goods" at the expense of destroying society, and this cannot be cured by merely altering the forms of political control.

Capitalism's virtue in delivering the goods would be acceptable to workers and community members only under one condition: that the goods the system delivers be valued as the ultimate source of individual welfare. The submission of the individual to his personal alienation is thus based on the ideological belief—capitalism's assertion—that material goods are the path to personal salvation; this belief is instilled and reinforced through media and schools. Yet it is doubtless false.

An individual's welfare and happiness is determined not by what he *has* in the form of individual commodities but by what he *is* and what he *does,* by his ability to undertake self-fulfilling *activities.* Commodities cannot do for you what you cannot do for yourself; they can act only as *instruments* in the process of human activity. The possibility of self-realizing activity depends as much on the *social contexts* open to the individual as on the means available to their performance. Thus the quality of community, work, and environment appear alongside of individual commodities as sources of individual welfare. An increase in the mass of goods available to the individual will enhance his well-being only insofar as they *expand the sphere of his activities* and only if the social roles involved in individual activity—roles defined by community, work, and environment—are themselves maintained or expanded. Economic growth cannot overcome the individual's alienation from these social spheres.

The individual's ability to undertake self-fulfilling activities depends on his own *level of personal psychic development,* in terms of physical, emotional, cognitive, aesthetic, and spiritual capacities. The individual alienated from himself, being alienated from growth-conducive social roles through his forced reduction to a purely efficient worker or child-raiser, is incapable of true fulfillment, and for him or her, commodities become a substitute for, rather than a complement to, personal activities. The individual discovers his alienation only by realizing this basic fact.

But the consciousness of alienation occurs not through the moral exhortations of the "converted" but the day-to-day experiences of people themselves, and a major force in this realization is the *process of economic growth.* Capitalist ideology holds that increasing personal income is the main path to happiness, that all we are not our money and status can be for us. Yet even taking account of inflation, incomes double every twenty-five or thirty years in the U.S., and we are not happier. On the contrary, social life continues to disintegrate and fragment. Economic growth itself gives the lie to the ethic of individual consumption as the sole social source of personal well-being. We cannot buy decent environment with increased income, the total supply of ecological balance is limited and declines through the normal operation of economic institutions, and the rich bid away this dwindling supply. We cannot buy decent community and decent work activities when their very destruction is the basis of capitalist growth.

So economic growth, the "virtue" of capitalism, the force in terms of which the system is justified and stabilized, is itself subject to a self-negating dialectic. If capitalist society justifies itself by delivering the goods, its very deliverance undercuts its justification; for once satisfied in this direction, individuals will make other demands on their social system, and such demands cannot be satisfied by a society wherein "all social value is reduced to exchange value."

A basic contradiction that capitalism faces, then, is the following: economic growth is a prerequisite to social stability; yet people have essentially satisfiable material needs, satisfiable in the sense that any further increase in material goods and services plays a minor part in securing their welfare regardless of whether they think it will or not; economic growth leads to the capacity for satisfying these material needs but cannot satisfy their other basic needs; and further economic growth will render the truth of this argument ever more manifest, ever closer to the daily experience of the worker. Therefore, economic growth, the prerequisite for stability, leads to instability.

BIBLIOGRAPHY

In addition to the works included in the body of this section, the editors also recommend the following.

Baran, Paul. *The Political Economy of Growth.* New York: Monthly Review Press, 1957.

Dobb, Maurice. *Papers on Capitalism, Development and Planning.* New York: International Publishers, 1967.

——. *Political Economy and Capitalism.* London: Routledge, Kegan Paul, 1937.

Domhoff, William. *Who Rules America?* Englewood, Cliffs, N.J.: Prentice-Hall, 1967.

Harrington, Michael. *The Accidental Century.* New York: Macmillan, 1965.

——. *Toward a Democratic Left.* New York: Macmillan, 1968.

Horowitz, David, ed. *Marx and Modern Economics.* New York: Monthly Review Press, 1968.

Kolko, Gabriel. *Wealth and Power in America.* New York: Praeger, 1962.

Magdoff, Harry. *The Age of Imperialism.* New York: Monthly Review Press, 1969.

Mandel, Ernest. *Marxist Economic Theory.* New York: Monthly Review Press, 1967.

Marcuse, Herbert. *Counterrevolution and Revolt.* Boston: Beacon Press, 1972.

——. *One-Dimensional Man.* Boston: Beacon Press, 1964.

Mills, C. Wright. *The Power Elite.* New York: Oxford University Press, 1956.

Nkrumah, Kwame. *Neo-Colonialism: Last Stage of Imperialism.* New York: International Publishers, 1965.

O'Connor, James. "The Fiscal Crisis of the State." In *Socialist Revolution,* January–February and March–April, 1970.

Perlo, Victor. *Empire of High Finance.* New York: International Publishers, 1957.

Robinson, Joan. *An Essay on Marxian Economics.* London: Macmillan, 1942.

Roszak, Theodore. *The Making of a Counter-Culture.* New York: Doubleday Anchor, 1969.

Strachey, John. *The Coming Struggle for Power.* New York: Covici, Friede, 1933.

——. *The Nature of Capitalist Crisis.* New York: Covici, Friede, 1935.

——. *The Theory and Practice of Socialism,* New York: Random House, 1936.

Sweezy, Paul. *The Theory of Capitalist Development.* New York: Monthly Review Press, 1942.

Veblen, Thorstein, *The Theory of the Leisure Class.* New York: Modern Library, 1934.

Williams, William A. *The Great Evasion.* Chicago: Quadrangle Paperbacks, 1964.